Account Title	Normal Balance	Financial Report Found On	Category	Permanent or Temporary
Medicare Tax Payable	Credit	Balance Sheet	Liability	Permanent
Merchandise Inventory	Debit	Balance Sheet; Income Statement	Current Asset; Cost of Goods Sold	Permanent
Mortgage Payable	Credit	Balance Sheet	Long-Term Liability	Permanent
Notes Payable	Credit	Balance Sheet	Current Liability	Permanent
Notes Receivable	Debit	Balance Sheet	Current Asset	Permanent
Organization Costs	Debit	Balance Sheet	Intangible Asset	Permanent
Patents	Debit	Balance Sheet	Intangible Asset	Permanent
Paid-In Capital from Treasury Stock	Credit	Balance Sheet	Stockholders' Equity	Permanent
Paid-In Capital in Excess of (. . .)	Credit	Balance Sheet	Stockholder's Equity	Permanent
Payroll Tax Expense	Debit	Income Statement	Operating Expense	Temporary
Petty Cash	Debit	Balance Sheet	Current Asset	Permanent
Premium on Bonds Payable	Credit	Balance Sheet	Long-Term Liability	Permanent
Prepaid Insurance	Debit	Balance Sheet	Current Asset	Permanent
Prepaid Rent	Debit	Balance Sheet	Current Asset	Permanent
Preferred Stock	Credit	Balance Sheet	Stockholders' Equity	Permanent
Purchases	Debit	Income Statement	Cost of Goods Sold	Temporary
Purchases Discount	Credit	Income Statement	Contra Cost of Goods Sold	Temporary
Purchases Returns and Allowances	Credit	Income Statement	Contra Cost of Goods Sold	Temporary
Retained Earnings	Credit	Statement of Retained Earnings; Balance Sheet	Stockholders' Equity	Permanent
Salaries Expense	Debit	Income Statement	Operating Expense	Temporary
Salaries Payable	Credit	Balance Sheet	Current Liability	Permanent
Sales	Credit	Income Statement	Revenue	Temporary
Sales Discount	Debit	Income Statement	Contra Revenue	Temporary
Sales Returns and Allowances	Debit	Income Statement	Contra Revenue	Temporary
Sales Tax Payable	Credit	Balance Sheet	Current Liability	Permanent
Social Security Tax Payable	Credit	Balance Sheet	Liability	Permanent
Stock Dividend Distributable	Credit	Balance Sheet	Stockholders' Equity	Permanent
Stock Subscriptions Receivable	Debit	Balance Sheet	Current Asset	Permanent
Supplies	Debit	Balance Sheet	Current Asset	Permanent
Treasury Stock	Debit	Balance Sheet	Contra Stockholder's Equity	Permanent
Unearned Revenue	Credit	Balance Sheet	Current Liability	Permanent
Vouchers Payable	Credit	Balance Sheet	Current Liability	Permanent
Withdrawals	Debit	Statement of Owner's Equity; Balance Sheet	Owners' Equity	Temporary

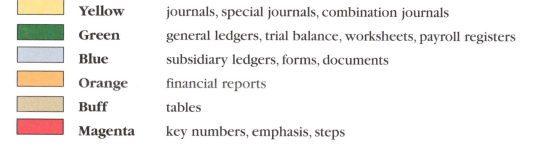

KEY TO USE OF COLOR IN TEXT

	Yellow	journals, special journals, combination journals
	Green	general ledgers, trial balance, worksheets, payroll registers
	Blue	subsidiary ledgers, forms, documents
	Orange	financial reports
	Buff	tables
	Magenta	key numbers, emphasis, steps

SEVENTH EDITION

COLLEGE ACCOUNTING

A PRACTICAL APPROACH

CHAPTERS 1–10

SEVENTH EDITION

COLLEGE ACCOUNTING

A PRACTICAL APPROACH

CHAPTERS 1–10

JEFFREY SLATER

NORTH SHORE COMMUNITY COLLEGE
BEVERLY, MASSACHUSETTS

PRENTICE HALL

UPPER SADDLE RIVER, NEW JERSEY 07458

Editorial/Production Credits
Editor in Chief: *P. J. Boardman*
Executive Editor: *Annie Todd*
Associate Editor: *Diane deCastro*
Director of Development: *Steve Deitmer*
Development Editor: *Mike Buchman*
Marketing Manager: *Beth Toland*
Director of Production: *Joanne Jay*
Managing Editor: *Bruce Kaplan*
Senior Production Manager: *Anne Graydon*
Copy Editor: *Sylvia Moore*
Proofreader: *Ann Koonce*
Design Manager: *Pat Smythe*
Interior Design: *Jill Yutkowitz, Lisa Delgado*
Art Design: *Ed Smith*
Cover Design: *Jill Yutkowitz*
Cover Art: *Dave Cutler*
Photo Permissions Supervisor: *Kay Dellosa*
Photo Permissions Editor: *Charles Morris*
Chapter-Opening Photos: *Jann Underwood*
Senior Manufacturing Supervisor: *Paul Smolenski*
Manufacturing Manager: *Vincent Scelta*
Compositor: *Progressive Information Technologies*

© 1999, 1996, by Prentice-Hall, Inc.
A Simon & Schuster Company
Upper Saddle River, New Jersey 07458

0-13-095489-6

Prentice-Hall International (UK) Limited, *London*
Prentice-Hall of Australia Pty. Limited, *Sydney*
Prentice-Hall Canada Inc., *Toronto*
Prentice-Hall Hispanoamericana, S.A., *Mexico*
Prentice-Hall of India Private Limited, *New Delhi*
Prentice-Hall of Japan, Inc., *Tokyo*
Simon & Schuster Asia Pte. Ltd., *Singapore*
Editora Prentice-Hall do Brasil, Ltda., *Rio de Janeiro*

Printed in the United States of America
10 9 8 7 6 5 4 3 2 1

To   SCUPPER
        MOLLY
            MAGGIE
                AMBER

With love, JEFF

BRIEF CONTENTS

CONTENTS

8 THE EMPLOYER'S TAX RESPONSIBILITIES: PRINCIPLES AND PROCEDURES 267

9 SPECIAL JOURNALS: SALES AND CASH RECEIPTS 312

The Big Picture 312

DUNKIN' DONUTS BOXES

COMPUTER WORKSHOPS

PREFACE

Today's accounting students are learning the skills that will help them succeed in business. The seventh edition of *College Accounting: A Practical Approach* by Jeffrey Slater helps students integrate these skills by infusing the tried-and-true Slater system with real-world applications. Each chapter begins with a "Big Picture" introduction that puts the subject in a practical context. A "Continuing Problem" at the end of each chapter lets students apply their skills to a practical case. Throughout the book, students read about real accounting applications in thirteen Dunkin' Donuts boxes that feature both local franchise operations and corporate support functions. And students are taught computer accounting skills using *Simply Accounting*™ and *Peachtree® Accounting* software.

THE REAL WORLD

Whether students will keep the books for their own small business or function within a corporation, developing an understanding of how accounting procedures are applied in a business setting is crucial to their success. That is why the seventh edition of *College Accounting: A Practical Approach* now brings the real world to the classroom through the following ***NEW features:***

To provide a conceptual overview of topics that will be discussed in the chapters, each chapter now opens with a short vignette called "The Big Picture." The scenarios come from the experiences of Tony Freedman, who started his own business (Eldorado Computer Center) in California upon graduation from a local community college. Tony keeps his own books and shares with students how he uses accounting procedures to run a successful and growing business.

Based on interviews with members of the accounting department at Dunkin' Donuts corporate headquarters, thirteen boxes have been specially crafted to illustrate how accounting procedures are used at both franchise stores and corporate headquarters. By reading about how useful the worksheet is to a shop owner throughout the year (Chapter 4), or how new IBM point-of-sale terminals help store owners generate more accurate Cash Summaries (Chapter 6), students will see how the skills they learn in class are applied by this well-known company.

The Computer Workshops following Chapters 3, 4, 5, 8, 10, and 13 have been updated for Version 5.0 of Simply Accounting. Also, a new Workshop has been added following Chapter 16 to show students how to set up a perpetual inventory system, which is used by most businesses to track and manage inventory. This commercial software package is used by small- to medium-sized businesses to keep their books and the Computer Workshops teach students to set up the manual systems they learn in the book in a computerized format. Many businesses use computers in some way to manage their accounting records, so students that possess computer skills are a very valuable asset!

A new supplement, *Peachtree® for College Accounting,* is available for student purchase with the seventh edition of *College Accounting: A Practical Approach.* Peachtree is the most widely-used commercial software package on the market and this supplement is designed to teach students how to convert the manual procedures they learn in Chapters 1 – 16 of the text into a computerized environment using Peachtree Accounting for Windows.

THE SLATER SYSTEM

Jeffrey Slater developed his renowned teaching system through 28+ years of classroom experience. Broad goals are presented at the start of each chapter. Students are then presented with material in small, manageable units followed by immediate self-checks and feedback. Each chapter is limited to a small number of units, so students review and apply concepts before they move on. In addition, cumulative reviews in each chapter help students solidify their learning.

Textbook Options

You can use the Slater System in several configurations of *College Accounting: A Practical Approach:*

◆ Chapters 1 – 10 *(0-13-095489-6)* OR
   Chapters 1 – 10 with Simply Accounting disks for Computer Workshops *(0-13-082554-9)*

◆ Chapters 1 – 15 *(0-13-095488-8)* OR
   Chapters 1 – 15 with Simply Accounting disks for Computer Workshops *(0-13-082555-7)*

◆ Chapters 1 – 26 *(0-13-788464-8)* OR
   Chapters 1 – 26 with Simply Accounting disks for Computer Workshops *(0-13-082557-3)*

◆ Chapters 1 – 15 paperback text with Study Guide and Working Papers *(0-13-095487-X)* OR
   Chapters 1 – 15 paperback text with Study Guide and Working Papers and Simply Accounting disks for Computer Workshops *(0-13-082556-5)*

SEVENTH EDITION HIGHLIGHTS AND CHANGES

The Slater System   The seventh edition retains the proven pedagogy that has made *College Accounting* a classic.

The Big Picture   New introductions open each chapter providing a conceptual preview and relating topics to an actual business, Eldorado Computer Center.

Continuing Problem   A new Continuing Problem runs through Chapters 1 – 16, asking students to apply skills to the business scenario set in the Big Picture.

Dunkin' Donuts Boxes   The real-world accounting issues facing franchise owners and corporate staff are presented in boxed features based on research of the nationally known company. Discussion questions tie the boxes to chapter concepts.

Quiz Tips   "Quiz Tips" provide additional guidance to help students complete the self-review activities at the end of each learning unit.

Check Figures   "Check Figures" provide quick feedback for students to monitor progress in all A and B problems.

Expanded Coverage of Perpetual Inventory   An Appendix to Chapter 12 now introduces perpetual inventory, the most prevalent method of tracking inventory in business today. Chapter 16 focuses on this method in depth.

Simply Accounting™ Computer Workshops   These popular workshop activities are updated for Version 5.0, and a new perpetual inventory workshop now follows Chapter 16.

Peachtree Accounting®   A new *Peachtree for College Accounting* supplement is tied directly to the text and allows students to learn how to apply accounting principles using Peachtree software.

Practical Accounting Tutor   The expanded, highly visual, interactive study guide allows students to review Chapters 1 – 10 at their own pace and includes a grading tool.

Self-Quiz Videotapes   New videotapes produced by the author recreate the Self-Review Quizzes at the end of each learning unit.

Real-World Applications   End-of-chapter materials, including "You Make the Call" sections, offer short cases that require critical thinking and cover ethical issues while stressing oral and written communications.

Extensive End-of-Chapter Framework   Each chapter offers extensive learning aides, including:

- Discussion Questions
- Mini Excrcises
- Exercises
- Problem sets A and B
- Real World Applications
- Accounting Recall: a cumulative review that offers a two-part quiz including vocabulary and theory. Forms and worked-out solutions are in the *Study Guide and Working Papers*.
- Continuing Problem: a cumulative problem that runs through Chapters 1 – 16, asking students to work through the entire business cycle for Eldorado Computer Center.

SUPPLEMENTS

For the Student

- Study Guide and Working Papers, Chs. 1 – 10 *(0-13-096153-1)*
- Study Guide and Working Papers, Chs. 1 – 15 *(0-13-096154-X)*
- Study Guide and Working Papers, Chs. 16 – 26 *(0-13-096155-8)*
- One-on-One Videos *(0-13-080876-8)*

- ◆ Practical Accounting Tutor CD-ROM *(0-13-080879-2)*
- ◆ A-1 Photography Practice Set — Manual *(0-13-080310-3)*
- ◆ A-1 Photography Practice Set — Computerized *(0-13-080319-7)*
- ◆ Who-Dun-It Bookstore Practice Set — Manual *(0-13-082027-X)*
- ◆ Runners Corporation Practice Set — Manual *(0-13-080316-2)*
- ◆ Runners Corporation Practice Set — Computerized *(0-13-080315-4)*
- ◆ Peachtree for College Accounting Practice Sets — Computerized *(0-13-982216-X)*

For the Instructor

- ◆ Instructor's Resource and Solutions Manual, Chs. 1 – 15 *(0-13-080866-0)*
- ◆ Instructor's Resource and Solutions Manual, Chs. 16 – 26 *(0-13-080867-9)*
- ◆ Solutions and Teaching Transparencies, Chapters 1 – 15 *(0-13-080873-3)*
- ◆ Solutions and Teaching Transparencies, Chapters 16 – 26 *(0-13-080874-1)*
- ◆ Solutions Manual for Who-Dun-It Bookstore Practice Set *(0-13-080872-5)*
- ◆ Solutions Manual for A-1 Photography/Runners Corporation Practice Sets *(0-13-080314-6)*
- ◆ Solutions Manual for Peachtree for College Accounting Practice Set *(0-13-099657-2)*
- ◆ Test Item File with Achievement Tests, Chs. 1 – 15 *(0-13-080868-7)*
- ◆ Test Item File with Achievement Tests, Chs. 16 – 26 *(0-13-080869-5)*
- ◆ Windows PH Custom Test *(0-13-080871-7)*
- ◆ Achievement Tests 1 – 15A *(0-13-080858-X)*
- ◆ Achievement Tests 1 – 15B *(0-13-080897-0)*
- ◆ Tips on Teaching College Accounting Video *(0-13-080875-X)*
- ◆ PowerPoint Transparencies *(0-13-080878-4)*

ACKNOWLEDGMENTS
Writers and Checkers

Tim Carse (SunGard EBS) — His work on Chapters 7 and 8

Paul A. Concilio (McLennan Community College) — Appendix to Chapter 12

Sylvia Hearing (Clackamas Community College) — Simply Accounting Computer Workshops

Mary McGarry (San Antonio College) — Dunkin' Donuts boxes

Kathleen Murphrey (San Antonio College) — Solution checking the text, Study Guide and Working Papers, and Instructor's Resource and Solutions Manual

Jann Underwood (Eldorado College) — The Big Picture and the Continuing Problem

Al Walczak (Linn Benton Community College) — Revising Chapter 16

Reviewers

Bill Reynolds, St. Charles County Community College

Charles N. Calvin, St. Charles County Community College

Dick D. Wasson, Southwestern College

Tom Kimberling, Ventura College

James Guyor, St. Clair County Community College

Noel McKeon, Florida Community College

Pete Rizzo, Heald Business College

Larry Ziegler, Highland College

Glen Rado, St. Phillips College

Sue Lynch, Florence-Darlington Technical College
Jeannelou Hodgens, Florence-Darlington Technical College
Charles J. Blumer, St. Charles County Community College
Marvin Dittman, Elgin Community College
Joan E. Cook, Milwaukee Area Technical College
Ray Lewis, San Antonio College
Delores G. Huerta, Del Mar College
Sophia B. Klopp, Palm Beach Community College
Albert J. Walczak, Linn-Benton Community College

Supplements Authors

Paul A. Concilio, McLennan Community College
Shari L. DeMarco, Bryant & Stratton Business College
Patricia Holmes, Des Moines Area Community College
Diane Mach, McLennan Community College
Larena McGinnity, Chadron State College
Errol Osteraa, Heald Business College
Lou Procopio, North Shore Community College
Barbara Roscher, McLennan Community College

Prentice Hall Staff

In addition to the people mentioned above, I would like to thank the dedicated Prentice Hall staff members who worked on this project: Diane DeCastro, Associate Editor, who did a tremendous amount of work in pulling together *both* the text and the supplements package; Annie Todd, Executive Editor, who worked on the last edition and served as a valuable resource on this edition; Elaine Oyzon-Mast, their Editorial Assistant; Beth Toland, Marketing Manager; Mike Buchman, Development Editor, and Steve Deitmer, Director of Development; Anne Graydon, Senior Production Editor, and Bruce Kaplan, Managing Editor; Paul Smolenski, Senior Manufacturing Supervisor; Pat Smythe, Design Manager, and Jill Yutkowitz, Designer; and last but not least, Richard Bretan, Supplements Production Manager.

—Jeff Slater

SEVENTH EDITION

COLLEGE ACCOUNTING

A PRACTICAL APPROACH

CHAPTERS 1–10

ACCOUNTING CONCEPTS AND PROCEDURES

An Introduction

THE BIG PICTURE

People start businesses for many reasons: to be their own boss; to be a success; to build their own financial empire; to bring a great idea to the market. But all businesses share one goal — to increase in value.

Tony Freedman, a graduate of Eldorado College, decided that he wanted to use his acquired skills as a computer technician and build his own business, Eldorado Computer Center. His technical skills would provide the services his customers needed, and his knowledge of accounting would show how his business was doing. He would provide added value to his customers and to his business at the same time. As he thought about his business, he asked these questions:

◆ What type of business organization shall I form?
◆ How much money will I need to start, and where will it come from?
◆ What will I charge my customers?
◆ What will my projected revenue and expenses be?

Tony had learned that accounting is the language of business because it helps translate events into numbers that show how a company is doing. He used this language to answer his questions and to write a business plan to open a sole proprietorship on July 1.

To the Student:

A business must have a way to track its financial activities. Accounting is the process of gathering, processing, reporting, and communicating this information. "The Big Picture" introduces each chapter by connecting accounting to the real world of business. At the end of each chapter, you will find the "Continuing Problem," which asks you to apply what you've learned in the chapter to a real business situation.

Accounting is the language of business; it provides information to managers, owners, investors, governmental agencies, and others inside and outside the organization. Accounting provides answers and insights to questions like these:

◆ Is Subway's cash balance sufficient?
◆ Should McDonald's expand its product line?
◆ Can American Airlines pay its debt obligations?
◆ What percentage of IBM's marketing budget is for television advertisement? How does this compare with the competition? What is the overall financial condition of IBM?

Smaller businesses also need answers to their financial questions:

◆ Did business increase enough over the last year to warrant hiring a new assistant?
◆ Should we spend more money to design, produce, and send out new brochures in an effort to create more business?

Accounting is as important to individuals as it is to businesses; it answers questions like

◆ Should I take out a loan for a new car or wait until I can afford to pay cash for it?
◆ Would my money work better in a savings bank or in a credit union savings plan?

Accounting is the process that analyzes, records, classifies, summarizes, reports, and interprets financial information to decision makers — whether individuals, small businesses, large corporations, or governmental agencies — in a timely fashion. It is important that students understand the "whys" of the accounting process. Just knowing the mechanics is not enough.

There are three main categories of business organization: (1) sole proprietorships, (2) partnerships, and (3) corporations. Let's define each of them and look at their advantages and disadvantages. This information also appears in Table 1-1.

Sole Proprietorship

A **sole proprietorship** is a business that has one owner. That person is both the owner and the manager of the business. An advantage of a sole proprietorship is that the owner makes all of the decisions for the business. A disadvantage is that if the business cannot pay its obligations, the business owner must pay them. This means that the owner could lose some of his personal assets (e.g., his house or his savings).

Sole proprietorships are easy to form. They end if the business closes or when the owner dies.

Partnership

A **partnership** is a form of business ownership that has at least two owners (partners). Each partner acts as an owner of the company. This is an advantage because the partners can share the decision making and the risks of the busi-

TABLE 1-1 TYPES OF BUSINESS ORGANIZATIONS

	Sole Proprietorship	Partnership	Corporation
Ownership	Business owned by one person.	Business owned by more than one person.	Business owned by stockholders.
Formation	Easy to form.	Easy to form.	More difficult to form.
Liability	Owner could lose personal assets to meet obligations of business.	Partners could lose personal assets to meet obligations of partnership.	Limited personal risk. Stockholders' loss is limited to their investment in the company.
Closing	Ends with death of owner or closing of business.	Ends with death of partner or exit of a partner.	Can continue indefinitely.

ness. A disadvantage is that, as in a sole proprietorship, the partners' personal assets could be lost if the partnership cannot meet its obligations.

Partnerships are easy to form. They end when a partner dies or leaves the partnership.

Corporation

Disney is an example of a corporation.

A **corporation** is a business owned by stockholders. The corporation may have only a few stockholders or it may have many stockholders. The stockholders are not personally liable for the corporation's debts, and they usually do not have input into the business decisions.

Corporations are more difficult to form than sole proprietorships or partnerships. Corporations can exist indefinitely.

CLASSIFYING BUSINESS ORGANIZATIONS

Whether we are looking at a sole proprietorship, a partnership, or a corporation, the business can be classified by what the business does to earn money. Companies are categorized as either service, merchandise, or manufacturing businesses.

A local cab company is a good example of a **service company** because it provides a service. The first part of this book focuses on service businesses.

Stores like Sears and J.C. Penney sell products. They are called merchandise companies. **Merchandise companies** can either make their own products or sell products that are made by another supplier. Companies like Mattel and General Motors that make their own products are called **manufacturers.** (See Table 1-2.)

TABLE 1-2 EXAMPLES OF SERVICE, MERCHANDISE, AND MANUFACTURING BUSINESSES

Service Businesses	Merchandise Businesses	Manufacturing Businesses
Pete's Taxi Service	Sears	Mattel
Jane's Painting Co.	J.C. Penney	General Motors
Dr. Wheeler, M.D.	L.L. Bean	Toro
Accountemps	Home Depot	Levi's
CellularOne Paging Services	Staples	Intel

DEFINITION OF ACCOUNTING

Accounting (also called the **accounting process**) is a system that measures the activities of a business in financial terms. It provides various reports and financial statements that show how the various transactions the business undertook (e.g., buying and selling goods) affected the business. It does this by performing the following functions:

◆ **Analyzing:** Looking at what happened and how the business was affected.
◆ **Recording:** Putting the information into the accounting system.
◆ **Classifying:** Grouping all of the same activities (e.g., all purchases) together.
◆ **Summarizing:** Explaining the results.
◆ **Reporting:** Issuing the reports that tell the results of the previous functions.
◆ **Interpreting:** Examining the reports to determine how the various pieces of information they contain relate to each other.

The system communicates the reports and financial statements to people who are interested in the information, such as the business's decision makers, investors, creditors, governmental agencies (e.g., the Internal Revenue Service), and so on.

As you can see, a lot of people use these reports. A set of procedures and guidelines were developed to make sure that everyone prepares and interprets them the same way. These guidelines are known as **generally accepted accounting principles (GAAP).**

Now let's look at the difference between bookkeeping and accounting. Keep in mind that we will use the terms "accounting" and "the accounting process" interchangeably.

DIFFERENCE BETWEEN BOOKKEEPING AND ACCOUNTING

Confusion often arises concerning the difference between bookkeeping and accounting. **Bookkeeping** is the recording (recordkeeping) function of the accounting process; a bookkeeper enters accounting information in the company's books. An accountant takes that information and prepares the financial reports that are used to analyze the company's financial position. Accounting involves many complex activities. Often, it includes the preparation of tax and financial reports, budgeting, and analyses of financial information.

Today, computers are used for routine bookkeeping operations that used to take weeks or months to complete. The text takes this into consideration by explaining how the advantages of the computer can be applied to a manual accounting system by using hands-on knowledge of how accounting works. Basic accounting knowledge is needed even though computers can do routine tasks.

LEARNING UNIT 1-1
The Accounting Equation

ASSETS, LIABILITIES, AND EQUITIES

Let's begin our study of accounting concepts and procedures by looking at a small business; Cathy Hall's law practice. Cathy decided to open her practice at the end of August. She consulted her accountant before she made her decision. The accountant told her some important things before she made this decision. First, he told her the new business would be considered a separate business entity whose finances had to be kept separate and distinct from Cathy's personal finances. The accountant went on to say that all transactions can be analyzed using the basic accounting equation: Assets = Liabilities + Owner's Equity.

Cathy had never heard of the basic accounting equation. She listened carefully as the accountant explained the terms used in the equation and how the equation works:

Assets

Cash, land, supplies, office equipment, buildings, and other properties of value *owned* by a firm are called **assets.**

Equities

The rights of financial claim to the assets are called **equities.** Equities belong to those who supply the assets. If you are the only person to supply assets to the firm, you have the sole rights, for financial claims, to them. For example, if you supply the law firm with $4,000 in cash and $3,000 in office equipment, your equity in the firm is $7,000.

Relationship Between Assets and Equities

The relationship between assets and equities is

| **Assets** | = | **Equities** |
| (Total value of items *owned* by business) | | (Total claims against the assets) |

The total dollar value of the assets of your law firm will be equal to the total dollar value of the financial claims to those assets, that is, equal to the total dollar value of the equities.

The total dollar value is broken down on the left-hand side of the equation to show the specific items of value owned by the business and on the right-hand side to show the types of claims against the assets owned.

Liabilities

A firm may have to borrow money to buy more assets; when this occurs it means the firm is **buying assets *on account*** (buy now, pay later). Suppose the law firm purchases a desk for $400 on account from Joe's Stationery, and the store is willing to wait 10 days for payment. The law firm has created a **liability:** an obligation to pay that comes due in the future. Joe's Stationery is called the **creditor.** This liability—the amount owed to Joe's Stationery—gives the store the right, or the financial claim, to $400 of the law firm's assets. When Joe's Stationery is paid, the store's rights to the assets of the law firm will end, since the obligation has been paid off.

Basic Accounting Equation

To best understand the various claims to a business's assets, accountants divide equities into two parts. The claims of creditors—outside persons or businesses—are labeled **liabilities.** The claim of the business's owner are labeled **owner's equity.** Let's see how the accounting equation looks now.

Elements of the basic accounting equation.

Assets =	**Equities**
	1. Liabilities: rights of creditors
	2. Owner's equity: rights of owner

Assets = Liabilities + Owner's Equity

The total value of all the assets of a firm equals the combined total value of the financial claims of the creditors (liabilities) and the claims of the owners (owner's equity). This is known as the **basic accounting equation.** The basic accounting equation provides a basis for understanding the conventional accounting system of a business. The equation records business transactions in a logical and orderly way that shows their impact on the company's assets, liabilities, and owner's equity.

Importance of Creditors

Another way of presenting the basic accounting equation is:

Assets − Liabilities = Owner's Equity

This form of the equation stresses the importance of creditors. The owner's rights to the business's assets are determined after the rights of the creditors are subtracted. In other words, creditors have first claim to assets. If a firm has no liabilities — and therefore no creditors — the owner has the total rights to assets. Another term for the owner's current investment, or equity, in the business's assets is **capital.**

As Cathy Hall's law firm engages in business transactions (paying bills, serving customers, and so on), changes will take place in the assets, liabilities, and owner's equity (capital). Let's analyze some of these transactions.

Transaction (A)   Aug. 28: Cathy invests $7,000 in cash and $800 of office equipment into the business.

On August 28, Cathy withdraws $7,000 from her personal bank account and deposits the money in the law firm's newly opened bank account. She also invests $800 of office equipment in the business. She plans to be open for business on September 1. With the help of her accountant, Cathy begins to prepare the accounting records for the business. We put this information into the basic accounting equation as follows:

ASSETS		= LIABILITIES +	OWNER'S EQUITY
Cash +	**Office Equipment** =		**Cathy Hall, Capital**
$7,000 +	$800	=	$7,800
	$7,800	= $7,800	

Note that the total value of the assets, cash, and office equipment — $7,800 — is equal to the combined total value of liabilities (none, so far) and owner's equity ($7,800). Remember, Hall has supplied all the cash and office equipment, so she has the sole financial claim to the assets. Note how the heading "Cathy Hall, Capital" is written under the owner's equity heading. The $7,800 is Cathy's investment, or equity, in the firm's assets.

Transaction (B)   Aug. 29: Law practice buys office equipment for cash, $900.

From the initial investment of $7,000 cash, the law firm buys $900 worth of office equipment (such as a desk), which lasts a long time, while **supplies** (such as pens) tend to be used up relatively quickly.

CH. 1 / ACCOUNTING CONCEPTS AND PROCEDURES: AN INTRODUCTION

	ASSETS		= LIABILITIES +	OWNER'S EQUITY
	Cash +	**Office Equipment** =		**Cathy Hall, Capital**
BEGINNING BALANCE	$7,000 +	$800 =		$7,800
TRANSACTION	−900	+900		
ENDING BALANCE	$6,100 +	$1,700 =		$7,800

$$\$7,800 = \$7,800$$

Shift in Assets

As a result of the last transaction, the law office has less cash but has increased its amount of office equipment. This is called a **shift in assets** — the makeup of the assets has changed, but the total of the assets remains the same.

Suppose you go food shopping at the supermarket with $100 and spend $60. Now you have two assets, food and money. The composition of the assets has been *shifted* — you have more food and less money than you did — but the *total* of the assets has not increased or decreased. The total value of the food, $60, plus the cash, $40, is still $100. When you borrow money from the bank, on the other hand, you have an increase in cash (an asset) and an increase in liabilities; overall there is an increase in assets, not just a shift.

An accounting equation can remain in balance even if only one side is updated. The key point to remember is that the left-hand-side total of assets must always equal the right-hand-side total of liabilities and owner's equity.

Transaction (C)   Aug. 30: Buys additional office equipment on account, $400.

The law firm purchases an additional $400 worth of chairs and desks from Wilmington Company. Instead of demanding cash right away, Wilmington agrees to deliver the equipment and to allow up to 60 days for the law practice to pay the invoice (bill).

This liability, or obligation to pay in the future, has some interesting effects on the basic accounting equation. Wilmington Company has accepted as payment a partial claim against the assets of the law practice. This claim exists until the law firm pays off the bill. This unwritten promise to pay the creditor is a liability called **accounts payable.**

	ASSETS		= LIABILITIES	+ OWNER'S EQUITY
	Cash +	**Office Equipment** =	**Accounts Payable** +	**Cathy Hall, Capital**
BEGINNING BALANCE	$6,100 +	$1,700 =		$7,800
TRANSACTION		+400	+$400	
ENDING BALANCE	$6,100 +	$2,100 =	$400	$7,800

$$\$8,200 = \$8,200$$

When this information is analyzed, we can see that the law practice has increased what it owes (accounts payable) as well as what it owns (office equipment) by $400. The law practice gains $400 in an asset but has an obligation to pay Wilmington Company at a future date.

The owner's equity remains unchanged. This transaction results in an increase of total assets from $7,800 to $8,200.

Finally, note that after each transaction the basic accounting equation remains in balance.

LEARNING UNIT 1-1 REVIEW

AT THIS POINT you should be able to

◆ List the functions of accounting. (pp. 2, 4)
◆ Define and explain the differences between sole proprietorships, partnerships, and corporations. (p. 3)
◆ Compare and contrast bookkeeping and accounting. (p. 4)
◆ Explain the role of the computer as an accounting tool. (p. 4)
◆ State the purpose of the accounting equation. (p. 5)
◆ Explain the difference between liabilities and owner's equity. (p. 6)
◆ Define capital. (p. 6)
◆ Explain the difference between a shift in assets and an increase in assets. (p. 7)

To test your understanding of this material, complete Self-Review Quiz 1-1. The blank forms you need are in the *Study Guide and Working Papers* for Chapter 1. The solution to the quiz immediately follows here in the text. If you have difficulty doing the problems, review Learning Unit 1-1 and the solution to the quiz. Videotapes are available to review these quizzes. Check with your instructor on availability.

Keep in mind that learning accounting is like learning to type — the more you practice, the better you become. You will not be an expert in one day. Be patient. It will all come together.

SELF-REVIEW QUIZ 1-1

(The blank forms you need are on page 1 of the *Study Guide and Working Papers*.)

Record the following transactions in the basic accounting equation:

Quiz Tip: Note that transaction 2 below is a shift in assets, while transaction 3 is an increase in assets. Keep asking yourself: What did the business get and who supplied it to the business? Remember, capital is not cash. Cash is an asset, while capital is part of owner's equity.

1. Pete O'Brien invests $14,000 to begin a real estate office.
2. The real estate office buys $600 of computer equipment for cash.
3. The real estate company buys $500 of additional computer equipment on account.

Solution to Self-Review Quiz 1-1

	ASSETS		=	LIABILITIES	+	OWNER'S EQUITY
	Cash	+ Computer Equipment	=	Accounts Payable	+	Pete O'Brien, Capital
1.	+$14,000					+$14,000
BALANCE	14,000		=			14,000
2.	−600	+$600				
BALANCE	13,400 +	600	=			14,000
3.		+500		+$500		
ENDING BALANCE	$13,400 +	$1,100	=	$ 500	+	$14,000
		$14,500 = $14,500				

LEARNING UNIT 1-2
The Balance Sheet

The balance sheet shows the company's financial position as of a particular date. (In our example, that date is at the end of August.)

In the first learning unit, the transactions for Cathy Hall's law office were recorded in the accounting equation. The transactions we recorded occurred before the law firm opened for business. A report called a **balance sheet** or **statement of financial position** can show the history of a company before it opened. The balance sheet is a formal report that presents the information from the ending balances of both sides of the accounting equation. Think of the balance sheet as a snapshot of the business's financial position as of a particular date.

Let's look at the balance sheet of Cathy Hall's law practice for August 31, 19XX, shown in Figure 1-1. The figures in the balance sheet come from the ending balances of the accounting equation for the law practice as shown in Learning Unit 1-1.

Note that in Figure 1-1 the assets owned by the law practice appear on the left-hand side and that liabilities and owner's equity appear on the right-hand side. Both sides equal $8,200. This *balance* between left and right gives the balance sheet its name. In later chapters we will be looking at other ways to set up a balance sheet.

POINTS TO REMEMBER IN PREPARING A BALANCE SHEET
The Heading

Do you remember the three elements that make up a balance sheet? Assets, liabilities, and owner's equity.

The heading of the balance sheet provides the following information:

◆ The company name: Cathy Hall, Attorney At Law.
◆ The name of the report: Balance Sheet.
◆ The date for which the report is prepared: August 31, 19XX.

Use of the Dollar Sign

Note that the dollar sign is not repeated each time a figure appears. As shown in the balance sheet for Cathy Hall's law practice, it usually is placed to the left of each column's top figure and to the left of the column's total.

FIGURE 1-1
The Balance Sheet

Remember: The balance sheet is a formal report.

	ASSETS	= LIABILITIES	+ OWNER'S EQUITY
	Cash + Office Equipment	= Accounts Payable	+ Cathy Hall, Capital
ENDING BALANCES	$6,100 + $2,100	= $400	+ $7,800

CATHY HALL, ATTORNEY AT LAW
BALANCE SHEET
AUGUST 31, 19XX

Assets		Liabilities and Owner's Equity	
Cash	$ 6 1 0 0 00	Liabilities	
Office Equipment	2 1 0 0 00	Accounts Payable	$ 4 0 0 00
		Owner's Equity	
		Cathy Hall, Capital	7 8 0 0 00
		Total Liabilities and	
Total Assets	$ 8 2 0 0 00	Owner's Equity	$ 8 2 0 0 00

CATHY HALL, ATTORNEY AT LAW BALANCE SHEET AUGUST 31, 19XX		
Assets		
Cash		$ 6 1 0 0 00
Office Equipment		2 1 0 0 00
Total Assets		$ 8 2 0 0 00

A single line means the numbers above it have been added or subtracted.

A double line indicates a total.

Distinguishing the Total

When adding numbers down a column, use a single line before the total and a double line beneath it. A single line means that the numbers above it have been added or subtracted. A double line indicates a total. It is important to align the numbers in the column; many errors occur because these figures are not lined up. These rules are the same for all accounting reports.

The balance sheet gives Cathy the information she needs to see the law firm's financial position before it opens for business. This information does not tell her, however, whether or not the firm will make a profit.

LEARNING UNIT 1-2 REVIEW

AT THIS POINT you should be able to

- ◆ Define and state the purpose of a balance sheet. (p. 9)
- ◆ Identify and define the elements making up a balance sheet. (p. 9)
- ◆ Show the relationship between the accounting equation and the balance sheet. (p. 9)
- ◆ Prepare a balance sheet in proper form from information provided. (p. 9)

SELF-REVIEW QUIZ 1-2

(The blank forms you need are on page 2 of the *Study Guide and Working Papers.*)

The date is November 30, 19XX. Use the following information to prepare in proper form a balance sheet for Janning Company:

Accounts Payable	$30,000
Cash	8,000
A. Janning, Capital	9,000
Office Equipment	31,000

Quiz Tip: The heading of a balance sheet answers the questions *who, what,* and *when.* Nov. 30, 19XX is the particular date.

Solution to Self-Review Quiz 1-2

JANNING COMPANY BALANCE SHEET NOVEMBER 30, 19XX				
Assets		Liabilities and Owner's Equity		
Cash	$ 8 0 0 0 00	Liabilities		
Office Equipment	31 0 0 0 00	Accounts Payable	$ 30 0 0 0 00	
		Owner's Equity		
		A. Janning, Capital	9 0 0 0 00	
		Total Liabilities and		
Total Assets	$ 39 0 0 0 00	Owner's Equity	$ 39 0 0 0 00	

Capital does not mean cash. The capital amount is the owner's current investment of assets in the business.

CH. 1 / ACCOUNTING CONCEPTS AND PROCEDURES: AN INTRODUCTION

LEARNING UNIT 1-3
The Accounting Equation Expanded: Revenue, Expenses, and Withdrawals

As soon as Cathy Hall's office opened, she began performing legal services for her clients and earning revenue for the business. At the same time, as a part of doing business, she incurred various expenses, such as rent.

When Cathy asked her accountant how these transactions fit into the accounting equation, he began by defining some terms.

Revenue   A service company earns **revenue** when it provides services to its clients. Cathy's law firm earned revenue when she provided legal services to her clients for legal fees. When revenue is earned, owner's equity is increased. In effect, revenue is a subdivision of owner's equity.

Assets are increased. The increase is in the form of cash if the client pays right away. If the client promises to pay in the future, the increase is called **accounts receivable.** When revenue is earned, the transaction is recorded as an increase in revenue and an increase in assets (either as cash and/or as accounts receivable, depending on whether it was paid right away or will be paid in the future).

Expenses   A business's **expenses** are the cost the company incurs in carrying on operations in its effort to create revenue. Expenses are also a subdivision of owner's equity; when expenses are incurred, they *decrease* owner's equity. Expenses can be paid for in cash or they can be charged.

Net Income/Net Loss   When revenue totals more than expenses, **net income** is the result; when expenses total more than revenue, **net loss** is the result.

Withdrawals   At some point Cathy Hall may need to withdraw cash or other assets from the business to pay living or other personal expenses that do not relate to the business. We will record these transactions in an account called **withdrawals.** Sometimes this account is called the *owner's drawing account.* Withdrawals is a subdivision of owner's equity that records personal expenses not related to the business. Withdrawals decrease owner's equity (see Fig. 1-2).

It is important to remember the difference between expenses and withdrawals. Expenses relate to business operations; withdrawals are the result of personal needs outside the normal operations of the business.

Now let's analyze the September transactions for Cathy Hall's law firm using an **expanded accounting equation** that includes withdrawals, revenues, and expenses.

When revenue is earned, it is recorded as an increase in Cathy's owner's equity and an increase in assets.

Accounts receivable is an asset. The law firm expects to be able to receive amounts owed from customers at a later date.

Remember: Accounts receivable results from earning revenue even when cash is not yet received.

Record an expense when it is incurred, whether it is paid then or is to be paid later.

FIGURE 1-2
Owner's Equity

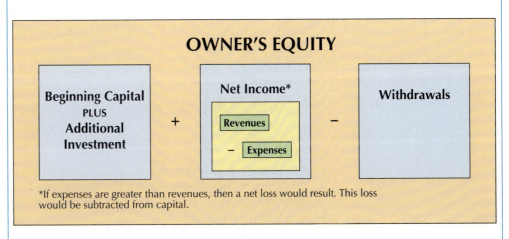

EXPANDED ACCOUNTING EQUATION

> **Transaction (D)** Sept. 1–30: Provided legal services for cash, $3,000.

Transactions A, B, and C were discussed earlier, when the law office was being formed in August. See Learning Unit 1-1.

	ASSETS			= LIABILITIES +		OWNER'S EQUITY			
	Cash +	Accts. Rec.	+ Office Equip.	= Accts. Pay.	+ C. Hall, Capital	− C. Hall, Withdr.	+ Revenue	− Expenses
BALANCE FORWARD	$6,100		+ $ 2,100 =	$ 400	+ $7,800			
TRANSACTION	+3,000						+$3,000	
ENDING BALANCE	$9,100		+ $ 2,100 =	$ 400	+ $7,800		+ $3,000	
			$11,200 =	$11,200				

In the law firm's first month of operation a total of $3,000 in cash was received for legal services performed. In the accounting equation the asset Cash is increased by $3,000. Revenue is also increased by $3,000, resulting in an increase in owner's equity.

A revenue column was added to the basic accounting equation. Amounts are recorded in the revenue column when they are earned. They are also recorded in the assets column, either under Cash and/or under Accounts Receivable. Do not think of revenue as an asset. It is part of owner's equity. It is the revenue that creates an inward flow of cash and accounts receivable.

> **Transaction (E)** Sept. 1–30: Provided legal services on account, $4,000.

	ASSETS			= LIABILITIES +		OWNER'S EQUITY			
	Cash +	Accts. Rec.	+ Office Equip.	= Accts. Pay.	+ C. Hall, Capital	− C. Hall, Withdr.	+ Revenue	− Expenses
BAL. FOR.	$9,100		+ $ 2,100 =	$ 400	+ $7,800		+ $3,000	
TRANS.		+$4,000					+4,000	
END. BAL.	$9,100 +	$4,000 +	$ 2,100 =	$ 400	+ $7,800		+ $7,000	
			$15,200 =	$15,200				

Cathy's law practice performed legal work on account for $4,000. The firm did not receive the cash for these earned legal fees; it accepted an unwritten promise from these clients that payment would be received in the future.

> **Transaction (F)** Sept. 1–30: Received $700 cash as partial payment from previous services performed on account.

During September some of Cathy's clients who had received services and promised to pay in the future decided to reduce what they owed the practice by $700 when their bills came due. This is shown as follows on the expanded accounting equation.

	ASSETS			= LIABILITIES +	OWNER'S EQUITY			
	Cash +	Accts. Rec.	+ Office Equip. =	Accts. Pay.	+ C. Hall, Capital	− C. Hall, Withdr.	+ Revenue	− Expenses
BALANCE FORWARD	$9,100 +	$4,000	+ $ 2,100 =	$ 400	+ $7,800		+ $7,000	
TRANSACTION	+700	−700						
ENDING BALANCE	$9,800 +	$3,300	+ $ 2,100 =	$ 400	+ $7,800		+ $7,000	
			$15,200 =	$15,200				

The law firm increased the asset Cash by $700 and reduced another asset, Accounts Receivable, by $700. The *total* of assets does not change. The right-hand side of the expanded accounting equation has not been touched because the total on the left-hand side of the equation has not changed. The revenue was recorded when it was earned, and the *same revenue cannot be recorded twice*. This transaction analyzes the situation *after* the revenue has been previously earned and recorded. Transaction (F) shows a shift in assets — more cash and less accounts receivable.

Transaction (G)   Sept. 1–30: Paid salaries expense, $600.

	ASSETS			= LIABILITIES +	OWNER'S EQUITY			
	Cash +	Accts. Rec.	+ Office Equip. =	Accts. Pay.	+ C. Hall, Capital	− C. Hall, Withdr.	+ Revenue	− Expenses
BAL. FOR.	$9,800 +	$3,300	+ $ 2,100 =	$ 400	+ $7,800		+ $7,000	
TRANS.	−600							+$600
END. BAL.	$9,200 +	$3,300	+ $ 2,100 =	$ 400	+ $7,800		+ $7,000 −	$600
			$14,600 =	$14,600				

As expenses increase, they decrease owner's equity. This incurred expense of $600 reduces the cash by $600. Although the expense was paid, the total of our expenses to date has *increased* by $600. Keep in mind that owner's equity decreases as expenses increase, so the accounting equation remains in balance.

Transaction (H)   Sept. 1–30: Paid rent expense, $700.

	ASSETS			= LIABILITIES +	OWNER'S EQUITY			
	Cash +	Accts. Rec.	+ Office Equip. =	Accts. Pay.	+ C. Hall, Capital	− C. Hall, Withdr.	+ Revenue	− Expenses
BAL. FOR.	$9,200 +	$3,300	+ $ 2,100 =	$ 400	+ $7,800		+ $7,000 −	$ 600
TRANS.	−700							+700
END. BAL.	$8,500 +	$3,300	+ $ 2,100 =	$ 400	+ $7,800		+ $7,000 −	$1,300
			$13,900 =	$13,900				

During September the practice incurred rent expenses of $700. This rent was not paid in advance; it was paid when it came due. The payment of rent reduces the asset Cash by $700 as well as increases the expenses of the firm, resulting in a decrease in owner's equity. The firm's expenses are now $1,300.

	ASSETS		= LIABILITIES +		OWNER'S EQUITY			
	Cash + Accts. Rec.	+ Office Equip. =	Accts. Pay.	+ C. Hall, Capital	− C. Hall, Withdr.	+ Revenue	− Expenses
BALANCE FORWARD	$8,500 + $3,300	+ $ 2,100 =	$ 400	+ $7,800		+ $7,000	− $1,300
TRANSACTION			+300				+300
ENDING BALANCE	$8,500 + $3,300	+ $ 2,100 =	$ 700	+ $7,800		+ $7,000	− $1,600
		$13,900 =	$13,900				

Cathy ran an ad in the local newspaper and incurred an expense of $300. This increase in expenses caused a corresponding decrease in owner's equity. Since Cathy has not paid the newspaper for the advertising yet, she owes $300. Thus her liabilities (Accounts Payable) increase by $300. Eventually, when the bill comes in and is paid, both Cash and Accounts Payable will be decreased.

	ASSETS		= LIABILITIES +		OWNER'S EQUITY			
	Cash + Accts. Rec.	+ Office Equip. =	Accts. Pay.	+ C. Hall, Capital	− C. Hall, Withdr.	+ Revenue	− Expenses
BAL. FOR.	$8,500 + $3,300	+ $ 2,100 =	$ 700	+ $7,800		+ $7,000	− $1,600
TRANS.	−200				+$200		
END. BAL.	$8,300 + $3,300	+ $ 2,100 =	$ 700	+ $7,800 −	$200	+ $7,000	− $1,600
		$13,700 =	$13,700				

By taking $200 for personal use, Cathy has *increased* her withdrawals from the business by $200 and decreased the asset Cash by $200. Note that as withdrawals increase, the owner's equity will *decrease*. Keep in mind that a withdrawal is *not* a business expense. It is a subdivision of owner's equity that records money or other assets an owner withdraws from the business for *personal* use.

Subdivision of Owner's Equity

Take a moment to review the subdivisions of owner's equity:

◆ As capital increases, owner's equity increases (see Transaction A).
◆ As withdrawals increase, owner's equity decreases (see Transaction J).
◆ As revenue increases, owner's equity increases (see Transaction D).
◆ As expenses increase, owner's equity decreases (see Transaction G).

Cathy Hall's Expanded Accounting Equation

The following is a summary of the expanded accounting equation for Cathy Hall's law firm.

Cathy Hall
Attorney at Law
Expanded Accounting Equation: A Summary

	ASSETS			= LIABILITIES +		OWNER'S EQUITY			
	Cash +	Accts. Rec.	+ Office Equip. =	Accts. Pay.	+ C. Hall, Capital	− C. Hall, Withdr.	+ Revenue	− Expenses
A.	$7,000		+$800 =		+$7,800			
BALANCE	7,000	+	800 =		7,800			
B.	−900		+900					
BALANCE	6,100	+	1,700 =		7,800			
C.			+400	+$400				
BALANCE	6,100	+	2,100 =	400 +	7,800			
D.	+3,000						+$3,000	
BALANCE	9,100	+	2,100 =	400 +	7,800	+	3,000	
E.		+$4,000					+ 4,000	
BALANCE	9,100 +	4,000 +	2,100 =	400 +	7,800	+	7,000	
F.	+700	−700						
BALANCE	9,800 +	3,300 +	2,100 =	400 +	7,800	+	7,000	
G.	−600							+$600
BALANCE	9,200 +	3,300 +	2,100 =	400 +	7,800	+	7,000 −	600
H.	−700							+700
BALANCE	8,500 +	3,300 +	2,100 =	400 +	7,800	+	7,000 −	1,300
I.				+300				+300
BALANCE	8,500 +	3,300 +	2,100 =	700 +	7,800	+	7,000 −	1,600
J.	−200					+$200		
END BALANCE	$8,300 +	$3,300 +	$2,100 =	$700 +	$7,800 −	$200 +	$7,000 −	$1,600

LEARNING UNIT 1-3 REVIEW

AT THIS POINT you should be able to

- Define and explain the difference between revenue and expenses. (p. 11)
- Define and explain the difference between net income and net loss. (p. 11)
- Explain the subdivision of owner's equity. (p. 14)
- Explain the effects of withdrawals, revenue, and expenses on owner's equity. (p. 14)
- Record transactions in an expanded accounting equation and balance the basic accounting equation as a means of checking the accuracy of your calculations. (p. 15)

SELF-REVIEW QUIZ 1-3

(The blank forms you need are on page 3 of the *Study Guide and Working Papers*.)

Record the following transactions into the expanded accounting equation for the Bing Company. Note that all titles have a beginning balance.

1. Received cash revenue, $3,000.
2. Billed customers for services rendered, $6,000.
3. Received a bill for telephone expenses (to be paid next month), $125.
4. Bob Bing withdrew cash for personal use, $500.
5. Received $1,000 from customers in partial payment for services performed in transaction 2.

Solution to Self-Review Quiz 1-3

	ASSETS			= LIABILITIES +		OWNER'S EQUITY			
	Cash +	Accts. Rec. +	Cleaning = Equip.	Accts. Pay.	+ B. Bing, Capital	− B. Bing, Withdr.	+ Revenue	− Expenses	
BEG. BALANCE	$10,000 +	$ 2,500 +	$6,500 =	$1,000	+ $11,800 −	$ 800 +	$ 9,000 −	$2,000	
1.	+3,000						+3,000		
BALANCE	13,000 +	2,500 +	6,500 =	1,000	+ 11,800 −	800 +	12,000 −	2,000	
2.		+6,000					+6,000		
BALANCE	13,000 +	8,500 +	6,500 =	1,000	+ 11,800 −	800 +	18,000 −	2,000	
3.				+125				+125	
BALANCE	13,000 +	8,500 +	6,500 =	1,125	+ 11,800 −	800 +	18,000 −	2,125	
4.	−500					+500			
BALANCE	12,500 +	8,500 +	6,500 =	1,125	+ 11,800 −	1,300 +	18,000 −	2,125	
5.	+1,000	−1,000							
END BALANCE	$13,500 +	$ 7,500 +	$6,500 =	$1,125	+ $11,800 −	$ 1,300 +	$18,000 −	$2,125	
			$27,500 =	$27,500					

LEARNING UNIT 1-4
Preparing Financial Reports

Cathy Hall would like to be able to find out whether her firm is making a profit, so she asks her accountant whether he can measure the firm's financial performance on a monthly basis. Her accountant replies that there are a number of financial reports that he can prepare, such as the income statement, which shows how well the law firm has performed over a specific period of time. The accountant can use the information in the income statement to prepare other reports.

THE INCOME STATEMENT

The income statement is prepared from data found in the revenue and expense columns of the expanded accounting equation.

An **income statement** is an accounting report that shows business results in terms of revenue and expenses. If revenues are greater than expenses, the report shows net income. If expenses are greater than revenues, the report shows net loss. An income statement can cover one, three, six, or twelve months. It cannot cover more than one year. The report shows the result of all revenues and expenses throughout the entire period and not just as of a specific date. The income statement for Cathy Hall's law firm is shown in Figure 1-3.

CATHY HALL, ATTORNEY AT LAW INCOME STATEMENT FOR MONTH ENDED SEPTEMBER 30, 19XX		
Revenue:		
Legal Fees		$ 7 0 0 0 00
Operating Expenses:		
Salaries Expense	$ 6 0 0 00	
Rent Expense	7 0 0 00	
Advertising Expense	3 0 0 00	
Total Operating Expenses		1 6 0 0 00
Net Income		$ 5 4 0 0 00

FIGURE 1-3
The Income Statement

The inside column of numbers ($600, $700, $300) is used to subtotal all expenses ($1,600) before subtracting from revenue.

If this statement of owner's equity is omitted, the information will be included in the owner's equity section of the balance sheet.

Points to Remember in Preparing an Income Statement

Heading   The heading of an income statement tells the same three things as all other accounting reports: the company's name, the name of the report, and the period of time the report covers.

The Set Up   As you can see on the income statement, the inside column of numbers ($600, $700, and $300) is used to subtotal all expenses ($1,600) before subtracting them from revenue ($7,000 − $1,600 = $5,400).

Operating expenses may be listed in alphabetical order, in order of largest amounts to smallest, or in a set order established by the accountant.

THE STATEMENT OF OWNER'S EQUITY

As we said, the income statement is a business report that shows business results in terms of revenue and expenses. But how does net income or net loss affect owner's equity? To find that out we have to look at a second type of report, the **statement of owner's equity.**

The statement of owner's equity shows for a certain period of time what changes occurred in Cathy Hall, Capital. The statement of owner's equity is shown in Figure 1-4.

The capital of Cathy Hall can be

Increased by:	Owner Investment
	Net Income (Revenue − Expenses)
Decreased by:	Owner Withdrawals
	Net Loss (Expenses Greater than Revenue)

FIGURE 1-4 Statement of Owner's Equity

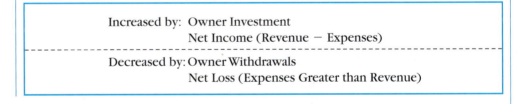

CATHY HALL, ATTORNEY AT LAW STATEMENT OF OWNER'S EQUITY FOR MONTH ENDED SEPTEMBER 30, 19XX			
Cathy Hall, Capital, September 1, 19XX		$ 7 8 0 0 00	
Net Income for September	$ 5 4 0 0 00		Comes from Income Statement
Less Withdrawals for September	2 0 0 00		
Increase in Capital		5 2 0 0 00	
Cathy Hall, Capital, September 30, 19XX		$ 13 0 0 0 00	

Remember, a withdrawal is *not* a business expense and thus is not involved in the calculation of net income or net loss on the income statement. It appears on the statement of owner's equity. The statement of owner's equity summarizes the effects of all the subdivisions of owner's equity (revenue, expenses, withdrawals) on beginning capital. The ending capital figure ($13,000) will be the beginning figure in the next statement of owner's equity.

Suppose that Cathy's law firm had operated at a loss in the month of September. Suppose instead of net income there was a net loss, and an additional investment of $700 was made on September 15. This is how the statement would look if this had happened.

CATHY HALL, ATTORNEY AT LAW STATEMENT OF OWNER'S EQUITY FOR MONTH ENDED SEPTEMBER 30, 19XX		
Cathy Hall, Capital, September 1, 19XX		$ 7 8 0 0 00
Additional Investment, September 15, 19XX		7 0 0 00
Total Investment for September		$ 8 5 0 0 00
Less: Net Loss for September	$ 4 0 0 00	
Withdrawals for September	2 0 0 00	
Decrease in Capital		6 0 0 00
Cathy Hall, Capital, September 30, 19XX		$ 7 9 0 0 00

THE BALANCE SHEET

Now let's look at how to prepare a balance sheet from the expanded accounting equation (see Fig. 1-5). As you can see, the asset accounts (cash, accounts receivable, and office equipment) appear on the left of the balance sheet. Accounts payable and Cathy Hall, Capital appear on the right. Notice that the $13,000 of capital can be calculated within the accounting equation, or read from the statement of owner's equity.

FIGURE 1-5 The Accounting Equation and the Balance Sheet

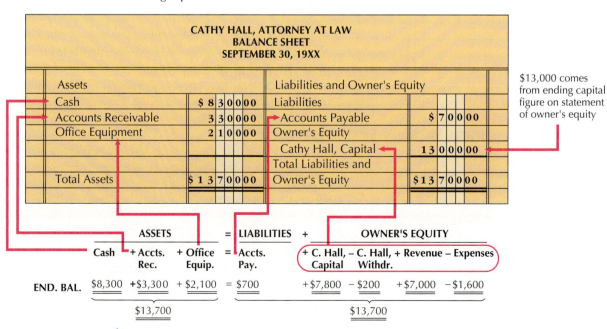

CH. 1 / ACCOUNTING CONCEPTS AND PROCEDURES: AN INTRODUCTION

TABLE 1-3   WHAT GOES ON EACH FINANCIAL REPORT

	Income Statement	Statement of Owner's Equity	Balance Sheet
Assets			X
Liabilities			X
Capital[†] (beg)		X	
Capital (end)		X	X
Withdrawals		X	
Revenues	X		
Expenses	X		

[†] Note Additional Investments go on the Statement of Owner's Equity.

Main elements of the income statement, the statement of owner's equity, and the balance sheet

In this chapter we have discussed three financial reports: the income statement, the statement of owner's equity, and the balance sheet. There is a fourth report, called the statement of cash flows, that will not be covered at this time. Let us review what elements of the expanded accounting equation go into each report, and the usual order in which the reports are prepared. Figure 1-5 presents a diagram of the accounting equation and the balance sheet. Table 1-3 summarizes the following points:

- The income statement is prepared first; it includes revenues and expenses and shows net income or net loss. This net income or net loss is used to update the next report, the statement of owner's equity.

- The statement of owner's equity is prepared second; it includes beginning capital and any additional investments, the net income or net loss shown on the financial statement, withdrawals, and the total, which is the **ending capital.** The balance in Capital comes from the statement of owner's equity.

- The balance sheet is prepared last; it includes the final balances of each of the elements listed in the accounting equation under Assets and Liabilities. The balance in Capital comes from the statement of owner's equity.

LEARNING UNIT 1-4 REVIEW

AT THIS POINT you should be able to

- Define and state the purpose of the income statement, the statement of owner's equity, and the balance sheet. (p. 16)
- Discuss why the income statement should be prepared first. (p. 17)
- Compare and contrast these three financial reports. (p. 19)
- Calculate a new figure for capital on the statement of owner's equity and the balance sheet. (p.17)
- Show what happens on a statement of owner's equity if there is a net loss. (p. 18)

SELF-REVIEW QUIZ 1-4

(The blank forms you need are on pages 4 and 5 of the *Study Guide and Working Papers.*)

From the following balances for Rusty Realty prepare:

1. Income statement for month ended November 30, 19XX.

Remember the TV ad in which Fred the Baker stumbles out of bed in the dark and drives to work—stopping only to wake up a rooster on the way! Fred is dedicated to making donuts (and the coffee and the bagels) fresh for the early morning customers at his Dunkin' Donuts store. Fred Baker, one of Dunkin' Donuts' newest shop owners, smiled as he thought of this commercial while he drove to work early one morning. Fred's name had been the source of lots of jokes—thousands of them—about his choice of companies, since it was also the name of the character in Dunkin' Donuts' long-running ad campaign. Like everyone else, Fred Baker was fond of Fred the Baker.

So what has this to do with accounting? Plenty, as it turns out. As one of Dunkin' Donuts' shop owners, Fred Baker wears two hats—his baker's cap and an accountant's green eyeshade. He makes the donuts, and he manages the accounts for his store. To learn how to do his job, Fred attended Dunkin' Donuts University. We'll share the financial lessons he learned there with you. The baking lessons—NO.

When you look at Fred's store, you are really seeing two businesses. Fred is the owner of his store, and he is a sole proprietor. He operates under an agreement with Dunkin' Donuts Inc. of Randolph, Massachusetts. Dunkin' Donuts Inc. supplies the business know-how and support (like training, national advertising, and recipes). Fred supplies capital (his investment) and his baking, management, and effort. Dunkin' Donuts Inc. and Fred operate interdependent businesses, and both rely on accounting information for their success.

Dunkin' Donuts Inc., in business since 1950, has grown dramatically over the years, to the point that it now has stores in 43 states and 20 countries. To manage this enormous service business requires very careful control of each of its 4,139 stores. At Dunkin' Donuts headquarters, Dwayne Goulding, Business Consultant for Fred's zone, monitors Fred's reports closely. It's his job to see that Fred makes money at making donuts, which in turn results in Dunkin' Donuts Inc. making money too.

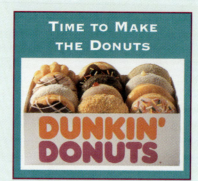

TIME TO MAKE THE DONUTS

DUNKIN' DONUTS.

Why does headquarters require accounting reports? Accounting reports give the information both Fred and the company need to make business decisions in a number of vital areas. For example:

1. Before Fred could buy his Dunkin' Donuts store, the company needed to know how much cash Fred had and his assets and liabilities. Fred prepared a personal Balance Sheet to give them this information.
2. Fred needs to know if his store is making a profit. He prepares an Income Statement to tell him that.
3. Dwayne needs to know if Fred's store is profitable and well run, compared to other shops in the zone. He compares the Income Statements of all shops to learn this. He also looks at competing businesses.
4. Fred must have the right amount of supplies on hand. If he has too few, he can't make the donuts. If he has too many, some may spoil. The Balance Sheet tells him what supplies are on hand. It also alerts Dwayne to potential problems Fred may have.
5. How often do Dunkin' Donuts stores report accounting information? Fred prepares a monthly Income Statement and Balance Sheet. He also prepares a daily Sales Report, which he summarizes every Saturday and sends to national headquarters. In addition, Fred does a weekly Payroll Report, which Dwayne reviews.

DISCUSSION QUESTIONS

1. What makes Fred a sole proprietor?
2. Why are Fred and Dunkin' Donuts interdependent businesses?
3. Why did Fred have to share his personal Balance Sheet with Dunkin' Donuts? Do you think most interdependent businesses do this?
4. What does Dunkin Donuts learn from Fred's Income Statement and Balance Sheet?

2. Statement of owner's equity for the month ended November 30, 19XX.

3. Balance sheet as of November 30, 19XX.

Cash	$4,000	R. Rusty, Capital	
Accounts Receivable	1,370	November 1, 19XX	$5,000
Store Furniture	1,490	R. Rusty, Withdrawals	100
Accounts Payable	900	Commissions Earned	1,500
		Rent Expense	200
		Advertising Expense	150
		Salaries Expense	90

Solution to Self-Review Quiz 1-4

Quiz Tip: Note that the inside column is only used for sub-totaling.

RUSTY REALTY
INCOME STATEMENT
FOR MONTH ENDED NOVEMBER 30, 19XX

Revenue:			
Commissions Earned			$ 1 5 0 0 0 0
Operating Expenses:			
Rent Expense	$ 2 0 0 0 0		
Advertising Expense	1 5 0 0 0		
Salaries Expense	9 0 0 0		
Total Operating Expenses		4 4 0 0 0	
Net Income		$ 1 0 6 0 0 0	

Subtotal Columns

The net income from the income statement is used to help build the statement of owner's equity.

RUSTY REALTY
STATEMENT OF OWNER'S EQUITY
FOR MONTH ENDED NOVEMBER 30, 19XX

R. Rusty, Capital, November 1, 19XX		$ 5 0 0 0 0 0
Net Income for November	$ 1 0 6 0 0 0	
Less Withdrawals for November	1 0 0 0 0	
Increase in Capital		9 6 0 0 0
R. Rusty, Capital, November 30, 19XX		$ 5 9 6 0 0 0

The new figure for capital from the statement of owner's equity is used as the capital figure on the balance sheet.

RUSTY REALTY
BALANCE SHEET
NOVEMBER 30, 19XX

Assets		Liabilities and Owner's Equity	
Cash	$ 4 0 0 0 0 0	Liabilities	
Accounts Receivable	1 3 7 0 0 0	Accounts Payable	$ 9 0 0 0 0
Store Furniture	1 4 9 0 0 0		
		Owner's Equity	
		R. Rusty, Capital	5 9 6 0 0 0
		Total Liabilities and	
Total Assets	$ 6 8 6 0 0 0	Owner's Equity	$ 6 8 6 0 0 0

COMPREHENSIVE DEMONSTRATION PROBLEM WITH SOLUTIONS TIPS

(The blank forms you need are on pages 6 and 7 of the *Study Guide and Working Papers.*)

Michael Brown opened his law office on June 1, 19XX. During the first month of operations Michael conducted the following transactions:

1. Invested $5,000 in cash into the law practice.
2. Paid $600 for office equipment.
3. Purchased additional office equipment on account, $1,000.
4. Performed legal services for clients receiving cash, $2,000.
5. Paid salaries, $800.
6. Performed legal services for clients on account, $1,000.
7. Paid rent, $1,200.
8. Withdrew $500 from his law practice for personal use.
9. Received $500 from customers in partial payment for legal services performed, transaction 6.

Assignment:

a. Record these transactions in the expanded accounting equation.

b. Prepare the financial statements at June 30 for Michael Brown, Attorney at Law.

Solution to Comprehensive Demonstration Problem

	ASSETS			= LIABILITIES +		OWNER'S EQUITY			
A.	Cash	+ Accts. Rec.	+ Office Equip.	= Accounts Payable	+ M. Brown, Capital	− M. Brown, Withdr.	+ Legal Fees	− Expenses
1.	+$5,000				+$5,000			
BAL.	5,000		=		5,000			
2.	−600		+$600					
BAL.	4,400	+	600 =		5,000			
3.			+1,000	+$1,000				
BAL.	4,400	+	1,600 =	1,000 +	5,000			
4.	+2,000						+$2,000	
BAL.	6,400	+	1,600 =	1,000 +	5,000		+ 2,000	
5.	−800							+$800
BAL.	5,600	+	1,600 =	1,000 +	5,000		+ 2,000 −	800
6.		+$1,000					+1,000	
BAL.	5,600 +	1,000 +	1,600 =	1,000 +	5,000		+ 3,000 −	800
7.	−1,200							+1,200
BAL.	4,400 +	1,000 +	1,600 =	1,000 +	5,000		+ 3,000 −	2,000
8.	−500					+$500		
BAL.	3,900 +	1,000 +	1,600 =	1,000 +	5,000 −	500	+ 3,000 −	2,000
9.	+500	−500						
END. BAL.	$4,400 +	$ 500 +	$1,600 =	$1,000 +	$5,000 −	$500	+ $3,000 −	$2,000
			$6,500 =	$6,500				

Solution Tips to Expanded Accounting Equation

A.

◆ **Transaction 1:** The business increased its cash by $5,000. Owner's Equity (capital) increased when Michael supplied the cash to the business.

◆ **Transaction 2:** There was a shift in assets when the equipment was purchased. The business lowered its cash by $600, and a new column — Equipment — was increased for the $600 of equipment that was bought. The amount of capital is not touched because the owner did not supply any new funds.

◆ **Transaction 3:** When creditors supply $1,000 of additional equipment, the business Accounts Payable shows the debt. The business had increased what it *owes* the creditors.

◆ **Transaction 4:** Legal Fees, a subdivision of owner's equity, is increased when the law firm provides a service even if no money is received. The service provides an inward flow of $2,000 cash, an asset. Remember, legal fees are *not* an asset. As legal fees increase, owner's equity increases.

◆ **Transaction 5:** The salary paid by Michael shows an $800 increase in expenses, and a corresponding decrease in owner's equity.

◆ **Transaction 6:** Michael did the work and earned the $1,000. That $1,000 is recorded as revenue. This time the legal fees create an inward flow of assets called Accounts Receivable for $1,000. Remember legal fees are *not* an asset. They are a subdivision of owner's equity.

◆ **Transaction 7:** The $1,200 rent expense reduces owner's equity as well as cash.

◆ **Transaction 8:** Withdrawals are for personal use. Here, business decreases cash of $500 while Michael increases $500. Withdrawals decrease the owner's equity.

◆ **Transaction 9:** This transaction does not reflect new revenue in the form of legal feels. It is only a shift in assets: more cash and less Accounts Receivable.

B-1.

Michael Brown, Attorney at Law
Income Statement
For Month Ended June 30, 19XX

Revenue:		
Legal Fees		$3,000
Operating expenses:		
Salaries expense	$ 800	
Rent expense	1,200	
Total operating expenses		2,000
Net income		$1,000

B-2.

Michael Brown, Attorney at Law
Income Statement
For Month Ended June 30, 19XX

Michael Brown, Capital, June 1, 19XX		$5,000
Net income for June	$1,000	
Less withdrawals for June	500	
Increase in Capital		500
Michael Brown, Capital, June 30, 19XX		$5,500

B-3.

Michael Brown, Attorney at Law
Balance Sheet
June 30, 19XX

Assets		*Liabilities and Owner's Equity*	
Cash	$4,400	Liabilities	
Accounts Receivable	500	Accounts Payable	$1,000
Office equipment	1,600	Owner's Equity	
		M. Brown, Capital	5,500
Total Assets	$6,500	Total Liabilities and Owner's Equity	$6,500

Solution Tips to Financial Reports

B-1. Income statement lists only Revenues and Expenses for a period of time. Inside column for subtotaling. Withdrawals are not listed here.

B-2. The statement of Owner's Equity takes the net income figure of $1,000 and adds it to Beginning Capital less any withdrawals. This new capital figure of $5,500 will go on the balance sheet. This report shows changes in Capital for a period of time.

B-3. The $4,400, $500, $1,600, and $1,000 came from the totals of the expanded accounting equation. The Capital figure of $5,500 came from the statement of Owner's Equity. This balance sheet reports Assets, Liabilities, and a new figure for Capital at a specific date.

SUMMARY OF KEY POINTS

Learning Unit 1-1

1. The functions of accounting involve analyzing, recording, classifying, summarizing, reporting, and interpreting financial information.
2. A sole proprietorship is a business owned by one person. A partnership is a business owned by two or more persons. A corporation is a business owned by stockholders.
3. Bookkeeping is the recording part of accounting.
4. The computer is a tool to use in the accounting process.
5. Assets = Liabilities + Owner's Equity is the basic accounting equation that aids in analyzing business transactions.
6. Liabilities represents amounts owed to creditors while capital represents what is invested by the owner.
7. Capital does not mean cash. Capital is the owner's current investment. The owner could have invested equipment that was purchased before the new business was started.
8. In a shift of assets, the composition of assets changes, but the total of assets does not change. For example, if a bill is paid by a customer, the firm increases cash (an asset) but decreases accounts receivable (an asset), so there is no overall increase in assets; total assets remain the same. When you borrow money from a bank, you have an increase in cash (an asset) and an increase in liabilities: overall there is an increase in assets, not just a shift.

Learning Unit 1-2

1. The balance sheet is a report written as of a particular date. It lists the assets, liabilities, and owner's equity of a business. The heading of the balance sheet answers the questions *who, what,* and *when* (as of a specific date).
2. The balance sheet is a formal report of a financial position.

Learning Unit 1-3

1. Revenue generates an inward flow of assets. Expenses generate an outward flow of assets or a potential outward flow. Revenue and expenses are subdivisions of owner's equity. Revenue is not an asset.
2. When revenue totals more than expenses, net income is the result; when expenses total more than revenue, net loss is the result.
3. Owner's equity can be subdivided into four elements: capital, withdrawals, revenue, and expenses.
4. Withdrawals decrease owner's equity; revenue increases owner's equity; expenses decrease owner's equity. A withdrawal is not a business expense; it is for personal use.

Learning Unit 1-4

1. The income statement is a report written for a specific period of time that lists earned revenue and expenses incurred to produce the earned revenue. The net income or net loss will be used in the statement of owner's equity.
2. The statement of owner's equity reveals the causes of a change in capital. This report lists any investments, net income (or net loss), and withdrawals. The ending figure for capital will be used on the balance sheet.
3. The balance sheet uses the ending balances of assets and liabilities from the accounting equation and the capital from the statement of owner's equity.
4. The income statement should be prepared first because the information on it as to net income or net loss is used to prepare the statement of owner's equity, which in turn provides information about capital for the balance sheet. In this way one builds upon the next, and it begins with the income statement.

KEY TERMS

Accounting A system that measures the business's activities in financial terms, provides written reports and financial statements about those activities, and communicates these reports to decision makers and others.

Accounts payable Amounts owed to creditors that result from the purchase of goods or services on account: a liability.

Accounts receivable An asset that indicates amounts owed by customers.

Assets Properties (resources) of value owned by a business (cash, supplies, equipment, land).

Balance sheet A report, as of a particular date, that shows the amount of assets owned by a business as well as the amount of claims (liabilities and owner's equity) against these assets.

Basic accounting equation Assets = Liabilities + Owner's Equity.

Bookkeeping The recording function of the accounting process.

Business entity In *accounting* it is assumed that a business is separate and distinct from the personal assets of the owner. Each unit or entity requires separate accounting functions.

Capital The owner's investment of equity in the company.

Corporation A type of business organization that is owned by stockholders. Stockholders usually are not personally liable for the corporation's debts.

Creditor Someone who has a claim to assets.

Ending capital Beginning Capital + Additional Investments + Net Income − Withdrawals = Ending Capital. Or: Beginning Capital + Additional Investments − Net Loss − Withdrawals = Ending Capital.

Equities The interest or financial claim of creditors (liabilities) and owners (owner's equity) who supply the assets to a firm.

Expanded accounting equation Assets = Liabilities + Capital − Withdrawals + Revenue − Expenses.

Expense A cost incurred in running a business by consuming goods or services in producing revenue; a subdivision of owner's equity. When expenses increase, there is a decrease in owner's equity.

Generally accepted accounting principles (GAAP) The procedures and guidelines that must be followed during the accounting process.

Income statement An accounting report that details the performance of a firm (revenue minus expenses) for a specific period of time.

Liabilities Obligations that come due in the future. Liabilities result in increasing the financial rights or claims of creditors to assets.

Manufacturing company Business that makes a product and sells it to its customers.

Merchandising company Business that buys a product from a manufacturing company to sell to its customers.

Net income When revenue totals more than expenses, the result is net income.

Net loss When expenses total more than revenue, the result is net loss.

Owner's equity Rights or financial claims to the assets of a business (in the accounting equation, assets minus liabilities).

Partnership A form of business organization that has at least two owners. The partners usually are personally liable for the partnership's debts.

Revenue An amount earned by performing services for customers or selling goods to customers; can be in the form of cash and/or accounts receivable; a subdivision of owner's equity — as revenue increases, owner's equity increases.

Service company Business that provides a service.

Shift in assets A shift that occurs when the composition of the assets has changed, but the total of the assets remains the same.

Sole proprietorship A type of business ownership that has one owner. The owner is personally liable for paying the business's debts.

Statement of financial position Another name for a balance sheet.

Statement of owner's equity A financial report that reveals the change in capital. The ending figure for capital is then placed on the balance sheet.

Supplies One type of asset acquired by a firm; has a much shorter life than equipment.

Withdrawals A subdivision of owner's equity that records money or other assets an owner withdraws from a business for personal use.

Blueprint of Financial Reports

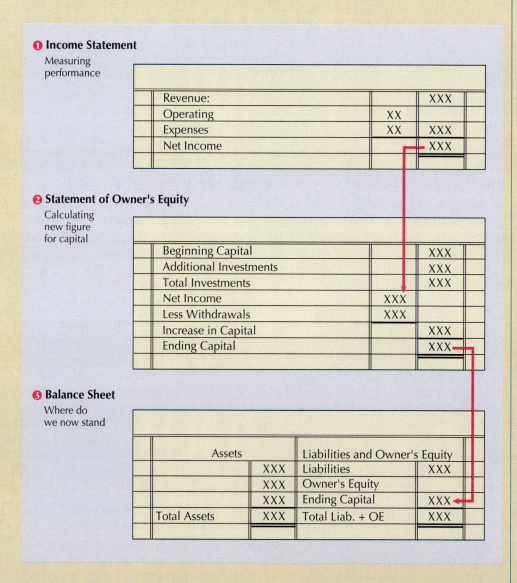

QUESTIONS, MINI EXERCISES, EXERCISES, AND PROBLEMS

Discussion Questions

1. What are the functions of accounting?
2. Define, compare, and contrast sole proprietorships, partnerships, and corporations.
3. How are businesses classified?
4. What is the relationship of bookkeeping to accounting?
5. List the three elements of the basic accounting equation.
6. Define capital.
7. The total of the left-hand side of the accounting equation must equal the total of the right-hand side. True or false? Please explain.
8. A balance sheet tells a company where it is going and how well it will perform. True or false? Please explain.
9. Revenue is an asset. True or false? Please explain.
10. What categories is owner's equity subdivided into?
11. A withdrawal is a business expense. True or false? Please explain.
12. As expenses increase they cause owner's equity to increase. Defend or reject.
13. What does an income statement show?
14. The statement of owner's equity only calculates ending withdrawals. True or false? Please explain.

Mini Exercises

(The blank forms you need are on page 9 of the *Study Guide and Working Papers.*)

Classifying Accounts

1. Classify each of the following items, as an Asset (A), Liability (L), or Part of Owner's Equity (OE).
   a. Land   _____
   b. Accounts Payable   _____
   c. P. Jean, Capital   _____
   d. Supplies   _____
   e. Cash   _____
   f. Computer Equipment   _____

The Accounting Equation

2. Complete
   a. A _____ _____ _____ results when the total of the assets remain the same but the makeup of the assets has changed.
   b. Assets − _____ = Owner's Equity.
   c. Capital does not mean _____.

Shift versus Increase in Assets

3. Identify which transaction results in a shift in assets (S) and which transaction causes an increase in assets (I).
   a. Ace Jewelry bought computer equipment for cash.
   b. Jake's Appliance bought office equipment on account.

The Balance Sheet

4. From the following, calculate what would be the total of assets on the Balance Sheet.

H. Anna, Capital	$8,000
Word Processing Equipment	600
Accounts Payable	2,000
Cash	9,400

The Accounting Equation Expanded

5. From the following, which are subdivisions of Owner's Equity?

    a. Land   _____

    b. B. Flynn, Capital   _____

    c. Accounts Receivable   _____

    d. B. Flynn, Withdrawals   _____

    e. Accounts Payable   _____

    f. Rent Expense   _____

    g. Office Equipment   _____

    h. Hair Salon Fees Earned   _____

Identifying Assets

6. Identify which of the following are *not* assets.

    a. Supplies   _____

    b. Accounts Payable   _____

    c. Legal Fees Earned   _____

    d. Accounts Receivable   _____

The Accounting Equation Expanded

7. Which of the following statements are false?

    a. _____ Revenue is an asset.

    b. _____ Revenue is a subdivision of Owner's Equity.

    c. _____ Revenue provides an inward flow of cash and/or Accounts Receivable.

    d. _____ Withdrawals are part of Total Assets.

Preparing Financial Reports

8. Indicate whether the following items would appear on the Income Statement (IS), Statement of Owner's Equity (OE), or Balance Sheet (BS).

    a. _____ B. Clo, Withdrawals

    b. _____ Supplies

    c. _____ Accounts Payable

    d. _____ Computer Equipment

    e. _____ Commission Fees Earned

    f. _____ Salaries Expense

    g. _____ B. Clo, Capital (Beg.)

    h. _____ Accounts Receivable

Preparing Financial Reports

9. Indicate next to each statement whether it refers to the Income Statement (IS), Statement of Owner's Equity (OE), or Balance Sheet (BS).

a. _____ Calculate new figure for Capital

b. _____ Prepared as of a particular date

c. _____ Statement that is prepared first

d. _____ Report Listing Revenues and Expenses

Exercises

(The forms you need are on pages 10–12 of the *Study Guide and Working Papers*.)

1-1. Complete the following table:

The accounting equation.

ASSETS = LIABILITIES + OWNER'S EQUITY

a. $7,000 = ? + $2,000
b. ? = $6,000 + $8,000
c. $10,000 = $4,000 + ?

Recording transactions into the accounting equation.

1-2. Record the following transactions in the basic accounting equation. Treat each one separately.

ASSETS = LIABILITIES + OWNER'S EQUITY

a. Jim invests $60,000 in company
b. Bought equipment for cash, $600
c. Bought equipment on account, $900

Preparing a balance sheet.

1-3. From the following, prepare a balance sheet for Avon's Cleaners at the end of November 19XX: Cash, $30,000; Cleaning Equipment, $8,000; Accounts Payable, $9,000; A. Avon, Capital?

Recording transactions into the expanded accounting equation.

1-4. Record the following transactions into the expanded accounting equation. The running balance may be omitted for simplicity.

ASSETS			= LIABILITIES +			OWNER'S EQUITY		
Cash +	Accounts Receivable	Computer Equipment	= Accounts Payable	+ B. Wong, Capital	− B. Wong, Withdrawals	+ Revenues	− Expenses	

a. Bill Wong invested $60,000 in a computer company.
b. Bought computer equipment on account, $7,000.
c. Bill Wong paid personal telephone bill from company checkbook, $200.
d. Received cash for services rendered, $14,000.
e. Billed customers for services rendered for month, $30,000.
f. Paid current rent expense, $4,000.
g. Paid supplies expense, $1,500.

Preparing the income statement, statement of owner's equity, and balance sheet.

1-5. From the following account balances, prepare in proper form (a) an income statement for June, (b) a statement of owner's equity, and (c) a balance sheet for French Realty.

Cash	$3,310
Accounts Receivable	1,490
Office Equipment	6,700
Accounts Payable	2,000
S. French, Capital, June 1	8,000
S. French, Withdrawals	40
Professional Fees	2,900

Salaries Expense	500
Utilities Expense	360
Rent Expense	500

Group A Problems

(The forms you need are on pages 13–19 of the *Study Guide and Working Papers.*)

The accounting equation.

1A-1. Maggie Kay decided to open Kay's Realty. Maggie completed the following transactions:

a. Invested $16,000 cash from her personal bank account into the business.

b. Bought equipment for cash, $4,000.

c. Bought additional equipment on account, $1,000.

d. Paid $400 cash to partially reduce what was owed from transaction C.

Check Figure:
Total Assets $16,600

Based on the above information, record these transactions into the basic accounting equation.

Preparing a balance sheet.

1A-2. Joyce Hill is the accountant for Green's Advertising Service. From the following information, her task is to construct a balance sheet as of September 30, 19XX, in proper form. Could you help her?

Building	$35,000
Accounts Payable	30,000
Green, Capital	29,000
Cash	10,000
Equipment	14,000

Check Figure:
Total Assets $59,000

Recording transactions in the expanded accounting equation.

1A-3. At the end of November, Rick Fox decided to open his own typing service. Analyze the following transactions he completed by recording their effects on the expanded accounting equation.

a. Invested $10,000 in his typing service.

b. Bought new office equipment on account, $4,000.

c. Received cash for typing services rendered, $500.

d. Performed typing services on account, $2,100.

e. Paid secretary's salary, $350.

f. Paid office supplies expense for the month, $210.

g. Rent expenses for office due but unpaid, $900.

h. Rick Fox withdrew cash for personal use, $400.

Check Figure:
Total Assets $15,640

Preparing an income statement, statement of owner's equity, and balance sheet.

1A-4. Jane West, owner of West's Stenciling Service, has requested that you prepare from the following balances (a) an income statement for June 19XX, (b) a statement of owner's equity for June, and (c) a balance sheet as of June 30, 19XX.

Cash	$2,300
Accounts Receivable	400
Equipment	685
Accounts Payable	310
J. West, Capital, June 1, 19XX	1,200
J. West, Withdrawals	300
Stenciling Fees	3,000
Advertising Expense	110
Repair Expense	25
Travel Expense	250
Supplies Expense	190
Rent Expense	250

Check Figure:
Total Assets $3,385

Comprehensive problem.

1A-5. John, a retired army officer, opened Tobey's Catering Service. As his accountant, analyze the transactions listed below and present in proper form.

1. The analysis of the transactions by utilizing the expanded accounting equation.

Check Figure:
Total Assets, Nov. 30 $24,060

2. A balance sheet showing the position of the firm before opening on November 1, 19XX.

3. An income statement for the month of November.

4. A statement of owner's equity for November.

5. A balance sheet as of November 30, 19XX.

19XX

Oct.   25 John Tobey invested $20,000 in the catering business from his personal savings account.
27 Bought equipment for cash from Munroe Co., $700
28 Bought additional equipment on account from Ryan Co., $1,000.
29 Paid $600 to Ryan Co. as partial payment of the October 28 transaction.

(You should now prepare your balance sheet as of October 31, 19XX)

Nov.   1 Catered a graduation and immediately collected cash, $2,400.
5 Paid salaries of employees, $690.
8 Prepared desserts for customers on account, $300.
10 Received $100 cash as partial payment of November 8 transaction.
15 Paid telephone bill, $60.
17 Paid his home electric bill from the company's checkbook, $90.
20 Catered a wedding and received cash, $1,800.
25 Bought additional equipment on account, $400.
28 Rent expense due but unpaid, $600.
30 Paid supplies expense, $400.

Group B Problems

(The forms you need are on pages 13–19 of the *Study Guide and Working Papers.*)

The accounting equation.

1B-1. Maggie Kay began a new business called Kay's Realty. The following transactions resulted:

a. Maggie invested $17,000 cash from her personal bank account into the realty company.

Check Figure:
Total Assets $18,000

b. Bought equipment on account, $1,800.

c. Paid $800 cash to partially reduce what was owed from transaction B.

d. Purchased additional equipment for cash, $3,000.

Record these transactions into the basic accounting equation.

Preparing a balance sheet.

1B-2. Joyce Hill has asked you to prepare a balance sheet as of September 30, 19XX, for Green's Advertising Service. Could you assist Joyce?

R. Green, Capital	$19,000
Accounts Payable	70,000
Equipment	41,000
Building	16,000
Cash	32,000

Check Figure:
Total Assets $89,000

Recording transactions in the expanded accounting equation.

1B-3. Rick Fox decided to open his own typing service company at the end of November. Analyze the following transactions by recording their effects on the expanded accounting equation.

a. Rick Fox invested $9,000 in the typing service.

b. Purchased new office equipment on account, $3,000.

c. Received cash for typing services rendered, $1,290.

d. Paid secretary's salary, $310.

e. Billed customers for typing services rendered, $2,690.

f. Paid rent expense for the month, $500.

g. Rick withdrew cash for personal use, $350.

h. Advertising expense due but unpaid, $100.

Check Figure:

Total Assets $14,820

Preparing an income statement, statement of owner's equity, and balance sheet.

1B-4. Jane West, owner of West's Stenciling Service, has requested that you prepare from the following balances (a) an income statement for June 19XX, (b) a statement of owner's equity for June, and (c) a balance sheet as of June 30, 19XX.

Cash	$2,043
Accounts Receivable	1,140
Equipment	540
Accounts Payable	45
J. West, Capital, June 1, 19XX	3,720
J. West, Withdrawals	360
Stenciling Fees	1,098
Advertising Expense	135
Repair Expense	45
Travel Expense	90
Supplies Expense	270
Rent Expense	240

Check Figure:

Total Assets $3,723

Comprehensive Problem.

1B-5. John Tobey, a retired army officer, opened Tobey's Catering Service. As his accountant, analyze the transactions and present the following information in proper form:

1. The analysis of the transactions by utilizing the expanded accounting equation.

2. A balance sheet showing the financial position of the firm before opening on November 1, 19XX.

3. An income statement for the month of November.

4. A statement of owner's equity for November.

5. A balance sheet as of November 30, 19XX.

Check Figure:

Total Assets, Nov. 30 $25,005

19XX

Oct.   25 John Tobey invested $17,500 in the catering business.

27 Bought equipment on account from Munroe Co., $900.

28 Bought equipment for cash from Ryan Co., $1,500.

29 Paid $300 to Munroe Co. as partial payment of the October 27 transaction.

Nov.   1 Catered a business luncheon and immediately collected cash, $2,000.

5 Paid salaries of employees, $350.

8 Provided catering services to Northwest Community College on account, $4,500.

10 Received from Northwest Community College $1,000 cash as partial payment of November 8 transaction.

15 Paid telephone bill, $95.

17 Tobey paid his home mortgage from the company's checkbook, $650.

20 Provided catering services and received cash, $1,800.

25 Bought additional equipment on account, $300.

28 Rent expense due but unpaid, $750.

30 Paid supplies expense, $600.

REAL WORLD APPLICATIONS

1R-1.

You have just been hired to prepare, if possible, an income statement for the year ended December 31, 19XX, for Logan's Window Washing Company. The problem is that Bill Logan kept only the following records (on the back of a piece of cardboard).

Money in:

Window cleaning	$11,376
My investment	1,200
Loan from brother-in-law	4,000

Money out:

Salaries	$5,080
Withdrawals	6,200
Supplies expense	1,400

What I owe or they owe me

A. People that work for me but I still owe salaries to $1,800

B. Owe bank interest of $300

C. Work done but clients still owe me $2,900

D. Advertising bill due but not paid $95

Assume that Logan's Window Washing Company records all revenues when earned and all expenses when incurred.

You feel that it is part of your job to tell Bill how to organize his records better. What would you tell him?

1R-2.

While Jon Lune was on a business trip, he asked Abby Slowe, the bookkeeper for Lune Co., to try to complete a balance sheet for the year ended December 31, 19XX. Abby, who had been on the job only two months, submitted the following.

LUNE CO. FOR THE YEAR ENDED DECEMBER 31, 19XX					
Building	$44,600 00	Accounts Payable	$127,604 00		
Land	72,935 00	Accounts Receivable	104,337 00		
Notes Payable	75,328 00	Auto	14,268 00		
Cash	10,016 00	Desks	6,825 00		
J. Lune, Capital	?	Total Equity	$250,034 00		

1. Could you help Abby fix as well as complete the balance sheet?

2. What written recommendations would you make about the bookkeeper? Should she be retained?

3. Suppose that (a) Jon Lune invested an additional $20,000 in cash as well as additional desks with a value of $8,000 and (b) Lune Co. bought an auto for $6,000 that was originally marked $8,000, paying $2,000 down and issuing a note for the balance. Could you prepare an updated balance sheet? Assume that these two transactions occurred on January 4.

YOU make the call

Critical Thinking/Ethical Case

(The forms you need are on page 8 of the Study Guide and Working Papers.)

1R-3.

Paul Kloss, Accountant for Lowe & Co., traveled to New York on company business. His total expenses came to $350. Paul felt that since the trip extended over the weekend he would "pad" his expense account with an additional $100 of expenses. After all, weekends represent his own time, not the company's. What would you do? Write your specific recommendations to Paul.

ACCOUNTING RECALL
A CUMULATIVE APPROACH

THIS EXAM REVIEWS CHAPTER 1

Your *Study Guide and Working Papers* has a form on page 23 to complete this exam, as well as solutions on page 26. The page references next to each question identify what page to turn back to if you answer the question incorrectly.

PART 1   Vocabulary Review

Match the terms to the appropriate definition or phrase.

Page Ref.

(6)	1. Capital	A. Prepared as of a particular date
(11)	2. Accounts receivable	B. A liability
(2)	3. Sole proprietorship	C. For personal use
(11)	4. Expense	D. Provides an inward flow of assets
(9)	5. Balance sheet	E. Company owned and managed by one person
(11)	6. Revenue	F. Amount owed by customers
(11)	7. Withdrawals	G. Owner's investment
(16)	8. Income statement	H. A cost of running a business
(7)	9. Accounts payable	I. Broken into four subdivisions
(5)	10. Owner's equity	J. Prepared for specific period of time

PART II   True or False (Accounting Theory)

(11)	11. Revenue is an asset.
(14)	12. The four subdivisions of owner's equity are capital, withdrawals, revenue, and expenses.
(14)	13. As expenses increase, owner's equity increases.
(18)	14. Accounts receivable goes on the income statement.
(17)	15. The statement of owner's equity calculates a new figure for capital.

CONTINUING PROBLEM

The following problem will continue from one chapter to the next carrying the balances forward of each month. Each chapter will focus on the learning experience of the chapter and add additional information as the business grows. Forms are on page 24 of the *Study Guide and Working Papers.*

Assignment

1. Set up an expanded accounting equation spreadsheet using the following accounts.

Assets	Liabilities	Owner's Equity
Cash	Accounts Payable	Freedman, Capital
Supplies		Freedman, Withdrawal
Computer Shop Equipment		Service Revenue
Office Equipment		Expenses (notate type)

2. Analyze and record each transaction in the expanded accounting equation.
3. Prepare the financial statements ending July 31 for Eldorado Computer Center.

On July 1, 19XX, Tony Freedman decided to begin his own computer service business. He named the business the Eldorado Computer Center. During the first month Tony conducted the following business transactions:

a) Invested $4,500 of his savings into the business
b) Paid $1,200 (check #8095) for the computer from Multi Systems, Inc.
c) Paid $600 (check # 8096) for office equipment from Office Furniture, Inc.
d) Set up a new account with Office Depot and purchased $250 in office supplies on credit
e) Paid July rent, $400 (check # 8087)
f) Repaired a system for a customer; collected $250
g) Collected $200 for system upgrade labor charge from a customer
h) Electric bill due but unpaid, $85
i) Collected $1,200 for services performed on Taylor Golf computers
j) Tony withdrew $100 (check # 8098) to take his wife Carol out in celebration of opening the new business

DEBITS AND CREDITS

Analyzing and Recording

Business Transactions

THE BIG PICTURE

As the owner of Eldorado Computer Center, Tony Freedman spends most of his time interacting with customers and performing services for them. Only some of Freedman's activities, however, are business transactions. In a business transaction an exchange takes place. Cash is paid for services. Credit is given to customers. Rent is paid for the use of space. Each transaction must be recorded in the accounts of Freedman's business.

In this chapter you will see how every transaction must affect at least two accounts. As you learned in Chapter 1, every account is categorized under a heading from the accounting equation: assets, liabilities, or owner's equity. When you analyze a transaction, you decide not only which accounts change in value, but also whether they increase or decrease. Remember the accounting equation must always be kept in balance, and the key to recording every transaction is the interpretation of what happened.

To analyze transactions accurately and to keep the accounting equation in balance, you will use T accounts and a system of debits and credits. The T account lets us write the value of a transaction as a credit or debit in a standard format. A T account can be easily totaled at any time. The rules for debits and credits assure us that if debits equal credits in every transaction, then the accounting equation will always balance. Whether you use a manual or a computerized accounting system, you must analyze transactions correctly to get correct results.

At the end of each monthly accounting period, Freedman conducts a trial balance, a test of the equality of debits and credits in all his accounts. He can then use the account balances to generate financial statements that he can compare from month to month.

- ◆ **Setting up and organizing a chart of accounts. (p. 41)**
- ◆ **Recording transactions in T accounts according to the rules of debit and credit. (p. 42)**
- ◆ **Preparing a trial balance. (p. 50)**
- ◆ **Preparing financial reports from a trial balance. (p. 52)**

In Chapter 1, we used the expanded accounting equation to document the financial transactions performed by Cathy Hall's law firm. Remember how long it was: the cash column had a long list of pluses and minuses, and there was no quick system of recording and summarizing the increases and decreases of cash or other items. Can you imagine the problem Compaq Computer or Dunkin' Donuts would have if they used the expanded accounting equation to track the thousands of business transactions they do each day?

LEARNING UNIT 2-1
The T Account

Let's look at the problem a little more closely. Each business transaction is recorded in the accounting equation under a specific **account.** There are different accounts for each of the subdivisions of the accounting equation — there are asset accounts; liabilities accounts, expense accounts, revenue accounts, and so on. What is needed is a way to record the increases and decreases in specific account *categories* and yet keep them together in one place. The answer is the **standard account** form (see Fig. 2-1). A standard account is a formal account that includes columns for date, explanation, posting reference, debit, and credit. Each account has a separate form and all transactions affecting that account are recorded on the form. All the business's account forms (which often are referred to as *ledger accounts*) are then placed in a **ledger.** Each page of the ledger contains one account. The ledger may be in the form of a bound or a loose-leaf book. If computers are used, the ledger may be part of a computer printout. For simplicity's sake, we will use the **T account** form. This form got its name because it looks like the letter T. Generally, T accounts are used for demonstration purposes.

FIGURE 2-1
The Standard Account Form is the source of the T account's Shape

Account Title							Account No.
Date	Item	PR	Debit	Date	Item	PR	Credit

Each T account contains three basic parts:

	1	
	Title of Account	
2 **Left side**		**Right side** **3**

All T accounts have this structure. In accounting, the left side of any T account is called the **debit** side.

Left side	
Dr. (debit)	

Just as the word *left* has many meanings, the word *debit* for now in accounting means a position, the left side of an account. Don't think of it as good (+) or bad (−).

Amounts entered on the left side of any account are said to be *debited* to an account. The abbreviation for debit (Dr.) is from the Latin *debere*.

The right side of any T account is called the **credit** side.

	Right side
	Cr. (credit)

Amounts entered on the right side of an account are said to be *credited* to an account. The abbreviation for credit (Cr.) is from the Latin *credere*.

At this point, do not associate the definition of debit and credit with the words *increase* or *decrease*. Think of debit or credit as only indicating a *position* (left or right side) of a T account.

BALANCING AN ACCOUNT

No matter which individual account is being balanced, the procedure used to balance it will be the same.

	Dr.	**Cr.**
Entries →	3,000	300
	500	400
Footings →	3,500	700
Balance	2,800	

In the "real" world, the T account would also include the date of the transaction. The date would appear to the left of the entry:

	Dr.		**Cr.**
4/2	3,000	4/3	300
4/20	500	4/25	400
	3,500		700
Bal.	2,800		

Note that on the debit (left) side the numbers add up to $3,500. On the credit (right) side the numbers add up to $700. The $3,500 and the $700 written in small type are called **footings.** Footings help in calculating the new (or ending) balance. The **ending balance** ($2,800) is placed on the debit or left side, since the balance of the debit side is greater than that of the credit side.

Remember, the ending balance does not tell us anything about increase or decrease. It only tells us that we have an ending balance of $2,800 on the debit side.

Sidebar (left margin):

Debit defined:

1. The *left* side of any T account.
2. A number entered on the left side of any account is said to be *debited* to an account.

Credit defined:

1. The *right* side of any T account.
2. A number entered on the right side of any account is said to be *credited* to an account.

Dollar signs are not used in standard accounts or T accounts. However, dollar signs are used in formal financial reports.

Footings aid in balancing an account. The ending balance is the difference between the footings.

If the balance was greater on the credit side, that is the side the ending balance would be on.

LEARNING UNIT 2-1 REVIEW

AT THIS POINT you should be able to

◆ Define ledger. (p. 37)
◆ State the purpose of a T account. (p. 38)
◆ Identify the three parts of a T account. (p. 38)
◆ Define debit. (p. 38)
◆ Define credit. (p. 38)
◆ Explain footings and calculate the balance of an account. (p. 38)

SELF-REVIEW QUIZ 2-1

(The blank forms you need are on page 27 of the *Study Guide and Working Papers*.)

Respond True or False to the following:

1.

Dr.	Cr.
1,000	100
50	50

The balance of the account is $900 Cr.

2. A credit always means increase.
3. A debit is the left side of any account.
4. A ledger can be prepared manually or by computer.
5. Footings replace the need for debits and credits.

Solutions to Self-Review Quiz 2-1

1. False   **2.** False   **3.** True   **4.** True   **5.** False

Quiz Tip:

Dr. + Dr. ——→ Add to get
Dr. balance

Cr. + Cr. ——→ Add to get
Cr. balance

Dr. − Cr. ——→ Subtract to get
balance for the
larger side.

LEARNING UNIT 2-2

Recording Business Transactions: Debits and Credits

Can you get a queen in checkers? In a baseball game does a runner rounding first base skip second base and run over the pitcher's mound to get to third? No — most of us don't do such things because we follow the rules of the game. Usually we learn the rules first and reflect on the reasons for them afterward. The same is true in accounting.

Instead of first trying to understand all the rules of debit and credit and how they were developed in accounting, it will be easier to learn the rules by "playing the game."

T ACCOUNT ENTRIES FOR ACCOUNTING IN THE ACCOUNTING EQUATION

Have patience. Learning the rules of debit and credit is like learning to play any game — the more you play, the easier it becomes. Table 2-1 shows the rules for the side on which you enter an increase or a decrease for each of the separate accounts in the accounting equation. For example, an increase is entered on the debit side in the asset account, but on the credit side for a liability account.

It might be easier to visualize these rules of debit and credit if we look at them in the T account form, using + to show increase and − to show decrease.

ASSETS	=	LIABILITIES	+	OWNER'S EQUITY						
Dr. | Cr.		Dr. | Cr.	+	Capital	− Withdrawals −	Revenue	− Expenses			
+ | −		− | +		Dr. | Cr.	Dr. | Cr.	Dr. | Cr.	Dr. | Cr.			
				− | +	+ | −	− | +	+ | −			

Rules for Assets Work in the Opposite Direction to Those for Liabilities
When you look at the equation you can see that the rules for assets work in the opposite direction to those for liabilities. That is, for assets the increases appear on the debit side and the decreases are shown on the credit side; the opposite is true for liabilities. As for the owner's equity, the rules for withdrawals and expenses, which *decrease* owner's equity, work in the opposite direction to the rules for capital and revenue, which *increase* owner's equity.

Assets	+ Withdrawals +	Expenses	=	Liabilities	+	Capital	+	Revenue
Dr. | Cr.	Dr. | Cr.	Dr. | Cr.		Dr. | Cr.		Dr. | Cr.		Dr. | Cr.
+ | −	+ | −	+ | −		− | +		− | +		− | +

This setup may help you visualize how the rules for withdrawals and expenses are just the opposite of those for capital and revenue.

A **normal balance of an account** is the side that increases by the rules of debit and credit. For example, the balance of cash is a debit balance, because an asset is increased by a debit. We will discuss normal balances further in Chapter 3.

Balancing the Equation   It is important to remember that any amount(s) entered on the debit side of a T account or accounts also must be on the credit side of another T account or accounts. This ensures that the total amount added to the debit side will equal the total amount added to the credit side, thereby keeping the accounting equation in balance.

Chart of Accounts   Our job is to analyze Cathy Hall's business transactions — the transactions we looked at in Chapter 1 — using a system of accounts guided by the rules of debits and credits that will summarize increases and decreases of individual accounts in the ledger. The goal is to prepare an income statement, statement of owner's equity, and balance sheet for Cathy Hall. Sound familiar? If this system works, the rules of debits and credits and the use of accounts will give us the same answers as in Chapter 1, but with greater ease.

Normal Balance

Dr.	Cr.
Assets	Liabilities
Expenses	Capital
Withdrawals	Revenue

Be sure to follow the rules of debits and credits when recording accounts. They were designed to keep the accounting equation in balance.

TABLE 2-1   RULES OF DEBIT AND CREDIT

Account Category	Increase (Normal Balance)	Decrease
Assets	Debit	Credit
Liabilities	Credit	Debit
Owner's Equity		
Capital	Credit	Debit
Withdrawals	Debit	Credit
Revenue	Credit	Debit
Expenses	Debit	Credit

TABLE 2-2 CHART OF ACCOUNTS FOR CATHY HALL, ATTORNEY AT LAW

Balance Sheet Accounts	
Assets	**Liabilities**
111 Cash	211 Accounts Payable
112 Accounts Receivable	**Owner's Equity**
121 Office Equipment	311 Cathy Hall, Capital
	312 Cathy Hall, Withdrawals

Income Statement Accounts	
Revenue	**Expenses**
411 Legal Fees	511 Salaries Expense
	512 Rent Expense
	513 Advertising Expense

The chart of accounts aids in locating and identifying accounts quickly.

Large companies may have up to four digits assigned to each title.

Cathy's accountant developed what is called a **chart of accounts.** The chart of accounts is a numbered list of all of the business's accounts. It allows accounts to be located quickly. In Cathy's business, for example, 100s are assets, 200s are liabilities, and so on. As you see in Table 2-2, each separate asset and liability has its own number. Note the chart may be expanded as the business grows.

THE TRANSACTION ANALYSIS: FIVE STEPS

We will analyze the transactions in Cathy Hall's law firm using a teaching device called a *transaction analysis chart* to record these five steps. (Keep in mind that the transaction analysis chart is not a part of any formal accounting system.) There are five steps to analyzing each business transaction:

Steps to analyze and record transactions. Steps 1 and 2 will come from the chart of accounts.

Remember the rules of debit and credit only tell us on which side to place information. Whether the debit or credit represents increases or decreases depends on the account category—assets, liabilities, capital, and so on. Think of a business transaction as an exchange—you get something and you give or part with something.

Step 1: Determine which accounts are affected. Example: cash, accounts payable, rent expense. A transaction always affects at least two accounts.

Step 2: Determine which categories the accounts belong to—assets, liabilities, capital, withdrawals, revenue, or expenses. Example: cash is an asset.

Step 3: Determine whether the accounts increase or decrease. Example: If you receive cash, that account is increasing.

Step 4: What do the rules of debits and credits say (Table 2-1)?

Step 5: What does the T account look like? Place amounts into accounts either on the left or right side depending on the rules in Table 2-1.

This is how the five-step analysis looks in chart form:

1	2	3	4	5
Accounts Affected	**Category**	**↓ or ↑ (decrease) (increase)**	**Rules of Dr. and Cr.**	**Appearance of T Accounts**

Let us emphasize a major point: *Do not try to debit or credit an account until you have gone through the first three steps of the transaction analysis.*

APPLYING THE TRANSACTION ANALYSIS TO CATHY HALL'S LAW PRACTICE

Transaction (A) August 28: Cathy Hall invests $7,000 cash and $800 of office equipment in the business

1 Accounts Affected	2 Category	3 ↓ ↑	4 Rules of Dr. and Cr.	5 Appearance of T Accounts
Cash	Asset	↑	Dr.	**Cash 111** (A) 7,000
Office Equipment	Asset	↑	Dr.	**Office Equipment 121** (A) 800
Cathy Hall, Capital	Capital	↑	Cr.	**Cathy Hall, Capital 311** 7,800 (A)

Note in column 3 of the chart: It doesn't matter if both arrows go up, as long as the sum of the debits equals the sum of the credits in the T accounts in column 5.

Note again that every transaction affects at least two T accounts, and that the total amount added to the debit side(s) must equal the total amount added to the credit side(s) of the T accounts of each transaction.

Analysis of Transaction A

Step 1: Which accounts are affected? The law firm receives its cash and office equipment, so three accounts are involved: Cash, Office Equipment, and Cathy Hall, Capital. These account titles come from the chart of accounts.

Step 2: Which categories do these accounts belong to? Cash and Office Equipment are assets. Cathy Hall, Capital, is capital.

Step 3: Are the accounts increasing or decreasing? The Cash and Office Equipment, both assets, are increasing in the business. The rights or claims of Cathy Hall, Capital, are also increasing, since she invested money and office equipment in the business.

Step 4: What do the rules say? According to the rules of debit and credit, an increase in assets (Cash and Office Equipment) is a debit. An increase in Capital is a credit. Note that the total dollar amount of debits will equal the total dollar amount of credits when the T accounts are updated in column 5.

Step 5: What does the T account look like? The amount for Cash and Office Equipment is entered on the debit side. The amount for Cathy Hall, Capital, goes on the credit side.

A transaction that involves more than one credit or more than one debit is called a **compound entry.** This first transaction of Cathy Hall's law firm is a compound entry; it involves a debit of $7,000 to Cash and a debit of $800 to Office Equipment (as well as a credit of $7,800 to Cathy Hall, Capital).

There is a name for this double-entry analysis of transactions, where two or more accounts are affected and the total of debits and credits is equal. It is called **double-entry bookkeeping.** This double-entry system helps in checking the recording of business transactions.

As we continue, the explanations will be brief, but do not forget to apply the five steps in analyzing and recording each business transaction.

Double-entry bookkeeping system: The total of all debits is equal to the total of all credits.

Transaction (B) **Aug. 29: Law practice bought office equipment for cash, $900.**

1 Accounts Affected	2 Category	3 ↓ ↑	4 Rules of Dr. and Cr.	5 T Account Update
Office Equipment	Asset	↑	Dr.	**Office Equipment 121** (A) 800 (B) 900
Cash	Asset	↓	Cr.	**Cash 111** (A) 7,000 | 900 (B)

Analysis of Transaction B

Step 1: The law firm paid cash for the office equipment it received. The accounts involved in the transaction are Cash and Office Equipment.

Step 2: The accounts belong to these categories: Office Equipment is an asset; Cash is an asset.

Step 3: The asset Office Equipment is increasing. The asset Cash is decreasing — it is being reduced in order to buy the office equipment.

Step 4: An increase in the asset Office Equipment is a debit; a decrease in the asset Cash is a credit.

Step 5: When the amounts are placed in the T accounts, the amount for Office Equipment goes on the debit side and the amount for Cash on the credit side.

Transaction (C) **Aug. 30: Bought more office equipment on account, $400.**

1 Accounts Affected	2 Category	3 ↓ ↑	4 Rules of Dr. and Cr.	5 T Account Update
Office Equipment	Asset	↑	Dr.	**Office Equipment 121** (A) 800 (B) 900 (C) 400
Accounts Payable	Liability	↑	Cr.	**Accounts Payable 211** | 400 (C)

Analysis of Transaction C

Step 1: The law firm receives office equipment by promising to pay in the future. An obligation or liability, Accounts Payable, is created.

Step 2: Office Equipment is an asset. Accounts Payable is a liability.

Step 3: The asset Office Equipment is increasing; the liability Accounts Payable is increasing because the law firm is increasing what it owes.

Step 4: An increase in the asset Office Equipment is a debit. An increase in the liability Accounts Payable is a credit.

Step 5: Enter the amount for Office Equipment on the debit side of the T account. The amount for the Accounts Payable goes on the credit side.

Transaction (D) Sept. 1–30: Provided legal services for cash, $3,000.

1 Accounts Affected	2 Category	3 ↓ ↑	4 Rules of Dr. and Cr.	5 T Account Update
Cash	Asset	↑	Dr.	**Cash 111** (A) 7,000 | 900 (B) (D) 3,000 |
Legal Fees	Revenue	↑	Cr.	**Legal Fees 411** | 3,000 (D)

Analysis of Transaction D

Step 1: The firm has earned revenue from legal services and receives $3,000 in cash.

Step 2: Cash is an asset. Legal Fees are revenue.

Step 3: Cash, an asset, is increasing. Legal Fees, or revenue, are also increasing.

Step 4: An increase in Cash, an asset, is debited. An increase in Legal Fees, or revenue, is credited.

Step 5: Enter the amount for Cash on the debit side of the T account. Enter the amount for Legal Fees on the credit side.

Transaction (E) Sept. 1–30: Provided legal services on account, $4,000.

1 Accounts Affected	2 Category	3 ↓ ↑	4 Rules of Dr. and Cr.	5 T Account Update
Accounts Receivable	Asset	↑	Dr.	**Accounts Receivable 112** (E) 4,000 |
Legal Fees	Revenue	↑	Cr.	**Legal Fees 411** | 3,000 (D) | 4,000 (E)

Analysis of Transaction E

Step 1: The law practice has earned revenue but has not yet received payment (cash). The amounts owed by these clients are called Accounts Receivable. Revenue is earned at the time the legal services are provided, whether payment is received then or will be received sometime in the future.

Step 2: Accounts Receivable is an asset. Legal Fees are revenue.

Step 3: Accounts Receivable is increasing because the law practice has increased the amount owed to it for legal fees that have been earned but not paid. Legal Fees, or revenue, are increasing.

Step 4: An increase in the asset Accounts Receivable is a debit. An increase in Revenue is a credit.

Step 5: Enter the amount for Accounts Receivable on the debit side of the T account. The amount for Legal Fees goes on the credit side.

Transaction (F) Sept. 1–30: Received $700 cash from clients for services rendered previously on account.

1 Accounts Affected	2 Category	3 ↓ ↑	4 Rules of Dr. and Cr.	5 T Account Update
Cash	Asset	↑	Dr.	**Cash 111** (A) 7,000 | 900 (B) (D) 3,000 | (F) 700 |
Accounts Receivable	Asset	↓	Cr.	**Accounts Receivable 112** (E) 4,000 | 700 (F)

Analysis of Transaction F

Step 1: The law firm collects $700 in cash from previous revenue earned. Since the revenue is recorded at the time it is earned, and not when the payment is made, in this transaction we are concerned only with the payment, which affects the Cash and Accounts Receivable accounts.

Step 2: Cash is an asset. Accounts Receivable is an asset.

Step 3: Since clients are paying what is owed, Cash (asset) is increasing and the amount owed (Accounts Receivable) is decreasing (the total amount owed by clients to Hall is going down). This transaction results in a shift in assets, more Cash for less Accounts Receivable.

Step 4: An increase in Cash, an asset, is a debit. A decrease in Accounts Receivable, an asset, is a credit.

Step 5: Enter the amount for Cash on the debit side of the T account. The amount for Accounts Receivable goes on the credit side.

Transaction (G) Sept. 1–30: Paid salaries expense, $600.

1 Accounts Affected	2 Category	3 ↓ ↑	4 Rules of Dr. and Cr.	5 T Account Update
Salaries Expense	Expense	↑	Dr.	**Salaries Expense 511** (G) 600 |
Cash	Asset	↓	Cr.	**Cash 111** (A) 7,000 | 900 (B) (D) 3,000 | 600 (G) (F) 700 |

Analysis of Transaction G

Step 1: The law firm pays $600 worth of salaries expense by cash.

Step 2: Salaries Expense is an expense. Cash is an asset.

Step 3: The Salaries Expense of the law firm is increasing, which results in a decrease in Cash.

Step 4: An increase in Salaries Expense, an expense, is a debit. A decrease in Cash, an asset, is a credit.

Step 5: Enter the amount for Salaries Expense on the debit side of the T account. The amount for Cash goes on the credit side.

Transaction (H)   Sept. 1–30: Paid rent expense, $700.

1 Accounts Affected	2 Category	3 ↓ ↑	4 Rules of Dr. and Cr.	5 T Account Update
Rent Expense	Expense	↑	Dr.	**Rent Expense 512** (H) 700	
Cash	Asset	↓	Cr.	**Cash 111** (A) 7,000 | 900 (B) (D) 3,000 | 600 (G) (F) 700 | 700 (H)

Analysis of Transaction H

Step 1: The law firm's rent expenses are paid in cash.

Step 2: Rent is an expense. Cash is an asset.

Step 3: The Rent Expense increases the expenses, and the payment for the Rent Expense decreases the cash.

Step 4: An increase in Rent Expense, an expense, is a debit. A decrease in Cash, an asset, is a credit.

Step 5: Enter the amount for Rent Expense on the debit side of the T account. Place the amount for Cash on the credit side.

Transaction (I)   Sept. 1–30: Received a bill for Advertising Expense
(to be paid next month), $300.

1 Accounts Affected	2 Category	3 ↓ ↑	4 Rules of Dr. and Cr.	5 T Account Update
Advertising Expense	Expense	↑	Dr.	**Advertising Expense 513** (I) 300 |
Accounts Payable	Liability	↑	Cr.	**Accounts Payable 211** | 400 (C) | 300 (I)

Analysis of Transaction I

Step 1: The advertising bill has come in and payment is due but has not yet been made. Therefore the accounts involved here are Advertising Expense and Accounts Payable; the expense has created a liability.

Step 2: Advertising Expense is an expense. Accounts Payable is a liability.

Step 3: Both the expense and the liability are increasing.

Step 4: An increase in an expense is a debit. An increase in a liability is a credit.

Step 5: Enter the amount for Advertising Expense on the debit side of the T Account. Enter amount for Accounts Payable on the credit side.

Transaction (J) Sept. 1–30: Hall withdrew cash for personal use, $200.

1 Accounts Affected	2 Category	3 ↓ ↑	4 Rules of Dr. and Cr.	5 T Account Update
Cathy Hall, Withdrawals	Withdrawals	↑	Dr.	**Cathy Hall, Withdrawals, 312** (J) 200 |
Cash	Asset	↓	Cr.	**Cash 111** (A) 7,000 | 900 (B) (D) 3,000 | 600 (G) (F) 700 | 700 (H) | 200 (J)

Analysis of Transaction J

Step 1: Cathy Hall withdraws cash from business for *personal* use. This withdrawal is not a business expense.

Step 2: This transaction affects Withdrawal and Cash accounts.

Step 3: Cathy has increased what she has withdrawn from the business for personal use. The business cash has been decreased.

Step 4: An increase in withdrawals is a debit. A decrease in cash is a credit. (*Remember:* Withdrawals go on the statement of owner's equity; expenses go on the income statement.)

Step 5: Enter the amount for Cathy Hall, Withdrawals on the debit side of the T account. The amount for Cash goes on the credit side.

Withdrawals are always increased by debits.

SUMMARY OF TRANSACTIONS FOR CATHY HALL

ASSETS		= LIABILITIES	+		OWNER'S EQUITY				
Cash 111	=	**Accounts Payable 211**	+	**Capital**	− **Withdrawals**	+ **Revenue**		− **Expenses**	
(A) 7,000 | 900 (B)		| 400 (C)	+	**Cathy Hall, Capital 311**	**Cathy Hall, Withdrawals 312**	**Legal Fees 411**		**Salaries Expense 511**	
(D) 3,000 | 600 (G)		| 300 (I)		−	+	−			
(F) 700 | 700 (H)				| 7,800 (A)	(J) 200 |	| 3,000 (D)		(G) 600 |	
| 200 (J)						| 4,000 (E)		**Rent Expense 512**	
Accounts Receivable 112								−	
(E) 4,000 | 700 (F)								(H) 700 |	
Office Equipment 121								**Advertising Expense 513**	
(A) 800 |								−	
(B) 900 |								(I) 300 |	
(C) 400 |									

LEARNING UNIT 2-2 REVIEW

AT THIS POINT you should be able to

◆ State the rules of debit and credit. (p. 40)
◆ List the five steps of a transaction analysis. (p. 41)
◆ Show how to fill out a transaction analysis chart. (p. 41)
◆ Explain double-entry bookkeeping. (p. 42)

SELF-REVIEW QUIZ 2-2

(The blank forms you need are on pages 27 and 28 of the *Study Guide and Working Papers*.)

O'Malley Company uses the following accounts from its chart of accounts: Cash (111), Accounts Receivable (112), Equipment (121), Accounts Payable (211), Bill O'Malley, Capital (311), Bill O'Malley, Withdrawals (312), Professional Fees (411), Utilities Expense (511), and Salaries Expense (512).

Record the following transactions into transaction analysis charts.

a. Bill O'Malley invested in the business $900 cash and equipment worth $600 from his personal assets.
b. Billed clients for services rendered, $9,000.
c. Utilities bill due but unpaid, $125.
d. Bill O'Malley withdrew cash for personal use, $120.
e. Paid salaries expense, $250.

Solution to Self-Review Quiz 2-2

A.

1 Accounts Affected	2 Category	3 ↓ ↑	4 Rules of Dr. and Cr.	5 T Account Update
Cash	Asset	↑	Dr.	**Cash 111** (A)　900
Equipment	Asset	↑	Dr.	**Equipment 121** (A)　600
Bill O'Malley, Capital	Capital	↑	Cr.	**Bill O'Malley, Capital 311** 1,500　(A)

B.

1 Accounts Affected	2 Category	3 ↓ ↑	4 Rules of Dr. and Cr.	5 T Account Update
Accounts Receivable	Asset	↑	Dr.	**Accounts Receivable 112** (B)　9,000
Professional Fees	Revenue	↑	Cr.	**Professional Fees 411** 9,000　(B)

Quiz Tip:

Column 1: Row titles must come from the chart of accounts. The order doesn't matter as long as the total of all debits equals the total of all credits.

When a business bills a client, it creates an asset—a claim for payment called an "account receivable."

48

C.

1 Accounts Affected	2 Category	3 ↓ ↑	4 Rules of Dr. and Cr.	5 T Account Update
Utilities Expense	Expense	↑	Dr.	Utilities Expense 511 (C) 125
Accounts Payable	Liability	↑	Cr.	Accounts Payable 211 125 (C)

Record an expense when it happens whether it is paid for or not.

D.

1 Accounts Affected	2 Category	3 ↓ ↑	4 Rules of Dr. and Cr.	5 T Account Update
Bill O'Malley, Withdrawals	Withdrawals	↑	Dr.	Bill O'Malley, Withdrawals 312 (D) 120
Cash	Asset	↓	Cr.	Cash 111 (A) 900 120 (D)

Think of withdrawals as always increasing.

E.

1 Accounts Affected	2 Category	3 ↓ ↑	4 Rules of Dr. and Cr.	5 T Account Update
Salaries Expense	Expense	↑	Dr.	Salaries Expense 512 (E) 250
Cash	Asset	↓	Cr.	Cash 111 (A) 900 120 (D) 250 (E)

Think of expenses as always increasing.

LEARNING UNIT 2-3
The Trial Balance and Preparation of Financial Reports

Let us look at all the transactions we have discussed, arranged by T accounts and recorded using the rules of debit and credit. (See the equation at the top of page 50.)

This grouping of accounts is much easier to use than the expanded accounting equation because all of the transactions that affect a particular account are in one place.

As we saw in Learning Unit 2-2, when all the transactions are recorded in the accounts, the total of all the debits should be equal to the total of all the credits. (If they are not, the accountant must go back and find the error by checking the numbers and adding every column again.)

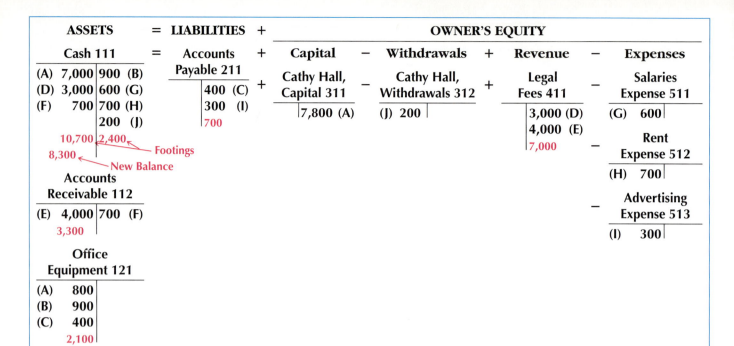

ASSETS	=	LIABILITIES	+	OWNER'S EQUITY					

ASSETS = **LIABILITIES** + **OWNER'S EQUITY**

Cash 111 = **Accounts Payable 211** + **Capital** − **Withdrawals** + **Revenue** − **Expenses**

Cash 111
- (A) 7,000 | 900 (B)
- (D) 3,000 | 600 (G)
- (F) 700 | 700 (H)
- | 200 (J)
- 10,700 | 2,400 ← Footings
- 8,300 ← New Balance

Accounts Payable 211
- | 400 (C)
- | 300 (I)
- | 700

Capital — Cathy Hall, Capital 311
- | 7,800 (A)

Withdrawals — Cathy Hall, Withdrawals 312
- (J) 200 |

Revenue — Legal Fees 411
- | 3,000 (D)
- | 4,000 (E)
- | 7,000

Expenses — Salaries Expense 511
- (G) 600 |

Accounts Receivable 112
- (E) 4,000 | 700 (F)
- 3,300

Rent Expense 512
- (H) 700 |

Office Equipment 121
- (A) 800 |
- (B) 900 |
- (C) 400 |
- 2,100

Advertising Expense 513
- (I) 300 |

THE TRIAL BALANCE

Footings are used to obtain the balance of each side of the T account. They are not needed if there is only one entry in the account.

Footings are used to obtain the balance of each side of every T account that has more than one entry. The footings are used to find the ending balance. The ending balances are used to prepare a **trial balance.** The trial balance is not a financial report, although it is used to prepare financial reports. The trial balance lists all of the accounts with their balances in the same order as they appear in the chart of accounts. It proves the accuracy of the ledger. For example, look at the Cash account above. The footing for the debit side is $10,700 and the footing for the credit side is $2,400. Since the debit side is larger, we subtract $2,400 from

Dunkin' Donuts shop owners have many accounts to deal with: food costs, payroll, rent, utilities, supplies, advertising, promotion, and—biggest of all—cash. It's critical for them to keep debits and credits straight. If not, both they and Dunkin' Donuts Inc. could lose a lot of money—fast.

Many of Dunkin' Donuts smaller shop owners keep their own accounts, while most of the larger shops use accountants. In some areas of the United States, some accountants actually specialize in handling Dunkin' Donuts accounts for individual shop owners. But many shop owners, especially those with just one shop, handle the books themselves, both to save money and to keep a finger on the pulse of their business.

The Balance Sheet for each shop must be submitted to the zone's Business Consultant on the last Saturday of each month at noon. Fred had once been late in sending the Balance Sheet because he mistakenly debited both cash and supplies when he paid for an order of paper cups. Fred had been angry at himself for having made such a basic error. Dwayne had been understanding, but

TIME TO PUT THE DEBITS ON THE LEFT . . .

had encouraged him to review the rules for recording debits and credits.

"It's only going to get harder, Fred," Dwayne had said. "Once you computerize your accounts, debits and credits are not as visible as they are with your paper system. You will only enter the payables, and the computer does the other side of the Balance Sheet. So a thorough knowledge of debits and credits is critical to understanding the [computerized] system. And the way you're growing the business, it won't be long before you'll want to switch to the computer."

DISCUSSION QUESTIONS

1. Why is the cash account so important in Fred's business?
2. Why do you think that most of the larger shops use accountants to do their books instead of doing them themselves?
3. Is the difference between debits and credits important to shop owners who don't do their own books?

FIGURE 2-2
Trial Balance for
Cathy Hall's Law Firm

Since this is not a formal report, there is no need to use dollar signs; however, the single and double lines under subtotals and final totals are still used for clarity.

CATHY HALL, ATTORNEY AT LAW TRIAL BALANCE SEPTEMBER 30, 19XX		
	Dr.	Cr.
Cash	8 3 0 0 00	
Accounts Receivable	3 3 0 0 00	
Office Equipment	2 1 0 0 00	
Accounts Payable		7 0 0 00
Cathy Hall, Capital		7 8 0 0 00
Cathy Hall, Withdrawals	2 0 0 00	
Legal Fees		7 0 0 0 00
Salaries Expense	6 0 0 00	
Rent Expense	7 0 0 00	
Advertising Expense	3 0 0 00	
Totals	15 5 0 0 00	15 5 0 0 00

As mentioned earlier, the ending balance of cash, $8,300, is a *normal balance* because it is on the side that increases the asset account.

Only the ending balance of each account is listed.

$10,700 to arrive at an *ending balance* of $8,300. Now look at the Rent Expense account. There is no need for a footing because there is only one entry. The amount itself is the ending balance. When the ending balance has been found for every account, we should be able to show that the total of all debits equals the total of all credits.

In the ideal situation, businesses would take a trial balance every day. The larger number of transactions most businesses conduct each day makes this impractical. Instead, trial balances are prepared periodically.

Keep in mind that the figure for capital might not be the beginning figure if any additional investment has taken place during the period. You can tell this by looking at the capital account in the ledger.

A more detailed discussion of the trial balance will be provided in the next chapter. For now, notice the heading, how the accounts are listed, the debits in the left column, the credits in the right, and the fact that the total of debits is equal to the total of credits.

A trial balance of Cathy Hall's accounts is shown in Figure 2-2.

PREPARING FINANCIAL REPORTS

The trial balance is used to prepare the financial reports. The diagram in Figure 2-3 on page 52 shows how financial reports can be prepared from a trial balance. Remember, financial reports do not have debit or credit columns. The left column is used only to subtotal numbers.

LEARNING UNIT 2-3 REVIEW

AT THIS POINT you should be able to

- ◆ Explain the role of footings. (p. 50)
- ◆ Prepare a trial balance from a set of accounts. (p. 50)
- ◆ Prepare financial reports from a trial balance. (p. 52)

SELF-REVIEW QUIZ 2-3

(The blank forms you need are on page 29 of the *Study Guide and Working Papers*.)

As the bookkeeper of Pam's Hair Salon, you are to prepare from the following accounts on June 30, 19XX (1) a trial balance as of June 30; (2)

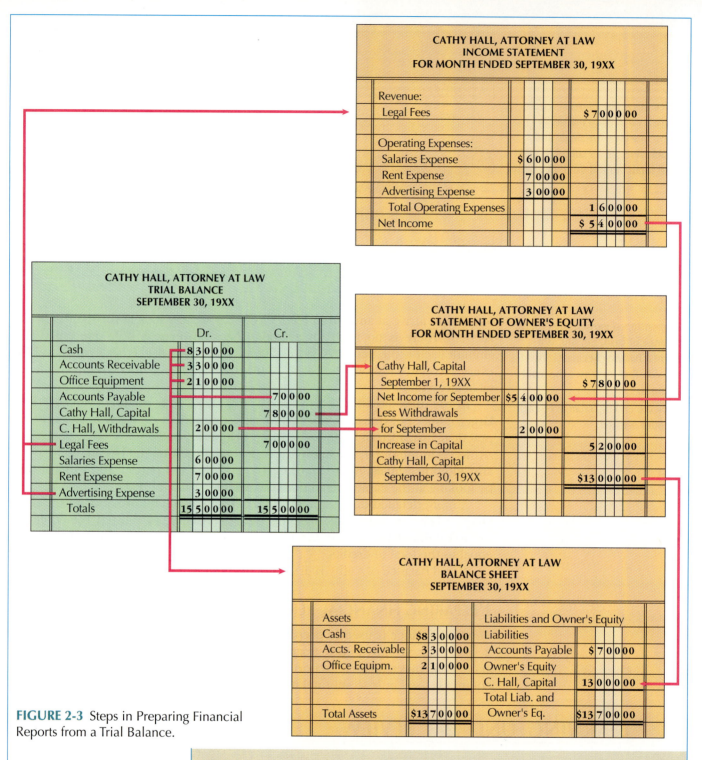

FIGURE 2-3 Steps in Preparing Financial Reports from a Trial Balance.

an income statement for the month ended June 30; (3) a statement of owner's equity for the month ended June 30; and (4) a balance sheet as of June 30, 19XX.

Cash 111		Accounts Payable 211		Salon Fees 411	
4,500	300	300	700		3,500
2,000	100				1,000
1,000	1,200				
300	1,300				
	2,600				

Accounts Receivable 131		Pam Jay, Capital 311		Rent Expense 511	
1,000	300		4,000*	1,200	

* No additional investments.

Salon Equipment 131

| 700 | |

Pam Jay, Withdrawals 321

| 100 | |

Salon Supplies Expense 521

| 1,300 | |

Salaries Expense 531

| 2,600 | |

Solution to Self-Review Quiz 2-3

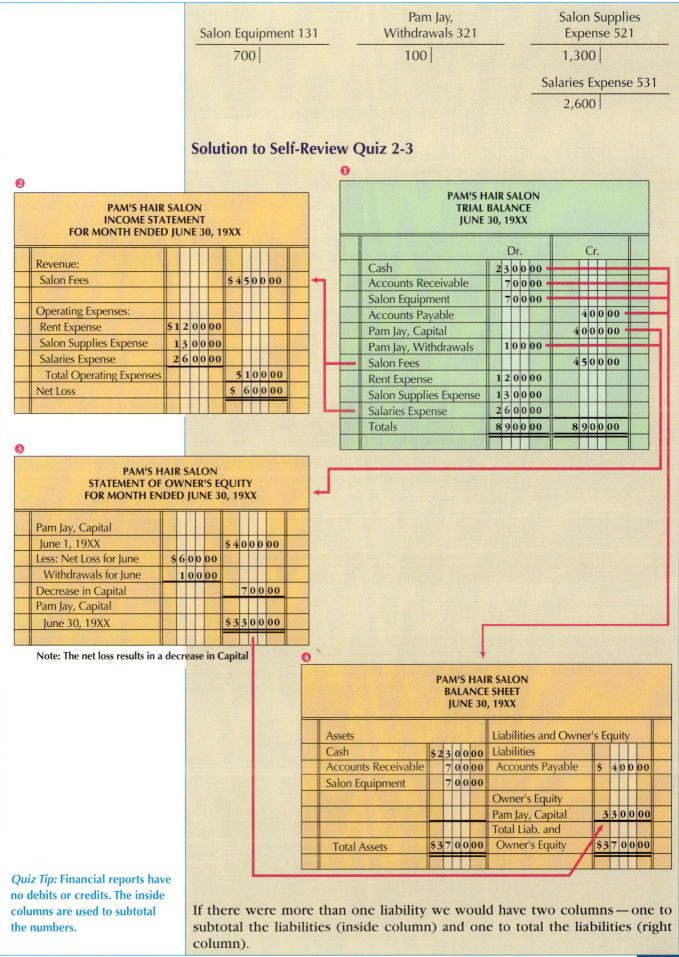

❷

PAM'S HAIR SALON
INCOME STATEMENT
FOR MONTH ENDED JUNE 30, 19XX

Revenue:			
Salon Fees			$4 50 0 00
Operating Expenses:			
Rent Expense	$1 2 0 0 00		
Salon Supplies Expense	1 3 0 0 00		
Salaries Expense	2 6 0 0 00		
Total Operating Expenses		5 1 0 0 00	
Net Loss		$ 6 0 0 00	

❶

PAM'S HAIR SALON
TRIAL BALANCE
JUNE 30, 19XX

	Dr.	Cr.
Cash	2 3 0 0 00	
Accounts Receivable	7 0 0 00	
Salon Equipment	7 0 0 00	
Accounts Payable		4 0 0 00
Pam Jay, Capital		4 0 0 0 00
Pam Jay, Withdrawals	1 0 0 00	
Salon Fees		4 5 0 0 00
Rent Expense	1 2 0 0 00	
Salon Supplies Expense	1 3 0 0 00	
Salaries Expense	2 6 0 0 00	
Totals	8 9 0 0 00	8 9 0 0 00

❸

PAM'S HAIR SALON
STATEMENT OF OWNER'S EQUITY
FOR MONTH ENDED JUNE 30, 19XX

Pam Jay, Capital			
June 1, 19XX		$4 0 0 0 00	
Less: Net Loss for June	$ 6 0 0 00		
Withdrawals for June	1 0 0 00		
Decrease in Capital		7 0 0 00	
Pam Jay, Capital			
June 30, 19XX		$3 3 0 0 00	

Note: The net loss results in a decrease in Capital

❹

PAM'S HAIR SALON
BALANCE SHEET
JUNE 30, 19XX

Assets		Liabilities and Owner's Equity	
Cash	$2 3 0 0 00	Liabilities	
Accounts Receivable	7 0 0 00	Accounts Payable	$ 4 0 0 00
Salon Equipment	7 0 0 00		
		Owner's Equity	
		Pam Jay, Capital	3 3 0 0 00
		Total Liab. and	
Total Assets	$3 7 0 0 00	Owner's Equity	$3 7 0 0 00

Quiz Tip: Financial reports have no debits or credits. The inside columns are used to subtotal the numbers.

If there were more than one liability we would have two columns — one to subtotal the liabilities (inside column) and one to total the liabilities (right column).

COMPREHENSIVE DEMONSTRATION PROBLEM WITH SOLUTION TIPS

(The blank forms you need are on pages 32–34 of the *Study Guide and Working Papers.*)

The chart of accounts of Mel's Delivery Service includes the following: Cash, 111; Accounts Receivable, 112; Office Equipment, 121; Delivery Trucks, 122; Accounts Payable, 211; Mel Free, Capital, 311; Mel Free, Withdrawals, 312; Delivery Fees Earned, 411; Advertising Expense, 511; Gas Expense, 512; Salaries Expense, 513; and Telephone Expense, 514. The following transactions resulted for Mel's Delivery Service during the month of July:

Transaction A: Mel invested $10,000 in the business from his personal savings account.

Transaction B: Bought delivery trucks on account, $17,000.

Transaction C: Advertising bill received but unpaid, $700.

Transaction D: Bought office equipment for cash, $1,200.

Transaction E: Received cash for delivery services rendered, $15,000.

Transaction F: Paid salaries expense, $3,000.

Transaction G: Paid gas expense for company trucks, $1,250.

Transaction H: Billed customers for delivery services rendered, $4,000.

Transaction I: Paid telephone bill, $300.

Transaction J: Received $3,000 as partial payment of transaction H.

Transaction K: Mel paid home telephone bill from company checkbook, $150.

As Mel's newly employed accountant, you must do the following:

1. Set up T accounts in a ledger.
2. Record transactions in the T accounts. (Place the letter of the transaction next to the entry.)
3. Foot the T accounts where appropriate.
4. Prepare a trial balance at the end of July.
5. Prepare from the trial balance, in proper form, (a) an income statement for the month of July, (b) a statement of owner's equity, and (c) a balance sheet as of July 31, 19XX.

Solution to Demonstration Problem

1, 2, 3.

GENERAL LEDGER

Cash 111				Acc. Payable 211			Advertising Expense 511		
(A) 10,000	1,200	(D)			17,000	(B)	(C)	700	
(E) 15,000	3,000	(F)			700	(C)			
(J) 3,000	1,250	(G)			17,700				
28,000	300	(I)							
22,100	150	(K)							
	5,900								

Acc. Receivable 112			
(H) 4,000	3,000	(J)	
1,000			

Mel Free, Capital 311	
	10,000 (A)

Gas Expense 512	
(G) 1,250	

Office Equipment 121	
(D) 1,200	

Mel Free, Withdrawals 312	
(K) 150	

Salaries Expense 513	
(F) 3,000	

Delivery Trucks 122	
(B) 17,000	

Delivery Fees Earned 411	
	15,000 (E)
	4,000 (H)
	19,000

Telephone Expense 514	
(I) 300	

Solution Tips to Recording Transactions

A.	Cash	A	↑	Dr.
	Mel Free, Capital	Cap.	↑	Cr.

F.	Salaries Expense	Exp.	↑	Dr.
	Cash	A	↓	Cr.

B.	Delivery Trucks	A	↑	Dr.
	Acc. Payable	L	↑	Cr.

G.	Gas Expense	Exp.	↑	Dr.
	Cash	A	↓	Cr.

C.	Advertising Expense	Exp.	↑	Dr.
	Acc. Payable	L	↑	Cr.

H.	Acc. Receivable	A	↑	Dr.
	Del. Fees Earned	Rev.	↑	Cr.

D.	Office Equipment	A	↑	Dr.
	Cash	A	↓	Cr.

I.	Tel. Expense	Exp.	↑	Dr.
	Cash	A	↓	Cr.

E.	Cash	A	↑	Dr.
	Del. Fees Earned	Rev.	↑	Cr.

J.	Cash	A	↑	Dr.
	Acc. Receivable	A	↓	Cr.

K.	Mel Free, Withd.	Withd.	↑	Dr.
	Cash	A	↓	Cr.

4.

Mel's Delivery Service
Trial Balance
July 31, 19XX

	Dr.	Cr.
Cash	22,100	
Accounts Receivable	1,000	
Office Equipment	1,200	
Delivery Trucks	17,000	
Accounts Payable		17,700

Mel Free, Capital		10,000
Mel Free, Withdrawals	150	
Delivery Fees Earned		19,000
Advertising Expense	700	
Gas Expense	1,250	
Salaries Expense	3,000	
Telephone Expense	300	
TOTALS	46,700	46,700

Solution Tips to Footings and Preparation of a Trial Balance

3. Footings: Cash   Add left side $28,000

Add right side $5,900

Take difference $22,100 and stay on side that is larger

Accounts Payable   Add $17,000 + $700 and stay on same side. Total is $17,700

4. Trial balance is a list of the ledger's ending balances. The list is in the same order as the chart of accounts. Each title has only one number listed either as a debit or credit balance.

5a.

Mel's Delivery Service
Income Statement
for Month Ended July 31, 19XX

Revenue:		
Delivery Fees Earned		$19,000
Operating Expenses:		
Advertising Expense	$700	
Gas Expense	1,250	
Salaries Expense	3,000	
Telephone Expense	300	
Total Operating Expenses		5,250
Net Income		$13,750

b.

Mel's Delivery Service
Statement of Owner's Equity
for Month Ended July 31, 19XX

Mel Free, Capital July 1, 19XX		$10,000
Net Income for July	$13,750	
Less Withdrawals for July	150	
Increase in Capital		13,600
Mel Free, Capital, July 31, 19XX		$23,600

c.

Mel's Delivery Service
Balance Sheet
July 31, 19XX

Assets		Liabilities and Owner's Equity	
Cash	$ 22,100	Liabilities	
Accounts Receivable	1,000	Accounts Payable	$17,700
Office Equipment	1,200		
Delivery Trucks	17,000	Owner's Equity	
		Mel Free, Capital	23,600
		Total Liabilities and	
Total Assets	**$41,300**	**Owner's Equity**	**$41,300**

Solution Tips to Prepare Financial Reports from a Trial Balance

			Trial Balance	
			Dr.	Cr.
Balance Sheet	<	Assets	X	
		Liabilities		X
Statement of Equity	<	Capital		X
		Withdrawals	X	
Income Statement	<	Revenues		X
		Expenses	X	
			XX	XX

Net income on the income statement of $13,750 goes on the statement of owner's equity.

Ending capital of $23,600 on the statement of owner's equity goes on the balance sheet as the new figure for capital.

Note: There are no debits or credits on Financial Reports. The inside column is used for subtotaling.

SUMMARY OF KEY POINTS

Learning Unit 2-1

1. A T account is a simplified version of a standard account.
2. A ledger is a group of accounts.
3. A debit is the left-hand position (side) of an account and a credit is the right-hand position (side) of an account.
4. A footing is the total of one side of an account: the ending balance is the difference between the footings.

Learning Unit 2-2

1. A chart of accounts lists the account titles and their numbers for a company.
2. The transaction analysis chart is a teaching device, not to be confused with standard accounting procedures.
3. A compound entry is a transaction involving more than one debit or credit.

Learning Unit 2-3

1. In double-entry bookkeeping, the recording of each business transaction affects two or more accounts, and the total of debits equals the total of credits.
2. A trial balance is a list of the ending balances of all accounts, listed in the same order as on the chart of accounts.

3. Any additional investments during the period result in capital on the trial balance not being the beginning figure for capital.

4. There are *no* debit or credit columns on the three financial reports.

KEY TERMS

Account An accounting device used in bookkeeping to record increases and decreases of business transactions relating to individual assets, liabilities, capital, withdrawals, revenue, expenses, and so on.

Chart of accounts A numbering system of accounts that lists the account titles and account numbers to be used by a company.

Compound entry A transaction involving more than one debit or credit.

Credit The right-hand side of any account. A number entered on the right side of any account is said to be credited to an account.

Debit The left-hand side of any account. A number entered on the left side of any account is said to be debited to an account.

Double-entry bookkeeping An accounting system in which the recording of each transaction affects two or more accounts, and the total of the debits is equal to the total of the credits.

Ending balance The difference between footings in a T account.

Footings The totals of each side of a T account.

Ledger A group of accounts that records data from business transactions.

Normal balance of an account The side of an account that increases by the rules of debit and credit.

Standard account A formal account that includes columns for date, explanation, posting reference, debit, and credit.

T account A skeleton version of a standard account, used for demonstration purposes.

Trial balance A list of the ending balances of all the accounts in a ledger. The total of the debits should equal the total of the credits.

BLUEPRINT FOR PREPARING FINANCIAL REPORTS FROM A TRIAL BALANCE

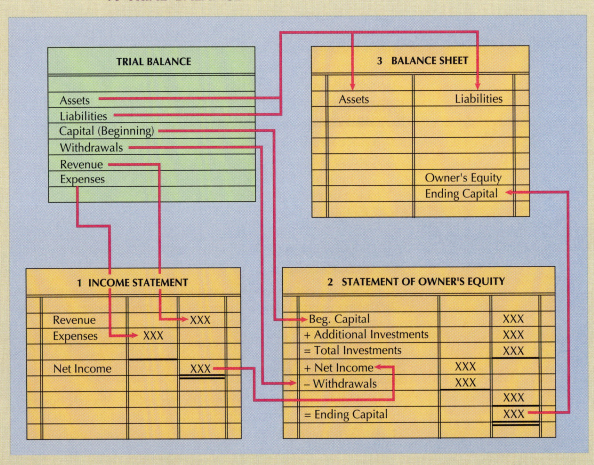

QUESTIONS, MINI EXERCISES, EXERCISES, AND PROBLEMS

Discussion Questions

1. Define a ledger.
2. Why is the left-hand side of an account called a debit?
3. Footings are used in balancing all accounts. True or false? Please explain.
4. What is the end product of the accounting process?
5. What do we mean when we say that a transaction analysis chart is a teaching device?
6. What are the five steps of the transaction analysis chart?
7. Explain the concept of double-entry bookkeeping.
8. A trial balance is a formal report. True or false? Please explain.
9. Why are there no debit or credit columns on financial reports?
10. Compare the financial statements prepared from the expanded accounting equation with those prepared from a trial balance.

Mini Exercises

(The blank forms you need are on page 36 in the *Study Guide and Working Papers*.)

The T Account

1. From the following, foot and balance each account.

Cash 110				R. Rich, Capital 311	
4/8	2,000	4/4	2,000	3/7	5,000
4/12	6,000			3/9	3,000
				4/12	6,000

Transaction Analysis

2. Complete the following:

Account	Category	↑	↓	Normal Balance
A. Cash				
B. Prepaid Rent				
C. Accounts Payable				
D. B. Block, Capital				
E. B. Block Withdrawals				
F. Legal Fees				
G. Salary Expense				

Transaction Analysis

3. Record the following transaction into the transaction analysis chart: Provided legal services for $4,000, receiving $3,000 cash with the remainder to be paid next month.

Accounts Affected	Category	↓	↑	Rules of Dr. and Cr.	T Accounts

Trial Balance

4. Rearrange the following titles in the order they would appear on a Trial Balance:

Selling Expense	Legal Fees
Accounts Receivable	D. Cope, Withdrawals
Accounts Payable	Rent Expense
D. Cope, Capital	Advertising Expense
Computer Equipment	Cash

Trial Balance/Financial Reports

5. From the following Trial Balance identify which report each title will appear on:

◆ Income Statement (IS)
◆ Statement of Owner's Equity (OE)
◆ Balance Sheet (BS)

Logan Co.
Trial Balance
Sept. 30, 19XX

		Dr.	Cr.
A. _____	Cash	390	
B. _____	Supplies	100	
C. _____	Office Equipment	200	
D. _____	Accounts Payable		100
E. _____	D. Heath, Capital		450
F. _____	D. Heath, Withdrawals	160	
G. _____	Fees Earned		290
H. _____	Hair Salon Fees		300
I. _____	Salaries Expense	130	
J. _____	Rent Expense	120	
K. _____	Advertising Expense	40	
	TOTALS	1,140	1,140

Exercises

(The blank forms you need are on page 37 in the *Study Guide and Working Papers.*)

Preparing a chart of accounts.

2-1. From the following, prepare a chart of accounts, using the same numbering system used in this chapter.

Word Processing Equipment	Professional Fees
Rent Expense	A. Sting, Capital
Accounts Payable	Cash
Accounts Receivable	Salaries Expense
Repair Expense	A. Sting, Withdrawals

Preparing a transaction analysis chart.

2-2. Record the following transaction into the transaction analysis chart: Heather Reese bought a new piece of office equipment for $11,000, paying $2,000 down and charging the rest.

2-3. Complete the table: For each account listed on the left, fill in what category it belongs to, whether increases and decreases in the account are marked on the debit or credit sides, and which financial report the account appears on. A sample is provided.

Accounts categorizing, rules, and on which reports they appear.

Accounts Affected	Category	↑	↓	Appears on which Financial Report
Supplies	Asset	Dr.	Cr.	Balance Sheet
Legal Fees Earned				
D. Long, Withdrawals				
Accounts Payable				
Salaries Expense				
Auto				

Rules of debits and credits

2-4. Given the following accounts, complete the table by inserting appropriate numbers next to the individual transaction to indicate which account is debited and which account is credited.

1. Cash	**6.** B. Baker, Withdrawals
2. Accounts Receivable	**7.** Plumbing Fees Earned
3. Equipment	**8.** Salaries Expense
4. Accounts Payable	**9.** Advertising Expense
5. B. Baker, Capital	**10.** Supplies Expenses

		Rules	
Transaction		**Dr.**	**Cr.**
Example:	A. Paid salaries expense.	8	1
	B. Bob paid personal utilities bill from company checkbook.		
	C. Advertising bill received but unpaid.		
	D. Received cash from plumbing fees.		
	E. Paid supplies expense.		
	F. Bob invested additional equipment into the business.		
	G. Billed customers for plumbing services rendered.		
	H. Received one-half the balance from transaction G.		
	I. Bought equipment on account.		

2-5. From the following trial balance of Hall's Cleaners, prepare the following:

◆ Income Statement
◆ Statement of Owner's Equity
◆ Balance Sheet

HALL'S CLEANERS TRIAL BALANCE JULY 31, 19XX		
	Dr.	Cr.
Cash	5 5 0 00	
Equipment	6 9 2 00	
Accounts Payable		4 5 5 00
J. Hall, Capital		8 0 0 00
J. Hall, Withdrawals	1 9 8 00	
Cleaning Fees		4 5 8 00
Salaries Expense	1 6 0 00	
Utilities Expense	1 1 3 00	
Totals	1 7 1 3 00	1 7 1 3 00

Group A Problems

(The forms you need are on pages 40–47 of the *Study Guide and Working Papers*.)

Use of a transaction analysis chart.

2A-1. The following transactions occurred in the opening and operation of Ted's Bookkeeping Service.

    a. Ted Williams opened the bookkeeping service by investing $6,000 from his personal savings account.
    b. Purchased store equipment on account, $3,000.
    c. Rent expense due but unpaid, $600.
    d. Received cash for bookkeeping services rendered, $800.
    e. Billed a client on account, $500.
    f. Ted Williams withdrew cash for personal use, $200.

Check Figure:
After F:

Cash	
6,000	200
800	

Complete the transaction analysis chart in the *Study Guide and Working Papers.* The chart of accounts includes Cash; Accounts Receivable; Store Equipment; Accounts Payable; Ted Williams, Capital; Ted Williams, Withdrawals; Bookkeeping Fees Earned; and Rent Expense.

Recording transactions into ledger accounts.

2A-2. Lee White opened a travel agency, and the following transactions resulted:

    a. Lee White invested $20,000 in the travel agency.
    b. Bought office equipment on account, $4,000.
    c. Agency received cash for travel arrangements that it completed for a client, $3,000.
    d. Lee White paid a personal bill from the company checkbook, $50.
    e. Paid advertising expense for the month, $700.
    f. Rent expense for the month due but unpaid, $900.
    g. Paid $800 as partial payment of what was owed from transaction **b.**

Check Figure:
After G:

	Cash		
(A)	20,000	50	(D)
(C)	3,000	700	(E)
		800	(G)

As Lee White's accountant, analyze and record the transactions in T account form. Set up the T accounts and label each entry with the letter of the transaction.

Chart of Accounts

Assets
Cash   111
Office Equipment   121
Liabilities
Accounts Payable   211
Owner's Equity
L. White, Capital   311
L. White, Withdrawals   312

Revenue
Travel Fees Earned   411
Expenses
Advertising Expense   511
Rent Expense   512

Preparing a trial balance from the T accounts.

2A-3. From the following T accounts of Mike's Window Washing Service, (a) record and foot the balances in the *Study Guide and Working Papers* where appropriate, and (b) prepare a trial balance in proper form for May 31, 19XX.

Check Figure:
Trial Balance Total   **$12,700**

Cash 111			
5,000 (A)	100	(D)
3,500 (G)	200	(E)
	400	(F)
	200	(H)
	900	(I)

Accounts Payable 211		
100 (D)	1,300	(C)

Fees Earned 411	
	6,500 (B)

Accounts Receivable 112	
6,500 (B)	3,500 (G)

Mike Frank, Capital 311	
	5,000 (A)

Rent Expense 511	
400 (F)	

Office Equipment 121	
1,300 (C)	
200 (H)	

Mike Frank, Withdrawals 312	
900 (I)	

Utilities Expense 512	
200 (E)	

2A-4. From the trial balance of Gracie Lantz, Attorney at Law, prepare (a) an

Check Figure:
Total Assets   **$6,400**

GRACIE LANTZ, ATTORNEY AT LAW TRIAL BALANCE MAY 31, 19XX	Dr.	Cr.
Cash	5 0 0 00	
Accounts Receivable	6 5 0 00	
Office Equipment	7 5 0 00	
Accounts Payable		4 3 0 00
Salaries Payable		6 7 5 00
G. Lantz, Capital		1 2 7 5 00
G. Lantz, Withdrawals	3 0 0 00	
Revenue from Legal Fees		1 3 5 0 00
Utilities Expense	3 0 0 00	
Rent Expense	4 5 0 00	
Salaries Expense	1 5 0 00	
Totals	7 6 0 0 00	7 6 0 0 00

income statement for the month of May, (b) a statement of owner's equity
for the month ended May 31, and (c) a balance sheet as of May 31, 19XX.

2A-5. The chart of accounts for Angel's Delivery Service is as follows:

Chart of Accounts

Assets	Revenue
Cash 111	Delivery Fees Earned 411
Accounts Receivable 112	**Expenses**
Office Equipment 121	Advertising Expense 511
Delivery Trucks 122	Gas Expense 512
Liabilities	Salaries Expense 513
Accounts Payable 211	Telephone Expense 514
Owner's Equity	
Alice Angel, Capital 311	
Alice Angel, Withdrawals 312	

Angel's Delivery Service completed the following transactions during the month of
March:

Transaction A: Alice Angel invested $16,000 in the delivery service from her
personal savings account.

Transaction B: Bought delivery trucks on account, $18,000.

Transaction C: Bought office equipment for cash, $600.

Transaction D: Paid advertising expense, $250.

Transaction E: Collected cash for delivery services rendered, $2,600.

Transaction F: Paid drivers' salaries, $900.

Transaction G: Paid gas expense for trucks, $1,200.

Transaction H: Performed delivery services for a customer on account, $800.

Transaction I: Telephone expense due but unpaid, $700.

Transaction J: Received $300 as partial payment of transaction H.

Transaction K: Alice Angel withdrew cash for personal use, $300.

As Alice's newly employed accountant, you must:

1. Set up T accounts in a ledger.
2. Record transactions in the T accounts. (Place the letter of the transaction next
   to the entry.)
3. Foot the T accounts where appropriate.
4. Prepare a trial balance at the end of March.
5. Prepare from the trial balance, in proper form, (a) an income statement for the
   month of March, (b) a statement of owner's equity, and (c) a balance sheet as
   of March 31, 19XX.

Group B Problems

(The forms you need are on pages 40–48 of the *Study Guide and Working
Papers.*)

2B-1. Ted Williams decided to open a bookkeeping service. Record the following
transactions into the transaction analysis charts:

Transaction A:	Ted invested $1,500 in the bookkeeping service from his personal savings account.
Transaction B:	Purchased store equipment on account, $900.
Transaction C:	Rent expense due but unpaid, $250.
Transaction D:	Performed bookkeeping services for cash, $1,200.
Transaction E:	Billed clients for bookkeeping services rendered, $700.
Transaction F:	Ted paid his home heating bill from the company checkbook, $275.

Check Figure:

After F:

Cash	
1,500	275
1,200	

Recording transactions into ledger accounts.

The chart of accounts for the shop includes Cash; Accounts Receivable; Store Equipment; Accounts Payable; Ted Williams, Capital; Ted Williams, Withdrawals; Bookkeeping Fees Earned; and Rent Expense.

2B-2. Lee White established a new travel agency. Record the following transactions for Lee in T account form. Label each entry with the letter of the transaction.

Transaction A:	Lee White invested $18,000 in the travel agency from her personal bank account.
Transaction B:	Bought office equipment on account, $6,000.
Transaction C:	Travel agency rendered service to Jensen Corp. and received cash, $1,200.
Transaction D:	Lee White withdrew cash for personal use, $200.
Transaction E:	Paid advertising expense, $600.
Transaction F:	Rent expense due but unpaid, $500.
Transaction G:	Paid $400 in partial payment of transaction B.

Check Figure:

After G:

	Cash		
(A)	18,000	200	(D)
(C)	1,200	600	(E)
		400	(G)

The chart of accounts includes Cash, 111; Office Equipment, 121; Accounts Payable, 211; L. White, Capital, 311; L. White, Withdrawals, 312; Travel Fees Earned, 411; Advertising Expense, 511; and Rent Expense, 512.

2B-3. From the following T accounts of Mike's Window Washing Service, (a) record and foot the balances in the *Study Guide* where appropriate and (b) prepare a trial balance for May 31, 19XX.

Preparing a trial balance from the T accounts.

Cash 111				Accounts Receivable 112		Office Equipment 121	
10,000 (A)	4,000	(C)		2,000 (G)		2,000	(B)
4,000 (F)	310	(D)				4,000	(C)
2,000 (G)	50	(E)					
	600	(H)					

Check Figure:

Trial Balance Total $20,000

Accounts Payable 211		Mike Frank, Capital 311		Mike Frank, Withdrawals 312	
	2,000 (B)		10,000 (A)	600 (H)	

Fees Earned 411		Rent Expense 511		Utilities Expense 512	
	4,000 (F)	310 (D)		50 (E)	
	4,000 (G)				

Preparing financial reports from the trial balance.

2B-4. From the trial balance of Gracie Lantz, Attorney at Law, prepare (a) an income from the statement for the month of May, (b) a statement of owner's equity for the month ended May 31, and (c) a balance sheet as of May 31, 19XX.

GRACIE LANTZ, ATTORNEY AT LAW
TRIAL BALANCE
MAY 31, 19XX

	Debit	Credit
Cash	6 0 0 0 00	
Accounts Receivable	2 4 0 0 00	
Office Equipment	2 4 0 0 00	
Accounts Payable		2 0 0 00
Salaries Payable		6 0 0 00
G. Lantz, Capital		4 0 0 0 00
G. Lantz, Withdrawals	2 0 0 0 00	
Revenue from Legal Fees		8 8 0 0 00
Utilities Expense	1 0 0 00	
Rent Expense	3 0 0 00	
Salaries Expense	4 0 0 00	
Totals	13 6 0 0 00	13 6 0 0 00

Check Figure:
Total Assets $10,800

Comprehensive Problem

Check Figure:
Trial Balance Total $84,300

2B-5. The chart of accounts of Angel's Delivery Service includes the following: Cash, 111; Accounts Receivable, 112; Office Equipment, 121; Delivery Trucks, 122; Accounts Payable, 211; Alice Angel, Capital, 311; Alice Angel, Withdrawals, 312; Delivery Fees Earned, 411; Advertising Expense, 511; Gas Expense, 512; Salaries Expense, 513; and Telephone Expense, 514. The following transactions resulted for Angel's Delivery Service during the month of March:

Transaction A:	Alice invested $40,000 in the business from her personal savings account.
Transaction B:	Bought delivery trucks on account, $25,000.
Transaction C:	Advertising bill received but unpaid, $800.
Transaction D:	Bought office equipment for cash, $2,500.
Transaction E:	Received cash for delivery services rendered, $13,000.
Transaction F:	Paid salaries expense, $1,850.
Transaction G:	Paid gas expense for company trucks, $750.
Transaction H:	Billed customers for delivery services rendered, $5,500.
Transaction I:	Paid telephone bill, $400.
Transaction J:	Received $1,600 as partial payment of transaction H.
Transaction K:	Alice paid home telephone bill from company checkbook, $88.

As Alice's newly employed accountant, you must

1. Set up T accounts in a ledger.
2. Record transactions in the T accounts. (Place the letter of the transaction next to the entry.)
3. Foot the T accounts where appropriate.
4. Prepare a trial balance at the end of March.
5. Prepare from the trial balance, in proper form, (a) an income statement for the month of March, (b) a statement of owner's equity, and (c) a balance sheet as of March 31, 19XX.

REAL WORLD APPLICATIONS

2R-1.
Andy Leaf is a careless bookkeeper. He is having a terrible time getting his trial balance to balance. Andy has asked for your assistance in preparing a correct trial balance. The following is the incorrect trial balance.

RANCH COMPANY
TRIAL BALANCE
JUNE 30, 19XX

	Dr.	Cr.
Cash	5 1 0 00	
Accounts Receivable		6 3 5 00
Office Equipment	3 6 0 00	
Accounts Payable	1 1 0 00	
Wages Payable	1 0 00	
H. Clo, Capital	6 3 5 00	
H. Clo, Withdrawals	1 4 4 0 00	
Professional Fees		2 2 4 0 00
Rent Expense		2 4 0 00
Advertising Expense	2 5 00	
Totals	3 0 9 0 00	3 1 1 5 00

Facts you have discovered:

◆ Debits to the Cash account were $2,640; credits to the Cash account were $2,150.

◆ Amy Hall paid $15 but was not updated in Accounts Receivable.

◆ A purchase of office equipment for $5 on account was never recorded in the ledger.

◆ Revenue was understated in the ledger by $180.

Show how these errors affected the ending balances for the accounts involved, and explain how the trial balance will indeed balance once they are corrected.

Tell Ranch Company how it can avoid this problem in the future. Write your recommendations.

2R-2.

Alice Groove, owner of Lonton Company, asked her bookkeeper how each of the following situations will affect the totals of the trial balance and individual ledger accounts.

◆ An $850 payment for a desk was recorded as a debit to Office Equipment, $85, and a credit to Cash, $85.

◆ A payment of $300 to a creditor was recorded as a debit to Accounts Payable, $300, and a credit to Cash, $100.

◆ The collection on an Accounts Receivable for $400 was recorded as a debit to Cash, $400, and a credit to J. Ray, Capital, $400.

◆ The payment of a liability for $400 was recorded as a debit to Accounts Payable, $40, and a credit to Supplies, $40.

◆ A purchase of equipment of $800 was recorded as a debit to Supplies, $800, and a credit to Cash, $800.

◆ A payment of $95 to a creditor was recorded as a debit to Accounts Payable, $95, and a credit to Cash, $59.

What did the bookkeeper tell her? Which accounts were overstated and understated? Which were correct? Explain in writing how mistakes can be avoided in the future.

YOU make the call

Critical Thinking/Ethical Case

2R-3.
Audrey Flet, the bookkeeper of ALN Co., was scheduled to leave on a three-week vacation at 5 o'clock on Friday. She couldn't get the company's trial balance to balance. At 4:30, she decided to put in fictitious figures to make it balance. Audrey told herself she would fix it when she got back from her vacation. Was Audrey right or wrong to do this? Why?

ACCOUNTING RECALL
A CUMULATIVE APPROACH

THIS EXAM REVIEWS CHAPTERS 1 AND 2

Your *Study Guide and Working Papers* (pages 51 and 55) have forms to complete this exam, as well as worked-out solutions. The page references next to each question identify what page to turn back to if you answer the question incorrectly.

PART 1   Vocabulary Review

Match the terms to the appropriate definition or phrase.

Page Ref.

(50)	1. Trial balance	A. Total remains the same
(38)	2. Debit	B. Entering numbers on right side
(40)	3. Normal balance	C. Subdivisions of owner's equity
(11)	4. Revenue	D. Group of accounts
(38)	5. Crediting	E. Numbering system
(9)	6. Balance sheet	F. Left side of an account
(7)	7. Shift in assets	G. Prepared as of a particular date
(40)	8. Chart of accounts	H. Not an asset
(37)	9. Ledger	I. Side of account that increases it
(11)	10. Capital, withdrawals, revenue, expenses	J. List of the ledger

PART II   True or False (Accounting Theory)

(38)	11. A debit always means increase.
(51)	12. There are no debit or credit columns on financial reports.
(50)	13. The trial balance lists only the ending figure for capital that goes on the balance sheet.
(40)	14. An increase in a withdrawal is a credit.
(50)	15. The trial balance is not a formal report.

CONTINUING PROBLEM

The Eldorado Computer Center created its chart of accounts as follows:

Chart of Accounts
As of June 1, 19XX

Assets
1000 Cash
1020 Accounts Receivable
1030 Supplies
1080 Computer Shop Equipment
1090 Office Equipment

Liabilities
2000 Accounts Payable

Owners Equity
3000 Freedman, Capital
3010 Freedman, Withdrawals

Revenue
4000 Service Revenue

Expenses
5010 Advertising Expense
5020 Rent Expense
5030 Utilities Expense
5040 Phone Expense
5050 Supplies Expense
5060 Insurance Expense
5070 Postage Expense

You will use this chart of accounts to complete the Continuing Problem.
The following problem continues from Chapter 1. The balances as of July 31 have been brought forward in your *Working Papers* on page 52.

Assignment:

1. Set up T accounts in a ledger.
2. Record the transactions (k) through (q) in the appropriate T accounts.
3. Foot the T accounts where appropriate.
4. Prepare a trial balance at the end of August.
5. Prepare from the trial balance an income statement, statement of owner's equity, and a balance sheet for the two months ending with August 31, 19XX.

k) Received the phone bill for the month of July, $155
l) Paid $150 (check #8099) for insurance for the month
m) Paid $200 (check #8100) of the amount due from transaction (d) in Chapter 1
n) Paid advertising expense for the month, $1,400 (check #8101)
o) Billed a client (Jeannine Sparks) for services rendered, $850
p) Collected $900 for services rendered
q) Paid the electric bill in full for the month of July [check #8102 — transaction (h), Chapter 1].
r) Paid cash (check #8103) for $50 in stamps
s) Purchased $200 worth of supplies from Computer Connection on credit

3

BEGINNING THE ACCOUNTING CYCLE

Journalizing, Posting, and the Trial Balance

THE BIG PICTURE

At Eldorado Computer Center, Tony Freedman uses the standard accounting practice of keeping a journal. Later, he copies (or "posts") transactions to a ledger. Each account is separate in the ledger, so it can be totaled. Like a personal diary, an accounting journal lets you capture information as it happens. You first analyze each transaction to determine which ledger accounts will be affected. Then you record your analysis — along with descriptive notes — in the journal.

Eldorado's journal lets Freedman look up transactions easily. He can also check his analysis at any time. If an error is discovered when he prepares the trial balance, he can trace his steps back to the original transaction and make corrections.

The Eldorado Computer Center deals with many different source documents, such as checks, calculator tapes, receipts, invoices, purchase orders, and deposit slips. When customers enter Tony's store, they complete a repair order authorizing the center to do the work. Once the work is completed, Tony issues a bill or "invoice." The customer may pay in cash, or Tony may extend credit. Either way, Tony records the invoice as a business transaction.

Of course people make mistakes in accounting records. Nonetheless, these records are kept in ink, not pencil. Corrections are shown clearly and initialed. This record shows a complete and trustworthy record of events.

◆ **Journalizing—analyzing and recording business transactions into a journal. (p. 71)**
◆ **Posting—transferring information from a journal to a ledger. (p. 80)**
◆ **Preparing a trial balance. (p. 86)**

The normal accounting procedures that are performed over a period of time are called the **accounting cycle.** The accounting cycle takes place in a period of time called an **accounting period.** An accounting period is the period of time covered by the income statement. Although it can be any time period up to one year (e.g., one month or three months), most businesses use a one-year accounting period. The year can be either a **calendar year** (January 1 through December 31) or a **fiscal year.**

A fiscal year is an accounting period that runs for any twelve consecutive months, so it can be the same as a calendar year. A business can choose any fiscal year that is convenient. For example, some retailers may decide to end their fiscal year when inventories and business activity are at a low point, such as after the Christmas season. This is called a **natural business year.** Using a natural business year allows the business to count its year-end inventory when it is easiest to do so.

Businesses would not be able to operate successfully if they only prepared financial reports at the end of their calendar or fiscal year. That is why most businesses prepare **interim reports** on a monthly, quarterly, or semiannual basis.

In this chapter, as well as in Chapters 4 and 5, we will follow Brenda Clark's new business, Clark's Word Processing Services. We will follow the normal accounting procedures that the business performs over a period of time. Clark has chosen to use a fiscal period of January 1 to December 31, which also is the calendar year.

The diagram (page 72) that follows lists the steps in the business accounting cycle for a manual and a computerized system. This diagram should be used as a reference figure. By the end of Chapter 5, every step in the manual accounting system will have been explained and illustrated.

This chapter covers Steps 1 to 4 of the accounting cycle. (See diagram on page p. 72.)

LEARNING UNIT 3-1

Analyzing and Recording Business Transactions into a Journal: Steps 1 and 2 of the Accounting Cycle

THE GENERAL JOURNAL

A business uses a journal to record transactions in chronological order. A ledger accumulates information from a journal. The journal and the ledger are in two different books.

Chapter 2 taught us how to analyze and record business transactions into T accounts, or ledger accounts. However, recording a debit in an account on one page of the ledger and recording the corresponding credit on a different page of the ledger can make it difficult to find errors. It would be much easier if all of the business's transactions were located in the same place. That is the function of the **journal** or **general journal.** Transactions are entered in the journal in chronological order (January 1, 8, 15, etc.), and then this recorded information is used to update the ledger accounts. In computerized accounting, a journal may be recorded on disk or tape.

We will use a general journal, the simplest form of a journal, to record the transactions of Clark's Word Processing Services. A transaction [debit(s) + credit(s)] that has been analyzed and recorded in a journal is called a **journal entry.** The process of recording the journal entry into the journal is called **journalizing.**

STEPS OF THE ACCOUNTING CYCLE

Manual Accounting System

9. Prepare a post-closing trial balance.

8. Journalize and post closing entries.

7. Journalize and post adjusting entries.

6. Prepare financial statements.

5. Prepare a worksheet.

4. Prepare a trial balance.

3. Post or transfer information from journal to ledger.

2. Analyze and record business transactions in a journal.

1. Business transactions occur and generate source documents.

Manual Accounting System

Computerized Accounting System

9. Trial balance is prepared automatically.

8. Closing procedures are usually completed automatically.

7. Financial statements are prepared automatically.

6. Record adjusting entries in a computerized journal; posting is automatic.

5. No worksheet is necessary.

4. Trial balance is prepared automatically.

3. Computer automatically posts information from journal to ledger.

2. Analyze and record business transactions in a computerized journal.

1. Business transactions occur and generate source documents.

Computerized Accounting System

Journal—book of original entry.

The journal is called the **book of original entry,** since it contains the first formal information about the business transactions. The ledger is known as the **book of final entry,** because the information the journal contains will be transferred to the ledger. Like the ledger, the journal may be a bound or loose-leaf book. Each of the journal pages looks like the one in Figure 3-1. The pages of the journal are numbered consecutively from page 1. Keep in mind that the journal and the ledger are separate books.

Relationship Between the Journal and the Chart of Accounts

The accountant must refer to the business's chart of accounts for the account name that is to be used in the journal. Every company has its own "unique" chart of accounts.

The chart of accounts for Clark's Word Processing Services appears on page 73. By the end of Chapter 5, we will have discussed each of these accounts.

Note that we will continue to use transaction analysis charts as a teaching aid in the journalizing process.

CLARK'S WORD PROCESSING SERVICES
GENERAL JOURNAL

Page 1

Date	Account Titles and Description	PR	Dr.	Cr.

FIGURE 3-1
The General Journal

Clark's Word Processing Services
Chart of Accounts

Assets (100–199)
111   Cash
112   Accounts Receivable
114   Office Supplies
115   Prepaid Rent
121   World Processing Equipment
122   Accumulated Depreciation,
      Word Processing Equipment

Liabilities (200–299)
211   Accounts Payable
212   Salaries Payable

Owner's Equity (300–399)
311   Brenda Clark, Capital
312   Brenda Clark, Withdrawals
313   Income Summary

Revenue (400–499)
411   Word Processing Fees

Expenses (500–599)
511   Office Salaries Expense
512   Advertising Expense
513   Telephone Expense
514   Office Supplies Expense
515   Rent Expense
516   Depreciation Expense,
      Word Processing Equipment

Journalizing the Transactions of Clark's Word Processing Services

Certain formalities must be followed in making journal entries:

◆ The debit portion of the transaction always is recorded first.

◆ The credit portion of a transaction is indented one-half inch and placed below the debit portion.

◆ The explanation of the journal entry follows immediately after the credit and one inch from the date column.

◆ A one-line space follows each transaction and explanation. This makes the journal easier to read, and there is less chance of mixing transactions.

◆ Finally, as always, the total amount of debits must equal the total amount of credits. The same format is used for each of the entries in the journal.

May 1, 19XX: Brenda Clark began the business by investing $10,000 in cash.

1 Accounts Affected	2 Category	3 ↓ ↑	4 Rules of Dr. and Cr.
Cash	Asset	↑	Dr.
Brenda Clark, Capital	Capital	↑	Cr.

CLARK'S WORD PROCESSING SERVICES
GENERAL JOURNAL

Page 1

Date			Account Titles and Description	PR	Dr.	Cr.
19XX May	1		Cash		10000 00	
			Brenda Clark, Capital			10000 00
			Initial investment of cash by owner			

For now the PR (posting reference) column is blank; we will discuss it later.

Let's now look at the structure of this journal entry. The entry contains the following information:

1. Year of the journal entry   19XX
2. Month of the journal entry   May
3. Day of journal entry   1
4. Name(s) of accounts debited   Cash
5. Name(s) of accounts credited   Brenda Clark, Capital
6. Explanation of transaction   Investment of cash
7. Amount of debit(s) $10,000
8. Amount of credit(s) $10,000

May 1: Purchased word processing equipment from Ben Co. for $6,000, paying $1,000 and promising to pay the balance within 30 days.

1 Accounts Affected	2 Category	3 ↓ ↑	4 Rules of Dr. and Cr.
Word Processing Equipment	Asset	↑	Dr.
Cash	Asset	↓	Cr.
Accounts Payable	Liability	↑	Cr.

Note that in this compound entry we have one debit and two credits—but the total amount of debits equals the total amount of credits.

This transaction affects three accounts. When a journal entry has more than two accounts, it is called a **compound journal entry.**

A journal entry that requires three or more accounts is called a compound journal entry.

		1	Word Processing Equipment		6000 00	
			Cash			1000 00
			Accounts Payable			5000 00
			Purchase of equipment from Ben Co.			

In this entry, only the day is entered in the date column. That is because the year and month were entered at the top of the page from the first transaction. There is no need to repeat this information until a new page is needed or a change of months occurs.

May 1: Rented office space, paying $1,200 in advance for the first three months.

1 Accounts Affected	2 Category	3 ↓ ↑	4 Rules of Dr. and Cr.
Prepaid Rent	Asset	↑	Dr.
Cash	Asset	↓	Cr.

Rent paid in advance is an asset.

In this transaction Clark gains an asset called prepaid rent and gives up an asset, cash. The prepaid rent does not become an expense until it expires.

		1	Prepaid Rent		1 2 0 0 00	
			Cash			1 2 0 0 00
			Rent paid in advance—3 mos.			

May 3: Purchased office supplies from Norris Co. on account, $600.

1 Accounts Affected	2 Category	3 ↓ ↑	4 Rules of Dr. and Cr.
Office Supplies	Asset	↑	Dr.
Accounts Payable	Liability	↑	Cr.

Supplies become an *expense* when used up.

Remember, supplies are an asset when they are purchased. Once they are used up or consumed in the operation of business, they become an expense.

		3	Office Supplies		6 0 0 00	
			Accounts Payable			6 0 0 00
			Purchase of supplies on account			
			from Norris			

May 7: Completed sales promotion pieces for a client and immediately collected $3,000.

1 Accounts Affected	2 Category	3 ↓ ↑	4 Rules of Dr. and Cr.
Cash	Asset	↑	Dr.
Word Processing Fees	Revenue	↑	Cr.

		7	Cash		3 0 0 0 00		
			Word Processing Fees			3 0 0 0 00	
			Cash received for services rendered				

May 15: Paid office salaries, $650.

1 Accounts Affected	2 Category	3 ↓ ↑	4 Rules of Dr. and Cr.
Office Salaries Expense	Expense	↑	Dr.
Cash	Asset	↓	Cr.

		15	Office Salaries Expense		6 5 0 00		
			Cash			6 5 0 00	
			Payment of office salaries				

May 18: Advertising bill from Al's News Co. comes in but is not paid, $250.

Remember, expenses are recorded when they are incurred, no matter when they are paid.

1 Accounts Affected	2 Category	3 ↓ ↑	4 Rules of Dr. and Cr.
Advertising Expense	Expense	↑	Dr.
Accounts Payable	Liability	↑	Cr.

		18	Advertising Expense		2 5 0 00		
			Accounts Payable			2 5 0 00	
			Bill in but not paid from Al's News				

Keep in mind that as withdrawals *increase,* owner's equity *decreases.*

May 20: Brenda Clark wrote a check on the bank account of the business to pay her home mortgage payment of $625.

1 Accounts Affected	2 Category	3 ↓ ↑	4 Rules of Dr. and Cr.
Brenda Clark, Withdrawals	Withdrawals	↑	Dr.
Cash	Asset	↓	Cr.

	20	Brenda Clark, Withdrawals		6 2 5 00		
		Cash			6 2 5 00	
		Personal withdrawal of cash				

May 22: Billed Morris Company for a sophisticated word processing job, $5,000.

Reminder: Revenue is recorded when it is earned, no matter when the cash is actually received.

1 Accounts Affected	2 Category	3 ↓ ↑	4 Rules of Dr. and Cr.
Accounts Receivable	Asset	↑	Dr.
Word Processing Fees	Revenue	↑	Cr.

	22	Accounts Receivable		5 0 0 0 00		
		Word Processing Fees			5 0 0 0 00	
		Billed Morris Co. for fees earned				

May 27: Paid office salaries, $650.

1 Accounts Affected	2 Category	3 ↓ ↑	4 Rules of Dr. and Cr.
Office Salaries Expense	Expense	↑	Dr.
Cash	Asset	↓	Cr.

CLARK'S WORD PROCESSING SERVICES
GENERAL JOURNAL

Page 2

Date		Account Titles and Description	PR	Dr.	Cr.
19XX May	27	Office Salaries Expense		6 5 0 00	
		Cash			6 5 0 00
		Payment of office salaries			

Note: Since we are on page 2 of the journal, the year and month are repeated.

May 28: Paid half the amount owed for word processing equipment purchased May 1 from Ben Co., $2,500.

1 Accounts Affected	2 Category	3 ↓ ↑	4 Rules of Dr. and Cr.
Accounts Payable	Liability	↓	Dr.
Cash	Asset	↓	Cr.

	28	Accounts Payable		2 5 0 0 00	
		Cash			2 5 0 0 00
		Paid half the amount owed Ben Co.			

May 29: Received and paid telephone bill, $220.

1	2	3		4
Accounts Affected	Category	↓	↑	Rules of Dr. and Cr.
Telephone Expense	Expense		↑	Dr.
Cash	Asset	↓		Cr.

	29	Telephone Expense		2 2 0 00	
		Cash			2 2 0 00
		Paid telephone bill			

This concludes the journal transactions of Clark's Word Processing Services. (See page 82 for a summary of all the transactions.)

LEARNING UNIT 3-1 REVIEW

AT THIS POINT you should be able to

- ◆ Define an accounting cycle. (p. 71)
- ◆ Define and explain the relationship of the accounting period to the income statement. (p. 71)
- ◆ Compare and contrast a calendar year to a fiscal year. (p. 71)
- ◆ Explain the term natural business year. (p. 71)
- ◆ Explain the function of interim reports. (p. 71)
- ◆ Define and state the purpose of a journal. (p. 71)
- ◆ Compare and contrast a book of original entry to a book of final entry. (p. 72)
- ◆ Differentiate between a chart of accounts and a journal. (p. 73)
- ◆ Explain a compound entry. (p. 74)
- ◆ Journalize a business transaction. (p. 75)

SELF-REVIEW QUIZ 3-1

(The blank forms you need are on pages 56–57 of the *Study Guide and Working Papers.*)

The following are the transactions of Lowe's Repair Service. Journalize the transactions in proper form. The chart of accounts includes Cash; Accounts Receivable; Prepaid Rent; Repair Supplies; Repair Equipment; Accounts Payable; A. Lowe, Capital; A. Lowe, Withdrawals; Repair Fees Earned; Salaries Expense; Advertising Expense; and Supplies Expense.

19XX
June 1 A. Lowe invested $6,000 cash and $4,000 of repair equipment in the business.
1 Paid two months' rent in advance, $1,200.
4 Bought repair supplies from Melvin Co. on account, $600. (These supplies have not yet been consumed or used up.)
15 Performed repair work, received $600 in cash, and had to bill Doe Co. for remaining balance of $300.
18 A. Lowe paid his home telephone bill, $50, with a check from the company.
20 Advertising bill for $400 from Jones Co. received but payment not due yet. (Advertising has already appeared in the newspaper.)
24 Paid salaries, $1,400.

Solution to Self-Review Quiz 3-1

LOWE'S REPAIR SERVICE
GENERAL JOURNAL

Page 1

Date			Account Titles and Description	PR	Dr.	Cr.
19XX June	1		Cash		6 000 00	
			Repair Equipment		4 000 00	
			A. Lowe, Capital			10 000 00
			Owner investment			
	1		Prepaid Rent		1 200 00	
			Cash			1 200 00
			Rent paid in advance—2mos.			
	4		Repair Supplies		600 00	
			Accounts Payable			600 00
			Purchase on account from Melvin Co.			
	15		Cash		600 00	
			Accounts Receivable		300 00	
			Repair Fees Earned			900 00
			Performed repairs for Doe Co.			
	18		A. Lowe, Withdrawals		50 00	
			Cash			50 00
			Personal withdrawal			
	20		Advertising Expense		400 00	
			Accounts Payable			400 00
			Advertising bill from Jones Co.			
	24		Salaries Expense		1 400 00	
			Cash			1 400 00
			Paid salaries			

Quiz Tip: All titles for the debits and credits come from the chart of accounts, debits against the date column and credits indented. The PR column is left blank in the journalizing process.

LEARNING UNIT 3-2
Posting to the Ledger: Step 3 of the Accounting Cycle

The general journal serves a particular purpose; it puts every transaction the business does in one place. There are things it cannot do, though. For example, if you were asked to find the balance of the cash account from the general journal, you would have to go through the entire journal and look for only the cash entries. Then you would have to add up the debits and credits for the cash account and determine the difference between the two.

What we really need to do to find balances of accounts is to transfer the information from the journal to the ledger. This is called **posting.** In the ledger we will accumulate an ending balance for each account so that we can prepare financial statements.

In Chapter 2, we used the T account form to make our ledger entries. T accounts are very simple, but they are not used in the real business world. They are only used for demonstration purposes. In practice, accountants often use a **four-column account form** that includes a column for the business's running balance. Figure 3-2 shows a standard four-column account. We will use that format in the text from now on.

Footings are not needed in four-column accounts.

POSTING

Now let's look at how to post the transactions of Clark's Word Processing Service from its journal. The diagram in Figure 3-3 shows how to post the cash line from the journal to the ledger. The steps in the posting process are numbered and illustrated in the figure.

Step 1: In the Cash account in the ledger, record the date (May 1, 19XX) and the amount of the entry ($10,000).

Step 2: Record the page number of the journal "GJ1" in the posting reference (PR) column of the Cash account.

Step 3: Calculate the new balance of the account. You keep a running balance in each account as you would in your checkbook. To do this you take the present balance in the account on the previous line and add or subtract the transaction as necessary to arrive at your new balance.

Step 4: Record the account number of Cash (111) in the posting reference (PR) column of the journal. This is called **cross referencing.**

The same sequence of steps occurs for each line in the journal. In a manual system like Clark's, the debits and credits in the journal may be posted in the order they were recorded, or all the debits may be posted first and then all the credits. If Clark used a computer system, the program menu would post at the press of a button.

FIGURE 3-2
Four-Column Account

Accounts Payable								Account No. 211
Date	Explanation	Post. Ref.	Debit	Credit	Balance Debit	Balance Credit		
19XX May 1		GJ1		5 0 0 0 00		5 0 0 0 00		
3		GJ1		6 0 0 00		5 6 0 0 00		
18		GJ1		2 5 0 00		5 8 5 0 00		
28		GJ2	2 5 0 0 00			3 3 5 0 00		

FIGURE 3-3

How to Post from Journal to Ledger

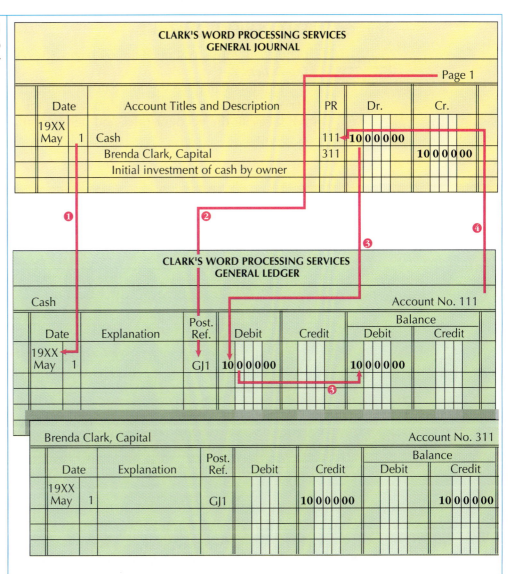

Using Posting References

The posting references are very helpful. In the journal, the PR column tells us which transactions have or have not been posted and also to which accounts they were posted. In the ledger, the posting reference leads us back to the original transaction in its entirety, so that we can see why the debit or credit was recorded and what other accounts were affected. (It leads us back to the original transaction by identifying the journal and the page in the journal from which the information came.)

LEARNING UNIT 3-2 REVIEW

AT THIS POINT you should be able to

◆ State the purpose of posting. (p. 80)
◆ Discuss the advantages of the four-column account. (p. 80)
◆ Identify the elements to be posted. (p. 81)
◆ From journalized transactions, post to the general ledger. (p. 81)

(The blank forms you need are on pages 58–63 of the *Study Guide and Working Papers.*)

The following are the journalized transactions of Clark's Word Processing Services. Your task is to post information to the ledger. The ledger in your workbook has all the account titles and numbers that were used from the chart of accounts.

CLARK'S WORD PROCESSING SERVICES
GENERAL JOURNAL

Page 1

Date		Account Titles and Description	PR	Dr.	Cr.
19XX May	1	Cash		10 00 00	
		Brenda Clark, Capital			10 00 00
		Initial investment of cash by owner			
	1	Word Processing Equipment		6 00 00	
		Cash			1 00 00
		Accounts Payable			5 00 00
		Purchase of equip. from Ben Co.			
	1	Prepaid Rent		1 20 00	
		Cash			1 20 00
		Rent paid in advance (3 months)			
	3	Office Supplies		6 00 00	
		Accounts Payable			6 00 00
		Purchase of supplies on acct. from Norris			
	7	Cash		3 00 00	
		Word Processing Fees			3 00 00
		Cash received for services rendered			
	15	Office Salaries Expense		6 50 00	
		Cash			6 50 00
		Payment of office salaries			
	18	Advertising Expense		2 50 00	
		Accounts Payable			2 50 00
		Bill received but not paid from Al's News			
	20	Brenda Clark, Withdrawals		6 25 00	
		Cash			6 25 00
		Personal withdrawal of cash			
	22	Accounts Receivable		5 00 00	
		Word Processing Fees			5 00 00
		Billed Morris Co. for fees earned			

CLARK'S WORD PROCESSING SERVICES
GENERAL JOURNAL

Page 2

Date		Account Titles and Description	PR	Dr.	Cr.
19XX May	27	Office Salaries Expense		65000	
		Cash			65000
		Payment of office salaries			
	28	Accounts Payable		250000	
		Cash			250000
		Paid half the amount owed Ben Co.			
	29	Telephone Expense		22000	
		Cash			22000
		Paid telephone bill			

Solution to Self-Review Quiz 3-2

Remember, the PR column remains empty until the entries have been posted.

CLARK'S WORD PROCESSING SERVICES
GENERAL JOURNAL

Page 1

Date		Account Titles and Description	PR	Dr.	Cr.
19XX May	1	Cash	111	1000000	
		Brenda Clark, Capital	311		1000000
		Initial investment of cash by owner			
	1	Word Processing Equipment	121	600000	
		Cash	111		100000
		Accounts Payable	211		500000
		Purchase of equip. from Ben Co.			
	1	Prepaid Rent	115	120000	
		Cash	111		120000
		Rent paid in advance (3 months)			
	3	Office Supplies	114	60000	
		Accounts Payable	211		60000
		Purchase of supplies on acct. from Norris			
	7	Cash	111	300000	
		Word Processing Fees	411		300000
		Cash received from services rendered			
	15	Office Salaries Expense	511	65000	
		Cash	111		65000
		Payment of office salaries			

(page 1, Clark's General Journal, cont. at top of p. 84)

	18	Advertising Expense	512	2 5 0 00			
		Accounts Payable	211			2 5 0 00	
		Bill received but not paid from Al's News					
	20	Brenda Clark, Withdrawals	312	6 2 5 00			
		Cash	111			6 2 5 00	
		Personal withdrawal of cash					
	22	Accounts Receivable	112	5 0 0 0 00			
		Word Processing Fees	411			5 0 0 0 00	
		Billed Morris Co. for fees earned					

CLARK'S WORD PROCESSING SERVICES
GENERAL JOURNAL

Page 2

Date		Account Titles and Description	PR	Dr.	Cr.
19XX May	27	Office Salaries Expense	511	6 5 0 00	
		Cash	111		6 5 0 00
		Payment of office salaries			
	28	Accounts Payable	211	2 5 0 0 00	
		Cash	111		2 5 0 0 00
		Paid half the amount owed Ben Co.			
	29	Telephone Expense	513	2 2 0 00	
		Cash	111		2 2 0 00
		Paid telephone bill			

CLARK'S WORD PROCESSING SERVICES
PARTIAL GENERAL LEDGER

Cash   Account No. 111

Date		Explanation	Post. Ref.	Debit	Credit	Balance Debit	Balance Credit
19XX May	1		GJ1	10 0 0 0 00		10 0 0 0 00	
	1		GJ1		1 0 0 0 00	9 0 0 0 00	
	1		GJ1		1 2 0 0 00	7 8 0 0 00	
	7		GJ1	3 0 0 0 00		10 8 0 0 00	
	15		GJ1		6 5 0 00	10 1 5 0 00	
	20		GJ1		6 2 5 00	9 5 2 5 00	
	27		GJ2		6 5 0 00	8 8 7 5 00	
	28		GJ2		2 5 0 0 00	6 3 7 5 00	
	29		GJ2		2 2 0 00	6 1 5 5 00	

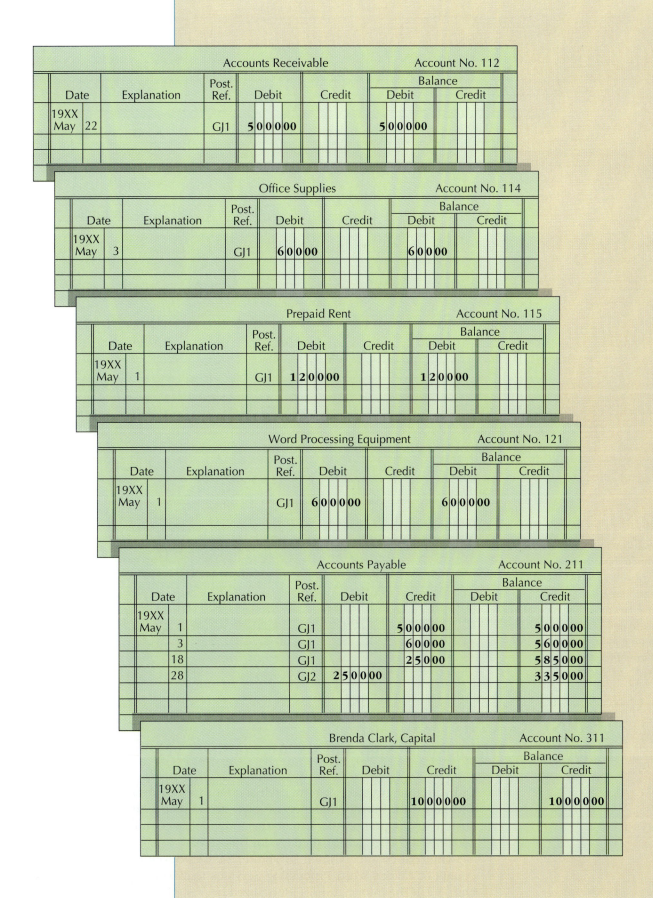

Accounts Receivable   Account No. 112

Date	Explanation	Post. Ref.	Debit	Credit	Balance Debit	Balance Credit
19XX May 22		GJ1	5 0 0 0 00		5 0 0 0 00	

Office Supplies   Account No. 114

Date	Explanation	Post. Ref.	Debit	Credit	Balance Debit	Balance Credit
19XX May 3		GJ1	6 0 0 00		6 0 0 00	

Prepaid Rent   Account No. 115

Date	Explanation	Post. Ref.	Debit	Credit	Balance Debit	Balance Credit
19XX May 1		GJ1	1 2 0 0 00		1 2 0 0 00	

Word Processing Equipment   Account No. 121

Date	Explanation	Post. Ref.	Debit	Credit	Balance Debit	Balance Credit
19XX May 1		GJ1	6 0 0 0 00		6 0 0 0 00	

Accounts Payable   Account No. 211

Date	Explanation	Post. Ref.	Debit	Credit	Balance Debit	Balance Credit
19XX May 1		GJ1		5 0 0 0 00		5 0 0 0 00
3		GJ1		6 0 0 00		5 6 0 0 00
18		GJ1		2 5 0 00		5 8 5 0 00
28		GJ2	2 5 0 0 00			3 3 5 0 00

Brenda Clark, Capital   Account No. 311

Date	Explanation	Post. Ref.	Debit	Credit	Balance Debit	Balance Credit
19XX May 1		GJ1		10 0 0 0 00		10 0 0 0 00

Brenda Clark, Withdrawals					Account No. 312		
		Post. Ref.	Debit	Credit	Balance		
Date	Explanation				Debit	Credit	
19XX May 20		GJ1	6 2 5 00		6 2 5 00		

Word Processing Fees					Account No. 411		
		Post. Ref.	Debit	Credit	Balance		
Date	Explanation				Debit	Credit	
19XX May 7		GJ1		3 0 0 0 00		3 0 0 0 00	
22		GJ1		5 0 0 0 00		8 0 0 0 00	

Office Salaries Expense					Account No. 511		
		Post. Ref.	Debit	Credit	Balance		
Date	Explanation				Debit	Credit	
19XX May 15		GJ1	6 5 0 00		6 5 0 00		
27		GJ2	6 5 0 00		1 3 0 0 00		

Advertising Expense					Account No. 512		
		Post. Ref.	Debit	Credit	Balance		
Date	Explanation				Debit	Credit	
19XX May 18		GJ1	2 5 0 00		2 5 0 00		

Telephone Expense					Account No. 513		
		Post. Ref.	Debit	Credit	Balance		
Date	Explanation				Debit	Credit	
19XX May 29		GJ2	2 2 0 00		2 2 0 00		

Quiz Tip: The Post Reference column in the ledger tells which page of the journal the information came from. The Post Reference column in the journal (the last to be filled in) tells what account number in the ledger the information was posted to.

LEARNING UNIT 3-3
Preparing the Trial Balance: Step 4 of the Accounting Cycle

Did you note in Quiz 3-2 how each account had a running balance figure? Did you know the normal balance of each account in Clark's ledger? As we discussed in Chapter 2, the list of the individual accounts with their balances taken from the ledger is called a **trial balance.**

The trial balance shown in Figure 3-4 was developed from the ledger accounts of Clark's Word Processing Services that were posted and balanced in Quiz 3-2. If the information is journalized or posted incorrectly, the trial balance will not be correct.

CLARK'S WORD PROCESSING SERVICE TRIAL BALANCE MAY 31, 19XX	Debit	Credit
Cash	6 1 5 5 00	
Accounts Receivable	5 0 0 0 00	
Office Supplies	6 0 0 00	
Prepaid Rent	1 2 0 0 00	
Word Processing Equipment	6 0 0 0 00	
Accounts Payable		3 3 5 0 00
Brenda Clark, Capital		10 0 0 0 00
Brenda Clark, Withdrawals	6 2 5 00	
Word Processing Fees		8 0 0 0 00
Office Salaries Expense	1 3 0 0 00	
Advertising Expense	2 5 0 00	
Telephone Expense	2 2 0 00	
Totals	21 3 5 0 00	21 3 5 0 00

The trial balance lists the accounts in the same order as in the ledger. The $6,155 figure of cash came from the ledger, p. 84.

FIGURE 3-4 Trial Balance

There are some things the trial balance will not show:

◆ The capital figure on the trial balance may not be the beginning capital figure. For instance, if Brenda Clark had made additional investments during the period, the additional investment would have been journalized and posted to the capital account. The only way to tell if the capital balance on the trial balance is the original balance is to check the ledger capital account to see whether any additional investments were made. This will be important when we make financial reports.

◆ There is no guarantee that transactions have been properly recorded. For example, the following errors would remain undetected: (1) a transaction that may have been omitted in the journalizing process; (2) a transaction incorrectly analyzed and recorded in the journal; (3) a journal entry journalized or posted twice.

The totals of a trial balance can balance and yet be incorrect.

WHAT TO DO IF A TRIAL BALANCE DOESN'T BALANCE

The trial balance of Clark's Word Processing Services shows that the total of debits is equal to the total of credits. But what happens if the trial balance is in balance, but the correct amount is not recorded in each ledger account? Accuracy in the journalizing and posting process will help ensure that no errors are made.

Even if there is an error, the first rule is "don't panic." Everyone makes mistakes, and there are accepted ways of correcting them. Once an entry had been made in ink, correcting an error in it must always show that the entry has been changed and who changed it. Sometimes the change has to be explained.

SOME COMMON MISTAKES

Correcting the trial balance: What to do if your trial balance doesn't balance.

Did you clear your adding machine?

If the trial balance does not balance, the cause could be something relatively simple. Here are some common errors and how they can be fixed:

◆ If the difference (the amount you are off) is 10, 100, 1,000, etc., there probably is a mathematical error in addition.

◆ If the difference is equal to an individual account balance in the ledger, the amount could have been omitted. It is also possible the figure was not posted from the general journal.

♦ Divide the difference by 2; then check to see if a debit should have been a credit and vice versa in the ledger or trial balance. Example: $150 difference ÷ 2 = $75. This means you may have placed $75 as a debit to an account instead of a credit or vice versa.

♦ If the difference is evenly divisible by 9, a **slide** or transposition may have occurred. A slide is an error resulting from adding or deleting zeros in writing numbers. For example, $4,175.00 may have been copied as $41.75. A **transposition** is the accidental rearrangement of digits of a number. For example, $4,175 might have been accidentally written as $4,157.

♦ Compare the balances in the trial balance with the ledger accounts to check for copying errors.

♦ Recompute balances in each ledger account.

♦ Trace all postings from journal to ledger.

If you cannot find the error after you have done all of this, take a coffee break. Then start all over again.

MAKING A CORRECTION BEFORE POSTING

Before posting, error correction is straightforward. Simply draw a line through the incorrect entry, write the correct information above the line, and write your initials near the change.

Correcting an Error in an Account Title   The following illustration shows an error and its correction in an account title:

	1	Word Processing Equipment		6 0 0 0 00		
		Cash			1 0 0 0 00	
		Accounts Payable ~~Accounts Receivable~~ *amp*			5 0 0 0 00	
		Purchase of equipment from Ben Co.				

Correcting a Numerical Error   Numbers are handled the same way as account titles, as the next change from 520 to 250 shows:

	18	Advertising Expense		2 5 0 00		
		Accounts Payable			*amp* 2 5 0 00 ~~5 2 0 00~~	
		Bill from Al's News				

Correcting an Entry Error   If a number has been entered in the wrong column, a straight line is drawn through it, and the number is then written in the correct column:

		1	Word Processing Equipment		6 0 0 0 00		
			Cash			1 0 0 0 00	
			Accounts Payable	*amp* ~~5 0 0 0 00~~		5 0 0 0 00	
			Purchase of equip. from Ben Co.				

MAKING A CORRECTION AFTER POSTING

It is also possible to correct an amount that is correctly entered in the journal but posted incorrectly to the ledger of the proper account. The first step is to draw a line through the error and write the correct figure above it. The next step is changing the running balance to reflect the corrected posting. Here, too, a line is drawn through the balance and the corrected balance is written above it. Both changes must be initialed.

			Word Processing Fees				Account No. 411	
Date	Explanation	Post. Ref.	Debit	Credit	Balance Debit		Balance Credit	
19XX May 7		GJ1		2 5 0 00			2 5 0 0 00	
22		GJ1		~~4 0 0 00~~ 1 0 0 00 *amp*			~~6 5 0 0 00~~ 3 5 0 0 00 *amp*	

CORRECTING AN ENTRY POSTED TO THE WRONG ACCOUNT

Drawing a line through an error and writing the correction above it is possible when a mistake has occurred within the proper account, but when an error involves a posting to the wrong account the journal must include a correction accompanied by an explanation. In addition, the correct information must be posted to the appropriate ledgers.

Suppose, for example, that as a result of tracing postings from journal entries to ledgers you find that a $180 telephone bill was incorrectly debited as an advertising expense. The following illustration shows how this is done.

Step 1: The journal entry is corrected and the correction is explained:

	GENERAL JOURNAL			Page 3	
Date	Account Titles and Description	PR	Dr.	Cr.	
19XX May 29	Telephone Expense	513	1 8 0 0 0		
	Advertising Expense	512		1 8 0 0 0	
	To correct error in which				
	Advertising Exp. was debited				
	for charges to Telephone Exp.				

Step 2: The Advertising Expense ledger account is corrected:

			Advertising Expense				Account No. 512	
Date	Explanation	Post. Ref.	Debit	Credit	Balance Debit		Balance Credit	
19XX May 18		GJ1	1 7 5 00		1 7 5 00			
23		GJ1	1 8 0 00		3 5 5 00			
29	Correcting entry	GJ3		1 8 0 00	1 7 5 00			

Step 3: The Telephone Expense ledger is corrected:

			Telephone Expense				Account No. 513	
Date	Explanation	Post. Ref.	Debit	Credit	Balance Debit		Balance Credit	
19XX May 29		GJ3	1 8 0 00		1 8 0 00			

LEARNING UNIT 3-3 REVIEW

AT THIS POINT you should be able to

◆ Prepare a trial balance with a ledger, using four-column accounts. (p. 87)
◆ Analyze and correct a trial balance that doesn't balance. (p. 87)
◆ Correct journal and posting errors. (p. 88)

SELF-REVIEW QUIZ 3-3

(The blank forms you need are on page 64 of the *Study Guide and Working Papers.*)

1.

MEMO
To: Al Vincent
From: Professor Jones
Re: Trial Balance
You have submitted to me an incorrect trial balance. Could you please re-work and turn in to me before next Friday?
Note: Individual amounts look OK.

A. RICE
TRIAL BALANCE
OCTOBER 31, 19XX

	Dr.	Cr.
Cash		8 0 6 0 00
Operating Expenses		1 7 0 0 00
A. Rice, Withdrawals		4 0 0 00
Service Revenue		5 4 0 0 00
Equipment	5 0 0 0 00	
Accounts Receivable	3 5 4 0 00	
Accounts Payable	2 0 0 0 00	
Supplies	3 0 0 00	
A. Rice, Capital		11 6 0 0 00

2. A $7,000 debit to office equipment was mistakenly journalized and posted on June 9, 19XX to office supplies. Prepare the appropriate journal entry to correct this error.

Solution to Self-Review Quiz 3-3

1.

Quiz Tip: Items in a trial balance are listed in the same order as in the ledger or the chart of accounts. Expect each account to have its normal balance (either debit or credit).

A. RICE
TRIAL BALANCE
OCTOBER 31, 19XX

	Dr.	Cr.
Cash	8 0 6 0 00	
Accounts Receivable	3 5 4 0 00	
Supplies	3 0 0 00	
Equipment	5 0 0 0 00	
Accounts Payable		2 0 0 0 00
A. Rice, Capital		11 6 0 0 00
A. Rice, Withdrawals	4 0 0 00	
Service Revenue		5 4 0 0 00
Operating Expenses	1 7 0 0 00	
Totals	19 0 0 0 00	19 0 0 0 00

2.

			GENERAL JOURNAL			Page 4
Date			Account Titles and Description	PR	Dr.	Cr.
19XX June	9		Office Equipment		7 0 0 0 00	
			Office Supplies			7 0 0 0 00
			To correct error in which office supplies			
			had been debited for purchase of			
			office equipment			

COMPREHENSIVE DEMONSTRATION PROBLEM WITH SOLUTION TIPS

(The blank forms you need are on pages 65–69 in the *Study Guide and Working Papers.*)

In March, Abby's Employment Agency had the following transactions:

19XX

Mar.	1	Abby Todd invested $5,000 in the new employment agency.
	4	Bought equipment for cash, $200.
	5	Earned employment fee commission, $200, but payment from Blue Co. will not be received until June.
	6	Paid wages expense, $300.
	7	Abby Todd paid her home utility bill from the company checkbook, $75.
	9	Placed Rick Wool at VCR Corporation, receiving $1,200 cash.
	15	Paid cash for supplies, $200.
	28	Telephone bill received but not paid, $180.
	29	Advertising bill received but not paid, $400.

The chart of accounts includes: Cash, 111; Accounts Receivable, 112; Supplies, 131; Equipment, 141; Accounts Payable, 211; A. Todd, Capital, 311; A. Todd, Withdrawals, 321; Employment Fees Earned, 411; Wage Expense, 511; Telephone Expense, 521; Advertising Expense, 531.

Your task is to:

a. Set up a ledger based on the chart of accounts.

b. Journalize (all p. 1) and post transactions.

c. Prepare a trial balance for March 31.

			ABBY'S EMPLOYMENT AGENCY					Page 1	

Date			Account Titles and Description	PR	Dr.	Cr.
19XX Mar.	1		Cash	111	5 0 0 0 00	
			A. Todd, Capital	311		5 0 0 0 00
			Owner investment			
	4		Equipment	141	2 0 0 00	
			Cash	111		2 0 0 00
			Bought equipment for cash			
	5		Accounts Receivable	112	2 0 0 00	
			Employment Fees Earned	411		2 0 0 00
			Fees on account from Blue Co.			
	6		Wage Expense	511	3 0 0 00	
			Cash	111		3 0 0 00
			Paid wages			
	7		A. Todd, Withdrawals	321	7 5 00	
			Cash	111		7 5 00
			Personal withdrawals			
	9		Cash	111	1 2 0 0 00	
			Employment Fees Earned	411		1 2 0 0 00
			Cash fees			
	15		Supplies	131	2 0 0 00	
			Cash	111		2 0 0 00
			Bought supplies for cash			
	28		Telephone Expense	521	1 8 0 00	
			Accounts Payable	211		1 8 0 00
			Telephone bill owed			
	29		Advertising Expense	531	4 0 0 00	
			Accounts Payable	211		4 0 0 00
			Advertising bill received			

GENERAL LEDGER

Cash   111

Date		PR	Dr.	Cr.	Balance Dr.	Balance Cr.
19XX March	1	GJ1	5,000		5,000	
	4	GJ1		200	4,800	
	6	GJ1		300	4,500	
	7	GJ1		75	4,425	
	9	GJ1	1,200		5,625	
	15	GJ1		200	5,425	

Accounts Receivable   112

Date		PR	Dr.	Cr.	Balance Dr.	Balance Cr.
19XX March	5	GJ1	200		200	

Supplies   131

Date		PR	Dr.	Cr.	Balance Dr.	Balance Cr.
19XX March	15	GJ1	200		200	

Equipment   141

Date		PR	Dr.	Cr.	Balance Dr.	Balance Cr.
19XX March	4	GJ1	200		200	

Accounts Payable   211

Date		PR	Dr.	Cr.	Balance Dr.	Balance Cr.
19XX March	28	GJ1		180		180
	29	GJ1		400		580

A. Todd, Capital   311

Date		PR	Dr.	Cr.	Balance Dr.	Balance Cr.
19XX March	1	GJ1		5,000		5,000

A. Todd, Withdrawals   321

Date		PR	Dr.	Cr.	Balance Dr.	Balance Cr.
19XX March	7	GJ1	75		75	

Employment Fees Earned   411

Date		PR	Dr.	Cr.	Balance Dr.	Balance Cr.
19XX March	5	GJ1		200		200
	9	GJ1		1,200		1,400

Wage Expense   511

Date		PR	Dr.	Cr.	Balance Dr.	Balance Cr.
19XX March	6	GJ1	300		300	

Telephone Expense   521

Date		PR	Dr.	Cr.	Balance Dr.	Balance Cr.
19XX March	28	GJ1	180		180	

Advertising Expense   531

Date		PR	Dr.	Cr.	Balance Dr.	Balance Cr.
19XX March	29	GJ1	400		400	

Solution Tips to Journalizing

1. When journalizing, the PR column is not filled in.
2. Write the name of the debit against the date column. Indent credits and list them below debits. Be sure total debits for each transaction equal total credits.
3. Skip a line between each transaction.

THE ANALYSIS OF THE JOURNAL ENTRIES

| March 1 | Cash | A | ↑ | Dr. | $5,000 |
| | A. Todd, Capital | Capital | ↑ | Cr. | $5,000 |

| 4 | Equipment | A | ↑ | Dr. | $ 200 |
| | Cash | A | ↓ | Cr. | $ 200 |

| 5 | Acc. Receivable | A | ↑ | Dr. | $ 200 |
| | Empl. Fees Earned | Rev. | ↑ | Cr. | $ 200 |

| 6 | Wage Expense | Exp. | ↑ | Dr. | $ 300 |
| | Cash | A | ↓ | Cr. | $ 300 |

| 7 | A. Todd, Withdrawals | Withd. | ↑ | Dr. | $ 75 |
| | Cash | A | ↓ | Cr. | $ 75 |

| 9 | Cash | A | ↑ | Dr. | $1,200 |
| | Empl. Fees Earned | Rev. | ↑ | Cr. | $1,200 |

| 15 | Supplies | A | ↑ | Dr. | $ 200 |
| | Cash | A | ↓ | Cr. | $ 200 |

| 28 | Telephone Expense | Exp. | ↑ | Dr. | $ 180 |
| | Accounts Payable | L | ↑ | Cr. | $ 180 |

| 28 | Advertising Expense | Exp. | ↑ | Dr. | $ 400 |
| | Accounts Payable | L | ↑ | Cr. | $ 400 |

Solution Tips to Posting

The PR column in the ledger cash account tells you from which page a journal information came (see page 1). After the ledger cash account is posted, Account Number 111 is put in the PR column of the journal. (This is called cross-referencing.)

Note how we keep a running balance in the cash account. A $5,000 dr. balance and a $200 credit entry result in a new debit balance of $4,800.

ABBY'S EMPLOYMENT AGENCY
TRIAL BALANCE
MARCH 31, 19XX

	Dr.	Cr.
Cash	5,425	
Accounts Receivable	200	
Supplies	200	
Equipment	200	
Accounts Payable		580
A. Todd, Capital		5,000
A. Todd, Withdrawals	75	
Employment Fees Earned		1,400
Wage Expense	300	
Telephone Expense	180	
Advertising Expense	400	
Totals	**6,980**	**6,980**

Solution Tip to Trial Balance

The trial balance lists the ending balance of each title in the order in which they appear in the ledger. The total of $6,980 on the left equals $6,980 on the right.

SUMMARY OF KEY POINTS

Learning Unit 3-1

1. The accounting cycle is a sequence of accounting procedures that are usually performed during an accounting period.
2. An accounting period is the time period for which the income statement is prepared. The time period can be any period up to one year.
3. A calendar year is from January 1 to December 31. The fiscal year is any twelve-month period. A fiscal year could be a calendar year but does not have to be.
4. Interim reports are statements that are usually prepared for a portion of the business's calendar or fiscal year (e.g., a month or a quarter).
5. A general journal is a book that records transactions in chronological order. Here debits and credits are shown together on one page. It is the book of original entry.
6. The ledger is a collection of accounts where information is accumulated from the postings of the journal. The ledger is the book of final entry.
7. Journalizing is the process of recording journal entries.
8. The chart of accounts provides the specific titles of accounts to be entered in the journal.

9. When journalizing, the post reference (PR) column is left blank.
10. A compound journal entry occurs when more than two accounts are affected in the journalizing process of a business transaction.

Learning Unit 3-2

1. Posting is the process of transferring information from the journal to the ledger.
2. The journal and ledger contain the same information but in a different form.
3. The four-column account aids in keeping a running balance of an account.
4. The normal balance of an account will be located on the side that increases it according to the rules of debits and credits. For example, the normal balances of liabilities occur on the credit side.
5. The mechanical process of posting requires care in transferring to the appropriate account the dates, post references, and amounts.

Learning Unit 3-3

1. A trial balance can balance but be incorrect. For example, an entire journal entry may not have been posted.
2. If a trial balance doesn't balance, check for errors in addition, omission of postings, slides, transpositions, copying errors, and so on.
3. Specific procedures should be followed in making corrections in journals and ledgers.

KEY TERMS

Accounting cycle For each accounting period, the process that begins with the recording of business transactions or procedures into a journal and ends with the completion of a post-closing trial balance.

Accounting period The period of time for which an income statement is prepared.

Book of final entry Book that receives information about business transactions from a book of original entry (a journal). Example: a ledger.

Book of original entry Book that records the first formal information about business transactions. Example: a journal.

Calendar year January 1 to December 31.

Compound journal entry A journal entry that affects more than two accounts.

Cross-referencing Adding to the PR column of the journal the account number of the ledger account that was updated from the journal.

Fiscal year The twelve-month period a business chooses for its accounting year.

Four-column account A running balance account that records debits and credits and has a column for an ending balance (debit or credit). Replaces the standard two-column account we used earlier.

General journal The simplest form of a journal, which records information from transactions in chronological order as they occur. This journal links the debit and credit parts of transactions together.

Interim reports Financial reports that are prepared for a month, quarter, or some other portion of the fiscal year.

Journal A listing of business transactions in chronological order. The journal links on one page the debit and credit parts of transactions.

Journal entry The transaction (debits and credits) that is recorded into a journal once it is analyzed.

Journalizing The process of recording a transaction entry into the journal.

Natural business year A business's fiscal year that ends at the same time as a slow seasonal period begins.

Posting The transferring, copying, or recording of information from a journal to a ledger.

Slide The error that results in adding or deleting zeros in the writing of a number. Example: 79,200 → 7,920.

Transposition The accidental rearrangement of digits of a number. Example: 152 → 125.

Trial balance An informal listing of the ledger accounts and their balances in the ledger that aids in proving the equality of debits and credits.

BLUEPRINT OF FIRST FOUR STEPS OF ACCOUNTING CYCLE

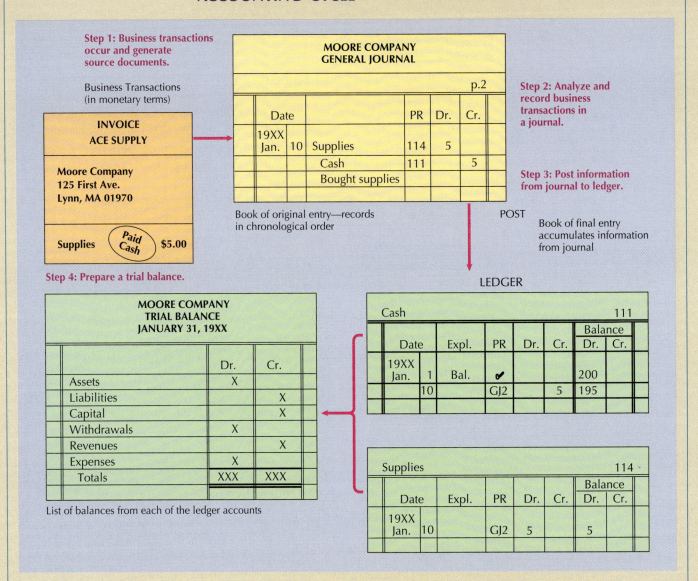

Step 1: Business transactions occur and generate source documents.

Business Transactions (in monetary terms)

INVOICE
ACE SUPPLY

Moore Company
125 First Ave.
Lynn, MA 01970

Supplies   *Paid Cash* $5.00

Step 2: Analyze and record business transactions in a journal.

MOORE COMPANY GENERAL JOURNAL

p.2

Date			PR	Dr.	Cr.
19XX Jan.	10	Supplies	114	5	
		Cash	111		5
		Bought supplies			

Book of original entry—records in chronological order

Step 3: Post information from journal to ledger.

POST

Book of final entry accumulates information from journal

Step 4: Prepare a trial balance.

MOORE COMPANY TRIAL BALANCE JANUARY 31, 19XX

	Dr.	Cr.
Assets	X	
Liabilities		X
Capital		X
Withdrawals	X	
Revenues		X
Expenses	X	
Totals	XXX	XXX

List of balances from each of the ledger accounts

LEDGER

Cash   111

Date	Expl.	PR	Dr.	Cr.	Balance Dr.	Cr.
19XX Jan. 1	Bal.	✔			200	
10		GJ2		5	195	

Supplies   114

Date	Expl.	PR	Dr.	Cr.	Balance Dr.	Cr.
19XX Jan. 10		GJ2	5		5	

QUESTIONS, MINI EXERCISES, EXERCISES, AND PROBLEMS

Discussion Questions

1. Explain the concept of the accounting cycle.
2. An accounting period is based on the balance sheet. Agree or disagree.
3. Compare and contrast a calendar year versus a fiscal year.
4. What are interim reports?
5. Why is the ledger called the book of final entry?
6. How do transactions get "linked" in a general journal?
7. What is the relationship of the chart of accounts to the general journal?
8. What is a compound journal entry?
9. Posting means updating the journal. Agree or disagree. Please comment.
10. The side that decreases an account is the normal balance. True or false?

11. The PR column of a general journal is the last item to be filled in during the posting process. Agree or disagree.
12. Discuss the concept of cross-referencing.
13. What is the difference between a transposition and a slide?

Mini Exercises

(The blank forms you need are on page 71 of the *Study Guide and Working Papers*.)

General Journal

1. Complete the following from the general journal of Ranger Co.

			RANGER COMPANY GENERAL JOURNAL					Page 1	
Date			Account Titles and Descriptions	PR	Dr.		Cr.		
19XX Aug	18		Cash		7 0 0 0 0 00				
			Equipment		2 0 0 00				
			B. Ranger, Capital				7 2 0 0 0 00		
			Initial Investment by Owner						

   a. Year of Journal Entry   _____
   b. Month of Journal Entry   _____
   c. Day of Journal Entry   _____
   d. Name(s) of Accounts Debited   _____
   e. Name(s) of Accounts Credited   _____
   f. Explanation of Transaction   _____
   g. Amount of Debit(s)   _____
   h. Amount of Credit(s)   _____
   i. Page of Journal   _____

General Journal

2. Provide the explanation for each of these general journal entries.

			GENERAL JOURNAL					Page 4	
Date			Account Titles and Descriptions	PR	Debit		Credit		
19XX July	9		Cash		7 0 0 0 0 00				
			Office Equipment		5 0 0 0 0 00				
			A. Rye, Capital				12 0 0 0 0 00		
			(A)						
	15		Cash		3 0 00				
			Accounts Receivable		6 0 00				
			Hair Fees Earned				9 0 00		
			(B)						
	20		Advertising Expense		4 0 00				
			Accounts Payable				4 0 00		
			(C)						

Posting and Balancing

3. Balance this four-column account. What function does the PR column serve? When will the Account 111 be used in the journalizing and posting process?

| Cash | | | | | Acct. 111 | |
| | | | | | Balance | |
Date	Explanation	PR	Dr.	Cr.	Dr.	Cr.
19XX						
June 4		GJ 1	15			
5		GJ 1	6			
9		GJ 2		4		
10		GJ 3	1			

The Trial Balance

4. The following Trial Balance was prepared *incorrectly.*
   a. Rearrange the accounts in proper order.
   b. Calculate the total of the Trial Balance. (Small numbers are used intentionally so you can do the calculations in your head.) Assume each account has a normal balance.

LARKIN CO.
TRIAL BALANCE
OCTOBER 31, 19XX

	Dr.	Cr.
B. Larkin, Capital	14	
Equipment	9	
Rent Expense		4
Advertising Expense		3
Accounts Payable		8
Taxi Fees	16	
Cash	17	
B. Larkin, Withdrawals	—	5
Totals	**56**	**19**

Correcting Entry

5. On May 1, 1998 a telephone expense for $180 was debited to Repair Expense. On June 12, 1999 this error was found. Prepare the corrected Journal Entry. When would a correcting entry *not* be needed?

Exercises

(The forms you need are on pages 72–77 of the *Study Guide and Working Papers.*)

Preparing journal entries.

3-1. Prepare journal entries for the following transactions that occurred during October:

19XX
Nov.   1   Ann Carter invested $20,000 cash and $2,000 of equipment into her new business.
        3   Purchased building for $60,000 on account.
        12 Purchased a truck from Lange Co. for $18,000 cash.
        18 Bought supplies from Green Co. on account, $700.

3-2. Record the following into the general journal of Fay's Repair Shop.

Preparing journal entries.

19XX
Jan.   1   Fay Hope invested $15,000 cash in the repair shop.
        5   Paid $7,000 for shop equipment.
        8   Bought from Lowell Co. shop equipment for $6,000 on account.
        14 Received $900 for repair fees earned.
        18 Billed Sullivan Co. $900 for services rendered.
        20 Fay withdrew $300 for personal use.

3-3. Post the following transactions to the ledger of King Company. The partial ledger of King Company is Cash, 111; Equipment, 121; Accounts Payable, 211; and A. King, Capital, 311. Please use four-column accounts in the posting process.

Posting

Date 19XX			PR	Dr.	Cr.
					Page 4
April	6	Cash		15 0 0 0 00	
		A. King, Capital			15 0 0 0 00
		Cash investment			
	14	Equipment		9 0 0 0 00	
		Cash			4 0 0 0 00
		Accounts Payable			5 0 0 0 00
		Purchase of equipment			

Journalizing, posting, and preparing a trial balance.

3-4. From the following transactions for Lowe Company for the month of July, (a) prepare journal entries (assume that it is p. 1 of the journal), (b) post to the ledger (use four-column account), and (c) prepare a trial balance.

19XX
July   1   Joan Lowe invested $6,000 in the business.
        4   Bought from Lax Co. equipment on account, $800.
        15 Billed Friend Co. for services rendered, $4,000.
        18 Received $5,000 cash for services rendered.
        24 Paid salaries expense, $1,800.
        28 Joan withdrew $400 for personal use.

Partial chart of accounts includes: Cash, 111; Accounts Receivable, 112; Equipment, 121; Accounts Payable, 211; J. Lowe, Capital, 311; J. Lowe, Withdrawals, 312; Fees Earned, 411; Salaries Expense, 511.

3-5. You have been hired to correct the following trial balance that has been recorded improperly from the ledger to the trial balance.

SUNG CO.
TRIAL BALANCE
MARCH 31, 19XX

	Dr.	Cr.
Accounts Payable	2 0 0 0 00	
A. Sung, Capital		6 5 0 0 00
A. Sung, Withdrawals		3 0 0 00
Services Earned		4 7 0 0 00
Concessions Earned	2 5 0 0 00	
Rent Expense	4 0 0 00	
Salaries Expense	2 5 0 0 00	
Miscellaneous Expense		1 3 0 0 00
Cash	10 0 0 0 00	
Accounts Receivable		1 2 0 0 00
Totals	17 4 0 0 00	14 0 0 0 00

3-6. On February 6, 19XX, Mike Sullivan made the following journal entry to record the purchase on account of office equipment priced at $1,400. This transaction had not yet been posted when the error was discovered. Make the appropriate correction.

Correcting entry

GENERAL JOURNAL

Date		Account Titles and Description	PR	Dr.	Cr.
19XX Feb.	6	Office Equipment		9 0 0 00	
		Accounts Payable			9 0 0 00
		Purchase of office equip. on account			

Group A Problems

(The forms you need are on pages 78–89 of the *Working Papers and Study Guide.*)

3A-1. Sue Vance operates Vance's Dog Grooming Center. As the bookkeeper, you have been requested to journalize the following transactions:

Journalizing

19XX
July
1 Paid rent for two months in advance, $3,000.
3 Purchased grooming equipment on account from Leek's Supply House, $2,500.
10 Purchased grooming supplies from Angel's Wholesale for $600 cash.
12 Received $1,400 cash from grooming fees earned.
20 Sue withdrew $400 for her personal use.
21 Advertising bill received from *Daily Sun* but unpaid, $120.
25 Paid cleaning expense, $90.
28 Paid salaries expense, $500.
29 Performed grooming work for $1,700, however, payment will not be received from Rick's Kennel until May.

Check Figure:

July 21

Dr. Advertising expense $120

Cr. Accounts Payable 120

30 Paid Leek's Supply House half the amount owed from July 3 transaction.

Your task is to journalize the above transactions. The chart of accounts for Vance's Dog Grooming Center is as follows:

Chart of Accounts

Assets	**Owner's Equity**
111 Cash	311 Sue Vance, Capital
112 Accounts Receivable	312 Sue Vance, Withdrawals
114 Prepaid Rent	**Revenue**
116 Grooming Supplies	411 Grooming Fees Earned
121 Grooming Equipment	**Expenses**
Liabilities	511 Advertising Expense
211 Accounts Payable	512 Salaries Expense
	514 Cleaning Expense

Comprehensive Problem: Journalizing, posting, and preparing a trial balance.

3A-2. On June 1, 19XX, Molly Taylor opened Taylor's Dance Studio. The following transactions occurred in June:

19XX
June
1 Molly Taylor invested $8,000 in the dance studio.
1 Paid three months' rent in advance, $1,000.
3 Purchased $700 of equipment from Astor Co. on account.
5 Received $900 cash for fitness-training workshop for dancers.
8 Purchased $300 of supplies for cash.
9 Billed Lester Co. $2,100 for group dance lesson for its employees.
10 Paid salaries of assistants, $400.
15 Molly Taylor withdrew $150 from the business for her personal use.
28 Paid electrical expense, $125.
29 Paid telephone bill for June, $190.

Your task is to

Check Figure:
Trial Balance Total $11,700

a. Set up the ledger based on the charts of accounts below.
b. Journalize (journal is p. 1) and post the June transactions.
c. Prepare a trial balance as of June 30, 19XX.

The chart of accounts for Taylor's Dance Studio is as follows:

Chart of Accounts

Assets	**Owner's Equity**
111 Cash	311 Molly Taylor, Capital
112 Accounts Receivable	312 Molly Taylor, Withdrawals
114 Prepaid Rent	**Revenue**
121 Supplies	411 Fees Earned
131 Equipment	**Expenses**
Liabilities	511 Electrical Expense
211 Accounts Payable	512 Salaries Expense
	531 Telephone Expense

3A-3. The following transactions occurred in June 19XX for A. French's Placement Agency:

19XX
June
1 A. French invested $9,000 cash in the placement agency.

1 Bought equipment on account from Hook Co., $2,000.

3 Earned placement fees of $1,600, but payment will not be received until July.

5 A. French withdrew $100 for his personal use.

7 Paid wages expense, $300.

9 Placed a client on a local TV show, receiving $600 cash.

15 Bought supplies on account from Lyon Co., $500.

28 Paid telephone bill for June, $160.

29 Advertising bill from Shale Co. received but not paid, $900.

The chart of accounts for A. French Placement Agency is as follows:

Chart of Accounts

Assets	Owner's Equity
111 Cash	311 A. French, Capital
112 Accounts Receivable	312 A. French, Withdrawals
131 Supplies	**Revenue**
141 Equipment	411 Placement Fees Earned
Liabilities	**Expenses**
211 Accounts Payable	511 Wage Expense
	512 Telephone Expense
	531 Advertising Expense

Your task is to

a. Set up the ledger based on the chart of accounts.

b. Journalize (p. 1) and post the June transactions.

c. Prepare a trial balance as of June 30, 19XX.

Group B Problems

(The forms you need are on pages 78–89 of the *Study Guide and Working Papers.*)

3B-1. In April Sue Vance opened a new dog grooming center. Please assist her by journalizing the following business transactions:

Check Figure:
April 21
Dr. Advertising expense $75
Cr. Accounts payable $75

19XX
April
1 Sue Vance invested $4,000 of grooming equipment as well as $6,000 cash in the new business.

3 Purchased grooming supplies on account from Rex Co., $500.

10 Purchased office equipment on account from Ross Stationery, $400.

12 Sue paid her home telephone bill from the company checkbook, $60.

20 Received $600 cash for grooming services performed.

21 Advertising bill received but not paid, $75.

25 Cleaning bill received but not paid, $90.

28 Performed grooming work for Jay Kennels, $700; however, payment will not be received until May.

29 Paid salaries expense, $400.

30 Paid Ross Stationery half the amount owed from April 10 transaction.

The chart of accounts for Vance's Dog Grooming Center includes: Cash, 111; Accounts Receivable, 112; Prepaid Rent, 114; Grooming Supplies, 116; Office Equipment, 120; Grooming Equipment, 121; Accounts Payable, 211; Sue Vance, Capital, 311; Sue Vance, Withdrawals, 312; Grooming Fees Earned, 411; Advertising Expense, 511; Salaries Expense, 512; and Cleaning Expense, 514.

Comprehensive Problem: Jour-nalizing, posting, and preparing a trial balance.

3B-2. In June the following transactions occurred for Taylor's Dance Studio.

19XX

June   1 Molly Taylor invested $6,000 in the dance studio.
        1 Paid four months rent in advance, $1,200.
        3 Purchased supplies on account from A.J.K., $700.
        5 Purchased equipment on account from Reese Company, $900.
        8 Received $1,300 cash for dance-training program provided to North-west Junior College.
        9 Billed Long Co. for dance lessons provided, $600.
       10 Molly withdrew $400 from the dance studio to buy a new chain saw for her home.
       15 Paid salaries expense, $400.
       28 Paid telephone bill, $118.
       29 Electric bill received but unpaid, $120.

Check Figure:
Total Trial Balance $9,620

Your task is to

a. Set up a ledger.

b. Journalize (all p. 1) and post the June transactions.

c. Prepare a trial balance as of June 30, 19XX.

Chart of accounts includes: Cash, 111; Accounts Receivable, 112; Prepaid Rent, 114; Supplies, 121; Equipment, 131; Accounts Payable, 211; M. Taylor, Capital, 311; M. Taylor, Withdrawals, 321; Fees Earned, 411; Electrical Expense, 511; Salaries Expense, 521; Telephone Expense, 531.

Comprehensive Problem: Jour-nalizing, posting, and preparing a trial balance.

3B-3. In June, A. French's Placement Agency had the following transactions:

19XX

June   1 A. French invested $6,000 in the new placement agency.
        2 Bought equipment for cash, $350.
        3 Earned placement fee commission, $2,100, but payment from Avon Co. will not be received until July.
        5 Paid wages expense, $400.
        7 A. French paid his home utility bill from the company checkbook, $69.
        9 Placed Jay Diamond on a national TV show, receiving $900 cash.
       15 Paid cash for supplies, $350.
       28 Telephone bill received but not paid, $185.
       29 Advertising bill received but not paid, $200.

Check Figure:
Total Trial Balance $9,385

The chart of accounts includes: Cash, 111; Accounts Receivable, 112; Supplies, 131; Equipment, 141; Accounts Payable, 211; A. French, Capital, 311; A. French, Withdrawals, 321; Placement Fees Earned, 411; Wage Expense, 511; Telephone Expense, 521; Advertising Expense, 531.

Your task is to

a. Set up a ledger based on the chart of accounts.

b. Journalize (all p. 1) and post transactions.

c. Prepare a trial balance for June 30, 19XX.

3R-1.

Paul Regan, bookkeeper of Hampton Co., has been up half the night trying to get his trial balance to balance. Here are his results:

HAMPTON CO. TRIAL BALANCE JUNE 30, 19XX	Dr.	Cr.
Office Sales		5 7 2 0 00
Cash in Bank	3 2 6 0 00	
Accounts Receivable	5 6 6 0 00	
Office Equipment	8 4 0 0 00	
Accounts Payable		4 1 6 0 00
D. Hole, Capital		11 5 6 0 00
D. Hole, Withdrawals		7 0 0 00
Wage Expense	2 6 0 0 00	
Rent Expense	9 4 0 00	
Utilities Expense	2 6 00	
Office Supplies	1 2 0 00	
Prepaid Rent	1 8 0 00	

Ken Small, the accountant, compared Paul's amounts in the trial balance with those in the ledger, recomputed each account balance, and compared postings. Ken found the following errors:

1. A $200 debit to D. Hole, Withdrawals, was posted as a credit.
2. D. Hole, Withdrawals, was listed on the trial balance as a credit.
3. A Note Payable account with a credit balance of $2,400 was not listed on the trial balance.
4. The pencil footings for Accounts Payable were debits of $5,320 and credits of $8,800.
5. A debit of $180 to Prepaid Rent was not posted.
6. Office Supplies bought for $60 was posted as a credit to Supplies.
7. A debit of $120 to Accounts Receivable was not posted.
8. A cash payment of $420 was credited to Cash for $240.
9. The pencil footing of the credits to Cash was overstated by $400.
10. The Utilities Expense of $260 was listed in the trial balance as $26.

Assist Paul Regan by preparing a correct trial balance. What advice could you give Ken about Paul? Can you explain the situation to Paul? Put your answers in writing.

3R-2.

Lauren Oliver, an accountant lab tutor, is having a debate with some of her assistants. They are trying to find out how each of the following five unrelated situations would affect the trial balance:

1. A $5 debit to cash in the ledger was not posted.
2. A $10 debit to Computer Supplies was debited to Computer Equipment.
3. An $8 debit to Wage Expense was debited twice to the account.
4. A $4 debit to Computer Supplies was debited to Computer Sales.
5. A $35 credit to Accounts Payable was posted as a $53 credit.

Could you indicate to Lauren the effect that each situation will have on the trial balance? If a situation will have no effect, indicate that fact. Put in writing how each of these situations could be avoided in the future.

YOU make the call

Critical Thinking/Ethical Case

3R-3.
Jay Simons, the accountant of See Co., would like to buy a new software package for his general ledger. He couldn't do it because all funds were frozen for the rest of the fiscal period. Jay called his friend at Joor Industries and asked whether he could copy their software. Why should or shouldn't Jay have done that?

ACCOUNTING RECALL
A CUMULATIVE APPROACH

THIS EXAM REVIEWS CHAPTERS 1 THROUGH 3

Your *Study Guide and Working Papers* have forms (pages 93 and 105) to complete this exam, as well as worked-out solutions. The page references next to each question identify what page to turn back to if you answer the question incorrectly.

PART 1   Vocabulary Review

Match the terms to the appropriate definition or phrase.
Page Ref.

(40)	1. Chart of Accounts	A. Process of recording transactions in a journal
(72)	2. Ledger	B. Rearrangement of digits
(88)	3. Slide	C. Book of original entry
(71)	4. Calendar year	D. Running balance
(88)	5. Transposition	E. Transferring information
(80)	6. Four-column account	F. January 1 to December 31
(71)	7. Journalizing	G. Adding or deleting numbers
(74)	8. Compound entry	H. Numbering system
(80)	9. Posting	I. More than two accounts
(71)	10. Journal	J. Book of final entry

PART II   True or False (Accounting Theory)

(72)	11.	The ledger is located in same book as a journal.
(81)	12.	The PR column of a general journal is completed after the posting to the ledger is complete.
(88)	13.	Correcting errors in journalizing can only be done before posting.
(71)	14.	A calendar year could be a fiscal year.
(87)	15.	A trial balance could balance but be incorrect.

CONTINUING PROBLEM

Tony's computer center is picking up in business, so he has decided to expand his bookkeeping system to a general journal/ledger system. The balances from August have been forwarded to the ledger accounts. The forms are in the *Study Guide and Working Papers*, pages 94–104.

Assignment:

1. Use the chart of accounts provided in Chapter 2 to record the following transactions.

Eldorado Computer Center
385 N. Escondido Blvd.
Escondido CA 92025
8104
September 1, -- 19xx ------
Pay To the Order of -- *Capital Management* ------ $ 1200.00 ------
One thousand and two hundred 00/100
First Union Bank
322 Glen Ave.
Escondido, CA 92025
memo *Prepaid Rent — Aug. Sept. Oct.*
0611 062 78 72
-------- *Tony Freedman* --------

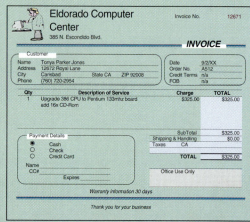

Eldorado Computer Center
385 N. Escondido Blvd.
Invoice No. 12671
INVOICE
Customer
Name: Tonya Parker Jones
Address: 12672 Royal Lane
City: Carlsbad State CA ZIP 92008
Phone: (760) 720-2954
Date: 9/2/XX
Order No. A512
Credit Terms: n/a
FOB: n/a

Qty	Description of Service	Charge	TOTAL
1	Upgrade 386 CPU to Pentium 133mhz board add 16x CD-Rom	$325.00	$325.00

SubTotal $325.00
Shipping & Handling $0.00
Taxes CA
TOTAL $325.00
Payment Details: Cash / Check / Credit Card
Warranty information 30 days
Thank you for your business

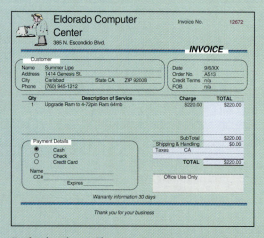

Eldorado Computer Center
385 N. Escondido Blvd.
Invoice No. 12672
INVOICE
Customer
Name: Summer Lipe
Address: 1414 Genesis St.
City: Carlsbad State CA ZIP 92008
Phone: (760) 945-1212
Date: 9/6/XX
Order No. A513
Credit Terms: n/a
FOB: n/a

Qty	Description of Service	Charge	TOTAL
1	Upgrade Ram to 4-72pin Ram 64mb	$220.00	$220.00

SubTotal $220.00
Shipping & Handling $0.00
Taxes CA
TOTAL $220.00
Payment Details: Cash / Check / Credit Card
Warranty information 30 days
Thank you for your business

Eldorado Computer Center
385 N. Escondido Blvd.
Escondido CA 92025
8105
September 8, -- 19xx ------
Pay To the Order of -- *Pacific Bell* ------ $ 155.00 ------
One hundred and fifty five 00/100
First Union Bank
322 Glen Ave.
Escondido, CA 92025
memo *August phone bill transaction (k) Chpt. 2*
0611 062 78 72
-------- *Tony Freedman* --------

Refer back to Chapter 2 transaction (k).

Jeannine Sparks
1919 Sierra St.
Escondido CA 92025
251
September 12, -- 19xx ------
Pay To the Order of -- *Eldorado Computer Center* ------ $ 850.00 ------
Eight Hundred and Fifty dollars 00/100
Bank First
322 Cardiff Ave.
Escondido, CA 92025
memo *Computer Fixed, Transaction (o) Chpt. 2*
0611 062 78 72
-------- *Jeannine Sparks* --------

Eldorado Computer Center
385 N. Escondido Blvd.
Escondido CA 92025
8106
September 15, -- 19xx ------
Pay To the Order of -- *Computer Connection* ------ $ 200.00 ------
Two hundred dollars and 00/100
First Union Bank
322 Glen Ave.
Escondido, CA 92025
memo *Account due from transaction (s) Chpt. 2*
0611 062 78 72
-------- *Tony Freedman* --------

Refer back to Chapter 2 transaction (s).

Eldorado Computer Center
385 N. Escondido Blvd.
Escondido CA 92025

8107

September 17, -- 19xx ------

Pay
To the
Order of— *Multi Systems, Inc* --- $ 1,200.00 -------

Twelve hundred dollars and 00/100

First Union Bank
322 Glen Ave.
Escondido, CA 92025

Purchase order 200
memo *Computer Equipment-Bench Workstations* --------- *Tony Freedman* ---------
0611 062 78 72

Purchased computer shop equipment.

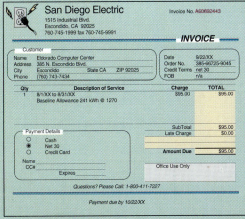

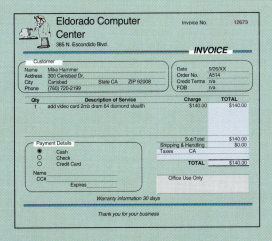

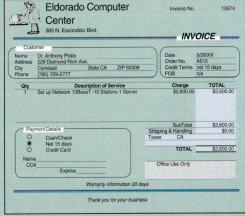

Refer back to Chapter 2 transaction (o).

2. Post all transactions to the general ledger accounts (the Prepaid Rent Account #1025 has been added to the chart of accounts).

3. Prepare a trial balance for Sept. 30, 19XX.

4. Prepare the financial statements for the three months ended September 30, 19XX.

COMPUTERIZED ACCOUNTING APPLICATION FOR CHAPTER 3

Journalizing, Posting, General Ledger, Trial Balance, and Chart of Accounts

Before starting on this assignment, read and complete the tasks discussed in Parts A, B, and F of the Computerized Accounting appendix at the back of this book.

How to Open the Company Data Files

1. Click on the Start button. Point to Programs; point to Simply Accounting; then click on Simply Accounting in the final menu presented.

2. The Simply Accounting copyright screen will appear briefly; then the Simply Accounting Open File dialog box will appear. Insert your Student Data Files disk into disk drive A. Enter the following path into the **File name** text box: A:\student\atlas.asc.

3. Click on the **Open** button. The program will respond with a request for the **Using Date for this Session.** The **Using** date is the date associated with the current work session. Once the **Using** date is advanced, it cannot be turned back to an earlier date.

4. Enter 12/31/97 into the **Using Date for this Session** text box; then click on the **OK** button. Click on the **OK** button in response to the message "The date entered is more than one week past your previous **Using** date of 12/1/97." When you start Simply Accounting, the file name for the company's data files (in this case Atlas) will appear in the title bar at the top of the Company Window. Your screen will look like this:

Note that the icons for Purchases, Payments, Sales, Receipts, Payroll, Transfers, and Adjustments Journals are shown with the no-entry symbol. The General Journal has no symbol. The Atlas Company will only be using the General Journal to record transactions.

How to Add Your Name to the Company Name

5. It is important for you to be able to identify the specific reports that you print for each assignment as your own, particularly if you are using a computer that shares a printer with other computers. Simply Accounting prints the name of the company you are working with at the top of each report. To personalize your reports so that you can identify both the company and your printed reports, the company name needs to be modified to include your name:

a. Click on the **Setup** menu; then click on Company Information. The Company Information dialog box will appear.

b. In the Company Information dialog box use the mouse to position the insertion point immediately before "Your Name" in the **Name** text box; drag through the "Your Name" text to highlight the text; then type your name. Your screen will look similar to the one shown below:

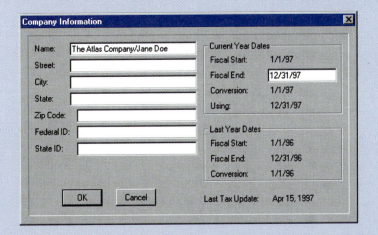

c. Click on the **OK** button to return to the Company Window.

How to Record a General Journal Entry

6. The owner of The Atlas Company has invested $10,000 in the business. Double-click on the General icon to open the General Journal dialog box. Enter the word "Memo" into the **Source** text box; press the TAB key; enter 12/1/97 into the **Date** text box; press the TAB key; enter "Initial investment of cash by owner" into the **Comment** text box; then press the TAB key.

The **Source** text box can be used for any reference number or notation you wish to associate with a general journal entry and the source document that authorizes the entry. The **Date** text box is used to record the date the transaction occurred. The **Comment** text box can be used for comments related to the journal entry in much the same way that an explanation is used when journal entries are recorded in a manual accounting system. Note that a flashing insertion point is positioned in the **Account** text box.

7. With the flashing insertion point positioned in the **Account** text box, press the ENTER key. The Select Account dialog box will appear. Double-click on 1110 Cash. The program will enter the account number and name into the **Account** text box, and the flashing insertion point will move to the **Debits** text box.

8. Enter 10000 into the **Debits** text box; then press the TAB key. Dollar amounts can be entered in several ways. For example, to enter $50.00, type 50, 50., or 50.00. To enter an amount containing a decimal point, type the decimal point as part of the amount. For example, enter five dollars and twenty-five cents as 5.25. Do not enter commas. The flashing insertion point will move to **Account** text box ready for the selection of the account to be credited for this entry.

9. With the flashing insertion point positioned in the **Account** text box, press the ENTER key to bring up the Select Account dialog box. Click on the down arrow button on the scroll bar to the right of the **Select account** listing to advance the display until 3110 Owner's, Capital appears. Double-click on 3110 Owner's, Capital. The program will offer the same amount as the **Debits** portion of the entry as a default amount in the **Credits** text box. The **Credits** amount remains highlighted.

10. Press the TAB key to accept the default **Credits** amount. This completes the data you need to enter into the General Journal dialog box to record the journal entry for the initial investment of cash by the owner. Your screen should look like this:

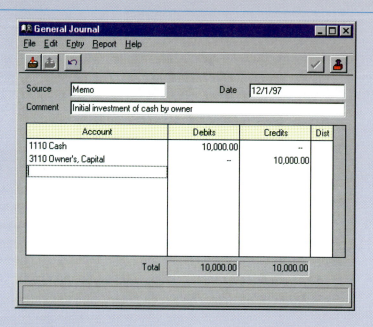

How to Review a Journal Entry

11. Before posting this transaction, you need to verify that the transaction data are correct by reviewing the journal entry. To review the entry, click on the General Journal Report menu; then click on Display General Journal Entry. The journal entry representing the data you have recorded in the General Journal dialog box is displayed. Review the journal entry for accuracy, noting any errors.

How to Edit an Entry Prior to Posting

12. Close the General Journal Entry window by clicking on the close button. If you have made an error, use the following editing techniques to correct the error.

Editing a General Journal Entry

◆ Move to the text box that contains the error by either pressing the TAB key to move forward through each text box or the SHIFT and TAB keys together to move to a previous text box. This will highlight the selected text box information so that you can change it. Alternatively, you can use the mouse to point to a text box and drag through the incorrect information to highlight it.

◆ Type the correct information; then press the TAB key to enter it.

◆ Note that when editing a dollar amount entered into the **Debits** or **Credits** text box, the program does not automatically change the corresponding **Debits** or **Credits** amount to agree with the new amount you have entered.

◆ If you have associated a transaction with an incorrect account, double-click on the incorrect account; then select the correct account from the Select Account dialog box. This will replace the incorrect account with the correct account.

◆ Note that the **Post** icon will be dimmed (unavailable) until the journal entry is in balance.

◆ To discard an entry and start over, click on the close button. Click on the **Yes** button in response to the question "Are you sure you want to discard this journal entry?"

◆ Review the journal entry for accuracy after any editing corrections.

◆ **It is IMPORTANT TO NOTE that the only way to edit a journal entry after it is posted is to reverse the entry and enter the correct journal entry.** To correct journal entries posted in error, see "Reversing an Entry Made in the General Journal Dialog Box" in Part C of the Computerized Accounting appendix.

How to Post an Entry

13. After verifying that the journal entry is correct, click on the **Post** icon to post this transaction. A blank General Journal dialog box is displayed, ready for additional General Journal transactions to be recorded.

Record Additional Transactions

14. Record the following additional journal entries (enter "Memo" into the **Source** text box for each transaction, then enter the **Date** listed for each transaction):

1997

Dec.
1 Paid rent for two months in advance, $400.
3 Purchased office supplies on account, $100.
9 Billed a customer for fees earned, $1,500.
13 Paid telephone bill, $180.
20 Owner withdrew $500 from the business.
27 Received $450 for fees earned.
31 Paid salaries expense, $700.

15. After you have posted the additional journal entries, click on the close button to close the General Journal dialog box. This will restore the Company Window screen, and the General Journal icon will remain highlighted.

How to Display and Print a General Journal

16. In the Company Window with the General Journal icon highlighted, click on the Reports menu; then click on Display General Journal. The General Journal Options dialog box will appear asking you to define the information you want displayed. Leave the **Current Year** and **By Posting Date** options buttons selected; leave the **All Ledger Entries** check box checked; enter 12/1/97 into the **Start** text box; leave the **Finish** text box date set at 12/31/97; then click on the **OK** button. The following General Journal Display will appear on your screen:

General Journal Display					_ □ ×
File Help					
12/1/97 to 12/31/97				Debits	Credits
12/1/97	J1	Memo, Initial investment of cash by owner			
		1110	Cash	10,000.00	-
		3110	Owner's, Capital	-	10,000.00
12/1/97	J2	Memo, Rent paid in advance (2 months)			
		1140	Prepaid Rent	400.00	-
		1110	Cash	-	400.00
12/3/97	J3	Memo, Purchased office supplies on account			
		1150	Office Supplies	100.00	-
		2110	Accounts Payable	-	100.00
12/9/97	J4	Memo, Billed customer for fees earned			
		1120	Accounts Receivable	1,500.00	-
		4110	Fees Earned	-	1,500.00
12/13/97	J5	Memo, Paid telephone bill			
		5150	Telephone Expense	180.00	-
		1110	Cash	-	180.00
12/20/97	J6	Memo, Personal withdrawal of cash			
		3120	Owner's, Withdrawals	500.00	-
		1110	Cash	-	500.00

17. The scroll bars can be used to advance the display to view other portions of the report. Note: You may display the entire General Journal Display window by clicking the maximize icon.

18. Click on the General Journal Display File menu; then click on Print to print the General Journal. If you experience any difficulties with your printer (for example, the type size is too small), refer to Part F of the Computerized Accounting appendix for information on how to adjust the print and display settings.

What to Do if You Posted an Incorrect Entry

19. Review your printed General Journal. If you have made an error in a posted journal entry, see "Reversing an Entry Made in the General Journal Dialog Box" in Part C of the Computerized Accounting appendix at the back of this book for information on how to correct the error.

How to Display and Print a General Ledger Report

20. Click on the close button to close the General Journal Display window; click on the Company Window Reports menu; point to Financials; then click on General Ledger. The General Ledger Report Options dialog box will appear. Leave the Current Year option button selected. Enter 12/1/97 into the **Start** text box; leave the **Finish** text box date set at 12/31/97; click on the **Select All** button, then click on the **OK** button. Your screen will look like this:

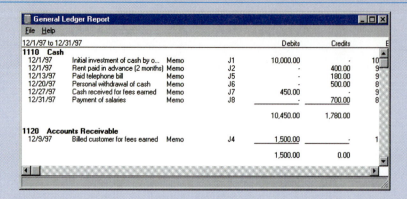

21. The scroll bars can be used to advance the display to view other portions of the report.

22. In the General Ledger Report click on the File menu; then click on Print to print the General Ledger report.

How to Display and Print a Trial Balance

23. Click on the close button to close the General Ledger Report window; click on the Company Window Reports menu; point to Financials; then click on Trial Balance. The Trial Balance Options dialog box will appear. Leave the Select a Report text box set at Current Year. Leave the **As at** date set at 12/31/97; then click on the **OK** button. Your screen will look like this:

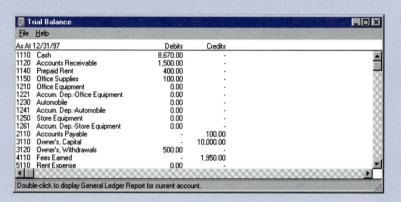

24. The scroll bar can be used to advance the display to view other portions of the report.

25. Click on the Trial Balance File menu; then click on Print to print the Trial Balance.

How to Display and Print a Chart of Accounts

26. Click on the close button to close the Trial Balance window; click on the Accounts icon under the General module column in the Company Window; click on the Company Window Reports menu; then click on Display Chart of Accounts. The Chart of Accounts window will appear. Move the mouse pointer opposite the Cash account. The mouse pointer will appear as a magnifying glass and the **Status Bar** will indicate that you can "Double-click to display General Ledger Report for current account." Your screen will look like this:

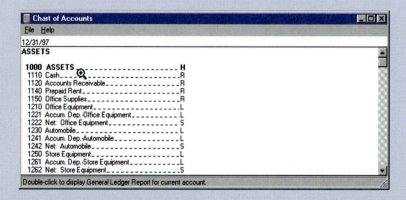

27. Double-click with your mouse. Your screen will look like this:

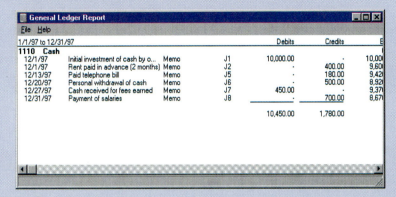

Simply Accounting's Drill-down Feature

28. Going deeper into the detail that supports a report in this manner is called "drill-down." You can drill-down to detailed supporting information on any Simply Accounting report where the mouse pointer changes to a magnifying glass. The **Status Bar** will tell you what information will appear when you double-click on an item in a report.

29. Click on the close button to close the General Ledger Report window: click on the Chart of Accounts File menu; then click on Print to print the Chart of Accounts.

30. Click on the close button to close the Chart of Accounts window and return to the Company Window.

How to Exit from the Program

31. Click on the Company Window File menu; then click on Exit to end the current work session and return to your Windows desktop. Your work will automatically be saved to your Student Data Files disk.

32. You can exit from Simply Accounting at any time during a current work session. Click on the Company Window File menu; then click on Exit. To resume working on an assignment, open the company data files; then leave the **Using Date for this Session** set at the default date offered.

How to Save your Work During a Current Work Session

33. To save your work during a lengthy current work session, click on the Company Window File menu. Click on Save; then continue with your current work session. It is a good practice to save your work about every 10 minutes when you are involved in a lengthy work session.

34. A Quick Reference Guide is in the Computerized Accounting appendix at the back of this textbook. You will find this guide useful for locating the page number on which frequently used Simply Accounting procedures are explained in detail.

Complete the Report Transmittal

35. Complete The Atlas Company Report Transmittal located in Appendix A in your *Study Guide and Working Papers.*

THE ACCOUNTING CYCLE CONTINUED

Preparing Worksheets and Financial Reports

THE BIG PICTURE

Revenue is increasing at Eldorado Computer Center. Tony Freedman can see the receipts from day to day. He has increased store hours, and now he's busier than ever making sure his customers are satisfied — so busy, in fact, that he was surprised when the fiscal year ended. "How well is the business doing?" Freedman wondered.

To answer that question he will have to prepare financial reports. But to prepare those reports he'll first have to gather information from his records and then make adjustments to be sure that he follows *GAAP*, "generally accepted accounting practices." Using the accrual method of accounting, GAAP's "revenue recognition principle" requires that revenue be recorded in the period in which it is earned. The GAAP "matching principle" requires that expenses be matched against the revenue generated. For instance, rental and utility expenses are recorded as they are used, not necessarily when they are paid.

Following these principles sometimes requires *adjustments*, actions that bring accounts up to date. They are internal transactions that do not involve an outside party. Adjusting entries usually are made at the end of the accounting period, but some businesses make them more frequently. Accounts commonly adjusted include: prepaid accounts, supplies, and long-term assets (which depreciate, or lose value, over time), interest, salaries, and taxes.

In this chapter you will learn to use a 10-column worksheet to help organize and check data in a trial balance. You'll make adjustments, adjust the trial balance, and complete the income-statement section and balance-sheet section of the worksheet. Using your worksheet, you will then prepare financial statements. These financial reports give a better picture of "how well the business is doing" than day-to-day receipts.

Learning Objectives	◆ Adjustments: prepaid rent, office supplies, depreciation on equipment, and accrued salaries. (p. 117) ◆ Preparation of adjusted trial balance on the worksheet. (p. 126) ◆ The income statement and balance sheet sections of the worksheet. (pp. 127–129) ◆ Preparing financial reports from the worksheet. (p. 132)

In the accompanying diagram, steps 1–4 show the parts of the manual accounting cycle that were completed for Clarke's Word Processing Services in the last chapter. This chapter continues the cycle with steps 5–6: the preparation of a worksheet and the three financial reports.

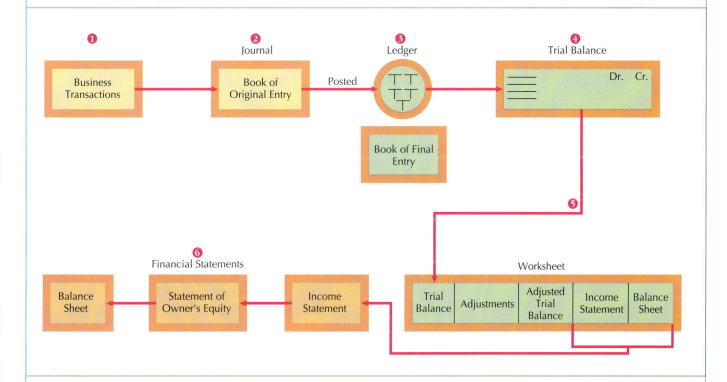

LEARNING UNIT 4-1
Step 5 of the Accounting Cycle: Preparing a Worksheet

The worksheet is not a formal report, so no dollar signs appear on it. Because it is a form, there are no commas, either.

As is true for all accounting reports, the heading includes the name of the company, the name of the report, the date, and the length of the accounting period.

An accountant uses a **worksheet** to organize and check data before preparing financial reports necessary to complete the accounting cycle. The most important function of the worksheet is to allow the accountant to find and correct errors before financial statements are prepared. In a way, a worksheet acts as the accountant's scratch pad. No one sees the worksheet once the formal reports are prepared. A sample worksheet is shown in Figure 4-1 on page 118.

The accounts listed on the far left of the worksheet are taken from the ledger. The rest of the worksheet has five sections: the trial balance, adjustments, adjusted trial balance, income statement, and balance sheet. Each of these sections is divided into debit and credit columns.

CLARK'S WORD PROCESSING SERVICES
WORKSHEET
FOR MONTH ENDING MAY 31, 19XX

Account Titles	Trial Balance		Adjustments		Adjusted Trial Balance		Income Statement	
	Dr.	Cr.	Dr.	Cr.	Dr.	Cr.	Dr.	Cr.
Cash	6 1 5 5 00							
Accounts Receivable	5 0 0 0 00							
Office Supplies	6 0 0 00							
Prepaid Rent	1 2 0 0 00							
Word Processing Equipment	6 0 0 0 00							
Accounts Payable		3 3 5 0 00						
Brenda Clark, Capital		10 0 0 0 00						
Brenda Clark, Withdrawals	6 2 5 00							
Word Processing Fees		8 0 0 0 00						
Office Salaries Expense	1 3 0 0 00							
Advertising Expense	2 5 0 00							
Telephone Expense	2 2 0 00							
	21 3 5 0 00	21 3 5 0 00						

FIGURE 4-1 Sample Worksheet

THE TRIAL BALANCE SECTION

We discussed how to prepare a trial balance in Chapter 2. Some companies prepare a separate trial balance; others, such as Clark's Word Processing Services, prepare the trial balance directly on the worksheet. A trial balance is taken on every account listed in the ledger that has a balance. Additional titles from the ledger are added as they are needed. (We will show this later.)

THE ADJUSTMENTS SECTION

Chapters 1–3 discussed transactions that occurred with outside suppliers and companies. In a real business, though, inside transactions also occur during the accounting cycle. These transactions must be recorded, too. At the end of the worksheet process, the accountant will have all of the business's accounts up-to-date and ready to be used to prepare the formal financial reports. By analyzing each of Clark's accounts on the worksheet, the accountant will be able to identify specific accounts that must be **adjusted,** to bring them up to date. The accountant for Clark's Word Processing Services needs to adjust the following accounts:

Adjusting is like fine-tuning your TV set.

- ◆ Office Supplies
- ◆ Prepaid Rent
- ◆ Word Processing Equipment
- ◆ Office Salaries Expense

Let's look at how to analyze and adjust each of these accounts.

Adjusting the Office Supplies Account

On May 31, the accountant found out that the company had only $100 worth of office supplies on hand. When the company had originally purchased the

$600 of office supplies, they were considered an asset. But as the supplies were used up, they became an expense.

- ◆ Office supplies available, $600.
- ◆ Office supplies left or on hand as of May 31, $100.
- ◆ Office supplies used up in the operation of the business for the month of May, $500.

As a result, the asset Office Supplies is too high on the trial balance (it should be $100, not $600). At the same time, if we don't show the additional expense of supplies used, the company's *net income* will be too high.

If Clark's accountant does not adjust the trial balance to reflect the change, the company's net income would be too high on the income statement and both sides (assets and owner's equity) of the balance sheet would be too high.

Now let's look at the adjustment for office supplies in terms of the transaction analysis chart.

The adjustment for supplies deals with the amount of supplies *used up.*

Adjustments affect both the income statement and balance sheet.

Office Supplies Exp. 514

500

This is supplies used up.

Office Supplies 114

600 | 500

100

This is supplies on hand.

For our discussion, the letter "A" is used to code the Office Supplies Expense because it is the first account to be adjusted.

Note: All accounts listed *below* the trial balance will be *increasing.*

Will go on income statement

Accounts Affected	Category	↓ ↑	Rules
Office Supplies Expense	Expense	↑	Dr.
Office Supplies	Asset	↓	Cr.

Will go on balance sheet

The office supplies expense account comes from the Chart of Accounts on page 73. Since it is not listed in the account titles, it must be listed below the trial balance. Let's see how we enter this adjustment on the worksheet:

CLARK'S WORD PROCESSING SERVICES
WORKSHEET
FOR MONTH ENDED MAY 31, 19XX

Account Titles	Trial Balance Dr.	Trial Balance Cr.	Adjustments Dr.	Adjustments Cr.
Cash	6 1 5 5 00			
Accounts Receivable	5 0 0 0 00			
Office Supplies	6 0 0 00			(A) 5 0 0 00
Prepaid Rent	1 2 0 0 00			
Word Processing Equipment	6 0 0 0 00			
Accounts Payable		3 3 5 0 00		
Brenda Clark, Capital		10 0 0 0 00		
Brenda Clark, Withdrawals	6 2 5 00			
Word Processing Fees		8 0 0 0 00		
Office Salaries Expense	1 3 0 0 00			
Advertising Expense	2 5 0 00			
Telephone Expense	2 2 0 00			
	21 3 5 0 00	21 3 5 0 00		
Office Supplies Expense			(A) 5 0 0 00	

A decrease in Office Supplies, $500.

An increase in Office Supplies Expense, $500.

The Office Supplies Expense account indicates the amount of supplies used up. It is listed below other trial balance accounts, since it was not on the original trial balance.

A debit will increase the account Office Supplies Expense; a credit will reduce the account Office Supplies.

Adjusting Prepaid Rent: On p. 119 the trial balance showed a figure for Prepaid Rent of $1,200. The amount of rent *expired* is the adjustment figure used to update Prepaid Rent and Rent Expense.

Place $500 in the debit column of the adjustments section on the same line as Office Supplies Expense. Place $500 in the credit column of the adjustments section on the same line as Office Supplies. The numbers in the adjustment column show what is used, *not* what is on hand.

Adjusting the Prepaid Rent Account

Back on May 1, Clark's Word Processing Services paid three months' rent in advance. The accountant realized that the rent expense would be $400 per month ($1,200 ÷ 3 months = $400).

Remember, when rent is paid in advance, it is considered an asset called *prepaid rent*. When the asset, prepaid rent, begins to expire or be used up it becomes an expense. Now it is May 31, and one month's prepaid rent has become an expense.

How is this handled? Should the account be $1,200, or is there really only $800 of prepaid rent left as of May 31? What do we need to do to bring prepaid rent to the "true" balance? The answer is that we must increase Rent Expense by $400 and decrease Prepaid Rent by $400.

Without this adjustment, the expenses for Clark's Word Processing Services for May will be too low, and the asset Prepaid Rent will be too high. If unadjusted amounts were used in the formal reports, the net income shown on the income statement would be too high, and both sides (assets and owner's equity) would be too high on the balance sheet. In terms of our transaction analysis chart, the adjustment would look like this:

Will go on income statement

Accounts Affected	Category	↓ ↑	Rules
Rent Expense	Expense	↑	Dr.
Prepaid Rent	Asset	↓	Cr.

Will go on balance sheet

Rent Expense 515

400	

Prepaid Rent 115

1,200	400 Adj.
800	

Like the Office Supplies Expense account, the Rent Expense account comes from the chart of accounts on p. 73.

The worksheet on page 121 shows how to enter an adjustment to Prepaid Rent.

Adjusting the Word Processing Equipment Account for Depreciation

Take this one slowly.

Original cost of $6,000 for word processing equipment remains *unchanged* after adjustments.

The life of the asset affects how it is adjusted. The two accounts we discussed above, Office Supplies and Prepaid Rent, involved things that are used up relatively quickly. Equipment—like word processing equipment—is expected to last much longer. Also, it is expected to help produce revenue over a longer period. That is why accountants treat it differently. The balance sheet reports the **historical cost,** or original cost, of the equipment. The original cost also is reflected in the ledger. The adjustment shows how the cost of the equipment is allocated (spread) over its expected useful life. This spreading is called **depreciation.** To depreciate the equipment, we have to figure out how much its cost goes down each month. Then we have to keep a running total of how that depreciation mounts up over time. The Internal Revenue Service (IRS) issues guidelines, tables, and formulas that must be used to estimate the amount of depreciation. Different methods can be used to calculate depreciation (see the Appendix at the end of the text). We will use the simplest method—straight-line depreciation—to calculate the depreciation of Clark Word Processing Services'

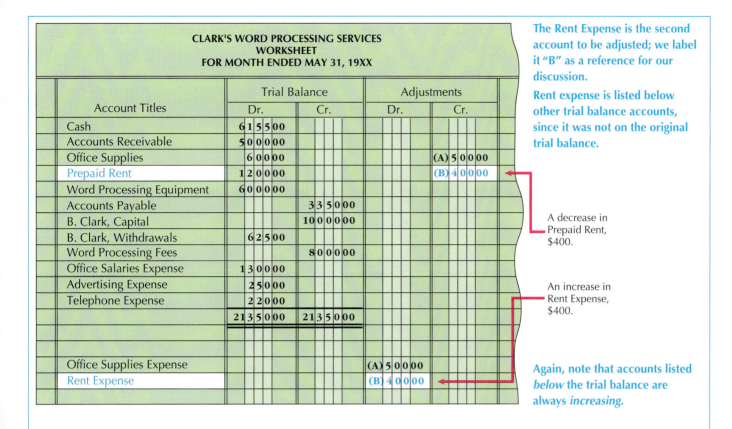

The Rent Expense is the second account to be adjusted; we label it "B" as a reference for our discussion.

Rent expense is listed below other trial balance accounts, since it was not on the original trial balance.

A decrease in Prepaid Rent, $400.

An increase in Rent Expense, $400.

Again, note that accounts listed *below* the trial balance are always *increasing.*

equipment. Under the straight-line method, equal amounts are taken over successive periods of time.

The calculation of depreciation for the year for Clark's Word Processing Services is as follows:

$$\frac{\text{cost of equipment} - \text{residual value}}{\text{estimated years of usefulness}}$$

According to the IRS, word processing equipment has an expected life of five years. At the end of that time, the property's value is called its "residual value." Think of **residual value** as the estimated value of the equipment at end of the fifth year. For Clark, the equipment has an estimated residual value of $1,200.

Assume equipment has a 5-year life.

Clark will record $960 of depreciation each year.

Depreciation is an expense reported on the income statement.

$$\frac{\$6,000 - \$1,200}{5 \text{ years}} = \frac{\$4,800}{5} = \$960 \text{ depreciation per year}$$

Our trial balance is for one month, so we must determine the adjustment for that month:

$$\frac{\$960}{12 \text{ months}} = \$80 \text{ depreciation per month}$$

This $80 is known as *Depreciation Expense* and will be shown on the income statement.

Next, we have to create a new account that can keep a running total of the depreciation amount apart from the original cost of the equipment. That account is called **Accumulated Depreciation.**

Accumulated Depreciation	
Dr.	**Cr.**

is a contra-asset account found on the balance sheet.

The Accumulated Depreciation account shows the relationship between the original cost of the equipment and the amount of depreciation that has been taken or accumulated over a period of time. This is a *contra-asset* account; it has the opposite balance of an asset such as equipment. Accumulated Depreciation will summarize, accumulate, or build up the amount of depreciation that is taken on the word processing equipment over its estimated useful life.

This is how this would look on a partial balance sheet of Clark's Word Processing Services.

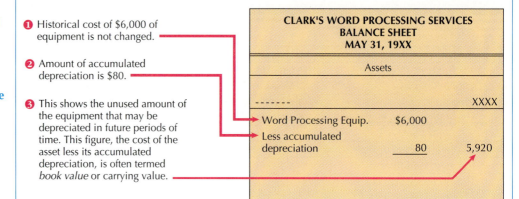

At end of June the accumulated depreciation will be $160, but historical cost will stay at $6,000.

Remember, book value is not the same as market value.

❶ Historical cost of $6,000 of equipment is not changed.

❷ Amount of accumulated depreciation is $80.

❸ This shows the unused amount of the equipment that may be depreciated in future periods of time. This figure, the cost of the asset less its accumulated depreciation, is often termed *book value* or carrying value.

CLARK'S WORD PROCESSING SERVICES
BALANCE SHEET
MAY 31, 19XX

Assets		
-------		XXXX
Word Processing Equip.	$6,000	
Less accumulated depreciation	80	5,920

Let's summarize the key points before going on to mark the adjustment on the worksheet:

1. Depreciation Expense goes on the income statement, which results in
   a. An increase in total expenses.
   b. A decrease in net income.
   c. Therefore, less to be paid in taxes.
2. Accumulated depreciation is a contra-asset account found on the balance sheet next to its related equipment account.
3. The original cost of equipment is not reduced; it stays the same until the equipment is sold or removed.
4. Each month the amount in the Accumulated Depreciation account grows larger, while the cost of the equipment remains the same.

Now, let's analyze the adjustment on the transaction analysis chart:

Taking depreciation does not result in any new payment of cash. The result of depreciation provides some tax savings.

Will go on income statement

Accounts Affected	Category	↓	↑	Rules
Depreciation Expense, Word Processing Equipment	**Expense**		↑	**Dr.**
Accumulated Depreciation, Word Processing Equipment	**Contra Asset**		↑	**Cr.**

Dep. Expense, W. P. 516

80

Accum. Dep., W. P. 122

80

Will go on balance sheet

Remember, the original cost of the equipment never changes: (1) the equipment account is not included among the affected accounts because the original cost of equipment remains the same; and (2) the original cost does not change. Even though the Accumulated Depreciation increases (as a credit), the equipment's **book value** decreases.

The worksheet on page 123 shows how we enter the adjustment for depreciation of word processing equipment.

Because this is a new business, neither account had a previous balance. Therefore, neither is listed in the account titles of the trial balance. We need to list both accounts below Rent Expense in the account titles section. On the worksheet, put $80 in the debit column of the adjustments section on the same line as Depreciation Expense, W. P. Equipment, and put $80 in the credit column

Note that the original cost of the equipment on the worksheet has *not* been changed ($6,000).

Next month (June in our example), accumulated depreciation will appear listed in the original trial balance.

CLARK'S WORD PROCESSING SERVICES
WORKSHEET
FOR MONTH ENDED MAY 31, 19XX

Account Titles	Trial Balance Dr.	Trial Balance Cr.	Adjustments Dr.	Adjustments Cr.
Cash	6155 00			
Accounts Receivable	5000 00			
Office Supplies	600 00			(A) 500 00
Prepaid Rent	1200 00			(B) 400 00
Word Processing Equipment	6000 00			
Accounts Payable		3350 00		
B. Clark, Capital		10000 00		
B. Clark, Withdrawals	625 00			
Word Processing Fees		8000 00		
Office Salaries Expense	1300 00			
Advertising Expense	250 00			
Telephone Expense	220 00			
	21350 00	21350 00		
Office Supplies Expense			(A) 500 00	
Rent Expense			(B) 400 00	
Depreciation Exp., W.P. Equip.			(C) 80 00	
Accum. Deprec., W.P. Equip.				(C) 80 00

An increase in Depreciation Expense, W.P. Equipment.

An increase in Accumulated Depreciation, W.P. Equipment.

The third account to be adjusted is assigned the letter "C."

Accumulated Depreciation

Dr.	Cr.
	History of amount of depreciation taken to date

Adjusting Salaries

of the adjustments section on the same line as Accumulated Depreciation, W. P. Equipment.

Next month, on June 30, $80 would be entered under Depreciation Expense, and Accumulated Depreciation would show a balance of $160. Remember, in May, Clark's was a new company, so no previous depreciation was taken.

Now let's look at the last adjustment for Clark's Word Processing Services.

Adjusting the Salaries Accrued Account

Clark's Word Processing Services paid $1,300 in Office Salaries Expense (see the trial balance of any previous worksheet in this chapter). The last salary checks for the month were paid on May 27. How can we update this account to show the salary expense as of May 31?

John Murray worked for Clark on May 28, 29, 30, and 31, but his next paycheck is not due until June 3. John earned $350 for these four days. Is the $350 an expense to Clark in May, when it was earned, or in June when it is due and is paid?

May						
S	M	T	W	T	F	S
						1
2	3	4	5	6	7	8
9	10	11	12	13	14	15
16	17	18	19	20	21	22
23	24	25	26	27	28	29
30	31					

Think back to Chapter 1, when we first discussed revenue and expenses. We noted then that revenue is recorded when it is earned, and expenses are recorded when they are incurred, not when they are actually paid off. This principle will be discussed further in a later chapter; for now it is enough to remember that we record revenue and expenses when they occur, because we want to match earned revenue with the expenses that resulted in earning those revenues. In this case, by working those four days, John Murray created some revenue for Clark in May. Therefore, the office salaries expense must be shown in May — the month the revenue was earned.

The results are:

Office Salaries Expense is increased by $350. This unpaid and unrecorded expense for salaries for which payment is not yet due is called **accrued salaries.** In effect, we now show the true expense for salaries ($1,650 instead of $1,300):

Office Salaries Expense	
1,300	
350	

The second result is that salaries payable is increased by $350. Clark's has created a liability called Salaries Payable, meaning that the firm owes money for salaries. When the firm pays John Murray, it will reduce its liability, Salaries Payable, as well as decrease its cash.

In terms of the transaction analysis chart, the following would be done:

Accounts Affected	Category	↓	↑	Rules
Office Salaries Expense,	Expense		↑	Dr.
Salaries Payable	Liability		↑	Cr.

How the adjustment for accrued salaries is entered is shown at the top of page 125.

The account Office Salaries Expense is already listed in the account titles, so $350 is placed in the debit column of the adjustments section on the same line as Office Salaries Expense. However, because the Salaries Payable is not listed in the account titles, it is added below the trial balance under Accumulated Depreciation, W. P. Equipment. Also, $350 is placed in the credit column of the adjustments section on the same line as Salaries Payable.

Now that we have finished all the adjustments that we intended to make, we total the adjustments section, as shown in Figure 4-2.

THE ADJUSTED TRIAL BALANCE SECTION

The adjusted trial balance is the next section on the worksheet. To fill it out, we must summarize the information in the trial balance and adjustments sections, as shown in Figure 4-3 on page 126.

Note that when the numbers are brought across from the trial balance to the adjusted trial balance, two debits will be added together and two credits will be added together. If the numbers include a debit and a credit, take the difference between the two and place it on the side that is larger.

Now that we have completed the adjustments and adjusted trial balance sections of the worksheet, it is time to move on to the income statement and the balance sheet sections. Before we do that though, look at the chart shown

Office Salaries Exp. 511

1,300	
350	

Salaries Payable 212

	350

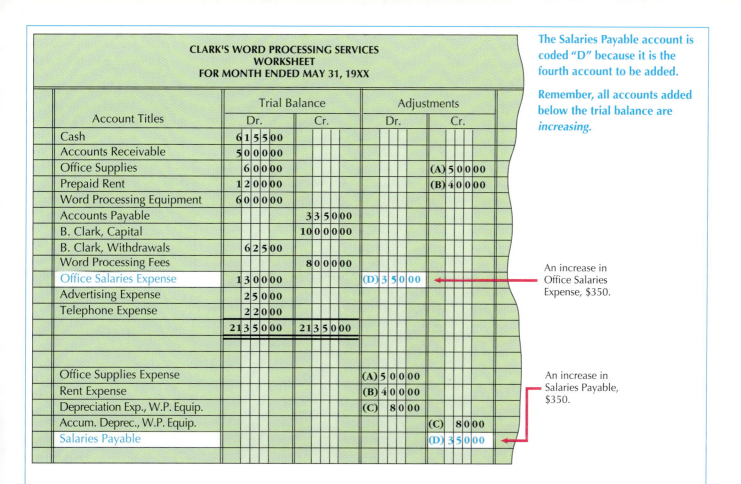

The Salaries Payable account is coded "D" because it is the fourth account to be added.

Remember, all accounts added below the trial balance are *increasing*.

An increase in Office Salaries Expense, $350.

An increase in Salaries Payable, $350.

CLARK'S WORD PROCESSING SERVICES
WORKSHEET
FOR MONTH ENDED MAY 31, 19XX

Account Titles	Trial Balance Dr.	Trial Balance Cr.	Adjustments Dr.	Adjustments Cr.
Cash	6 1 5 5 00			
Accounts Receivable	5 0 0 0 00			
Office Supplies	6 0 0 00			(A) 5 0 0 00
Prepaid Rent	1 2 0 0 00			(B) 4 0 0 00
Word Processing Equipment	6 0 0 0 00			
Accounts Payable		3 3 5 0 00		
B. Clark, Capital		10 0 0 0 00		
B. Clark, Withdrawals	6 2 5 00			
Word Processing Fees		8 0 0 0 00		
Office Salaries Expense	1 3 0 0 00		(D) 3 5 0 00	
Advertising Expense	2 5 0 00			
Telephone Expense	2 2 0 00			
	21 3 5 0 00	21 3 5 0 00		
Office Supplies Expense			(A) 5 0 0 00	
Rent Expense			(B) 4 0 0 00	
Depreciation Exp., W.P. Equip.			(C) 8 0 00	
Accum. Deprec., W.P. Equip.				(C) 8 0 00
Salaries Payable				(D) 3 5 0 00

FIGURE 4-2
The Adjustments Section of the Worksheet

CLARK'S WORD PROCESSING SERVICES
WORKSHEET
FOR MONTH ENDED MAY 31, 19XX

Account Titles	Trial Balance Dr.	Trial Balance Cr.	Adjustments Dr.	Adjustments Cr.
Cash	6 1 5 5 00			
Accounts Receivable	5 0 0 0 00			
Office Supplies	6 0 0 00			(A) 5 0 0 00
Prepaid Rent	1 2 0 0 00			(B) 4 0 0 00
Word Processing Equipment	6 0 0 0 00			
Accounts Payable		3 3 5 0 00		
B. Clark, Capital		10 0 0 0 00		
B. Clark, Withdrawals	6 2 5 00			
Word Processing Fees		8 0 0 0 00		
Office Salaries Expense	1 3 0 0 00		(D) 3 5 0 00	
Advertising Expense	2 5 0 00			
Telephone Expense	2 2 0 00			
	21 3 5 0 00	21 3 5 0 00		
Office Supplies Expense			(A) 5 0 0 00	
Rent Expense			(B) 4 0 0 00	
Depreciation Exp., W.P. Equip.			(C) 8 0 00	
Accum. Deprec., W.P. Equip.				(C) 8 0 00
Salaries Payable				(D) 3 5 0 00
			1 3 3 0 00	1 3 3 0 00

FIGURE 4-3 The Adjusted Trial Balance Section of the Worksheet

CLARK'S WORD PROCESSING SERVICES
WORKSHEET
FOR MONTH ENDED MAY 31, 19XX

Account Titles	Trial Balance Dr.	Trial Balance Cr.	Adjustments Dr.	Adjustments Cr.	Adjusted Trial Balance Dr.	Adjusted Trial Balance Cr.
Cash	6155 00				6155 00	
Accounts Receivable	5000 00				5000 00	
Office Supplies	600 00			(A) 500 00	100 00	
Prepaid Rent	1200 00			(B) 400 00	800 00	
Word Processing Equipment	6000 00				6000 00	
Accounts Payable		3350 00				3350 00
Brenda Clark, Capital		10000 00				10000 00
Brenda Clark, Withdrawals	625 00				625 00	
Word Processing Fees		8000 00				8000 00
Office Salaries Expense	1300 00		(D) 350 00		1650 00	
Advertising Expense	250 00				250 00	
Telephone Expense	220 00				220 00	
	21350 00	21350 00				
Office Supplies Expense			(A) 500 00		500 00	
Rent Expense			(B) 400 00		400 00	
Depreciation Exp., W.P. Equip.			(C) 80 00		80 00	
Accum. Deprec., W.P. Equip.				(C) 80 00		80 00
Salaries Payable				(D) 350 00		350 00
			1330 00	1330 00	21780 00	21780 00

Callout annotations:

- If no adjustment is made, just carry over amount from trial balance on same side.
- Supplies were $600 but we used up $500, leaving us with a $100 balance in supplies. Note: If there are a debit and a credit, take the *difference* between the two and place it on the side that is larger.
- Note: Equipment is *not* adjusted here.
- Two debits are added together. If two credits, they also would have been added together.
- Carry these amounts over to adjusted trial balance in the same positions.
- *Note:* The total of the left (debit) must equal the total of the right (credit) ($21,780).

TABLE 4-1 NORMAL BALANCES AND ACCOUNT CATEGORIES

Account Titles	Category	Normal Balance on Adjusted Trial Balance	Income Statement Dr.	Income Statement Cr.	Balance Sheet Dr.	Balance Sheet Cr.
Cash	Asset	Dr.			X	
Accounts Receivable	Asset	Dr.			X	
Office Supplies	Asset	Dr.			X	
Prepaid Rent	Asset	Dr.			X	
Word Proc. Equip.	Asset	Dr.			X	
Accounts Payable	Liability	Cr.				X
Brenda Clark, Capital	Capital	Cr.				X
Brenda Clark, Withdrawals	Withdrawal	Dr.			X	
Word Proc. Fees	Revenue	Cr.		X		
Office Salaries Exp.	Expense	Dr.	X			
Advertising Expense	Expense	Dr.	X			
Telephone Expense	Expense	Dr.	X			
Office Supplies Exp.	Expense	Dr.	X			
Rent Expense	Expense	Dr.	X			
Dep. Exp., W. P. Equip.	Expense	Dr.	X			
Acc. Dep., W. P. Equip.	Contra Asset	Cr.				X
Salaries Payable	Liability	Cr.				X

in Table 4-1. This table should be used as a reference to help you in filling out the next two sections of the worksheet.

Keep in mind that the numbers from the adjusted trial balance are carried over to one of the last four columns of the worksheet before the bottom section is completed.

THE INCOME STATEMENT SECTION

As shown in Figure 4-4 on page 128, the income statement section lists only revenue and expenses from the adjusted trial balance. Note that accumulated depreciation and salaries payable do not go on the income statement. Accumulated depreciation is a contra-asset found on the balance sheet. Salaries payable is a liability found on the balance sheet.

The revenue ($8,000) and all the individual expenses are listed in the income statement section. The revenue is placed in the credit column of the income statement section because it has a credit balance. The expenses have debit balances, so they are placed in the debit column of the income statement section. The following steps must be taken after the debits and credits are placed in the correct columns:

In the worksheet, net income is placed in the debit column of the income statement. Net loss goes on the credit column.

Step 1: Total the debits and credits.

Step 2: Calculate the balance between the debit and credit columns and place the difference on the smaller side.

Step 3: Total the columns.

The worksheet in Figure 4-4 shows that the label Net Income is added in the account title column on the same line as $4,900. When there is a net income, it will be placed in the debit column of the income statement section of the worksheet. If there is a net loss, it is placed in the credit column. The $8,000 total indicates that the two columns are in balance.

The difference between $3,100 Dr. and $8,000 Cr. indicates a net income of $4,900. Do not think of the Net Income as a Dr. or Cr. The $4,900 is placed in the debit column to balance both columns to $8,000. Actually, the credit side is larger by $4,900.

CLARK'S WORD PROCESSING SERVICES
WORKSHEET
FOR MONTH ENDED MAY 31, 19XX

Account Titles	Adjusted Trial Balance		Income Statement	
	Dr.	Cr.	Dr.	Cr.
Cash	6 1 5 5 00			
Accounts Receivable	5 0 0 0 00			
Office Supplies	1 0 0 00			
Prepaid Rent	8 0 0 00			
Word Processing Equipment	6 0 0 0 00			
Accounts Payable		3 3 5 0 00		
B. Clark, Capital		10 0 0 0 00		
B. Clark, Withdrawals	6 2 5 00			
Word Processing Fees		8 0 0 0 00		8 0 0 0 00
Office Salaries Expense	1 6 5 0 00		1 6 5 0 00	
Advertising Expense	2 5 0 00		2 5 0 00	
Telephone Expense	2 2 0 00		2 2 0 00	
Office Supplies Expense	5 0 0 00		5 0 0 00	
Rent Expense	4 0 0 00		4 0 0 00	
Depreciation Exp., W.P. Equip.	8 0 00		8 0 00	
Accum. Deprec., W.P. Equip.		8 0 00		
Salaries Payable		3 5 0 00		
	21 7 8 0 00	21 7 8 0 00	3 1 0 0 00	8 0 0 0 00
Net Income			4 9 0 0 00	
			8 0 0 0 00	8 0 0 0 00

FIGURE 4-4 The Income Statement Section of the Worksheet

Remember: The ending figure for capital is not on the worksheet.

To see whether additional investments occurred for the period you must check the capital account in the ledger.

The amounts come from the adjusted trial balance, except the $4,900, which was carried over from the income statement section.

THE BALANCE SHEET SECTION

To fill out the balance sheet section of the worksheet, the following are carried over from the adjusted trial balance section: assets, contra-assets, liabilities, capital, and withdrawals. Because the beginning figure for capital* is used on the worksheet, the net income is brought over to the credit column of the balance sheet so both columns balance.

Let's now look at the completed worksheet in Figure 4-5 to see how the balance sheet section is completed. Note how the net income of $4,900 is brought over to the credit column of the worksheet. The figure for capital is also on the credit column, while the figure for withdrawals is on the debit column. By placing the net income in the credit column both sides total $18,680. If a net loss were to occur it would be placed in the debit column of the balance sheet column.

Now that we have completed the worksheet, we can go on to the three financial reports. But first let's summarize our progress.

---

* We assume no additional investments during the period.

FIGURE 4-5 The Completed Worksheet

CLARK'S WORD PROCESSING SERVICES
WORKSHEET
FOR MONTH ENDED MAY 31, 19XX

Account Titles	Trial Balance Dr.	Trial Balance Cr.	Adjustments Dr.	Adjustments Cr.	Adjusted Trial Balance Dr.	Adjusted Trial Balance Cr.	Income Statement Dr.	Income Statement Cr.	Balance Sheet Dr.	Balance Sheet Cr.
Cash	6155 00				6155 00				6155 00	
Accounts Receivable	5000 00				5000 00				5000 00	
Office Supplies	600 00			(A) 500 00	100 00				100 00	
Prepaid Rent	1200 00			(B) 400 00	800 00				800 00	
Word Processing Equipment	6000 00				6000 00				6000 00	
Accounts Payable		3350 00				3350 00				3350 00
B. Clark, Capital		10000 00				10000 00				10000 00
B. Clark, Withdrawals	625 00				625 00				625 00	
Word Processing Fees		8000 00				8000 00		8000 00		
Office Salaries Expense	1300 00		(D) 350 00		1650 00		1650 00			
Advertising Expense	250 00				250 00		250 00			
Telephone Expense	220 00				220 00		220 00			
	21350 00	21350 00								
Office Supplies Expense			(A) 500 00		500 00		500 00			
Rent Expense			(B) 400 00		400 00		400 00			
Depreciation Exp., W.P. Equip.			(C) 80 00		80 00		80 00			
Accum. Deprec., W.P. Equip.				(C) 80 00		80 00				80 00
Salaries Payable				(D) 350 00		350 00				350 00
			1330 00	1330 00	21780 00	21780 00	3100 00	8000 00	18680 00	13780 00
Net Income							4900 00			4900 00
							8000 00	8000 00	18680 00	18680 00

LEARNING UNIT 4-1 REVIEW

AT THIS POINT you should be able to

◆ Define and explain the purpose of a worksheet. (p. 117)
◆ Explain the need as well as the process for adjustments. (p. 118)
◆ Explain the concept of depreciation. (p. 120)
◆ Explain the difference between depreciation expense and accumulated depreciation. (p. 121)
◆ Prepare a worksheet from a trial balance and adjustment data. (p. 129)

SELF-REVIEW QUIZ 4-1

From the accompanying trial balance and adjustment data, complete a worksheet for P. Logan Co. for the month ended Dec. 31, 19XX. (You can use the blank fold-out worksheet located at the end of the *Study Guide and Working Papers*.)

Note: The numbers used on this quiz may seem impossibly small, but we have done that on purpose, so that at this point you don't have to worry about arithmetic, just about preparing the worksheet correctly.

P. LOGAN TRIAL BALANCE DECEMBER 31, 19XX	Dr.	Cr.
Cash	1500	
Accounts Receivable	300	
Prepaid Insurance	300	
Store Supplies	500	
Store Equipment	600	
Accumulated Depreciation, Store Equipment		400
Accounts Payable		200
P. Logan, Capital		1400
P. Logan, Withdrawals	300	
Revenue from Clients		2500
Rent Expense	200	
Salaries Expense	800	
	4500	4500

Adjustment Data:

a. Depreciation Expense, Store Equipment, $1.
b. Insurance Expired, $2
c. Supplies on hand, $1.
d. Salaries owed but not paid to employees, $3.

Solution to Self-Review Quiz 4-1

Quiz Tip: The adjustment for supplies of $4 represents the amount *used up*. The *on hand* amount of $1 ends up on the adjusted trial balance.

Don't adjust this line! Store Equipment always contains the historical cost.

P. LOGAN COMPANY
WORKSHEET
FOR MONTH ENDED DECEMBER 31, 19XX

Account Titles	Trial Balance Dr.	Trial Balance Cr.	Adjustments Dr.	Adjustments Cr.	Adjusted Trial Balance Dr.	Adjusted Trial Balance Cr.	Income Statement Dr.	Income Statement Cr.	Balance Sheet Dr.	Balance Sheet Cr.
Cash	1500				1500				1500	
Accounts Receivable	300				300				300	
Prepaid Insurance	300			(B) 200	100				100	
Store Supplies	500			(C) 400	100				100	
Store Equipment	600				600				600	
Accum. Depr., Store Equipment		400		(A) 100		500				500
Accounts Payable		200				200				200
P. Logan, Capital		1400				1400				1400
P. Logan, Withdrawals	300				300				300	
Revenue from Clients		2500				2500		2500		
Rent Expense	200				200		200			
Salaries Expense	800		(D) 300		1100		1100			
	4500	4500								
Depr. Exp., Store Equipment			(A) 100		100		100			
Insurance Expense			(B) 200		200		200			
Supplies Expense			(C) 400		400		400			
Salaries Payable				(D) 300		300				300
			1000	1000	4900	4900	2000	2500	2900	2400
Net Income							500			500
							2500	2500	2900	2900

Note that Accumulated Depreciation is listed in trial balance, since this is not a new company. Store Equipment has already been depreciated $4.00 from an earlier period.

LEARNING UNIT 4-2

Step 6 of the Accounting Cycle: Preparing the Financial Statements from the Worksheet

The formal financial reports can be prepared from the worksheet completed in Learning Unit 4-1. Before beginning, we must check that the entries on the worksheet are correct and in balance. To do this, we have to be sure that (1) all entries are recorded in the appropriate column, (2) the correct amounts are entered in the proper places, (3) the addition is correct across the columns (i.e., from the trial balance to the adjusted trial balance to the financial reports), and (4) the columns are added correctly.

PREPARING THE INCOME STATEMENT

The first report to be prepared for Clark's Word Processing Services is the income statement. When preparing the income statement, it is important to remember that:

1. Every figure on the formal report is on the worksheet. Figure 4-6 shows where each of these figures goes on the income statement.
2. There are no debit or credit columns on the formal report.
3. The inside column on financial reports is used for subtotaling.
4. Withdrawals do not go on the income statement; they go on the statement of owner's equity.

Take a moment to look at the income statement in Figure 4-6. Note which items go where from the income statement section of the worksheet onto the formal report.

PREPARING THE STATEMENT OF OWNER'S EQUITY

Figure 4-7 is the statement of owner's equity for Clark's. The figure shows where the information comes from on the worksheet. It is important to remember that if there were additional investments, the figure on the worksheet for capital would not be the beginning figure for capital. Checking the ledger account for capital will tell you whether the amount is correct. Note how net income and withdrawals aid in calculating the new figure for capital.

PREPARING THE BALANCE SHEET

In preparing the balance sheet (p. 134), remember that the balance sheet section totals on the worksheet ($18,680) do *not* match the totals on the formal balance sheet ($17,975). This is because information is grouped differently on the formal report. First, in the formal report Accumulated Depreciation ($80) is subtracted from Word Processing Equipment, reducing the balance. Second, Withdrawals ($625) are subtracted from Owner's Equity, reducing the balance further. These two reductions (−$80 − $625 = −$705) represent the difference between the worksheet and the formal version of the balance sheet ($17,975 − $18,680 = −$705). Figure 4-8 on page 134 shows how to prepare the balance sheet from the worksheet.

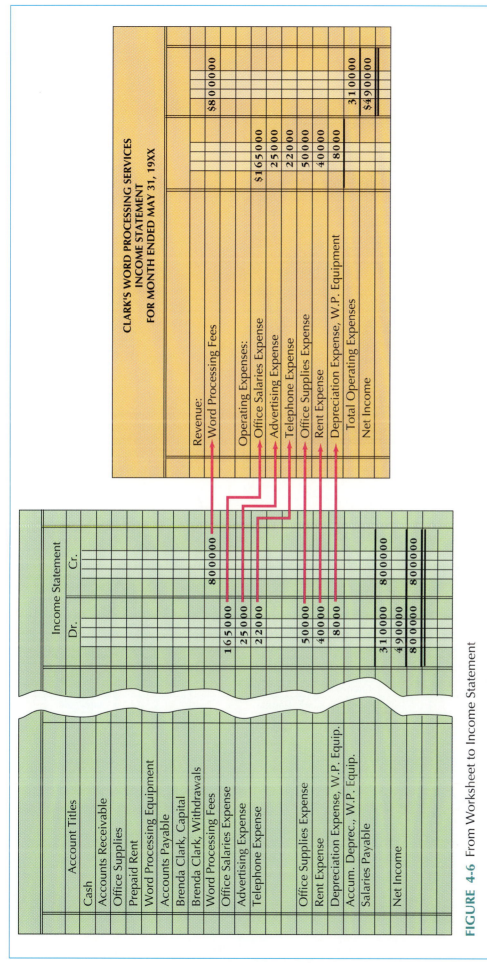

CLARK'S WORD PROCESSING SERVICES
INCOME STATEMENT
FOR MONTH ENDED MAY 31, 19XX

Revenue:		
Word Processing Fees		$800000
Operating Expenses:		
Office Salaries Expense	$165000	
Advertising Expense	25000	
Telephone Expense	22000	
Office Supplies Expense	50000	
Rent Expense	40000	
Depreciation Expense, W.P. Equipment	8000	
Total Operating Expenses		310000
Net Income		$490000

Income Statement

Account Titles	Dr.	Cr.
Cash		
Accounts Receivable		
Office Supplies		
Prepaid Rent		
Word Processing Equipment		
Accounts Payable		
Brenda Clark, Capital		
Brenda Clark, Withdrawals		
Word Processing Fees		800000
Office Salaries Expense	165000	
Advertising Expense	25000	
Telephone Expense	22000	
Office Supplies Expense	50000	
Rent Expense	40000	
Depreciation Expense, W.P. Equip.	8000	
Accum. Deprec., W.P. Equip.		
Salaries Payable		
	310000	800000
Net Income	490000	
	800000	800000

FIGURE 4-6 From Worksheet to Income Statement

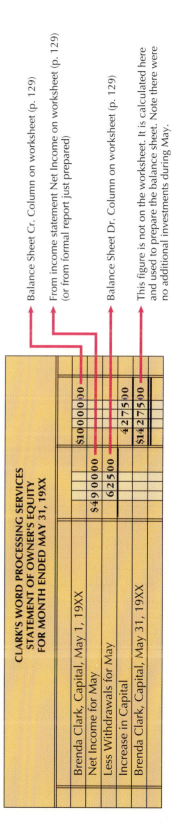

CLARK'S WORD PROCESSING SERVICES
STATEMENT OF OWNER'S EQUITY
FOR MONTH ENDED MAY 31, 19XX

Brenda Clark, Capital, May 1, 19XX		$1000000
Net Income for May	$490000	
Less Withdrawals for May	62500	
Increase in Capital		427500
Brenda Clark, Capital, May 31, 19XX		$1427500

Balance Sheet Cr. Column on worksheet (p. 129)

From income statement Net Income on worksheet (p. 129) (or from formal report just prepared)

Balance Sheet Dr. Column on worksheet (p. 129)

This figure is not on the worksheet. It is calculated here and used to prepare the balance sheet. Note there were no additional investments during May.

FIGURE 4-7 Completing a Statement of Owner's Equity

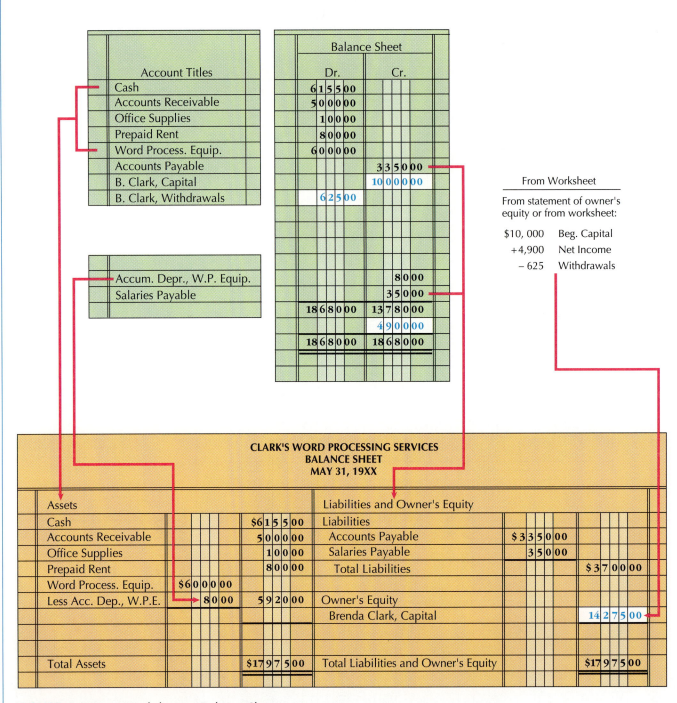

FIGURE 4-8 From Worksheet to Balance Sheet

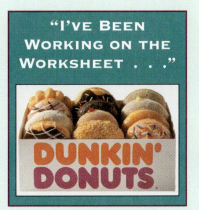

red has dreams. Big ones. He wants to grow his business to the point where he can start another Dunkin' Donuts shop. To do that, Fred realizes that he will have to manage his current shop more efficiently. His donuts and muffins are widely praised, and his bagel line is so successful that he has hired more help. But along with this success has come more paperwork. Fred now spends hours on his accounts. What to do?

Dunkin' Donuts' Business Consultant, Dwayne Goulding, knows that Fred needs to reduce the time he spends handling his accounts. Dwayne has suggested that Fred hire an accountant, or that he switch to a computerized accounting system, as many owners have done recently. Fred has been hesitant to do either, because he wants to control the finances himself. And save money. And he fears computers. What to do?

Seeing Fred's dilemma, Dwayne encourages him to contact his zone's Advisory Council. This Advisory Council, like hundreds across the country, offers fellow Dunkin' Donuts shop owners from the same zone a chance to get together to share ways to improve their operations and discuss common problems. They work with Dwayne and the rest of the Dunkin' Donuts managerial team to keep their interdependent businesses running smoothly and profitably.

"I'VE BEEN WORKING ON THE WORKSHEET . . ."

When Fred approaches the Council, they are very supportive. "I've been there, Fred, so I know how you feel," said Joe Franklin, from two towns away. "First, you're on the right track when you prepare a worksheet. It's too easy to mess up if you try to skip this step. Next, you might want to try keeping a clean copy of last month's worksheet. Even though you don't have to submit it to Dwayne, you frequently have to go back and refer to it when questions come up on your Income Statement or Balance Sheet. When your worksheet is all crossed out and doodled on, like this one is, you can't find info fast. Also, you may need your worksheets at tax time. I sure found that out the hard way!"

DISCUSSION QUESTIONS

1. What is an Advisory Council? Why do you think that Dwayne recommended that Fred seek their advice?
2. Why do you think that some small business owners fear computerization and equate it with a loss of financial control?
3. Why is a clear worksheet helpful even after that month's statements have been prepared?

LEARNING UNIT 4-2 REVIEW

AT THIS POINT you should be able to

◆ Prepare the three financial reports from a worksheet. (p. 132)
◆ Explain why totals of the formal balance sheet don't match totals of balance sheet columns on the worksheet. (p. 132)

SELF-REVIEW QUIZ 4-2

(The forms you need are located on pages 107 and 108 of the *Study Guide and Working Papers.*)

From the worksheet on page 131 for P. Logan, please prepare (1) an income statement for December; (2) a statement of owner's equity; and (3) a balance sheet for December 31, 19XX. No additional investments took place during the period.

P. LOGAN
INCOME STATEMENT
FOR THE MONTH ENDED DECEMBER 31, 19XX

Revenue:			
Revenue from clients			$25 00
Operating Expenses:			
Rent Expense	$2 00		
Salaries Expense	11 00		
Depreciation Expense, Store Equipment	1 00		
Insurance Expense	2 00		
Supplies Expense	4 00		
Total Operating Expenses		20 00	
Net Income		$5 00	

P. LOGAN
STATEMENT OF OWNER'S EQUITY
FOR THE MONTH ENDED DECEMBER 31, 19XX

P. Logan, Capital, December 1, 19XX			$14 00
Net Income for December	$5 00		
Less Withdrawals for December	3 00		
Increase in Capital		2 00	
P. Logan, Capital, December 31, 19XX		$16 00	

P. LOGAN
BALANCE SHEET
DECEMBER 31, 19XX

Assets				Liabilities and Owner's Equity			
Cash			$15 00	Liabilities			
Accounts Receivable			3 00	Accounts Payable	$2 00		
Prepaid Insurance			1 00	Salaries Payable	3 00		
Store Supplies			1 00	Total Liabilities		$5 00	
Store Equipment	$6 00			Owner's Equity			
Less Acc. Dep., St. Eq.	5 00		1 00	P. Logan, Capital		16 00	
				Total Liabilities and			
Total Assets			$21 00	Owner's Equity		$21 00	

COMPREHENSIVE DEMONSTRATION PROBLEM WITH SOLUTION TIPS

(The blank forms you need are on pages 109 and 110 of the *Study Guide and Working Papers.*)

From the following trial balance and additional data complete (1) a worksheet and (2) the three financial reports (numbers are intentionally small so you may concentrate on the theory).

FROST COMPANY
TRIAL BALANCE
DECEMBER 31, 19XX

	Dr.	Cr.
Cash	14	
Accounts Receivable	4	
Prepaid Insurance	5	
Plumbing Supplies	3	
Plumbing Equipment	7	
Accumulated Depreciation, Plumbing Equipment		5
Accounts Payable		1
J. Frost, Capital		12
J. Frost, Withdrawals	3	
Plumbing Fees		27
Rent Expense	4	
Salaries Expense	5	
Totals	45	45

Adjustment Data:

a. Insurance Expired $3
b. Plumbing Supplies on Hand $1
c. Depreciation Expense, Plumbing Equipment $1
d. Salaries owed but not paid to employees $2

Solution Tips to Building a Worksheet

1. Adjustments (Used up)

a.

Insurance Expense	Expense	↑	Dr.	$3
Prepaid Insurance	Asset	↓	Cr.	$3

Expired means used up

b.

Plumbing Supplies Expense	Expense	↑	Dr.	$2
Plumbing Supplies	Asset	↓	Cr.	$2

$3 − 1 = $2 *used up*

on hand

(cont. on p. 139)

FROST COMPANY
WORKSHEET
FOR MONTH ENDED DECEMBER 31, 19XX

Account Titles	Trial Balance Dr.	Trial Balance Cr.	Adjustments Dr.	Adjustments Cr.	Adjusted Trial Balance Dr.	Adjusted Trial Balance Cr.	Income Statement Dr.	Income Statement Cr.	Balance Sheet Dr.	Balance Sheet Cr.
Cash	1400				1400				1400	
Accounts Receivable	400				400				400	
Prepaid Insurance	500			(A) 300	200				200	
Plumbing Supplies	300			(B) 200	100				100	
Plumbing Equipment	700				700				700	
Accum. Depr., Plumb. Equip.		500		(C) 100		600				600
Accounts Payable		100				100				100
J. Frost, Capital		1200				1200				1200
J. Frost, Withdrawals	300				300				300	
Plumbing Fees		2700				2700		2700		
Rent Expense	400				400		400			
Salaries Expense	500		(D) 200		700		700			
	4500	4500								
Insurance Expense			(A) 300		300		300			
Plumbing Supplies Expense			(B) 200		200		200			
Depr. Exp. Plumb. Equip.			(C) 100		100		100			
Salaries Payable				(D) 200		200				200
			800	800	4800	4800	1700	2700	3100	2100
Net Income							1000			1000
							2700	2700	3100	3100

c.

Depreciation Expense, Plumbing Equipment	Expense	↑	Dr.	$1
Accumulated Depreciation, Plumbing Equipment	Contra Asset	↑	Cr.	$1

The original cost of equipment of $7 is not "touched."

d.

Salaries Expense,	Expense	↑	Dr.	$2
Salaries Payable	Liability	↑	Cr.	$2

2. Last four columns of worksheet prepared from adjusted trial balance.
3. Capital of $12 is the old figure. Net income of $10 (revenue − expenses) is brought over to same side as capital on the balance sheet Cr. column to balance columns.

FROST COMPANY
INCOME STATEMENT
FOR MONTH ENDED DECEMBER 31, 19XX

Revenue:		
Plumbing Fees		$27
Operating Expenses:		
Rent Expense	$4	
Salaries Expense	7	
Insurance Expense	3	
Plumbing Supplies Expense	2	
Depreciation Expense, Plumbing Equipment	1	
Total Operating Expenses		17
Net Income		$10

FROST COMPANY
STATEMENT OF OWNER'S EQUITY
FOR MONTH ENDED DECEMBER 31, 19XX

J. Frost Capital, Dec. 1, 19XX		$12
Net Income for December	$10	
Less Withdrawals for December	3	
Increase in Capital		7
J. Frost, Capital Dec. 31, 19XX		$19

FROST COMPANY
BALANCE SHEET
DECEMBER 31, 19XX

Assets			Liabilities and Owner's Equity		
Cash		$14	Liabilities		
Accounts Receivable		4	Accounts Payable	$1	
Prepaid Insurance		2	Salaries Payable	2	
Plumbing Supplies		1	Total Liabilities		$ 3
Plumbing Equipment	$7				
Less Accumulated Dep.	6	1	Owner's Equity		
			J. Frost, Capital		19
			Total Liabilities and		
Total Assets		$22	Owner's Equity		$22

Solution Tips for Preparing Financial Reports from a Worksheet

Inside columns of the three financial reports are used for subtotal. There are no debits or credits on the formal reports.

REPORT

◆ **Income Statement** From Income Statement columns of worksheet for revenue and expenses.

◆ **Statement of Owner's Equity** From Balance Sheet Cr. column for old figure for Capital. Net Income from Income Statement. From Balance Sheet Dr. column for Withdrawal figure.

◆ **Balance Sheet** From Balance Sheet Dr. column for Assets. From Balance Sheet Cr. Column for liabilities and Accumulated Depreciation. New Figure for Capital from Statement of Owner's Equity.

Note how plumbing equipment $7 and Accumulated Depreciation $6 are rearranged on the formal balance sheet. The total assets of $22 is not on the worksheet. Remember there are no debits or credits on formal reports.

SUMMARY OF KEY POINTS

Learning Unit 4-1

1. The worksheet is not a formal report.
2. Adjustments update certain accounts so that they will be up to their latest balance before financial reports are prepared. Adjustments are the result of internal transactions.
3. Adjustments will affect both the income statement and the balance sheet.
4. Accounts listed *below* the account titles on the trial balance of the worksheet are *increasing*.
5. The original cost of a piece of equipment is not adjusted, historical cost is not lost.
6. Depreciation is the process of spreading the original cost of the asset over its expected useful life.
7. Accumulated depreciation is a contra-asset on the balance sheet that summarizes, accumulates, or builds up the amount of depreciation that an asset has accumulated.
8. Book value is the original cost less accumulated depreciation.
9. Accrued salaries are unpaid and unrecorded expenses that are accumulating but for which payment is not yet due.
10. Revenue and Expenses go on income statement sections of the worksheet. Assets, contra-assets, liabilities, capital, and withdrawals go on balance sheet sections of the worksheet.

Learning Unit 4-2

1. The formal reports prepared from a worksheet do not have debit or credit columns.
2. Revenue and expenses go on the income statement. Beginning capital plus net income less withdrawals (or: beginning capital minus net loss, less withdrawals) go on the statement of owner's equity. Be sure to check capital account in ledger to see if any additional investments took place. Assets, contra-assets, liabilities, and the new figure for capital go on the balance sheet.

KEY TERMS

Accrued salaries Salaries that are earned by employees but unpaid and unrecorded during the period (and thus need to be recorded by an adjustment) and will not come due for payment until the next accounting period.

Accumulated depreciation A contra-asset account that summarizes or accumulates the amount of depreciation that has been taken on an asset.

Adjusting The process of calculating the latest up-to-date balance of each account at the end of an accounting period.

Book value Cost of equipment less accumulated depreciation.

Depreciation The allocation (spreading) of the cost of an asset (such as an auto or equipment) over its expected useful life.

Historical cost The actual cost of an asset at time of purchase.

Residual value Estimated value of an asset after all the allowable depreciation has been taken.

Worksheet A columnar device used by accountants to aid them in completing the accounting cycle. It is not a formal report. Often called a spreadsheet.

BLUEPRINT OF STEPS 5 AND 6 OF THE ACCOUNTING CYCLE

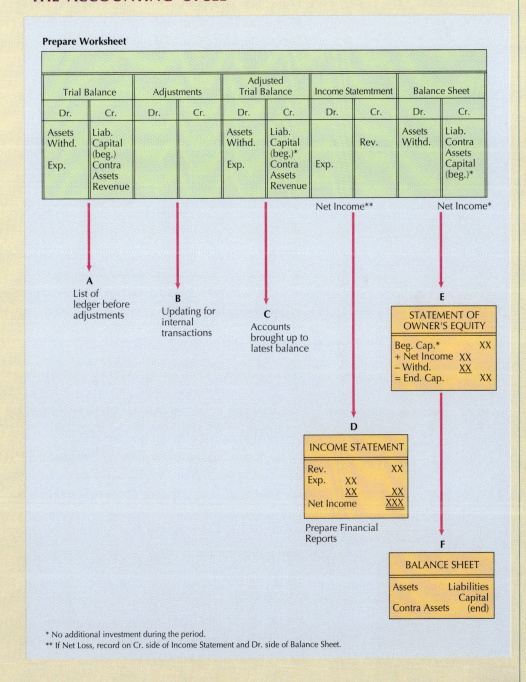

Prepare Worksheet

	Trial Balance		Adjustments		Adjusted Trial Balance		Income Statemtment		Balance Sheet	
	Dr.	Cr.	Dr.	Cr.	Dr.	Cr.	Dr.	Cr.	Dr.	Cr.
	Assets Withd. Exp.	Liab. Capital (beg.) Contra Assets Revenue			Assets Withd. Exp.	Liab. Capital (beg.)* Contra Assets Revenue	Exp.	Rev.	Assets Withd.	Liab. Contra Assets Capital (beg.)*

Net Income** (Income Statement) / Net Income* (Balance Sheet)

A
List of ledger before adjustments

B
Updating for internal transactions

C
Accounts brought up to latest balance

D

INCOME STATEMENT

Rev.		XX
Exp.	XX	
	XX	XX
Net Income		XXX

Prepare Financial Reports

E

STATEMENT OF OWNER'S EQUITY

Beg. Cap.*		XX
+ Net Income	XX	
– Withd.		XX
= End. Cap.		XX

F

BALANCE SHEET

Assets	Liabilities
	Capital
Contra Assets	(end)

* No additional investment during the period.
** If Net Loss, record on Cr. side of Income Statement and Dr. side of Balance Sheet.

QUESTIONS, MINI EXERCISES, EXERCISES, AND PROBLEMS

Discussion Questions

1. Worksheets are required in every company's accounting cycle. Please agree or disagree and explain why.
2. What is the purpose of adjusting accounts?
3. What is the relationship of internal transactions to the adjusting process?
4. Explain how an adjustment can affect both the income statement and balance sheet. Please give an example.
5. Why do we need the accumulated depreciation account?
6. Depreciation expense goes on the balance sheet. True or false. Why?
7. Each month the cost of accumulated depreciation grows while the cost of equipment goes up. Agree or disagree. Defend your position.
8. Define accrued salaries.
9. Why don't the formal financial reports contain debit or credit columns?
10. Explain how the financial reports are prepared from the worksheet.

Mini Exercises

(The blank forms you need are on pages 112–113 of the *Study Guide and Working Papers.*)

Adjustment for Supplies

1. *Before Adjustment*

Supplies	Supplies Expense
400	

Given: At year end an inventory of supplies showed $50.
a. How much is the adjustment for supplies?
b. Draw a transaction analysis box for this adjustment.
c. What will the balance of supplies be on the Adjusted Trial Balance?

Adjustment for Prepaid Rent

2. *Before Adjustment*

Prepaid Rent	Rent Expense
700	

Given: At year end rent expired is $300.
a. How much is the adjustment for Prepaid Rent?
b. Draw a transaction analysis box for this adjustment.
c. What will be the balance of Prepaid Rent on the Adjusted Trial Balance?

Adjustment for Depreciation

3. *Before Adjustment*

Equip.	Acc. Dep., Equip.	Dep. Exp., Equip.
6,000	1,000	

Given: At year end depreciation on Equipment is $1,000.
a. Which of the three T Accounts above is not affected?
b. Which Title is a contra-asset?

c. Draw a transaction analysis box for this adjustment.

d. What will be the balance of these three accounts on the Adjusted Trial Balance?

Adjustment for Accrued Salaries

4. *Before Adjustment*

Salaries Expense	Salaries Payable
900	

Given: Accrued Salaries, $200.

a. Draw a transaction analysis box for this adjustment.

b. What will be the balance of these two accounts on the Adjusted Trial Balance?

Worksheet

5. From the following Adjusted Trial Balance titles of a worksheet identify in which column each account will be listed on the last four columns of the worksheet.

(ID) Income Statement Dr. Column

(IC) Income Statement Cr. Column

(BD) Balance Sheet Dr. Column

(BC) Balance Sheet Cr. Column

	ATB	IS	BS
A. Supplies	~~ ~~	_____	_____
B. Acc. Receivable	~~ ~~	_____	_____
C. Cash	~~ ~~	_____	_____
D. Prepaid Rent	~~ ~~	_____	_____
E. Equipment	~~ ~~	_____	_____
F. Acc. Depreciation	~~ ~~	_____	_____
G. B., Capital	~~ ~~	_____	_____
H. B., Withdrawals	~~ ~~	_____	_____
I. Taxi Fees	~~ ~~	_____	_____
J. Advertising Expense	~~ ~~	_____	_____
K. Off. Supplies Expense	~~ ~~	_____	_____
L. Rent Expense	~~ ~~	_____	_____
M. Depreciation Expense	~~ ~~	_____	_____
N. Salaries Payable	~~ ~~	_____	_____

6. From the following Balance Sheet (which was made from the worksheet and other financial reports) explain why the lettered numbers were not found on the worksheet. *Hint:* There are no debits or credits on the formal financial reports.

H. WELLS
BALANCE SHEET
DECEMBER 31, 19XX

Assets			Liabilities and Owner's Equity			
Cash		$ 6	Liabilities			
Acc. Receivable		2	Accounts Payable	$2		
Supplies		2	Salaries, Payable	1		
Equipment	$10		Total Liabilities		$ 3	(B)
Less Acc. Dep.	4	6	Owner's Equity			
			H. Wells, Capital		13	(C)
			Total Liability and			
(A) Total Assets		$16	Owner's Equity		$16	(D)

(The blank forms you need are on pages 114–116 of the *Study Guide and Working Papers.*)

4-1. Complete the following table.

Account	Category	Normal Balance	Which Financial Report(s) Found
Salary Expense			
Prepaid Insurance			
Equipment			
Accumulated Depreciation			
A. Jax, Capital			
A. Jax, Withdrawals			
Salaries Payable			
Depreciation Expense			

Categorizing accounts.

Reviewing adjustments and the transaction analysis charts.

4-2. Use transaction analysis charts to analyze the following adjustments:
   a. Depreciation on equipment, $500.
   b. Rent expired, $200.

4-3. From the following adjustment data, calculate the adjustment amount and record appropriate debits or credits:

Recording adjusting entries.

   a. Supplies purchased, $600.
      Supplies on hand, $200.
   b. Store equipment, $10,000.
      Accumulated depreciation before adjustment, $900.
      Depreciation expense, $100.

Preparing a worksheet.

4-4. From the following trial balance and adjustment data, complete a worksheet for J. Trent as of December 31, 19XX:

   a. Depreciation expense, equipment $2.00
   b. Insurance expired   1.00
   c. Store supplies on hand   4.00
   d. Wages owed, but not paid for (they   5.00
      are an expense in the old year)

J. TRENT
TRIAL BALANCE
DECEMBER 31, 19XX

	Dr.	Cr.
Cash	9 00	
Accounts Receivable	2 00	
Prepaid Insurance	7 00	
Store Supplies	6 00	
Store Equipment	7 00	
Accumulated Depreciation, Equipment		2 00
Accounts Payable		4 00
J. Trent, Capital		17 00
J. Trent, Withdrawals	6 00	
Revenue from Clients		24 00
Rent Expense	4 00	
Wage Expense	6 00	
	47 00	47 00

4-5. From the completed worksheet in Exercise 4-4, prepare

    a. An income statement for December.

    b. A statement of owner's equity for December.

    c. A balance sheet as of December 31, 19XX.

Group A Problems

(The blank forms you need are on pp. 117–120 of the *Study Guide and Working Papers.*)

4A-1.

SILVER'S FITNESS CENTER TRIAL BALANCE DECEMBER 31, 19XX		
	Debit	Credit
Cash in Bank	4 1 0 0 00	
Accounts Receivable	5 0 0 0 00	
Gym Supplies	5 4 0 0 00	
Gym Equipment	7 2 0 0 00	
Accumulated Depreciation, Gym Equipment		3 7 5 0 00
J. Silver, Capital		10 7 0 0 00
J. Silver, Withdrawals	3 0 0 0 00	
Gym Fees		11 3 0 0 00
Rent Expense	9 0 0 00	
Advertising Expense	1 5 0 00	
	25 7 5 0 00	25 7 5 0 00

Given the following adjustment data on December 31:

    a. Gym supplies on hand, $1,500.

    b. Depreciation taken on gym equipment, $800.

Complete a partial worksheet up to the adjusted trial balance.

4A-2. On the next page is the trial balance for Fred's Plumbing Service for December 31, 19XX.

Adjustment data to update the trial balance:

    a. Rent expired, $500.

    b. Plumbing supplies on hand (remaining), $100.

    c. Depreciation expense, plumbing equipment, $200.

    d. Wages earned by workers but not paid or due until January, $350.

Your task is to prepare a worksheet for Fred's Plumbing Service for the month of December.

FRED'S PLUMBING SERVICE
TRIAL BALANCE
DECEMBER 31, 19XX

	Dr.	Cr.
Cash in Bank	3 6 0 6 00	
Accounts Receivable	7 0 0 00	
Prepaid Rent	8 0 0 00	
Plumbing Supplies	7 4 2 00	
Plumbing Equipment	1 4 0 0 00	
Accumulated Depreciation, Plumbing Equipment		1 0 6 0 00
Accounts Payable		4 4 2 00
Fred Jack, Capital		3 2 5 0 00
Plumbing Revenue		4 3 5 6 00
Heat Expense	4 0 0 00	
Advertising Expense	2 0 0 00	
Wage Expense	1 2 6 0 00	
	9 1 0 8 00	9 1 0 8 00

4A-3. The following is the trial balance for Kevin's Moving Co.

KEVIN'S MOVING CO.
TRIAL BALANCE
OCTOBER 31, 19XX

	Dr.	Cr.
Cash	5 0 0 0 00	
Prepaid Insurance	2 5 0 0 00	
Moving Supplies	1 2 0 0 00	
Moving Truck	11 0 0 0 00	
Accumulated Depreciation, Moving Truck		9 0 0 0 00
Accounts Payable		2 7 6 8 00
K. Hoff, Capital		5 4 4 2 00
K. Hoff, Withdrawals	1 4 0 0 00	
Revenue from Moving		9 0 0 0 00
Wage Expense	3 7 1 2 00	
Rent Expense	1 0 8 0 00	
Advertising Expense	3 1 8 00	
	26 2 1 0 00	26 2 1 0 00

Adjustment data to update trial balance:

a. Insurance expired, $700.

b. Moving supplies on hand, $900.

c. Depreciation on moving truck, $500.

d. Wages earned but unpaid, $250.

Your task is to

1. Complete a worksheet for Kevin's Moving Co. for the month of October.

2. Prepare an income statement for October, a statement of owner's equity for October, and a balance sheet as of October 31, 19XX.

4A-4.

Adjustment data to update trial balance:

a. Insurance expired, $700.

b. Repair supplies on hand, $3,000.

c. Depreciation on repair equipment, $200.

d. Wages earned but unpaid, $400.

Your task is to

1. Complete a worksheet for Dick's Repair Service for the month of November.

2. Prepare an income statement for November, a statement of owner's equity for November, and a balance sheet as of November 30, 19XX.

Comprehensive Problem

Check Figure:

Net Income $1,830

DICK'S REPAIR SERVICE TRIAL BALANCE NOVEMBER 30, 19XX		
	Dr.	Cr.
Cash	3 2 0 0 00	
Prepaid Insurance	4 0 0 0 00	
Repair Supplies	4 6 0 0 00	
Repair Equipment	3 0 0 0 00	
Accumulated Depreciation, Repair Equipment		7 0 0 00
Accounts Payable		5 5 7 0 00
D. Horn, Capital		3 8 0 0 00
Revenue from Repairs		7 0 0 0 00
Wages Expense	1 8 0 0 00	
Rent Expense	3 6 0 00	
Advertising Expense	1 1 0 00	
	17 0 7 0 00	17 0 7 0 00

Group B Problems

(The blank forms you need are on pages 117–120 of the *Study Guide and Working Papers.*)

4B-1.

Completing a partial worksheet up to adjusted trial balance.

Check Figure:

Total of Adjusted Trial Balance $18,600

SILVER'S FITNESS CENTER TRIAL BALANCE DECEMBER 31, 19XX		
	Dr.	Cr.
Cash	2 0 0 0 00	
Accounts Receivable	2 0 0 0 00	
Gym Supplies	4 2 0 0 00	
Gym Equipment	8 0 0 0 00	
Accumulated Depreciation, Gym Equipment		5 7 0 0 00
J. Silver, Capital		11 0 0 0 00
J. Silver, Withdrawals	1 0 0 0 00	
Gym Fees		1 4 0 0 00
Rent Expense	8 0 0 00	
Advertising Expense	1 0 0 00	
	18 1 0 0 00	18 1 0 0 00

Please complete a partial worksheet up to the adjusted trial balance using the following adjustment data:

a. Gym supplies on hand, $2,600.

b. Depreciation taken on gym equipment, $500.

4B-2. Given the following trial balance and adjustment data of Fred's Plumbing Service, your task is to prepare a worksheet for the month of December.

Completing a worksheet.

Check Figure:
Net Income $673

FRED'S PLUMBING SERVICE
TRIAL BALANCE
DECEMBER 31, 19XX

	Dr.	Cr.
Cash in Bank	3 9 6 00	
Accounts Receivable	2 8 4 00	
Prepaid Rent	4 0 0 00	
Plumbing Supplies	3 1 0 00	
Plumbing Equipment	1 0 0 0 00	
Accumulated Depreciation, Plumbing Equipment		2 0 0 00
Accounts Payable		3 4 6 00
Fred Jack, Capital		4 5 6 00
Plumbing Revenue		4 6 8 0 00
Heat Expense	6 3 2 00	
Advertising Expense	1 2 0 0 00	
Wage Expense	1 4 6 0 00	
Total	5 6 8 2 00	5 6 8 2 00

Adjustment data:

a. Plumbing supplies on hand, $60.
b. Rent expired, $150.
c. Depreciation on plumbing equipment, $200.
d. Wages earned but unpaid, $115.

4B-3. Using the following trial balance and adjustment data of Kevin's Moving Co., prepare

1. A worksheet for the month of October.
2. An income statement for October, a statement of owner's equity for October, and a balance sheet as of October 31, 19XX.

Comprehensive Problem

Check Figure:
Net Loss $1,628

KEVIN'S MOVING CO.
TRIAL BALANCE
OCTOBER 31, 19XX

	Dr.	Cr.
Cash	3 9 2 0 00	
Prepaid Insurance	3 2 8 8 00	
Moving Supplies	1 4 0 0 00	
Moving Truck	10 6 5 8 00	
Accumulated Depreciation, Moving Truck		3 6 6 0 00
Accounts Payable		1 3 1 2 00
K. Hoff, Capital		17 4 8 2 00
K. Hoff, Withdrawals	4 2 4 0 00	
Revenue from Moving		8 1 6 2 00
Wages Expense	5 7 1 2 00	
Rent Expense	1 0 8 0 00	
Advertising Expense	3 1 8 00	
	30 6 1 6 00	30 6 1 6 00

Adjustment Data:

a. Insurance expired $600
b. Moving supplies on hand $310

     c. Depreciation on moving truck $580

     d. Wages earned but unpaid $410

4B-4. As the bookkeeper of Dick's Repair Service, use the information that follows to prepare

    1. A worksheet for the month of November.

    2. An income statement for November, a statement of owner's equity for November, and a balance sheet as of November 30, 19XX.

Comprehensive Problem

Check Figure:

Net Income $1,012

DICK'S REPAIR SERVICE TRIAL BALANCE NOVEMBER 30, 19XX		
	Dr.	Cr.
Cash	3 2 0 4 00	
Prepaid Insurance	4 0 0 0 00	
Repair Supplies	7 7 0 00	
Repair Equipment	3 1 0 6 00	
Accumulated Depreciation, Repair Equipment		6 5 0 00
Accounts Payable		1 9 0 4 00
D. Horn, Capital		6 2 5 8 00
Revenue from Repairs		5 6 3 4 00
Wages Expense	1 6 0 0 00	
Rent Expense	1 5 6 0 00	
Advertising Expense	2 0 6 00	
	14 4 4 6 00	14 4 4 6 00

Adjustment Data:

    a. Insurance expired $300

    b. Repair supplies on hand $170

    c. Depreciation on repair equipment $250

    d. Wages earned but unpaid $106

REAL WORLD APPLICATIONS

4R-1.

MEMO

To: Hal Hogan, Bookkeeper

From: Pete Tennant, V. P.

Re: Adjustments for year ended December 31, 19XX

Hal, here is the information you requested. Please supply me with the adjustments needed ASAP. Also, please put in writing why we need to do these adjustments.

Thanks.

Attached to memo:

a. Insurance data:

Policy No.	Date of Policy Purchase	Policy Length	Cost
100	November 1 of previous year	4 years	$480
200	May 1 of current year	2 years	600
300	September 1 of current year	1 year	240

b. Rent data: Prepaid rent had a $500 balance at beginning of year. An additional $400 of rent was paid in advance in June. At year end, $200 of rent had expired.

c. Revenue data: Accrued storage fees of $500 were earned but uncollected and unrecorded at year end.

4R-2.

> *Hint: Unearned Rent is a liability on the balance sheet.*

On Friday, Harry Swag's boss asks him to prepare a special report, due on Monday at 8:00 A.M. Harry gathers the following material in his briefcase:

	Dec. 31	
	19X1	**19X2**
Prepaid Advertising	$300	$600
Interest Payable	150	350
Unearned Rent	500	300

Cash paid for:	Advertising	$1,900
	Interest	1,500
Cash received for:	Rent	2,300

As his best friend, could you help Harry show the amounts that are to be reported on the 19XX income statement for (a) Advertising Expense, (b) Interest Expense, and (c) Rent Fees Earned. Please explain in writing why unearned rent is considered a liability.

 make the call

Critical Thinking/Ethical Case

4R-3.

Janet Fox, President of Angel Co., went to a tax seminar. One of the speakers at the seminar advised the audience to put off showing expenses until next year because doing so would allow them to take advantage of a new tax law. When Janet returned to the office, she called in her accountant, Frieda O'Riley. She told Frieda to forget about making any adjustments for salaries in the old year so more expenses could be shown in the new year. Frieda told her that putting off these expenses would not follow generally accepted accounting procedures. Janet said she should do it anyway. You make the call. Write your specific recommendations to Frieda.

ACCOUNTING RECALL
A CUMULATIVE APPROACH

THIS EXAM REVIEWS CHAPTERS 1 THROUGH 4

Pages 125 and 129 of the *Study Guide and Working Papers* have the forms to complete this exam, as well as worked-out solutions. The page references next to each question identify what page to turn back to if you answer the question incorrectly.

PART 1   Vocabulary Review

Match the terms to the appropriate definition or phrase.

Page Ref.

(120)	1. Prepaid rent	A. Estimated value of an asset after all depreciation taken
(123)	2. Accrued salaries	
(122)	3. Depreciation expense	B. Earned but unpaid
(121)	4. Accumulated depreciation	C. Actual cost at time of purchase

(40)	5. Normal balance	D. Columnar device
(121)	6. Residual value	E. Rent paid in advance
(5)	7. An Asset	F. Cost — accumulated depreciation
(117)	8. Worksheet	G. Supplies
(122)	9. Book value	H. Shown on the income statement
(122)	10. Historical cost	I. Side that increases it
		J. Contra asset

PART II True or False (Accounting Theory)

(118)　11. Adjustments are the result of external transactions.

(119)　12. Adjustments affect only the balance sheet.

(122)　13. Accumulated depreciation and equipment will both go on the balance sheet.

(121)　14. The normal balance of accumulated depreciation is a debit.

(132)　15. All financial reports could be prepared from a worksheet.

CONTINUING PROBLEM

At the end of September, Tony took a complete inventory of his supplies and found the following:

5 dozen ¼″ screws at a cost of $8.00 a dozen

2 dozen ½″ screws at a cost of $5.00 a dozen

2 cartons of computer inventory paper at a cost of $14 a carton

3 feet of coaxial cable at a cost of $4.00 per foot

After speaking to his accountant, he found that a reasonable depreciation amount for each of his long-term assets is as follows:

Computer purchased July 5, 19XX	Depreciation $33 a month
Office Equipment purchased July 17, 19XX	Depreciation $10 a month
Computer Workstations purchased Sept. 17, 19XX	Depreciation $20 a month

Tony uses the straight-line method of depreciation and declares no salvage value for any of the assets. If any long-term asset is purchased in the first fifteen days of the month, he will charge depreciation for the full month. If an asset is purchased on the sixteenth of the month, or later, he will not charge depreciation in the month it was purchased.

August and September's rent has now expired.

Assignment:

Use your trial balance from the completed problem in Chapter 3 and the above adjusting information to complete the worksheet for the three months ended September 30, 19XX. From the worksheets prepare the financial statements. (See pp. 126–127 in your *Study Guide and Working Papers*.)

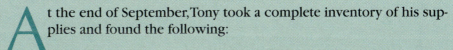

COMPUTERIZED ACCOUNTING APPLICATION FOR CHAPTER 4

PART A: Compound Journal Entries, Adjusting Entries, and Financial Reports

PART B: Backup Procedures

Before starting on this assignment, read and complete the tasks discussed in Parts A, B, and F of the Computerized Accounting appendix at the back of this book and complete the Computerized Accounting Application assignment at the end of Chapter 3.

PART A: Compound Journal Entries, Adjusting Entries, and Financial Reports

Open the Company Data Files

1. Click on the Start button. Point to Programs; point to Simply Accounting; then click on Simply Accounting in the final menu presented. The Simply Accounting Open File dialog box will appear.

2. Insert your Student Data Files disk into disk drive A. Enter the following path into the **File name** text box: A:\student\zell.asc

3. Click on the **Open** button; enter 12/31/97 into the **Using Date for this Session** text box; then click on the **OK** button. Click on the **OK** button in response to the message "The date entered is more than one week past your previous Using date of 12/1/97." The Company Window for Zell will appear.

Add Your Name to the Company Name

4. Click on the Company Window Setup menu; then click on Company Information. The Company Information dialog box will appear. Insert your name in place of the text "Your Name" in the **Name** text box. Click on the **OK** button to return to the Company Window.

How to Record a Compound Journal Entry

5. In the Computerized Accounting Application assignment in Chapter 3 you learned how to record journal entries in the General Journal dialog box. Compound journal entries can also be recorded in the General Journal dialog box. The owner of The Zell Company has made an investment in the business consisting of $5,000 in cash and an automobile valued at $12,000. Open the General Journal dialog box. Enter the word Memo into the **Source** text box; press the TAB key; enter 12/1/97 into the **Date** text box; press the TAB key; enter "Initial investment by owner" into the **Comment** text box; then press the TAB key. The flashing insertion point will be positioned in the **Account** text box.

6. With the flashing insertion point positioned in the **Account** text box, press the ENTER key. The Select Account dialog box will appear. Double-click on 1110 Cash; enter 5000 into the **Debits** text box; then press the TAB key.

7. Press the ENTER key to bring up the Select Account dialog box. Double-click on 1230 Automobile. The program will offer 5000.00 as a default amount in the **Credits** text box. The **Credits** amount remains highlighted. You do not want to accept the default. To override the default, enter − 12000 (Be sure to enter the minus sign!); then press the TAB key. The 12000.00 amount will move to the **Debits** text box.

8. Press the ENTER key to bring up the Select Account dialog box; then double-click on 3110 Owner's Capital. The program will offer the total of the **Debits** portion of the compound journal entry (17000.00) as a default amount in the **Credits** text box. The **Credits** amount remains highlighted. Press the TAB key

to accept the default **Credits** amount. This completes the data you need to enter into the General Journal dialog box to record the compound journal entry for the initial investment by the owner. Your screen should look like this:

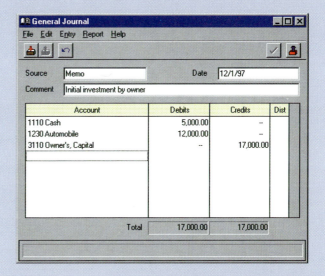

Review the Compound Journal Entry

9. Click on the General Journal Report menu; then click on Display General Journal Entry. Review the compound journal entry for accuracy, noting any errors.

10. Close the General Journal Entry window; then make any editing corrections required.

Post the Entry

11. After verifying that the compound journal entry is correct, click on the **Post** icon to post this transaction.

Record Additional Transactions

12. Record the following additional journal entries (enter "Memo" into the **Source** text box for each transaction; then enter the Date listed for each transaction):

1997
Dec.
  1 Paid rent for two months in advance, $500.
  3 Purchased office supplies ($200) and office equipment ($1,100) both on account.
  9 Billed a customer for fees earned, $2,000.
 13 Paid telephone bill, $150.
 20 Owner withdrew $475 from the business for personal use.
 27 Received $600 for fees earned.
 30 Paid salaries expense, $800.

Display and Print a General Journal and Trial Balance

13. After you have posted the additional journal entries, close the General Journal; then print the following reports:

  a. General Journal (By posting date, All ledger entries, Start: 12/1/97, Finish: 12/31/97).

  b. Trial Balance As at 12/31/97.

14. Review your printed reports. If you have made an error in a posted journal entry, see "Reversing an Entry Made in the General Journal Dialog Box" in Part C of the Computerized Accounting appendix for information on how to correct the error.

How to Record Adjusting Journal Entries

15. Open the General Journal; then record adjusting journal entries based on the following adjustment data (*Source:* Memo; *Date:* 12/31/97; *Comment:* Adjusting entry):

  a. One month's rent has expired.

  b. An inventory shows $25 of office supplies remaining.

  c. Depreciation on office equipment, $50.

  d. Depreciation on automobile, $150.

16. After you have posted the adjusting journal entries, close the General Journal;
then print the following reports:

    a. General Journal (By posting date, All ledger entries, Start: 12/31/97, Finish:
12/31/97).

    b. General Ledger Report (Start: 12/1/97, Finish: 12/31/97, Select All).

    c. Trial Balance As at 12/31/97.

17. Review your printed reports. If you have made an error in a posted journal entry, see "Reversing an Entry Made in the General Journal Dialog Box" in Part C
of the Computerized Accounting appendix for information on how to correct
the error.

**How to Display and Print an
Income Statement**

18. Click on the Company Window Reports menu; point to Financials; then click
on Income Statement. The Income Statement Options dialog box will appear
asking you to define the information you want displayed. Leave the Select a Report text box set at Current Year. Leave the **Start** text box date set at 1/1/97;
leave the **Finish** text box date set at 12/31/97; then click on the **OK** button.
Your screen will look like this:

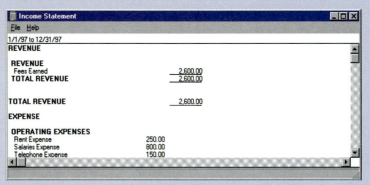

19. The scroll bar can be used to advance the display to view other portions of the
report.

20. Click on the Income Statement File menu; then click on Print to print the Income Statement.

**How to Display and Print a
Balance Sheet**

21. Close the Income Statement window; click on the Company Window Reports
menu; point to Financials; then click on Balance Sheet. The Balance Sheet Options dialog box will appear asking you to define the information you want displayed. Leave the Select a Report text box set at Current Year. Leave the **As at**
date set as 12/31/97; then click on the **OK** button. Your screen will look like
this:

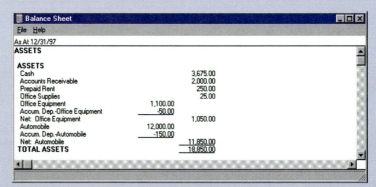

22. Use the scroll bar to advance the display to the Owner's Equity section of the
Balance Sheet. Note that the program has included the Statement of Owner's
Equity information directly in the Owner's Equity section of the Balance Sheet.

23. Click on the Balance Sheet File menu; click on Print to print the Balance Sheet;
then close the Balance Sheet window to return to the Company Window.

Exit from the Program

24. Click on the Company Window File menu; then click on Exit to end the current work session and return to your Windows desktop.

PART B: Backup Procedures

Companies that use computerized accounting systems make frequent backup copies of their accounting data for two major reasons:

1. To ensure that they have a copy of the accounting data in case the current data becomes damaged.
2. To permit the printing of historical reports after the **Using** date has been advanced to a new month.

The methods used to make backup copies of company data files vary greatly. Large companies may backup daily using sophisticated high-speed tape backup devices while small companies may backup weekly on floppy disks using the backup program supplied with their operating system or applications software.

Normally all backup copies of a company's data files are stored on a secondary storage medium separate from the original data files in case the original secondary storage medium becomes damaged. However, for the purposes of this introduction to computerized accounting systems, you will be using the working copy of your Student Data Files disk to store backup copies of a company's data files. You will be using a backup method known as the Save As method.

How to Make a Backup Copy of a Company's Data Files

1. Click on the Start button. Point to Programs; point to Simply Accounting; then click on Simply Accounting in the final menu presented. The Simply Accounting Open File dialog box will appear.
2. Insert your Student Data Files disk into disk drive A. Enter the following path into the **File name** text box: A:\student\zell.asc
3. Click on the **Open** button; leave the **Using date for this session** set at 12/31/97; then click on the **OK** button. The Company Window for Zell will appear on your screen.
4. Click on the Company Window File menu; then click on Save As. The Save As dialog box will appear. Enter the following new file name into the **File name** text box: A:\student\zelldec.asc
5. Click on the **Save** button. Note that the company name in the Company Window has changed from Zell to Zelldec. Click on the Company Window File menu again; then click on Save As. Enter the following new file name into the **File name** text box: A:\student\zell.asc
6. Click on the **Save** button. Click on the **Yes** button to confirm that you want to replace the existing file. Note that the company name in the Company Window has changed back from Zelldec to Zell.
7. You now have two sets of company data files for The Zell Company on your Student Data Files disk. The current data is stored under the file name zell.asc. The backup data for December is stored under the file name zelldec.asc.

Exit from the Program

8. Click on the Company Window File menu; then click on Exit to end the current work session and return to your Windows desktop.
9. For information on when you might want to use the backup copy of a company's data files, see Part E of the Computerized Accounting appendix in the back of this book.

Complete the Report Transmittal

10. Complete The Zell Company Report Transmittal located in Appendix A in your *Study Guide and Working Papers.*

THE ACCOUNTING CYCLE COMPLETED

Adjusting, Closing, and Post-Closing Trial Balance

THE BIG PICTURE

As Tony Freedman began to prepare for his busiest season, he thought it might be a good time to end the fiscal year for Eldorado Computer Center and record the adjusting entries before closing the books.

Under GAAP, every business is required to complete an accounting cycle within 12 months of doing business. Freedman has chosen to end his cycle using a fiscal year date of September 30. He chose this date because it was a good time to complete inventory and take time to analyze his books. As Christmas gets closer he knows there will be a lot of potential new business because it's the "giving" season.

Adjusting entries must be recorded and posted to the permanent books to reflect the changes. This will bring each ledger account up to date with the balances reflected on the financial statements.

The final step ends with closing the books. This process closes the temporary accounts (revenue, expenses, and withdrawals) into the permanent account (capital). Remember that owner's equity is made up with several temporary accounts that reflect how the business is doing. Profits (when revenue exceeds expenses) from the business increase the worth of a business. On the other hand, a net loss will decrease the worth of a business. Similarly, when an owner personally withdraws assets from the business, that too will decrease the value of the business. Closing the books is simply a process of moving the temporary account balances to the permanent account.

In Chapters 3 and 4 we completed these steps of the manual accounting cycle for Clark's Word Processing Services:

Step 1: Business transactions occurred and generated source documents.

Step 2: Business transactions were analyzed and recorded into a journal.

Step 3: Information was posted or transferred from journal to ledger.

Step 4: A trial balance was prepared.

Step 5: A worksheet was completed.

Step 6: Financial statements were prepared.

This chapter covers the following steps. This will complete Clark's accounting cycle for the month of May:

Step 7: Journalizing and posting adjusting entries.

Step 8: Journalizing and posting closing entries.

Step 9: Preparing a post-closing trial balance.

Remember, for ease of presentation we are using a month as the accounting cycle for Clark. In the "real" world, the cycle can be any time period that does not exceed one year.

LEARNING UNIT 5-1
Journalizing and Posting Adjusting Entries: Step 7 of the Accounting Cycle

RECORDING JOURNAL ENTRIES FROM THE WORKSHEET

The information in the worksheet is up to date. The financial reports prepared from that information can give the business's management and other interested parties a good idea of where the business stands as of a particular date. The problem is that the worksheet is an informal report. The information concerning the adjustments has not been placed into the journal, or posted to the ledger accounts. This means that the books are not up to date and ready for the next accounting cycle to begin. For example, the ledger shows $1,200 of prepaid rent (p. 85), but the balance sheet we prepared in Chapter 4 shows an $800 balance. Essentially, the worksheet is a tool for preparing financial reports. Now we must use the adjustment columns of the worksheet as a basis for bringing the ledger up to date. We do this by **adjusting journal entries** (see Figs. 5-1, 5-2). Again, the updating must be done before the next accounting period starts. For Clark's Word Processing Services, the next period begins on June 1.

At this point, many ledger accounts are not up to date.

Purpose of adjusting entries.

Figure 5-2 shows the adjusting journal entries for Clark taken from the adjustments section of the worksheet. Once the adjusting journal entries are posted to the ledger, the accounts making up the financial statements that were prepared from the worksheet will equal the updated ledger. (Keep in mind that this is the same journal we have been using.) Let's look at some simplified T accounts to show how Clark's ledger looked before and after the adjustments were posted (see Adjustments A–D on pp. 118–124).

Account Titles	Trial Balance		Adjustments	
	Dr.	Cr.	Dr.	Cr.
Cash	6155 00			
Accounts Receivable	5000 00			
Office Supplies	600 00			(A) 500 00
Prepaid Rent	1200 00			(B) 400 00
Word Processing Equipment	6000 00			
Accounts Payable		3350 00		
Brenda Clark, Capital		10000 00		
Brenda Clark, Withdrawals	625 00			
Word Processing Fees		8000 00		
Office Salaries Expense	1300 00		(D) 350 00	
Advertising Expense	250 00			
Telephone Expense	220 00			
	21350 00	21350 00		
Office Supplies Expense			(A) 500 00	
Rent Expense			(B) 400 00	
Depreciation Exp., W.P. Equip.			(C) 80 00	
Accum. Deprec., W.P. Equip.				(C) 80 00
Salaries Payable				(D) 350 00
			1330 00	1330 00

Adjustment (A)

Before Posting:

Office Supplies 114
600 |

Office Supplies Expense 514
|

After Posting:

Office Supplies 114
600 | 500

Office Supplies Expense 514
500 |

FIGURE 5-2
Adjustments A–D in the
adjustments section of the
worksheet must be recorded
in the journal and posted to
the ledger.

CLARK'S WORD PROCESSING SERVICES
GENERAL JOURNAL

Page 2

Date		Account Titles and Description	PR	Dr.	Cr.
		Adjusting Entries			
May	31	Office Supplies Expense	514	500 00	
		Office Supplies	114		500 00
	31	Rent Expense	515	400 00	
		Prepaid Rent	115		400 00
	31	Depreciation Expense, W.P. Equip.	516	80 00	
		Accumulated Depreciation, W.P. Equip.	122		80 00
	31	Office Salaries Expense	511	350 00	
		Salaries Payable	212		350 00

Adjustment (B)

Before Posting:

Prepaid Rent 115	Rent Expense 515
1,200	

After Posting:

Prepaid Rent 115	Rent Expense 515
1,200	400	400	

Adjustment (C)

Before Posting:

Word Processing Equipment 121	Depreciation Expense, W. P. Equipment 516	Accumulated Depreciation, W. P. Equipment 122
6,000		

After Posting:

Word Processing Equipment 121	Depreciation Expense, W. P. Equipment 516	Accumulated Depreciation, W. P. Equipment 122
6,000	80	80

The first adjustment in (C) shows the same balances for Depreciation Expense and Accumulated Depreciation. However, in subsequent adjustments the Accumulated Depreciation balance will keep getting larger, but the debit to Depreciation Expense and the credit to Accumulated Depreciation will be the same. We will see why in a moment.

Adjustment (D)

Before Posting:

Office Salaries Expense 511	Salaries Payable 212
650	
650	

After Posting:

Office Salaries Expense 511	Salaries Payable 212
650	350
650	
350	

LEARNING UNIT 5-1 REVIEW

AT THIS POINT you should be able to

◆ Define and state the purpose of adjusting entries. (p. 157)
◆ Journalize adjusting entries from the worksheet. (p. 158)
◆ Post journalized adjusting entries to the ledger. (p. 159)
◆ Compare specific ledger accounts before and after posting of the journalized adjusting entries. (p. 159)

SELF-REVIEW QUIZ 5-1

(The blank forms you need are on pages 129–130 of the *Study Guide and Working Papers.*)

Turn to the worksheet of P. Logan (p. 131) and (1) journalize and post the adjusting entries and (2) compare the adjusted ledger accounts before and after the adjustments are posted. T accounts are provided in your study guide with beginning balances.

Solution to Self-Review Quiz 5-1

Turn to the worksheet of P. Logan (p. 131)

	Date		Account Titles and Description	PR	Dr.	Cr.
						Page 2
			Adjusting Entries			
	Dec.	31	Depreciation Expense, Store Equip.	511	1 00	
			Accumulated Depreciation, Store Equip.	122		1 00
		31	Insurance Expense	516	2 00	
			Prepaid Insurance	116		2 00
		31	Supplies Expense	514	4 00	
			Store Supplies	114		4 00
		31	Salaries Expense	512	3 00	
			Salaries Payable	212		3 00

Quiz Tip: These journalized entries come from the Adjustments column of the worksheet.

PARTIAL LEDGER

Before Posting

Depreciation Expense, Store Equipment 511

Accumulated Depreciation, Store Equipment 122 — | 4

Prepaid Insurance 116 — 3 |

Insurance Expense 516

Store Supplies 114 — 5 |

Supplies Expense 514

Salaries Expense 512 — 8 |

Salaries Payable 212

After Posting

Depreciation Expense, Store Equipment 511 — 1 |

Accumulated Depreciation Store Equipment 122 — | 4 \ 1

Prepaid Insurance 116 — 3 | 2

Insurance Expense 516 — 2 |

Store Supplies 114 — 5 | 4

Supplies Expense 514 — 4 |

Salaries Expense 512 — 8 \ 3 |

Salaries Payable 212 — | 3

LEARNING UNIT 5-2

Journalizing and Posting Closing Entries: Step 8 of the Accounting Cycle

To make recording of the next period's transactions easier, a mechanical step, called *closing*, is taken by Clark's accountant. Closing is intended to end — or close off — the revenue, expense, and withdrawal accounts at the end of the accounting period. The information needed to complete closing entries will be found in the income statement and balance sheet sections of the worksheet.

To make it easier to understand this process, we will first look at the difference between temporary (nominal) accounts and permanent (real) accounts.

Here is the expanded accounting equation we used in an earlier chapter:

Assets = Liabilities + Capital − Withdrawals + Revenues − Expenses

Permanent accounts are found on the balance sheet.

Three of the items in that equation — assets, liabilities, and capital — are known as **real** or **permanent accounts** because their balances are carried over from one accounting period to another. The other three items — withdrawals, revenue, and expenses — are called **nominal** or **temporary accounts,** because their balances are not carried over from one accounting period to another. Instead, their "balances" are set at zero at the beginning of each accounting period. This allows us to accumulate new data about revenue, expenses, and withdrawals, in the new accounting period. The process of closing summarizes the effects of the temporary accounts on capital for that period using **closing journal entries.** When the closing process is complete, the accounting equation will be reduced to:

Assets = Liabilities + Ending Capital

After all closing entries are journalized and posted to the ledger; all temporary accounts have a zero balance in the ledger. Closing is a step-by-step process.

If you look back to page 134 in Chapter 4, you will see that we already calculated the new capital on the balance sheet to be $14,275 for Clark's Word Processing Services. But before the mechanical closing procedures are journalized and posted, the capital account of Clark in the ledger is only $10,000 (Chapter 3, p. 85). Let's look now at how to journalize and post closing entries.

HOW TO JOURNALIZE CLOSING ENTRIES

There are four steps to be performed in journalizing closing entries:

An Income Summary is a temporary account located in the chart of accounts under owner's equity. It does not have a normal balance of a debit or a credit.

Step 1: Clear the revenue balance and transfer it to Income Summary. **Income Summary** is a temporary account in the ledger needed for closing. At the end of the closing process there will be no balance in Income Summary.

Revenue ⟶ Income Summary

Step 2: Clear the individual expense balances and transfer them to Income Summary.

Expenses ⟶ Income Summary

Sometimes, closing the accounts is referred to as "clearing the accounts."

Step 3: Clear the balance in Income Summary and transfer it to Capital.

Income Summary ⟶ Capital

Step 4: Clear the balance in Withdrawals and transfer it to Capital.

Withdrawals ⟶ Capital

Figure 5-3 on page 162 is a visual representation of these four steps. Keep in mind that this information must first be journalized and then posted to the appropriate ledger accounts. The worksheet presented in Figure 5-4 on page 162, contains all the figures we will need for the closing process.

Step 1: Clear Revenue Balance and Transfer to Income Summary

Here is what is in the ledger before closing entries are journalized and posted:

Word Processing Fees 411	Income Summary 313
8,000	

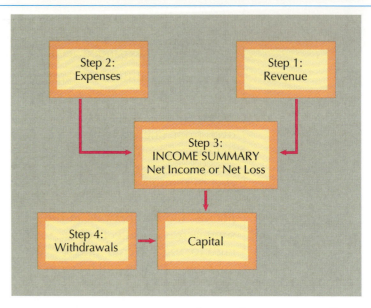

FIGURE 5-3 Four Steps in Journalizing Closing Entries. All numbers can be found on the worksheet in Figure 5-4.

The income statement section on the worksheet below shows that the Word Processing Fees have a credit balance of $8,000. To close or clear this to zero, a debit of $8,000 is needed. But if we add an amount to the debit side, we must also add a credit—so we add $8,000 on the credit side of the Income Summary.

FIGURE 5-4 Closing Figures on the Worksheet

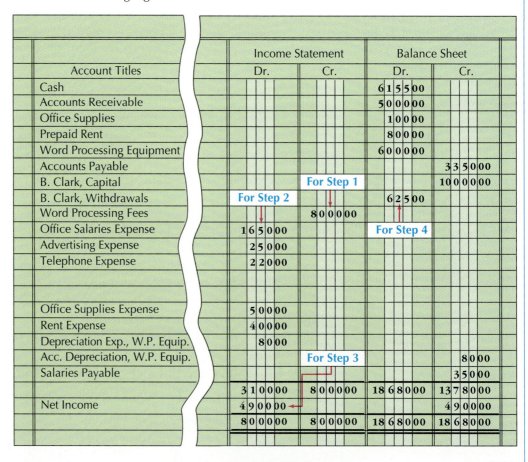

Account Titles	Income Statement Dr.	Income Statement Cr.	Balance Sheet Dr.	Balance Sheet Cr.
Cash			6 1 5 5 00	
Accounts Receivable			5 0 0 0 00	
Office Supplies			1 0 0 00	
Prepaid Rent			8 0 0 00	
Word Processing Equipment			6 0 0 0 00	
Accounts Payable				3 3 5 0 00
B. Clark, Capital		For Step 1		10 0 0 0 00
B. Clark, Withdrawals	For Step 2		6 2 5 00	
Word Processing Fees		8 0 0 0 00		
Office Salaries Expense	1 6 5 0 00	For Step 4		
Advertising Expense	2 5 0 00			
Telephone Expense	2 2 0 00			
Office Supplies Expense	5 0 0 00			
Rent Expense	4 0 0 00			
Depreciation Exp., W.P. Equip.	8 0 00			
Acc. Depreciation, W.P. Equip.		For Step 3		8 0 00
Salaries Payable				3 5 0 00
	3 1 0 0 00	8 0 0 0 00	18 6 8 0 00	13 7 8 0 00
Net Income	4 9 0 0 00			4 9 0 0 00
	8 0 0 0 00	8 0 0 0 00	18 6 8 0 00	18 6 8 0 00

The following is the journalized closing entry for Step 1:

	May	31	Word Processing Fees	411	8 0 0 0 00				
			Income Summary	313			8 0 0 0 00		

This is what Word Processing Fees and Income Summary should look like in the ledger after the first step of closing entries is journalized and posted:

Word Processing Fees 411
8,000	8,000
Closing	Revenue

Income Summary 313
	8,000
	Revenue

Note that the revenue balance is cleared to zero and transferred to Income Summary, a temporary account also located in the ledger.

Step 2: Clear Individual Expense Balances and Transfer the Total to Income Summary

Here is what is in the ledger for each expense before Step 2 of closing entries is journalized and posted. Each expense is listed on the worksheet in the debit column of the income statement section on page 162.

Office Salaries Expense 511
650
650
350

Advertising Expense 512
250

Telephone Expense 513
220

Office Supplies Expense 514
500

Rent Expense 515
400

Depreciation Expense, W. P. Equipment 516
80

The income statement section of the worksheet lists all the expenses as debits. If we want to reduce each expense to zero, each one must be credited. The following is the journalized closing entry for Step 2:

		31	Income Summary	313	3 1 0 0 00				
			Office Salaries Expense	511			1 6 5 0 00		
			Advertising Expense	512			2 5 0 00		
			Telephone Expense	513			2 2 0 00		
			Office Supplies Expense	514			5 0 0 00		
			Rent Expense	515			4 0 0 00		
			Depreciation Expense, W.P.Equip.	516			8 0 00		

The following is what individual expenses and Income Summary should look like in the ledger after Step 2 of closing entries is journalized and posted:

Remember, the worksheet is a tool. The accountant realizes that the information about the total of the expenses will be transferred to the Income Summary.

The $3,100 is the total of the expenses on the worksheet.

Office Salaries Expense 511	Advertising Expense 512
650 Closing 1,650	250 Closing 250
650	
350	

Telephone Expense 513	Office Supplies Expense 514
220 Closing 220	500 Closing 500

Rent Expense 515	Depreciation Expense, W. P. Equipment 516
400 Closing 400	80 Closing 80

Income Summary 313

Expenses	Revenue
Step 2 3,100	8,000 Step 1

Step 3: Clear Balance in Income Summary (Net Income) and Transfer It to Capital

This is how the Income Summary and B. Clark, Capital, accounts look before Step 3:

Income Summary 313	B. Clark, Capital 311
3,100 8,000	10,000
4,900	

Note that the balance of Income Summary (Revenue minus Expenses or $8,000 - $3,100) is $4,900. That is the amount we must clear from the Income Summary account and transfer to the B. Clark, Capital, account.

In order to transfer the balance of $4,900 from Income Summary (check the bottom debit column of the income statement section on the worksheet in Fig. 5-4) to Capital, it will be necessary to debit Income Summary for $4,900 (the difference between the revenue and expenses) and credit or increase Capital of B. Clark for $4,900.

This is the journalized closing entry for Step 3:

The opposite would take place if the business had a net loss.

31	Income Summary	313	4 9 0 0 00			
	B. Clark, Capital	311			4 9 0 0 00	

This is what the Income Summary and B. Clark, Capital, accounts will look like in the ledger after Step 3 of closing entries is journalized and posted:

At the end of these three steps, the Income Summary has a zero balance. If we had a net loss the end result would be to decrease capital. Entry would be debit capital and credit income summary for the loss.

Income Summary 313

Total of Expenses → 3,100 | 8,000 ← Revenue
Debit to close account → 4,900 | 4,900 ← Net Income

B. Clark, Capital 311

10,000
4,900 ← Net Income

Step 4: Clear the Withdrawals Balance and Transfer it to Capital

Next, we must close the withdrawals account. The B. Clark, Withdrawals, and B. Clark, Capital, accounts now look like this:

```
   B. Clark, Withdrawals 312        B. Clark, Capital 311
   625           |                          | 10,000
                 |                          |  4,900
```

To bring the Withdrawals account to a zero balance, and summarize its effect on Capital, we must credit Withdrawals and debit Capital.

Remember, withdrawals are a nonbusiness expense and thus not transferred to Income Summary. The closing entry is journalized as follows:

					Dr.	Cr.
	31	B. Clark, Capital	311		625 00	
		B. Clark, Withdrawals	312			625 00

At this point the B. Clark, Withdrawals, and B. Clark, Capital, accounts would look like this in the ledger.

```
   B. Clark, Withdrawals 312             B. Clark, Capital 311
      625 | Closing  625           625 | 10,000
                               Withdrawals | Beg. Balance
                                           |  4,900
                                             Net Income
```

Note that the $10,000 is a beginning balance since no additional investments were made during the period.

Now let's look at a summary of the closing entries.

		SUMMARY OF CLOSING ENTRIES				
Date		Account Titles and Description	PR	Dr.	Cr.	
		Closing Entries				
19XX						
May	31	Word Processing Fees	411	8000 00		
		Income Summary	313		8000 00	
	31	Income Summary	313	3100 00		
		Office Salaries Expense	511		1650 00	
		Advertising Expense	512		250 00	
		Telephone Expense	513		220 00	
		Office Supplies Expense	514		500 00	
		Rent Expense	515		400 00	
		Depreciation Expense, W.P. Equip.	516		80 00	
	31	Income Summary	313	4900 00		
		B. Clark, Capital	311		4900 00	
	31	B. Clark, Capital	311	625 00		
		B. Clark, Withdrawals	312		625 00	

The following is the complete ledger for Clark's Word Processing Services (see Fig. 5-5). Note how the word "adjusting" or "closing" is written in the explanation column of individual ledgers, as for example in the one for Office Supplies. If the goals of closing have been achieved, only permanent accounts will have balances carried to the next accounting period. All temporary accounts should have zero balances.

FIGURE 5-5
Complete Ledger

CLARK'S WORD PROCESSING SERVICES
GENERAL LEDGER

Cash   Account No. 111

Date		Explanation	Post. Ref.	Debit	Credit	Balance Debit	Balance Credit
19XX May	1		GJ1	10 000 00		10 000 00	
	1		GJ1		1 000 00	9 000 00	
	1		GJ1		1 200 00	7 800 00	
	7		GJ1	3 000 00		10 800 00	
	15		GJ1		650 00	10 150 00	
	20		GJ1		625 00	9 525 00	
	27		GJ2		650 00	8 875 00	
	28		GJ2		2 500 00	6 375 00	
	29		GJ2		220 00	6 155 00	

Accounts Receivable   Account No. 112

Date		Explanation	Post. Ref.	Debit	Credit	Balance Debit	Balance Credit
19XX May	22		GJ1	5 000 00		5 000 00	

Office Supplies   Account No. 114

Date		Explanation	Post. Ref.	Debit	Credit	Balance Debit	Balance Credit
19XX May	3		GJ1	600 00		600 00	
	31	Adjusting	GJ2		500 00	100 00	

CH. 5 / THE ACCOUNTING CYCLE COMPLETED: ADJUSTING, CLOSING, AND POST-CLOSING TRIAL BALANCE

(Fig. 5.5 cont.)

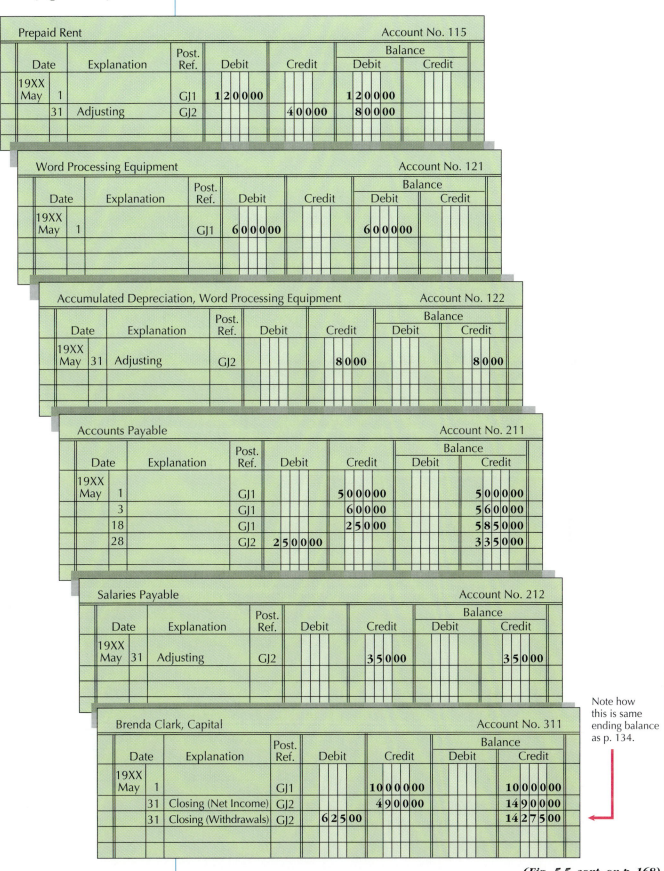

Prepaid Rent — Account No. 115

Date	Explanation	Post. Ref.	Debit	Credit	Balance Debit	Balance Credit
19XX May 1		GJ1	1 2 0 0 00		1 2 0 0 00	
31	Adjusting	GJ2		4 0 0 00	8 0 0 00	

Word Processing Equipment — Account No. 121

Date	Explanation	Post. Ref.	Debit	Credit	Balance Debit	Balance Credit
19XX May 1		GJ1	6 0 0 0 00		6 0 0 0 00	

Accumulated Depreciation, Word Processing Equipment — Account No. 122

Date	Explanation	Post. Ref.	Debit	Credit	Balance Debit	Balance Credit
19XX May 31	Adjusting	GJ2		8 0 00		8 0 00

Accounts Payable — Account No. 211

Date	Explanation	Post. Ref.	Debit	Credit	Balance Debit	Balance Credit
19XX May 1		GJ1		5 0 0 0 00		5 0 0 0 00
3		GJ1		6 0 0 00		5 6 0 0 00
18		GJ1		2 5 0 00		5 8 5 0 00
28		GJ2	2 5 0 0 00			3 3 5 0 00

Salaries Payable — Account No. 212

Date	Explanation	Post. Ref.	Debit	Credit	Balance Debit	Balance Credit
19XX May 31	Adjusting	GJ2		3 5 0 00		3 5 0 00

Brenda Clark, Capital — Account No. 311

Date	Explanation	Post. Ref.	Debit	Credit	Balance Debit	Balance Credit
19XX May 1		GJ1		1 0 0 0 0 00		1 0 0 0 0 00
31	Closing (Net Income)	GJ2		4 9 0 0 00		1 4 9 0 0 00
31	Closing (Withdrawals)	GJ2	6 2 5 00			1 4 2 7 5 00

Note how this is same ending balance as p. 134.

(Fig. 5-5 cont. on p. 168)

(Fig. 5.5 cont.)

Brenda Clark, Withdrawals   Account No. 312

Date		Explanation	Post. Ref.	Debit	Credit	Balance Debit	Balance Credit
19XX May	20		GJ1	6 2 5 00		6 2 5 00	
	31	Closing	GJ2		6 2 5 00	—	—

Income Summary   Account No. 313

Date		Explanation	Post. Ref.	Debit	Credit	Balance Debit	Balance Credit
19XX May	31	Closing (Revenue)	GJ2		8 0 0 0 00		8 0 0 0 00
	31	Closing (Expenses)	GJ2	3 1 0 0 00			4 9 0 0 00
	31	Closing (Net Income)	GJ2	4 9 0 0 00		—	—

Word Processing Fees   Account No. 411

Date		Explanation	Post. Ref.	Debit	Credit	Balance Debit	Balance Credit
19XX May	7		GJ1		3 0 0 0 00		3 0 0 0 00
	22		GJ1		5 0 0 0 00		8 0 0 0 00
	31	Closing	GJ2	8 0 0 0 00		—	—

Office Salaries Expense   Account No. 511

Date		Explanation	Post. Ref.	Debit	Credit	Balance Debit	Balance Credit
19XX May	15		GJ1	6 5 0 00		6 5 0 00	
	27		GJ2	6 5 0 00		1 3 0 0 00	
	31	Adjusting	GJ2	3 5 0 00		1 6 5 0 00	
	31	Closing	GJ2		1 6 5 0 00	—	—

Advertising Expense   Account No. 512

Date		Explanation	Post. Ref.	Debit	Credit	Balance Debit	Balance Credit
19XX May	18		GJ1	2 5 0 00		2 5 0 00	
	31	Closing	GJ2		2 5 0 00	—	—

(Fig. 5.5 cont.)

Telephone Expense   Account No. 513

Date	Explanation	Post. Ref.	Debit	Credit	Balance Debit	Balance Credit
19XX May 29		GJ2	2 2 0 00		2 2 0 00	
31	Closing	GJ2		2 2 0 00		

Office Supplies Expense   Account No. 514

Date	Explanation	Post. Ref.	Debit	Credit	Balance Debit	Balance Credit
19XX May 31	Adjusting	GJ2	5 0 0 00		5 0 0 00	
31	Closing	GJ2		5 0 0 00	—	—

Rent Expense   Account No. 515

Date	Explanation	Post. Ref.	Debit	Credit	Balance Debit	Balance Credit
19XX May 31	Adjusting	GJ2	4 0 0 00		4 0 0 00	
31	Closing	GJ2		4 0 0 00	—	—

Depreciation Expense, Word Processing Equipment   Account No. 516

Date	Explanation	Post. Ref.	Debit	Credit	Balance Debit	Balance Credit
19XX May 31	Adjusting	GJ2	8 0 00		8 0 00	
31	Closing	GJ2		8 0 00	—	—

LEARNING UNIT 5-2 REVIEW

AT THIS POINT you should be able to

◆ Define closing. (p.160)
◆ Differentiate between temporary (nominal) and permanent (real) accounts. (p. 161)
◆ List the four mechanical steps of closing. (p. 161)
◆ Explain the role of the Income Summary account. (p. 161)
◆ Explain the role of the worksheet in the closing process. (p. 161)

SELF-REVIEW QUIZ 5-2

(The blank forms you need are on pages 131–132 of the *Study Guide and Working Papers.*)

Go to the worksheet for P. Logan on p. 131. Then (1) journalize and post the closing entries and (2) calculate the new balance for P. Logan, Capital.

Solution to Self-Review Quiz 5-2

		Closing Entries				
Dec.	31	Revenue from Clients	410	25 00		
		Income Summary	312		25 00	
	31	Income Summary	312	20 00		
		Rent Expense	518		2 00	
		Salaries Expense	512		11 00	
		Depreciation Expense, Store Equip.	510		1 00	
		Insurance Expense	516		2 00	
		Supplies Expense	514		4 00	
	31	Income Summary	312	5 00		
		P. Logan, Capital	310		5 00	
	31	P. Logan, Capital	310	3 00		
		P. Logan, Withdrawals	311		3 00	

PARTIAL LEDGER

P. Logan, Capital 310
3	14
	5
	16

Revenue from Clients 410
25	25

Supplies Expense 514
4	4

P. Logan, Withdrawals 311
3	3

Dep. Exp., Store Equip. 510
1	1

Insurance Expense 516
2	2

Income Summary 312
20	25
5	5

Salaries Expense 512
11	11

Rent Expense 518
2	2

Quiz Tip: No calculations are needed in the closing process. ALL numbers come from the worksheet. Income summary is a temporary account in the ledger.

P. Logan, Capital		$14
Net Income	$5	
Less Withdrawals	3	
Increase in Capital		2
P. Logan, Capital (ending)		$16

The doorbell rang at 1 A.M. "The cavalry has arrived!" said the giant in the doorway. "You're a real friend in need, Lou," said Fred gratefully, as he opened the door. "I've been over and over this, and I can't get it to balance. And my monthly closing is due to Dwayne at noon tomorrow! I hate to bother you so late, but . . ." Fred had called Lou Jacobs, his roommate at Dunkin' Donuts University. Lou had ridden hard to the rescue—one and a half hours on the Expressway.

"You look as if you haven't slept in days, Fred," interrupted Lou. "This is what friends are for. Let me at those accounts! You put a pot of coffee on. I'll start with payroll, because you hired someone this month."

Dunkin' Donuts company policy calls for a closing every month, on the last Saturday, before noon. This way comparisons between shops are most valid. Dunkin' Donuts University stresses to all shop owners that the monthly closing grows more difficult as the year progresses. Errors get harder to find, and accuracy becomes ever more critical. There is, unfortunately, no set way to find errors, and even no set place to start. Lou chose payroll because it is one of the largest expenses and because of the new hire.

At 2:45 A.M. Lou woke Fred, who was dozing. "I think I've got it, Fred! It looks like you messed up on ad-

CLOSING TIME

justing the Salaries Expense account. I looked at the Payroll Register and compared the total to the Salaries Payable account. It didn't match! Remember, you hired Maria Sanchez on the 26th, so you have to increase *both* the Salaries Expense *and* the Salaries Payable lines, because she has accrued wages. Salaries Expense is a debit and Salaries Payable is a credit. You skipped the payable. Now, If you make this adjusting entry in the General Journal, the worksheet will balance."

Fred's sigh of relief turned into a big yawn, and they both laughed. "Thank heavens *you* stayed awake in Accounting class!," said Fred, with another huge yawn.

DISCUSSION QUESTIONS

1. How would the adjustment be made if Maria Sanchez received $6.50 per hour and worked 25 hours? Where would you place her accrued wages?
2. Fred bought six new uniforms for Maria Sanchez for $72 each, but forgot to post it to the Uniforms account. How much will the closing balance be off? In what way will it be off?
3. Why does Dunkin' Donuts require a monthly closing from each shop, no matter how much—or little—business each does?

LEARNING UNIT 5-3
The Post-Closing Trial Balance: Step 9 of the Accounting Cycle and the Cycle Reviewed

PREPARING A POST-CLOSING TRIAL BALANCE

The post-closing trial balance helps prove the accuracy of the adjusting and closing process. It contains the true ending figure for capital.

The last step in the accounting cycle is the preparation of a **post-closing trial balance,** which lists only permanent accounts in the ledger and their balances after adjusting and closing entries have been posted. This post-closing trial balance aids in checking whether the ledger is in balance. This checking is important to do because so many new postings go to the ledger from the adjusting and closing process.

The procedure for taking a post-closing trial balance is the same as for a trial balance, except that, since closing entries have closed all temporary accounts, the post-closing trial balance will contain only permanent accounts (balance sheet). Keep in mind, however, that adjustments have occurred.

THE ACCOUNTING CYCLE REVIEWED

Table 5-1 on the next page lists the steps we completed in the manual accounting cycle for Clark's Word Processing Services for the month of May:

TABLE 5-1 STEPS OF THE MANUAL ACCOUNTING CYCLE

Steps	Explanation
1. Business transactions occur and generate source documents.	Cash register tape, sales tickets, bills, checks, payroll cards.
2. Analyze and record business transactions into a journal.	Called journalizing.
3. Post or transfer information from journal to ledger.	Copying the debits and credits of the journal entries into the ledger acounts.
4. Prepare a trial balance.	Summarizing each individual ledger account and listing those accounts to test for mathematical accuracy in recording transactions.
5. Prepare a worksheet.	A multicolumn form that summarizes accounting information to complete the accounting cycle.
6. Prepare financial statements.	Income statement, statement of owner's equity, and balance sheet.
7. Journalize and post adjusting entries.	Use figures in the adjustment columns of worksheet.
8. Journalize and post closing entries.	Use figures in the income statement and balance sheet sections of worksheet.
9. Prepare a post-closing trial balance.	Prove the mathematical accuracy of the adjusting and closing process of the accounting cycle.

Insight: Most companies journalize and post adjusting and closing entries only at the end of their fiscal year. A company that prepares interim reports may complete only the first six steps of the cycle. Worksheets allow the preparation of interim reports without the formal adjusting and closing of the books. If this happens, footnotes on the interim report will indicate the extent to which adjusting and closing were completed.

Insight: To prepare a financial report for April, the data needed can be obtained by subtracting the worksheet accumulated totals from the end of March from the worksheet prepared at the end of April. In this chapter, we chose a month that would show the completion of an entire cycle for Clark's Word Processing Services.

LEARNING UNIT 5-3 REVIEW

AT THIS POINT you should be able to

◆ Prepare a post-closing trial balance. (p. 171)
◆ Explain the relationship of interim reports to the accounting cycle. (p. 172)

SELF-REVIEW QUIZ 5-3

(The blank forms you need are on page 132 of the *Study Guide and Working Papers*.)

From the ledger on page 166, prepare a post-closing trial balance.

Solution to Self-Review Quiz 5-3

Quiz Tip: The post-closing trial balance contains only permanent accounts because all temporary accounts have been closed. All temporary accounts are summarized in the capital account.

CLARK'S WORD PROCESSING SERVICES
POST-CLOSING TRIAL BALANCE
MAY 31, 19XX

	Dr.	Cr.
Cash	6 1 5 5 00	
Accounts Receivable	5 0 0 0 00	
Office Supplies	1 0 0 00	
Prepaid Rent	8 0 0 00	
Word Processing Equipment	6 0 0 0 00	
Accumulated Depreciation, Word Processing Equip.		8 0 00
Accounts Payable		3 3 5 0 00
Salaries Payable		3 5 0 00
Brenda Clark, Capital		14 2 7 5 00
Totals	18 0 5 5 00	18 0 5 5 00

COMPREHENSIVE DEMONSTRATION PROBLEM WITH SOLUTION TIPS

(The blank forms you need are on pages 133–141 of the *Study Guide and Working Papers.*)

From the following transactions for Rolo Co. complete the entire accounting cycle. The Chart of Accounts includes:

Assets
111   Cash
112   Accounts Receivable
114   Prepaid Rent
115   Office Supplies
121   Office Equipment
122   Accumulated Depreciation, Office Equipment

Liabilities
211   Accounts Payable
212   Salaries Payable

Owner's Equity
311   Rolo Kern, Capital
312   Rolo Kern, Withdrawals
313   Income Summary

Revenue
411   Fees Earned

Expenses
511   Salaries Expense
512   Advertising Expense
513   Rent Expense
514   Office Supplies Expense
515   Depreciation Expense, Office Equipment

We will use unusually small numbers to simplify calculation and emphasize the theory.

19XX
Jan.   1   Rolo Kern invested $1,200 cash and $100 of office equipment to open Rolo Co.

1   Paid rent for three months in advance, $300

4   Purchased office equipment on account, $50

6   Bought office supplies for cash, $40

8   Collected $400 for services rendered

12   Rolo paid his home electric bill from the company checkbook, $20

14   Provided $100 worth of services to clients who will not pay till next month

16   Paid salaries, $60

18   Advertising bill received for $70 but will not be paid until next month

Adjustment Data on January 31

a. Supplies on hand $6
b. Rent Expired $100
c. Depreciation, Office Equipment $20
d. Salaries Accrued $50

JOURNALIZING TRANSACTIONS AND POSTING TO LEDGER, ROLO COMPANY

General Journal						Page 1
Date		Account Titles and Description	PR	Dr.	Cr.	
19XX Jan	1	Cash	111	1 2 0 0 00		
		Office Equipment	121	1 0 0 00		
		R. Kern, Capital	311		1 3 0 0 00	
		Initial Investment				
	1	Prepaid Rent	114	3 0 0 00		
		Cash	111		3 0 0 00	
		Rent Paid in Advance—3 mos.				
	4	Office Equipment	121	5 0 00		
		Accounts Payable	211		5 0 00	
		Purchased Equipment on Account				
	6	Office Supplies	115	4 0 00		
		Cash	111		4 0 00	
		Supplies purchased for cash				
	8	Cash	111	4 0 0 00		
		Fees Earned	411		4 0 0 00	
		Services rendered				
	12	R. Kern, Withdrawals	312	2 0 00		
		Cash	111		2 0 00	
		Personal payment of a bill				
	14	Accounts Receivable	112	1 0 0 00		
		Fees Earned	411		1 0 0 00	
		Services rendered on account				
	16	Salaries Expense	511	6 0 00		
		Cash	111		6 0 00	
		Paid salaries				
	18	Advertising Expense	512	7 0 00		
		Accounts Payable	211		7 0 00	
		Advertising bill, but not paid				

Solution Tips to Journalizing and Posting Transactions

Jan 1	Cash	Asset	↑	Dr.	$1,200
	Office Equipment	Asset	↑	Dr.	$ 100
	R. Kern, Capital	Capital	↑	Cr.	$1,300

2	Prepaid Rent	Asset	↑	Dr.	$ 300
	Cash	Asset	↓	Cr.	$ 300

| 4 | Office Equipment | Asset | ↑ | Dr. | $ 50 |
| | Accounts Payable | Liability | ↑ | Cr. | $ 50 |

| 6 | Office Supplies | Asset | ↑ | Dr. | $ 40 |
| | Cash | Asset | ↓ | Cr. | $ 40 |

| 8 | Cash | Asset | ↑ | Dr. | $ 400 |
| | Fees Earned | Revenue | ↑ | Cr. | $ 400 |

| 12 | R. Kern, Withdrawals | Withdrawals | ↑ | Dr. | $ 20 |
| | Cash | Asset | ↓ | Cr. | $ 20 |

| 14 | Accounts Receivable | Asset | ↑ | Dr. | $ 100 |
| | Fees Earned | Revenue | ↑ | Cr. | $ 100 |

| 16 | Salaries Expense | Expense | ↑ | Dr. | $ 70 |
| | Cash | Asset | ↓ | Cr. | $ 70 |

| 18 | Advertising Expense | Expense | ↑ | Dr. | $ 70 |
| | Accounts Payable | Liability | ↑ | Cr. | $ 70 |

Note: All account titles come from the chart of accounts. When journalizing, the PR column of the general journal is blank. It is in the posting process that we update the ledger. The PR column in the ledger accounts tells us from what journal page the information came. After the title in ledger is posted to, we fill in the PR column of the journal telling us to what account number the information was transferred.

COMPLETING THE WORKSHEET

See worksheet on page 177.

Solution Tips to the Trial Balance and Completion of the Worksheet

After the posting process is complete from the journal to the ledger, we take the ending balance in each account and prepare a Trial Balance on the worksheet. If a title has no balance, it is not listed on the trial balance. New titles on the worksheet will be added below as needed.

ROLO CO
WORKSHEET
FOR MONTH ENDED JANUARY 31, 19XX

Account Titles	Trial Balance Dr.	Trial Balance Cr.	Adjustments Dr.	Adjustments Cr.	Adjusted Trial Balance Dr.	Adjusted Trial Balance Cr.	Income Statement Dr.	Income Statement Cr.	Balance Sheet Dr.	Balance Sheet Cr.
Cash	118000				118000				118000	
Accounts Receivable	10000				10000				10000	
Prepaid Rent	30000			(B) 10000	20000				20000	
Office Supplies	4000			(A) 3400	600				600	
Office Equipment	15000				15000				15000	
Accounts Payable		12000				12000				12000
R. Kern, Capital		130000				130000				130000
R. Kern, Withdrawals	2000				2000				2000	
Fees Earned		50000				50000		50000		
Salaries Expense	6000		(D) 5000		11000		11000			
Advertising Expense	7000				7000		7000			
	192000	192000								
Office Supplies Expense			(A) 3400		3400		3400			
Rent Expense			(B) 10000		10000		10000			
Depr. Exp., Office Equip.			(C) 2000		2000		2000			
Acc. Dep., Office Equip.				(C) 2000		2000				2000
Salaries Payable				(D) 5000		5000				5000
			20400	20400	199000	199000	33400	50000	165600	149000
Net Income							16600			16600
							50000	50000	165600	165600

ADJUSTMENTS

Office Supplies Expense	Expense	↑	Dr.	$ 34	($40 − $6)
Office Supplies	Asset	↓	Cr.	$ 34	

On hand of $6 is not the Adjustment. Need to calculate amount used up.

Rent Expense	Expense	↑	Dr.	$100
Prepaid Rent	Asset	↓	Cr.	$100

Expired.

Depr. Exp., Office Equip.	Expense	↑	Dr.	$ 20
Accum. Dep., Office Equip.	Contra-Asset	↑	Cr.	$ 20

Do not touch original cost of equipment.

Salaries Expense	Expense	↑	Dr.	$ 50
Salaries Payable	Liability	↑	Cr.	$ 50

Owed but not paid.

Note: This information is on the worksheet but has *not* been updated in the ledger. (This will happen when we journalize and post adjustments at end of cycle.)

Note that the last four columns of the worksheet come from numbers on the Adjusted Trial Balance.

We move the Net Income of $166 to the Balance Sheet credit column since the capital figure is the old one on the worksheet.

PREPARING THE FORMAL FINANCIAL REPORTS

ROLO CO.
INCOME STATEMENT
FOR MONTH ENDED JANUARY 31, 19XX

Revenue:		
Fees Earned		$500 00
Operating Expenses		
Salaries Expense	$110 00	
Advertising Expense	70 00	
Office Supplies Expense	34 00	
Rent Expense	100 00	
Depreciation Expense, Office Equipment	20 00	
Total Operating Expenses		334 00
Net Income		$166 00

ROLO CO.
STATEMENT OF OWNER'S EQUITY
FOR MONTH ENDED JANUARY 31, 19XX

R. Kern, Capital, January 1, 19XX		$1300 00
Net Income for January	$166 00	
Less Withdrawals for January	20 00	
Increase in Capital		146 00
R. Kern, Capital, January 31, 19XX		$1446 00

ROLO CO.
BALANCE SHEET
JANUARY 31, 19XX

Assets			Liabilities & Owner's Equity		
Cash		$1 1 8 0 00	Liabilities		
Accounts Receivable		1 0 0 00	Accounts Payable	$1 2 0 00	
Prepaid Rent		2 0 0 00	Salaries Payable	5 0 00	
Office Supplies		6 00	Total Liabilities		$ 1 7 0 00
Office Equipment	$1 5 0 00		Owner's Equity		
Less Accum. Depr.	2 0 00	1 3 0 00	R. Kern, Capital		1 4 4 6 00
			Total Liabilities &		
Total Assets		$16 1 6 00	Owner's Equity		$16 1 6 00

Solution Tips to Preparing the Financial Reports

The reports are prepared from the worksheet. (Many of the ledger accounts are not up to date.) The Income Statement lists revenue and expenses. The net income figure of $166 is used to update the Statement of Owner's Equity. The Statement of Owner's Equity calculates a new figure for Capital, $1,446 (Beginning Capital + Net Income − Withdrawals). This new figure is then listed on the Balance Sheet (Assets, Liabilities, and a new figure for Capital).

JOURNALIZING AND POSTING ADJUSTING AND CLOSING ENTRIES

See journal at top of page 180.

Solution Tips to Journalizing and Posting Adjusting and Closing Entries

ADJUSTMENTS

The adjustments from the worksheet are journalized (same journal) and posted to the ledger. Now ledger accounts will be brought up to date. Remember, we have already prepared the financial reports from the worksheet. Our goal now is to get the ledger up to date.

CLOSING

Note Income Summary is a temporary account located in the ledger.

Goals:

1. Wipe out all temporary accounts in the ledger to zero balances.
2. Get a new figure for capital in the ledger.

General Journal						Page 2
Date		Account Titles and Description	PR	Dr.	Cr.	
		ADJUSTING ENTRIES				
Jan.	31	Office Supplies Expense	514	3400		
		Office Supplies	115		3400	
	31	Rent Expense	513	10000		
		Prepaid Rent	114		10000	
	31	Depr. Expense, Office Equipment	515	2000		
		Accum. Depr., Office Equip.	122		2000	
	31	Salaries Expense	511	5000		
		Salaries Payable	212		5000	
		CLOSING ENTRIES				
Step 1 →	31	Fees Earned	411	50000		
		Income Summary	313		50000	
Step 2 →	31	Income Summary	313	33400		
		Salaries Expense	511		11000	
		Advertising Expense	512		7000	
		Office Supplies Expense	514		3400	
		Rent Expense	513		10000	
		Depr. Expense, Office Equip.	515		2000	
Step 3 →	31	Income Summary	313	16600		
		R. Kern, Capital	311		16600	
Step 4 →	31	R. Kern, Capital	311	2000		
		R. Kern, Withdrawals	312		2000	

Closing { Step 1, Step 2, Step 3, Step 4 }

STEPS IN THE CLOSING PROCESS

Where do I get my information for closing?

Step 1: Close revenue to Income Summary.

Step 2: Close individual expenses to Income Summary.

Step 3: Close balance of Income Summary to capital. (This really is the net income figure on the worksheet.)

Step 4: Close balance of withdrawals to capital.

All the journal closing entries (no new calculations needed since all figures are on the worksheet) are posted. The result in the ledger is that all temporary accounts have a zero balance.

GENERAL LEDGER

Cash   111

Date	PR	Dr.	Cr.	Balance Dr.	Balance Cr.
1/1	GJ1	1,200		1,200	
1/1	GJ1		300	900	
1/6	GJ1		40	860	
1/8	GJ1	400		1,260	
1/12	GJ1		20	1,240	
1/16	GJ1		60	1,180	

Accounts Receivable   112

Date	PR	Dr.	Cr.	Balance Dr.	Balance Cr.
1/14	GJ1	100		100	

Prepaid Rent   114

Date	PR	Dr.	Cr.	Balance Dr.	Balance Cr.
1/1	GJ1	300		300	
1/31Adj.	GJ2		100	200	

Office Supplies   115

Date	PR	Dr.	Cr.	Balance Dr.	Balance Cr.
1/6	GJ1	40		40	
1/31Adj	GJ2		34	6	

Office Equipment   121

Date	PR	Dr.	Cr.	Balance Dr.	Balance Cr.
1/1	GJ1	100		100	
1/4	GJ1	50		150	

Accumulated Depreciation, Equipment   122

Date	PR	Dr.	Cr.	Balance Dr.	Balance Cr.
1/31Adj.	GJ2		20		20

Accounts Payable   211

Date	PR	Dr.	Cr.	Balance Dr.	Balance Cr.
1/4	GJ1		50		50
1/18	GJ1		70		120

Salaries Payable   212

Date	PR	Dr.	Cr.	Balance Dr.	Balance Cr.
1/31Adj.	GJ2		50		50

Rolo Kern, Capital   311

Date	PR	Dr.	Cr.	Balance Dr.	Balance Cr.
1/1	GJ1		1,300		1,300
1/31Clos.	GJ2		166		1,466
1/31Clos.	GJ2	20			1,446

Rolo Kern, Withdrawals   312

Date	PR	Dr.	Cr.	Balance Dr.	Balance Cr.
1/12	GJ1	20		20	
1/31Clos.	GJ2		20	—	

Income Summary   313

Date	PR	Dr.	Cr.	Balance Dr.	Balance Cr.
1/31Clos.	GJ2		500		500
1/31Clos.	GJ2	334			166
1/31Clos.	GJ2	166		—	—

Fees Earned					411
				Balance	
Date	PR	Dr.	Cr.	Dr.	Cr.
1/8	GJ1		400		400
1/14	GJ1		100		500
1/31 Clos.	GJ2	500		——	——

Rent Expense					513
				Balance	
Date	PR	Dr.	Cr.	Dr.	Cr.
1/31 Adj.	GJ2	100		100	
1/31 Clos.	GJ2		100	——	——

Salaries Expense					511
				Balance	
Date	PR	Dr.	Cr.	Dr.	Cr.
1/16	GJ1	60		60	
1/31 Adj.	GJ2	50		110	
1/31 Clos.	GJ2		110	——	——

Office Supplies Expense					514
				Balance	
Date	PR	Dr.	Cr.	Dr.	Cr.
1/31 Adj.	GJ2	34		34	
1/31 Clos.	GJ2		34	——	——

Advertising Expense					512
				Balance	
Date	PR	Dr.	Cr.	Dr.	Cr.
1/18	GJ1	70		70	
1/31 Clos.	GJ2		70	——	——

Depreciation Expenses Office Equipment					515
				Balance	
Date	PR	Dr.	Cr.	Dr.	Cr.
1/31 Adj.	GJ2	20		20	
1/31 Clos.	GJ2		20	——	——

These are all permanent accounts.

ROLO CO.
POST-CLOSING TRIAL BALANCE
JANUARY 31, 19XX

	Dr.	Cr.
Cash	1 1 8 0 00	
Accounts Receivable	1 0 0 00	
Prepaid Rent	2 0 0 00	
Office Supplies	6 00	
Office Equipment	1 5 0 00	
Accum. Dep., Office Equipment		2 0 00
Accounts Payable		1 2 0 00
Salaries Payable		5 0 00
R. Kern, Capital		1 4 4 6 00
TOTAL	1 6 3 6 00	1 6 3 6 00

Solution Tips for the Post-Closing Trial Balance

The Post-Closing Trial Balance is a list of the ledger *after* adjusting and closing entries have been completed. Note the figure for capital $1,446 is the new figure.

Beginning Capital	$1,300
+ Net Income	166
− Withdrawals	20
= Ending Capital	$1,446

Next accounting period we will enter new amounts in the Revenues, Expenses, and Withdrawal accounts. For now, the post-closing trial balance is only made up of permanent accounts.

SUMMARY OF KEY POINTS

Learning Unit 5-1

1. After formal financial reports have been prepared, the ledger has still not been brought up to date.
2. Information for journalizing adjusting entries comes from the adjustments section of the worksheet.

Learning Unit 5-2

1. Closing is a mechanical process that aids the accountant in recording transactions for the next period.
2. Assets, liabilities, and capital are permanent (real) accounts; their balances are carried over from one accounting period to another. Withdrawals, revenue, and expenses are temporary (nominal) accounts; their balances are *not* carried over from one accounting period to another.
3. Income Summary is a temporary account in the general ledger and does not have a normal balance. It will summarize revenue and expenses and transfer the balance to capital. Withdrawals do not go into Income Summary, because they are *not* business expenses.
4. All information for closing can be obtained from the worksheet or ledger.
5. When closing is complete, all temporary accounts in the ledger will have a zero balance, and all this information will be updated in the capital account.
6. Closing entries are usually done only at year end. Interim reports can be prepared from worksheets that are prepared monthly, quarterly, etc.

Learning Unit 5-3

1. The post-closing trial balance is prepared from the ledger accounts after the adjusting and closing entries have been posted.
2. The accounts on the post-closing trial balance are all permanent titles.

KEY TERMS

Adjusting journal entries   Journal entries that are needed in order to update specific ledger accounts to reflect correct balances at the end of an accounting period.

Closing journal entries   Journal entries that are prepared to (a) reduce or clear all temporary accounts to a zero balance, or (b) update capital to a new balance.

Income Summary   A temporary account in the ledger that summarizes revenue and expenses and transfers its balance (net income or net loss) to capital. Does not have a normal balance.

Permanent accounts (real)   Accounts whose balances are carried over to the next accounting period. Examples: assets, liabilities, capital.

Post-closing trial balance   The final step in the accounting cycle that lists only permanent accounts in the ledger and their balances after adjusting and closing entries have been posted.

Temporary accounts (nominal)   Accounts whose balances at end of an accounting period are not carried over to the next accounting period. These accounts — revenue, expenses, withdrawals — help summarize a new or ending figure for capital to begin the next accounting period. Keep in mind that Income Summary is also a temporary account.

BLUEPRINT OF CLOSING PROCESS FROM THE WORKSHEET

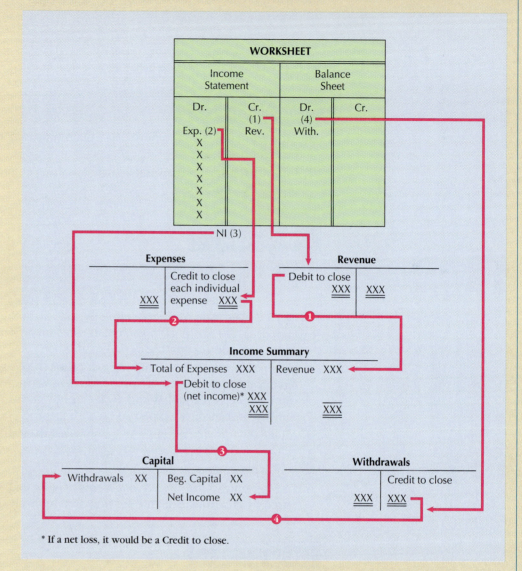

* If a net loss, it would be a Credit to close.

THE CLOSING STEPS

1. Close revenue balance to Income Summary.
2. Close each *individual* expense and transfer *total* of all expenses to Income Summary.
3. Transfer balance in Income Summary (Net Income or Net Loss) to Capital.
4. Close Withdrawals to Capital.

QUESTIONS, MINI EXERCISES, EXERCISES, AND PROBLEMS

Discussion Questions

1. When a worksheet is completed, what balances are found in the general ledger?
2. Why must adjusting entries be journalized even though the formal reports have already been prepared?

3. "Closing slows down the recording of next year's transactions." Defend or reject this statement with supporting evidence.
4. What is the difference between temporary and permanent accounts?
5. What are the two major goals of the closing process?
6. List the four steps of closing.
7. What is the purpose of Income Summary and where is it located?
8. How can a worksheet aid the closing process?
9. What accounts are usually listed on a post-closing trial balance?
10. Closing entries are always prepared once a month. Agree or disagree. Why?

Mini Exercises

(The blank forms you need are on pages 143–144 of the *Study Guide and Working Papers*.)

Journalizing and Posting Adjusting Entries

1. Post the following Adjusting Entries (be sure to cross-reference back to Journal) that came from the Adjustment columns of the worksheet.

Ledger Accounts Before Adjusting Entries Posted

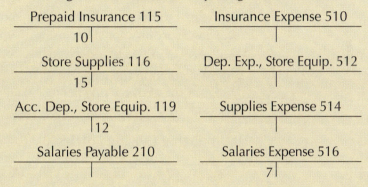

Prepaid Insurance 115	Insurance Expense 510
10	

Store Supplies 116	Dep. Exp., Store Equip. 512
15	

Acc. Dep., Store Equip. 119	Supplies Expense 514
12	

Salaries Payable 210	Salaries Expense 516
	7

	General Journal			Page 3	
Date	Account Titles and Description	PR	Dr.	Cr.
Dec. 31	Insurance Expense		6 00	
	Prepaid Insurance			6 00
31	Supplies Expense		3 00	
	Store Supplies			3 00
31	Depr. Exp., Store Equipment		7 00	
	Accum. Depr., Store Equipment			7 00
31	Salaries Expense		4 00	
	Salaries Payable			4 00

Steps of Closing and Journalizing Closing Entries

2.

```
                     Worksheet

            IS                      BS

     Dr.       Cr.         Dr.        Cr.
     (2)       Rev. (1)    Withd.     (4)
     E
     X
     P
     E
     N
     S
     E
     S
     ___       ___
```

NI (3)

Goals of Closing:

1. Temporary accounts in the ledger should have a zero balance.

2. New figure for capital in closing.

Note: All closing can be done from the worksheet. Income Summary is a temporary account in the ledger.

From the above worksheet explain the four steps of closing. Keep in mind that each *individual* expense normally would be listed in the closing process.

Journalizing Closing Entries

3. From the following accounts, journalize the closing entries (assume December 31).

Mel Blanc, Capital 310		Gas Expense 510	
	30	5	

Mel Blanc, Withdr. 312		Advertising Exp. 512	
6		4	

Income Summary 314		Dep. Exp., Taxi 516	
		6	

Taxi Fees 410	
	18

Posting to Income Summary

4. Draw a T Account of Income Summary and post to it all entries from Question 3 that affect it. Is Income Summary a temporary or permanent account?

Posting to Capital

5. Draw a T Account for Mel Blanc, Capital, and post to it all entries from Question 3 that affect it. What is the final balance of the capital account?

Exercises

(The blank forms you need are on pages 145–147 of the *Study Guide and Working Papers.*)

5-1. From the adjustments section of a worksheet presented here, prepare adjusting journal entries for end of December.

Journalize adjusting entries

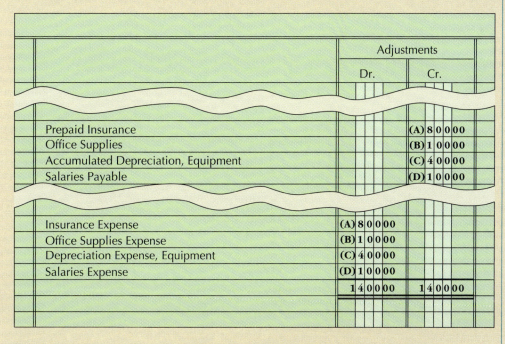

	Adjustments	
	Dr.	Cr.
Prepaid Insurance		(A) 8 0 0 00
Office Supplies		(B) 1 0 0 00
Accumulated Depreciation, Equipment		(C) 4 0 0 00
Salaries Payable		(D) 1 0 0 00
Insurance Expense	(A) 8 0 0 00	
Office Supplies Expense	(B) 1 0 0 00	
Depreciation Expense, Equipment	(C) 4 0 0 00	
Salaries Expense	(D) 1 0 0 00	
	1 4 0 0 00	1 4 0 0 00

5-2. Complete the following table by placing an X in the correct column.

Temporary vs. permanent accounts.

	Temporary	Permanent	Will be Closed
Ex. Accounts Receivable		X	
1. Income Summary			
2. A. Rose, Capital			
3. Salary Expense			
4. A. Rose, Withdrawals			
5. Fees Earned			
6. Accounts Payable			
7. Cash			

Closing entries.

5-3. From the following T accounts, journalize the four closing entries on December 31, 19XX.

J. King, Capital	
	14,000

Rent Expense	
5,000	

J. King, Withdrawals	
4,000	

Wage Expense	
7,000	

Income Summary	

Insurance Expense	
1,200	

Fees Earned	
	33,000

Dep. Expense, Office Equipment	
900	

Reconstructing closing entries.

5-4. From the following posted T accounts, reconstruct the closing journal entries for December 31, 19XX.

M. Foster, Capital			Insurance Expense	
Withdrawals 100	2,000 (Dec. 1)		50	Closing 50
	700 Net Income			

M. Foster, Withdrawals			Wage Expense	
	100	Closing 100	100	Closing 100

Income Summary			Rent Expense	
Expenses 600	Revenue 1,300		200	Closing 200
700	Net Income 700			

Salon Fees			Depreciation Expense, Equipment	
Closing 1,300	1,300		250	Closing 250

Post-closing trial balance.

5-5. From the following accounts (not in order), prepare a post-closing trial balance for Wey Co. on December 31, 19XX. **Note:** These balances are **before** closing.

Accounts Receivable	$18,875
Legal Supplies	14,250
Office Equipment	59,700
Repair Expense	2,850
Salaries Expense	1,275
P. Wey, Capital	63,450
P. Wey, Withdrawals	1,500
Legal Fees Earned	12,000
Accounts Payable	45,000
Cash	22,000

Group A Problems

(The blank forms you need are on pages 148–165 of the *Study Guide and Working Papers.*)

5A-1. Given the following data for Marc's Consulting Service:

Review in preparing a worksheet and journalizing adjusting and closing entries.

Check Figure:
Net Income $4,600

MARC'S CONSULTING SERVICE TRIAL BALANCE JUNE 30, 19XX		
	Dr.	Cr.
Cash	18 0 0 0 00	
Accounts Receivable	6 0 0 0 00	
Prepaid Insurance	4 0 0 00	
Supplies	1 5 0 0 00	
Equipment	3 0 0 0 00	
Accumulated Depreciation, Equipment		9 0 0 00
Accounts Payable		10 0 0 00
M. Key, Capital		12 3 0 0 00
M. Key, Withdrawals	3 0 0 00	
Consulting Fees Earned		9 0 0 0 00
Salaries Expense	1 4 0 0 00	
Telephone Expense	1 0 0 0 00	
Advertising Expense	6 0 0 00	
	32 2 0 0 00	32 2 0 0 00

Adjustment Data:

a. Insurance expired $300.

b. Supplies on hand $700.

c. Depreciation on equipment $100.

d. Salaries earned by employees but not to be paid till July $200.

Your task is to

1. Prepare a worksheet.
2. Journalize adjusting and closing entries.

Journalizing and posting adjusting and closing entries. Preparing a post-closing trial balance.

Check Figure:
Post-closing Trial Balance $3,504

5A-2. Enter beginning balance in each account in your working papers from the trial balance columns of the worksheet. From the worksheet on page 190, (1) journalize and post adjusting and closing entries after entering beginning balance in each account in the ledger, and (2) prepare from the ledger a post-closing trial balance for the month of March.

Comprehensive review of the entire accounting cycle, Chapters 1–5.

5A-3. As the bookkeeper of Pete's Plowing, you have been asked to complete the entire accounting cycle for Pete from the following information:

19XX

Check Figure:
Net Income $15,780

Jan.

1 Pete invested $7,000 cash and $6,000 worth of snow equipment into the plowing company.

1 Paid rent for three months in advance for garage space, $2,000.

4 Purchased office equipment on account from Ling Corp., $7,200.

6 Purchased snow supplies for $700 cash.

8 Collected $15,000 from plowing local shopping centers.

12 Pete Mack withdrew $1,000 from the business for his own personal use.

20 Plowed North East Co. parking lots, payment not to be received until March, $5,000.

26 Paid salaries to employees, $1,800.

28 Paid Ling Corp. one-half amount owed for office equipment.

29 Advertising bill received from Bush Co. but will not be paid until March, $900.

30 Paid telephone bill, $210.

Adjustment Data:

a. Snow supplies on hand $400.

b. Rent expired $600.

c. Depreciation on office equipment $120.
($7,200 ÷ 5 yr. = $1,440/12 = $120)

d. Depreciation on snow equipment $100.
($6,000 ÷ 5 = $1,200/12 mo. = $100)

e. Accrued salaries $190.

POTTER CLEANING SERVICE
WORKSHEET
FOR MONTH ENDED MARCH 31, 19XX

Account Titles	Trial Balance Dr.	Trial Balance Cr.	Adjustments Dr.	Adjustments Cr.	Adjusted Trial Balance Dr.	Adjusted Trial Balance Cr.	Income Statement Dr.	Income Statement Cr.	Balance Sheet Dr.	Balance Sheet Cr.
Cash	400 00				400 00				400 00	
Prepaid Insurance	520 00			(A) 180 00	340 00				340 00	
Cleaning Supplies	144 00			(B) 100 00	44 00				44 00	
Auto	2720 00				2720 00				2720 00	
Accum. Depr. Auto		860 00		(C) 150 00		1010 00				1010 00
Accounts Payable		224 00				224 00				224 00
B. Potter, Capital		540 00				540 00				540 00
B. Potter, Withdrawals	460 00				460 00				460 00	
Cleaning Fees		4680 00	(D) 160 00			4680 00		4680 00		
Salaries Expense	1440 00				1600 00		1600 00			
Telephone Expense	264 00				264 00		264 00			
Advertising Expense	196 00				196 00		196 00			
Gas Expense	160 00				160 00		160 00			
	6304 00	6304 00								
Insurance Expense			(A) 180 00		180 00		180 00			
Cleaning Supplies Expense			(B) 100 00		100 00		100 00			
Depr. Expense Auto			(C) 150 00		150 00		150 00			
Salaries Payable				(D) 160 00		160 00				160 00
			590 00	590 00	6614 00	6614 00	2650 00	4680 00	3964 00	1934 00
Net Income							2030 00			2030 00
							4680 00	4680 00	3964 00	3964 00

Chart of Accounts

Assets
111 Cash
112 Accounts Receivable
114 Prepaid Rent
115 Snow Supplies
121 Office Equipment
122 Accumulated Depreciation, Office Equipment
123 Snow Equipment
124 Accumulated Depreciation, Snow Equipment

Liabilities
211 Accounts Payable
212 Salaries Payable

Owner's Equity
311 Pete Mack, Capital
312 Pete Mack, Withdrawals
313 Income Summary

Revenue
411 Plowing Fees

Expenses
511 Salaries Expense
512 Advertising Expense
513 Telephone Expense
514 Rent Expense
515 Snow Supplies Expense
516 Depreciation Expense, Office Equipment
517 Depreciation Expense, Snow Equipment

Group B Problems

(The blank forms you need are on pages 148–165 of the *Study Guide and Working Papers.*)

5B-1.

Review in preparing a worksheet and journalizing and closing entries.

> **MEMO**
>
> To: Ron Ear
>
> From: Sue French
>
> Re: Accounting Needs
>
> Please prepare ASAP from the following information (attached) (1) a worksheet along with (2) journalized adjusting and closing entries.

Check Figure:
Net Income $3,530

MARC'S CONSULTING SERVICE
TRIAL BALANCE
JUNE 30, 19XX

	Dr.	Cr.
Cash	10 1 5 0 00	
Accounts Receivable	5 0 0 0 00	
Prepaid Insurance	7 0 0 00	
Supplies	3 0 0 00	
Equipment	12 9 5 0 00	
Accumulated Depreciation, Equipment		4 0 0 0 00
Accounts Payable		5 7 5 0 00
M. Key, Capital		15 1 5 0 00
M. Key, Withdrawals	4 0 0 00	
Consulting Fees Earned		5 2 0 0 00
Salaries Expense	4 5 0 00	
Telephone Expense	7 0 00	
Advertising Expense	8 0 00	
	30 1 0 0 00	30 1 0 0 00

Adjustment Data:

a.	Insurance expired	$100.
b.	Supplies on hand	$20.
c.	Depreciation on equipment	$200.
d.	Salaries earned by employees but not due to be paid till July	$490.

Journalizing and posting adjusting and closing entries. Preparing a post-closing trial balance.

Check Figure:
Post-closing Trial Balance $3,294

Comprehensive review of entire accounting cycle. Review of Chapters 1–5.

5B-2. Enter beginning balance in each account in your working papers from the trial balance columns of the worksheet. From the worksheet on page 193, (1) journalize and post adjusting and closing entries after entering beginning balances in each account in the ledger, and (2) prepare from the ledger a post-closing trial balance at end of March.

5B-3. From the following transactions as well as additional data, please complete the entire accounting cycle for Pete's Plowing (use the chart of accounts on page 191).

19XX
Jan.

Check Figure:
Net Income $9,610

1 To open the business, Pete invested $8,000 cash and $9,600 worth of snow equipment.
1 Paid rent for five months in advance, $3,000.
4 Purchased office equipment on account from Russell Co., $6,000.
6 Bought snow supplies, $350.
8 Collected $7,000 for plowing during winter storm emergency.
12 Pete paid his home telephone bill from the company checkbook, $70.
20 Billed Eastern Freight Co. for plowing fees earned but not to be received until March, $6,500.
24 Advertising bill received from Jones Co. but will not be paid until next month, $350.
26 Paid salaries to employees, $1,800.
28 Paid Russell Co. one-half of amount owed for office equipment.
29 Paid telephone bill of company, $165.

Adjustment Data:

a.	Snow supplies on hand	$200.
b.	Rent expired	$600.
c.	Depreciation on office equipment ($6,000/4 yr = $1,500 ÷ 12 = $125)	$125.
d.	Depreciation on snow equipment ($9,600 ÷ 2 = $4,800 ÷ 12 = $400)	$400.
e.	Salaries accrued	$300.

REAL WORLD APPLICATIONS

5R-1. Ann Humphrey needs a loan from the Charles Bank to help finance her business. She has submitted to the Charles Bank the following unadjusted trial balance. As the loan officer, you will be meeting with Ann tomorrow. Could you make some specific written suggestions to Ann regarding her loan report?

Cash in Bank	770	
Accounts Receivable	1,480	
Office Supplies	3,310	
Equipment	7,606	
Accounts Payable		684
A. Humphrey, Capital		8,000
Service Fees		17,350
Salaries	11,240	

POTTER CLEANING SERVICE
WORKSHEET
FOR MONTH ENDED MARCH 31, 19XX

Account Titles	Trial Balance Dr.	Trial Balance Cr.	Adjustments Dr.	Adjustments Cr.	Adjusted Trial Balance Dr.	Adjusted Trial Balance Cr.	Income Statement Dr.	Income Statement Cr.	Balance Sheet Dr.	Balance Sheet Cr.
Cash	1 7 2 4 00				1 7 2 4 00				1 7 2 4 00	
Prepaid Insurance	3 5 0 00			(A) 2 0 0 00	1 5 0 00				1 5 0 00	
Cleaning Supplies	8 0 0 00			(B) 6 0 0 00	2 0 0 00				2 0 0 00	
Auto	1 2 2 0 00				1 2 2 0 00				1 2 2 0 00	
Accumulated Depreciation, Auto		6 6 0 00		(C) 1 5 0 00		8 1 0 00				8 1 0 00
Accounts Payable		6 7 4 00				6 7 4 00				6 7 4 00
B. Potter, Capital		2 4 8 0 00				2 4 8 0 00				2 4 8 0 00
B. Potter, Withdrawals	6 0 0 00				6 0 0 00				6 0 0 00	
Cleaning Fees		3 7 0 0 00				3 7 0 0 00		3 7 0 0 00		
Salaries Expense	2 0 0 0 00		(D) 1 7 5 00		2 1 7 5 00		2 1 7 5 00			
Telephone Expense	2 8 4 00				2 8 4 00		2 8 4 00			
Advertising Expense	2 7 6 00				2 7 6 00		2 7 6 00			
Gas Expense	2 6 0 00				2 6 0 00		2 6 0 00			
	7 5 1 4 00	7 5 1 4 00								
Insurance Expense			(A) 2 0 0 00		2 0 0 00		2 0 0 00			
Cleaning Supplies Expense			(B) 6 0 0 00		6 0 0 00		6 0 0 00			
Depreciation Expense, Auto			(C) 1 5 0 00		1 5 0 00		1 5 0 00			
Salaries Payable				(D) 1 7 5 00		1 7 5 00				1 7 5 00
			1 1 2 5 00	1 1 2 5 00	7 8 3 9 00	7 8 3 9 00	3 9 4 5 00	3 7 0 0 00	3 8 9 4 00	4 1 3 9 00
Net Loss								2 4 5 00	2 4 5 00	
							3 9 4 5 00	3 9 4 5 00	4 1 3 9 00	4 1 3 9 00

Utilities Expense	842	
Rent Expense	360	
Insurance Expense	280	
Advertising Expense	146	
Totals	26,034	26,034

5R-2. Janet Smother is the new bookkeeper who replaced Dick Burns, owing to his sudden illness. Janet finds on her desk a note requesting that she close the books and supply the ending capital figure. Janet is upset, since she can only find the following:

    a. Revenue and expense accounts all were zero balance.

    b. Income Summary

       14,360 | 19,300

    c. Owner withdrew $8,000.

    d. Owner beginning capital was $34,400.

Could you help Janet accomplish her assignment? What written suggestions should Janet make to her supervisor so that this situation will not happen again?

YOU make the call

Critical Thinking/Ethical Case

5R-3. Todd Silver is the purchasing agent for Moore Co. One of his suppliers, Gem Co., offers Todd a free vacation to France if he buys at least 75 percent of Moore's supplies from Gem Co. Todd, who is angry because Moore Co. has not given him a raise in over a year, is considering the offer. Write your recommendation to Todd.

ACCOUNTING RECALL
A CUMULATIVE APPROACH

THIS EXAM REVIEWS CHAPTERS 1 THROUGH 5

Page 170 and 179 of the *Study Guide and Working Papers* has forms to complete this exam, as well as worked-out solutions. The page references next to each question identify what page to turn back to if you answer the question incorrectly.

PART 1   Vocabulary Review

Match the terms to the appropriate definition or phrase.

Page Ref.

(160)	1. Closing entries	A. Updates specific ledger accounts
(122)	2. Book value	B. A temporary account usually with
(161)	3. Income summary	debit balance
(121)	4. Contra-asset	C. A permanent account
(119)	5. Supplies	D. Lists only permanent account
(71)	6. Journal	E. Clears all temporary accounts

(172)	7. Post-closing trial balance	F. Book of original entry
(157)	8. Adjusting journal entries	G. A temporary account in the ledger
(81)	9. Ledger	H. Cost — accumulated depreciation
(11)	10. Withdrawals	I. Book of final entry
		J. Accumulated depreciation

(161) 11. Income summary has a normal balance of a debit.

(161) 12. After closing, all temporary accounts will be cleared to zero balance.

(161) 13. Closing entries cannot be made from a worksheet.

(128) 14. The worksheet shows the beginning figure for capital.

(157) 15. Financial reports are prepared after journalizing and posting adjusting and closing entries.

CONTINUING PROBLEM

Tony has decided to end the Eldorado Computer Center's first year as of September 30, 19XX. Below is an updated chart of accounts.

Assets
1000 Cash
1020 Accounts Receivable
1025 Prepaid Rent
1030 Supplies
1080 Computer Shop Equip.
1081 Accum. Depr. CS Equip.
1090 Office Equipment
1091 Accum. Depr. Office Equip.

Liabilities
2000 Accounts Payable

Owner's Equity
3000 T. Freedman, Capital
3010 T. Freedman, W/D
3020 Income Summary

Revenue
4000 Service Revenue

Expenses
5010 Advertising Expense
5030 Utilities Expense
5050 Supplies Expense
5070 Postage Expense
5090 Depr. Exp. Office Equip.
5020 Rent Expense
5040 Phone Expense
5060 Insurance Expense
5080 Depr. Exp. C.S. Equip.

Assignment:

(See pp. 171–178 in your *Study Guide and Working Papers*.)

1. Journalize the adjusting entries from Chapter 4.
2. Post the adjusting entries to the ledger.
3. Journalize the closing entries.
4. Post the closing entries to the ledger.
5. Prepare a post-closing trial balance.

Valdez Realty

Reviewing the Accounting Cycle Twice

This comprehensive review problem requires you to complete the accounting cycle for Valdez Realty twice. This will allow you to review Chapters 1–5 while reinforcing the relationships between all parts of the accounting cycle. By completing two cycles, you will see how the ending June balances in the ledger are used to accumulate data in July. (The blank forms you need are on pages 180–200 of the *Study Guide and Working Papers.*)

The following chart shows the steps of the accounting cycle and the pages in the text where each step is covered. You can use it to review the accounting cycle before you start and as a reference while you are working.

Steps in the Accounting Cycle	Pages in Text Where Covered
1. Business transactions occur and generate source documents.	**1.** p. 72
2. Analyze and record business transactions into a journal.	**2.** p. 73
3. Post or transfer information from journal to ledger.	**3.** p. 81
4. Prepare a trial balance.	**4.** p. 87
5. Prepare a worksheet.	**5.** p. 117
6. Prepare financial statements.	**6.** p. 132
7. Journalize and post adjusting entries.	**7.** p. 157
8. Journalize and post closing entries.	**8.** p. 160
9. Prepare a post-closing trial balance.	**9.** p. 171

First, let's look at the chart of accounts for Valdez Realty (top of page 197).

On June 1 Juan Valdez opened a real estate office called Valdez Realty. The following transactions were completed for the month of June:

19XX
June   1   Juan Valdez invested $7,000 cash in the real estate agency along with
            $3,000 of office equipment.
        1   Rented office space and paid three months rent in advance, $2,100.

Valdez Realty
Chart of Accounts

Assets
111 Cash
112 Accounts Receivable
114 Prepaid Rent
115 Office Supplies
121 Office Equipment
122 Accumulated Depreciation,
      Office Equipment
123 Automobile
124 Accumulated Depreciation,
      Automobile

Liabilities
211 Accounts Payable
212 Salaries Payable

Owner's Equity
311 Juan Valdez, Capital
312 Juan Valdez, Withdrawals
313 Income Summary

Revenue
411 Commissions Earned

Expenses
511 Rent Expense
512 Salaries Expense
513 Gas Expense
514 Repairs Expense
515 Telephone Expense
516 Advertising Expense
517 Office Supplies Expense
518 Depreciation Expense,
      Office Equipment
519 Depreciation Expense,
      Automobile
524 Miscellaneous Expense

1 Bought an automobile on account, $12,000.
4 Purchased office supplies for cash, $300.
5 Purchased additional office supplies on account, $150.
6 Sold a house and collected a $6,000 commission.
8 Paid gas bill, $22.
15 Paid the salary of the office secretary, $350.
17 Sold a building lot and earned a commission, $6,500. Payment is to be received on July 8.
20 Juan Valdez withdrew $1,000 from the business to pay personal expenses.
21 Sold a house and collected a $3,500 commission.
22 Paid gas bill, $25.
24 Paid $600 to repair automobile.
30 Paid the salary of the office secretary, $350.
30 Paid the June telephone bill, $510.
30 Received advertising bill for June, $1,200. The bill is to be paid on July 2.

Required Work for June:

1. Journalize transactions and post to ledger accounts.
2. Prepare a trial balance in the first two columns of the worksheet and complete the worksheet using the following adjustment data:
   a. One month's rent had expired.
   b. An inventory shows $50 of office supplies remaining.
   c. Depreciation on office equipment, $100.
   d. Depreciation on automobile, $200.
3. Prepare a June income statement, statement of owner's equity, and balance sheet.
4. From the worksheet, journalize and post adjusting and closing entries (p. 3 of journal).
5. Prepare a post-closing trial balance.

During July, Valdez Realty completed these transactions:

19XX

July   1 Purchased additional office supplies on account, $700.

        2 Paid advertising bill for June.

        3 Sold a house and collected a commission, $6,600.

        6 Paid for gas expense, $29.

        8 Collected commission from sale of building lot on June 17.

     12 Paid $300 to send employees to realtor's workshop.

     15 Paid the salary of the office secretary, $350.

     17 Sold a house and earned a commission of $2,400. Commission to be received on August 10.

     18 Sold a building lot and collected a commission of $7,000.

     22 Sent a check for $40 to help sponsor a local road race to aid the poor. (This is not to be considered an advertising expense, but it is a business expense.)

     24 Paid for repairs to automobile, $590.

     28 Juan Valdez withdrew $1,800 from the business to pay personal expenses.

     30 Paid the salary of the office secretary, $350.

     30 Paid the July telephone bill, $590.

     30 Advertising bill for July, $1,400. The bill is to be paid on August 2.

Required Work for July:

1. Journalize transactions in a general journal (p. 4) and post to ledger accounts.

2. Prepare a trial balance in the first two columns of the worksheet and complete the worksheet using the following adjustment data:

   a. One month's rent had expired.

   b. An inventory shows $90 of office supplies remaining.

   c. Depreciation on office equipment, $100.

   d. Depreciation on automobile, $200.

3. Prepare a July income statement, statement of owner's equity, and balance sheet.

4. From the worksheet, journalize and post adjusting and closing entries (p. 6 of journal).

5. Prepare a post-closing trial balance.

COMPUTERIZED ACCOUNTING APPLICATION FOR VALDEZ REALTY MINI PRACTICE SET (CHAPTER 5)

Closing Process and Post-Closing Trial Balance

Before starting on this assignment, read and complete the tasks discussed in Parts A, B, and F of the Computerized Accounting appendix at the back of this book and complete the Computerized Accounting Application assignments at the end of Chapters 3 and 4.

This comprehensive review problem requires you to complete the accounting cycle for Valdez Realty twice. This will allow you to review Chapters 1 – 5 while reinforcing the relationships between all parts of the accounting cycle. By completing two cycles, you will see how the ending June balances in the ledger are used to accumulate data in July.

PART A: The June Accounting Cycle

On June 1, Juan Valdez opened a real estate office called Valdez Realty.

Open the Company Data Files

1. Click on the Start button. Point to Programs; point to Simply Accounting; then click on Simply Accounting in the final menu presented. The Simply Accounting Open File dialog box will appear.

2. Insert your Student Data Files disk into disk drive A. Enter the following path into the **File name** text box: A:\student\valdez.asc

3. Click on the **Open** button, enter 6/30/97 into the **Using Date for this Session** text box; then click on the **OK** button. Click on the **OK** button in response to the message "The date entered is more than one week past your previous **Using** date of 6/1/97." The Company Window for Valdez will appear.

Add Your Name to the Company Name

4. Click on the Company Window Setup menu; then click on Company Information. The Company Information dialog box will appear. Insert your name in place of the text "Your Name" in the **Name** text box. Click on the **OK** button to return to the Company Window.

Record June Transactions

5. Open the General Journal dialog box; then record the following journal entries (enter "Memo" into the **Source** text box for each transaction; then enter the **Date** listed for each transaction):

1997

June		
	1	Juan Valdez invested $7,000 cash in the real estate agency along with $3,000 in office equipment.
	1	Rented office space and paid three months rent in advance, $2,100.
	1	Bought an automobile on account, $12,000.
	4	Purchased office supplies for cash, $300.
	5	Purchased additional office supplies on account, $150.
	6	Sold a house and collected a $6,000 commission.
	8	Paid gas bill, $22.
	15	Paid the salary of the office secretary, $350.
	17	Sold a building lot and earned a commission, $6,500. Expected receipt 7/8/97.
	20	Juan Valdez withdrew $1,000 from the business to pay personal expenses.
	21	Sold a house and collected a $3,500 commission.
	22	Paid gas bill, $25.
	24	Paid $600 to repair automobile.

30 Paid the salary of the office secretary, $350.

30 Paid the June telephone bill, $510.

30 Received advertising bill for June, $1,200. The bill is to be paid on 7/2/97.

Print Reports

6. After you have posted the journal entries, close the General Journal; then print the following reports:

   a. General Journal (By posting date, All ledger entries, Start: 6/1/97, Finish: 6/30/97).

   b. Trial Balance As at 6/30/97.

   Review your printed reports. If you have made an error in a posted journal entry, see "Reversing an Entry Made in the General Journal Dialog Box" in Part C of the Computerized Accounting appendix for information on how to correct the error.

Record June Adjusting Entries

7. Open the General Journal; then record adjusting journal entries based on the following adjustment data (Source: Memo; Date: 6/30/97; Comment: Adjusting entry):

   a. One month's rent has expired.

   b. An inventory shows $50 of office supplies remaining.

   c. Depreciation on office equipment, $100.

   d. Depreciation on automobile, $200.

Print Reports

8. After you have posted the adjusting journal entries, close the General Journal; then print the following reports:

   a. General Journal (By posting date, All ledger entries, Start: 6/1/97, Finish: 6/30/97).

   b. Trial Balance As at 6/30/97.

   c. General Ledger Report (Start: 6/1/97, Finish: 6/30/97, Select All).

   d. Income Statement (Start: 6/1/97, Finish: 6/30/97).

   e. Balance Sheet As at 6/30/97.

   Review your printed reports. If you have made an error in a posted journal entry, see "Reversing an Entry Made in the General Journal Dialog Box" in Part C of the Computerized Accounting appendix for information on how to correct the error.

How to Close the Accounting Records

9. Simply Accounting has the capability of performing the first three steps of the closing process automatically.

Done automatically by the program.	**Step 1:**	Clear Revenue Balance and Transfer to Income Summary.
	Step 2:	Clear Individual Expense Balances and Transfer the Total to Income Summary.
	Step 3:	Clear Balance in Income Summary and Transfer it to Capital.

It does not have the capability of performing the fourth step of the closing process automatically, so you will need to record this closing journal entry.

You need to record this closing entry.	**Step 4:**	Clear the Withdrawals Balance and Transfer it to Capital.

Record Entry to Close Withdrawals Account

10. Open the General Journal; then record the closing journal entry for Juan Valdez's Withdrawals account.

11. After you have posted the closing entry for Juan Valdez's Withdrawals account, close the General Journal to return to the Company Window.

Make a Backup Copy of June Accounting Records.

12. Click on the Company Window File menu; click on Save As; then enter the following new file name into the **File name** text box: A:\student\valdjune.asc

13. Click on the **Save** button. Note that the company name in the Company Window has changed from Valdez to Valdjune. Click on the Company Window File menu again; then click on Save As. Enter the following new file name into the **File name** text box:A:\student\valdez.asc

14. Click on the **Save** button. Click on the **Yes** button to confirm that you want to replace the existing file. Note that the company name in the Company Window has changed back from Valdjune to Valdez.

15. You now have two sets of company data files for Valdez Realty on your Student Data Files disk. The current data is stored under the file name valdez.asc. The backup data for June is stored under the file name valdjune.asc.

Important Information About the Closing Process.

16. The next instruction will ask you to advance the **Using** date to a new month. It is this procedure that instructs the program to complete the first three steps in the closing process. It is important that you make a backup copy of a company's data files prior to advancing the **Using** date to a new month. When you advance the **Using** date to a new month the program will permanently remove all journal entries from all Journals and all individual postings of journal entries to the general ledger accounts. You will not be able to display or print a General Journal or General Ledger report based on dates in the prior month, nor will you be able to record journal entries for dates in the prior month. If for some reason you need to print a General Journal or General Ledger, or record a transaction that occurred in the prior month, you can do so by using the backup copy of the company's data files that you created prior to advancing the **Using** date. See Part E of the Computerized Accounting appendix at the end of this book for information on how and when to use a backup copy of a company's data files.

How to Advance the Using Date

17. Click on the Company Window Maintenance menu; then click on Advance Using Date. Click on the **No** button in response to the question "Would you like to backup now?" Enter 7/1/97 into the **New Using Date** text box; then click on the **OK** button. Click on the **OK** button in response to the message "You have entered both a new calendar quarter and a new fiscal year. If you proceed, the program will zero all employees' quarter-to-date payroll information, move the current year's data into last year, close all Revenue and Expense account balances into the Retained Earnings integration account, and set the new fiscal year's dates. Print all employee reports and make a backup before proceeding."

18. The warning message stated that the revenue and expense accounts would be closed to an account titled Retained Earnings. This is the account that corporations use to accumulate earnings. Valdez Realty is a sole proprietorship, and the program will correctly close the revenue and expense accounts to Income Summary and close Income Summary to the Juan Valdez, Capital account even though the message used a different account name. The backup you created using the Save As method will serve as the backup suggested in the warning message.

Print a Post-closing Trial Balance

19. Print a post-closing Trial Balance As at 7/1/97.

Exit from the Program

20. Click on the Company Window File menu; then click on Exit to end the current work session and return to your Windows desktop.

Complete the Report Transmittal

21. Complete the Valdez Realty Report Transmittal for June located in Appendix A of your *Study Guide and Working Papers.*

PART B: The July Accounting Cycle

Open the Company Data Files

1. Click on the Start button. Point to Programs: point to Simply Accounting; then click on Simply Accounting in the final menu presented. The Simply Accounting Open File dialog box will appear.

2. Insert your Student Data Files disk into disk drive A. Enter the following path into the **File name** text box:A:\student\valdez.asc

3. Click on the **Open** button; enter 7/31/97 into the **Using Date for this Session** text box; then click on the **OK** button. Click on the **OK** button in

response to the message "The date entered is more than one week past your previous **Using** date of 7/1/97." The Company Window for Valdez Realty will appear.

Modify the Fiscal End Date

4. Click on the Company Window Setup menu; then click on Company Information. The Company Information dialog box will appear. Enter 7/31/97 as the new **Fiscal End** date; then click on the **OK** button.

Record July Transactions

5. Open the General Journal dialog box; then record the following journal entries (enter "Memo" into the **Source** text box for each transaction; then enter the **Date** listed for each transaction):

1997
July
  1 Purchased additional office supplies on account, $700.
  2 Paid advertising bill for June.
  3 Sold a house and collected a commission, $6,600.
  6 Paid for gas expense, $29.
  8 Collected commission from sale of building lot on 6/17/97.
  12 Paid $300 to send employees to realtor's workshop.
  15 Paid the salary of the office secretary, $350.
  17 Sold a house and earned a commission of $2,400. Expected receipt 8/10/97.
  18 Sold a building lot and collected a commission of $7,000.
  22 Sent a check for $40 to help sponsor a local road race to aid the poor. (This is not to be considered an advertising expense, but it is a business expense.)
  24 Paid for repairs to automobile, $590.
  28 Juan Valdez withdrew $1,800 from the business to pay personal expenses.
  30 Paid the salary of the office secretary, $350.
  30 Paid the July telephone bill, $590.
  30 Advertising bill for July, $1,400. The bill is to be paid on 8/2/97.

Print Reports

6. After you have posted the journal entries, close the General Journal; then print the following reports:

  a. General Journal (By posting date, All ledger entries, Start: 7/1/97, Finish: 7/31/97).

  b. Trial Balance As at 7/31/97.

Review your reports. If you have made an error in a posted journal entry, see "Reversing an Entry Made in the General Journal Dialog Box" in Part C of the Computerized Accounting appendix for information on how to correct the error.

Record July Adjusting Entries

7. Open the General Journal; then record adjusting journal entries based on the following adjustment data (Source: Memo; Date: 7/31/97; Comment: Adjusting entry):

  a. One month's rent has expired.

  b. An inventory shows $90 of office supplies remaining.

  c. Depreciation on office equipment, $100.

  d. Depreciation on automobile, $200.

Print Reports

8. After you have posted the adjusting journal entries, close the General Journal; then print the following reports:

  a. General Journal (By posting date, All ledger entries, Start: 7/1/97, Finish: 7/31/97).

  b. Trial Balance As at 7/31/97.

  c. General Ledger Report (Start: 7/1/97, Finish: 7/31/97, Select All).

  d. Income Statement (Start: 7/1/97, Finish: 7/31/97).

  e. Balance Sheet As at 7/31/97.

Review your reports. If you have made an error in a posted journal entry, see "Reversing an Entry Made in the General Journal Dialog Box" in Part C of the Computerized Accounting appendix for information on how to correct the error.

Record Entry to Close With-drawals Account

9. Record the closing journal entry for Juan Valdez's Withdrawals account.

10. After you have posted the closing entry for Juan Valdez's Withdrawals account, close the General Journal to return to the Company Window.

Make a Backup Copy of July Accounting Records

11. Click on the Company Window File menu; click on Save As; then enter the following new file name into the **File name** text box:A:\student\valdjuly.asc

12. Click on the **Save** button. Note that the company name in the Company Window has changed from Valdez to Valdjuly. Click on the Company Window File menu again; then click on Save As. Enter the following new file name into the **File name** text box:A:\student\valdez.asc

13. Click on the **Save** button. Click on the **Yes** button in response to the question "Replace existing file?" Note that the company name in the Company Window has changed back from Valdjuly to Valdez.

14. You now have three sets of company data files for Valdez Realty on your Student Data Files disk. The current data is stored under the file name valdez.asc. The backup data for June is stored under the file name valdjune.asc and the backup data for July is stored under the file name valdjuly.asc.

Advance the Using Date

15. Click on the Company Window Maintenance menu; then click on Advance Using Date. Click on the **No** button in response to the question "Would you like to backup now?" Enter 8/1/97 into the **New Using Date** text box; then click on the **OK** button. Click on the **OK** button in response to the warning message. The backup you created using the Save As method will serve as the backup suggested in the warning message.

Print a Post-closing Trial Balance

16. Print a post-closing Trial Balance As at 8/1/97.

Exit from the Program

17. Click on the Company Window File menu; then click on Exit to end the current work session and return to your Windows desktop.

Complete the Report Transmittal

18. Complete the Valdez Realty Report Transmittal for July located in Appendix A of your *Study Guide and Working Papers*.

BANKING PROCEDURES AND CONTROL OF CASH

THE BIG PICTURE

As Tony Freedman planned for the upcoming months, he thought about the problems he'd had managing cash. In particular, he often ran short of change and frequently lost track of small cash purchases. Eldorado Computer Center was currently using one checking account for paying bills and making deposits. Maybe new banking technology was the solution, Tony thought; so he prepared some questions to ask of a customer service representative at his bank:

◆ Should I have an ATM card for my business versus a small cash account kept on site?
◆ Is there an advantage to having an on-line machine for ATM or credit card transactions for my customers?
◆ Is there a benefit to banking on line?

The bank's customer service representative responded:

Using an ATM card certainly has advantages when you want to make deposits or withdraw cash outside of banking hours, and it beats standing in long teller lines during banking hours. However, an ATM card will not solve your problem of making change for customers at your place of business or small cash expenditures on an as-needed basis.

There is an advantage to having an on-line debit machine for your business. For a small monthly expense, your customers can make payments from their checking accounts without writing a check. The bank will clear the transaction only if the funds are available, which eliminates your possible expense of accepting non-sufficient checks. Some of our customers choose to handle their banking transactions via the computer. They like not having to leave their home or their office for most banking transactions—although there are still some security measures to be concerned with.

Even though technology offered some new options that Tony might make use of in the future, he decided that basic accounting was the answer to his current cash control woes. First he would reconcile his cash ledger accounts for the past four months with his bank statements. He also decided that it would be necessary to establish a petty cash fund.

<table>
<tr><td>

Learning Objectives

</td><td>

◆ **Depositing, writing, and endorsing checks for a checking account. (p. 205)**
◆ **Reconciling a bank statement. (p. 211)**
◆ **Establishing and replenishing a petty cash fund; setting up an auxiliary petty cash record. (p. 216)**
◆ **Establishing and replenishing a change fund. (p.220)**
◆ **Handling transactions involving cash short and over. (p. 220)**

</td></tr>
</table>

The internal control policies of a company will depend on things such as number of employees, company size, sources of cash, etc.

In the first five chapters of this book, we analyzed the accounting cycle for businesses that perform personal services (for example, word processing or legal services). In this chapter, we turn our attention to Debbie's Wholesale Stationery Company, a merchandising company that earns revenue by selling goods (or merchandise) to customers. When Debbie found that her business was increasing, she became concerned that she was not monitoring the business's cash closely enough. To try and remedy the situation, Debbie and her accountant decided to develop a system of **internal controls.**

After studying the situation carefully, Debbie began a series of procedures that were to be followed by all company employees. These are the new company policies that Debbie's Wholesale Stationery Company put into place:

1. Responsibilities and duties of employees will be divided. For example, the person receiving the cash, whether at the register or by opening the mail, will not record this information into the accounting records. The accountant, for his part, will not be handling the cash receipts.
2. All cash receipts of Debbie's Wholesale will be deposited into the bank the same day they arrive.
3. All cash payments will be made by check (except petty cash, which will be discussed later in this chapter).
4. Employees will be rotated. This allows workers to become acquainted with the work of others as well as to prepare for a possible changeover of jobs.
5. Debbie Lawrence will sign all checks after receiving authorization to pay from the departments concerned.
6. At time of payment, all supporting invoices or documents will be stamped paid. That will show when the invoice or document is paid as well as the number of the check used.
7. All checks will be prenumbered. This will control the use of checks and make it difficult to use a check fraudulently without its being revealed at some point.

Now let's look at how Debbie's Wholesale implemented these policies.

LEARNING UNIT 6-1
Bank Procedures, Checking Accounts, and Bank Reconciliations

Before Debbie's Wholesale opened on April 1, 19XX, Debbie had a meeting at Security National Bank to discuss the steps in opening up and using a checking account for the company.

OPENING A CHECKING ACCOUNT

Purpose of a signature card.

The bank manager gave Debbie a signature card to fill out. The signature card included space for signature(s), business and home addresses, references, type of account, etc. Because Debbie would be signing all of the checks for her company, she was the only employee who had to sign the card. The bank keeps the signature card in its files. When checks are presented for payment, the bank checks it to validate Debbie's signature. This helps avoid possible forgeries.

Once the account was opened, Debbie received a set of checks and **deposit tickets** that were preprinted with the business's name, address, and account number (see Fig. 6-1). Debbie's Wholesale was to use the deposit tickets when it received cash or checks from any source and deposited them into the checking account.

In a deposit ticket, check amounts are listed separately along with the code number of city and bank on which they are drawn. The code can be found in the upper right corner of a check (see Fig. 6-3 on p. 208). The top part of the fraction (53-393) is known as the *American Banker's Association Transit Number:* 53 identifies the large city or state the bank is located in; 393 identifies the bank.

The lower part of the fraction (113) is split in two; 1 represents the First Federal Reserve District; 13 is a routing number used by the Federal Reserve Bank. This is the way the code number appears on a check.

Deposit tickets usually come in duplicate. The bank keeps one copy, and the company keeps the other so it can verify that the items making up the deposit have actually been deposited correctly. The bank manager told Debbie

FIGURE 6-1 A Deposit Ticket

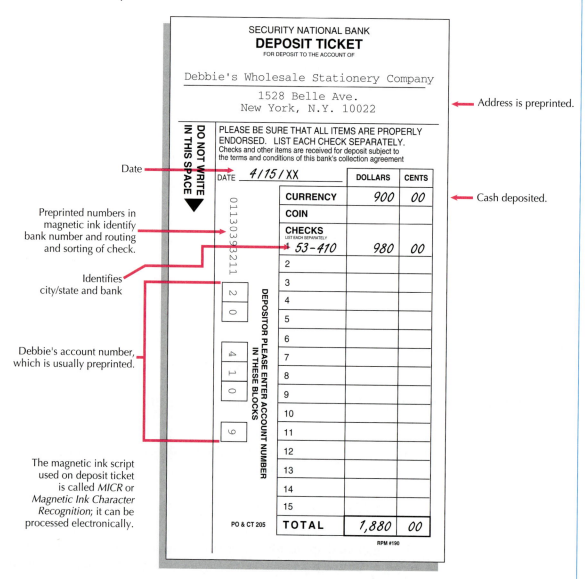

CH. 6 / BANKING PROCEDURES AND CONTROL OF CASH

that she could give the deposits to a bank teller or she could use an automated teller machine **(ATM).** The ATM could also be used for withdrawing cash, transferring funds, or paying bills.

Often, Debbie makes her deposits after business hours, when the bank is closed. When this happens, she puts the deposit into a locked bag (provided by the bank) and places the bag in the night depository. The bank will credit Debbie's account in the morning, when the deposit is processed. All payments of money are by written check (except petty cash), and all money (checks) received is deposited in the bank account.

Many checking accounts earn interest. However, for our purposes, we will assume that the checking account for Debbie's Wholesale does not pay interest. Also assume that the checking account has a monthly service charge, and that there is no individual charge for each check written.

When a bank credits your account, it is increasing the balance.

CHECK ENDORSEMENT

Checks have to be *endorsed* (signed) by the person to whom the check is made out before they can be deposited or cashed. **Endorsement** is the signing or stamping of one's name on the back left-hand side of the check.

This signature means that the drawer has transferred the right to deposit or cash the check to someone else (the bank). The bank can then collect the money from the person or company that issued the check.

Endorsements can be made by using a rubber stamp instead of a handwritten signature.

Three different types of endorsement can be used (see Fig. 6-2). The first is a **blank endorsement.** A blank endorsement does not specify that a particular person or firm must endorse it. It can be further endorsed by someone else. The bank will pay the last person who signs the check. This type of endorsement is not very safe. If the check is lost, the person who finds it can sign it and get the money.

FIGURE 6-2
Types of Check Endorsement

Types of Check Endorsement

Debbie Lawrence
204109

Blank Endorsement

A signature on the back left side of a check of the person or firm the check is payable to. This can be *further* endorsed by someone else–the bank will give the money to the last person who signs the check. This is not a very safe type of endorsement. If the check is lost, anyone who picks it up can sign it and get the money.

Pay to the order of
Security National Bank.
Debbie's Wholesale Stationery Co.
204109

Full Endorsement

This is a safer type of endorsement, since the person or company signing (or stamping) the back of the check indicates the name of the company or person to whom the check is to be paid. Only the person or company named in the endorsement can transfer the check to someone else.

Payable to the order of
Security National Bank
for deposit only.
Debbie's Wholesale Stationery Co.
204109

Restrictive Endorsement

This is the safest endorsement for businesses. Debbie's Wholesale stamps the back of the check so that it must be deposited in the firm's account. This limits any further use to the check (it can only be deposited in the specified account).

FIGURE 6-3 A Company Check

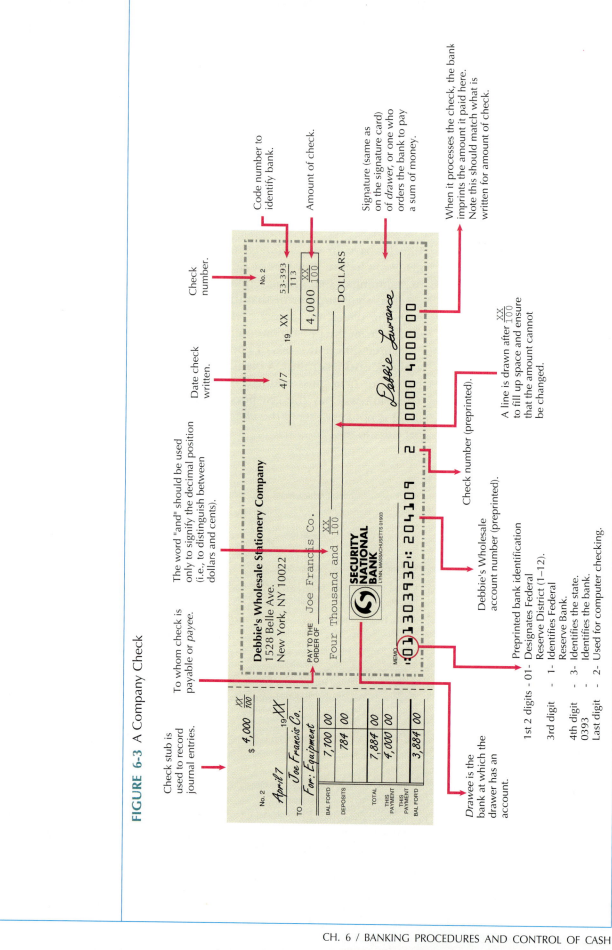

Check stub is used to record journal entries.

To whom check is payable or payee.

The word "and" should be used only to signify the decimal position (i.e., to distinguish between dollars and cents).

Check number.

Date check written.

Code number to identify bank.

Amount of check.

Signature (same as on the signature card) of *drawer*, or one who orders the bank to pay a sum of money.

When it processes the check, the bank imprints the amount it paid here. Note this should match what is written for amount of check.

A line is drawn after $\frac{XX}{100}$ to fill up space and ensure that the amount cannot be changed.

Check number (preprinted).

Check number (preprinted).

Debbie's Wholesale account number (preprinted).

Preprinted bank identification

1st 2 digits - 01- Designates Federal Reserve District (1–12).
3rd digit - 1- Identifies Federal Reserve Bank.
4th digit - 3- Identifies the state.
0393 - - Identifies the bank.
Last digit - 2- Used for computer checking.

Drawee is the bank at which the drawer has an account.

The second type of endorsement is a **full endorsement.** The person or company signing (or stamping) the back of the check indicates the name of the company or the person to whom the check is to be paid. Only the person or company named in the endorsement can transfer the check to someone else.

Restrictive endorsements are the third type of endorsement. This is the safest endorsement for businesses. Debbie's Wholesale stamps the back of the check, so that it must be deposited in the firm's account. This limits any further use of the check.

THE CHECKBOOK

When Debbie opened her business's checking account, she received checks. These checks could be used to buy things for the business or to pay bills or salaries.

A **check** is a written order signed by a **drawer** (the person who writes the check) instructing a **drawee** (the person who pays the check) to pay a specific sum of money to the **payee** (the person to whom the check is payable). Figure 6-3 (p. 208) shows a check issued by Debbie's Wholesale Stationery Company. Debbie Lawrence is the drawer; Security National Bank is the drawee; and Joe Francis Company is the payee.

Look at the check in Figure 6-3. Notice that certain things, such as the company's name and address and the check number, are preprinted. Other things you should notice are (1) the line drawn after $\frac{xx}{100}$ is to fill up the empty space and ensure that the amount cannot be changed and (2) the word "and" should be used only to differentiate between dollars and cents.

Figure 6-3 includes a check stub. The check stub is used to record transactions, and it is kept for future reference. The information found on the stub includes the beginning balance ($7,100), the amount of any deposits ($784), the total amount in the account ($7,884), the amount of the check being written ($4,000), and the ending balance ($3,884). The check stub should be filled out before the check is written.

If the written amount on the check doesn't match the amount expressed in figures, Security National Bank may either pay the amount written in words, return the check unpaid, or contact the drawer to see what was meant.

Many companies use checkwriting machines to type out the information on the check. This prevents anyone from making fraudulent changes on handwritten checks.

During the same time period, in-company records must be kept for all transactions affecting Debbie's Wholesale Stationery Company's checkbook balance. Figure 6-4 (p. 210) shows these records. Note that the bank deposits ($14,324) minus the checks written ($6,994) give an ending checkbook balance of $7,330.

MONTHLY RECORDKEEPING: THE BANK'S STATEMENT OF ACCOUNT AND IN-COMPANY RECORDS

Each month, Security National Bank will send Debbie's Wholesale Stationery Company a Statement of Account. This statement reflects all of the activity in the account during that period. It begins with the beginning balance of the account at the start of the month, along with the checks the bank has paid and any deposits received (see Fig. 6-5, p. 210). Any other charges or additions to the bank balance are indicated by codes found on the statement. All checks that have been paid by the bank are sent back to Debbie's Wholesale. These are called **cancelled checks** because they have been processed by the bank and are no longer negotiable. The ending balance in Figure 6-5 is $6,919.

BANK DEPOSITS MADE FOR APRIL

Date of Deposit	Amount	Received From
April 1	$8,000	Debbie Lawrence, Capital
4	784	Check — Hal's Clothing
16	1,880	Cash sales/Check — Bevans Company
22	1,960	Check — Roe Company
27	500	Sale of equipment
30	1,200	Cash sales

Total deposits for month: $14,324

CHECKS WRITTEN FOR MONTH OF APRIL

Date	Check No.	Payment To	Amount	Description
April 2	1	Peter Blum	$ 900	Insurance paid in advance
7	2	Joe Francis Co.	4,000	Paid equipment
9	3	Rick Flo Co.	800	Cash purchases
12	4	Thorpe Co.	594	Paid purchases
28	5	Payroll	700	Salaries

Total amount of checks written: $6,994

Cash/checks deposited	$14,324
Checks paid	− 6,994
Balance in company checkbook	$ 7,330

FIGURE 6-4
Transactions Affecting
Checkbook Balance

FIGURE 6-5 A Bank Statement

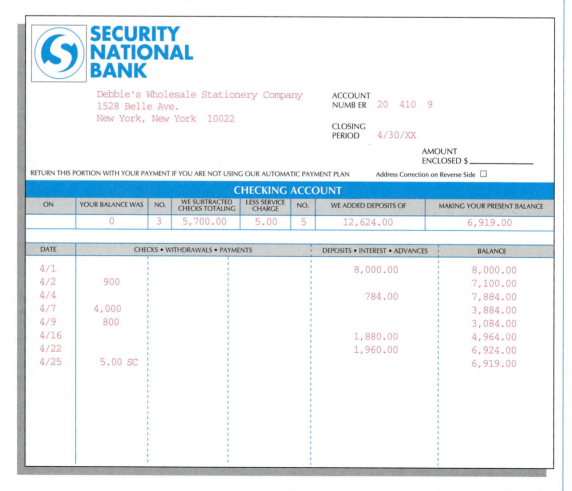

THE BANK RECONCILIATION PROCESS

The problem is that the ending bank balance of $6,919 does not agree with the amount in Debbie's checkbook, $7,330, or the balance in the cash amount in the ledger, $7,330. Such differences are caused partly by the time a bank takes to process a company's transactions. A company records a transaction when it occurs. A bank cannot record a deposit until it receives the funds, and it cannot pay a check until the check is presented by the payee. In addition, the bank statement will report fees and transactions that the company did not know about.

Debbie's accountant has to find out why there is a $411 difference between the balances and how the records can be brought into balance. The process of reconciling the bank balance on the bank statement versus the company's checkbook balance is called a **bank reconciliation.** Bank reconciliations involve several steps, including calculating the deposits in transit and the outstanding checks. The bank reconciliation usually is done on the back of the **bank statement** (see Fig. 6-6). However, it can also be done by computer software.

Deposits in Transit

In comparing the list of deposits received by the bank with the checkbook, the accountant notices that the two deposits made on April 27 and 30 for $500 and $1,200 were not on the bank's statement. The accountant realizes that in order to prepare this statement, the bank only included information about Debbie's Wholesale Stationery up to April 25. These two deposits made by Debbie were not shown on the monthly bank statement, since they arrived at the bank after the statement was printed. Thus, timing becomes a consideration in the reconciliation process. The deposits not yet added onto the bank balance are called **deposits in transit.** These two deposits need to be added to the bank balance

Deposits in transit: These un-recorded deposits could result if a deposit were placed in a night depository on the last day of the month.

Keep in mind that both the bank and the depositor can make mistakes that will not be discovered until the reconciliation process.

FIGURE 6-6
Bank Reconciliation Using Back of Bank Statement

CHECKS OUTSTANDING				
NUMBER	AMOUNT		1. Enter balance shown on this statement	6,919 00
4	594 00			
5	700 00		2. If you have made deposits since the date of this statement add them to the above balance.	1,700 00
			3. SUBTOTAL	8,619 00
			4. Deduct total of checks outstanding	1,294 00
			5. ADJUSTED BALANCE This should agree with your checkbook.	7,325 00
TOTAL OF CHECKS OUTSTANDING	1,294 00			

TO VERIFY YOUR CHECKING BALANCE
1. Sort checks by number or by date issued and compare with your check stubs and prior outstanding list. Make certain all checks paid have been recorded in your checkbook. If any of your checks were not included with this statement, list the numbers and amounts under "CHECKS OUTSTANDING".
2. Deduct the Service Charge as shown on the statement from your checkbook balance.
3. Review copies of charge advices included with this statement and check for proper entry in your checkbook.

IF THE ADJUSTED BALANCE DOES NOT AGREE WITH YOUR CHECKBOOK BALANCE, THE FOLLOWING SUGGESTIONS ARE OFFERED FOR YOUR ASSISTANCE.

- Recheck additions and subtractions in your checkbook and figures to the left.
- Make certain checkbook balances have been carried forward properly.
- Verify deposits recorded on statement against deposits entered in checkbook.
- Compare amount on each checkbook stub.

shown on the bank statement. Debbie's checkbook is not affected, since the two deposits have already been added to its balance. The bank has no way of knowing that the deposits are coming until they are received.

Outstanding Checks

The first thing the accountant does when the bank statement is received is put the checks in numerical order (1, 2, 3, etc.). In doing so, the accountant notices that two payments were not made by the bank and two checks, no. 4 and no. 5, were not returned by the bank.

Debbie's books showed that these two checks had been deducted from the checkbook balance. However, these **outstanding checks** were not yet presented to the bank for payment or deducted from the bank balance. When these checks do reach the bank, the bank will reduce the amount of the balance.

Service Charges

Debbie's accountant also notices a bank service charge of $5. This means Debbie's checkbook balance should be lowered by $5.

Nonsufficient Funds

An **NSF (nonsufficient funds)** check is a check that has been returned because the drawer did not have enough money in its account to pay the check. Accountants are continually on the lookout for NSF (nonsufficient funds) checks. If there is an NSF funds check, it means that there is less money in the checking account than was thought. Debbie's Wholesale will have to (1) lower the checkbook balance and (2) try to collect the amount from the customer. The bank would notify Debbie's Wholesale of an NSF (or other deductions) check by a **debit memorandum.** Think of a debit memorandum as a deduction from the depositor's balance.

If the bank acts as a collecting agent for Debbie's Wholesale, say in collecting notes, it will charge Debbie a small fee, and the net amount collected will be added to Debbie's bank balance. The bank will send to Debbie a **credit memorandum** verifying the increase in the depositor's balance.

A journal entry is also needed to bring the ledger accounts of cash and service charge expense up to date. Any adjustment to the checkbook balance results in a journal entry. The following entry was made to accomplish this:

April	30	Service Charge Expense			5 00		
		Cash					5 00
		Bank service charge for April					

Example of a More Comprehensive Bank Reconciliation

The bank reconciliation of Debbie's Stationery was not as complicated as it is for many other companies. Let's take a moment to look at the bank reconciliation for Monroe Company, which is based on the following:

Checkbook balance: $3,978.

Balance reported by bank: $5,230.

Recorded in journal check no. 108 for $54 *more* than amount of check when store equipment was purchased.

Bank collected a note ($2,000) for Monroe, charging a collection fee of $10.

Margin notes

Checks #4 and #5 are outstanding.

Checks outstanding are checks drawn by the depositor but not yet presented to the bank for payment by the payee.

Debit memorandum:
Deducted from balance

Credit memorandum:
Addition to balance

Adjustments to the checkbook balance must be journalized and posted. This keeps the depositor's ledger accounts (especially cash) up to date.
This charge could be recorded as a miscellaneous expense.

A bounced check for $252 (NSF) has to be covered by Monroe. The bank has lowered Monroe's balance by $252 (see Fig. 6-7 on p. 214).

Bank service charge of $10.

Deposits in transit, $1,084.

Checks not yet processed by the bank:

Check	Amount
191	$204
198	250
201	100

MONROE COMPANY
BANK RECONCILIATION AS OF JUNE 30, 19XX

Checkbook Balance			Balance per Bank	
Checkbook Balance		$3,978	Bank Statement Balance	$5,230
Add:			Add:	
Error in recording			Deposits in Transit	1,084
Check no. 108	$54			$6,314
Proceeds of a note*				
less collection				
charge by bank	1,990	2,044	Deduct:	
		$6,022	Check no. 191..$204	
			198.. 250	
Deduct:			201.. 100	554
NSF Check	$252			
Bank Service				
Charge	10	262		
Reconciled Balance		$5,760	Reconciled Balance	$5,760

Note that every time an adjustment is made in the reconciliation process to the checkbook balance, a journal entry is needed. Monroe Company has to make the following journal entries:

Date		Account Title and Description	PR	Dr.	Cr.
19XX June	30	Cash		1990 00	
		Collection Expense		10 00	
		Notes Receivable*			2000 00
		Note collected			
	30	Cash		54 00	
		Store Equipment			54 00
		Error recording check no. 108			
	30	Accounts Receivable		252 00	
		Cash			252 00
		Alvin Sooth NSF check			
	30	Miscellaneous Expense		10 00	
		Cash			10 00
		Bank service charge			

* We will discuss Notes Receivable in a later chapter—for now, think of it as a kind of written Accounts Receivable.

Debit:	Monroe Co. 170 Roe Rd. Dallas, TX 75208	Valley Bank
2/4–10–60811		Date: 6/30/XX
NSF Check – Alvin Sooth		$252.00
		Approved JS

FIGURE 6-7
Sample Debit Memorandum

TRENDS IN BANKING

Electronic Funds Transfer

Banking services on the Internet was cleared by U.S. regulators in 1995. Today banking by computer continues to expand.

Many financial institutions have developed or are developing ways to transfer funds electronically, without the use of paper checks. Such systems are called **electronic funds transfers (EFT).** Most EFTs are established to save money and avoid theft.

Automatic payroll deposits are an example of an EFT. This is how it works: The company asks its employees if they would like their paychecks deposited automatically into their checking accounts. Employees who agree to do this are asked to sign an authorization form. The bank, on receiving computer-coded payroll data, adds each worker's payroll amount to his or her checking account. Employees who do not sign the authorization continue to get paper checks that they must cash themselves.

Another good example is the automatic teller machine (ATM). In some states, ATMs now issue postage stamps, railroad tickets, and grocery coupons. **Debit cards** are still another example of an EFT. If a customer buys a service or a product with a debit card, the amount of the purchase is deducted directly from the customer's bank account.

Check Truncation (Safekeeping)

Some banks do not return cancelled checks to the depositor but use a procedure called **check truncation** or **safekeeping.** What this means is that the bank holds a cancelled check for a specific period of time (usually 90 days) and then keeps a microfilm copy handy and the original check is destroyed. In Texas, for example, some credit unions and savings and loan institutions do not send back checks. Instead, the check date, number, and amount are listed on the bank statement. If the customer needs a copy of a check, the bank will provide the check or a photocopy for a small fee. (Photocopies are accepted as evidence in Internal Revenue Service tax returns and audits.)

Truncation cuts down on the amount of "paper" that is returned to customers and thus provides substantial cost savings. It is estimated that over 60 million checks are written each day in the United States.

LEARNING UNIT 6-1 REVIEW

AT THIS POINT you should be able to

◆ Define and explain the need for deposit tickets. (p. 206)
◆ Explain where the American Bankers' Association transit number is located on the check and what its purpose is. (p. 206)

- List as well as compare and contrast the three common types of check endorsement. (p. 207)
- Explain the structure of a check. (p. 208)
- Define and state the purpose of a bank statement. (p. 210)
- Explain deposits in transit, checks outstanding, service charge, and NSF. (p. 217)
- Explain the difference between a debit memorandum and a credit memorandum. (p. 212)
- Explain how to do a bank reconciliation. (p. 213)
- Explain electronic funds transfer and check truncation. (p. 214)

SELF-REVIEW QUIZ 6-1

(The blank forms you need are on page 201 of the *Study Guide and Working Papers.*)

Indicate, by placing an X under it, the heading that describes the appropriate action for each of the following situations:

Situation	Add to Bank Balance	Deduct from Bank Balance	Add to Checkbook Balance	Deduct from Checkbook Balance
1. Bank service charge				
2. Deposits in transit				
3. NSF check				
4. A $50 check was written and recorded by the company as $60				
5. Proceeds of a note collected by the bank				
6. Check outstanding				

Solution to Self-Review Quiz 6-1

Situation	Add to Bank Balance	Deduct from Bank Balance	Add to Checkbook Balance	Deduct from Checkbook Balance
1				X
2	X			
3				X
4			X	
5			X	
6		X		

Quiz Tip: Deposits in transit are added to the bank balance while checks outstanding are subtracted from the bank balance.

LEARNING UNIT 6-2
The Establishment of Petty Cash and Change Funds

Petty Cash is an asset on the balance sheet.

Debbie realized how time-consuming and expensive it would be to write checks for small amounts to pay for postage, small supplies, etc., so she set up a **petty cash fund.** Similarly, she established a *change fund* to make cash transactions more convenient. This unit will explain how to manage petty cash and change funds.

SETTING UP THE PETTY CASH FUND

The *petty cash fund* is an account dedicated to paying small day-to-day expenses. These petty cash expenses are recorded in an auxiliary record and later summarized, journalized, and posted. Debbie estimated that the company would need a fund of $60 to cover small expenditures during the month of May. This petty cash was not expected to last longer than one month. She gave one of her employees responsibility for overseeing the fund. This person is called the *custodian.*

The check for $60 is drawn to the order of the custodian, cashed, and the proceeds turned over to John Sullivan, the custodian.

Debbie named her office manager, John Sullivan, as custodian. In other companies the cashier or secretary may be in charge of petty cash. Check no. 6 was drawn to the order of the custodian and cashed to establish the fund. John keeps the petty cash fund in a small tin box in the office safe.

Shown here is the transaction analysis chart for the establishment of a $60 petty cash fund, which would be journalized on May 1, 19XX as follows:

Petty Cash is an asset, which is established by writing a new check. The Petty Cash account is debited only once unless a greater or lesser amount of petty cash is needed on a regular basis.

Accounts Affected	Category	↑ ↓	Rules
Petty Cash	Asset	↑	Dr.
Cash (checks)	Asset	↓	Cr.

GENERAL JOURNAL					Page 1	
Date		Account Title and Description	PR	Dr.	Cr.	
19XX May	1	Petty Cash		60 00		
		Cash			60 00	
		Establishment				

Note the new asset called *Petty Cash,* which was created by writing check no. 6, reduced the asset Cash. In reality, the total assets stay the same; what has occurred is a shift from the asset Cash (check no. 6) to a new asset account called Petty Cash.

The Petty Cash account is not debited or credited again if the size of the fund is not changed. If the $60 fund is used up quickly, the fund should be increased. If the fund is too large, the Petty Cash account should be reduced. We will take a closer look at this when we discuss replenishment of petty cash.

MAKING PAYMENTS FROM THE PETTY CASH FUND

John Sullivan has the responsibility for filling out a **petty cash voucher** for each cash payment made from the petty cash fund. The petty cash vouchers are numbered in sequence.

FIGURE 6-8
Petty Cash Voucher

Petty Cash Voucher No. 1

Date: May 2, 19XX   Amount: $3.00
Paid To: Al's Cleaning
For: Cleaning

                                    Approved By: John Sullivan

                                    Payment Received By: Debbie Lawrence

Debit Account No.: 619

Note that when the voucher (shown in Fig. 6-8) is completed, it will include:

◆ The voucher number (which will be in sequence)
◆ The date
◆ The person or organization to whom the payment was made
◆ The amount of payment
◆ The reason for payment: cleaning
◆ The signature of the person who approved the payment
◆ The signature of the person who received the payment from petty cash
◆ The account to which the expense will be charged.

The completed vouchers are placed in the petty cash box. No matter how many vouchers John Sullivan fills out, *the total of (1) the vouchers in the box and (2) the cash on hand should equal the original amount of petty cash with which the fund was established ($60).*

Assume that at the end of May the following items are documented by petty cash vouchers in the petty cash box as having been paid by John Sullivan:

19XX
May   2 Cleaning package, $3.00
         5 Postage stamps, $9.00
         8 First-aid supplies, $15.00
         9 Delivery expense, $6.00
        14 Delivery expense, $15.00
        27 Postage stamps, $6.00

John records this information in the **auxiliary petty cash record** shown in Figure 6-9 (p. 218). It is not a required record but an aid to John—an auxiliary record that is not essential but is quite helpful as part of the petty cash system. You may want to think of the auxiliary petty cash record as an optional worksheet. Let's look at how to replenish the petty cash fund.

HOW TO REPLENISH THE PETTY CASH FUND

No postings are done from the auxiliary book because it is not a journal. At some point the summarized information found in the auxiliary petty cash record is used as a basis for a journal entry in the general journal and eventually posted to appropriate ledger accounts to reflect up-to-date balances.

This $54 of expenses (see Figure 6-9) is recorded in the general journal (Fig. 6-10 on p. 219) and a new check, no. 17, for $54 is cashed and returned to John Sullivan. In replenishment, old expenses are updated in journal and ledger to show where money has gone. Auxiliary before replenishment. The petty cash box now once again reflects $60 cash. The old vouchers that were used are stamped to indicate that they have been processed and the fund replenished.

A new check is written in the replenishment process, which is payable to the custodian, cashed by Sullivan, and the cash placed in the petty cash box.

Date	Voucher No.	Description	Receipts	Payments	Postage Expense	Delivery Expense	Sundry Account	Sundry Amount
							Category of Payments	
19XX May 1		Establishment	60 00					
2	1	Cleaning		3 00			Cleaning	3 00
5	2	Postage		9 00	9 00			
8	3	First Aid		15 00			Misc.	15 00
9	4	Delivery		6 00		6 00		
14	5	Delivery		15 00		15 00		
27	6	Postage		6 00	6 00			
		Total	60 00	54 00	15 00	21 00		18 00

FIGURE 6-9 Auxiliary Petty Cash Record

Note that in the replenishment process the debits are a summary of the totals (except sundry, since individual items are different) of expenses or other items from the auxiliary petty cash record. Posting of these specific expenses will assure that the expenses will not be understated on the income statement. The credit to cash allows us to draw a check for $54 to put money back in the petty cash box. The $60 in the box now agrees with the petty cash account balance. The end result is that our petty cash box is filled, and we have justified which accounts the petty cash money was spent for. Think of replenishment as a single, summarizing entry.

Remember, if at some point the petty cash fund is to be greater than $60, a check can be written that will increase Petty Cash and decrease Cash. If the Petty Cash account balance is to be reduced, we can credit or reduce Petty Cash. But for our present purpose Petty Cash will remain at $60.

The auxiliary petty cash record after replenishment would look as follows (keep in mind no postings are made from the auxiliary):

AUXILIARY PETTY CASH RECORD

Date	Voucher No.	Description	Receipts	Payments	Postage Expense	Delivery Expense	Sundry Account	Sundry Amount
							Category of Payments	
19XX May 1		Establishment	60 00					
2	1	Cleaning		3 00			Cleaning	3 00
5	2	Postage		9 00	9 00			
8	3	First Aid		15 00			Misc.	15 00
9	4	Delivery		6 00		6 00		
14	5	Delivery		15 00		15 00		
27	6	Postage		6 00	6 00			
		Total	60 00	54 00	15 00	21 00		18 00
		Ending Balance		6 00				
			60 00	60 00				
		Ending Balance	6 00					
31		Replenishment	54 00					
31		Balance (New)	60 00					

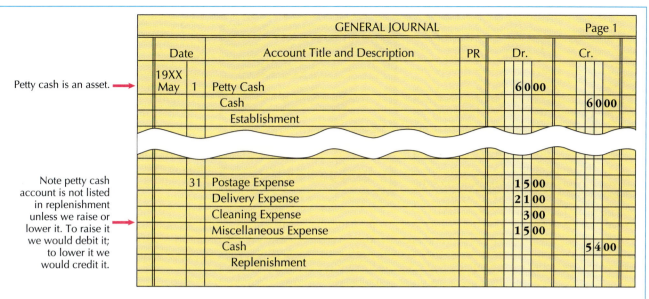

	Date		Account Title and Description	PR	Dr.	Cr.
	19XX May	1	Petty Cash		6 0 00	
			Cash			6 0 00
			Establishment			
		31	Postage Expense		1 5 00	
			Delivery Expense		2 1 00	
			Cleaning Expense		3 00	
			Miscellaneous Expense		1 5 00	
			Cash			5 4 00
			Replenishment			

Petty cash is an asset. →

Note petty cash account is not listed in replenishment unless we raise or lower it. To raise it we would debit it; to lower it we would credit it. →

FIGURE 6-10 Establishment and Replenishment of Petty Cash Fund

Figure 6-11, below, may help you put the sequence together.

Before concluding this unit, let's look at how Debbie will handle setting up a change fund and problems with cash shortages and overages.

SETTING UP A CHANGE FUND AND INSIGHT INTO CASH SHORT AND OVER

If a company like Debbie's Stationery expects to have many cash transactions occurring, it may be a good idea to establish a **change fund.** This is a fund that is placed in the cash register drawer and used to make change for customers who pay cash. Debbie decides to put $120 in the change fund, made up of various denominations of bills and coins. Let's look at a transaction analysis chart and the journal entry (on p. 220) for this sort of procedure.

FIGURE 6-11 Which transactions involve petty cash and how to record them.

Date		Description	New Check Written	Petty Cash Voucher Prepared	Recorded in Auxiliary Petty Cash Record	
19XX Jan.	1	Establishment of petty cash for $60	X		X	Dr. petty cash / Cr. cash
	2	Paid salaries, $2,000	X			
	10	Paid $10 from petty cash for Band-Aids		X	X	No journal entries
	19	Paid $8 from petty cash for postage		X	X	
	24	Paid light bill, $200	X			
	29	Replenishment of petty cash to $60	X		X	Dr. individual expenses / Cr. cash

Has nothing to do with petty cash (amounts too great). →

In this step the old expenses are listed in general journal and a new check is written to → replenish. All old vouchers removed from petty cash box.

Dunkin' Donuts is urging its shop owners to get rid of their cash registers and switch to a new IBM point-of-sale terminal. With these new machines, clerks just use a touch screen to punch in the number and type of items bought. This is faster than using the old cash registers and easier to learn. Training staff to handle cash is a critical component of a cash business like Dunkin' Donuts. Every sale must be recorded—and recorded correctly. Cash control is built into the new IBM system, which also provides the owners with information that will help them spot problems and track trends.

Fred was pleased when he heard about the new system at the company's annual convention in Orlando, Florida. Register training was a recurring problem for him and for most store owners. Now the terminals in the store would be easier to learn. They are linked, so he would be able to see consolidated data quickly. But the chore of closing out the cash drawer at the end of a shift remained. And it was still a critical control point.

"I gotta remember that," said Fred, thinking back to the convention, "when I explain how to close out her cash register drawer to Sally again. Even though she messes up my Cash Summary almost every day, getting

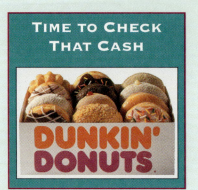

TIME TO CHECK THAT CASH

mad sure hasn't helped. Maybe if I go through it with her step-by-step." Fred had spent hours figuring out a discrepancy between the cash in the drawer and the register tape. Sally had forgotten to void a mistaken entry for $99.99. Fred had first suspected that Sally had made a huge error in counting change.

Nodding happily to himself, Fred treated himself to one of his glazed donuts. Doing the daily Cash Summary normally gave Fred a sense of accomplishment (when Sally wasn't working). And the monthly chore of reconciling the shop's bank account had been no problem. The cash on the monthly financials that he submitted to Dwayne were right on the money.

DISCUSSION QUESTIONS

1. How would Fred catch a discrepancy in the cash account?
2. How would Fred record a loss?
3. Why is cash register training so important to a service business like Fred's?
4. Why does Dunkin' Donuts invest time, money, and effort in investigating new cash handling systems like the IBM point-of-sale terminals?

Accounts Affected	Category	↑	↓	Dr./Cr.
Change Fund	Asset	↑		Dr.
Cash	Asset		↓	Cr.

April	1	Change Fund		1 2 0 00	
		Cash			1 2 0 00
		Establish change fund			

At the close of the business day Debbie will place the amount of the change fund back in the safe in the office. She will set up the change fund (the same $120) in the appropriate denominations for the next business day. She will deposit in the bank the *remainder* of the cash taken in for the day.

Now, in the next section, we'll look at how to record errors that are made in making change, called **cash short and over.**

Cash Short and Over

In a local pizza shop the total sales for the day did not match the amount of cash on hand. Errors often happen in making change. To record and summarize the differences in cash, an account called *cash short and over* is used. This account will record both overages (too much money) and shortages (not enough money). Lets first look at the account (in T account form).

Beg. change fund
+ Cash register total
= Cash should have on hand
− Counted cash
= Shortage or overage of cash

Cash Short and Over

Dr.	Cr.
shortage	overage

All shortages will be recorded as debits and all overages will be recorded as credits. This account is temporary. If the ending balance of the account is a debit (a shortage) it is considered a miscellaneous expense that would be reported on the income statement. If the balance of the account is a credit (an overage) it is considered as other income reported on the income statement. Let's look at how the cash short and over account could be used to record shortages or overages in sales as well as in the petty cash process.

Example 1: Shortages and Overages in Sales:

Dec. 5 pizza shop rang up sales of $560 for the day but only had $530 in cash.

Accounts Affected	Category	↑ ↓	Dr./Cr.
Cash	Asset	↑	Debit $530
Cash Short and Over	Misc. Exp.	↑	Debit $30
Sales	Revenue	↑	Credit $560

The journal entry would look as follows:

Dec	5	Cash		5 3 0 00	
		Cash Short and Over		3 0 00	
		Sales			5 6 0 00
		Cash shortage			

Note the shortage $30 is a debit and would be recorded on the income statement as a miscellaneous expense.

What would the entry look like if the pizza shop showed a $50 overage?

Accounts Affected	Category	↑ ↓	Dr./Cr.
Cash	Asset	↑	Debit $610
Cash Short and Over	Other Income	↑	Credit $50
Sales	Revenue	↑	Credit $560

The journal entry would be as follows:

Dec	5	Cash		6 1 0	
		Cash Short and Over			5 0 00
		Sales			5 6 0 00
		Cash shortage			

Note the cash short and over account would be reported as other income on the income statement. Now let's look at how to use this cash short and over account to record petty cash transactions.

Example 2: Cash Short and Over in Petty Cash

A local computer company had established petty cash for $200. Today, November 30, the petty cash box had $160 in vouchers as well as $32 in coin and currency. What would be the journal entry to replenish petty cash? Assume the vouchers were made up of $90 for postage and $70 for supplies expense.

If you add up the vouchers and cash in the box, cash is short by $8.

Accounts Affected	Category	↑	↓	Dr./Cr.
Postage Expense	Expense	↑		Debit $90
Supplies Expense	Expense	↑		Debit $70
Cash Short and Over	Misc. Expense	↑		Debit $8
Cash	Asset		↓	Credit $168

The journal entry is as follows:

Nov	8	Postage Expense			9 0 00					
		Supplies Expense			7 0 00					
		Cash Short and Over			8 00					
		Cash						1 6 8 00		

If there had been an overage, the cash short and over would be a credit as other income. Note in Self-Review Quiz 6-2 the Solution shows how a fund shortage would be recorded in the auxiliary record.

LEARNING UNIT 6-2 REVIEW

AT THIS POINT you should be able to

- ◆ State the purpose of a petty cash fund. (p. 216)
- ◆ Prepare a journal entry to establish a petty cash fund. (p.216)
- ◆ Prepare a petty cash voucher. (p. 217)
- ◆ Explain the relationship of the auxiliary petty cash record to the petty cash process. (p. 217)
- ◆ Prepare a journal entry to replenish Petty Cash to its original amount. (p. 218)
- ◆ Explain why individual expenses are debited in the replenishment process. (p. 218)
- ◆ Explain how a change fund is established. (p. 220)
- ◆ Explain how Cash Short and Over could be a miscellaneous expense. (p.221)

SELF-REVIEW QUIZ 6-2

(The blank forms you need are on pages 201–202 of the *Study Guide and Working Papers*.)

As the custodian of the petty cash fund it is your task to prepare entries to establish the fund on October 1, as well as to replenish the fund on October 31. Please keep an auxiliary petty cash record.

19XX
Oct. 1 Establish petty cash fund for $90, check no. 8.
      5 Voucher 11, delivery expense, $21.
      9 Voucher 12, delivery expense, $15.
     10 Voucher 13, office repair expense, $24.
     17 Voucher 14, general expense, $12.
     30 Replenishment of petty cash fund, $78, check no. 108. (Check would be payable to the custodian.)

Solution to Self-Review Quiz 6-2

GENERAL JOURNAL					Page 6	
Date		Account Title and Description	PR	Dr.	Cr.	
19XX Oct.	1	Petty Cash		90 00		
		Cash			90 00	
		Establishment, Check 8				
	31	Delivery Expense		36 00		
		General Expense		12 00		
		Office Repair Expense		24 00		
		Cash Short and Over		6 00		
		Cash			78 00	
		Replenishment, Check 108				

AUXILIARY PETTY CASH RECORD

Date		Voucher No.	Description	Receipts	Payments	Delivery Expense	General Expense	Sundry Account	Amount
19XX Oct.	1		Establishment	90 00					
	5	11	Delivery		21 00	21 00			
	9	12	Delivery		15 00	15 00			
	10	13	Repairs		24 00			Office Repair	24 00
	17	14	General		12 00		12 00		
	25		Fund Shortage		6 00			Cash Short and Over	6 00
			Totals	90 00	78 00	36 00	12 00		30 00
			Ending Balance		12 00				
					90 00				
	30		Ending Balance	12 00					
	31		Replenishment	78 00					
Nov.	1		New Balance	90 00					

Quiz Tip:

How to calculate shortage:

$21 + $15 + $24 + $12 = $72 of vouchers

Replenished with $78 check. Thus there was a $6 shortage.

Note how cash short and over was entered in the auxiliary petty cash record.

Summary of key points

Learning Unit 6-1

1. Restrictive endorsement limits any further negotiation of a check.
2. Check stubs are filled out before a check is written.
3. The payee is the person the check is payable to. The drawer is the one who orders the bank to pay a sum of money. The drawee is the bank that the drawer has an account with.
4. The process of reconciling the bank balance with the company's balance is called the bank reconciliation. The timing of deposits, when the bank statement was issued, etc., often results in differences between the bank balance and the checkbook balance.
5. Deposits in transit are added to the bank balance.
6. Checks outstanding are subtracted from the bank balance.
7. NSF means that a check has insufficient funds to be credited (deposited) to a checking account; therefore, the amount is not included in the bank balance and thus the checking account balance is lowered.
8. When a bank debits your account they are deducting an amount from your balance. A credit to the account is an increase to your balance.
9. All adjustments to the checkbook balance require journal entries.

Learning Unit 6-2

1. Petty Cash is an asset found on the balance sheet.
2. The auxiliary petty cash record is an auxiliary book; thus no postings are done from this book. Think of it as an optional worksheet.
3. When a petty cash fund is established, the amount is entered as a debit to Petty Cash and a credit to Cash.
4. At time of replenishment of the petty cash fund, all expenses are debited (by category) and a credit to Cash (a new check) results. This replenishment, when journalized and posted, updates the ledger from the journal.
5. The only time the Petty Cash account is used is to establish the fund to begin with or bring the fund to a higher or lower level. If the petty cash level is deemed sufficient, all replenishments will debit specific expenses and credit cash (new check written). The asset Petty Cash account balance will remain unchanged.
6. A change fund is an asset that is used to make change for customers.
7. Cash Short and Over is an account that is either a miscellaneous expense or miscellaneous income, depending on whether the ending balance is shortage or overage.

KEY TERMS

ATM Automatic teller machine.

Auxiliary petty cash record A supplementary record for summarizing petty cash information.

Bank reconciliation This is the process of reconciling the checkbook balance with the bank balance given on the bank statement.

Bank statement A report sent by a bank to a customer indicating the previous balance, individual checks processed, individual deposits received, service charges, and ending bank balance.

Cancelled check A check that has been processed by a bank and is no longer negotiable.

Cash Short and Over The account that records cash shortages and overages. If ending balance is a debit, it is recorded on the income statement as a miscellaneous expense; if it is a credit, it is recorded as miscellaneous income.

Change fund Fund made up of various denominations that are used to make change for customers.

Check A form used to indicate a specific amount of money that is to be paid by the bank to a named person or company.

Check truncation (safekeeping) Procedure whereby checks are not returned to drawer with the bank statement but are instead kept at the bank for a certain amount of time before being first transferred to microfilm and then destroyed.

Credit memorandum Increase in depositor's balance.

Debit card A card similar to a credit card, except that the amount of a purchase is deducted directly from the customer's bank account.

Debit memorandum Decrease in depositor's balance.

Deposits in transit Deposits that were made by customers of a bank but did not reach, or were not processed by, the bank before the preparation of the bank statement.

Deposit ticket A form provided by a bank for use in depositing money or checks into a checking account.

Drawee Bank that drawer has an account with.

Drawer Person who writes a check.

Endorsement *Blank* — could be further endorsed. *Full* — restricts further endorsement to only the person or company named. *Restrictive* — restricts any further endorsement.

EFT (electronic funds transfer) An electronic system that transfers funds without use of paper checks.

Internal control A system of procedures and methods to control a firm's assets as well as monitor its operations.

NSF (nonsufficient funds) Notation indicating that a check has been written on an account that lacks sufficient funds to back it up.

Outstanding checks Checks written by a company or person that were not received or not processed by the bank before the preparation of the bank statement.

Payee The person or company the check is payable to.

Petty cash fund Fund (source) that allows payment of small amounts without the writing of checks.

Petty cash voucher A petty cash form to be completed when money is taken out of petty cash.

BLUEPRINT OF A BANK RECONCILIATION

Checkbook Balance		Balance Per Bank	
Ending Balance per Books	$XXX	Ending Bank Statement Balance (last figure on bank statement)	$XXX
Add:		Add:	
Recording of errors that understate balance	$XXX	Deposits in transit (amount not yet credited by bank)	$XXX
Proceeds of notes collected by bank or other items credited (added) by bank but not yet updated in checkbook	XXX	Bank errors	XXX
	XXX		XXX

(Cont. on page 226)

Deduct:		Deduct:		
Recording of errors that over-state balance	XXX	List of outstand-ing checks (amount not yet debited by bank)	XXX	
Service charges	XXX			
Printing charges	XXX	Bank errors	XXX	
NSF, check, etc., or other items debited (charged) by bank but not yet updated in checkbook	XXX			XXX
	XXX			
Reconciled Balance (Adjusted Balance)	$XXX	Reconciled Balance (Adjusted Balance)		$XXX

QUESTIONS, MINI EXERCISES, EXERCISES, AND PROBLEMS

Discussion Questions

1. What is the purpose of internal control?
2. What is the advantage of having preprinted deposit tickets?
3. Explain the difference between a blank endorsement and a restrictive endorsement.
4. Explain the difference between payee, drawer, and drawee.
5. Why should check stubs be filled out first, before the check itself is written?
6. A bank statement is sent twice a month. True or false? Please explain.
7. Explain the end product of a bank reconciliation.
8. Why are checks outstanding subtracted from the bank balance?
9. An NSF results in a bank issuing the depositor a credit memorandum. Agree or disagree. Please support your response.
10. Why do adjustments to the checkbook balance in the reconciliation process need to be journalized?
11. What is EFT?
12. What is meant by check truncation or safekeeping?
13. Petty cash is a liability. Accept or reject. Explain.
14. Explain the relationship of the auxiliary petty cash record to the recording of the cash payment.
15. At time of replenishment, why are the totals of individual expenses debited?
16. Explain the purpose of a change fund.
17. Explain how Cash Short and Over can be a miscellaneous expense.

Mini Exercises

(The blank forms you need are on page 204 in the *Study Guide and Working Papers*.)

Bank Reconciliation

1. Indicate what effect each situation will have on the bank reconciliation process:

   1. Add to bank balance
   2. Deduct from bank balance
   3. Add to checkbook balance
   4. Deduct from checkbook balance

   _____ a. $5 bank service charge
   _____ b. $100 deposit in transit
   _____ c. $30 NSF check
   _____ d. A $15 check was written and recorded as $25
   _____ e. Bank collected a $1,000 note less $50 collection fee
   _____ f. Check no. 111 was outstanding for $55

Journal Entries in Reconciliation Process

2. Which of the transactions in Mini Exercise 1 would require a journal entry?

Bank Reconciliation

3. From the following, construct a bank reconciliation for Woody Co. as of May 31, 19XX.

Checkbook balance	$10
Bank statement balance	15
Deposits in transit	5
Outstanding checks	15
Bank service charge	5

Petty Cash

4. Indicate what effect each situation will have:

   1. New check written
   2. Recorded in general journal
   3. Petty cash voucher prepared
   4. Recorded in auxiliary petty cash record

   _____ a. Established petty cash   _____ d. Paid $3.00 for stamps from petty cash
   _____ b. Paid $1,000 bill
   _____ c. Paid $2 for band-aids   _____ e. Paid electric bill, $250
           from petty cash   _____ f. Replenished petty cash

Replenishment of Petty Cash

5. Petty cash was originally established for $20. During the month $5 was paid out for band-aids and $6 for stamps. During replenishment custodian discovered balance in petty cash was $8. Record using a general journal entry the replenishment of petty cash back to $20.

Increasing Petty Cash

6. In Mini Exercise 5, if the custodian decided to raise the level of petty cash to $30, what would be the journal entry to replenish (use a general journal entry)?

Exercises

(The blank forms you need are on pages 205–206 of the *Study Guide and Working Papers.*)

Bank reconciliation.

6-1. From the following information, construct a bank reconciliation for Norry Co. as of July 31, 19XX. Then prepare journal entries if needed.

Checkbook balance	$420	Outstanding checks	95
Bank statement balance	300	Bank service charge	15
Deposits (in transit)	200	(debit memo)	

Establishing and replenishing petty cash.

6-2. In general journal form, prepare journal entries to establish a petty cash fund on July 1 and replenish it on July 31.

19XX
July   1   A $40 petty cash fund is established.
        31   At end of month $12 cash plus the following paid vouchers exist: donations expense, $10; postage expense, $7; office supplies expense, $7; miscellaneous expense, $4.

Cash shortage in replenishment.

6-3. If in Exercise 6-2 cash on hand is $11, prepare the entry to replenish the petty cash on July 31.

Cash overage in replenishment.

6-4. If in Exercise 6-2 cash on hand is $13, prepare the entry to replenish the petty cash on July 31.

Calculate cash shortage with Change Fund.

6-5. At the end of the day the clerk for Pete's Variety Shop noticed an error in the amount of cash he should have. Total cash sales from the sales tape were $1,100 while the total cash in the register was $1,056. Pete keeps a $30 change fund in his shop. Prepare an appropriate general journal entry to record the cash sale as well as reveal the cash shortage.

Group A Problems

(The blank forms you need are on pages 207–214 of the *Study Guide and Working Papers.*)

Preparing a bank reconciliation including collection of a note.

Check Figure:
Reconciled Balance $6,460

6A-1. Rose Company received a bank statement from Macy Bank indicating a bank balance of $6,950. Based on Rose's check stubs, the ending checkbook balance was $5,825. Your task is to prepare a bank reconciliation for Rose Company as of July 31, 19XX, from the following information (journalize entries as needed):
   a. Checks outstanding: no. 124, $600; no. 126, $850
   b. Deposits in transit, $960
   c. Bank service charge, $18
   d. Macy Bank collected a note for Rose, $660, less a $7 collection fee.

Preparing a bank reconciliation with NSF using back side of a bank statement.

Check Figure:
Reconciled Balance $6,270

6A-2. From the bank statement on page 229, please (1) complete the bank reconciliation for Rick's Deli found on the reverse of the bank statement, and (2) journalize the appropriate entries as needed.
   a. A deposit of $3,000 is in transit.
   b. Rick's Deli has an ending checkbook balance of $6,600.
   c. Checks outstanding: no. 111, $600; no. 119, $1,200; no. 121, $330
   d. Jim Rice's check for $300 bounced due to lack of sufficient funds.

Establishment and replenishment of petty cash.

Check Figure:
Cash Replenishment $36

6A-3. The following transactions occurred in April for Merry Co.:

19XX
April   1   Issued check no. 14 for $80 to establish a petty cash fund.
       5   Paid $5 from petty cash for postage, voucher no. 1.
       8   Paid $10 from petty cash for office supplies, voucher no. 2.

(For Problem 6A-2)

JAMES NATIONAL BANK
RIO MEAN BRAND
BUGNA, TEXAS

RICK'S DELI
8811 2ND ST.
BUGNA, TEXAS

Old Balance	Checks in Order of Payment		Deposits	Date	New Balance
6,000				2/2	6,000
	90.00	210.00		2/3	5,700
	150.00		300.00	2/10	5,850
	600.00		600.00	2/15	5,850
	300.00	NSF	300.00	2/20	5,850
	1,200.00		1,200.00	2/24	5,850
	600.00	30.00 SC	180.00	2/28	5,400

15 Issued check no. 15 to Reliable Corp. for $200 from past purchases on account.

17 Paid $8 from petty cash for office supplies, voucher no. 3.

20 Issued check no. 16 to Roger Corp., $600 from past purchases on account.

24 Paid $4 from petty cash for postage, voucher no. 4.

26 Paid $9 from petty cash for local church donation, voucher no. 5 (this is a miscellaneous payment).

28 Issued check no. 17 to Roy Kloon to pay for office equipment, $700.

30 Replenish petty cash, check no. 18.

Your task is to

1. Record the appropriate entries in the general journal as well as the auxiliary petty cash record as needed.

2. Be sure to replenish the petty cash fund on April 30 (check no. 18).

Establishing and replenishing petty cash including a cash shortage.

6A-4. From the following, record the transactions into Logan's auxiliary petty cash record and general journal (p. 2) as needed:

19XX
Oct.

1 A check was drawn (no. 444) payable to Roberta Floss, petty cashier, to establish a $100 petty cash fund.

5 Paid $14 for postage stamps, voucher no. 1.

9 Paid $12 for delivery charges on goods for resale, voucher no. 2.

12 Paid $8 for donation to a church (Miscellaneous Expense), voucher no. 3.

14 Paid $9 for postage stamps, voucher no. 4.

17 Paid $8 for delivery charges on goods for resale, voucher no. 5.

27 Purchased computer supplies from petty cash for $8, voucher no. 6.

28 Paid $4 for postage, voucher no. 7.

29 Drew check no. 618 to replenish petty cash and a $3 shortage.

Check Figure:

Cash Replenishment $66

Group B Problems

(The blank forms you need are on pages 207–214 of the *Study Guide and Working Papers*.)

Preparing a bank reconciliation including collection of a note.

6B-1. As the bookkeeper of Rose Company you received the bank statement from Macy Bank indicating a balance of $9,185. The ending checkbook balance was $8,215. Prepare the bank reconciliation for Rose Company as of July 31, 19XX, and prepare journal entries as needed based on the following:

Check Figure:

Reconciled Balance $10,940

a. Deposits in transit, $3,600

b. Bank service charges, $29

c. Checks outstanding: no. 111, $590; no. 115, $1,255

d. Macy Bank collected a note for Rose, $2,760, less a $6 collection fee.

Preparing a bank reconciliation with NSF using back side of a bank statement.

Check Figure:

Reconciled Balance $756

6B-2. Based on the following, please (1) complete the bank reconciliation for Rick's Deli found on the reverse of the bank statement below, and (2) journalize the appropriate entries as needed.

a. Checks outstanding: no. 110, $80; no. 116, $160; no. 118, $52.

b. A deposit of $416 is in transit.

c. The checkbook balance of Rick's Deli shows an ending balance of $798.

d. Jim Rice's check for $40 bounced due to lack of sufficient funds.

Establishment and replenishment of petty cash.

JAMES NATIONAL BANK
RIO MEAN BRAND
BUGNA, TEXAS

RICK'S DELI
8811 2ND ST.
BUGNA, TEXAS

Old Balance	Checks in Order of Payment		Deposits	Date	New Balance
718				4/2	718.00
	12.00	36.00		4/3	670.00
	20.00		40.00	4/10	690.00
	80.00		80.00	4/15	690.00
	40.00	NSF	40.00	4/20	690.00
	160.00		160.00	4/24	690.00
	80.00	2.00 SC	24.00	4/28	632.00

6B-3. From the following transactions, (1) record the entries as needed in the general journal of Merry Co. as well as the auxiliary petty cash record, and (2) replenish the petty cash fund on April 30 (check no. 8).

19XX
April   1 Issued check no. 4 for $60 to establish a petty cash fund.
          5 Paid $9 from petty cash for postage, voucher no. 1.
          8 Paid $12 from petty cash for office supplies, voucher no. 2.
         15 Issued check no. 5 to Reliable Corp. for $400 from past purchases on account.

Check Figure:

Cash Replenishment $46

         17 Paid $7 from petty cash for office supplies, voucher no. 3.
         20 Issued check no. 6 to Roger Corp, $300 from past purchases on account.
         24 Paid $6 from petty cash for postage, voucher no. 4.
         26 Paid $12 from petty cash for local church donation, voucher no. 5 (this is a miscellaneous payment).
         28 Issued check no. 7 to Roy Kloon to pay office equipment, $800.
         30 Replenish petty cash.

Establishing and replenishing petty cash including a cash shortage.

6B-4. From the following, record the transactions into Logan's auxiliary petty cash record and general journal (p. 2) as needed:

19XX
Oct.   1 Roberta Floss, the petty cashier, cashed a check, no. 444, to establish a $90 petty cash fund.
          5 Paid $16 for postage stamps, voucher no. 1.

9 Paid $14 for delivery charges on goods for resale, voucher no. 2.

12 Paid $6 for donation to a church (Miscellaneous Expense), voucher no. 3.

14 Paid $10 for postage stamps, voucher no. 4.

17 Paid $7 for delivery charges on goods for resale, voucher no. 5.

27 Purchased computer supplies from petty cash for $9, voucher no. 6.

28 Paid $3 for postage, voucher no. 7.

29 Drew check no. 618 to replenish petty cash and a $4 shortage.

Check Figure:

Cash Replenishment $69

REAL WORLD APPLICATIONS

6R-1.

Karen Johnson, the bookkeeper of Hoop Co., has appointed Jim Pool as the petty cash custodian. The following transactions occurred in November:

19XX

Nov. 25 Check no. 441 was written and cashed to establish a $50 petty cash fund.

27 Paid $8.50 delivery charge for goods purchased for resale.

29 Purchased office supplies for $12 from petty cash.

30 Purchased postage stamps for $15 from petty cash.

On December 3 Jim received the following internal memo:

MEMO

TO: Jim Pool

FROM: Karen Johnson

RE: Petty Cash

Jim, I'll need $5 for postage stamps. By the way, I noticed that our petty cash account seems to be too low. Let's increase its size to $100.

Could you help Jim replenish petty cash on December 3 by providing him with a general journal entry? Support your answer and indicate in writing whether Karen was correct.

6R-2.

Ginger Company has the policy of depositing all receipts and making all payments by check. On receiving the bank statement, Bill Free, a new bookkeeper, is quite upset that the balance in cash in the ledger is $4,209.50 while the ending bank balance is $4,440.50. Bill is convinced the bank has made an error. Based on the following facts, is Bill's concern warranted? What other written suggestions could you offer Bill in the bank reconciliation process?

a. The Nov. 30 cash receipts, $611, had been placed in the bank's night depository after banking hours and consequently did not appear on the bank statement as a deposit.

b. Two debit memorandums and a credit memorandum were included with the returned check. None of the memorandums had been recorded at the time of the reconciliation. The first debit memorandum had a $130 NSF check written by Abby Ellen. The second was a $6.50 debit memorandum for service charges. The credit memorandum was for $494 and represented the proceeds less a $6 collection fee from a $500 non-interest-bearing note collected for Ginger Company by the bank.

c. It was also found that checks no. 942 for $71.50 and no. 947 for $206.50, both written and recorded on Nov. 28, were not among the cancelled checks returned.

d. Bill found that check no. 899 was correctly drawn for $1,094, in payment for a new cash register. However, this check had been recorded as though it were for $1,148.

e. The October bank reconciliation showed two checks outstanding on September 30, no. 621 for $152.50 and no. 630 for $179.30. Check no. 630 was returned with the November bank statement, but check no. 621 was not.

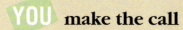 **make the call**

Critical Thinking/Ethical Case

6R-3.

Jerry Ary, the bookkeeper of Logan Co., received a bank statement from Ajax Bank. Jerry noticed a $200 mistake made by the bank in the company's favor. Jerry called his supervisor, who said that as long as it benefits the company, he should not tell the bank about the error. You make the call. Write your specific recommendations to Jerry.

ACCOUNTING RECALL
A CUMULATIVE APPROACH

THIS EXAM REVIEWS CHAPTERS 1 THROUGH 6

Your *Study Guide and Working Papers* (pp. 218 and 230) have forms to complete this exam, as well as worked-out solutions. The page references next to each question identify what page to turn back to if you answer the question incorrectly.

PART 1   Vocabulary Review

Match the terms to the appropriate definition or phrase.

Page Ref.

(161)	1. Permanent account	A.	A supplementary record
(207)	2. Blank endorsement	B.	Revenues, Expenses, Withdrawals
(209)	3. Payee	C.	A process of reconciling
(161)	4. Temporary accounts	D.	Assets, Contra-assets, Liabilities, Capital
(212)	5. Outstanding checks	E.	Person or company to whom the check is payable
(211)	6. Bank reconciliation		
(217)	7. Auxiliary petty cash record	F.	Lacks sufficient funds
		G.	Contra-asset on the Balance Sheet
(122)	8. Accumulated depreciation	H.	Add to bank balance
(211)	9. Deposits in transit	I.	Checks written but not processed by bank
(212)	10. NSF	J.	Could be further endorsed

PART II   True or False (Accounting Theory)

(216)   11. Petty cash is a liability.

(217)   12. The auxiliary petty cash record is a journal.

(161)   13. The closing process reduces all temporary accounts to a zero balance.

(212)   14. NSF results in lowering the bank balance in the reconciliation process.

(219)   15. In replenishment, the old expenses are shown and a new check is written.

CONTINUING PROBLEM

The books have been closed for the first year of business for Eldorado Computer Center. The company ended up with a marginal profit for the first three months in operation. Tony expects faster growth as he enters into a busy season.

Following is a list of transactions for the month of October. Petty Cash Account #1010 and Miscellaneous Expense Account #5100 have been added to the chart of accounts.

Assignment:

(See pp. 219–220 in your *Study Guide and Working Papers*.)

1. Record the transactions in general journal or petty cash format.
2. Post the transactions to the general ledger accounts.
3. Prepare a trial balance.

Oct.   1 Paid rent for November, December, and January, $1,200 (check #8107)

2 Established a petty cash fund for $100

4 Collected $3,600 from a cash customer for building five systems

5 Collected $2,600, the amount due from A. Pitale's invoice #12674, customer on account

6 Purchased $25 worth of stamps, using petty cash voucher #101

7 Withdrew $2,000 (check #8108) for personal use.

8 Purchased $22 worth of supplies, using petty cash voucher #102

12 Paid the newspaper carrier $10, using petty cash voucher #103

16 Paid the amount due on the September phone bill, $65 (check #8109)

17 Paid the amount due on the September electric bill, $95 (check #8110)

22 Performed computer services for Taylor Golf; billed the client $4,200 (invoice #12675)

23 Paid $20 for computer paper, using petty cash voucher #104

30 Took $15 out of petty cash for lunch, voucher #105

31 Replenished the petty cash. Coin and currency in drawer $8.00

Since Tony was so busy trying to close his books, he forgot to reconcile his last three months of bank statements. What follows on pages 234 and 235 is a list of all deposits and checks written for the past three months (Each entry is identified by chapter, transaction date, or transaction letter.) and bank statements for July through September. The statement for October won't arrive until the first week of November.

Chapter	Transaction	Payor/Payee	Amount
		DEPOSITS	
1	(a)	Tony Freedman	$4,500
1	(f)	Cash customer	250
1	(i)	Taylor Golf	1200
1	(g)	Cash customer	200
2	(p)	Cash customer	900
3	Sept. 2	Tonya Parker Jones	325
3	Sept. 6	Summer Lipe	220
3	Sept. 12	Jeannine Sparks	850
3	Sept. 26	Mike Hammer	140

Chapter	Transaction	Check #	Payor/Payee	Amount
			CHECKS	
1	(b)	8095	Multi Systems	$1200
1	(c)	8096	Office Furniture, Inc.	600
1	(e)	8097	Capital Management	400
1	(j)	8098	Tony Freedman	100
2	(l)	8099	Insurance Protection, Inc.	150
2	(m)	8100	Office Depot	200
2	(n)	8101	Computer Edge Magazine	1400
2	(q)	8102	San Diego Electric	85
2	(r)	8103	U.S. Postmaster	50
3	Sept. 1	8104	Capital Management	1200
3	Sept. 8	8105	Pacific Bell USA	155
3	Sept. 15	8106	Computer Connection	200
3	Sept. 16	8107	Multi Systems, Inc.	1200

BANK STATEMENT
First Union Bank 322 Glen Ave. Escondido, CA 92025

Eldorado Computer Center   *Statement Date: July 22 , 19XX*

Checks Paid:

Date paid	Number	Amount	Date received	Amount
7-4	8095	1200.00	7-1	4500.00
7-7	8096	600.00	7-10	250.00
7-15	8097	400.00	7-20	1200.00
Total 3 checks paid for $2,200.00			7-21	200.00
			Total Deposits	**$6,150.00**

Ending Balance on July 22 — $3,950.00

Received Statement July 29, 19XX.

BANK STATEMENT
First Union Bank 322 Glen Ave. Escondido, CA 92025

Eldorado Computer Center   *Statement Date: August 21 , 19XX*

Checks Paid: **Deposits and Credits:**

Date paid	Number	Amount	Date received	Amount
8-2	8098	100.00	8-12	900.00
8-3	8099	150.00		
8-10	8100	200.00		
8-15	8101	1400.00		
8-20	8102	85.00	**Total Deposits**	**$900.00**
Total 5 checks paid for $1935.00				

Beginning balance on July 22 — $3,950.00   *Ending balance on August 21 — $2,915.00*

Received statement August 27, 19XX.

BANK STATEMENT
First Union Bank 322 Glen Ave. Escondido, CA 92025

Eldorado Computer Center   *Statement Date: September 20 , 19XX*

Checks Paid:			Deposits and Credits:	
Date paid	Number	Amount	Date received	Amount
9-2	8103	50.00	9-4	325.00
9-6	8104	1200.00	9-7	220.00
9-12	8105	155.00	9-14	850.00

Total 3 checks paid for $1405.00   *Total Deposits $1,395.00*

Beginning balance on August 21   *Ending balance on September 20*
$2,915.00   *$2,905.00*

Received statement September 29, 19XX.

Assignment:

1. Compare the Computer Center's deposits and checks with the bank statements, and complete a bank reconciliation as of September 30.

PAYROLL CONCEPTS AND PROCEDURES

Employee Taxes

THE BIG PICTURE

The Eldorado Computer Center ended its first year so successfully that owner Tony Freedman decided to hire two employees. He would pay them based on an hourly wage, using time cards to track the hours they worked. Freedman knew that this would involve significant expense and effort. In many companies the cost of payroll is more than half of total expenses. Beyond the cost of wages, however, a business becomes responsible for complying with rules that govern payroll deductions.

In addition to paying wages on time, the business must deduct taxes and other amounts. It must account for this money very strictly and pass it on to the proper agency according to government rules and regulations. These regulations are constantly changing, and the person handling payroll must be aware of all changes in order to stay in compliance with the law.

Some companies choose an outside service to prepare the payroll and issue the checks. Much of the work is done with computer accounting payroll software. Since Freedman will have only two employees (in addition to himself), he has decided to take the task on himself to save the expense of hiring an outside service.

In this chapter you will learn how to calculate hourly wages and overtime. You will also learn the basic rules and procedures for making payroll deductions, withholding taxes, and paying taxes withheld.

Learning Objectives	◆ Calculating overtime pay, FICA deductions for Social Security and Medicare, and federal income tax withholding. (p. 237) ◆ Preparing a payroll register. (p. 244) ◆ Journalizing and posting the payroll entry from the payroll register. (p. 251) ◆ Maintaining an individual employee earnings record. (p. 254)

Payroll can be a significant factor in running a business. Besides the money issue, business expenses (including payroll) must comply with a growing number of federal and state payroll regulations. That is why it is important to completely understand the step-by-step process involved in manual payroll systems. An accurate payroll system has (1) continual checks and balances and (2) strong internal control.

In this chapter we will take a close look at the employees of Fred's Market and see how their payroll is calculated; how it is affected by federal, state, and local taxes and deductions; and how the accountant for Fred's Market handles a weekly payroll. (In Chapter 8 we will continue to look at Fred's Market, but from the employer's point of view rather than that of the employees.)

LEARNING UNIT 7-1
Introduction to Payroll

A number of laws and regulations at the federal and state level govern payroll. We will look at several of them here.

FAIR LABOR STANDARDS ACT AND OVERTIME PAY

The **Fair Labor Standards Act** (also known as **Federal Wage and Hour Law**) applies to all employers involved directly or indirectly in **interstate commerce.** "Interstate commerce" is defined as one business communicating or doing business with another business in some other state. Since simple activities such as mailing or making long-distance phone calls are considered activities that pass the interstate commerce test, nearly all employers must comply with the law.

Two of the most important requirements of the Fair Labor Standards Act are that workers (1) must receive a minimum hourly rate of pay and (2) be paid at a higher rate of pay for any hours beyond 40 worked during a week. Once a worker reaches 40 hours, he or she must be paid at least time and a half (or 1.5 times the worker's regular rate of pay). Some employers, such as retailers, may pay double time (or 2 times the worker's regular rate of pay) to employees who work on a national holiday. This is commonly known as *overtime pay* (or premium pay).

Not all employers are subject to the 40-hour standard: restaurants, hotels, and the like are not required to pay overtime until a worker has worked more than 44 hours in one week. Also, workers who are considered to be executives, professionals, or administrative personnel of a company are exempt from the 40-hour requirement.

Two methods are commonly used to calculate overtime for a worker. Both are contained in the regulations to the Fair Labor Standards Act. Let's say that a person whose standard rate of pay is $6 an hour worked four hours of overtime. He works in an industry where overtime is considered beyond 40 hours. His pay would be calculated as follows:

> The Fair Labor Standards Act also deals with such issues as employing minors under the age of 18, recordkeeping, and the concept of equal pay for equal work, regardless of sex.

> Depending on the industry, either 40 or 44 hours represents the total hours worked before considering overtime.

METHOD 1

$$\begin{array}{rll}
\text{Total hours} \times \text{Regular rate} = & 44 \times \$6 = & \$264 \\
+ \text{ Overtime hours} \times \tfrac{1}{2} \text{ rate} = & 4 \times \$3 = & \underline{12} \\
\text{Total pay} = & & \underline{\underline{\$276}}
\end{array}$$

METHOD 2

$$\begin{array}{rll}
\text{Regular hours} \times \text{Regular rate} = & 40 \times \$6 = & \$240 \\
+ \text{ Overtime hours} \times 1\tfrac{1}{2} \text{ rate} = & 4 \times \$9 = & \underline{36} \\
\text{Total pay} = & & \underline{\underline{\$276}}
\end{array}$$

Using Method 1, the employer is clearly able to see that pure overtime wages cost $12 over the regular cost of labor. Because it is the more common method, we will use Method 2, which calculates the overtime rates at time and a half.

WITHHOLDING FOR FEDERAL INCOME TAXES (FIT)

Many rules and regulations govern the federal income taxes that a person must pay. Here, however, we will discuss only those that relate to withholding.

Every U.S. citizen must pay income tax each year. The tax is due on April 15 of the year after the tax year. (For example, taxes for 1997 are due on April 15, 1998; taxes for 1998 are due on April 15, 1999, etc.) Instead of each individual or company paying the tax due on April 15, employers are required to withhold taxes for each employee, deposit them in a special account, and then send them to the government at regular intervals. The funds sent to the government are called **payroll tax deposits.** We will discuss the specifics of payroll tax deposits in Chapter 8.

To facilitate this, the employer must have each employee fill out a **Form W-4** (an **Employee's Withholding Allowance Certificate**), which is kept on file by the employer (see Fig. 7-1). Using the Form W-4 along with the special withholding tables provided by the Internal Revenue Service (or IRS), an employer can determine the amount of **federal income tax withholding** (or

FIGURE 7-1 Form W-4, Employee's Withholding Allowance Certificate

FIT) required. The FIT takes the employee's gross earnings, marital state, and number of exemptions claimed into consideration. An **exemption** (or **allowance**) represents the specific income that will be considered *non*taxable for FIT purposes.

Usually a worker is entitled to an allowance for himself or herself, one for his or her spouse (unless the spouse is working and claiming an allowance), and one for each dependent (e.g., a child) for whom the worker is providing more than one-half the support in a given year.

To properly calculate federal income tax withholding, the employee uses the **wage bracket table** in an IRS publication known as Circular E or *Employer's Tax Guide* (Publication 15). The wage bracket tables in this publication show the amount of federal income tax to be withheld for individuals who are paid weekly, biweekly, semimonthly, or monthly. These periods of time used to determine how much an employee earns are called **pay** (or **payroll**) **periods.** There are separate tables for married persons and for single persons (see Figs. 7-2 and 7-3, respectively, on pages 240–241).

Let's assume that an employee who has filled out a Form W-4 stating that he is married and has three withholding allowances earns $1,175 each week. Using the first table in Figure 7-2 (called MARRIED Persons — WEEKLY Payroll Period) we go down the left-hand column until we arrive at $1,170 in the column labeled "At least." Notice that the column to the immediate right of the first column says "But less than" $1,180. The $1,175 amount falls between these two amounts. Since the employee claims three allowances, we slide over to the right. Where the three allowances intersect with the "At least" $1,170, we see a federal withholding tax of $166. If the employee had earned $1,169, his or her tax would have been $164.

WITHHOLDING FOR FEDERAL INSURANCE CONTRIBUTIONS ACT (FICA)

The **Federal Insurance Contributions Act** (better known as **FICA**) helps fund the payments related to (1) monthly retirement benefits for those over 62 years of age, (2) medical benefits after age 65, (3) benefits for workers who have become disabled, and (4) benefits for families of deceased workers who were covered by the federal Social Security Act. Under this act, passed into law in 1935, employees, self-employed persons, and employers must all pay a FICA tax. The employer must match the amounts contributed by each employee. The employer's share of these taxes will be further discussed in Chapter 8.

FICA taxes are broken down into two parts: Social Security and Medicare. Employers must calculate and report each of these taxes separately to the government and to each employee. Employees are notified on their paycheck stubs and on their Form W-2, which they will receive after the end of the tax year.

Each year rates and maximum dollar amounts are set for Social Security. For example, in 1937, the first year FICA tax was collected, the rate was 1 percent on the first $3,000 of an employee's earnings during the year. This meant that the most an employee could contribute to Social Security that year was $30.

It is important to realize that the rate and the maximum dollar amount of earnings subject to FICA taxes, called a wage base limit, continually change. For this text, we use $65,400 as the wage base limit for Social Security (Old Age, Survivors, and Disability Insurance). There is no wage base limit for Medicare (Hospital Insurance). This means that the employee and employer pay 1.45 percent on all of the employee's earnings for the year. As of this writing, the rate of tax for Social Security is 6.2 percent (both the employee and employer would pay this). For Medicare, the rate is 1.45 percent.[1]

---

[1] 1997 Social Security rate is 6.2 percent on a base of $65,400. The 1998 rate is 6.2 percent on a base of $68,400.

MARRIED Persons—WEEKLY Payroll Period

If the wages are—		And the number of withholding allowances claimed is—										
At least	But less than	0	1	2	3↓	4	5	6	7	8	9	10
		The amount of income tax to be withheld is—										
$740	$750	$93	$86	$79	$72	$65	$58	$51	$44	$37	$30	$23
750	760	95	88	81	74	67	60	53	45	38	31	24
760	770	96	89	82	75	68	61	54	47	40	33	26
770	780	98	91	84	77	70	63	56	48	41	34	27
780	790	99	92	85	78	71	64	57	50	43	36	29
790	800	101	94	87	80	73	66	59	51	44	37	30
800	810	102	95	88	81	74	67	60	53	46	39	32
810	820	105	97	90	83	76	69	62	54	47	40	33
820	830	108	98	91	84	77	70	63	56	49	42	35
830	840	111	100	93	86	79	72	65	57	50	43	36
840	850	114	101	94	87	80	73	66	59	52	45	38
850	860	116	103	96	89	82	75	68	60	53	46	39
860	870	119	106	97	90	83	76	69	62	55	48	41
870	880	122	109	99	92	85	78	71	63	56	49	42
880	890	125	112	100	93	86	79	72	65	58	51	44
890	900	128	114	102	95	88	81	74	66	59	52	45
900	910	130	117	104	96	89	82	75	68	61	54	47
910	920	133	120	107	98	91	84	77	69	62	55	48
920	930	136	123	110	99	92	85	78	71	64	57	50
930	940	139	126	112	101	94	87	80	72	65	58	51
940	950	142	128	115	102	95	88	81	74	67	60	53
950	960	144	131	118	105	97	90	83	75	68	61	54
960	970	147	134	121	108	98	91	84	77	70	63	56
970	980	150	137	124	110	100	93	86	78	71	64	57
980	990	153	140	126	113	101	94	87	80	73	66	59
990	1,000	156	142	129	116	103	96	89	81	74	67	60
1,000	1,010	158	145	132	119	106	97	90	83	76	69	62
1,010	1,020	161	148	135	122	108	99	92	84	77	70	63
1,020	1,030	164	151	138	124	111	100	93	86	79	72	65
1,030	1,040	167	154	140	127	114	102	95	87	80	73	66
1,040	1,050	170	156	143	130	117	104	96	89	82	75	68
1,050	1,060	172	159	146	133	120	106	98	90	83	76	69
1,060	1,070	175	162	149	136	122	109	99	92	85	78	71
1,070	1,080	178	165	152	138	125	112	101	93	86	79	72
1,080	1,090	181	168	154	141	128	115	102	95	88	81	74
1,090	1,100	184	170	157	144	131	118	104	96	89	82	75
1,100	1,110	186	173	160	147	134	120	107	98	91	84	77
1,110	1,120	189	176	163	150	136	123	110	99	92	85	78
1,120	1,130	192	179	166	152	139	126	113	101	94	87	80
1,130	1,140	195	182	168	155	142	129	116	102	95	88	81
1,140	1,150	198	184	171	158	145	132	118	105	97	90	83
1,150	1,160	200	187	174	161	148	134	121	108	98	91	84
1,160	1,170	203	190	177	164	150	137	124	111	100	93	86
→1,170	1,180	206	193	180	[166]	153	140	127	114	101	94	87
1,180	1,190	209	196	182	169	156	143	130	116	103	96	89
1,190	1,200	212	198	185	172	159	146	132	119	106	97	90
1,200	1,210	214	201	188	175	162	148	135	122	109	99	92
1,210	1,220	217	204	191	178	164	151	138	125	112	100	93
1,220	1,230	220	207	194	180	167	154	141	128	114	102	95
1,230	1,240	223	210	196	183	170	157	144	130	117	104	96
1,240	1,250	226	212	199	186	173	160	146	133	120	107	98
1,250	1,260	228	215	202	189	176	162	149	136	123	110	99
1,260	1,270	231	218	205	192	178	165	152	139	126	112	101
1,270	1,280	234	221	208	194	181	168	155	142	128	115	102
1,280	1,290	237	224	210	197	184	171	158	144	131	118	105
1,290	1,300	240	226	213	200	187	174	160	147	134	121	108
1,300	1,310	242	229	216	203	190	176	163	150	137	124	110
1,310	1,320	245	232	219	206	192	179	166	153	140	126	113
1,320	1,330	248	235	222	208	195	182	169	156	142	129	116
1,330	1,340	251	238	224	211	198	185	172	158	145	132	119
1,340	1,350	254	240	227	214	201	188	174	161	148	135	122
1,350	1,360	256	243	230	217	204	190	177	164	151	138	124
1,360	1,370	259	246	233	220	206	193	180	167	154	140	127
1,370	1,380	262	249	236	222	209	196	183	170	156	143	130
1,380	1,390	265	252	238	225	212	199	186	172	159	146	133

$1,390 and over   Use Table 1(b) for a **MARRIED person** on page 29. Also see the instructions on page 27.

FIGURE 7-2 Wage Bracket Tables—Married Persons. The federal income tax (FIT) withholding for a married person earning $1,175 per week with 3 exemptions is $166.

SINGLE Persons—WEEKLY Payroll Period

If the wages are—		And the number of withholding allowances claimed is—										
At least	But less than	0	1	2	3	4	5	6	7	8	9	10
		The amount of income tax to be withheld is—										
$600	$610	$102	$89	$75	$62	$55	$48	$41	$34	$27	$20	$13
610	620	105	91	78	65	57	49	42	35	28	21	14
620	630	107	94	81	68	58	51	44	37	30	23	16
630	640	110	97	84	71	60	52	45	38	31	24	17
640	650	113	100	87	73	61	54	47	40	33	26	19
650	660	116	103	89	76	63	55	48	41	34	27	20
660	670	119	105	92	79	66	57	50	43	36	29	22
670	680	121	108	95	82	69	58	51	44	37	30	23
680	690	124	111	98	85	71	60	53	46	39	32	25
690	700	127	114	101	87	74	61	54	47	40	33	26
700	710	130	117	103	90	77	64	56	49	42	35	28
710	720	133	119	106	93	80	67	57	50	43	36	29
720	730	135	122	109	96	83	69	59	52	45	38	31
730	740	138	125	112	99	85	72	60	53	46	39	32
740	750	141	128	115	101	88	75	62	55	48	41	34
750	760	144	131	117	104	91	78	65	56	49	42	35
760	770	147	133	120	107	94	81	67	58	51	44	37
770	780	149	136	123	110	97	83	70	59	52	45	38
780	790	152	139	126	113	99	86	73	61	54	47	40
790	800	155	142	129	115	102	89	76	63	55	48	41
800	810	158	145	131	118	105	92	79	65	57	50	43
810	820	161	147	134	121	108	95	81	68	58	51	44
820	830	163	150	137	124	111	97	84	71	60	53	46
830	840	166	153	140	127	113	100	87	74	61	54	47
840	850	169	156	143	129	116	103	90	77	63	56	49
850	860	172	159	145	132	119	106	93	79	66	57	50
860	870	175	161	148	135	122	109	95	82	69	59	52
870	880	177	164	151	138	125	111	98	85	72	60	53
880	890	180	167	154	141	127	114	101	88	75	62	55
890	900	183	170	157	143	130	117	104	91	77	64	56
900	910	186	173	159	146	133	120	107	93	80	67	58
910	920	189	175	162	149	136	123	109	96	83	70	59
920	930	191	178	165	152	139	125	112	99	86	73	61
930	940	194	181	168	155	141	128	115	102	89	75	62
940	950	197	184	171	157	144	131	118	105	91	78	65
950	960	200	187	173	160	147	134	121	107	94	81	68
960	970	203	189	176	163	150	137	123	110	97	84	71
970	980	206	192	179	166	153	139	126	113	100	87	73
980	990	209	195	182	169	155	142	129	116	103	89	76
990	1,000	212	198	185	171	158	145	132	119	105	92	79
1,000	1,010	215	201	187	174	161	148	135	121	108	95	82
1,010	1,020	218	203	190	177	164	151	137	124	111	98	85
1,020	1,030	221	206	193	180	167	153	140	127	114	101	87
1,030	1,040	224	210	196	183	169	156	143	130	117	103	90
1,040	1,050	227	213	199	185	172	159	146	133	119	106	93
1,050	1,060	230	216	201	188	175	162	149	135	122	109	96
1,060	1,070	233	219	204	191	178	165	151	138	125	112	99
1,070	1,080	237	222	207	194	181	167	154	141	128	115	101
1,080	1,090	240	225	210	197	183	170	157	144	131	117	104
1,090	1,100	243	228	214	199	186	173	160	147	133	120	107
1,100	1,110	246	231	217	202	189	176	163	149	136	123	110
1,110	1,120	249	234	220	205	192	179	165	152	139	126	113
1,120	1,130	252	237	223	208	195	181	168	155	142	129	115
1,130	1,140	255	241	226	211	197	184	171	158	145	131	118
1,140	1,150	258	244	229	214	200	187	174	161	147	134	121
1,150	1,160	261	247	232	218	203	190	177	163	150	137	124
1,160	1,170	264	250	235	221	206	193	179	166	153	140	127
1,170	1,180	268	253	238	224	209	195	182	169	156	143	129
1,180	1,190	271	256	241	227	212	198	185	172	159	145	132
1,190	1,200	274	259	245	230	215	201	188	175	161	148	135
1,200	1,210	277	262	248	233	218	204	191	177	164	151	138
1,210	1,220	280	265	251	236	222	207	193	180	167	154	141
1,220	1,230	283	268	254	239	225	210	196	183	170	157	143
1,230	1,240	286	272	257	242	228	213	199	186	173	159	146
1,240	1,250	289	275	260	245	231	216	202	189	175	162	149

$1,250 and over Use Table 1(a) for a **SINGLE person** on page 29. Also see the instructions on page 27.

FIGURE 7-3 Wage Bracket Tables—Single Persons

Thus, the most an employee could contribute for Social Security tax from January 1 through December 31 (known as a **calendar year**) would be $4,054.80, calculated as follows:

$$Base \quad Rate$$
$$\$65,400 \times .062 = \$4,054.80$$

Let's look at how two different employees would be taxed. Employee A earns $75,000 for the year while Employee B earns $125,000. Both employees have earned over $65,400, the Social Security wage base limit, so both will pay the maximum Social Security tax. However, they will pay different amounts for Medicare tax.

Employee A	Earnings	Wage Base Limit	Rate	
Social Security	$75,000	$65,400	$\times$ .062 =	$4,054.80
Medicare	$75,000	None	$\times$ .0145 =	1,087.50
				= $5,142.30

Employee B	Earnings	Wage Base Limit	Rate	
Social Security	$125,000	$65,400	$\times$ .062 =	$4,054.80
Medicare	$125,000	None	$\times$ .0145 =	1,812.50
				= $5,867.30

Please note that every employee pays Social Security tax up to the wage base limit, which is subject to change each year. Every employee pays Medicare tax on every dollar earned—there is no wage base limit for Medicare.

STATE AND CITY INCOME TAXES (SIT)

Employees in 41 states also have to pay a state income tax. The rates and rules vary too much for us to discuss them here, but all states that tax income publish charts and tables like those of the federal government. This allows employers to calculate the proper amount of **state income tax withholding.**

Many counties and/or cities also tax income. Such county and/or city income taxes are in addition to federal and state taxes.

WORKERS' COMPENSATION INSURANCE

Workers' Compensation Insurance protects employees against losses due to injury or death incurred while on the job. Each employer (in cooperation with an insurance agent) must estimate the cost of the insurance. The premium must be paid in advance. In Chapter 8 we will look at how the premium is calculated as well as specific tax responsibilities of the employer. Keep in mind that this tax is on the employer, not on the employee.

LEARNING UNIT 7-1 REVIEW

AT THIS POINT you should be able to

- ◆ Explain the purpose of the Federal Wage and Hour Law. (p. 237)
- ◆ Calculate overtime pay. (p. 238)
- ◆ Complete a W-4 form. (p. 238)
- ◆ Explain the term "claiming an allowance." (p. 239)

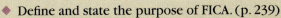

- ◆ Define and state the purpose of FICA. (p. 239)
- ◆ Calculate the FICA deductions for Social Security and Medicare. (p. 242)
- ◆ Utilize a wage bracket table to arrive at deductions from federal income tax. (p. 239)
- ◆ Explain the purpose of Workers' Compensation Insurance. (p. 242)

SELF-REVIEW QUIZ 7-1

(The forms you need are on page 231 of the *Study Guide and Working Papers*.)

John Small earns $1,300 each week as a software engineer. To date this year, before the current payroll, he earned a total of $65,000. Please calculate the amount of FICA tax for Social Security and Medicare, federal income tax, and state income tax deducted in the current pay period.

- ◆ FICA: Social Security is 6.2 percent on $65,400; Medicare is 1.45 percent with no wage base limit.
- ◆ John is married, claiming two allowances (please use Figure 7-2).
- ◆ The state income tax rate is 8 percent.
- ◆ No other deductions are taken out by John's employer.

Solution to Self-Review Quiz 7-1

This is how John's tax would be calculated:

FICA: Social Security:	$ 400 × .062	= $ 24.80
Medicare	$1,300 × .0145	= $ 18.85
Federal income tax		$216.00 by IRS table
State income tax	$1,300 × .08	= $104.00

The wage base limit for Social Security is $65,400. John has earned—and been taxed on—$65,000. Therefore, in the current pay period, he only has to pay Social Security tax on $400 of his pay; the remaining $900 is not taxed for that purpose. However, John's total check of $1,300 is taxed for Medicare since there is no wage base limit for this tax.

LEARNING UNIT 7-2
The Payroll Process

Fred Stone, owner of Fred's Market, has five employees working for him. They are:

Bob Jones	$16 per hour
Abby King	$14 per hour
Susan O'Mally	$1,375 salary per week
Pat Regan	$900 salary per week
Jim Zott	$1,380 salary per week

Fred does not receive a salary since he is the owner of the sole proprietorship, but he does plan to eventually withdraw portions of the profit.

RECORDING PAYROLL DATA IN THE PAYROLL REGISTER

Fred's Market pays its employees on a weekly basis. The **payroll register** shown in Figure 7-4 on pages 244–245 contains the payroll information for the week of November 25. The payroll register is a multicolumn form used specifically for the purpose of recording the earnings of the employees of a business for a given pay period. Let's look closely at each column to see how the numbers were determined.

FIGURE 7-4 Payroll Register for Fred's Market

FRED'S MARKET
PAYROLL REGISTER
NOVEMBER 25, 19XX

Employee Name	Allowances and Marital Status	Cumulative Earnings	Salary per Week	No. of Hrs.	Wages per Hour	Earnings Regular	Earnings Overtime	Earnings Gross	Cumulative Earnings	Taxable Earnings Federal Unemployment	Taxable Earnings Soc. Sec.	Taxable Earnings Medicare
Jones, Bob	S-0	68000 00	—	39	16 00	624 00		624 00	7424 00	200 00	624 00	624 00
King, Abby	S-1	66000 0	—	44	14 00	560 00	84 00	644 00	7244 00	400 00	644 00	644 00
O'Mally, Susan	M-3	64625 00	1375 00			1375 00		1375 00	66000 00	———	775 00 (1)	1375 00
Regan, Pat	M-1	42300 00	900 00			900 00		900 00	43200 00	———	900 00	900 00
Zott, Jim	M-2	64860 00	1380 00			1380 00		1380 00	66240 00	———	540 00	1380 00
TOTALS		185185 00	3655 00			4839 00	84 00	4923 00	190108 00	600 00	3483 00	4923 00
Discussions in this chapter are keyed to these letters	(A)	(B)	(C)			(D)	(E)	(F)	(G)	(H)	(I)	(J)

(1) $65,400
    −64,625
    $ 775

FIGURE 7-4 (cont.)

FRED'S MARKET
PAYROLL REGISTER
NOVEMBER 25, 19XX

	FICA		Deductions			Net Pay	Check No.	Distribution of Expense Accounts	
	Soc. Sec.	Medicare	Federal Income Tax	State Income Tax	Medical Insurance			Office Salaries Expense	Market Wages Expense
	(2)	(3)							
	3869	905	10700	3120	2200	41606	840		62400
	3993	934	10000	3220	2200	44053	841		64400
	4805	1994	22200	6875	4400	97226	842	137500	
	5580	1305	11700	4500	4400	62515	843	90000	
	3348	2001	23800	6900	4400	97551	844	138000	
	21595	7139	78400	24615	17600	342951		365500	126800
	(K)	(L)	(M)	(N)	(O)	(P)	(Q)	(R)	(S)

Discussions in this chapter are keyed to these letters

② $624 x .062
③ $624 x .0145

Note: Figure 7-4 should be used as a reference guide for both Chapters 7 and 8.

(A) Allowance and Marital Status

As previously mentioned, employees must complete Form W-4 (see Fig. 7-1 on p. 238). The form indicates the employee's marital status so that the correct amount of federal income tax withholding can be calculated. Remember, individual workers completing the form are entitled to claim one allowance for themselves and one for each dependent.

Fred's bookkeeper uses information from Form W-4 to determine how much money for federal income tax (column M). When more allowances are claimed, less tax is deducted from the employee's earnings when the check is issued. The opposite is also true: the fewer the allowances, the larger the deduction.

> **Example:** Bob Jones is single and claims zero allowances. A high amount of federal income taxes are taken out with each paycheck. If Bob overpays FIT, he may receive a refund at year end after he files his individual income tax return.

(B) Cumulative Earnings

This column represents each employee's cumulative earnings for the calendar year *before* the new payroll period. As we will show later, the cumulative figure can be obtained from the employee's individual earnings record.

Salary per Week, Number of Hours, and Wages per Hour

> **Example:** Abby King has earnings $6,600 before this payroll in the calendar year.

(C) Salary per Week, Number of Hours, and Wages per Hour

The weekly salary or hours worked with rate of pay per hour provides the basis for computing the gross earnings of the employees.

> **Example:** Bob Jones is paid $16 per hour and worked 39 hours for this pay period.

(D) Earnings

To calculate the regular earnings for an employee paid by the hour, multiply the number of hours (40 or less) times the rate per hour. Salaried employee amounts are listed with no calculations.

> **Example:** Bob Jones has earned $624 for this pay period.
>
> | Hours worked | | Rate per hour | | Regular pay |
> |:---:|:---:|:---:|:---:|:---:|
> | 39 | $\times$ | $16 | = | $624 |

(E) Overtime

After 40 hours, hourly employees earn overtime pay (time and a half). *Note:* salaried employees do not receive overtime.

Example: Abby King has worked 4 hours of overtime at a rate of $21 per hour.

$$\underset{\$14}{\text{Hourly rate}} \times \underset{1.5}{\text{Time and a half}} = \underset{\$21}{\text{Overtime rate}}$$

$$\underset{\$21}{\text{Overtime rate}} \times \underset{4}{\text{Overtime hours}} = \underset{\$84}{\text{Overtime earnings}}$$

(F) Gross Earnings

Gross earnings is the total amount that has been earned (including overtime) before any deductions. We will use these numbers to fill columns (R) and (S).

Example: Abby King's gross earnings are $644.

$$\underset{\$560}{\text{Regular pay}} + \underset{\$84}{\text{Overtime}} = \underset{\$644}{\text{Gross pay}}$$

(G) Cumulative Earnings

This column provides an up-to-date picture of how much each employee has earned *after* this pay period for the calendar year. This column tells whether an employee has reached the Social Security tax wage base limit.

Example: Pat Regan has now earned a total of $43,200 for this calendar year.

$$\underset{\$42,300}{\substack{\text{Cumulative earnings} \\ \text{before pay period}}} + \underset{\$900}{\substack{\text{Gross earnings for} \\ \text{the pay period}}} = \underset{\$43,200}{\substack{\text{Cumulative earnings} \\ \text{to date}}}$$

(H) Taxable Earnings: Unemployment Insurance

In the next chapter we will see that certain taxes for state and federal unemployment insurance are paid only by the employer. Federal unemployment taxes, which are based on **taxable earnings,** are paid on the first $7,000 of earnings of each employee. The first $7,000 that each employee earns during the year is the wage base limit for federal unemployment insurance purposes. *This column doesn't show the tax amount: it shows the earnings that are subject to being taxed.*

Example: Before this payroll, Bob Jones has cumulative earnings of $6,800. In this pay period, he earns $624. Since the employer pays these unemployment taxes on the first $7,000 of earnings, only $200 will be taxed (we will provide tax rates in next chapter) of the $624.

Total taxable earnings for unemployment taxes per employee	$7,000
Cumulative earnings before pay period for Jones	6,800
Taxable earnings	$ 200

Now look at the lines on the payroll register for Susan O'Mally, Pat Regan, and Jim Zott. No federal unemployment insurance tax needs to be paid for any of these employees because each of them had earned $7,000 before this pay period.

(I) Taxable Earnings FICA: Social Security

All employees are taxed for Social Security until they have earned $65,400 for the calendar year. This column shows the amount of earnings that will be taxed for Social Security. It *does not* show the actual tax.

> **Example:** Susan O'Mally has earned $64,625 before this pay period. Since she has earned more than the maximum of $65,400 after this payroll, only $775 will be taxed for Social Security:
>
> $$\begin{array}{r} \$65{,}400 \\ -\ 64{,}625 \\ \hline \$\ \ \ \ 775 \end{array}$$

(J) Taxable Earnings FICA: Medicare

All employee earnings are subject to the FICA Medicare tax.

(K) FICA Deduction—Social Security

The rate for Social Security is 6.2 percent on $65,400. In column (I) we see the taxable earnings for Social Security. By multiplying the 6.2 percent times the taxable earnings for each employee, we arrive at the Social Security tax.

> **Example:** For this pay period for Jim Zott only $540 of the $1,380 is taxable for Social Security (column I)
>
> $$\begin{array}{r} \$65{,}400 \\ -\ 64{,}860 \\ \hline \$\ \ \ \ 540 \times .062 = \$33.48 \end{array}$$

(L) FICA Deduction—Medicare

The rate for Medicare is 1.45 percent on all employee earnings.

> **Example:** Jim Zott's whole earnings of $1,380 is multiplied times 1.45 percent to arrive at a Medicare tax of $20.01.
>
> $$\$1{,}380 \times .0145 = \$20.01$$

(M) Federal Income Tax

Federal income tax does not have a cutoff point. Employees are taxed on the total amount of their earnings for the year. The amount of tax withheld depends upon the person's (1) income, (2) marital status, and (3) number of exemptions claimed. Withholding tables are provided in *Circular E* of the *Employer's Tax Guide* published by the IRS.

> **Example:** Susan O'Mally is married, earning $1,375 per week, and claims three allowances. Using Figure 7-2 (p. 240), we get a tax of $222.

At the end of the year, the employee must prepare a federal tax return (Form 1040) and file it with the IRS. If too much tax has been withheld, the employee can request a refund; if too little has been taken out, the employee must pay the amount due when his or her tax return is filed. Various tax deductions and tax credits affect the amount of tax due.

(N) State Income Tax

Assume a 5 percent state income tax rate. Like federal income tax, there is no cutoff point. All of the employee's earnings are taxed.

> **Example:** Pat Regan's state income tax is $45.
>
> | Gross pay | | Tax rate | | State income tax |
> |-----------|---|----------|---|------------------|
> | $900 | × | .05 | = | $45 |

(O) Medical Insurance

Fred's Market deducts $22 from hourly workers and $44 from salaried workers to pay for **medical insurance.**

(P) Net Pay

Net pay, or *take home pay,* is gross pay less deductions. Gross pay is what we wished we had; net pay is what we are stuck with.

> **Example:** Abby King, who is single, has worked a 44-hour week this pay period. Therefore, her gross earnings for the week are $644. Abby has one allowance. She will take home $429.53 as her net pay. This is what Abby's check showed.
>
> | | | | |
> |---|---|---:|---:|
> | Gross Pay | | | $644.00 |
> | *Less:* | FICA — Social Security | $ 39.93 | |
> | | FICA — Medicare | 9.34 | |
> | | Federal Income Tax | 100.00 | |
> | | State Income Tax | 32.20 | |
> | | Medical Insurance | 22.00 | 203.47 |
> | Net Pay | | | $440.53 |

(Q) Check Number

When the payroll is paid, the check number is recorded in the payroll register.

(R & S) Distribution of Expense Accounts

These two columns identify the specific accounts to which the total gross earnings of $4,923 [column (F)] will be charged. For Fred's Market some employee earnings are allocated to office salaries and some to market wages. (We will show how this is done in the next unit when data from the payroll register is used to journalize and post the payroll entry.)

LEARNING UNIT 7-2 REVIEW

AT THIS POINT you should be able to

◆ Explain and prepare a payroll register. (p. 244)
◆ Explain the purpose of the taxable earnings columns and how they relate to the cumulative earnings columns. (p. 247)

SELF-REVIEW QUIZ 7-2

(The forms you need are on pages 231–232 of the *Study Guide and Working Papers*.)

Ryan Leter is an hourly employee who is paid weekly. He is paid overtime at a rate of 1.5 times his hourly pay for any hours he works over 40 each week. Ryan Leter has cumulative earnings of $64,600 before this pay period. This week he earns $1,200. Calculate his net pay, assuming the following facts:

1. FICA: Social Security, 6.2 percent on $65,400; Medicare, 1.45 percent with no wage base limit.
2. He is married claiming two allowances (use the table in Figure 7-2).
3. State income tax rate is 7 percent.
4. No other deductions are taken out by his employer.

Solutions to Self-Review Quiz 7-2

1. FICA: Social Security — $800 × .062 = $49.60;
   Medicare — $1,200 × .0145 = $17.40.
2. Federal income tax is $188 by table.
3. State income tax is $84.
   Thus, his net pay = $861 ($1,200 − $49.60 − $17.40 − $188 − $84).

Quiz Tip: Only the first $800 of Leter's wages is subject to social security tax ($65,400 − $64,600).

LEARNING UNIT 7-3
Recording and Paying the Payroll

Since the payroll register is a multicolumn form used only to record payroll data, we must take the data from the payroll register and prepare a journal entry in the general journal to record the payroll and then post to the specific accounts in the general ledger. Refer to the payroll register shown in Figure 7-4, pp. 244–245.

For Fred's Market, the payroll for the week ending on November 25, 19XX is recorded in the general journal as follows:

General Journal					
Nov	25	Office Salaries Expense	3 6 5 5 00		
		Market Wages Expense	1 2 6 8 00		
		FICA — Social Security Payable		2 1 5 95	
		FICA — Medicare Payable		7 1 39	
		Federal Income Tax Payable		7 8 4 00	
		State Income Tax Payable		2 4 6 15	
		Medical Insurance Payable		1 7 6 00	
		Wages and Salaries Payable		3 4 2 9 51	
		Records payroll from payroll			
		register for week ended Nov. 25			

Note that the debits to **Office Salaries Expense** and **Market Wages Expense** come from the totals of the distribution of expense accounts on the payroll register (p. 245). The credits to **FICA—Social Security Payable** and **FICA—Medicare Payable,** the FIT Payable, SIT Payable, and Medical Insurance Payable are from the totals of these deductions on the payroll register. Keep in mind that these deductions are liabilities. The credit to **Wages and Salaries Payable** (a liability account) is from the total of the net pay column on the payroll register. The ledger of Fred's Market will look as follows *after* the posting process has been completed:

Wages and Salaries Payable 202		FICA—Social Security Payable 203		FICA—Medicare Payable 204
	3,429.51		215.95		71.39
Liability on the balance sheet		Liability on the balance sheet		Liability on the balance sheet

Federal Income Tax Payable 205		State Income Tax Payable 206		Medical Insurance Payable 207
	784.00		246.15		176.00
Liability on the balance sheet		Liability on the balance sheet		Liability on the balance sheet

Office Salaries Expense 601		Market Wages Expense 602
3,655.00		1,268.00
Expense on the income statement		Expense on the income statement

Figure 7-5 on page 252 summarizes this process.

PAYROLL CHECKING ACCOUNTS: PAYING THE PAYROLL

Fred's Market pays payroll by check from a special payroll checking account. The account is called Payroll Checking Cash. Most medium- to large-size firms have a separate checking account *for payroll checks* and a regular checking account for all other checks. Employers use a payroll checking account for paychecks for two reasons: 1) it gives them better internal control over the amounts deposited for a pay period, and 2) it allows for easier reconciliation of the account at the end of each month.

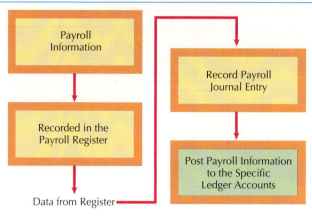

FIGURE 7-5 The Payroll Recording and Posting Process (see p. 253.)

A deposit for the total net amount of the payroll is placed in this separate checking account. When all the checks are written, the payroll checking account balance should be zero. The following journal entries would result in paying the payroll.

Payroll Checking Cash   ←——— Separate account for payroll
   Cash   set up.

Wages and Salaries Payable   ←——— Payroll paid and balance in
   Payroll Checking Cash   Payroll Checking is zero.

The checks from Fred's Market provide space to list amounts earned along with deductions, as shown in Figure 7-6 for Susan O'Mally. Keep in mind that if

FIGURE 7-6
Check from Fred's Market.

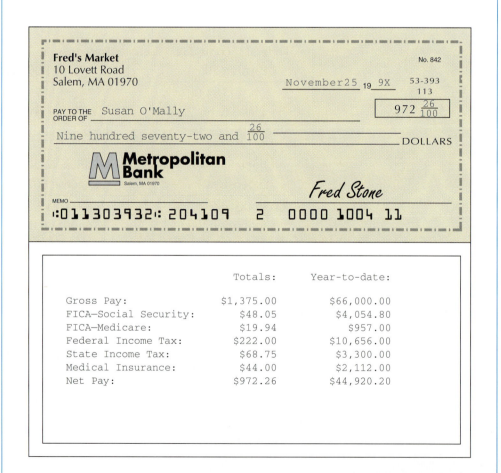

	Totals:	Year-to-date:
Gross Pay:	$1,375.00	$66,000.00
FICA—Social Security:	$48.05	$4,054.80
FICA—Medicare:	$19.94	$957.00
Federal Income Tax:	$222.00	$10,656.00
State Income Tax:	$68.75	$3,300.00
Medical Insurance:	$44.00	$2,112.00
Net Pay:	$972.26	$44,920.20

the account Payroll Checking Cash is not used, payroll can be paid by debiting Wages and Salaries Payable and crediting Cash.

THE INDIVIDUAL EMPLOYEE EARNINGS RECORD

Before concluding this chapter, it is important to look at how Fred keeps an individual record of each person's earnings and deductions, as required to meet federal employment laws and state regulations.

Fred maintains a summary of each employee's earnings, deductions, net pay for each payroll period, and cumulative earnings during the year. Figure 7-7 on page 254 is a partial **individual employee earnings record** for Susan O'Mally. This record will help Fred gather information to pay taxes and report quarterly and yearly payroll amounts. Individual employee earnings records generally break the calendar year into quarters, showing quarterly totals and year-to-date totals for earnings and taxes withheld. Keep in mind that each quarter is 13 weeks.

Note in the record for Susan that in the fourth quarter in week 48, she pays no more tax for Social Security since she is over the maximum $65,400. However, she will continue to pay Medicare on all of her earnings.

Figure 7-8 reviews the payroll function for Fred.

FIGURE 7-8 Payroll Function for Fred's Market

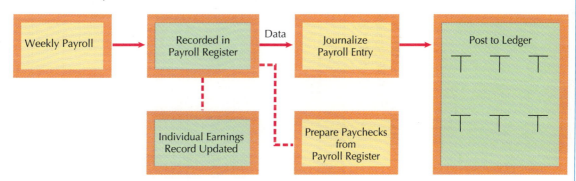

LEARNING UNIT 7-3 REVIEW

AT THIS POINT you should be able to

- Explain how to enter payroll information into the general journal from the payroll register. (p. 250)
- Journalize entries to pay a payroll. (p. 251)
- Update an individual employee earnings record. (p. 254)

SELF-REVIEW QUIZ 7-3

(The forms you need are on page 232 of the *Study Guide and Working Papers.*) Indicate which of the following statements are false:

(Cont. on p. 255)

FIGURE 7-7 Employee Individual Earnings Record

INDIVIDUAL EMPLOYEE EARNINGS RECORD
FOR SUSAN O'MALLEY
FOURTH QUARTER, 19XX

Week #	Hours Worked Regular	Hours Worked Overtime	Total Earnings	Deductions Soc. Sec.	Medicare	Fed. Inc. Tax	State Inc. Tax	Med. Ins.	Net Pay	Check No.	Cumulative Pay
											53625.00
40			1375.00	85.25	19.94	222.00	68.75	44.00	935.06	710	55000.00
41			1375.00	85.25	19.94	222.00	68.75	44.00	935.06	750	56375.00
42			1375.00	85.25	19.94	222.00	68.75	44.00	935.06	780	57750.00
43			1375.00	85.25	19.94	222.00	68.75	44.00	935.06	812	59125.00
44			1375.00	85.25	19.94	222.00	68.75	44.00	935.06	830	60500.00
45			1375.00	85.25	19.94	222.00	68.75	44.00	935.06	842	61875.00
46			1375.00	85.25	19.94	222.00	68.75	44.00	935.06	871	63250.00
47			1375.00	85.25	19.94	222.00	68.75	44.00	935.06	893	64625.00
48			1375.00	48.05	19.94	222.00	68.75	44.00	972.26	915	66000.00
Total 4th Quarter			17875.00	730.05	259.22	2886.00	893.75	572.00	12533.98		
Total for Year			71500.00	4054.80	1036.88	11544.00	3575.00	2288.00	49001.32		

All Dunkin' Donuts shops keep a master file of employee information, containing every employee's name, address, phone number, Social Security number, rate of pay, hours worked per week, and W-4 form. Different shop owners offer different rates of pay, depending on local conditions. They offer different benefits as well. They employ mostly part-time workers, usually with a core of full-timers. Fred, for example, pays clerks with less than one year's experience the minimum wage. He offers health and dental insurance. Some of the bigger shop owners also offer profit sharing to employees with a minimum of five years of service. The frequency of pay varies by state, and sometimes by city or county. So, of course, do tax rates.

All this information must be recorded and reported to the various state, local, and federal authorities—and to Dunkin' Donuts headquarters, through the zone's Business Consultant.

Scheduling workers and keeping payroll records are Fred's least-favorite jobs. He was pleased to hear Dwayne announce at an Advisory Council meeting that

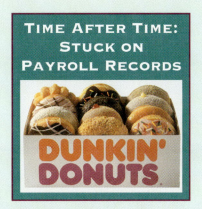

TIME AFTER TIME: STUCK ON PAYROLL RECORDS

the company's new IBM terminals will offer an electronic scheduling package.

"Wow! That will really help, Dwayne!" said Fred joyously. "No more different colors of ink just to keep track of who will work when! Now we can plan around the exam schedules of the part-timers without a hassle! Scheduling will be my favorite module in the new system!"

"Sure," said Molly Harris, another shop owner. "Now you can concentrate on payroll records. What fun!"

Fred groaned.

DISCUSSION QUESTIONS

1. What payroll records does Fred need to keep for his donut shop?
2. What other information might Fred want in order to schedule working hours for each employee?
3. How does the payroll register help Fred prepare the payroll? Consult the process outlined on page 253.

---

1. The use of a payroll register to record a company's payroll is optional.
2. FICA—Social Security Payable is a liability on the income statement.
3. Wages and Salaries Expense has a normal credit balance.
4. Individual employee earnings records are used by employees to keep track of their wages.
5. Every calendar quarter has 13 weeks.

Quiz Tip: **There are four quarters in a year.**

Solution to Self-Review Quiz 7-3

Statements 1, 2, 3, and 4 are false.

SUMMARY OF KEY POINTS

Learning Unit 7-1

1. The Fair Labor Standards Act states that a worker (1) will receive a minimum hourly rate of pay and (2) will work a maximum of 40 hours during the week at the regular rate of pay with time and a half after 40 hours.
2. In order for the rules of the Fair Labor Standards Act to apply to an employer, the employer must be involved in interstate commerce.
3. The employee and employer equally contribute to Social Security tax an amount that is based on a given yearly rate and wage base for a calendar year. Only Social Security tax has a wage base limit of $65,400 as of this writing. Medicare has no wage base limit, so an employee and employer will pay this tax on all of the employee's earnings during the calendar year.
4. Tax tables for federal income tax withholding can be found in IRS *Circular E, Employer's Tax Guide* (also known as Publication 15).

Learning Unit 7-2

1. Gross pay less deductions equals net pay.
2. The taxable earnings columns do not show the tax. They show amount of earnings to be taxed for unemployment taxes, Social Security, and Medicare. Note that FICA is made up of two taxes, Social Security and Medicare.

Learning Unit 7-3

1. A payroll register provides the data for journalizing the payroll entry in the general journal.
2. Deductions for payroll represent liabilities for the employer until paid.
3. The account distribution columns of the payroll register indicate which accounts will be debited to record the total payroll wages and salaries expense when a journal entry is prepared.
4. The accounts *FICA – Social Security Payable* and *FICA – Medicare Payable* accumulate the tax liabilities of both the employer and the employee for Medicare and Social Security.
5. Paying a payroll results in debiting *Wages and Salaries Payable* and crediting *Cash* (or Payroll Checking Cash).
6. The individual employee earnings records are updated soon after the payroll register is prepared.

KEY TERMS

Allowance (also called exemption) A certain dollar amount of a person's income that will be considered nontaxable for income tax withholding purposes.

Calendar year A one-year period beginning on January 1 and ending on December 31. Employers must use a calendar year for payroll purposes, even if the employer uses a fiscal year for financial statements and for any other reasons.

Fair Labor Standards Act (Federal Wage and Hour Law) A law the majority of employers must follow that contains rules stating the minimum hourly rate of pay and the maximum number of hours a worker will work before being paid time and a half for overtime hours worked. This law also has other rules and regulations that employers must follow for payroll purposes.

Federal income tax withholding Amount of federal income tax withheld by the employer from the employee's gross pay; the amount withheld is determined by the employee's gross pay, the pay period, the number of allowances claimed by the employee on the W-4 form, and by the marital status indicated on the W-4 form.

FICA (Federal Insurance Contributions Act) Part of the Social Security Act of 1935, this law requires that a tax be levied on both the employer and employee up to a certain maximum rate and wage base for Social Security tax purposes. Furthermore, there is a tax for Medicare purposes with no employer or employee wage base maximum.

FICA–Medicare Payable A liability account that accumulates tax for Medicare.

FICA–Social Security Payable A liability account that accumulates tax for Social Security.

Gross earnings Amount of pay received before any deductions.

Individual employee earnings record An accounting document that summarizes the total amount of wages paid and the deductions for the calendar year. It aids in preparing governmental reports. A new record is prepared for each employee each year.

Interstate commerce Test that is applied to determine whether an employer must follow the rules of the Fair Labor Standards Act. If an employer communicates or does business with another business in some other state it is usually considered to be involved in interstate commerce.

Market Wages Expense An account that records from the payroll register gross wages earned by employees of a market (grocery) outlet.

Medical insurance A deduction from employee's paycheck for health insurance.

Net pay Gross pay less deductions. Net pay (or *take home pay*) is what the worker actually takes home.

Office Salaries Expense An account that records from the payroll gross salaries earned by employees of an office.

Pay (or payroll) period A length of time used by an employer to calculate the amount of an employee's earnings. Pay periods can be weekly, biweekly (once every two weeks), semimonthly (twice each month), or monthly.

Payroll register A multicolumn form that can be used to record payroll data. The data in the payroll register is then used to prepare the general journal entry to record the paying of employees for a pay period.

Payroll tax deposits Amounts an employer pays to the government for payroll taxes. We will discuss these deposits in more detail in Chapter 8.

State income tax withholding Amount of state income tax withheld by the employer from the employee's gross pay.

Taxable earnings Shows amount of earnings subject to a tax. This *does not* show the tax itself.

W-4 (Employee's Withholding Allowance Certificate) A form filled out by employees used by employers to supply needed information about the number of allowances claimed, marital status, etc. The form is used for payroll purposes to determine federal income tax withholding from an employee's paycheck.

Wage bracket tables Various charts in IRS Circular E providing information about deductions for federal income tax based on earnings and data supplied on the W-4 form.

Wages and Salaries Payable A liability account that shows net pay for payroll before employees are paid. Account zeros out after employees are paid.

Workers' Compensation Insurance Insurance required by employers to protect their employees against losses due to injury or death incurred while on the job.

Questions, Mini Exercises, Exercises, and Problems

Discussion Questions

1. What is the purpose of the Fair Labor Standards Act (also called Federal Wage and Hour Law)?
2. Explain how to calculate overtime.
3. Define and state the purpose of completing a W-4 form (called the *Employee's Withholding Allowance Certificate*).
4. The more allowances an employee claims on a W-4 form the more take home pay the employee gets with each paycheck. Please comment.
5. Why should a business prepare a payroll register before employees are paid? Please explain.

(Cont. on p. 259)

BLUEPRINT FOR RECORDING, POSTING, AND PAYING THE PAYROLL

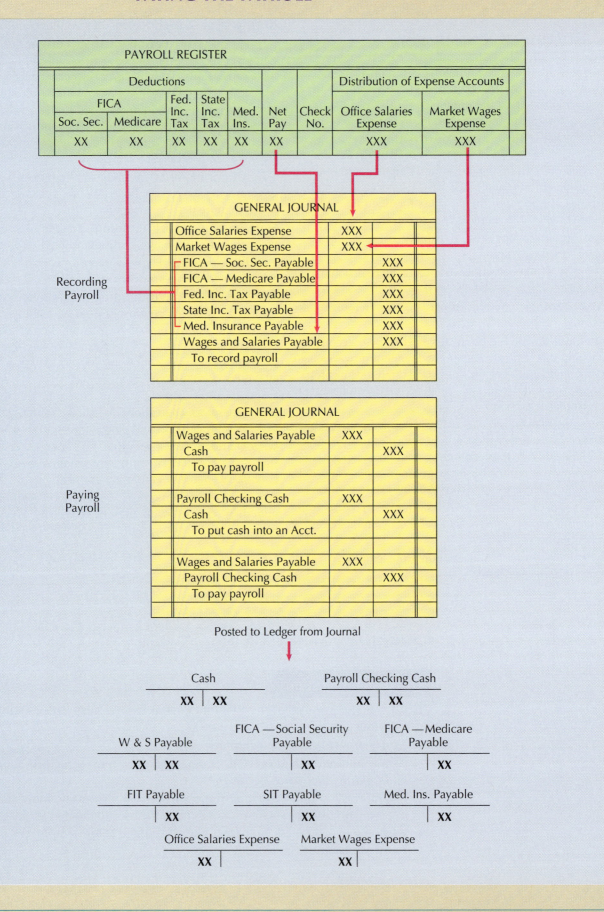

6. True or false: the taxable earnings column of a payroll register records the amount of tax due.

7. Define and state the purpose of FICA taxes.

8. Explain how to calculate Social Security and Medicare.

9. Do you agree or disagree with the following statement: the employer doesn't have to contribute to Social Security.

10. Explain how federal and state income tax withholding are determined.

11. What is a calendar year?

12. True or false: an employer must always use a calendar year for payroll purposes.

13. What purpose does the individual employee earnings record serve?

14. Why does payroll information center on 13-week quarters?

15. Please draw a diagram showing how the following items relate to each other: (A) a weekly payroll; (B) a payroll register; (C) individual employees' earnings; (D) general journal entries for payroll; (E) a payroll checking account.

16. If you earned $130,000 this year, you would pay more Social Security and Medicare tax than your partner who earned $75,000. Do you agree or disagree? Please provide calculations to support your answer.

Mini Exercises

(The forms you need are on page 234 of the *Study Guide and Working Papers.*)

Calculating Gross Earnings

1. Calculate the total wages earned (assume an overtime rate of time and a half over 40 hours).

Employee	Hourly Rate	No. of Hours Worked
A. Dawn Slow	$10	37
B. Jill Jones	12	50

FICA

2. Pete Martin, single claiming 1, has cumulative earnings before this weekly pay period of $80,000. Assuming he is paid $1,200 this week, what will his deduction be for FIT and FICA (Medicare and Social Security)? Use tables and rates in text.

Net Pay

3. Calculate Pete's Net Pay from 2 above. State income tax is 5 percent and death insurance is $40.

Payroll Register

4. From the following identify:
   1. Total of gross pay — comes from distribution of expense accounts
   2. A deduction
   3. Net Pay
   _____ A. Office Salaries Expense and Wages Expense
   _____ B. FICA — SS Payable
   _____ C. FICA — Medicare Payable
   _____ D. Federal Income Tax Payable
   _____ E. Medical Insurance Payable
   _____ F. Wages and Salaries Payable

Payroll Account

5. From the following indicate if the title is:

    1. An Asset   **4.** Appears in the Income Statement
    2. A Liability   **5.** Appears on the Balance Sheet
    3. An Expense

       _____ **a.** FICA — Social Security Payable
       _____ **b.** Office Salaries Expense
       _____ **c.** Federal Income Tax Payable
       _____ **d.** FICA — Medicare Payable
       _____ **e.** Wages and Salaries Payable

Exercises

(The forms you will need are on pages 235 – 236 of the *Study Guide and Working Papers.*)

Calculating wages with overtime.

7-1. Calculate the total wages earned for each employee (assume an overtime rate of time and a half over 40 hours):

Employee	Hourly Rate	No. of Hours Worked
Bob Role	$ 8	35
Jill West	12	44
Dale Aster	11	46

Tax table.

7-2. Compute the Net Pay for each employee using the federal income tax withholding tables in Figure 7-2 (Assume the following for FICA: Social Security tax is 6.2 percent on a wage base limit of $65,400; Medicare is 1.45 percent on all earnings; the payroll is paid weekly; there is no state income tax).

Employee	Status	Claiming	Cumulative Pay	This Week's Pay
Alvin Cell	Married	1	$50,000	$1,190
Angel Lowe	Single	0	$64,300	$1,200

7-3. Complete the table:

Categorizing accounts.

	Category	↑	Normal Balance	Account Appears on Which Financial Report?
Medical Insurance Payable				
Wages and Salaries Payable				
Office Salaries Expense				
Market Wages Expense				
FICA—Social Security Payable				
Federal Income Tax Payable				
State Income Tax Payable				

7-4. The following weekly payroll journal entry was prepared by Luster Company from its payroll register. Which columns of the payroll register has the data come from? How does the *taxable earnings* column of the payroll register relate to this entry?

Payroll register and the journal entry.

Oct.	7	Shop Salaries Expense		4 0 0 00		
		Factory Wages Expense		2 0 0 00		
		FICA–Social Security Payable				3 7 2 00
		FICA–Medicare Payable				8 7 00
		Federal Income Tax Payable				1 2 0 0 00
		State Income Tax Payable				1 2 5 6 00
		Union Dues Payable				1 1 0 00
		Wages and Salaries Payable				2 9 7 5 00

7-5. The following amounts have been taken from the weekly payroll register for the Debra Company on October 9, 19XX. Using the same account title headings that we have used in this chapter, please prepare the general journal entry to record the payroll for Debra Company for October 9.

Recording payroll by journal entry.

Factory Wages Expense	$3,579.00
Office Salaries Expense	1,597.00
Deduction for FICA — Social Security	296.15
Deduction for FICA — Medicare	75.05
Deduction for federal income tax	1,112.84
Deduction for state income tax	258.80
Deduction for union dues	350.00

Group A Problems

(The forms you need are on pages 237–241 of the *Study Guide and Working Papers*.)

7A-1. From the following information, please complete the chart for gross earnings for the week. (Assume an overtime rate of time and one half over 40 hours.)

Calculating gross earnings with overtime.
Check Figure:
d. $660 Gross Earnings

	Hourly Rate	No. of Hours Worked	Gross Earnings
a. Joe Jackson	$ 6	40	
b. Edna Kane	8	47	
c. Dick Wall	10	42	
d. Pat Green	12	50	

7A-2. March Company has five salaried employees. Your task is to record the following information into a payroll register.

Completing a payroll register.

Employee	Allowance and Marital Status	Cumulative Earnings Before this Payroll	Weekly Salary	Department
Kool, Alice	M-1	$42,000	$1,200	Sales
Lose, Bob	S-1	30,000	680	Office
Moore, Linda	M-2	59,200	1,240	Office
Relt, Rusty	M-3	64,000	1,270	Sales
Veel, Larry	S-0	29,000	610	Sales

Assume the following:

1. FICA: Social Security, 6.2 percent on $65,400; Medicare, 1.45 percent on all earnings.
2. Each employee contributes $25 per week for union dues.
3. State income tax is 6 percent of gross pay.
4. FIT is calculated from tables in Figures 7-2 and 7-3.

Check Figure:

Net Pay $3,382.49

Completing a payroll register and journalizing the payroll entry.

7A-3. The bookkeeper of Gore Co. gathered the following data from individual employees' earnings records and daily time cards. Your task is to (1) complete a payroll register on December 12 and (2) journalize the appropriate entry to record the payroll.

Employee	Allowance and Marital Status	Cumulative Earnings Before this Payroll	M	T	W	T	F	Hourly Rate of Pay	Department
Boy, Pete	M-1	$64,100	5	11	9	8	8	$18	Sales
Heat, Donna	S-0	15,000	8	10	9	9	4	16	Office
Pyle, Ray	M-3	66,000	8	10	10	10	10	16	Sales
Vent, Joan	S-1	19,000	8	8	8	8	8	20	Office

Daily Time columns: M, T, W, T, F

Assume the following:

1. FICA: Social Security, 6.2 percent on $65,400; Medicare, 1.45 percent on all earnings.
2. Federal income tax is calculated from tables in Figures 7-2 and 7-3.
3. Each employee contributes $25 per week for health insurance.
4. Overtime is paid at a rate of time and a half over 40 hours.

Check Figure:

Net Pay $2,309.64

Payroll register completed; journalizing and posting.

7A-4. Gary Nelson, Accountant, has gathered the following data from the time cards and individual employee earnings records. Your task is to

1. On December 5, 19XX, prepare a payroll register for this weekly payroll.
2. Journalize (p. 4) in the general journal and post to the general ledger accounts.

Employee	Allowance and Marital Status	Cumulative Earnings Before this Payroll	Weekly Salary	Check No.	Department
Aulson, Andy	M-3	$30,000	$ 950	30	Factory
Flynn, Jacki	M-1	50,000	$1,000	31	Office
Moore, Jeff	M-2	60,000	1,200	32	Factory
Sullivan, Alison	M-1	65,000	1,300	33	Office

Check Figure:

Net Pay $3,235.87

Assume the following:

1. FICA: Social Security, 6.2 percent on $65,400; Medicare, 1.45 percent on all earnings.
2. Federal income tax is calculated from tables in Figure 7-2.
3. State income tax is 5 percent of gross pay.
4. Union dues are $10 per week.

Group B Problems

(The forms you need are on pages 237–241 in the *Study Guide and Working Papers.*)

Calculating gross earnings with overtime.

7B-1. From the following information, please complete the chart for gross earnings for the week. (Assume an overtime rate of time and one half over 40 hours.)

		Hourly Rate	No. of Hours Worked	Gross Earnings
a.	Joe Jackson	$ 5	40	
b.	Edna Kane	9	47	
c.	Dick Wall	12	36	
d.	Pat Green	14	55	

Check Figure:

d. Gross Pay $875

Completing a payroll register.

7B-2. March Company has five salaried employees. Your task is to record the following information into a payroll register.

Employee	Allowance and Marital Status	Cumulative Earnings Before this Payroll	Weekly Salary	Department
Kool, Alice	M-1	$45,150	$1,290	Sales
Lose, Bob	S-1	22,575	645	Office
Moore, Linda	M-2	59,300	1,240	Office
Relt, Rusty	M-3	64,500	1,300	Sales
Veel, Larry	S-0	21,875	625	Sales

Check Figure:

Net Pay $3,468.65

Assume the following:

1. FICA: Social Security, 6.2 percent on $65,400; Medicare, 1.45 percent on all earnings.
2. Each employee contributes $25 per week for union dues.
3. State income tax is 6 percent of gross pay.
4. FIT is calculated from tables in Figures 7-2 and 7-3.

Completing a payroll entry and journalizing the payroll entry.

7B-3. The bookkeeper of Gore Co. gathered the following data from individual employees' earnings records and daily time cards. Your task is to (1) complete a payroll register on December 12 and (2) journalize the appropriate entry to record the payroll.

Employee	Allowance and Marital Status	Cumulative Earnings Before this Payroll	M	T	W	T	F	Hourly Rate of Pay	Department
Boy, Pete	S-1	$64,900	12	11	7	7	7	$16	Sales
Heat, Donna	S-0	19,000	8	9	9	9	5	16	Office
Pyle, Ray	M-3	67,550	10	10	10	10	5	20	Sales
Vent, Joan	S-1	13,500	6	8	8	8	8	19	Office

Daily Time: M, T, W, T, F

Check Figure:

Net Pay $2,323.36

Assume the following:

1. FICA: Social Security, 6.2 percent on $65,400; Medicare, 1.45 percent on all earnings.
2. Federal income tax is calculated from tables in Figures 7-2 and 7-3.
3. Each employee contributes $25 per week for health insurance.
4. Overtime is paid at a rate of time and a half over 40 hours.

Payroll entry completed; journalizing and posting.

7B-4. Gary Nelson, Accountant, has gathered the following data from the time cards and individual employee earnings records. Your task is to

1. On December 5, 19XX, prepare a payroll register for this weekly payroll.
2. Journalize (p. 4) in the general journal and post to the general ledger accounts.

Employee	Allowance and Marital Status	Cumulative Earnings Before this Payroll	Weekly Salary	Check No.	Department
Aulson, Andy	M-3	$30,000	$ 800	30	Factory
Flynn, Jacki	M-1	50,000	$1,100	31	Office
Moore, Jeff	M-2	60,000	1,050	32	Factory
Sullivan, Alison	M-1	65,000	1,200	33	Office

Assume the following:

1. FICA: Social Security, 6.2 percent on $65,400; Medicare 1.45 percent on all earnings.
2. Federal income tax is calculated from tables in Figure 7-2.
3. State income tax is 6 percent of gross pay.
4. Union dues are $15 per week.

REAL WORLD APPLICATIONS

7R-1.

Small Company, a sole proprietorship, has two employees, Jim Roy and Janice Alter. The owner of Small Co. is Bert Ryan. During the current pay period, Jim worked 48 hours and Janice 56. The reason for these extra hours is that both Jim and Janice worked their regular 40-hour workweek, plus Jim worked 8 extra hours on Sunday while Janice worked 8 extra hours on Saturday and Sunday. Their contract with Small Co. is that they are each paid an hourly rate of $8 per hour with all hours over 40 to be time and a half and double time on Sunday. Bert, the owner, feels he is also entitled to a salary, since he works as many hours. He plans to pay himself $425.

As the accountant for Small Co., (1) calculate the gross pay for Jim and Janice and (2) write a letter to Bert Ryan with your recommendations regarding his salary.

7R-2.

Marcy Moore works for Moose Company during the day and GTA Company at night. Both her employers have deducted FICA taxes for Social Security and Medicare. At year end Marcy has earned $58,000 at her job at Moose Company and $8,000 at GTA.

At a party she tells Bill Barnes, an accountant, who tells her she has paid too much Social Security tax and that she is entitled to a refund or credit on her tax return she files for the year. Bill suggests she call the Internal Revenue Service's toll-free number and ask for taxpayer assistance. Assume Social Security of 6.2 percent on $65,400 and Medicare of 1.45 percent on all of Marcy's earnings during the year.

As Marcy's friend, (1) check to see if indeed she has overpaid any FICA tax, and (2) write a brief note to her and show her your calculations to support your answer.

 make the call

Critical Thinking/Ethical Case

7R-3.

Russ Todd works for a delicatessen. As the bookkeeper Russ has been asked by the owner to keep two separate books for meals tax. The owner has asked Todd to hire someone on the weekends to punch in false tapes that can be submitted to the state. These tapes would show low sales and thus less liability for meals tax payments. You make the call. Write down your specific recommendations to Russ.

ACCOUNTING RECALL
A CUMULATIVE APPROACH

THIS EXAM REVIEWS CHAPTERS 1 THROUGH 7

Your *Study Guide and Working Papers* (pages 244–255) have forms to complete this exam, as well as worked-out solutions. The page references next to each question identify what page to turn back to if you answer the question incorrectly.

PART 1   Vocabulary Review

Match the terms to the appropriate definition or phrase.

Page Ref.

(247)	1. Taxable earnings columns	A. Gross pay less deductions
(217)	2. Petty cash	B. In payroll register records, gross payroll
(212)	3. NSF	
(239)	4. Exemption	C. Liability accounts for social security and medicare
(161)	5. Closing	
(251)	6. Office salaries expense	D. An asset
(240)	7. Wage bracket tables	E. Does not show tax
(249)	8. Net pay	F. Found in Circular E
(254)	9. Employee individual earnings record	G. Result of a bounced check
		H. Not taxable
(251)	10. FICA — Social Security payable, and FICA — Medicare payable	I. Helps get updated figure for Capital in ledger
		J. Broken down into quarters

PART II   True or False (Accounting Theory)

(216)   11. Petty cash is a liability.

(243)   12. A payroll register is always the same for each company.

(247)   13. The taxable earnings column of a payroll register shows earnings that are subject to being taxed.

(254)   14. Wages and Salaries Payable records gross pay.

(122)   15. Accumulated depreciation is a contra-asset on the balance sheet.

CONTINUING PROBLEM

n preparing for next year, Freedman has hired two employees to work hourly, assisting with some troubleshooting and repair work.

Assignment:

(See pp. 245 – 254 in your *Study Guide and Working Papers*.)

1. Record the following transactions in general journal format, and post to the general ledger.
2. Prepare a payroll register.
3. Prepare a trial balance as of November 30, 19XX.

   Assume the following transactions:

   a) The following accounts have been added to the chart of accounts: Wage Expense #5110; FICA-Social Security Payable #2020; FICA-Medicare Payable #2030; FIT Payable #2040; State Income Tax Payable #2050; and Wages Payable #2010.

   b) FICA-Social Security is taxed at 6.2 percent up to $65,400 in earnings; and Medicare at 1.45 percent on all earnings.

   c) State income tax is 2 percent of gross pay.

   d) Both employees have no federal income tax taken out of their pay.

   e) Each employee earns $10 an hour and is paid $1\frac{1}{2}$ times their salary for hours worked in excess of 40 weekly.

Nov		
	1	Billed Vita Needle Company $6,800; invoice #12675 for services rendered
	3	Billed Accu Pac, Inc. $3,900; invoice #12676 for services rendered
	5	Purchased new shop benches $1,400 on account from System Design Furniture
	7	Paid the two employee wages: Lance Kumm, 38 hours, and Anthony Hall, 42 hours
	9	Received the phone bill, $150.
	12	Collected $500 of the amount due from Taylor Golf
	14	Paid the two employee wages: Lance Kumm, 25 hours, and Anthony Hall, 36 hours.
	18	Collected $800 of the amount due from Taylor Golf.
	20	Purchased a fax machine for the office from Multi Systems on credit, $450.
	21	Paid the two employee wages: Lance Kumm, 26 hours, and Anthony Hall, 35 hours

8

THE EMPLOYER'S TAX RESPONSIBILITIES

Principles and Procedures

THE BIG PICTURE

The goals for Eldorado Computer Center this year are to increase earnings, expand into additional locations, and increase revenue by 30 percent. Freedman realizes that company growth will eventually mean hiring more people. Therefore, although his revenue will increase, his operating expenses will also increase because of the additional payroll expenses he will incur.

After studying Chapter 8, you will understand these extra expenses. They include employer payroll taxes and worker's compensation insurance, which the law requires the employer to pay. Although Freedman is not offering benefits to his part-time employees at this time, he realizes that this too could become an additional operating expense.

Quarterly and annual federal tax returns must be submitted as well, similar to the personal income tax return that you are required to submit once a year. And most states require the employer to pay state unemployment insurance (SUTA) for each employee.

<table>
<tr>
<td>

Learning
Objectives

</td>
<td>

◆ **Calculating and journalizing employer payroll tax expenses. (p. 268)**
◆ **Completing the Employer's Quarterly Federal Tax Return and Deposit Coupon (Forms 941 and 8109) and paying tax obligations for FICA tax (Social Security and Medicare) and federal income tax. (p. 273)**
◆ **Preparing Forms W-2, W-3, 940-EZ, and estimates of workers' compensation insurance premiums. (p. 282)**

</td>
</tr>
</table>

I n Chapter 7 we looked at how Fred's Market computed and recorded payroll data about its *employees*. This chapter focuses on specific tax responsibilities of the *employer*.

LEARNING UNIT 8-1
The Employer's Payroll Tax Expense

When opening a business, every employer must get a federal **employer identification number** (also known as an **EIN**) for purposes of reporting earnings, taxes, etc. When Fred opened Fred's Market, he filled out **Form SS-4** to obtain his EIN. The SS-4 form asks for the following information:

1. Name of applicant.
2. Trade name of business.
3. Address or place of business.
4. County in which business is located.
5. Name of the principle officer or owner of the business.
6. Type of business (sole proprietor, partnership, etc.).
7. The reason for applying for an EIN.
8. The date the business began.
9. The closing month of the accounting year.
10. First date that the business will pay its employees.
11. The potential number of employees in the coming year.
12. Main activity or nature of the business.

Fred's payroll tax obligations are recorded in the general journal when the payroll is recorded. Fred's Market is responsible for (1) Social Security and Medicare tax (or FICA), (2) federal unemployment tax (FUTA), and (3) state unemployment tax (SUTA). The total of these taxes are recorded in the **Payroll Tax Expense** account in the general ledger.

Let's look at how Fred calculates the amount of each tax.

CALCULATING THE EMPLOYER'S PAYROLL TAXES
FICA (Federal Insurance Contributions Act)

It is the responsibility of Fred's Market to match whatever its employees pay into FICA on a dollar-for-dollar basis each pay period. The accounts in the ledger, *FICA-Social Security Payable* and *FICA-Medicare Payable*, record the tax for *both* the employee and the employer. To determine the amount of FICA Fred's Market owes, we must use the FICA taxable earnings columns for Social Security and Medicare from the payroll register discussed in Chapter 7 and reproduced here for your convenience as Figure 8-1.

FRED'S MARKET
PAYROLL REGISTER
NOVEMBER 25, 19XX

Employee Name	Allowances and Marital Status	Cumulative Earnings	Salary per Week	No. of Hrs.	Wages per Hour	Earnings Regular	Earnings Overtime	Earnings Gross	Cumulative Earnings	Taxable Earnings Federal Unemploy-ment	Taxable Earnings Soc. Sec.	Taxable Earnings Medicare
Jones, Bob	S-0	6800 00	—	39	16 00	624 00		624 00	7424 00	200 00	624 00	624 00
King, Abby	S-1	6600 00	—	44	14 00	560 00	84 00	644 00	7244 00	400 00	644 00	644 00
O'Mally, Susan	M-3	64625 00	1375 00			1375 00		1375 00	66000 00	—	775 00 ①	1375 00
Regan, Pat	M-1	42300 00	900 00			900 00		900 00	43200 00	—	900 00	900 00
Zott, Jim	M-2	64860 00	1380 00			1380 00		1380 00	66240 00	—	540 00	1380 00
TOTALS		185185 00	3655 00			4839 00	84 00	4923 00	190108 00	600 00	3483 00	4923 00
Discussions in this chapter are keyed to these letters	(A)	(B)	(C)			(D)	(E)	(F)	(G)	(H)	(I)	(J)

①
$65,400
−64,625
$ 775

FIGURE 8-1 Partial Payroll for Fred's Market

The payroll register shows that $3,483 [column (I)] of wages is subject to Social Security tax, while in column (J) we see $4,923 of wages is subject to tax for Medicare.

$$\text{Social Security} \qquad \$3,483 \times .062 = \$215.95$$
$$\text{Medicare} \qquad \$4,923 \times .0145 = \$ 71.38$$

The employer must match the FICA contribution of the employee for Social Security *and* Medicare taxes.

FICA-Social Security Payable 203	FICA-Medicare Payable 204
215.95 (employee)	71.38 (employee)
215.95 (employer)	71.38 (employee)

FUTA (Federal Unemployment Tax Act)

Unemployment insurance is a joint effort on the part of the federal government, all 50 states, and U.S. territories. Each state is required to run its own unemployment program for its unemployed workers. The state programs are approved and monitored by the federal government.

To raise money for these unemployment programs, the federal government levies taxes on employers under a law called the **Federal Unemployment Tax Act (FUTA).** This law (1) induces states to create their own unemployment programs, and (2) allows the federal government to monitor state programs. As mentioned in Chapter 7, the FUTA tax currently is 6.2 percent of wages paid during the year and the wage base limit is $7,000.

Generally, the federal government allows employers a credit against FUTA tax as long as the employer has paid all monies due to the state unemployment fund on time. This credit, called the **normal FUTA tax credit,** cannot exceed 5.4 percent. So, an employer who is entitled to the normal FUTA credit will pay a net amount of eight-tenths of one percent, as shown below:

6.2%	FUTA tax
− 5.4%	normal FUTA tax credit
.8%	net FUTA tax for federal purposes

In effect the federal law says to employees, "Comply with your state's unemployment tax laws and your total tax will not exceed a maximum of 6.2 percent: 0.8 percent to the federal government, and a state rate that will vary up to a maximum of 5.4 percent. Remember that employers alone are responsible for paying FUTA tax; it is never deducted from employees' wages.

In Learning Unit 8-3, we will look at how to complete the federal report and the deposit requirements for FUTA tax. For now, let's calculate the amount of accumulated federal unemployment tax for Fred's Market based on the unemployment column under taxable earnings in the payroll register. Remember the $600 in column H represents the amount of earnings taxable for federal unemployment.

To calculate the FUTA tax, we multiply the FUTA taxable earnings times the net FUTA tax rate.

Taxable FUTA Earnings		FUTA Rate		FUTA Tax	FUTA Tax Payable 209
$600	×	.008	=	$4.80	4.80

FUTA tax is paid after the end of a calendar year if the total tax owed is less than $100 for the year. If the amount owed is more than $100, the tax is paid on a quarterly basis, no later than the end of the month following the end of the quarter.

SUTA (State Unemployment Tax Acts)

To support state unemployment programs, all states charge employers a certain percent in taxes under the **State Unemployment Tax Act (SUTA).** Generally, employers pay more in SUTA tax than FUTA tax.

Each state has its own state unemployment wage base limit. Currently, these limits range from a low of $7,000 to a high of $25,000. The limits vary according to the needs of each state unemployment fund and are subject to change. For the current rate in your state, check with the state department of labor and employment.

The states vary the percentage rates charged to employers. The differences are based on the total amount of contributions the employer makes into the state fund and the dollar amount of unemployment claim money paid out of the fund to former employees of the employer. For example, employers who do not lay off employees during slack seasons (such as after the Christmas season or at the end of a ski resort season) owe a smaller percentage for state unemployment tax purposes. The variance, which is called an **experience** or **merit rating,** motivates employers to stabilize their workforce.

Fred's current state unemployment tax rate is 5.4 percent of the first $7,000 paid to each of Fred's employees during the calendar year. From the taxable earnings column (H) of the payroll register in Figure 8-1, we multiply $600 by the SUTA rate of 5.4 percent.

$$\underset{\$600}{\text{Taxable Earnings}} \times \underset{.054}{\text{SUTA Rate}} = \underset{\$32.40}{\text{SUTA Tax}} \qquad \frac{\text{SUTA Tax Payable 208}}{|32.40}$$

SUTA taxes are paid after the end of each **calendar quarter.** Employers are required to complete a state unemployment tax report and pay any SUTA tax due at this time.

JOURNALIZING PAYROLL TAX EXPENSE

Before showing the general journal entry to record Fred's Market payroll tax expense, let's review the categories and rules that affect the specific payroll ledger accounts used to record this expense.

Accounts Affected	Category	↑ ↓	Rules
Payroll Tax Expense	**Expense**	↑	**Dr.**
FICA—Social Security Payable	**Liability**	↑	**Cr.**
FICA—Medicare Payable	**Liability**	↑	**Cr.**
State Unemployment Tax Payable (SUTA)	**Liability**	↑	**Cr.**
Federal Unemployment Tax Payable (FUTA)	**Liability**	↑	**Cr.**

The total of employer's portion of FICA for Social Security and Medicare tax, FUTA, and SUTA equals the total of Fred's payroll tax expense.

The Journal Entry

The following is the general journal entry recording Fred's payroll tax expense for the weekly payroll ending November 25. (We will look carefully at the general ledger entries in Learning Unit 8-2.)

Nov	25	Payroll Tax Expense	610	3 2 4 53			
		FICA — Social Security Payable	203		2 1 5 95	←	$3,483 × .062 = $215.95
		FICA — Medicare Payable	204		7 1 38	←	$4,923 × .0145 = $71.38
		SUTA Tax Payable	208		3 2 40	←	$600 × .054 = $32.40
		FUTA Tax Payable	209		4 80	←	$600 × .008 = $4.80
		Records employer's payroll tax					

In Learning Unit 8-2 we'll look at how to complete the form that goes with the payment of FICA tax (Social Security and Medicare) of the employee *and* the employer along with the amounts of federal income tax deducted from employees' paychecks. It is important to keep in mind that FUTA and SUTA taxes also have separate report forms to be completed, which we will look at in Learning Unit 8-3.

LEARNING UNIT 8-1 REVIEW

AT THIS POINT you should be able to

◆ Explain the purpose of the Form SS-4. (p. 268)
◆ Explain the use of the taxable earnings column in calculating the employer's payroll tax expense. (p. 270)
◆ Calculate the employer's payroll taxes. (p. 268)
◆ Explain the difference between FUTA and SUTA taxes. (p. 270)
◆ Explain when FUTA and SUTA taxes are paid. (p. 270)
◆ Journalize the employer's payroll tax expense. (p. 272)

SELF-REVIEW QUIZ 8-1

(The forms you need are on page 256 of the *Study Guide and Working Papers*.)

Given the following, prepare the general journal entry to record the payroll tax expense for Bill Co. for the weekly payroll of July 8. Assume the following: (a) SUTA is paid at a rate of 5.6 percent on the first $7,000 of earnings; (b) FUTA is paid at the net rate of .8 percent on the first $7,000 of earnings; (c) FICA rate for Social Security is 6.2 percent on $65,400, and Medicare is 1.45 percent on all earnings.

Employee	Cumulative Pay Before This Week's Payroll	Gross Pay For Week
Bill Jones	$6,000	$800
Julie Warner	6,600	400
Al Brooks	7,900	700

Solution to Self-Review Quiz 8-1

	July	8	Payroll Tax Expense					2 2 2 15					
			FICA — Social Security Payable							1 1 7 80			
			FICA — Medicare Payable							2 7 55			
			SUTA Tax Payable							6 7 20			
			FUTA Tax Payable							9 60			
			Record employer's payroll tax										

FICA:
SS: $1,900 × .062 = $117.80
Med: 1,900 × .0145 = 27.55
SUTA: 1,200 × .056 = 67.20
FUTA: 1,200 × .008 = 9.60
$222.15

Quiz Tip: Al Brooks earned more than $7,000; thus his employer takes no SUTA or FUTA taxes on the $700 of Al's gross pay.

LEARNING UNIT 8-2
Form 941: Completing the Employer's Quarterly Federal Tax Return and Paying Tax Obligations for FICA Tax and Federal Income Tax

In this unit, we will look at Fred's Market's last calendar quarter (October, November, and December). Our goals are (1) determining the timing for paying FICA (for both the employees and the employer) and federal income tax (or FIT) and (2) completing **Form 941,** the **Employer's Quarterly Federal Tax Return.**

Before getting into specific deposit rules and form completions, let's look at Figure 8-2, which is a worksheet that Fred's accountant prepared to monitor Fred's Market deposit requirements for the taxes reported on Form 941—Social Security, Medicare, and federal income taxes. These so-called **Form 941 taxes,** will be discussed later in this Learning Unit. (The worksheet in Figure 8-2 has nothing to do with unemployment taxes, which follow different rules.)

Do note on the worksheet that the quarter is 13 weeks. Since Form 941 requires FICA information to be separated by Social Security and Medicare, you can see how helpful the worksheet can be. Note in week 47 that some wages are not taxable for Social Security since the $65,400 wage base limit was met. However, *all* wages for Medicare are taxable since there is no wage base limit for this tax. This worksheet can be built from the information in each individual's employee's earnings record and the weekly payroll registers.

Now let's look at the deposit rules Fred's Market must follow regarding Form 941 taxes (which are FICA and FIT).

DEPOSITING FORM 941 TAXES

The amount of tax due must be deposited in what is called an authorized depository in Fred's area or a Federal Reserve Bank. Authorized depositories are banks that have been authorized by the Federal Reserve system to accept payroll tax deposits from their own checking account customers. Federal Reserve banks can accept payroll tax deposits from any business, no matter where the business maintains its checking account.

Payroll Period	Week #	Earnings	FIT	Taxable FICA Wages for Soc. Sec.	Medicare	FICA Soc. Sec. EE + ER	Medicare EE + ER	Total Tax	Cumulative Tax
Oct.	40	4819.00	756.00	4819.00	4819.00	597.56	139.75	1493.31	1493.31
	41	5013.25	810.00	5013.25	5013.25	621.64	145.38	1577.02	3070.33
	42	4819.00	756.00	4819.00	4819.00	597.56	139.75	1493.31	4563.64
	43	4892.75	768.00	4892.75	4892.75	606.70	141.89	1516.59	6080.23
		19544.00	3090.00	19544.00	19544.00	2424.46	566.77	6080.23	
Nov.	44	4819.00	756.00	4819.00	4819.00	597.56	139.75	1493.31	7573.54
	45	5007.15	809.00	5007.15	5007.15	620.89	145.21	1575.10	9148.64
	46	5152.50	832.00	5152.50	5152.50	638.91	149.42	1620.33	10768.97
	47	4923.00	784.00	3483.00	4923.00	431.89*	142.77*	1358.66	12127.63
		19901.65	3181.00	18461.65	19901.65	2289.25*	577.15*	6047.40	
Dec.	48	5090.50	822.00	1464.50	5090.50	181.60	147.62	1151.22	13278.85
	49	5121.75	827.00	1495.75	5121.75	185.47	148.53	1161.00	14439.85
	50	5629.00	909.00	2003.00	5629.00	248.37	163.24	1320.61	15760.46
	51	5700.75	921.00	2074.00	5700.75	257.18	165.32	1343.50	17103.96
	52	4819.00	756.00	1193.00	4819.00	147.93	139.75	1043.68	18147.64
		26361.00	4235.00	8230.25	26361.00	1020.55	764.46	6020.01	
Totals for the Quarter		65806.65	10506.00	46235.90	65806.65	5733.26*	1908.38*	18147.64	

*Off one or two cents due to rounding

FIGURE 8-2 Fred's Accountant has Prepared this Worksheet to Track the Form 941 Payroll Taxes for Fred's Market During the Last Quarter

Types of Payroll Tax Depositors

For payroll tax deposit purposes, employers are classified as either **monthly** or **semiweekly depositors.** A monthly depositor is an employer who only has to deposit Form 941 taxes on the fifteenth day of every month. Semi-weekly depositors must deposit their Form 941 taxes once or twice each week.

The employer's classification depends on the dollar amount of the Form 941 taxes it has paid in the past. The IRS has developed a rule known as the **look-back period** rule, to determine how to classify an employer for payroll tax deposits. Under this rule, the IRS will *look back* to a time period that begins on July 1 and ends the following June 30 of the past year. (For example, to determine the employer's status for 1997, the IRS will look at the period between July 1, 1995 and June 30, 1996.) If, during this look-back time period, the employer has paid under $50,000 of Form 941 taxes, the IRS considers the employer to be a *monthly depositor.* If the employer has paid $50,000 or more during this period, it is considered to be a *semiweekly depositor.* Figure 8-3 shows how the look-back period works for payroll purposes.

Fred's Market is a semiweekly depositor because it made in excess of $50,000 in FICA and FIT deposits during the look-back period. If Fred's Market had made less than $50,000 in payroll tax deposits during the look-back period, it would have been classified as a monthly depositor.

New employers are automatically classified as monthly depositors until they have been in business long enough to have a look-back period for evaluation purposes. The employer's status is reevaluated every year.

Rules for Monthly Depositors   The rules for monthly depositors are fairly simple. They are:

1. The employee and employer Social Security and Medicare taxes and the employees' FIT accumulated during any month must be deposited by the fifteenth of the next month.
2. If the fifteenth of the month is a Saturday, Sunday, or bank holiday, the employer must make the payroll tax deposit on the next banking day.

Rules for Semiweekly Depositors   Semiweekly depositors like Fred's Market may have to make up to two payroll tax deposits every week, depending on when employees are paid. For this purpose, each seven-day week begins on Wednesday and ends on the following Tuesday. The seven-day week is broken into two payday time periods: Wednesday through Friday, and Saturday through Tuesday. In addition, the following rules apply:

1. If the company's payday occurs on Wednesday, Thursday, or Friday, the payroll tax deposit is due on the following Wednesday. If the company's payday occurs

> The IRS examines the amount of Form 941 taxes paid during the period beginning on July 1 and ending on June 30 to determine whether the employer is a monthly depositor or a semi-weekly depositor. This is called the look-back period rule.

FIGURE 8-3 The level of payroll taxes paid during the look-back period determines how often employer deposits payroll taxes.

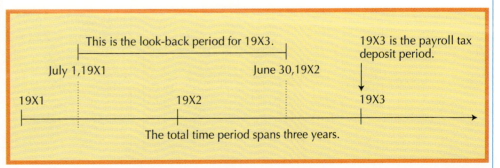

	Monday	Tuesday	Wednesday	Thursday	Friday	Saturday	Sunday
The payday occurs this week →			■ If the payday occurs on one of these days, the deposit will be due Wednesday of the next week.			★ If the payday occurs on Saturday or Sunday, or...	
	★ ...Monday or Tuesday, then payroll tax deposit will be due and payable on Friday of this week.		■ Deposit day for Wednesday–Friday payday		★ Deposit day for Saturday–Tuesday payday		

FIGURE 8-4 The payday determines when the tax deposit is due.

on Saturday, Sunday, Monday, or Tuesday, the payroll tax deposit is due on the following Friday. Thus, if an employer pays its employees on a Thursday and a Monday, it must make two payroll tax deposits—one on Wednesday for the Thursday payday, and one on Friday for the Monday payday.

2. If a bank holiday occurs after the end of the payday time-period but before the day the payroll tax deposit is due, the employer gets one extra day in which to make the deposit. So, a deposit due on a Wednesday will be due on Thursday, and a Friday deposit will be due on the following Monday.

As a general rule, the depositor always has three banking days in which to make the payroll tax deposit. The diagram in Figure 8-4 shows how these rules are applied.

Here is how the rules apply to Fred's Market. First, look back at Figure 8-2 (p. 274) to locate the dates of each weekly payday. Next, look at Figure 8-5, which shows a calendar for the last quarter of the year.

Note that each payday falls on a Friday. Because Fred's Market is a semi-weekly payroll tax depositor, its Form 941 payroll tax deposits are due on the following Wednesday. Fred's first payday in October falls on October 7. Its first payroll tax deposit will be due on October 12. Another deposit will be due on every Wednesday from that date until the end of the year. However, if we look at week 51 in Figure 8-2 (p. 274), the payday for this week is December 23, which is two days before Christmas. Christmas is a bank holiday, but in looking at the December calendar in Figure 8-5, we see that it falls on a Sunday. Under the law, Monday, December 26 then becomes the legal holiday. Fred must then apply the rule regarding a holiday that falls between a payday and the tax deposit day, and will make the Form 941 tax deposit on Thursday, December 29.

FIGURE 8-5 Last calendar quarter for Fred's Market shows paydays falling on Fridays.

○ = Paydays
△ = Tax Deposit Days

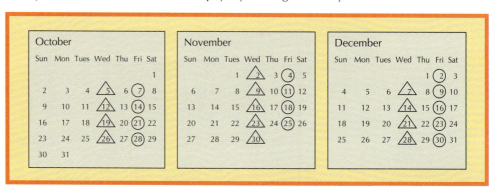

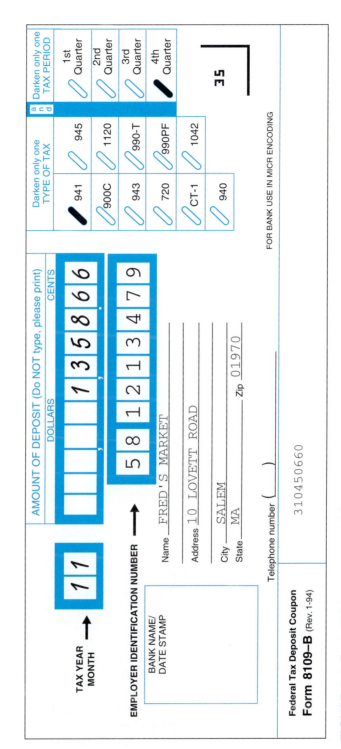

FIGURE 8-6 Form 8109.

Completion of Form 8109 to Accompany Deposits

Fred's accountant informed Fred that the check that is written for the amount of the Form 941 payroll tax deposit each week must be accompanied by IRS **Form 8109,** Federal Tax Deposit Coupon.

Fred received a book of coupons when he got the EIN for Fred's Market. Figure 8-6 on page 277 shows Form 8109 completed for the week 47 Form 941 payroll tax deposit. Note that the dollar amount found at the top of the form ($1,358.66) is the same as the amount found in the "Total Tax" column for week 47 in Figure 8-2.

In looking at Figure 8-6 you will see that in the upper-right-hand corner the "Type of Tax" and "Tax Period" must be indicated by darkening the appropriate oval using a No. 2 pencil. Fred's bookkeeper has darkened the "941" and "4th Quarter" ovals for the week 47 payday.

Journalizing and Posting Payroll Tax Deposits

Payment of the payroll tax deposit for week 47 is made in the general journal as follows:

Accounts Affected	Category	↑	↓	Rules
FICA—Social Security Payable	Liability		↓	Dr.
FICA—Medicare Payable	Liability		↓	Dr.
Federal Income Tax Payable	Liability		↓	Dr.
Cash	Asset		↓	Cr.

FRED'S MARKET
GENERAL JOURNAL

Nov	30	FICA — Social Security Payable	203	4 3 1 89	
		FICA — Medicare Payable	204	1 4 2 77	
		Federal Income Tax Payable	205	7 8 4 00	
		Cash	111		1 3 5 8 66
		To record the Form 941 tax deposit for week			
		#47 payroll on November 25, 19XX			

Now let's look at the partial general ledger of Fred's Market to get a better understanding of how specific payroll accounts in the ledger are updated regarding FICA (Social Security and Medicare) and FIT. Note in the *FICA-Social Security* and *Medicare Payable* accounts (shown on p. 279) how the posting came from the general journal for the employees' and employer's share of FICA tax.* The general journal is also used when the payroll tax deposit is made, recording a debit to the *FICA-Social Security* and *Medicare Payable* accounts as well as the *Federal Income Tax Payable* account.

Under the Form 941 payroll tax deposit rules, the general journal entries to record the payroll are made weekly each Friday, while the entries to record the payment of the payroll taxes are made each Wednesday after the Friday payday. Check Figure 8-2 (p. 274) to see how the Form 941 tax liability has been recorded and then paid in the partial general ledger accounts shown on page 279.

---

* *Note:* each credit would actually be 2 credits — one from the employee and one from the employer.

FICA–Social Security Payable				203
Date	PR	Dr.	Cr.	Cr. Bal.
19XX				
Nov. 4	GJ28		597 56	597 56
9	GJ28	597 56		0
11	GJ28		620 89	620 89
16	GJ28	620 89		0
18	GJ29		638 91	638 91
23	GJ29	638 91		0
25	GJ29		431 89	431 89
30	GJ29	431 89		0

FICA–Medicare Payable				204
Date	PR	Dr.	Cr.	Cr. Bal.
19XX				
Nov. 4	GJ28		139 75	139 75
9	GJ28	139 75		0
11	GJ28		145 21	145 21
16	GJ28	145 21		0
18	GJ29		149 42	149 42
23	GJ29	149 42		0
25	GJ29		142 77	142 77
30	GJ29	142 77		0

FORM 941: EMPLOYER'S QUARTERLY FEDERAL TAX RETURN

Fred's accountant used the worksheet in Figure 8-2 in preparing Form 941 for the last quarter for Fred's Market (see Fig. 8-7 on the next page). The top section of the form identifies the taxpayer (Fred's Market), its address, the date the quarter ended, and Fred's Market's EIN. The postal code for the state where Fred's Market is located is filled in on the left-hand side of the form.

This is how Fred's accountant filled out Form 941 using the dollar amounts from Figure 8-2:*

Line 1a: This line is only filled in for the first quarter of the year. It is left blank for the last quarter.

2: Total gross pay: $65,806.65 ($19,544.00 + $19,901.65 + $26,361.00)

3: Total income tax: $10,506.00 ($3,090.00 + $3,181.00 + $4,235.00)

4: No adjustment — this line is only used in special situations.

5: The same amount as is found on line 3: $10,506.00.

6a: The wages subject to Social Security tax are multiplied by 12.4 percent (6.2 percent for the employee and 6.2 percent for the employer). Total taxable wages are $46,235.90 ($19,544.00 + $18,461.65 + $8,230.25). Note that this line is different from Line 2 because of the $65,400 Social Security wage base limit. The tax is $5,733.25.

6b: No employees of Fred's Market receive any tip income, so this line is left blank.

7: Taxable wages for Medicare are $65,806.65 ($19,544.00 + $19,901.65 + $26,361.00). Note that this line *will* be the same as Line 2 because all earnings are subject to Medicare tax. The tax is $1,908.39 (1.45% for the employee and 1.45% for the employer).

8: Total of Social Security and Medicare is $7,641.64 ($5,733.25 + $1,908.39).

9: Due to rounding of the dollar amounts, additional cents might be added to Line 9 as an adjustment. The amount must be written on Line 9. The goal here is to have Line 13 equal Line 17(d), found at the bottom of the form. For this problem no adjustment is needed.

10: This line is the sum of Line 8 as adjusted by Line 9.

11: This line is the sum of Lines 5 and 10 added together.

12: If Fred's Market advanced any Earned Income to its employees, it would deduct the amount on this line.

13: This line is the net of Line 11 as adjusted by any amount found on Line 12.

14: Total of the deposits made by Fred for the last quarter is $18,147.64, under the semiweekly deposit rule. Note that the last Form 941 tax deposit

Fraction of cents: If there is a difference between the total tax on Line 8 and the total deducted from your employees' wages or tips because of fractions of cents added or dropped in collecting the tax, report the difference on Line 9. Use the center column on Line 9 with a + or − sign to show the amount of the adjustment.

* Note that the rounding results in a one cent difference for *both* Social Security and Medicare.

Form 941 — Employer's Quarterly Federal Tax Return

Form **941**

Department of the Treasury
Internal Revenue Service

4141

▶ See separate instructions for information on completing this return.

Please type or print.

OMB No. 1545-0029

Enter state code for state in which deposits made . ▶ M:A (see page 2 of instructions).

Name (as distinguished from trade name)
Fred Stone

Trade name, if any
Fred's Market

Address (number and street)
10 Lovett Road

Date quarter ended
December 31,

Employer identification number
58-12134791

City, state, and ZIP code
Salem, MA   01970

T	
FF	
FD	
FP	
I	
T	

If address is different from prior return, check here ▶

IRS Use

1 1 1 1 1 1 1 1 1 1   2   3 3 3 3 3 3   4 4 4
5 5 5   6   7   8 8 8 8 8   9 9   10 10 10 10 10 10 10 10 10 10

If you do not have to file returns in the future, check here ▶ ☐ and enter date final wages paid ▶

If you are a seasonal employer, see **Seasonal employers** on page 2 and check here (see instructions) ▶ ☐

1	Number of employees (except household) employed in the pay period that includes March 12th ▶	1		
2	Total wages and tips subject to withholding, plus other compensation	2	65,806	65
3	Total income tax withheld from wages, tips, and sick pay	3	10,506	00
4	Adjustment of withheld income tax for preceding quarters of calendar year	4		
5	Adjusted total of income tax withheld (line 3 as adjusted by line 4—see instructions) . . .	5	10,506	00
6a	Taxable social security wages . . . . . . $ 46,235.90 × 12.4% (.124) =	6a	5,733	25
b	Taxable social security tips . . . . $ × 12.4% (.124) =	6b		
7	Taxable Medicare wages and tips . . . . $ 65,806.65 × 2.9% (.029) =	7	1,908	39*
8	Total social security and Medicare taxes (add lines 6a, 6b, and 7). Check here if wages are not subject to social security and/or Medicare tax . . . . ▶ ☐	8	7,641	64
9	Adjustment of social security and Medicare taxes (see instructions for required explanation) Sick Pay $ _____ ± Fractions of Cents $ _____ ± Other $ _____ =	9		
10	Adjusted total of social security and Medicare taxes (line 8 as adjusted by line 9—see instructions)	10	7,641	64
11	**Total taxes** (add lines 5 and 10)	11	18,147	64
12	Advance earned income credit (EIC) payments made to employees, if any	12		
13	Net taxes (subtract line 12 from line 11). **This should equal line 17, column (d) below** (or line D of Schedule B (Form 941))	13	18,147	64
14	Total deposits for quarter, including overpayment applied from a prior quarter	14	18,147	64
15	**Balance due** (subtract line 14 from line 13). Pay to Internal Revenue Service	15	-0-	

16 **Overpayment,** if line 14 is more than line 13, enter excess here ▶ $ _____
and check if to be: ☐ Applied to next return   **OR**   ☐ Refunded.

- **All filers:** If line 13 is less than $500, you need not complete line 17 or Schedule B.
- **Semiweekly depositors:** Complete Schedule B and check here . . . . ▶ ☒
- **Monthly depositors:** Complete line 17, columns (a) through (d) and check here . . . . . ▶ ☐

17	Monthly Summary of Federal Tax Liability.			
	(a) First month liability	**(b)** Second month liability	**(c)** Third month liability	**(d)** Total liability for quarter
	6,080.23	6,047.40	6,020.01	18,147.64

Sign Here

Under penalties of perjury, I declare that I have examined this return, including accompanying schedules and statements, and to the best of my knowledge and belief, it is true, correct, and complete.

Signature ▶ *Fred Stone*

Print Your Name and Title ▶ Fred Stone, Owner

Date ▶ 1/31/9X

FIGURE 8-7 Employer's Quarterly Federal Tax Return

---

* Note that due to rounding in Figure 8-2 (page 274), we are off by one cent. Thus we are using $1908.39 instead of $1908.38. If any adjustment were needed, it would be entered on line 9. Here no adjustment is needed.

is made after the year ends, but is allowed to be taken as a last quarter deposit because it applies to the December 30 payday.

15: There is no balance due to Fred's.

16: There is no overpayment for Fred's. Note that directly below Line 16 are two boxes that only are checked under certain circumstances. The accountant will check off the box for semiweekly depositors and prepare Form 941 Schedule B, which is an itemized listing of the semiweekly deposits made for the last quarter. This schedule is not shown here.

17: This line is broken into four sections. The first three sections labeled (a), (b), and (c) are the monthly Form 941 liability. These amounts are found in the column "Total Tax" at the end of October, November, and December in Figure 8-2. Note that the sum of (a), (b), and (c) will equal (d). Recall that the amount found on Line 13 must equal the amount found in box 17(d).

LEARNING UNIT 8-2 REVIEW

AT THIS POINT you should be able to

◆ Explain which taxes are reported on Form 941. (p. 273)
◆ Understand how employers are classified as payroll tax depositors. (p. 275)
◆ Explain the summary of Form 941 payroll tax deposit rules for monthly depositors. (p. 275)
◆ Explain the summary of Form 941 payroll tax deposit rules for semiweekly depositors. (p. 275)
◆ Prepare and explain the purpose of Form 8109. (p. 278)
◆ Record the general journal entry to pay FICA (Social Security and Medicare) and federal income taxes when a payroll tax deposit is made. (p. 278)
◆ Review how the general journal entries are posted into the general ledger to record the paying of employees and the paying of payroll taxes. (p. 279)
◆ Complete an Employer's Quarterly Federal Tax Return from a worksheet. (p. 280)

SELF-REVIEW QUIZ 8-2

(The blank forms you need are on page 257 of the *Study Guide and Working Papers*.)

Carol Ann's Import Chalet is a business that employs five full-time employees and four part-time employees. The accountant for Carol Ann's has determined that the business is a monthly depositor. The accountant prepared a worksheet showing the following payroll tax liabilities for the month of October:

Date	Social Security (EE + ER)	Medicare (EE + ER)	FIT
10/7	$ 486.56	$169.05	$ 829.00
10/14	632.15	165.01	901.00
10/21	579.43	131.05	734.00
10/28	389.99	142.24	765.00
Totals	$2,088.13	$607.35	$3,229.00

1. What is the dollar amount of the Form 941 tax deposit and when must it be made under the monthly deposit rule. Use Fig. 8-5 (p. 276) for the date.

2. Assume that Carol Ann's is classified as a semiweekly depositor. Please calculate the amount of each Form 941 tax deposit and when it would be made by completing the table on the next page (Use Fig. 8-5 for the dates):

Payday Date	Date of Deposit	Amount of Deposit
10/7	?	?
10/14	?	?
10/21	?	?
10/28	?	?

Quiz Tip: The tax for 941 is:

FICA–SS: employee and employer

FICA–MED: employee and employer

FIT: employee, only

Solutions to Self-Review Quiz 8-2

1. As a monthly depositor, Carol Ann's deposit date would be Tuesday, November 15. The total amount of the deposit would be $5,924.48 ($2,088.13 + $607.35 + $3,229.00).

2. As a semiweekly depositor, Carol Ann's deposit schedule would be completed as follows:

Payday Date	Date of Deposit	Amount of Deposit
10/7	10/12	$1,484.61
10/14	10/19	1,698.16
10/21	10/26	1,444.48
10/28	11/2*	1,297.23*

* Note that this deposit will be made in November given the calendar dates found in Figure 8-5.

LEARNING UNIT 8-3
W-2, W-3, Form 940-EZ, and Workers' Compensation

W-2: WAGE AND TAX STATEMENT

Form W-2, Wage and Tax Statement is a multipart form that is prepared by the employer each year. Fred's Market is required to give (or mail) copies of Form W-2 to each person who was employed in the past year. These forms must be distributed by January 31 of the following year. Employees use the figures on Form W-2 to compute the amount of income tax they must pay. One copy of the form must be attached to his or her federal income tax return; other copies must be attached to state and local tax returns.

Anyone who stopped working for Fred before the end of that year may be given a Form W-2 at any time after the employment ends. If the former employee asks for it, the employer must supply completed copies within 30 days of the request or the final wage payment, whichever is later.

Additional copies of Form W-2 are sent to the Social Security Administration and state and local governments. The employer retains a copy of the W-2 form for each employee for its records.

Figure 8-8 shows the W-2 that Susan O'Mally received from Fred's Market. The information was obtained from her individual employee earnings record. Note that Social Security wages and taxes are shown separately from the amounts reported for Medicare wages and taxes. That is because there is a wage base limit for the Social Security tax, but not for the Medicare tax.

W-3: Transmittal of Income and Tax Statements

Form W-3, Transmittal of Income and Tax Statements, is prepared and sent by the employer to the Social Security Administration along with copies of

a Control number	22222	Void ☐	For Official Use Only ▶ OMB No. 1545-0008	

b Employer's identification number 58-12134791	1 Wages, tips, other compensation 71,500.00	2 Federal income tax withheld 11,544.00
c Employer's name, address, and ZIP code Fred's Market 10 Lovett Road Salem, MA 01920	3 Social security wages 65,400.00	4 Social security tax withheld 4,054.80
	5 Medicare wages and tips 71,500.00	6 Medicare tax withheld 1,036.88
	7 Social security tips	8 Allocated tips
d Employee's social security number 021-36-9494	9 Advance EIC payment	10 Dependent care benefits
e Employee's name (first, middle initial, last) Susan O'Mally 80 Garfield Street Marblehead, MA 01945	11 Nonqualified plans	12 Benefits included in box 1
	13 See Instrs. for box 13	14 Other

15 Statutory employee ☐	Deceased ☐	Pension plan ☐	Legal rep. ☐	942 emp. ☐	Subtotal ☐	Deferred compensation ☐

f Employee's address and ZIP code

16 State	Employer's state I.D. No.	17 State wages, tips, etc.	18 State income tax	19 Locality name	20 Local wages, tips, etc.	21 Local income tax
MA	6 21-8966-4	71,500	3,575.00			

Cat. No. 10134D — Department of the Treasury—Internal Revenue Service

Form W-2 Wage and Tax Statement 199X

Copy A For Social Security Administration

For Paperwork Reduction Act Notice, see separate instructions.

FIGURE 8-8 Completed Form W-2

each employees' Form W-2. The W-3 form reports the total amounts of wages, tips, and compensation paid to employees; the total federal income tax withheld; the total Social Security and Medicare taxes withheld; and some other information.

Employers are required to send Form W-3 and Forms W-2 to the Social Security Administration for FICA tax purposes. The Social Security Administration, under a special agreement with the IRS, makes all information found on individual W-2 forms electronically available to the IRS so that it can check to verify the accuracy of the employer's 941 Forms and individual employees' federal income tax returns.

The information used to complete the W-3 form in Figure 8-9 came from a summary of the individual employee earnings records that Fred's accountant prepared after the end of the year (see Fig. 8-10 on page 284).

Form 940-EZ: Employer's Annual Federal Unemployment Tax Return

There are two types of federal unemployment tax returns. **Form 940-EZ, Employer's Annual Federal Unemployment Tax Return** is used by a business that only employs workers in one state. Businesses that employ workers in several states (multistate employers) must file a **Form 940.** Form 940 asks for additional information that is not required on Form 940-EZ.

Fred's Market must file Form 940-EZ. After the first year it files this form, the IRS will send Fred a preaddressed Form 940-EZ, near the close of each calendar year. Form 940-EZ must be filed no later than January 31 unless all required

DO NOT STAPLE

a Control number	33333	For Official Use Only ▶ OMB No. 1545-0008	

b Kind of Payer ▶	941 ☒ Military ☐ 943 ☐ CT-1 ☐ 942 ☐ Medicare govt. emp. ☐	1 Wages, tips, other compensation 252,668.00	2 Federal income tax withheld 40,664.00

		3 Social security wages 240,208.00	4 Social security tax withheld 14,892.90
c Total number of statements 5	d Establishment number	5 Medicare wages and tips 252,668.00	6 Medicare tax withheld 3,663.82
e Employer's identification number 58-12134791		7 Social security tips	8 Allocated tips
f Employer's name Fred's Market 10 Lovett Road Salem, MA 01970		9 Advance EIC payments	10 Dependent care benefits
		11 Nonqualified plans	12 Deferred compensation
		13 Adjusted total social security wages and tips	
		14 Adjusted total Medicare wages and tips	
g Employer's address and ZIP code			
h Other EIN used this year		15 Income tax withheld by third-party payer	
i Employer's state I.D. No. 6 21-8966-4			

Under penalties of perjury, I declare that I have examined this return and accompanying documents, and, to the best of my knowledge and belief, they are true, correct, and complete.

Signature ▶ *Fred Stor*   Title ▶ Owner   Date ▶ 1/31/XX

Telephone number (617) 555-1212

Form **W-3 Transmittal of Wage and Tax Statements 199X**   Department of the Treasury / Internal Revenue Service

FIGURE 8-9 Completed Form W-3

FUTA deposits have been made during the year, in which case the return can be filed by February 10. The completed form is shown in Figure 8-11.

FUTA   As we saw earlier, the FUTA tax rate is .8 percent (or eight tenths of one percent) on the first $7,000 of each employee's gross pay. If Fred's accumulated FUTA tax liability is $100 or more during the calendar year, Fred must make a FUTA tax deposit with a Federal Reserve bank or a bank authorized to

FIGURE 8-10 Employee Earnings Record Summary

Employee	Total Earnings	FICA Taxable Earnings Soc. Sec.	FICA Taxable Earnings Medicare	FICA Tax Soc. Sec.	FICA Tax Medicare	FIT
Jones, Bob	$29,120.00	$29,120.00	$29,120.00	$1,805.44	$422.24	$525.200
King, Abby	33,488.00	33,488.00	33,488.00	2,076.26	485.58	577.200
O'Mally, Susan	71,500.00	65,400.00	71,500.00	4,054.80	1,036.88	1,154.400
Regan, Pat	46,800.00	46,800.00	46,800.00	2,901.60	678.60	717.600
Zott, Jim	71,760.00	65,400.00	71,760.00	4,054.80	1,040.52	1,092.000
	$252,668.00	$240,208.00	$252,668.00	$14,892.90	$3,663.82	$40,664.00

Form 940-EZ

Department of the Treasury
Internal Revenue Service

Employer's Annual Federal Unemployment (FUTA) Tax Return

OMB No. 1545-1110

199X

	FF
T	FD
	FP
	I
	T

Name (as distinguished from trade name)   Calendar year
Fred Stone   199X

Trade name, if any
Fred's Market

Address and ZIP code
10 Lovett Road, Salem, MA 01970

Employer identification number
58 : 12134791

If incorrect, make any necessary changes. ▶

Follow the chart under Who May Use Form 940-EZ on page 2. If you cannot use Form 940-EZ, you must use Form 940 instead.

A   Enter the amount of contributions paid to your state unemployment fund. (See instructions for line A on page 4.) ▶ $ ......1,890..|00..

B   (1) Enter the name of the state where you have to pay contributions ▶ ..MASSACHUSETTS...........

(2) Enter your state reporting number as shown on state unemployment tax return. ▶ 281-615

If you will not have to file returns in the future, check here (see Who Must File, on page 2) **complete, and sign the return** . . . ▶ ☐

If this is an Amended Return check here .... ▶ ☐

Part I   Taxable Wages and FUTA Tax

1	Total payments (including payments shown on lines 2 and 3) during the calendar year for services of employees	1	252,668	00

2   Exempt payments. (Explain all exempt payments, attaching additional sheets if necessary.) ▶ _____ | 2 | |

3   Payments for services of more than $7,000. Enter only amounts over the first $7,000 paid to each employee. Do not include any exempt payments from line 2. Do not use your state wage limitation. The $7,000 amount is the Federal wage base. Your state wage base may be different | 3 | 217,668 | 00 |

4	Total exempt payments (add lines 2 and 3)	4	217,668	00
5	**Total taxable wages** (subtract line 4 from line 1)	5	35,000	00
6	**FUTA tax.** Multiply the wages on line 5 by .008 and enter here. (If the result is over $100, also complete Part II.) .	6	280	00
7	Total FUTA tax deposited for the year, including any overpayment applied from a prior year (from your records) ▶	7	280	00
8	**Amount you owe** (subtract line 7 from line 6). This should be $100 or less. Pay to "Internal Revenue Service". ▶	8	-0-	
9	**Overpayment** (subtract line 6 from line 7). Check if it is to be: ☐ Applied to next return, or ☐ Refunded ▶	9		

Part II   Record of Quarterly Federal Unemployment Tax Liability (Do not include state liability.) Complete only if line 6 is over $100.

Quarter	First (Jan. 1 – Mar. 31)	Second (Apr. 1 – June 30)	Third (July 1 – Sept. 30)	Fourth (Oct. 1 – Dec. 31)	Total for year
Liability for quarter	280.00	-0-	-0-	-0-	280.00

Under penalties of perjury, I declare that I have examined this return, including accompanying schedules and statements, and, to the best of my knowledge and belief, it is true, correct, and complete, and that no part of any payment made to a state unemployment fund claimed as a credit was, or is to be, deducted from the payments to employees.

Signature ▶ *Fred Stone*   Title (Owner, etc.) ▶ Owner   Date ▶ 2/10/XX

Cat. No. 10983G   Form **940-EZ** (1993)

FIGURE 8-11 Completed Form 940-EZ

take payroll tax deposits. The FUTA tax deposit rule is quite simple: if the amount of FUTA tax owed is $100 or more during any calendar quarter, the employer must deposit the amount due no later than one month after the quarter ends.

At the end of the first quarter Fred owes $280 for FUTA taxes. Fred's accountant has prepared a schedule showing how the tax was computed by taking each employee's weekly earnings times the amount earned each payday. (See Table 8-1 below for the calculations.) If an employee earned over the $7,000 FUTA wage base limit, only the first $7,000 will be taxable for FUTA purposes. Note that all of Fred's employees earned over the $7,000 FUTA limit during the first quarter of the year. Remember, because all of the employees of Fred's Market earned over $7,000 during the first quarter of the year, no further FUTA tax is due for the rest of the year. Please see Part II of the Form 940-EZ in Figure 8-11.

Since Fred owes $280 in FUTA taxes, he will make the FUTA tax deposit on April 30 to comply with the FUTA deposit rule. The general journal entry is prepared as shown below.

			FRED'S MARKET GENERAL JOURNAL			
*	April	30	FUTA Payable	212	2 8 0 00	
			SUTA Payable	213	1 8 9 0 00	
			Cash	111		2 1 7 0 00
			To record the FUTA and SUTA tax			
			deposits for the first quarter of the year.			

* Note this could be two separate entries.

SUTA   Fred must also pay state unemployment tax to Massachusetts. The SUTA tax is also due one month after the quarter ends, on April 30. Fred will pay out $1,890 in tax, based on a SUTA percentage rate of 5.4 percent on the first $7,000 that each of his employees have earned ($35,000 × .054 = $1,890).

The amount of SUTA Fred pays is shown on Lines A and B of Form 940-EZ.

WORKERS' COMPENSATION INSURANCE

Fred's Market is required to have **workers' compensation insurance** to insure its employees against losses due to accidental injury or death incurred while on the job. Fred is required to estimate the cost of this insurance and pay the premium in advance.

The premium for workers' compensation insurance is based on the total estimated gross payroll and the rate is calculated per $100 of weekly payroll. At year end, the actual payroll is compared to the estimated payroll, and Fred either will receive credit for overpayment or be responsible for paying additional premiums.

TABLE 8-1   COMPUTATION OF FUTA TAX FOR A YEAR

Employee	Amount Earned During Quarter					Amount Taxable for FUTA
Jones, Bob	13 Weeks	×	$624	per Week	=	$8,112	$7,000
King, Abby	13 Weeks	×	$560			$7,280	$7,000
O'Mally, Susan	13 Weeks	×	$1,375			$17,875	$7,000
Regan, Pat	13 Weeks	×	$900			$11,700	$7,000
Zott, Jim	13 Weeks	×	$1,380			$17,940	$7,000
						$35,000 × .008 = $280

These are the facts on which Fred's insurance cost was calculated:

1. Estimated payroll for Fred: $230,000.
2. Two grades of workers: Office and stockroom.
3. Rate per $100 of payroll: Office, 14 cents; stockroom, $1.90.
4. Estimated payroll: Office, $150,000; stockroom, $80,000.

This is how the estimated premium was calculated:

Office:	$150,000/$100 = 1,500 × $ .14 =	$ 210
Stockroom:	$80,000/$100 = 800 × $1.90 =	1,520
	Total Estimated Premium:	$1,730

Accounts Affected	Category	↑ ↓	Dr./Cr.
Prepaid Insurance, Worker's Compensation	**Asset**	↑	**Dr.**
Cash	**Asset**	↓	**Cr.**

Fred would have to pay $1,730 in advance. At the end of the year, his records show that his office payroll was $155,000 and his stockroom payroll was $87,542.

Give those amounts, Fred's actual premium should be $1,880.30 calculated as follows:

Office:	$155,000/$100 = 1,550 × $ .14 =	$ 217.00
Stockroom:	$87,542/$100 = 875.42 × $1.90 =	1,663.30
	Total Estimated Premium:	$1,880.30

Since the actual premium is $150.30 higher than the estimate, Fred must pay this amount in January together with the estimated premium for the next year.

The $150.30 adjustment takes place on December 31 by debiting *Workers' Compensation Insurance Expense* and crediting *Workers' Compensation Insurance Payable.*

Accounts Affected	Category	↑ ↓	Dr./Cr.
Workers' Compensation Insurance Expense	**Expense**	↑	**Dr.**
Workers' Compensation Insurance Payable	**Liability**	↑	**Cr.**

LEARNING UNIT 8-3 REVIEW

AT THIS POINT you should be able to

- Prepare a W-2 form. (p. 283)
- Explain the difference between a W-2 form and a W-3 form. (p. 283)
- Prepare a 940-EZ form. (p. 285)
- Explain the difference between a Form 940-EZ and a Form 940. (p. 283)
- Calculate estimated premium for workers' compensation. (p. 286)
- Prepare journal entries to record as well as adjust the premiums for workers' compensation insurance. (p. 287)

SELF-REVIEW QUIZ 8-3

(The forms you need are on page 257 of the *Study Guide and Working Papers.*)
Are the following questions true or false?

1. W-4's must be received by employees by January 31 of the following year.
2. Form W-3 is sent to the Social Security Administration yearly.

3. A Form 940 is prepared by a business that employs workers in only one state.

4. The Employer's Annual Federal Unemployment Tax Return records the employer's FICA and FIT tax liabilities.

5. A FUTA tax liability of $100 must be paid 10 days after the quarter ends.

6. Premiums for Workers' Compensation Insurance may be adjusted based on actual payroll figures.

Solutions to Self-Review Quiz 8-3

1. **False.** W-2 forms must be sent to each employee by January 31 of the next year. The W-4 form is filled out by a new employee and is used for calculating federal and state income taxes.

2. **True.**

3. **False.** The Form 940 will be prepared by a business that employs workers in more than one state. Form 940-EZ will be prepared by an employer with workers in only one state.

4. **False.** The Employer's Annual Federal Unemployment Tax Return records and reports the FUTA tax liability. The Form 941 records and reports the FICA and FIT tax liabilities.

5. **False.** A FUTA tax liability of $100 must be paid one month after the quarter ends.

6. **True.**

Quiz Tip: If you are getting refunds for FIT, you may want to change your withholding.

"As an employer, Fred, what are your tax responsibilities?" asked George Olsen, president of the local Kiwanis club. They were at one of the luncheons sponsored by the club every month. Fred had been asked to join a panel discussion on The Role of Small Business in Our Local Economy. Luckily, George had told the panelists the questions in advance, so Fred had his answers ready.

"Well, of course, I pay city, state, and U.S. government taxes myself. I also have to file city, state, and federal withholding taxes for each of my employees. I have to withhold state unemployment taxes, as well as FICA, which is another name for Social Security and Medicare taxes, for each of them. I pay workers' compensation, too," said Fred quickly.

"That's funny," said a voice from the audience. "My brother-in-law has a Dunkin' Donuts shop in the southern part of the state, and he doesn't pay any city taxes. What's going on here?"

"Naturally, the situation is slightly different for Dunkin' Donuts shop owners in different cities and towns in our state," said Fred confidently. "Not all cities have city income taxes. Different states have different regulations about worker's comp, as well."

"Oh, right," said the voice, sounding embarrassed.

"What happens at the corporate level at Dunkin' Donuts, Fred?" asked George Olsen, shifting the topic diplomatically.

A TAXING TIME

"That's a really big operation, as you can imagine," said Fred. "We have corporate employees in some 20 states and countries, so a portion of the payroll function is not handled in-house. Instead it is outsourced to ADP, an international payroll processing service. They generate the checks and handle the tax reporting to the various cities, states, and countries. The corporate employees manage all the other aspects of the payroll process, from collecting information on hours worked to analysis of the labor dollars."

"Thanks, Fred," said George, "Now let's move on to Eva Jonet, who is going to tell us about advertising her new nail salon."

Fred nodded and breathed a sigh of relief as Eva took the microphone from him. He much preferred baking to public speaking!

DISCUSSION QUESTIONS

1. George had warned Fred not to use technical language in preparing his remarks, so Fred didn't mention Form 941 taxes. Define Form 941 taxes.

2. Fred is classified as a monthly depositor of Form 941 taxes. Why?

3. Assume that Fred owed $2,679.90 in Form 941 taxes for November. When would it be due? What would happen if that day were a Sunday?

CHAPTER REVIEW

SUMMARY OF KEY POINTS

Learning Unit 8-1

1. The Payroll Tax Expense for the employer is made up of FICA tax (Social Security and Medicare) and the state and federal unemployment insurance taxes.
2. The maximum amount of credit given for state unemployment taxes paid against the FUTA tax is 5.4 percent. This is known as the normal FUTA tax credit.
3. The Payroll Tax Expense is recorded at the time the payroll is recorded.

Learning Unit 8-2

1. Federal Form 941 is prepared and filed no later than one month after the calendar quarter ends. It reports the amount of Social Security, Medicare, and Federal Income taxes withheld from employees and the Social Security and Medicare taxes due from the employer during the quarter.
2. Social Security, Medicare, and federal income taxes are known as *Form 941 taxes*.
3. The total amount of Form 941 taxes paid by a business during a specific period of time determines how often the business will have to make its payroll tax deposits. This time period is called a *look-back period.*
4. Businesses will make their payroll tax deposits either monthly or semiweekly when paying Form 941 taxes.
5. Different deposit rules apply to monthly and semiweekly depositors.
6. Form 941 payroll tax deposits must be made using Form 8109 known as the Federal Tax Deposit Coupon.

Learning Unit 8-3

1. Information to prepare W-2 forms can be obtained from the individual employee earnings records.
2. The Form W-3 is used by the Social Security Administration in verifying that taxes have been withheld as reported on individual employee W-2 forms.
3. Form 940-EZ is prepared by January 31, after the end of the previous calendar year. This form can be filed by February 10 if all required deposits have been made by January 31.
4. If the amount of FUTA taxes is equal to or more than $100 during any calendar quarter, the deposit must be made no later than one month after the quarter ends. If the amount is less than $100, no deposit is required until the liability reaches the $100 point.
5. Workers' Compensation Insurance (the estimated premium) is paid at the beginning of the year by the employer to protect against potential losses to its employees due to accidental death or injury incurred while on the job.

Key Terms

Calendar Quarter A three-month time period. There are four calendar quarters in a calendar year (January 1 through December 31). The first quarter is January through March, the second is April through June, the third is July through September, and the fourth is October through December.

Employer identification number (EIN) This number assigned by the IRS is used by an employer when recording and paying payroll and income taxes.

Experience/merit rating A percentage rate that is assigned to a business by the state in calculating state unemployment taxes. The rate is based on the employment record and amount of contributions paid into the state unemployment fund. The lower the rating, the less tax that must be paid.

Federal Insurance Contributions Act (FICA) Part of the Social Security law that requires employees and employers to pay Social Security taxes and Medicare taxes.

Federal Unemployment Tax Act (FUTA) A tax paid by employers to the federal government. The 1997 rate is .8 percent after applying the normal FUTA tax credit (see below) on the first $7,000 of earnings of each employee.

Form 940, Employer's Annual Federal Unemployment Tax Return One version of the form used by employers at the end of the year to report the amount of unemployment tax due for the calendar year. This version of the form is used by an employer with workers in more than one state. If more than $100 is cumulatively owed in a quarter, it should be paid quarterly, one month after the end of the quarter. Normally payment is due January 31 after the calendar year, or February 10 if deposits have already been made by an employer.

Form 940-EZ, Employer's Annual Federal Unemployment Tax Return The other version of the form used by employers at the end of the year to report the amount of unemployment tax due for the calendar year. The "EZ" version of this form is used by an employer with workers in only one state.

Form 941, Employer's Quarterly Federal Tax Return A tax report that a business will complete after the end of each calendar quarter indicating the total FICA (Social Security and Medicare) owed plus the amount of federal income tax withheld from employees' pay for the quarter. If federal tax deposits have been made timely, the total amount deposited should equal the amount due on Form 941. If there is a difference, a payment may be due.

Form 941 taxes Another term used to describe Social Security, Medicare, and federal income taxes. This name comes from the form used to report these taxes.

Form 8109 A coupon that is completed and sent along with payments of tax deposits relating to either Forms 940-EZ or 941. This form can also be used to deposit other types of taxes a business may owe the federal government.

Form W-2, Wage and Tax Statement A form completed by the employer at the end of the calendar year to provide a summary of gross earnings and deductions to each employee. At least two copies go to the employee, one copy to the IRS, one copy to any state where employees' income taxes have been withheld, one copy to the Social Security Administration, and one copy into the records of the business.

Form W-3, Transmittal of Income and Tax Statements A form completed by the employer to verify the number of W-2's and amounts withheld as shown on them. This form is sent to a Social Security Administration data processing center along with copies of each employee's W-2 forms.

Look-back Period A period of time used to determine if a business will make its Form 941 tax deposits on a monthly or semiweekly basis. The IRS has defined this period as July 1 through June 30 of the year prior to the year in which Form 941 tax deposits will be made.

Monthly Depositor A business classified as a monthly depositor will make its payroll tax deposits only once each month for the amount of Form 941 due from the prior month.

Normal FUTA Tax Credit A credit given to employers who pay their state unemployment taxes on time. The credit is usually 5.4 percent, which is applied against a 6.2 percent rate. The result is a net FUTA tax of .8 percent.

Payroll Tax Expense The general ledger account that records the total of the employer's FICA (Social Security and Medicare), SUTA, and FUTA tax responsibilities.

Semiweekly depositor A business classified as a semiweekly depositor may make its payroll tax deposits up to twice in one week. Semiweekly depositors will make a minimum of one Form 941 payroll tax deposit each week.

SS-4 Form The form filled out by an employer in order to get an employer identification number. The form is sent to the IRS, who assigns the number to the business.

State Unemployment Tax Act (SUTA) A tax usually paid only by employers to the state for employee unemployment insurance.

Workers' Compensation Insurance Insurance paid for, in advance, by an employer to protect its employees against loss due to injury or death incurred during employment.

BLUEPRINT OF FORM 941 TAX DEPOSIT RULES

10 Questions and Answers About Depositing Social Security, Medicare, and Federal Income Taxes to the Government

Here is a summary of questions and answers that will help you to understand the payroll tax deposit rules for Form 941 taxes.

1. **What are Form 941 taxes?** This term is used to describe the amount of Social Security, Medicare, and federal income tax paid by employees, and the amount of Social Security and Medicare taxes that are matched and paid by an employer. The total of these taxes are known as Form 941 taxes because they are reported on Form 941 each quarter.

2. **When does an employer deposit Form 941 taxes?** How often an employer deposits Form 941 taxes depends on how the employer is classified for this purpose. The IRS classifies an employer as either a *monthly* or *semiweekly depositor* based on the amount of Form 941 taxes paid during a time-period known as a *look-back period.*

3. **When is a look-back period?** This time period is a fiscal year that begins on July 1 and ends on June 30 of the year before the calendar year when the deposits will be made. For example, for the 1998 calendar year, an employer's look-back period will begin on July 1, 1996 and end June 30, 1997.

4. **What is the dollar amount used to classify an employer for Form 941 tax deposits?** The key dollar amount used to determine if an employer is a *monthly* or *semiweekly* depositor is $50,000 in Form 941 taxes. Two rules apply here:

   a. If the total amount deposited in Form 941 taxes is less than $50,000 during the look-back period, the employer is considered a *monthly tax depositor.*

   b. If the total amount deposited in Form 941 taxes is $50,000 or more during the look-back period, the employer is considered a *semiweekly tax depositor.*

5. **How do employers deposit Form 941 taxes?** An employer will fill out a Form 8109 (Federal Tax Deposit Coupon) and give this form with a check to a bank authorized to receive payroll tax deposits or to a Federal Reserve Bank. Generally authorized banks will only take checks written from an account maintained at that same bank. So, an employer usually cannot make a Form 941 deposit at bank A using a check written from an account maintained at bank B. A Federal Reserve Bank will accept a check from any U.S. bank for payroll tax deposit purposes.

6. **When do monthly depositors make their deposits?** A monthly depositor will figure the total amount of Form 941 taxes owed in a calendar month and then pay this amount by the fifteenth of the next month. So, if an employer owes $3,125 in Form 941 taxes for the month of June, it will deposit this same amount no later than July 15 of the same year.

7. **When do semiweekly depositors make their deposits?** These rules are a little more complicated. A semiweekly depositor may have to make up to two Form 941 deposits each week. When a tax deposit is due depends on when the employees are paid. To keep the rules consistent, the IRS has taken a calendar week and divided it into two payday time-periods. It is easiest to think of a two-week period of time when discussing these time periods: *Wednesday, Thursday, and Friday* of week one; and, *Saturday and Sunday* of week one and *Monday and Tuesday* of week two.

   Two deposit rules apply to these two time-periods. We can call these rules the **Wednesday** and **Friday rules.**

   a. **Wednesday rule:** If employees are paid during the week one Wednesday – Friday period, the tax deposit will be due on Wednesday of week two.

b. Friday rule: If employees are paid anytime from Saturday or Sunday of week one, or Monday or Tuesday of week two, the tax deposit will be due on Friday of week two.

What these rules mean is that the payroll tax deposit will be due three banking days after the payday time-period ends. For the Wednesday rule, the deposit is due three banking days after Friday of week one, on the following Wednesday (in week two). For the Friday rule, the deposit is due three banking days after Tuesday of week two, on Friday of week two.

8. **What is a *banking day?*** This term refers to any day that a bank is open to the public for business. This means that Saturdays, Sundays, and legal holidays are not banking days.

9. **How do legal holidays affect payroll tax deposits?** If a legal holiday occurs after the last day of a payday time-period, the employer will get one extra day to make its Form 941 tax deposit as follows:

   a. **For monthly depositors:** If the fifteenth of the month is a Saturday, Sunday, or legal holiday, the deposit will be due and payable on the next banking day.

   b. **For semiweekly depositors:** A deposit due on Wednesday will be due on Thursday of the same week, and a Friday deposit will be due on Monday of the following week. Remember that the employer will always have three banking days after the last day of either payday time-period to make its payroll tax deposit.

10. **What happens if an employer is late with its Form 941 tax deposit?** If a Form 941 tax deposit is not made the day it should be deposited, the employer may be assessed a fine for lateness and even charged interest depending on how late the deposit is.

QUESTIONS, MINI EXERCISES, EXERCISES, AND PROBLEMS

Discussion Questions

1. What taxes make up *Payroll Tax Expense?*

2. Explain how an employer can receive a credit against the FUTA tax due.

3. Explain what an experience or merit rating is, and how it affects the amount paid by an employer for state unemployment insurance.

4. How is an employer classified as a monthly or semiweekly depositor for Form 941 tax purposes?

5. What is the purpose of Form 8109?

6. How often is Form 941 completed?

7. Please comment on the following statement: The amount found on Line 20(d) of Form 941 must always be the same amount found on Line 16 of the form.

8. Bill Smith leaves his job on July 9. He requests a copy of his W-2 form when he leaves. His boss tells him to wait until January of next year. Please discuss whether Bill's boss is correct in making this statement.

9. Why would one employer prepare a Form 940 while another would prepare a 940-EZ?

10. Employer "A" has a FUTA tax liability of $67.49 on March 31 of the current year. When does the employer have to make the deposit for this liability?

11. Employer "B" has a FUTA tax liability of $553.24 on January 31 of the current year. When does the employer have to make the deposit for this liability?

12. Why is the year-end adjusting entry needed for Workers' Compensation Insurance?

Mini Exercises

(The forms you need are on page 259 of the *Study Guide and Working Papers.*)

Account Classifications

1. Complete the following table:

Accounts Affected	Category	↑	Rules
a. Payroll Tax Expense			
b. FICA-SS Payable			
c. FICA-Medicare Payable			
d. State Unemployment Tax Payable			
e. Federal Unemployment Tax Payable			

Exempt Wages

2. Given: Pete Bole cumulative earnings before this pay period $6,800; gross pay for week $500. How much of *this* week's pay will be subject to taxes for: FICA-Medicare; FICA-Social Security; SUTA; FUTA. Assume base and rates in text.

Look-Back Periods

3. Label the following Look-Back Periods for 1998 by months

A	B	C	D
1996		1997	

Monthly versus Semiweekly Depositor

4. In November 1997, Pete also is trying to find out if he is a monthly or semiweekly depositor for FICA (SS + Med.) and Federal Income Tax for 1998. Please advise based on the following taxes owed:

1996	Quarter 3	$28,000
	Quarter 4	12,000
1997	Quarter 1	3,000
	Quarter 2	10,000

Paying the Tax

5. Complete the following table:

Depositor	Four Quarter Look-Back Period Tax Liability	Payroll Paid	Tax Paid by
Monthly	$28,000	Nov.	A.
Semiweekly	$66,000	On Wed.	B.
		On Thur.	C.
		On Fri.	D.
		On Sat.	E.
		On Sun.	F.
		On Mon.	G.

(The forms you need are on pages 260–262 of the *Study Guide and Working Papers.*)

Journalizing the payroll tax

8-1. From the following information, prepare a general journal entry to record the payroll tax expense for Asty Company for the payroll of August 9:

Employee	Cumulative Earnings Before Weekly Payroll	Gross Pay For Week
J. Kline	$3,500	$900
A. Met	6,600	750
D. Ring	7,900	300

The FICA tax rate for Social Security is 6.2 percent on $65,400, and Medicare is 1.45 percent on all earnings. Federal unemployment tax is .8 percent (.008 when expressed as a decimal) on the first $7,000 earned by each employee. The experience or merit rating for Asty Co. is 5.6 percent on the first $7,000 of employee earnings for state unemployment purposes.

Change in merit rating

8-2. Using 8-1 above, the state changed Asty's experience/merit rating to 4.9 percent. What effect would this change have on the total payroll tax expense?

Change in payroll tax expense

8-3. Using exercise 8-1, if D. Ring earned $2,000 for the week instead of $300, what effect would this change have on the total payroll tax expense?

Journalizing payment of deposit

8-4. At the end of January 19XX, the total amount of Social Security, $610, and Medicare, $200, was withheld as tax deductions from the employees of Cornfield Acres Inc. Federal income tax of $3,000 was also deducted from their paychecks. Cornfield Acres has been classified as a monthly depositor of Form 941 taxes. Indicate when this payroll tax deposit is due and provide a general journal entry to record the payment.

Calculating total payroll tax expense

8-5. The total wage expense for Howie Co. was $150,000. Of this total, $30,000 was beyond the Social Security wage base limit and not subject to this tax. All earnings are subject to Medicare tax, and $60,000 was beyond the federal and state unemployment wage base limits and not subject to unemployment taxes. Please calculate the total payroll tax expense for Howie Co. given the following rates and wage base limits:

a. FICA tax rate — Social Security, 6.2 percent; Medicare, 1.45 percent.

b. State unemployment tax rate, 5.9 percent.

c. Federal unemployment tax rate (after credit), .8 percent.

Determining when tax deposits are due

8-6. Carol's Grocery Store made the following Form 941 payroll tax deposits during the look-back period of July 1, 19X1 through June 30, 19X2:

Quarter Ended	Amount Paid in 941 Taxes
September 30, 19X1	$13,783.26
December 31, 19X1	14,893.22
March 31, 19X2	14,601.94
June 30, 19X2	15,021.01

Should Carol's Grocery Store make Form 941 tax deposits monthly or semiweekly for 19X3?

Determining when tax deposits are due

8-7. If Carol's Grocery Store downsized its operation during the second quarter of 19X2 and as a result paid only $6,121.93 in Form 941 taxes for the quarter that ended on June 30, 19X2, should Carol's Grocery make its Form 941 payroll tax deposits monthly or semiweekly for 19X3?

8-8. From the following accounts, record the payment of (a) July 3 payment for FICA (Social Security and Medicare) and federal income taxes; (b) July 30 payment of state unemployment tax; and (c) July 30 deposit of FUTA tax that may be required. Please prepare general journal entries from the following T accounts:

Journal entry to record payment of taxes

FICA-Social Security Payable 203		FICA-Medicare Payable 204	
	June 30 400 (EE)		June 30 100 (EE)
	400 (ER)		100 (ER)

FIT Payable 205		FUTA Tax Payable 206	
	June 30 3,005		June 30 119

SUTA Tax Payable 207	
	June 30 411

FUTA

8-9. At the end of the first quarter of 19XX, you have been asked to determine the FUTA tax liability for Oscar Company as well as to record any payment of tax liability. The following information has been supplied to you: FUTA tax rate is .8 percent on the first $7,000 each employee earns during the year.

Employee	Gross Pay Per Week
J. King	$400
A. Lane	500
B. Move	600
C. Slade	900

Workers compensation

8-10. From the following data, estimate the annual premium and record it by preparing a general journal entry:

Type of Work	Estimated Payroll	Rate per $100
Office	$15,000	$ .17
Sales	42,000	1.90

Group A Problems

(The forms you need are on pages 263-269 of the *Study Guide and Working Papers*.)

Journal entry to record payroll tax expense

8A-1. For the week of April 8 at Kane's Hardware, the partial payroll summary shown below is taken from the individual employee earnings records. Both Jill Reese and Jeff Vatack have earned more than $7,000 before this payroll.

Your task is to:

1. Complete the table.
2. Prepare a journal entry to record the payroll tax expense for Kane's. Use the federal income tax withholding tables in Figures 7-2 and 7-3 (Chapter 7 — pp. 240–242) to figure the amount of income tax withheld. Please show the calculations for FICA taxes.

Check Figure:

Payroll Tax Expense $483.62

Employee	Allowance and Marital Status	Gross	FICA Soc. Sec.	Medicare	Federal Income Tax
Al Jones	S-1	$ 600			
Janice King	S-0	850			
Alice Long	S-2	750			
Jill Reese	M-0	1,060			
Jeff Vatack	M-2	1,365			

Assume: FICA tax rate for Social Security is 6.2 percent up to $65,400 in earnings (no one has earned this much as of April 8); Medicare is 1.45 percent on all earnings. The state unemployment tax rate is 5.1 percent on the first $7,000 of earnings, and the federal unemployment tax rate is .8 percent of the first $7,000 of earnings. In cases where the amount of FICA tax calculates to one-half cent, round up to the next cent.

8A-2. The following is the monthly payroll of Hogan Co., owned by Dean Hogan. Employees are paid on the last day of each month.

Employer's tax responsibilities

JANUARY

Employee	Monthly Earnings	Year-to-Date Earnings	FICA		Federal Income Tax
			Soc. Sec.	Medicare	
Sam Koy	$1,800	$1,800	$111.60	$ 26.10	$ 241
Joy Lane	3,150	3,150	195.30	45.68	361
Amy Hess	4,100	4,100	254.20	59.45	500
	$9,050	$9,050	$561.10	$131.23	$1,102

FEBRUARY

Employee	Monthly Earnings	Year-to-Date Earnings	FICA		Federal Income Tax
			Soc. Sec.	Medicare	
Sam Koy	$1,975	$ 3,775	$122.45	$ 28.64	$ 265
Joy Lane	2,900	6,050	179.80	42.05	325
Amy Hess	3,775	7,875	234.05	54.74	426
	$8,650	$17,700	$536.30	$125.43	$1,016

MARCH

Check Figure:

Deposit of SUTA Tax $1,195.58

Employee	Monthly Earnings	Year-to-Date Earnings	FICA		Federal Income Tax
			Soc. Sec.	Medicare	
Sam Koy	$ 3,200	$ 6,975	$198.40	$ 46.40	$ 608
Joy Lane	4,080	10,130	252.96	59.16	558
Amy Hess	4,250	12,125	263.50	61.63	545
	$11,530	$29,230	$714.86	$167.19	$1,711

Hogan Company is located at 2 Roundy Road, Marblehead, MA 01945. Employer identification number is 29-3458821. FICA tax rate for Social Security is 6.2 percent up to $65,400 in earnings during the year; Medicare is 1.45 percent on all earnings. The SUTA tax rate is 5.7 percent on the first $7,000. The FUTA tax rate is .8 percent on the first $7,000 of earnings. Hogan Company is classified as a monthly depositor for Form 941 taxes.

Your task is to:

1. Journalize entries to record the employer's payroll tax expense for each pay period in the general journal.
2. Journalize entries for the payment of each tax liability including SUTA tax in the general journal.

Journal entries and Form 941

Check Figure:

Total Liability for Quarter $8,301.22

8A-3. Ed Ward, accountant of Hogan Company, has been requested to complete Form 941 for the first quarter of the current year. Using Problem 8A-2, Ed gathers the needed data. Ed has suddenly been called away to an urgent budget meeting and has requested you to assist him by preparing the Form 941 for the first quarter. Please note that the difference in the tax liability, a few cents, should be adjusted in the middle column of Line 9 — this difference is due to the rounding of FICA tax amounts.

Journal entries and Form 941

Check Figure:

Dec. 31 Payroll Tax Expense $736.67

8A-4. The following is the monthly payroll for the last three months of the year for Henson's Sporting Goods Shop, 1 Roe Road, Lynn, MA 01945. The shop is a sole proprietorship owned and operated by Bill Henson. The employer ID number for Henson's Sporting Goods is 28-93118921.

The employees at Henson's are paid once each month on the last day of the month. Pete Avery is the only employee who has contributed the maximum into Social Security. None of the other employees will reach the Social Security wage base limit by the end of the year. Assume the rate for Social Security to be 6.2 percent with a wage base maximum of $65,400, and the rate for Medicare to be 1.45 percent on all earnings. Henson's is classified as a monthly depositor for Form 941 payroll tax deposit purposes.

OCTOBER

Check Figure:

Dec. 31 Payroll Tax Expense
$736.67

Employee	Monthly Earnings	Year-to-Date Earnings	FICA Soc. Sec.	Medicare	Federal Income Tax
Pete Avery	$ 2,950	$ 61,450	$182.90	$ 42.78	$ 530
Janet Lee	3,590	40,150	222.58	52.06	427
Sue Lyons	3,800	43,900	235.60	55.10	536
	$10,340	$145,500	$641.08	$149.94	$1,493

NOVEMBER

Employee	Monthly Earnings	Year-to-Date Earnings	FICA Soc. Sec.	Medicare	Federal Income Tax
Pete Avery	$ 3,180	$ 64,630	$197.16	$ 46.11	$ 597
Janet Lee	3,772	43,922	233.86	54.69	468
Sue Lyons	3,891	47,791	241.24	56.42	559
	$10,843	$156,343	$672.26	$157.22	$1,624

DECEMBER

Employee	Monthly Earnings	Year-to-Date Earnings	FICA Soc. Sec.	Medicare	Federal Income Tax
Pete Avery	$ 4,250	$ 68,880	$ 47.74	$ 61.63	$ 902
Janet Lee	3,800	47,722	235.60	55.10	479
Sue Lyons	4,400	52,191	272.80	63.80	704
	$12,450	$168,793	$556.14	$180.53	$2,085

Your task is to:

1. Journalize entries to record the employer's payroll tax expense for each pay period in the general journal.
2. Journalize entries for the payment of each tax for FICA tax (Social Security and Medicare) and federal income tax given that Henson's is a monthly Form 941 tax depositor.
3. Complete Form 941 for the fourth quarter of the current year.

Form 940-EZ

Check Figure:

Total Exempt Payments
$147,793

8A-5. Using the information from Problem 8A-4 above, please complete a Form 940-EZ for Henson's Sporting Goods for the current year. Additional information needed to complete the form is as follows:

a. FUTA tax deposit for first quarter, $168.00
b. SUTA rate, 5.7 percent; state reporting number, 025-319-2.

   Please note that there were no FUTA tax deposits for the second, third, or fourth quarters of the year. Henson's has three employees for the year who all earned over $7,000.

Group B Problems

(The forms you need are on pages 263 - 269 of the *Study Guide and Working Papers*.)

Journal entry to record payroll tax expense

8B-1. For the week of April 8 at Kane's Hardware, the following partial payroll summary is taken from the individual employee earnings records. Both Jill Reese and Jeff Vatack have earned more than $7,000 before this payroll.

Your task is to:

1. Complete the table.
2. Prepare a journal entry to record the payroll tax expense for Kane's. Use the federal income tax withholding tables in Figures 7-2 and 7-3 (Chapter 7) to figure the amount of income tax withheld. Please show the calculations for FICA taxes.

Employee	Allowance and Marital Status	Gross	FICA Soc. Sec.	Medicare	Federal Income Tax
Al Jones	S-1	$ 620			
Janice King	S-2	890			
Alice Long	S-0	750			
Jill Reese	M-1	1,100			
Jeff Vatack	M-2	1,340			

Assume: FICA tax rate for Social Security is 6.2 percent up to $65,400 in earnings (no one has earned this much as of April 8); Medicare is 1.45 percent on all earnings. The state unemployment tax rate is 5.2 percent on the first $7,000 of earnings, and the federal unemployment tax rate is .8 percent of the first $7,000 of earnings. In cases where the FICA tax calculates to one-half cent, round up to the next cent.

8B-2. The following is the monthly payroll of Hogan Co., owned by Dean Hogan. Employees are paid on the last day of each month.

JANUARY

Employee	Monthly Earnings	Year-to-Date Earnings	FICA Soc. Sec.	Medicare	Federal Income Tax
Sam Koy	$1,675	$1,675	$103.85	$ 24.29	$217
Joy Lane	3,000	3,000	186.00	43.50	343
Amy Hess	3,590	3,590	222.58	52.06	396
	$8,265	$8,265	$512.43	$119.85	$956

FEBRUARY

Employee	Monthly Earnings	Year-to-Date Earnings	FICA Soc. Sec.	Medicare	Federal Income Tax
Sam Koy	$1,975	$ 3,650	$122.45	$ 28.64	$ 265
Joy Lane	2,900	5,900	179.80	42.05	325
Amy Hess	3,775	7,365	234.05	54.74	426
	$8,650	$16,915	$536.30	$125.43	$1,016

MARCH

Employee	Monthly Earnings	Year-to-Date Earnings	FICA Soc. Sec.	Medicare	Federal Income Tax
Sam Koy	$ 3,220	$ 6,870	$199.64	$ 46.69	$ 608
Joy Lane	4,000	9,900	248.00	58.00	535
Amy Hess	4,300	11,665	266.60	62.35	556
	$11,520	$28,435	$714.24	$167.04	$1,699

Hogan Company is located at 2 Roundy Road, Marblehead, MA 01945. Employer identification number is 29-3458821. FICA tax rate for Social Security is 6.2 percent up to $65,400 in earnings during the year; Medicare is 1.45 percent on all earnings. The SUTA tax rate is 5.7 percent on the first $7,000. The FUTA tax rate is .8 percent on the first $7,000 of earnings. Hogan Company is classified as a monthly depositor for Form 941 taxes.

Your task is to:

1. Journalize entries to record the employer's payroll tax expense for each pay period in the general journal.

2. Journalize entries for the payment of each tax liability including SUTA tax in the general journal.

Journal entries and Form 941

Check Figure:
Liability for Quarter $8,021.58

8B-3. Ed Ward, accountant of Hogan Company, has been requested to complete Form 941 for the first quarter of the current year. Using Problem 8B-2, Ed gathers the needed data. Ed has suddenly been called away to an urgent budget meeting and has requested you to assist him by preparing the Form 941 for the first quarter. Please note that the difference in the tax liability, a few cents, should be adjusted in the middle column of Line 9 — this difference is due to the rounding of FICA tax amounts.

Journal entries and Form 941

8B-4. The following is the monthly payroll for the last three months of the year for Henson's Sporting Goods Shop, 1 Roe Road, Lynn, MA 01945. The shop is a sole proprietorship owned and operated by Bill Henson. The employer ID number for Henson's Sporting Goods is 28-93118921.

The employees at Henson's are paid once each month on the last day of the month. Pete Avery is the only employee who has contributed the maximum into Social Security. None of the other employees will reach the Social Security wage base limit by the end of the year. Assume the rate for Social Security to be 6.2 percent with a wage base maximum of $65,400, and the rate for Medicare to be 1.45 percent on all earnings. Henson's is classified as a monthly depositor for Form 941 payroll taxes.

OCTOBER

Employee	Monthly Earnings	Year-to-Date Earnings	FICA Soc. Sec.	FICA Medicare	Federal Income Tax
Pete Avery	$ 2,950	$ 62,600	$182.90	$ 42.78	$ 530
Janet Lee	3,590	41,075	222.58	52.06	427
Sue Lyons	3,800	44,000	235.60	55.10	536
	$10,340	$147,675	$641.08	$149.94	$1,493

NOVEMBER

Check Figure:
Dec 31 Payroll Tax Expense
$654.51

Employee	Monthly Earnings	Year-to-Date Earnings	FICA Soc. Sec.	FICA Medicare	Federal Income Tax
Pete Avery	$ 3,000	$ 65,600	$173.60	$ 43.50	$ 552
Janet Lee	3,650	44,725	226.30	52.93	439
Sue Lyons	3,710	47,710	230.02	53.80	503
	$10,360	$158,035	$629.92	$150.23	$1,494

DECEMBER

Employee	Monthly Earnings	Year-to-Date Earnings	FICA Soc. Sec.	FICA Medicare	Federal Income Tax
Pete Avery	$ 4,250	$ 69,850	—	$ 61.63	$ 902
Janet Lee	3,850	48,575	$238.70	55.83	490
Sue Lyons	3,900	51,610	241.80	56.55	559
	$12,000	$170,035	$480.50	$174.01	$1,951

Your task is to:

1. Journalize entries to record the employer's payroll tax expense for each pay period in the general journal.

2. Journalize entries for the payment of each tax for FICA tax (Social Security and Medicare) and federal income tax.

3. Complete Form 941 for the fourth quarter of the current year.

8B-5. Using the information from Problem 8B-4 above, please complete a 940-EZ form for Henson's Sporting Goods for the current year. Additional information needed to complete the form is as follows:

   a. FUTA tax deposit for first quarter, $168.

   b. SUTA tax rate, 5.7 percent; state reporting number, 025-319-2.

     Please note that there were no FUTA tax deposits for the third or fourth quarters of the year. Henson's has three employees for the year who all earned over $7,000.

REAL WORLD APPLICATIONS

8R-1.

Sunshine School Supplies is a leading manufacturer of back-to-school kits and other items used by students in elementary and middle schools. Each summer Sunshine needs additional help to assemble, pack, and ship school items sold in stores around the country. Sunshine's company policy has been to hire 30 additional workers for 12 weeks during the summer. Each employee works 40 hours per week and earns $6 per hour. At the end of August these additional workers are laid off.

   Sunshine's state unemployment rate has risen to 5.4 percent with no experience/merit rating allowed due to these layoffs in the last few years.

   Miriam Holtz, who is the president of Sunshine, asks for your help to find a way to reduce Sunshine's 5.4 state unemployment rate. When Miriam called the state department of labor and employment, she was told that Sunshine's unemployment rate could drop to 4.1 percent if it stopped laying off workers.

   Miriam has thought about using temporary employment agency workers during the summer months as a way to obtain the help the company needs and at the same time stop the seasonal layoffs.

   Miriam asks you if this is a good idea. She gives you the following facts to use in analyzing this idea:

1. Five hundred workers who are permanent employees of Sunshine earn in excess of $7,000 each by September of each year.
2. A temporary employment agency told Miriam it would charge Sunshine $7.00 per hour for each worker it supplied during the summer.
3. The current federal unemployment tax rate is .8 percent up to the first $7,000 each employee earns during a year.
4. The current SUTA wage base limit is the first $7,000 each employee earns during a year.
5. Sunshine pays a FICA tax rate of 6.2 percent for Social Security and 1.45 percent for Medicare. The Social Security wage base limit is $65,400; there is no wage base limit for Medicare.

   Please write a short memo to Miriam Holtz that shows your analysis of two options: (1) Continue to hire 30 additional workers for the summer and then lay them off; and, (2) have the temporary employment agency provide 30 additional workers for the summer.

   In your memo be sure to show the financial effect of both options in terms of the tax calculations on employee earnings for SUTA, FUTA, and FICA. For option (1) be sure to include the SUTA and FUTA tax effects for *both* the permanent and temporary workers. At the end of your memo please provide Miriam with your conclusion so she can make a good decision for her company.

8R-2.

Cathy Johnson has just been hired as a bookkeeper for the Small Fry Dog Toy Company. She recently graduated from the local community college with an associates degree in business. She took several accounting courses at school but was unable to take the school's payroll accounting course.

Cathy is confused about payroll tax forms and their purpose. She wants to learn more about the forms the business must prepare and send in to the government.

You are the accountant for Small Fry. Your boss has asked you to help teach Cathy about the forms and why they are used. The boss feels it is best to give Cathy a brief written summary about the following forms:

1. Form 941
2. Form 940-EZ
3. Form 8109
4. Form W-2
5. Form W-3

Please write a brief report to Cathy to help her to understand the following points about these payroll tax forms:

a. The purpose of each form.
b. What is reported on each form.
c. When each form is sent to the government.
d. Where the amounts found on each form come from in the accounting system.

make the call
Critical Thinking/Ethical Case

8R-3.
Abby Ross works in the Payroll Department for Lange Co. as a junior accountant. Abby also is going to school for an advanced degree in accounting. After work each day she uses the company's photocopy machine to make extra copies of her assignments. Should she be photocopying personal material on a company machine? You make the call. Write down your specific recommendations to Abby.

ACCOUNTING RECALL
A CUMULATIVE APPROACH

THIS EXAM REVIEWS CHAPTERS 1 THROUGH 8

Your *Study Guide and Working Papers* have forms (pp. 274 and 279) to complete this exam, as well as worked-out solutions. The page references next to each question identify what page to turn back to if you answer the question incorrectly.

PART 1   Vocabulary Review

Match the terms to the appropriate definition or phrase.

Page Ref.
(212)   1. Checks outstanding   A. Total of employer's tax
(271)   2. SUTA   responsibilities

(268)	3. SS-4	B. Used up
(271)	4. Payroll tax expense	C. Four quarters
(255)	5. Quarter	D. Merit rating
(282)	6. W-2	E. Federal employer identification
(280)	7. 941	number
(275)	8. Look-back periods	F. FICA (EE + ER) + FIT
(248)	9. Medicare — tax payable	G. 13 weeks
(281)	10. Adjustments	H. Not processed by bank
		I. A liability
		J. Provides summary of gross earnings

PART II   True or False (Accounting Theory)

(271)	11. SUTA is not part of Payroll Tax Expense.
(212)	12. NSF means check did not have sufficient funds.
(278)	13. Quarterly return (941) records taxes for FIT and SUTA.
(270)	14. FUTA is always paid once a year.
(171)	15. The post-closing trial balance is the last step of the Accounting Cycle.

CONTINUING PROBLEM

As December comes to an end, Tony Freedman wants to take care of his payroll obligations. He will complete Form 941 for the first quarter of the current year and Form 940-EZ for federal unemployment taxes. Freedman will make the necessary deposits and payments associated with his payroll.

Assignment:

(See pp. 275 – 278 in your *Study Guide and Working Papers*.)

1. Record the payroll tax expense entry in general journal format for the quarter, using the information in the Chapter 7 problem.
2. Journalize entries for the payment of each tax liability including SUTA tax in the general journal. Freedman is classified as a quarterly depositor.
3. Prepare Form 941 for the first quarter. Eldorado Computer Center's employer identification number is 35-41325881.
4. Complete Form 940 for Eldorado Computer Center. FUTA tax ceiling is $7,000 and SUTA tax ceiling is $10,000 in cumulative wages for each employee. The Eldorado Computer Center's FUTA rate is .8 percent and SUTA rate is 2.7 percent. No deposits have been made.

   Hint: Sometimes the amount of Social Security taxes paid by the employee for the quarter will not equal the employee's tax liability because of rounding. Any overage/difference should be reported on line 9 of Form 941.

Pete's Market

Completing Payroll Requirements for First Quarter and Preparing Form 941

This Mini Practice Set will aid in putting the pieces of payroll together. In this project, you are the bookkeeper and will have the responsibility of recording payroll in the payroll register, paying the payroll, recording the employer's tax responsibilities, and paying tax deposits, as well as completing the quarterly report. (The forms you need are on pages 278-283 of the *Study Guide and Working Papers*.)

Pete's Market, owned by Pete Reel, is located at 4 Sun Avenue, Swampscott, MA 01970. His employer identification number is 42-4583312. Please assume the following:

1. FICA: Social Security, 6.2 percent on $65,400; Medicare, 1.45 percent on all earnings.
2. SUTA: 4.9 percent (due to favorable merit rating) on $7,000.
3. FUTA: .8 percent on first $7,000.
4. Employees are paid monthly. The payroll is recorded the last day of each month and is paid on the first day of the next month.
5. FIT table provided with problem from IRS Circular E, *Employer's Tax Guide* (see p. 241).
6. State income tax is 8 percent.

The following are the employees of Pete's Market along with their monthly salary exemptions, etc.

SALARY PER MONTH

		January	February	March	
Fred Flynn	S-0	$2,500	$2,590	$2,475	(Sales Salaries)
Mary Jones	S-2	3,000	3,000	4,000	(Market Salaries)
Lilly Vron	S-1	3,000	3,000	4,260	(Sales Salaries)

Partial Ledger Accounts as of December 31, 19XX

FICA-Social Security Payable 210	
	410.90 (EE)
	410.90 (ER)

FICA-Medicare Payable 212		
	100	(EE)
	100	(ER)

FIT Payable 220
600

SIT Payable 225
150

FUTA Payable 230
88

SUTA Payable 240
155

Using the general journal and payroll register provided, please complete the following:

19XX
Jan. 15 Record the entry for the deposit of Social Security, Medicare, and FIT from last month's payroll. (For simplicity we will not record the payment of state income tax.)

	31	Pay state unemployment tax due from last quarter.
	31	Pay federal unemployment tax owed.
	31	Complete payroll register for January payroll, journalize payroll entry, and journalize entry for employer's payroll tax expense.
Feb.	1	Transfer cash for the January Net Pay from Cash to Payroll Checking Cash.
	1	Pay payroll.
	15	Pay taxes due for Social Security, Medicare, and FIT.
	28	Complete payroll register for February payroll. Journalize payroll entry as well as journalize entry for employer's payroll tax expense.
Mar.	1	Transfer cash for the February Net Pay from Cash to Payroll Checking Cash.
	1	Pay payroll.
	15	Pay taxes due for Social Security, Medicare, and FIT.
	31	Complete payroll register for March payroll. Journalize payroll entry as well as journalize entry for employer's payroll tax expense.
Apr.	1	Transfer cash for the March Net Pay from Cash to Payroll Checking Cash.
	1	Pay payroll.
	15	Pay taxes due for Social Security, Medicare, and FIT.
	30	Pay federal unemployment tax due for quarter 1.
	30	Pay state unemployment tax due for quarter 1.
	30	Complete Form 941 for the first quarter.

If the wages are—		And the number of withholding allowances claimed is—										
At least	But less than	0	1	2	3	4	5	6	7	8	9	10
		The amount of income tax to be withheld is—										
$2,440	$2,480	$396	$338	$281	$245	$214	$184	$153	$122	$92	$61	$31
2,480	2,520	407	350	292	251	220	190	159	128	98	67	37
2,520	2,560	418	361	304	257	226	196	165	134	104	73	43
2,560	2,600	429	372	315	263	232	202	171	140	110	79	49
2,600	2,640	440	383	326	269	238	208	177	146	116	85	55
2,640	2,680	452	394	337	280	244	214	183	152	122	91	61
2,680	2,720	463	406	348	291	250	220	189	158	128	97	67
2,720	2,760	474	417	360	302	256	226	195	164	134	103	73
2,760	2,800	485	428	371	314	262	232	201	170	140	109	79
2,800	2,840	496	439	382	325	268	238	207	176	146	115	85
2,840	2,880	508	450	393	336	279	244	213	182	152	121	91
2,880	2,920	519	462	404	347	290	250	219	188	158	127	97
2,920	2,960	530	473	416	358	301	256	225	194	164	133	103
2,960	3,000	541	484	427	370	312	262	231	200	170	139	109
3,000	3,040	552	495	438	381	324	268	237	206	176	145	115
3,040	3,080	564	506	449	392	335	278	243	212	182	151	121
3,080	3,120	575	518	460	403	346	289	249	218	188	157	127
3,120	3,160	586	529	472	414	357	300	255	224	194	163	133
3,160	3,200	597	540	483	426	368	311	261	230	200	169	139
3,200	3,240	608	551	494	437	380	322	267	236	206	175	145
3,240	3,280	620	562	505	448	391	334	277	242	212	181	151
3,280	3,320	631	574	516	459	402	345	288	248	218	187	157
3,320	3,360	642	585	528	470	413	356	299	254	224	193	163
3,360	3,400	653	596	539	482	424	367	310	260	230	199	169
3,400	3,440	664	607	550	493	436	378	321	266	236	205	175
3,440	3,480	676	618	561	504	447	390	333	275	242	211	181
3,480	3,520	687	630	572	515	458	401	344	287	248	217	187
3,520	3,560	698	641	584	526	469	412	355	298	254	223	193
3,560	3,600	709	652	595	538	480	423	366	309	260	229	199
3,600	3,640	720	663	606	549	492	434	377	320	266	235	205
3,640	3,680	732	674	617	560	503	446	389	331	274	241	211
3,680	3,720	743	686	628	571	514	457	400	343	285	247	217
3,720	3,760	754	697	640	582	525	468	411	354	297	253	223
3,760	3,800	765	708	651	594	536	479	422	365	308	259	229
3,800	3,840	776	719	662	605	548	490	433	376	319	265	235
3,840	3,880	788	730	673	616	559	502	445	387	330	273	241
3,880	3,920	799	742	684	627	570	513	456	399	341	284	247
3,920	3,960	810	753	696	638	581	524	467	410	353	295	253
3,960	4,000	821	764	707	650	592	535	478	421	364	307	259
4,000	4,040	832	775	718	661	604	546	489	432	375	318	265
4,040	4,080	844	786	729	672	615	558	501	443	386	329	272
4,080	4,120	855	798	740	683	626	569	512	455	397	340	283
4,120	4,160	866	809	752	694	637	580	523	466	409	351	294
4,160	4,200	877	820	763	706	648	591	534	477	420	363	305
4,200	4,240	889	831	774	717	660	602	545	488	431	374	317
4,240	4,280	902	842	785	728	671	614	557	499	442	385	328
4,280	4,320	914	854	796	739	682	625	568	511	453	396	339
4,320	4,360	926	865	808	750	693	636	579	522	465	407	350
4,360	4,400	939	876	819	762	704	647	590	533	476	419	361
4,400	4,440	951	888	830	773	716	658	601	544	487	430	373
4,440	4,480	964	900	841	784	727	670	613	555	498	441	384
4,480	4,520	976	913	852	795	738	681	624	567	509	452	395
4,520	4,560	988	925	864	806	749	692	635	578	521	463	406
4,560	4,600	1,001	937	875	818	760	703	646	589	532	475	417
4,600	4,640	1,013	950	887	829	772	714	657	600	543	486	429
4,640	4,680	1,026	962	899	840	783	726	669	611	554	497	440
4,680	4,720	1,038	975	911	851	794	737	680	623	565	508	451
4,720	4,760	1,050	987	924	862	805	748	691	634	577	519	462
4,760	4,800	1,063	999	936	874	816	759	702	645	588	531	473
4,800	4,840	1,075	1,012	949	885	828	770	713	656	599	542	485
4,840	4,880	1,088	1,024	961	898	839	782	725	667	610	553	496
4,880	4,920	1,100	1,037	973	910	850	793	736	679	621	564	507
4,920	4,960	1,112	1,049	986	922	861	804	747	690	633	575	518
4,960	5,000	1,125	1,061	998	935	872	815	758	701	644	587	529
5,000	5,040	1,137	1,074	1,011	947	884	826	769	712	655	598	541

$5,040 and over   Use Table 4(a) for a **SINGLE person** on page 29. Also see the instructions on page 27.

COMPUTER WORKSHOP

COMPUTERIZED ACCOUNTING APPLICATION FOR PETE'S MARKET MINI PRACTICE SET (CHAPTER 8)

Completing Payroll Requirements for First Quarter and Preparing Form 941

Before starting on this assignment, read and complete the tasks discussed in Parts A, B, and F of the Computerized Accounting appendix at the end of this book and complete the Computerized Accounting Application assignments for Chapter 3, Chapter 4, and the Valdez Realty Mini Practice Set (Chapter 5).

Pete's Market, owned by Pete Reel, is located at 4 Sun Avenue, Swampscott, Massachusetts, 01970. His employer identification number is 42-4583312. The educational version of Simply Accounting packaged with this text uses the state and federal tax laws in effect on April 15, 1997. Federal Income Tax (FIT), State Income Tax (SIT), Social Security, Medicare, FUTA, and SUTA are all calculated automatically by the program based on the following assumptions and built-in tax rates:

1. FICA: Social Security, 6.2 percent on $65,400; Medicare, 1.45 percent on all earnings.

2. SUTA: 4.9 percent on the first $10,800 in earnings.

3. FUTA: .8 percent on the first $7,000 in earnings.

4. Employees are paid monthly. The payroll is recorded and paid on the last day of each month. The cash amount for the first quarter's net pay has been transferred from the Cash account to the Payroll Checking Cash account.

5. FIT is calculated automatically by the program based on the marital status and number of exemptions claimed by each employee.

6. SIT for Massachusetts is calculated automatically by the program based on the marital status and number of exemptions claimed by each employee.

The Payroll Journal in Simply Accounting is designed to work with the General Ledger module in an integrated fashion. When transactions are recorded in the Payroll Journal, the program automatically updates the employee records, records the journal entry, and posts all accounts affected in the general ledger.

The following are the employees of Pete's Market and their monthly wages for the first payroll quarter:

	January	February	March
Fred Flynn	$2,500	$2,590	$2,475
Mary Jones	3,000	3,000	4,000
Lilly Vron	3,000	3,000	4,260

The trial balance for Pete's Market as at 1/1/97 appears below:

		Debits	Credits
1010	Cash	65,183.37	—
1020	Payroll Checking Cash	19,780.67	—
2310	FIT Payable	—	1,415.94
2320	SIT Payable	—	535.50
2330	Social Security Tax Payable	—	1,116.00
2335	Medicare Tax Payable	—	261.00
2340	FUTA Payable	—	48.00

2350	SUTA Payable	—	1,587.60
3560	Pete Reel, Capital	—	80,000.00
		84,964.04	84,964.04

Open the Company Data Files

1. Click on the Start button. Point to Programs; point to Simply Accounting; then click on Simply Accounting in the final menu presented. The Simply Accounting Open File dialog box will appear.

2. Insert your Student Data Files disk into disk drive A. Enter the following path into the **File name** text box: A:\student\pete.asc

3. Click on the **Open** button; enter 1/31/97 into the **Using Date for this Session** text box; then click on the **OK** button. Click on the **OK** button in response to the message "The date entered is more than one week past your previous **Using date** of 1/1/97." The Company Window for Pete will appear.

Add Your Name to the Company Name

4. Click on the Company Window Setup menu; then click on Company Information. The Company Information dialog box will appear. Insert your name in place of the text "Your Name" in the **Name** text box. Click on the **OK** button to return to the Company Window.

Record Payment of December Payroll Liabilities and Taxes

5. Open the General Journal dialog box; then record the following general journal entries (Enter "Memo" into the **Source** text box for each transaction; then enter the **Date** listed for each transaction.):

1997
Jan. 15 Record the compound journal entry for the deposit of Social Security, Medicare, and FIT from last month's payroll. (For simplicity we will not record the payment of state income tax.)
     31 Record the payment of SUTA from last quarter.
     31 Record the payment of FUTA tax owed.

How to Record Payroll Journal Entries

6. Close the General Journal; then double-click on the Payroll Journal icon. The Payroll Journal dialog box will appear.

7. Click on the arrow button to the right of the **To the Order of** text box. Click on Fred Flynn's name; then press the TAB key.

8. Click on the **Wages** text box; enter 2500; then press the TAB key. This completes the data you need to enter into the Payroll Journal dialog box to record the payroll journal entry for Fred Flynn's January payroll check. Your screen should look like this:

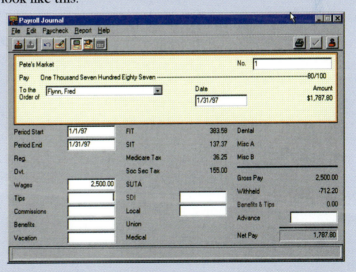

How to Review a Payroll Journal Entry

9. Before posting this transaction, you need to verify that the transaction data are correct by reviewing the payroll journal entry. To review the entry, click on the Payroll Journal Report menu; then click on Display Payroll Journal Entry. The journal entry representing the data you have recorded in the Payroll Journal dialog box is displayed.

Note that the program has combined the journal entry to record and pay the payroll with the journal entry to record the employer's payroll tax expense into a single compound journal entry. Also note that the program uses four individual payroll tax expense accounts (Social Security Tax Expense, Medicare Tax Expense, FUTA Expense, and SUTA Expense) in place of a single Payroll Tax Expense account. Review the payroll entry for accuracy noting any errors.

How to Edit a Payroll Journal Entry Prior to Posting

10. Close the Payroll Journal Entry window. If you have made an error, use the following editing techniques to correct the error:

Editing a Payroll Journal Entry

◆ Move to the text box that contains the error by either pressing the TAB key to move forward through each text box or the SHIFT and TAB keys together to move to a previous text box. This will highlight the selected text box information so that you can change it. Alternatively, you can use the mouse to point to a text box and drag through the incorrect information to highlight it.

◆ Type the correct information; then press the TAB key to enter it.

◆ If you have associated the transaction with an incorrect employee, re-select the correct employee from the employee list display after clicking on the arrow button to the right of the **To the Order of** text box.

◆ To discard an entry and start over, click on the close button. Click on the **Yes** button in response to the question "Are you sure you want to discard this journal entry?"

◆ Review the journal entry for accuracy after any editing corrections.

◆ **It is IMPORTANT TO NOTE that the only way to edit a payroll journal entry after it is posted is to reverse the entry and enter the correct journal entry.** To correct payroll journal entries posted in error, see Part C of the Computerized Accounting appendix in the back of this book.

How to Post a Payroll Entry

11. After verifying that the payroll journal entry is correct, click on the **Post** icon to post this transaction. A blank Payroll Journal dialog box is displayed, ready for additional Payroll Journal transactions to be recorded.

Record Remaining January Payroll

12. Record the January payroll journal entries for Mary Jones and Lilly Vron.

13. After you have posted the additional payroll journal entries, close the Payroll Journal dialog box. This will restore the Company Window screen, and the Payroll Journal icon will remain highlighted.

How to Display and Print an Employee Detail Report

14. Click on the Company Window Reports menu; point to payroll and then click on Employee. The Employee Report Options dialog box will appear. Click on the **Select All** button; click on the **Detail** option button; leave the **Start** date set at 1/1/97; leave the **Finish** date set at 1/31/97; leave the FIT, SIT, Medicare, and Soc. Sec. check boxes checked; then click on the **OK** button. Your screen will look like this:

Print Reports

15. Click on the Employee Detail File menu; then click on Print to print the report. Close the Employee Detail window and return to the Company Window. Print the following reports:

a. General Journal (By posting date; All ledger entries; Start: 1/1/97, Finish: 1/31/97).

b. Trial Balance As at 1/31/97.

The program can display and print separate Journal Reports that list transactions recorded in a specific Journal (General, Purchases, Payments, Sales, Receipts, Payroll, Transfers, or Adjustments) and the program can display and print a single General Journal report that lists transactions recorded in all Journals. To display or print a General Journal report that includes all transactions recorded in all Journals, check the **All Ledger Entries** check box in the General Journal options dialog box. To save time and reduce the amount of printing involved in the Computer Workshop assignments, always check the **All Ledger Entries** check box.

> Review your printed reports. If you have made an error in a posted journal entry, see Part C of the Computerized Accounting appendix (Reversing an Entry Made in the General Journal or Payroll Journal Dialog Box) for information on how to correct the error.

Make a January Backup Copy

16. Click on the Company Window File menu; click on Save As; then enter the following new file name into the **File name** text box: A:\student\petejan.asc

17. Click on the **Save** button. Note that the company name in the Company Window has changed from Pete to Petejan. Click on the Company Window File menu again; then click on Save As. Enter the following new file names into the **File name** text box: A:\student\pete.asc

18. Click on the **Save** button. Click on the **Yes** button in response to the question "Replace existing file?" Note that the company name in the Company Window has changed back from Petejan to Pete.

19. You now have two sets of company data files for Pete's Market on your Student Data Files disk. The current data is stored under the file name pete.asc. The January backup data is stored under the file name petejan.asc

Advance Dates

20. Click on the Company Window Maintenance menu; then click on Advance Using Date. Click on the **No** button in response to the question "You have never backed up your data. Would you like to backup now?" Enter 2/1/97 into the **New Using Date** text box; then click on the **OK** button. Click on the **OK** button in response to the warning message. The backup you created using the Save As method will serve as the backup suggested in both warning messages.

21. Click on the Company Window Setup menu; then click on Company Information. The Company Information dialog box will appear. Enter 2/28/97 as the new **Fiscal end** date; then click on the **OK** button.

22. Click on the Company Window Maintenance menu; then click on Advance Using Date. Click on the **No** button in response to the question "You have never backed up your data. Would you like to backup now?" Enter 2/28/97 into the **New Using Date** text box; then click on the **OK** button. Click on the **OK** button in response to the warning message.

Record Payment of January Payroll Liabilities and Taxes

23. Record the following general journal entry:

1997
Feb.   15   Record the compound journal entry for the deposit of Social Security, Medicare, and FIT from last month's payroll.

Record February Payroll

24. Record the February payroll journal entries for Fred Flynn, Mary Jones, and Lilly Vron.

Print Reports

25. Print the following reports:

a. Employee Detail (Select All; Start: 2/1/97; Finish: 2/28/97).

b. General Journal (By posting date; All ledger entries; Start: 2/1/97; Finish: 2/28/97).

c. Trial Balance As at 2/28/97.

Make a February Backup Copy	**26.** Click on the Company Window File menu; click on Save As; then enter the following new file name into the **File name** text box: A:\student\petefeb.asc
	27. Click on the **Save** button. Note that the company name in the Company Window has changed from Pete to Petefeb. Click on the Company Window File menu again; then click on Save As. Enter the following new file name into the **File name** text box: A:\student\pete.asc
	28. Click on the **Save** button. Click on the **Yes** button in response to the question "Replace existing file?" Note that the company name in the Company Window has changed back from Petefeb to Pete.
	29. You now have three sets of company data files for Pete's Market on your Student Data Files disk. The current data is stored under the file name pete.asc. The January backup data is stored under the file name petejan.asc and the February backup data is stored under the file name petefeb.asc.
Advance Dates	**30.** Click on the Company Window Maintenance menu; then click on Advance Using Date. Click on the **No** button in response to the question "You have never backed up your data. Would you like to backup now?" Enter 3/1/97 into the **New Using Date** text box; then click on the **OK** button. Click on the **OK** button in response to the warning message. The backup you created using the Save As method will serve as the backup suggested in both warning messages.
	31. Click on the Company Window Setup menu; then click on Company Information. The Company Information dialog box will appear. Enter 3/31/97 as the new **Fiscal end** date; then click on the **OK** button.
	32. Click on the Company Window Maintenance menu; then click on Advance Using Date. Click on the **No** button in response to the question "You have never backed up your data. Would you like to backup now?" Enter 3/31/97 into the **New Using Date** text box; then click on the **OK** button. Click on the **OK** button in response to the warning message.
Record Payment of February Payroll Liabilities and Taxes	**33.** Record the following general journal entry:

1997
Mar.   15   Record the compound journal entry for the deposit of Social Security, Medicare, and FIT from last month's payroll.

Record March Payroll	**34.** Record the March payroll journal entries for Fred Flynn, Mary Jones, and Lilly Vron.
Print Reports	**35.** Print the following reports:
	a. Employee Detail (Select All; Start: 3/1/97; Finish: 3/31/97).
	b. General Journal (By posting date; All ledger entries; Start: 3/1/97; Finish: 3/31/97).
	c. Trial Balance As at 3/31/97.
How to Display and Print 941 Summary Reports	**36.** Click on the Company Window Reports menu; point to Payroll; then click on 941 Summary. The 941 Summary Options dialog box will appear. Leave the **FIT** option button checked; click on the **Select All** button; then click on the **OK** button. The 941 FIT Summary display will appear. Click on the 941 FIT Summary File menu; then click on Print to print the report.
	37. Close the 941 FIT Summary window; click on the Company Window Reports menu; point to Payroll; then click on 941 Summary. The 941 Summary Options dialog box will appear. Click on the **SS/Med Tax** option button; click on the **Select All** button; then click on the **OK** button. The 941 Social Security/Medicare Summary display will appear. Click on the 941 Social Security/Medicare Summary File menu; click on Print to print the report; then close the 941 Social Security/Medicare Summary window.
Make a March Backup Copy	**38.** Click on the Company Window File menu; click on Save As; then enter the following new file name into the **File Name** text box: A:\student\petemar.asc
	39. Click on the **Save** button. Note that the company name in the Company Window has changed from Pete to Petemar. Click on the Company Window File

menu again; then click on Save As. Enter the following new file name into the **File Name** text box: A:\student\pete.asc

40. Click on the **Save** button. Click on the **Yes** button in response to the question "Replace existing file?" Note that the company name in the Company Window has changed back from Petemar to Pete.

41. You now have four sets of company data files for Pete's Market on your Student Data Files disk. The current data is stored under the file name pete.asc. The January backup data is stored under the file name petejan.asc, the February backup data is stored under the file name petefeb.asc, and the March backup data is stored under the file name petemar.asc.

Advance Dates

42. Click on the Company Window Maintenance menu; then click on Advance Using Date. Click on the **No** button in response to the question "You have never backed up your data. Would you like to backup now?" Enter 4/1/97 into the **New Using Date** text box; then click on the **OK** button. Click on the **OK** button in response to the warning message. The backup you created using the Save As method will serve as the backup suggested in both warning messages.

43. Click on the Company Window Maintenance menu again; then click on Advance Using Date. Click on the **No** button in response to the question "You have never backed up your data. Would you like to backup now?" Enter 4/30/97 into the **New Using Date** text box; then click on the **OK** button. Click on the **OK** button in response to the warning message.

Record Payment of March Payroll Liabilities and Taxes

44. Record the following general journal entries:

1997
Apr. 15 Record the compound journal entry for the deposit of Social Security, Medicare, and FIT from last month's payroll.
      30 Record the payment of SUTA from last quarter.
      30 Record the payment of FUTA tax owed.

Print Reports

45. Print the following reports:
    a. General Journal (By posting date; All ledger entries; Start: 4/1/97, Finish: 4/30/97).
    b. Trial Balance As at 4/30/97.

Exit from the Program

46. Click on the Company Window File menu; then click on Exit to end the current work session and return to your Windows desktop.

Complete the Report Transmittal and Form 941

47. Complete the Pete's Market Report Transmittal and Form 941 located in Appendix A of your *Study Guide and Working Papers*.

SPECIAL JOURNALS

Sales and Cash Receipts

THE BIG PICTURE

In reviewing the records last month for the Eldorado Computer Center, Tony Freedman discovered that his retail business has increased his revenue and profits. He also discovered that it is important to keep accurate detailed records of sales transactions. He decided to experiment with some specialized journals to track his sales activity and receipt of cash payments.

The cash receipts journal will assist Freedman in trimming down the number of entries he has to post daily for the business. Since controlling cash is one of the most important things a business must do in order to avoid financial difficulty, cash transactions must be posted accurately. The retail side of his business has increased the cash inflow, and also, by its very nature, the increased potential of loss or theft. Protecting this cash requires implementing some internal control procedures to avoid loss or theft.

The other specialized journal Tony has decided to experiment with is the sales journal. This journal will allow him to keep track of his sales to customers on credit. Freedman has extended more credit to his customers, and he wants to keep a closer look at his sales on account. He wants to know how he is collecting from those sales.

In this chapter you will learn the importance of protecting your cash and collecting your accounts receivable from the credit customers. The schedule of accounts receivable prepared at the end of the month will give you a detail of what dollar amount is owed by each customer. The ease of posting from specialized journals will help reduce the potential for errors when you have a lot of repetitive transactions.

In Chapters 9 and 10 we will take a look at how merchandise companies operate. Chapter 9 focuses on sellers of goods; Chapter 10 discusses buyers. Let's first look at Chou's Toy Shop to get an overview of merchandise terms and journal entries. After that, we will take an in-depth look at how Art's Wholesale Clothing Company keeps its books.

LEARNING UNIT 9-1
Chou's Toy Shop: Seller's View of a Merchandise Company

Chou's Toy Shop is a **retailer.** It buys toys, games, bikes, etc., from manufacturers and **wholesalers** and resells these goods (or **merchandise**) to its customers. The shelving, display cases, and so on are called "fixtures" or "equipment." These items are not for resale.

GROSS SALES

Gross sales: Revenue earned from sale of merchandise to customers.

Each cash or charge sale made at Chou's Toy Shop is rung up at the register. Suppose the shop had $3,000 in sales on July 18. Of that amount, $1,800 were cash sales and $1,200 were charges. This is how the account that recorded those sales would look:

Sales (Gross)

Dr.	Cr.
	3,000 ← Revenue account with a credit balance

This account is a revenue account with a credit balance and will be found on the income statement. Here is the journal entry for the day. **Note:** We will talk about sales tax later.

Accounts Affected	Category	↑ ↓	Rules	T-Account Update
Cash	Asset	↑	Dr.	**Cash** 1,800 |
Accounts Receivable	Asset	↑	Dr.	**Accounts Receivable** 1,200 |
Sales	Revenue	↑	Cr.	**Sales** | 3,000

July	18	Cash			1 8 0 0 00		
		Accounts Receivable			1 2 0 0 00		
		Sales				3 0 0 0 00
		Sales for July 18				

SALES RETURNS AND ALLOWANCES

It would be great for Chou if all the customers were completely satisfied, but that rarely is the case. On July 19, Michelle Reese brought back a doll she bought on account for $50. She told Chou that the doll was defective and she wanted either a price reduction or a new doll. They agreed on a $10 price reduction. Michelle now owes Chou $40. The account called **Sales Returns and Allowances (SRA)** would record this information.

Sales Returns and Allowances

Contra-revenue account with a debit balance → Dr. | Cr.
10 |

This account is a contra-revenue account with a debit balance. It will be recorded on the income statement. This is how the journal entry would look:

Accounts Affected	Category	↑	↓	Rules	T Account Update
Sales Returns and Allowances	**Contra-revenue**	↑		**Dr.**	**Sales Ret. & Allow.** Dr. | Cr. 10 |
Accounts Receivable, Michelle Reese	**Asset**		↓	**Cr.**	**Accounts Receivable** Dr. | Cr. 1,200 | 10

Look at how the sales returns and allowances increase.

July	19	Sales Returns and Allowances			1 0 00		
		Accounts Receivable, Michelle Reese				1 0 00
		Issued credit memorandum				

SALES DISCOUNT

Chou gives a 2 percent **sales discount** to customers who pay their bills early. He wants his customers to know about this policy, so he posted the following sign at the cash register:

Sales Discount Policy

2/10, n/30	2% discount is allowed off price of bill if paid within the first 10 days or full amount is due within 30 days
n/10, EOM	No discount, full amount of bill is due within 10 days after the end of the month.

Note the **discount period** is the time when a discount is granted. The discount period is less time than the **credit period,** which is the length of time allowed to pay back the amount owed on the bill.

If Michelle pays her $40 bill early she will get an $.80 discount. This is the account that records this information:

Sales Discount

Contra-revenue ➡ account with a debit balance.

Dr.	Cr.
.80	

This is how Michelle's discount is calculated:

$$.02 \times \$40 = \$.80$$

Michelle pays her bill on July 24. She is entitled to the discount because she paid her bill within 10 days. Let's look at how Chou would record this on his books.

Accounts Affected	Category	↑	↓	Rules	T Account Update
Cash	Asset	↑		Dr.	Cash Dr. | Cr. 39.20 |
Sales Discount	Contra-revenue	↑		Dr.	Sales Discount Dr. | Cr. .80 |
Accounts Receivable	Asset		↓	Cr.	Accounts Receivable Dr. | Cr. 1,200 | 40

July	24	Cash			39 20			
		Sales Discount			80			
		Accounts Receivable, Michelle Reese					40 00	

Although Michelle pays $39.20, her Accounts Receivable is credited for the full amount, $40.

In the examples so far we have not shown any transactions with sales tax. Note the actual or **net sales** for Chou would be **gross sales** less sales returns and allowances less any sales discounts. Let's look at how Chou would record his monthly sales if sales tax were charged.

SALES TAX PAYABLE

None of the examples shown above show state sales tax. Still, like it or not, Chou must collect that tax from his customers and send it to the state. Sales tax represents a liability to Chou.

Assume the state Chou's is located in charges a 5 percent sales tax. Remember, Chou's sales on July 18 were $3,000. Chou must figure out the sales tax on the purchases. For this purpose, let's assume that there were only two sales on that date: the cash sale ($1,800) and the charge sale ($1,200).

The sales tax on the cash purchase is calculated as follows:

$$\$1,800 \times .05 = \$90 \text{ tax}$$
$$\$1,800 + \$90 \text{ tax} = \$1,890 \text{ cash}$$

Here is how the sales tax on the charge sale is computed:

$$\$1,200 \times .05 = \$60 \text{ tax} + \$1,200 \text{ charge} = \$1,260 \text{ Accounts Receivable}$$

This is how it would be recorded:

Accounts Affected	Category	↑	↓	Rules	T Account Update
Cash	Asset	↑		Dr.	Cash Dr. | Cr. 1,890 |
Accounts Receivable	Asset	↑		Dr.	Accounts Receivable Dr. | Cr. 1,260 |
Sales Tax Payable	Liability	↑		Cr.	Sales Tax Payable Dr. | Cr. | 90 | 60
Sales	Revenue	↑		Cr.	Sales Dr. | Cr. | 3,000

July	18	Cash		1 8 9 0 00		
		Accounts Receivable		1 2 6 0 00		
		Sales Tax Payable			1 5 0 00	
		Sales			3 0 0 0 00	
		July 18 Sales				

In a later unit in this chapter, we will show you how to record a credit memorandum with sales tax.

LEARNING UNIT 9-1 REVIEW

AT THIS POINT you should be able to

- Explain the purpose of a contra-revenue account. (p. 314)
- Explain how to calculate net sales. (p. 315)
- Define, journalize, and explain gross sales, sales returns and allowances, and sales discounts. (p. 314)
- Journalize an entry for sales tax payable. (p. 316)

SELF-REVIEW QUIZ 9-1

(The forms you need can be found on page 285 of the *Study Guide and Working Papers*.)

Which of the following statements are false?

1. Sales Returns and Allowances is a contra-asset account.
2. Sales Discount has a normal balance of a debit.
3. Sales Tax Payable is a liability.
4. Sales Discount is a contra-asset.
5. Credit terms are standard in all industries.

Solution to Self-Review Quiz 9-1

Numbers 1, 4, and 5 are false.

LEARNING UNIT 9-2
The Sales Journal and Accounts Receivable Subsidiary Ledger

SPECIAL JOURNALS

Now let's examine how Art's Wholesale Clothing Company keeps its books. Art's business conducts many transactions. The following partial general journal shows the journal entries Art's must make for these sales on account transactions.

ART'S WHOLESALE CLOTHING COMPANY GENERAL JOURNAL					
April	3	Accounts Receivable, Hal's		8 0 0 00	
		Sales			8 0 0 00
		Sales on Account			
	6	Accounts Receivable, Bevans		1 6 0 0 00	
		Sales			1 6 0 0 00
		Sales on Account			
	18	Accounts Receivable, Roe		2 0 0 0 00	
		Sales			2 0 0 0 00
		Sales on Account			

This method is not very efficient. However, if Art's Wholesale Company kept a **special journal** for each type of transaction he conducts, the number of postings and recordings required for each transaction would be reduced. After carefully looking at the situation with his accountant, Art decided to use the following special journals:

For a discussion of recording of credit cards in special journals see appendix.

Special Journal Type	What It Records	
Sales journal	Sale of merchandise on account	Covered in this chapter
Cash receipts journal	Receiving cash from any source	
Purchases journal	Buying merchandise or other items on account	Covered in next chapter
Cash payments journal (cash disbursement journal)	Paying of cash for any purpose	

Subsidiary ledgers

In the same way Art's Wholesale Clothing Company needs more than just a general journal, the business needs more than just a general ledger. For example, so far in this text, the only title we have used for recording amounts owed to the seller has been Accounts Receivable. Art could have replaced the Accounts Receivable title in the general ledger with the following list of customers who owe him money:

- Accounts Receivable, Bevans Company
- Accounts Receivable, Hal's Clothing
- Accounts Receivable, Mel's Department Store
- Accounts Receivable, Roe Company

As you can see, this would not be manageable if Art had 1,000 credit customers. To solve this problem, Art sets up a separate **accounts receivable subsidiary ledger.** Such a special ledger, often simply called a **subsidiary ledger,** contains a single type of account, such as credit customers. An account is opened for each customer and the accounts are arranged alphabetically.

The diagram in Figure 9-1 shows how the accounts receivable subsidiary ledger fits in with the general ledger. To clarify the difference in updating the general ledger versus the subsidiary ledger we will *post* to the general ledger and *record* to the subsidiary ledger. The word "post" refers to information that is moved from the journal to the general ledger; the word "record" refers to information that is transferred from the journal into the individual customer's account in the subsidiary ledger.

The accounts receivable subsidiary ledger, or any other subsidiary ledger, can be in the form of a card file, a binder notebook, or computer tapes or disks. It will not have page numbers. The accounts receivable subsidiary ledger is organized alphabetically based on customers' names and addresses; new customers can be added and inactive customers deleted.

The general ledger is *not* in the same book as the accounts receivable subsidiary ledger.

Proving: At the end of the month, the sum of the accounts receivable subsidiary ledger will equal the ending balance in accounts receivable, the controlling account in the general ledger.

FIGURE 9-1 Partial General Ledger of Art's Wholesale Clothing Company and Accounts Receivable Subsidiary Ledger

PARTIAL GENERAL LEDGER

ACCOUNTS RECEIVABLE SUBSIDIARY LEDGER

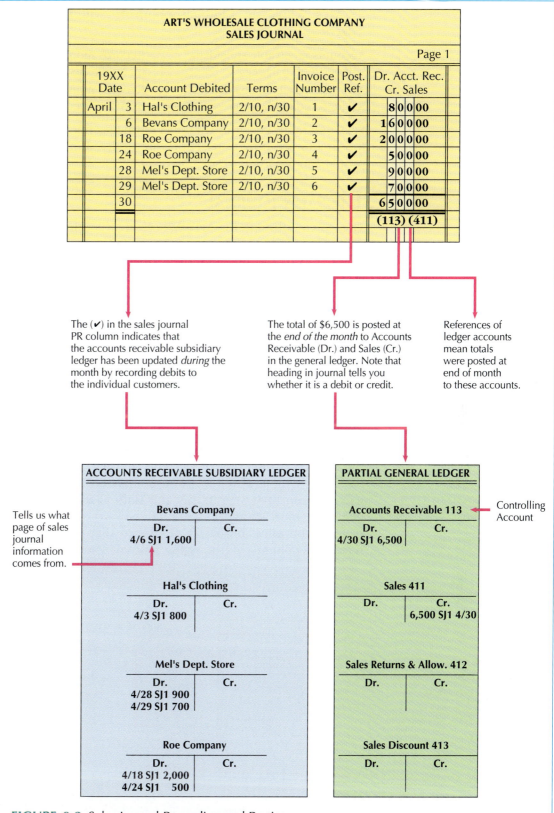

FIGURE 9-2 Sales Journal Recording and Postings

When using an accounts receivable subsidiary ledger, the title Accounts Receivable in the general ledger is called the **controlling account,** since it summarizes or controls the accounts receivable subsidiary ledger. At the end of the month the total of the individual accounts in the accounts receivable ledger will equal the ending balance in Accounts Receivable in the general ledger.

Art's Wholesale Clothing Company will use the following subsidiary ledgers:

Accounts receivable subsidiary ledger (debit balance)	Records money owed by credit customers	Covered in this chapter
Accounts payable subsidiary ledger (credit balance)	Records money owed by Art to creditors	Covered in next chapter

Let's now look closer at the sales journal, general ledger, and subsidiary ledger for Art's to see how transactions are updated in the special journal as well as posted and recorded to specific titles.

THE SALES JOURNAL

The **sales journal** for Art's Wholesale Clothing Company records all sales made on account to customers. Figure 9-2 on page 319 shows the sales journal at the end of the first month in operation, along with the recordings to the accounts receivable ledger and posting to the general ledger. Keep in mind that the reason the balances in the accounts receivable subsidiary ledger are *debit* balances is that the customers listed *owe* Art's Wholesale money. For some other companies, a sales journal might have multiple revenue account columns.

Look at the first transaction listed in the sales journal. It shows that on April 3 Art's Wholesale Clothing Company sold merchandise on account to Hal's Clothing for $800. The bill or **sales invoice** for this sale is shown in Figure 9-3.

Recording from the Sales Journal to the Accounts Receivable Subsidiary Ledger

As shown on the first line of the sales journal in Figure 9-2, the information on the invoice is recorded in the sales journal. However, the *PR column is left blank*. As soon as possible we now update the accounts receivable subsidiary ledger. To do this, we pull out the Hal's Clothing file card and update it: the debit side must show the $800 he owes Art along with the date (April 3) and page of the sales journal (p. 1). Once that is done, place a ✓ in the post-reference column of the sales journal. The accounts receivable subsidiary

Recording to the accounts receivable subsidiary ledger occurs daily.

Hal's Clothing	
Dr.	Cr.
4/3 SJ1	
800	

✓ means accounts receivable ledger has been updated.

FIGURE 9-3
Sales Invoice

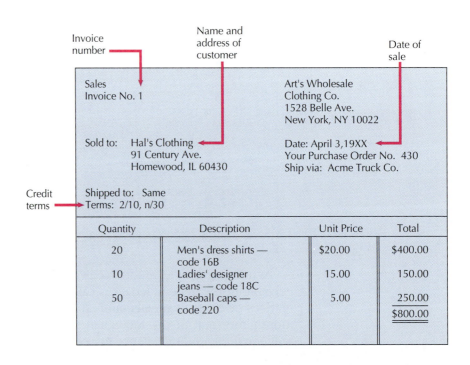

Invoice number

Name and address of customer

Date of sale

Sales Invoice No. 1

Art's Wholesale Clothing Co.
1528 Belle Ave.
New York, NY 10022

Sold to: Hal's Clothing
91 Century Ave.
Homewood, IL 60430

Date: April 3, 19XX
Your Purchase Order No. 430
Ship via: Acme Truck Co.

Credit terms

Shipped to: Same
Terms: 2/10, n/30

Quantity	Description	Unit Price	Total
20	Men's dress shirts — code 16B	$20.00	$400.00
10	Ladies' designer jeans — code 18C	15.00	150.00
50	Baseball caps — code 220	5.00	250.00
			$800.00

ledger shows us Hal's outstanding balance at any moment in time. We do not have to go through all the invoices. Note how the sales journal only needs one line instead of the three lines that would have been required in a general journal.

Posting at End of Month from the Sales Journal to the General Ledger

The sales journal is totaled ($6,500) at the end of the month. Looking back at page 319, you can see that the heading of Art's sales journal is a debit to accounts receivable and a credit to sales. Therefore, at the end of the month the $6,500 total is posted to Accounts Receivable (debit) *and* to Sales (credit) in the general ledger. In the general ledger we record the date (4/30), the initials of the journal (SJ), the page of the sales journal (1), and appropriate debit or credit ($6,500). Once the account in the general ledger is updated, we place below the totals in the sales journal the account numbers to which the information was posted (in this case accounts 113 and 411).

Sales Tax

Art's Wholesale Clothing Company does not have to deal with sales tax because it sells goods wholesale. However, if Art's was a retail company, it would have to pay sales tax.

Let's look at how Munroe Menswear Company, a retailer, handles sales tax on a purchase made by Jones Company. Figure 9-4 shows Munroe's sales journal.

Also, a new account, **Sales Tax Payable,** must be created. That account is a liability account in the general ledger with a credit balance. The customer owes Munroe the sale amount plus the tax.

Keep in mind that if sales discounts are available, they are not calculated on the sales tax. The discount is on the selling price less any returns before the tax. For example, if Jones receives a 2 percent discount, he pays the following:

$5,000 × .02 = $100 savings →

$5,250	Total owed (tax is $250)
−100	Savings (discount)
$5,150	Amount paid

Recording to the general ledger occurs at end of month.

Acc. Rec. 113

Dr.	Cr.
4/30 SJ1	
6,500	

Sales 411

Dr.	Cr.
	6,500 SJ1
	4/30

Sales Tax Payable

	XXX

A liability in general ledger.

FIGURE 9-4
Munroe Sales Journal

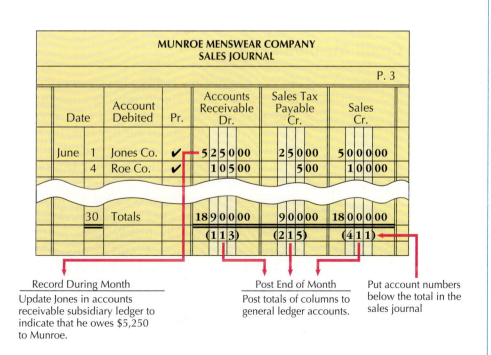

Record During Month
Update Jones in accounts receivable subsidiary ledger to indicate that he owes $5,250 to Munroe.

Post End of Month
Post totals of columns to general ledger accounts.

Put account numbers below the total in the sales journal

LEARNING UNIT 9-2 REVIEW

AT THIS POINT you should be able to

- Define and state the purposes of special journals. (p. 317)
- Define and state the purposes of the accounts receivable subsidiary ledger. (p. 318)
- Define and state the purpose of the controlling account, Accounts Receivable. (p. 318)
- Journalize, record, or post sales on account to a sales journal and its related accounts receivable and general ledgers. (p. 319)

SELF-REVIEW QUIZ 9-2

(The forms you need are on page 285 of the *Study Guide and Working Papers.*) Which of the following statements are false?

1. Special journals completely replace the general journal.
2. Special journals aid the division of labor.
3. The subsidiary ledger makes the general ledger less manageable.
4. The subsidiary ledger is separate from the general ledger.
5. The controlling account is located in the accounts receivable subsidiary ledger.
6. The total(s) of a sales journal are posted to the general ledger at the end of the month.
7. The accounts receivable subsidiary ledger is arranged in alphabetical order.
8. Transactions recorded into a sales journal are recorded only weekly to the accounts receivable subsidiary ledger.

Quiz Tip: The normal balance of the accounts receivable subsidiary ledger is a debit.

Solution to Self-Review Quiz 9-2

Numbers 1, 3, 5, and 8 are false.

LEARNING UNIT 9-3
The Credit Memorandum

At the beginning of this chapter we introduced the Sales Returns and Allowances account. Merchandising businesses often use this account to handle transactions involving goods that have already been sold. For example, if a customer returns the goods he has bought, his account will be credited for the amount he paid; if a customer gets an allowance because the goods he purchased were damaged, his account will be credited for the amount of the allowance. In both of these examples, the company's sales revenue decreases. That is why the account is called a contra-revenue account: the sales revenue decreases and the normal balance is a debit.

A credit memorandum *reduces* accounts receivable.

Remember, no sales tax was involved because Art's is a wholesale company.

Companies usually handle sales returns and allowances by means of a **credit memorandum.** Credit memoranda inform customers that the amount of the goods returned or the amount allowed for damaged goods has been subtracted (credited) from the customer's ongoing account with the company.

A sample credit memorandum from Art's Wholesale Clothing Company appears in Figure 9-5. It shows that on April 12 credit memo No. 1 was issued to Bevans Company for defective merchandise that had been returned. (Figure 9-2

**Art's Wholesale
Clothing Co.
1528 Belle Ave.
New York, NY 10022**

Credit
Memorandum No. _1_
Date: _April 12_
Credit to Bevans Company
                110 Aster Rd.
                Cincinnati, Ohio 45227
We credit your account as follows:
Merchandise returned 60 model 8 B men's dress gloves—$600

FIGURE 9-5
Credit Memorandum

Sales Returns and Allowances	
Dr.	Cr.
+	−

A contra-revenue account

Note that the Sales Returns and Allowances account is increasing, which in turn reduces sales revenue and reduces amount owed by customer (accounts receivable).

shows that Art's Wholesale Clothing Company sold Bevans Company $1,600 of merchandise on April 6.)

Let's assume that Art's Clothing has high-quality goods and does not expect many sales returns and allowances. Based on this assumption, no special journal for sales returns and allowances will be needed. Instead, any returns and allowances will be recorded in the general journal, and all postings and recordings will be done when journalized. Let's look at a transaction analysis chart before we journalize, record, and post this transaction.

Accounts Affected	Category	↑	↓	Rules
Sales Returns and Allowances	Contra-revenue account	↑		Dr.
Accounts Receivable, Bevans Co.	Asset		↓	Cr.

JOURNALIZING, RECORDING, AND POSTING THE CREDIT MEMORANDUM

The credit memorandum results in two postings to the general ledger and one recording to the accounts receivable subsidiary ledger (see Fig. 9-6 on page 324).

Note in the PR column next to Accounts Receivable, Bevans Co., that there is a diagonal line with the account number 113 above and a ✓ below. This is to show that the amount of $600 has been credited to Accounts Receivable in the controlling account in the general ledger *and* credited to the account of Bevans Company in the accounts receivable subsidiary ledger.

If the accountant for Art's Wholesale Clothing Company decided to develop a special journal for sales allowances and returns, the entry for a credit memorandum such as the one we've been discussing would look like this:

Remember, sales discounts are *not* taken on returns.

SALES RETURNS AND ALLOWANCES JOURNAL					
Date	Credit Memo No.	Account Credited	PR	Sales Ret. and Allow. – Dr. Accts. Rec. – Cr.	
19XX April 12	1	Bevans Company	✔	6 0 0 00	

During the month the
subsidiary ledger is updated

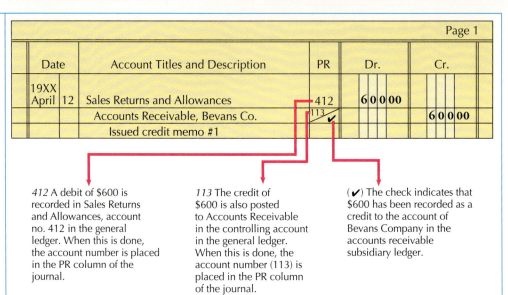

		Date	Account Titles and Description	PR	Dr.	Cr.		Page 1
	19XX							
	April	12	Sales Returns and Allowances	412	6 0 0 00			
			Accounts Receivable, Bevans Co.	113 ✔		6 0 0 00		
			Issued credit memo #1					

412 A debit of $600 is recorded in Sales Returns and Allowances, account no. 412 in the general ledger. When this is done, the account number is placed in the PR column of the journal.

113 The credit of $600 is also posted to Accounts Receivable in the controlling account in the general ledger. When this is done, the account number (113) is placed in the PR column of the journal.

(✔) The check indicates that $600 has been recorded as a credit to the account of Bevans Company in the accounts receivable subsidiary ledger.

FIGURE 9-6
Postings and Recordings for the Credit Memorandum into the Subsidiary and General Ledger.

THE CREDIT MEMORANDUM WITH SALES TAX

Figure 9-4 (p. 321) shows the sales journal for Munroe Menswear Company. Remember, since Munroe is a retail company, its customers must pay sales tax. Let's assume that on June 8 Roe returns $50 worth of the $100 of merchandise he bought earlier in the month. Let's analyze and journalize the credit memo that Munroe issued. Keep in mind that the customer is no longer responsible for paying for either the returned merchandise or the tax on it.

Accounts Affected	Category	↑ ↓	Rules	T Account Update			
Sales Returns and Allowances	Contra-revenue	↑	Dr.	**Sales Ret. & Allow.** Dr. | Cr. 50 |			
Sales Tax Payable ($5 tax on $100) ($2.50 tax on $50)	Liability	↓	Dr.	**Sales Tax Payable** Dr. | Cr. 2.50 |			
Accounts Receivable, Roe	Asset	↓	Cr.	**Acc. Rec.** Dr. | Cr. | 52.50	**Roe Co.** Dr. | Cr. 105 | 52.50		

	June	8	Sales Returns and Allowances		5 0 00		
			Sales Tax Payable		2 50		
			Accounts Receivable, Roe Co.			5 2 50	
			Received credit memo				

This journal entry requires three postings to the general ledger and one recording to Roe in the accounts receivable subsidiary ledger. Note since Roe returned half of his merchandise he was able to reduce what he pays for sales tax by half (from $5 to $2.50).

AT THIS POINT you should be able to

◆ Explain Sales Tax Payable in relation to Sales Discount. (p. 324)
◆ Explain, journalize, post, and record a credit memorandum with or without sales tax. (p. 324)

SELF-REVIEW QUIZ 9-3

(The forms you need are on pages 285–287 of the *Study Guide and Working Papers*.)

Journalize the following transactions into the sales journal or general journal for Moss Co. Record to the accounts receivable subsidiary ledger and post to general ledger accounts as appropriate. Use the same journal headings that we used for Art's Wholesale Clothing Company. (All sales carry credit terms of 2/10, n/30.) There is no tax.

19XX

May   1   Sold merchandise on account to Jane Company, invoice no. 1, $600.
      5   Sold merchandise on account to Ralph Company, invoice no. 2, $2,500.
    20   Issued credit memo no. 1 to Jane Company for $200 due to defective merchandise returned.

Solution to Self-Review Quiz 9-3

Quiz Tip: Total of accounts receivable subsidiary ledger $400 +$2,500 does indeed equal the balance in the controlling account, accounts receivable $2,900 at end of month, in the general ledger.

MOSS COMPANY SALES JOURNAL

Page 1

Date			Account Debited	Terms	Invoice No.	Post Ref.	Dr. Acct. Rec. Cr. Sales
19XX May	1		Jane Company	2/10, n/30	1	✔	6 0 0 00
	5		Ralph Company	2/10, n/30	2	✔	2 5 0 0 00
	31						3 1 0 0 00
							(112) (411)

MOSS COMPANY GENERAL JOURNAL

Page 1

Date		Account Titles and Description	PR	Dr.	Cr.
19XX May	20	Sales Ret. and Allowances	412	2 0 0 00	
		Acct. Rec., Jane Company	112 ✔		2 0 0 00
		Issued credit memo #1			

Controlling Account →

PARTIAL GENERAL LEDGER

Note the unusual credit balance of $200 due to the return. Why? Because total of sales journal is not posted till end of month.

Accounts Receivable Account No. 112

Date		Explanation	Post. Ref.	Debit	Credit	Balance Debit	Balance Credit
19XX May	20		GJ1		200 00		200 00
	31		SJ1	3100 00		2900 00	

Sales Account No. 411

Date		Explanation	Post. Ref.	Debit	Credit	Balance Debit	Balance Credit
19XX May	31		SJ1		3100 00		3100 00

Sales Returns and Allowances Account No. 412

Date		Explanation	Post. Ref.	Debit	Credit	Balance Debit	Balance Credit
19XX May	20		GJ1	200 00		200 00	

ACCOUNTS RECEIVABLE SUBSIDIARY LEDGER

Customers owe Moss money and thus have a debit balance.

NAME Jane Company
ADDRESS 118 Morris Rd., Boston, MA 01935

Date		Explanation	Post. Ref.	Debit	Credit	Dr. Balance
19XX May	1		SJ1	600 00		600 00
	20		GJ1		200 00	400 00

NAME Ralph Company
ADDRESS 31 Norris Rd., Boston, MA 01935

Date		Explanation	Post. Ref.	Debit	Credit	Dr. Balance
19XX May	5		SJ1	2500 00		2500 00

LEARNING UNIT 9-4
Cash Receipts Journal and Schedule of Accounts Receivable

A **cash receipts journal** is another special journal often used in a merchandising operation. The cash receipts journal records the receipt of cash (or checks) from any source. The number of columns in the cash receipts journal depends on how frequently certain types of transactions occur. Figure 9-7 shows the headings in the cash receipts journal for Art's Wholesale, describes the purpose of each column, and tells when to update the accounts receivable ledger as well as general ledger.

The following transactions occurred and affected the cash receipts journal for Art's Clothing in April:

19XX
April   1   Art Newner invested $8,000 in the business.
        4   Received check from Hal's Clothing for payment of invoice no. 1 less discount.
        15 Cash sales for first half of April, $900.

FIGURE 9-7 Cash Receipts Journal

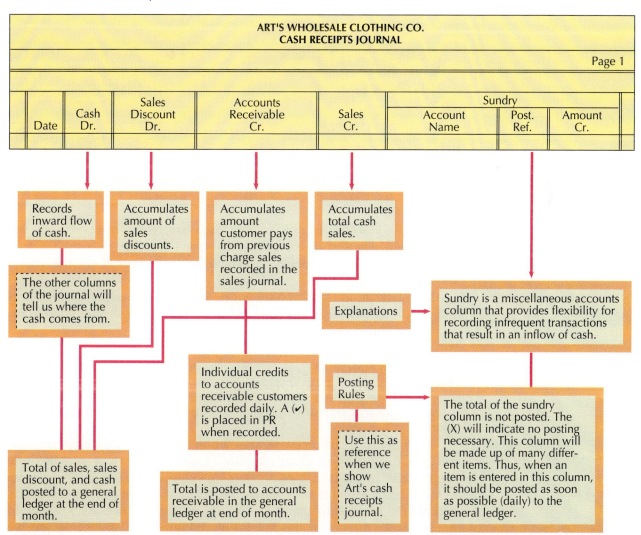

16 Received check from Bevans Company in settlement of invoice no. 2 less returns and discount.
22 Received check from Roe Company for payment of invoice no. 3 less discount.
27 Sold store equipment, $500.
30 Cash sales for second half of April, $1,200.

Benefits of a Cash Receipts Journal

Before we look at how these transactions will look in the cash receipts journal, let's see how the April 4 transaction would look if it were put into a general journal. This will illustrate the benefits of using a cash receipts journal.

19XX
April   4   Received check from Hal's Clothing for payment of invoice no. 1 less discount. (Keep in mind the sales journal showed the invoice at $800 on April 3.)

Accounts Affected	Category	↓ ↑	Rules	T Account Update		
Cash	**Asset**	↑	**Dr.**	**Cash**		
				Dr. | Cr.		
				784 |		
Sales Discount	**Contra-revenue**	↑	**Dr.**	**Sales Discount**		
				Dr. | Cr.		
				16 |		
Accounts Receivable, Hal's Clothing	**Asset**	↓	**Cr.**	**Acc. Rec.**		**Hal's Clothing**
				Dr. | Cr.		Dr. | Cr.
				800 | 800		800 | 800

April	4	Cash			784 00			
		Sales Discount			16 00			
		Accounts Receivable, Hal's Clothing					800 00	

If a general journal was used there would have to be three postings and one recording. Using a cash receipts journal (see Fig. 9-7, p. 327), the totals of cash sales discount and accounts receivable are not posted till the end of the month.

The diagram in Figure 9-8 on pages 329–330 shows the cash receipts journal for the end of April along with the recordings in the accounts receivable subsidiary ledger and posting to the general ledger.

JOURNALIZING, RECORDING, AND POSTING FROM THE CASH RECEIPTS JOURNAL

Now let's look at how the April 4 transaction is recorded in the cash receipts journal.

When payment is received, Art's Wholesale updates the cash receipts journal (see p. 329) by entering the date (April 4), cash debit of $784, sales discount debit of $16, credit to accounts receivable of $800, and which account name (Hal's Clothing) is to be credited. The terms of sale indicate that Hal's Clothing is entitled to the discount and no longer owes Art's Wholesale the $800 balance. As soon as this line is entered into the cash receipts journal, Art's

Hal's Clothing is located in the Accounts Receivable Subsidiary Ledger.

Remember, subsidiary ledgers can be in the form of a card file, a binder notebook, or computer tapes or disks.

FIGURE 9-8
Cash Receipts Journal
and Posting

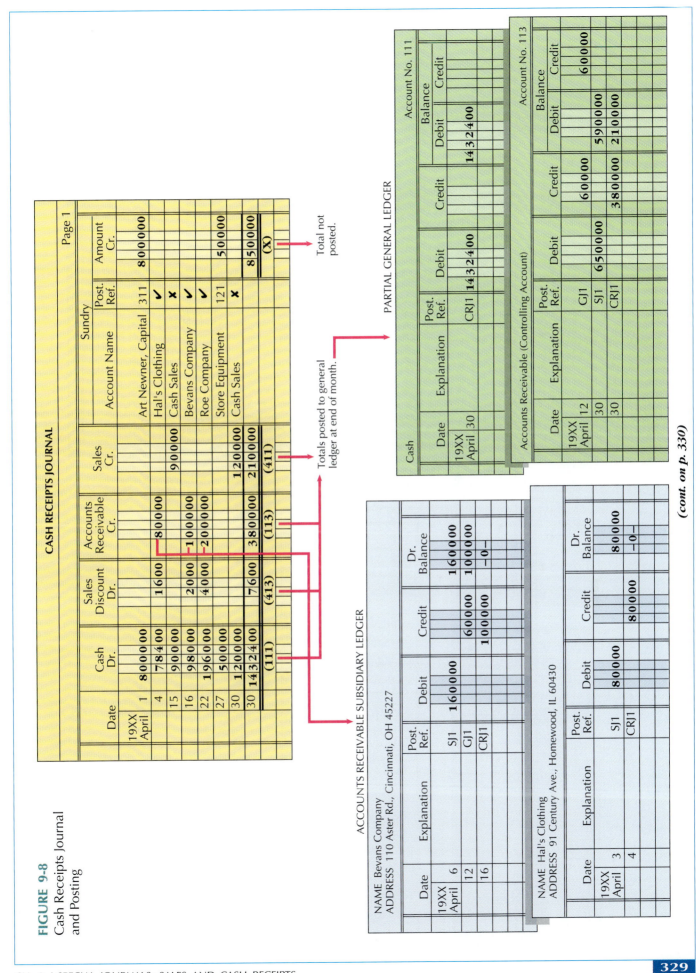

(cont. on p. 330)

FIGURE 9-8 (cont.)

PARTIAL GENERAL LEDGER

Store Equipment Account No. 121

Date	Explanation	Post. Ref.	Debit	Credit	Balance Debit	Balance Credit
19XX April 1	Balance	✔			400000	
27		CRJ1		50000	350000	

Art Newner, Capital Account No. 311

Date	Explanation	Post. Ref.	Debit	Credit	Balance Debit	Balance Credit
19XX April 1		CRJ1		800000		800000

Sales Account No. 411

Date	Explanation	Post. Ref.	Debit	Credit	Balance Debit	Balance Credit
19XX April 30		SJ1		650000		650000
30		CRJ1		210000		860000

Sales Discount Account No. 413

Date	Explanation	Post. Ref.	Debit	Credit	Balance Debit	Balance Credit
19XX April 30		CRJ1	7600		7600	

ACCOUNTS RECEIVABLE SUBSIDIARY LEDGER

NAME Mel's Dept. Store
ADDRESS 181 Foss Rd., Swampscott, MA 01907

Date	Explanation	Post. Ref.	Debit	Credit	Dr. Balance
19XX April 28		SJ1	90000		90000
29		SJ1	70000		160000

NAME Roe Company
ADDRESS 18 Rantool St., Beverly, MA 01915

Date	Explanation	Post. Ref.	Debit	Credit	Dr. Balance
19XX April 18		SJ1	200000		200000
22		CRJ1		200000	-0-
24		SJ1	50000		50000

Wholesale will update the card file of Hal's Clothing. Note in the accounts receivable subsidiary ledger of Hal's Clothing how the date (April 4), post reference (CRJ1), and credit amount ($800) are recorded. The balance in the accounts receivable ledger is zero. The last step of this transaction is to go back to the cash receipts journal and put a ✓ in the post reference column.

In looking back at this cash receipts journal, note that:

◆ All totals of cash receipts journal *except* **sundry** were posted to the general ledger at the end of the month.

◆ Art Newner, Capital, and Store Equipment were posted to the general ledger when entered in the sundry column. For now in the general ledger it was assumed that the equipment account had a beginning balance of $4,000.

◆ The cash sales were not posted when entered (thus the X to show no posting is needed). The sales and cash totals are posted at the *end* of the month.

◆ A (✓) means information was recorded daily to the accounts receivable subsidiary ledger.

◆ The Account Name column was used to describe each transaction.

We can prove the accuracy of recording transactions of the cash receipts journal by totaling the columns with debit balances and credit balances. This process, called **crossfooting,** is done before the totals are posted.

If a bookkeeper was using more than one page for the cash receipts journal, the balances on the bottom of one page would be brought forward to the next page. Let's crossfoot the cash receipts journal of Art's Wholesale (Fig. 9-8, p. 329).

Debit Columns		Credit Columns		
Cash	+ Sales Discount =	Accounts Receivable	+ Sales	+ Sundry
$14,324	+ $76	= $3,800	+ $2,100	+ $8,500
	$14,400	= $14,400		

Recording Sales Tax

Consider the following situation. It involves Ryan Stationery, a retail stationer that must charge 5 percent sales tax to its customers. Hope Co. bought on July 1 $600 of equipment for cash from Ryan.

Here is how the transaction would be recorded in the general journal:

Accounts Affected	Category	↑	↓	Rules	T Account Update
Cash	Asset	↑		Dr.	Cash 630 |
Sales Tax Payable	Liability	↑		Cr.	Sales Tax Payable | 30
Sales	Revenue	↑		Cr.	Sales | 600

July	1	Cash			630 00			
		Sales Tax Payable					30 00	
		Sales					60 0 00	
		Cash Sale						

Sundry: Miscellaneous accounts column(s) in a special journal, which record transactions that seldom occur.

The last step is to put a ✓ back in the PR of the cash receipts journal to show the accounts receivable ledger is up to date.

Crossfooting special journals makes it easier to look for journalizing or posting errors.

Proving the cash receipts journal.

The total of sales tax payable would be posted to Sales Tax Payable in the general ledger at the end of the month.

This is how the transaction would be recorded in a cash receipts journal.

						Sundry		
CASH RECEIPTS JOURNAL								
Date	Cash Dr.	Sales Discount Dr.	Accounts Receivable Cr.	Sales Tax Payable Cr.	Sales Cr.	Acct.	Post Ref.	Amt.
July 1	630 00			30 00	600 00		✗	

The total of the sales tax as a result of cash sales would be posted to Sales Tax Payable in the general ledger at the end of the month. It represents a liability of the merchant to forward the tax to the government. Remember, no cash discounts are taken on the sales tax.

Now let's prove the accounts receivable subsidiary ledger to the controlling account—accounts receivable—at the end of April for Art's Wholesale Clothing Company.

SCHEDULE OF ACCOUNTS RECEIVABLE

The **schedule of accounts receivable** is an alphabetical list of the companies that have an outstanding balance in the accounts receivable subsidiary ledger. This total should be equal to the balance of the accounts receivable controlling account in the general ledger at the end of the month.

Let's examine the schedule of accounts receivable for Art's Wholesale Clothing Company:

Schedule is listed in alphabetical order.

ART'S WHOLESALE CLOTHING COMPANY SCHEDULE OF ACCOUNTS RECEIVABLE APRIL 30, 19XX	
Mel's Dept. Store	$1 600 00
Roe Company	500 00
Total Accounts Receivable	$ 2 100 00

The balance of the controlling account, Accounts Receivable ($2,100), in the general ledger (p. 329) does indeed equal the sum of the individual customer balances in the accounts receivable ledger ($2,100) as shown in the schedule of accounts receivable. The schedule of accounts receivable can help forecast potential cash inflows as well as possible credit and collection decisions.

LEARNING UNIT 9-4 REVIEW

AT THIS POINT you should be able to

◆ Journalize, record, and post transactions using a cash receipts journal with or without sales tax. (p. 328)
◆ Prepare a schedule of accounts receivable. (p. 332)

SELF-REVIEW QUIZ 9-4

(The forms you need are on pages 288–290 of the *Study Guide and Working Papers*.)

Journalize, crossfoot, record, and post when appropriate the following transactions into the cash receipts journal of Moore Co. Use the same headings as for Art's Wholesale Clothing.

ACCOUNTS RECEIVABLE SUBSIDIARY LEDGER		
NAME	BALANCE	INVOICE NO.
Irene Welch	$500	1
Janis Fross	200	2

PARTIAL GENERAL LEDGER

	Acct. No.	Balance
Cash	110	$600
Accounts Receivable	120	700
Store Equipment	130	600
Sales	410	700
Sales Discount	420	

19XX

May 1 Received check from Irene Welch for invoice no. 1 less 2 percent discount.

8 Cash sales collected, $200.

15 Received check from Janis Fross for invoice no. 2 less 2 percent discount.

19 Sold store equipment at cost, $300.

Solution to Self-Review Quiz 9-4

MOORE COMPANY
CASH RECEIPTS JOURNAL

Page 2

Date	Cash Dr.	Sales Discount Dr.	Accounts Receivable Cr.	Sales Cr.	Sundry — Account Name	Post. Ref.	Sundry — Amount Cr.
19XX May 1	490 00	10 00	500 00		Irene Welch	✔	
8	200 00			200 00	Cash Sales	✘	
15	196 00	4 00	200 00		Janis Fross	✔	
19	300 00				Store Equipment	130	300 00
31	1186 00	14 00	700 00	200 00			300 00
	(110)	(420)	(120)	(410)			(X)

Crossfooting: $1,200 = $1,200

PARTIAL GENERAL LEDGER

Cash — Account No. 110

Date	Explanation	Post. Ref.	Debit	Credit	Balance Debit	Balance Credit
19XX May 1	Balance	✔			600 00	
31		CRJ2	1186 00		1786 00	

Accounts Receivable — Account No. 120

Date	Explanation	Post. Ref.	Debit	Credit	Balance Debit	Balance Credit
19XX May 1	Balance	✔			700 00	
31		CRJ2		700 00		

Quiz Tip: Sum of all debits equals sum of all credits

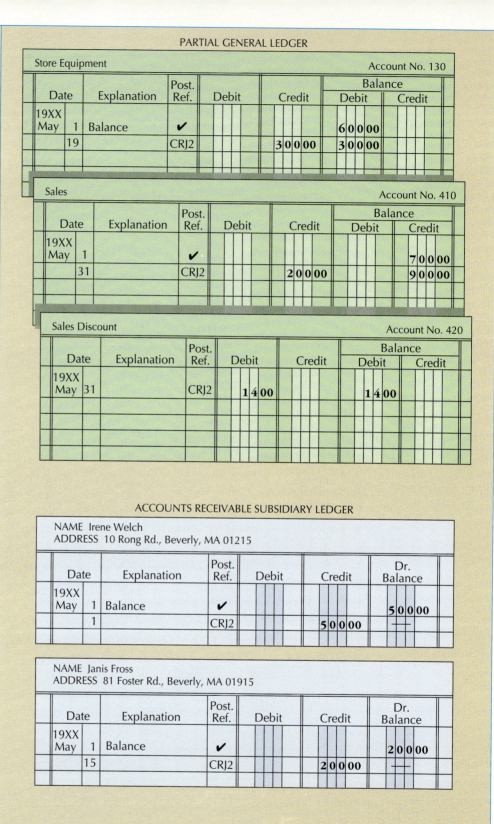

PARTIAL GENERAL LEDGER

Store Equipment — Account No. 130

Date		Explanation	Post. Ref.	Debit	Credit	Balance Debit	Balance Credit
19XX May	1	Balance	✔			6000 00	
	19		CRJ2		3000 00	3000 00	

Sales — Account No. 410

Date		Explanation	Post. Ref.	Debit	Credit	Balance Debit	Balance Credit
19XX May	1		✔				7000 00
	31		CRJ2		2000 00		9000 00

Sales Discount — Account No. 420

Date		Explanation	Post. Ref.	Debit	Credit	Balance Debit	Balance Credit
19XX May	31		CRJ2	14 00		14 00	

ACCOUNTS RECEIVABLE SUBSIDIARY LEDGER

NAME Irene Welch
ADDRESS 10 Rong Rd., Beverly, MA 01215

Date		Explanation	Post. Ref.	Debit	Credit	Dr. Balance
19XX May	1	Balance	✔			500 00
	1		CRJ2		500 00	—

NAME Janis Fross
ADDRESS 81 Foster Rd., Beverly, MA 01915

Date		Explanation	Post. Ref.	Debit	Credit	Dr. Balance
19XX May	1	Balance	✔			200 00
	15		CRJ2		200 00	—

Quiz Tip: The total of the sundry column $300 is not posted. Only individual amounts are posted to the general ledger during the month.

COMPREHENSIVE DEMONSTRATION PROBLEM WITH SOLUTION TIPS

(The forms you need are on pages 291-294 of the *Study Guide and Working Papers*.)

a. Journalize, record, and post as needed, the following transactions to the sales, cash receipts, and general journal. All terms are 2/10, n/30.

b. Prepare a schedule of Accounts Receivable.

Solution Tips to Journalizing

	19XX		
CRJ	July	1	Walter Lantze invested $2,000 into the business.
SJ		1	Sold merchandise on account to Panda Co., invoice no. 1 — $300.
SJ		2	Sold merchandise on account to Buzzard Co., invoice no. 2 — $600.
CRJ		3	Cash sale — $400.
GJ		9	Issued Credit Memorandum no. 1 to Panda Co. for defective merchandise — $100.
CRJ		10	Received check from Panda Co. for invoice no. 1 less returns and discount.
CRJ		16	Cash sale — $500.
SJ		19	Sold merchandise on account to Panda Co. — $550, invoice no. 3.

Record immediately to subsidiary ledger.

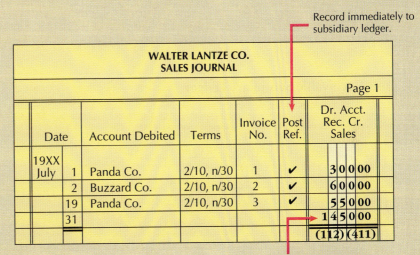

WALTER LANTZE CO.
SALES JOURNAL

Page 1

Date		Account Debited	Terms	Invoice No.	Post Ref.	Dr. Acct. Rec. Cr. Sales
19XX July	1	Panda Co.	2/10, n/30	1	✔	3 0 0 00
	2	Buzzard Co.	2/10, n/30	2	✔	6 0 0 00
	19	Panda Co.	2/10, n/30	3	✔	5 5 0 00
	31					1 4 5 0 00
						(112) (411)

Total posted at end of month to General Ledger Accounts.

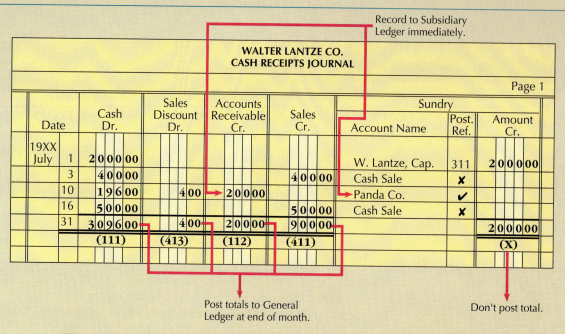

Record to Subsidiary Ledger immediately.

WALTER LANTZE CO.
CASH RECEIPTS JOURNAL

Page 1

Date	Cash Dr.	Sales Discount Dr.	Accounts Receivable Cr.	Sales Cr.	Sundry Account Name	Post. Ref.	Amount Cr.
19XX July 1	2 000 00				W. Lantze, Cap.	311	2 000 00
3	40 000			40 000	Cash Sale	✗	
10	19 600	4 00	200 00		Panda Co.	✓	
16	50 000			50 000	Cash Sale	✗	
31	3 096 00	4 00	200 00	900 00			2 000 00
	(111)	(413)	(112)	(411)			(X)

Post totals to General Ledger at end of month.

Don't post total.

	GENERAL JOURNAL			Page 1	
Date	Account Title and Description	PR	Dr.	Cr.
19XX July 9	Sales Returns and Allowances	412	1 00 00	
	Accounts Receivable, Panda Co.	112 ✓		1 00 00
	Issued credit memo #1			

Post immediately to General Ledger.

Record immediately to Subsidiary Ledger.

Accounts Receivable Subsidiary Ledger is usually a debit balance.

Accounts Receivable Subsidiary Ledger

Buzzard Co.

Date	PR	Debit	Credit	Dr. Balance
19XX July 2	SJ1	600 00		600 00

Panda Co.

Date	PR	Debit	Credit	Dr. Balance
19XX July 1	SJ1	300 00		300 00
9	GJ1		100 00	200 00
10	CRJ1		200 00	—
19	SJ1	550 00		550 00

General Ledger

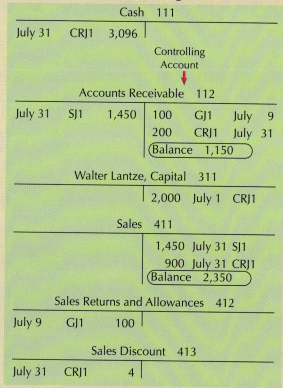

Cash   111

| July 31 | CRJ1 | 3,096 | |

Controlling Account

Accounts Receivable   112

July 31	SJ1	1,450	100	GJ1	July 9
			200	CRJ1	July 31
		Balance 1,150			

Walter Lantze, Capital   311

| | | | 2,000 | July 1 | CRJ1 |

Sales   411

			1,450	July 31	SJ1
			900	July 31	CRJ1
			Balance 2,350		

Sales Returns and Allowances   412

| July 9 | GJ1 | 100 | |

Sales Discount   413

| July 31 | CRJ1 | 4 | |

The controlling account at end of the month equals the sum of the Accounts Receivable Subsidiary Ledger.

LANTZE CO. SCHEDULE OF ACCOUNTS RECEIVABLE JULY 31, 19XX		
Buzzard Co.	$	600 00
Panda Co.		550 00
Total Accounts Receivable	$	1150 00

SUMMARY OF KEY POINTS

Learning Unit 9-1

1. Sales Returns and Allowances and Sales Discount are contra-revenue accounts.
2. Net Sales = Gross Sales − Sales Returns and Allowances − Sales Discounts.
3. Discounts are not taken on sales tax, freight, or goods returned. The discount period is shorter than the credit period.

Learning Unit 9-2

1. A general journal is still used with special journals.
2. A sales journal records sales on account.
3. The accounts receivable subsidiary ledger, organized in alphabetical order, is not in the same book as Accounts Receivable, the controlling account in the general ledger.
4. At the end of the month the total of all customers' ending balances in the accounts receivable subsidiary ledger should be equal to the ending balance in Accounts Receivable, the controlling account in the general ledger.

Learning Unit 9-3

1. The ✓ in the post-reference column of the sales journal means a customer's account in the accounts receivable ledger (or the accounts receivable subsidiary ledger) (on the debit side) has been updated (or recorded) during the month.
2. At the end of the month the total(s) of the sales journal is posted to general ledger accounts.
3. Sales Tax Payable is a liability found in the general ledger.
4. When a credit memorandum is issued, the result is that Sales Returns and Allowances is increasing, and Accounts Receivable is decreasing. When we record this into a general journal we assume that all parts of the transaction will be posted to the general ledger and recorded in the subsidiary ledger when the entry is journalized.

Learning Unit 9-4

1. The cash receipts journal records receipt of cash from any source.
2. The sundry column records the credit part of a transaction that does not occur frequently. Never post the *total* of sundry. Post items in sundry column to the general ledger when entered.
3. A ✓ in the post reference column of the cash receipts journal means that the accounts receivable ledger (or the accounts receivable subsidiary ledger) has been updated (recorded) with a credit.

4. An X in the cash receipts journal post-reference column means no posting was necessary, since the totals of these columns will be posted at the end of the month.

5. Crossfooting means proving that the total of debits and the total of credits are equal in the special journal, thus verifying the accuracy of recording.

6. A schedule of accounts receivable is a listing of the ending balances of customers in the accounts receivable subsidiary ledger. This total should be the same balance as found in the controlling account, Accounts Receivable, in the general ledger.

KEY TERMS

Accounts receivable subsidiary ledger A book or file that contains in alphabetical order the individual records of amounts owed by various credit customers.

Cash receipts journal A special journal that records all transactions involving the receipt of cash from any source.

Controlling account—Accounts Receivable The Accounts Receivable account in the general ledger, after postings are complete, shows a firm the total amount of money owed to it. This figure is broken down in the accounts receivable ledger, where it indicates specifically who owes the money.

Credit memorandum A piece of paper sent by the seller to a customer who has returned merchandise previously purchased on credit. The credit memorandum indicates to the customer that the seller is reducing the amount owed by the customer.

Credit period Length of time allowed for payment of goods sold on account.

Crossfooting The process of proving that the total debit columns of a special journal are equal to the total credit columns of a special journal.

Discount period A period shorter than the credit period when a discount is available to encourage early payment of bills.

Gross sales The revenue earned from sale of merchandise to customers.

Merchandise Goods brought into a store for resale to customers.

Net sales Gross sales less sales returns and allowances less sales discounts.

Retailers Merchants who buy goods from wholesalers for resale to customers.

Sales discount account A contra-revenue account that records cash discounts granted to customers for payments made within a specific period of time.

Sales invoice A bill sent to customer(s) reflecting a sale on credit.

Sales journal A special journal used to record only sales made on account.

Sales Returns and Allowances (SRA) account A contra-revenue account that records price adjustments and allowances granted on merchandise that is defective and has been returned.

Sales Tax Payable account An account in the general ledger that accumulates the amount of sales tax owed. It has a credit balance.

Schedule of accounts receivable A list of the customers, in alphabetical order, that have an outstanding balance in the accounts receivable ledger (or the accounts receivable subsidiary ledger). This total should be equal to the balance of the Accounts Receivable controlling account in the general ledger at the end of the month.

Special journal A journal used to record similar groups of transactions. Example: The sales journal records all sales on account.

Subsidiary ledger A ledger that contains accounts of a single type. Example: The accounts receivable subsidiary ledger records all credit customers.

Sundry Miscellaneous accounts column(s) in a special journal, which records part of transactions that do not occur too often.

Wholesalers Merchants who buy goods from suppliers and manufacturers for sale to retailers.

QUESTIONS, MINI EXERCISES, EXERCISES, AND PROBLEMS

Discussion Questions

1. Explain the purpose of a contra-revenue account.
2. What is the normal balance of sales discount?
3. Give two examples of contra-revenue accounts.

4. What is the difference between a discount period and a credit period?

5. Explain the terms A. 2/10, n/30; B. n/10, EOM.

6. If special journals are used, what purpose will a general journal serve?

7. Compare and contrast the controlling account Accounts Receivable to the accounts receivable subsidiary ledger.

8. Why is the accounts receivable subsidiary ledger organized in alphabetical order?

9. When is a sales journal used?

10. What is an invoice? What purpose does it serve?

11. Why is sales tax a liability to the business?

12. Sales discounts are taken on sales tax. Agree or disagree and tell why.

13. When a seller issues a credit memorandum (assume no sales tax), what accounts will be affected?

14. Explain the function of a cash receipts journal.

15. When is the sundry column of the cash receipts journal posted?

16. Explain the purpose of a schedule of accounts receivable.

Mini Exercises

(The forms you need are on pages 296–297 of the *Study Guide and Working Papers.*)

Overview

1. Complete the table below for Sales, Sales Returns and Allowances, and Sales Discounts.

Accounts Affected	Category	↓ ↑	Temporary or Permanent

Calculating Net Sales

2. Given the following, calculate net sales:

Gross sales	$20
Sales Returns and Allowances	2
Sales Discounts	1

Sales Journal and General Journal

3. Match the following to the three journal entries (more than one number can be used)

> 1. Journalized into Sales Journal.
> 2. Record immediately to Subsidiary Ledger.
> 3. Post totals from Sales Journal at end of month to General Ledger.
> 4. Journalized in General Journal.
> 5. Record and post immediately to Subsidiary and General Ledger.

a. ____ Sold merchandise on account to Ree Co., invoice no. 1 — $50.

b. ____ Sold merchandise on account to Flynn Co., invoice no. 2 — $100.

c. ____ Issued credit memorandum no. 1 to Flynn Co. for defective merchandise — $25.

(cont. on p. 341)

BLUEPRINT OF SALES AND CASH RECEIPTS JOURNALS

SUMMARY OF HOW TO POST AND RECORD
Single-Column Sales Journal

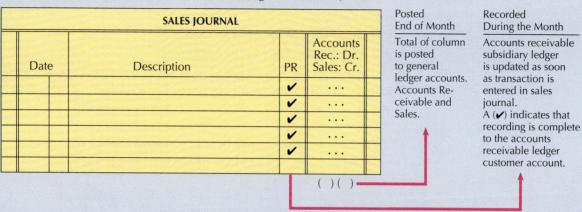

SALES JOURNAL				
Date	Description	PR	Accounts Rec.: Dr. Sales: Cr.	
		✔	...	
		✔	...	
		✔	...	
		✔	...	
		✔	...	

( )( )

Posted End of Month
Total of column is posted to general ledger accounts. Accounts Receivable and Sales.

Recorded During the Month
Accounts receivable subsidiary ledger is updated as soon as transaction is entered in sales journal.
A (✔) indicates that recording is complete to the accounts receivable ledger customer account.

Multicolumn Sales Journal

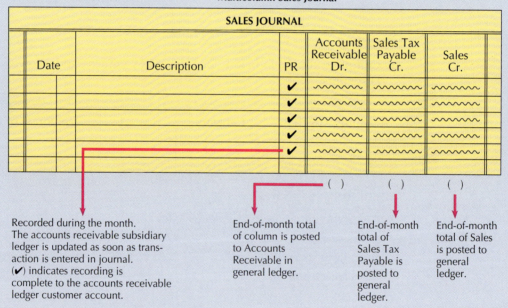

				Accounts Receivable Dr.	Sales Tax Payable Cr.	Sales Cr.	
SALES JOURNAL							
Date	Description		PR				
			✔	〰	〰	〰	
			✔	〰	〰	〰	
			✔	〰	〰	〰	
			✔	〰	〰	〰	
			✔	〰	〰	〰	

( ) ( ) ( )

Recorded during the month. The accounts receivable subsidiary ledger is updated as soon as transaction is entered in journal. (✔) indicates recording is complete to the accounts receivable ledger customer account.

End-of-month total of column is posted to Accounts Receivable in general ledger.

End-of-month total of Sales Tax Payable is posted to general ledger.

End-of-month total of Sales is posted to general ledger.

Issuing a Credit Memo without Sales Tax Recorded in a General Journal

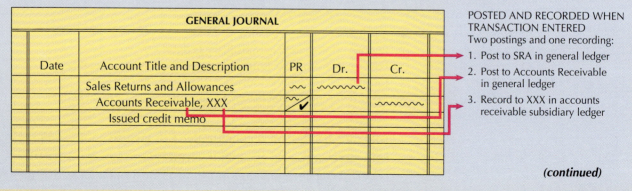

GENERAL JOURNAL				
Date	Account Title and Description	PR	Dr.	Cr.
	Sales Returns and Allowances	〰	〰	
	Accounts Receivable, XXX	⁄✔		〰
	Issued credit memo			

POSTED AND RECORDED WHEN TRANSACTION ENTERED
Two postings and one recording:
1. Post to SRA in general ledger
2. Post to Accounts Receivable in general ledger
3. Record to XXX in accounts receivable subsidiary ledger

(continued)

Issuing a Credit Memo with Sales Tax Recorded in a General Journal

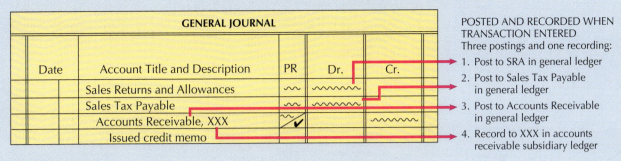

	GENERAL JOURNAL				POSTED AND RECORDED WHEN TRANSACTION ENTERED

POSTED AND RECORDED WHEN TRANSACTION ENTERED
Three postings and one recording:
1. Post to SRA in general ledger
2. Post to Sales Tax Payable in general ledger
3. Post to Accounts Receivable in general ledger
4. Record to XXX in accounts receivable subsidiary ledger

The Cash Receipts Journal

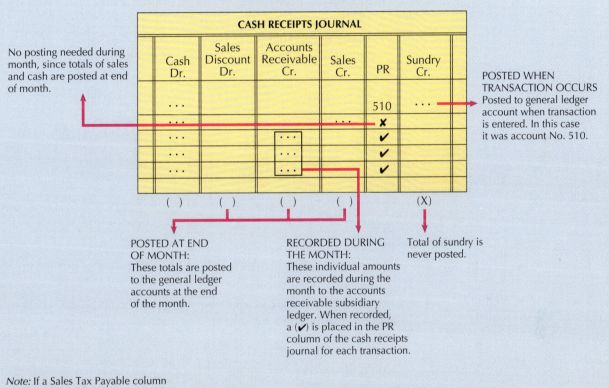

No posting needed during month, since totals of sales and cash are posted at end of month.

POSTED WHEN TRANSACTION OCCURS
Posted to general ledger account when transaction is entered. In this case it was account No. 510.

POSTED AT END OF MONTH:
These totals are posted to the general ledger accounts at the end of the month.

RECORDED DURING THE MONTH:
These individual amounts are recorded during the month to the accounts receivable subsidiary ledger. When recorded, a (✔) is placed in the PR column of the cash receipts journal for each transaction.

Total of sundry is never posted.

Note: If a Sales Tax Payable column were added, total of column would be posted at end of month.

Credit Memorandum

4. Draw a transactional analysis box for the following credit memorandum: Issued credit memorandum to Bob Corp. for defective merchandise — $50.

Sales and Cash Receipts Journal

5. Match the following to the four journal entries (a number can be used more than once).

1. Journalized into Sales Journal.
2. Journalized into Cash Receipts Journal.
3. Record immediately to Subsidiary Ledger.
4. Totals of Special Journals will be posted at end of month (except Sundry column).
5. Post to General Ledger immediately.
6. Journalize into General Journal.

a. ____ Sold merchandise on account to Ally Co., invoice no. 10 — $40.
b. ____ Received check from Moore Co. — $100 less 2 percent discount.
c. ____ Cash Sales — $100.
d. ____ Issued credit memorandum no. 2 to Ally Co. for defective merchandise — $20.

6. From the following, prepare a schedule of Accounts Receivable for Blue Co., for May 31, 19XX.

Accounts Receivable Subsidiary Ledger

Bon Co.
5/6 SJ1   100

Peke Co.
5/20 SJ1   30 | 5/27 CRJ1   10

Green Co.
5/9 SJ1   10

General Ledger

Accounts Receivable
5/31 SJ1   140 | 5/31 CRJ1   10

Exercises

(The forms you need are on pages 298–300 of the *Study Guide and Working Papers*.)

Recording to accounts receivable ledger and posting to general ledger.

9-1. From the following sales journal, record to the accounts receivable subsidiary ledger and post to the general ledger accounts as appropriate.

SALES JOURNAL					
					P. 1
Date	Account Debited	Invoice No.	PR		Dr. Accts. Receivable Cr. Sales
19XX April 18	Kevin Stone Co.	1			4 0 0 00
19	Bill Valley Co.	2			6 0 0 00

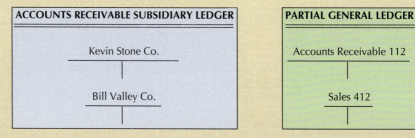

ACCOUNTS RECEIVABLE SUBSIDIARY LEDGER

Kevin Stone Co.

Bill Valley Co.

PARTIAL GENERAL LEDGER

Accounts Receivable 112

Sales 412

9-2. Journalize, record, and post when appropriate the following transactions into the sales journal (same heading as Exercise 9-1) and general journal (p. 1) (all sales carry terms of 2/10, n/30):

Journalizing, recording, and posting that includes credit memorandum.

19XX
May   16   Sold merchandise on account to Ronald Co., invoice no. 1, $1,000.
      18   Sold merchandise on account to Bass Co., invoice no. 2, $1,700.
      20   Issued credit memorandum no. 1 to Bass Co. for defective merchandise, $700.

Use the following account numbers: Accounts Receivable, 112; Sales, 411; Sales Returns and Allowances, 412.

Journalizing transaction into cash receipts journal.

9-3. From Exercise 9-2, journalize in the cash receipts journal the receipt of check from Ronald Co. for payment of invoice no. 1 on May 24. Use the same headings as for Art's Wholesale Clothing (on p. 329).

Journalizing, recording, and posting sales and cash receipts journal; schedule of accounts receivable.

9-4. From the following transactions for Edna Co., when appropriate, journalize, record, post, and prepare a schedule of accounts receivable. Use the same journal headings (all p. 1) and chart of accounts (use Edna Cares, Capital) that Art's Wholesale Clothing used in the text. You will have to set up your own accounts receivable subsidiary ledger and partial general ledger as needed. All sales terms are 2/10, n/30.

19XX
June   1   Edna Cares invested $3,000 in the business.
       1   Sold merchandise on account to Boston Co., invoice no. 1, $700.
       2   Sold merchandise on account to Gary Co., invoice no. 2, $900.
       3   Cash sale, $200.
       8   Issued credit memorandum no. 1 to Boston for defective merchandise, $200.
      10   Received check from Boston for invoice no. 1 less returns and discount.
      15   Cash sale, $400.
      18   Sold merchandise on account to Boston Co., invoice no. 3, $600.

9-5. From the following facts calculate what Ann Frost must pay Blue Co. for the purchase of a dining room set. Sale terms are 2/10, n/30.

Sales tax and cash discount calculation.

   a. Sales ticket price before tax, $4,000 — dated April 5.
   b. Sales tax, 7 percent.
   c. Returned one defective chair for credit of $400 on April 8.
   d. Paid bill on April 13.

Group A Problems

(The forms you need are on pages 301–320 of the *Study Guide and Working Papers*.)

Multicolumn journal: Journalizing and posting to general ledger, recording to accounts receivable subsidiary ledger, and preparing a schedule of accounts receivable.

9A-1. Jill Blue has opened Max Co., a wholesale grocery and pizza company. The following transactions occurred in June:

19XX
June   1   Sold grocery merchandise to Joe Kase Co. on account, $400, invoice no. 1.
       4   Sold pizza merchandise to Sue Moore Co. on account, $600, invoice no. 2.
       8   Sold grocery merchandise to Long Co. on account, $700, invoice no. 3.
      10   Issued credit memorandum no. 1 to Joe Kase for $150 of grocery merchandise returned due to spoilage.
      15   Sold pizza merchandise to Sue Moore Co. on account, $160, invoice no. 4.

Check Figure:
Schedule of Accounts Receivable
$3,210

19 Sold grocery merchandise to Long Co. on account, $300, invoice no. 5.

25 Sold pizza merchandise to Joe Kase Co. on account, $1,200, invoice no. 6.

Required:

1. Journalize the transactions in the appropriate journals.

2. Record to the accounts receivable subsidiary ledger and post to general ledger as appropriate.

3. Prepare a schedule of accounts receivable.

9A-2. The following transactions of Ted's Auto Supply occurred in November (your working papers have balances as of Nov. 1 for certain general ledger and accounts receivable ledger accounts):

19XX

Multicolumn sales journal: Use of sales tax; journalizing and posting to general ledger and recording to accounts receivable ledger; and preparing a schedule of accounts receivable.

Check Figure:
Schedule of Accounts Receivable $13,045

Nov. 1 Sold auto parts merchandise to R. Volan on account, $1,000, invoice no. 60, plus 5 percent sales tax.

5 Sold auto parts merchandise to J. Seth on account, $800, invoice no. 61, plus 5 percent sales tax.

8 Sold auto parts merchandise to Lance Corner on account, $9,000, invoice no. 62, plus 5 percent sales tax.

10 Issued credit memorandum no. 12 to R. Volan for $500 for defective auto parts merchandise returned from Nov. 1 transaction. (Be careful to record the reduction in sales tax payable as well.)

12 Sold auto parts merchandise to J. Seth on account, $600, invoice no. 63, plus 5 percent sales tax.

Required:

1. Journalize the transactions in the appropriate journals.

2. Record to the accounts receivable subsidiary ledger and post to general ledger as appropriate.

3. Prepare a schedule of accounts receivable.

9A-3. Mark Peaker owns Peaker's Sneaker Shop. (In your working papers balances as of May 1 are provided for the accounts receivable and general ledger accounts.) The following transactions occurred in May:

19XX

Comprehensive Problem: Recording transactions into sales, cash receipts, and general journals. Recording to accounts receivable subsidiary ledger and posting to general ledger. Preparing a schedule of accounts receivable.

Check Figure:
Schedule of Accounts Receivable $5,700

May 1 Mark Peaker invested an additional $12,000 in the sneaker store.

3 Sold $700 of merchandise on account to B. Dale, sales ticket no. 60, terms 1/10, n/30.

4 Sold $500 of merchandise on account to Ron Lester, sales ticket no. 61, terms 1/10, n/30.

9 Sold $200 of merchandise on account to Jim Zon, sales ticket no. 62, terms 1/10, n/30.

10 Received cash from B. Dale in payment of May 3 transaction, sales ticket no. 60, less discount.

20 Sold $3,000 of merchandise on account to Pam Pry, sales ticket no. 63, terms 1/10, n/30.

22 Received cash payment from Ron Lester in payment of May 4 transaction, sales ticket no. 61.

23 Collected cash sales, $3,000.

24 Issued credit memorandum no. 1 to Pam Pry for $2,000 of merchandise returned from May 20 sales on account.

26 Received cash from Pam Pry in payment of May 20, sales ticket no. 63. (Don't forget about the credit memo and discount.)

28 Collected cash sales, $7,000.

30 Sold sneaker rack equipment for $300 cash. (Beware.)

30 Sold merchandise priced at $4,000, on account to Ron Lester, sales ticket no. 64, terms 1/10, n/30.

31 Issued credit memorandum no. 2 to Ron Lester for $700 of merchandise returned from May 30 transaction, sales ticket no. 64.

Required:

1. Journalize the transactions.
2. Record to the accounts receivable subsidiary ledger and post to general ledger as needed.
3. Prepare a schedule of accounts receivable.

9A-4. Bill Murray opened Bill's Cosmetic Market on April 1. There is a 6 percent sales tax on all cosmetic sales. Bill offers no sales discounts. The following transactions occurred in April:

19XX

April

1 Bill Murray invested $8,000 in the Cosmetic Market from his personal savings account.

5 From the cash register tapes, lipstick cash sales were $5,000 plus sales tax.

5 From the cash register tapes, eye shadow cash sales were $2,000 plus sales tax.

8 Sold lipstick on account to Alice Koy Co., $300, sales ticket no. 1, plus sales tax.

9 Sold eye shadow on account to Marika Sanchez Co., $1,000, sales ticket no. 2, plus sales tax.

15 Issued credit memorandum no. 1 to Alice Koy Co. for $150 for lipstick returned. (Be sure to reduce sales tax payable for Bill.)

19 Marika Sanchez Co. paid half the amount owed from sales ticket no. 2, dated April 9.

21 Sold lipstick on account to Jeff Tong Co., $300, sales ticket no. 3, plus sales tax.

24 Sold eye shadow on account to Rusty Neal Co., $800, sales ticket no. 4, plus sales tax.

25 Issued credit memorandum no. 2 to Jeff Tong Co. for $200 for lipstick returned from sales ticket no. 3, dated April 21.

29 Cash sales taken from the cash register tape showed:
1. Lipstick — $1,000 + $60 sales tax collected.
2. Eye shadow — $3,000 + $180 sales tax collected.

29 Sold lipstick on account to Marika Sanchez Co., $400, sales ticket no. 5, plus sales tax.

30 Received payment from Marika Sanchez Co. of sales ticket no. 5, dated April 29.

Required:

1. Journalize the above in the sales journal, cash receipts journal, or general journal.
2. Record to the accounts receivable subsidiary ledger and post to general ledger when appropriate.
3. Prepare a schedule of accounts receivable for the end of April.

Comprehensive problem: Using sales tax in recording transactions into sales, cash receipts, and general journals. Recording to accounts receivable subsidiary ledger and posting to general ledger. Crossfooting and preparing a schedule of accounts receivable.

Check Figure:

Schedule of Accounts Receivable $1,643

Group B Problems

(The forms you need are on pages 301–320 of the *Study Guide and Working Papers.*)

9B-1. The following transactions occurred for Max Co. for the month of June:

June 1 Sold grocery merchandise to Joe Kase Co. on account, $800, invoice no. 1.
      4 Sold pizza merchandise to Sue Moore Co. on account, $550, invoice no. 2.
      8 Sold grocery merchandise to Long Co. on account, $900, invoice no. 3.
     10 Issued credit memorandum no. 1 to Joe Kase for $160 of grocery merchandise returned due to spoilage.
     15 Sold pizza merchandise to Sue Moore Co. on account, $700, invoice no. 4.
     19 Sold grocery merchandise to Long Co. on account, $250, invoice no. 5.

Multicolumn journal: Journalizing and posting to general ledger, recording to accounts receivable subsidiary ledger, and preparing a schedule of accounts receivable.

Check Figure:
Schedule of Accounts Receivable $3,040

Required:

1. Journalize the transactions in the appropriate journals.
2. Record to the accounts receivable subsidiary ledger and post to general ledger as appropriate.
3. Prepare a schedule of accounts receivable.

9B-2. In November the following transactions occurred for Ted's Auto Supply (your working papers have balances as of Nov. 1 for certain general ledger and accounts receivable ledger accounts):

19XX

Multicolumn sales journal: Use of sales tax; journalizing and posting to general ledger and recording to accounts receivable subsidiary ledger; and preparing a schedule of accounts receivable.

Check Figure:
Schedule of Accounts Receivable $22,600

Nov. 1 Sold merchandise to R. Volan on account, $4,000, invoice no. 70, plus 5 percent sales tax.
      5 Sold merchandise to J. Seth on account, $1,600, invoice no. 71, plus 5 percent sales tax.
      8 Sold merchandise to Lance Corner on account, $15,000, invoice no. 72, plus 5 percent sales tax.
     10 Issued credit memorandum no. 14 to R. Volan for $2,000 for defective merchandise returned from Nov. 1 transaction. (Be careful to record the reduction in sales tax payable as well.)
     12 Sold merchandise to J. Seth on account, $1,400, invoice no. 73, plus 5 percent sales tax.

Required:

1. Journalize the transactions in the appropriate journals.
2. Record to the accounts receivable subsidiary ledger and post to general ledger as appropriate.
3. Prepare a schedule of accounts receivable.

9B-3. (In your working papers all the beginning balances needed are provided for the accounts receivable subsidiary and general ledger.) The following transactions occurred for Peaker's Sneaker Shop:

19XX

Check Figure:
Schedule of Accounts Receivable $8,000

Comprehensive Problem: Recording transactions into sales, cash receipts, and general journals. Recording to accounts receivable subsidiary ledger and posting to general ledger. Preparing a schedule of accounts receivable.

May   1 Mark Peaker invested an additional $14,000 in the sneaker store.
      3 Sold $2,000 of merchandise on account to B. Dale, sales ticket no. 60, terms 1/10, n/30.
      4 Sold $900 of merchandise on account to Ron Lester, sales ticket no. 61, terms 1/10, n/30.
      9 Sold $600 of merchandise on account to Jim Zon, sales ticket no. 62, terms 1/10, n/30.
     10 Received cash from B. Dale in payment of May 3 transaction, sales ticket no. 60, less discount.
     20 Sold $4,000 of merchandise on account to Pam Pry, sales ticket no. 63, terms 1/10, n/30.
     22 Received cash payment from Ron Lester in payment of May 4 transaction, sales ticket no. 61.
     23 Collected cash sales, $6,000.

24 Issued credit memorandum no. 1 to Pam Pry for $500 of merchandise returned from May 20 sales on account.

26 Received cash from Pam Pry in payment of May 20 sales ticket no. 63. (Don't forget about the credit memo and discount.)

28 Collected cash sales, $12,000.

30 Sold sneaker rack equipment for $200 cash. (Beware.)

30 Sold $6,000 of merchandise on account to Ron Lester, sales ticket no. 64, terms 1/10, n/30.

31 Issued credit memorandum no. 2 to Ron Lester for $800 of merchandise returned from May 30 transaction, sales ticket no. 64.

Required:

1. Journalize the transactions in the appropriate journals.

2. Record and post as appropriate.

3. Prepare a schedule of accounts receivable.

9B-4. Bill's Cosmetic Market began operating in April. There is a 6 percent sales tax on all cosmetic sales. Bill offers no discounts. The following transactions occurred in April:

19XX

April 1 Bill Murray invested $10,000 in the Cosmetic Market from his personal account.

5 From the cash register tapes, lipstick cash sales were $5,000 plus sales tax.

5 From the cash register tapes, eye shadow cash sales were $3,000 plus sales tax.

8 Sold lipstick on account to Alice Koy Co., $400, sales ticket no. 1, plus sales tax.

9 Sold eye shadow on account to Marika Sanchez Co., $900, sales ticket no. 2, plus sales tax.

15 Issued credit memorandum no. 1 to Alice Koy Co. for lipstick returned, $200. (Be sure to reduce sales tax payable for Bill.)

19 Marika Sanchez Co. paid half the amount owed from sales ticket no. 2, dated April 9.

21 Sold lipstick on account to Jeff Tong Co., $600 sales ticket no. 3, plus sales tax.

24 Sold eye shadow on account to Rusty Neal Co., $1,000, sales ticket no. 4, plus sales tax.

25 Issued credit memorandum no. 2 to Jeff Tong Co. for $300, for lipstick returned from sales ticket no. 3, dated April 21.

29 Cash sales taken from the cash register tape showed:
  1. Lipstick — $4,000 + $240 sales tax collected.
  2. Eye shadow — $2,000 + $120 sales tax collected.

29 Sold lipstick on account to Marika Sanchez Co., $700, sales ticket no. 5 plus sales tax.

30 Received payment from Marika Sanchez Co. of sales ticket no. 5, dated April 29.

Required:

1. Journalize, record, and post as appropriate.

2. Prepare a schedule of accounts receivable for the end of April.

Comprehensive Problem: Using sales tax in recording transactions into sales, cash receipts, and general journals. Recording to accounts receivable subsidiary ledger and posting to general ledger, and preparing a schedule of accounts receivable.

Check Figure:

Schedule of Accounts Receivable $2,067

REAL WORLD APPLICATIONS

9R-1.

Ronald Howard has been hired by Green Company to help reconstruct the sales journal, general journal, and cash receipts journal, which were recently destroyed in a fire. The owner of Green has supplied him with the following data. Please ignore dates, invoice numbers, etc., and enter the entries into the reconstructed sales journal, general journal, and cash receipts journal. What written recommendation should Ron make so reconstruction will not be needed in the future?

Accounts Receivable Subsidiary Ledger

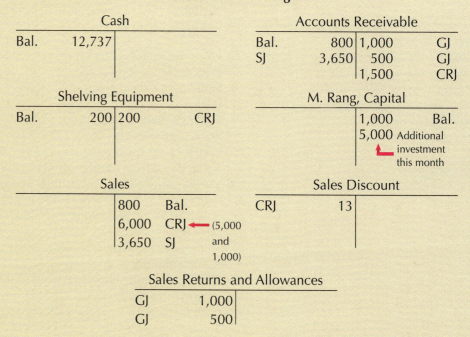

Partial General Ledger

9R-2.

The bookkeeper of Floore Company records credit sales in a sales journal and returns in a general journal. The bookkeeper did the following:

1. Recorded an $18 credit sale as $180 in the sales journal.
2. Correctly recorded a $40 sale in the sales journal but posted it to B. Blue's account as $400 in the accounts receivable ledger.
3. Made an additional error in determining the balance of J. B. Window Co. in the accounts receivable ledger.
4. Posted a sales return that was recorded in the general journal to the Sales Returns and Allowance account and the Accounts Receivable account but forgot to record it to the B. Katz Co.
5. Added the total of the sales column incorrectly.

6. Posted a sales return to the Accounts Receivable account but not to the Sales Returns and Allowances account. Accounts Receivable ledger was recorded correctly.

Could you inform the bookkeeper in writing as to when each error will be discovered?

 make the call

Critical Thinking/Ethical Case

9R-3.

Amy Jak is the National Sales Manager of Rowe Co. In order to get sales up to the projection for the old year, Amy asked the accountant to put the first two weeks of sales in January back into December. Amy told the accountant that this secret would only be between them. Should Amy move the new sales into the old sales year? You make the call. Write down your specific recommendations to Amy.

ACCOUNTING RECALL
A CUMULATIVE APPROACH

THIS EXAM REVIEWS CHAPTERS 1 THROUGH 9

Your *Study Guide and Working Papers* has forms (pp. 325 and 331) to complete this exam, as well as worked-out solutions. The page references next to each question identify what page to turn back to if you answer the question incorrectly.

PART 1 Vocabulary Review

Match the terms to the appropriate definition or phrase.

Page Ref.

(318)	1. Accounts receivable subsidiary ledger	A. The results of a cash discount
		B. Records sales on account
(327)	2. Sundry	C. A contra-revenue account
(251)	3. Medicare payable	D. Clears temporary accounts
(161)	4. Closing	E. In alphabetical order
(211)	5. Deposit in transit	F. Miscellaneous
(323)	6. Sales returns and allowances	G. Records receipt of cash
		H. A liability
(319)	7. Controlling account	I. Deposits not received by the bank
(320)	8. Sales journal	J. Accounts receivable
(329)	9. Cash receipts journal	
(314)	10. Sales discount	

(216)   11. Petty cash is a liability.

(319)   12. The controlling account balance at end of month will equal the sum of the subsidiary ledger.

(323)   13. Issuing a credit memo results in sales returns and allowances decreasing.

(248)   14. There is no tax base for Medicare.

(319)   15. A (✓) means the controlling account has been updated.

CONTINUING PROBLEM

Freedman will use two specialized journals for recording business transactions in the month of January. To assist you in recording the transactions, at the end of this problem is the Schedule of Accounts Receivable as of December 31 and an updated chart of accounts with the current balance listed for each account.

Assignment:

(See p. 326 in your *Study Guide and Working Papers.*)

1. Journalize the transactions in the appropriate journals (cash receipts, sales journal, or general journal).
2. Record in the accounts receivable subsidiary ledger and post to the general ledger as appropriate. A partial general ledger is included in the *Working Papers.*
3. Prepare a schedule of accounts receivable as of January 31, 19X1.

The January transactions are as follows.

Jan 1 Sold $700 worth of merchandise to Taylor Golf on credit, sales invoice #5000; terms are 2/10/n30

10 Sold $3,000 worth of merchandise on account to Anthony Pitale, sales invoice #5001; terms are 2/10/n30

11 Received $3,000 from Accu Pac, Inc. toward payment of their balance; no discount allowed

12 Collected $2,000 cash sales.

19 Sold $4,000 worth of merchandise on account to Vita Needle, sales invoice #5002, terms are 4/10/n30.

20 Collected balance in full from invoice #5001, Anthony Pitale.

29 Issued credit memorandum to Taylor Golf for $400 worth of merchandise returned, invoice #5000.

29 Collect full payment from Vita Needle, invoice #5002.

Schedule of Accounts Receivable
Eldorado Computer Center
December 31, 19XX

Taylor Golf	$ 2,900.00
Vita Needle	6,800.00
Accu Pac	$ 3,900.00
Total Amount Due	**$13,600.00**

CHART OF ACCOUNTS AND CURRENT BALANCES AS OF 12/31/XX

Account #	Account Name	Debit Balance	Credit Balance
1000	Cash	$ 3,336.65	
1010	Petty Cash	100	
1020	Accounts Receivable	13,600	
1025	Prepaid Rent	1,600	
1030	Supplies	132	
1040	Merchandise Inventory	0	
1080	Computer Shop Equipment	3,800	
1081	Accumulated Depr. CS Equip.		$ 99
1090	Office Equipment	1,050	
1091	Accumulated Depr. Office Equip.		20
2000	Accounts Payable		2,050
2010	Wages Payable		0
2020	FICA-SS Payable		0
2030	FICA-Medicare Payable		0
2040	FIT Payable		0
2050	SIT Payable		0
2060	FUTA Payable		0
2070	SUTA Payable		0
3000	Freedman Capital		7,406
3010	Freedman Withdrawals	2,015	
3020	Income Summary		0
4000	Service Revenue		18,500
4010	Sales		0
4020	Sales Returns and Allowances	0	
4030	Sales Discounts	0	
5010	Advertising Expense	0	
5020	Rent Expense	0	
5030	Utilities Expense	0	
5040	Phone Expense	150	
5050	Supplies Expense	0	
5060	Insurance Expense	0	
5070	Postage Expense	25	
5080	Depreciation Exp. C.S. Equipment	0	
5090	Depreciation Exp. Office Equipment	0	
5100	Miscellaneous Expense	10	
5110	Wage Expense	2,030	
5120	Payroll Tax Expense	226.35	
5130	Interest Expense	0	
5140	Bad Debt Expense	0	
6000	Purchases	0	
6010	Purchases Returns and Allowances		0
6020	Purchases Discounts		0
6030	Freight In	0	

SPECIAL JOURNALS

Purchases and Cash Payments

10

THE BIG PICTURE

Tony Freedman was delighted to see the difference he made in using the specialized sales and cash receipts journal last month. He has decided to continue his efforts in using two more specialized journals: a purchases journal to track the merchandise Eldorado Computer Center is selling, and a cash payments journal.

You have learned how specialized journals can benefit the company in easing the posting of transactions. In this chapter you will learn how to use a purchases and cash payment journal.

A purchases journal is used to record purchases of merchandise on account, and the cash payments journal is used to record all cash payments. Each creditor you purchase merchandise from will have an individual ledger account showing the volume of business you are giving that creditor on account. The schedule of accounts payable, like the schedule of accounts receivable, will show a detailed list of each creditor and the amount owed.

Freedman has two primary objectives for using all of the specialized journals. One is to increase efficiency, and the other is to improve accuracy and detail.

◆ Calculating net purchases. (p. 356)
◆ Journalizing transactions in a purchases journal. (p. 360)
◆ Posting from a purchases journal to the accounts payable subsidiary ledger and the general ledger. (p. 360)
◆ Preparing, journalizing, recording, and posting a debit memorandum. (p. 361)
◆ Journalizing and posting from a cash payments journal. (p. 365)
◆ Preparing a schedule of accounts payable. (p. 367)

Chapter 9 focused on the sellers in merchandise companies. This chapter will look at the buyers. Many of the concepts and rules related to special journals will carry over to this chapter.

LEARNING UNIT 10-1
Chou's Toy Shop: Buyer's View of a Merchandise Company

PURCHASES

Chou brings merchandise into his toy store for resale to customers. The account that records the cost of this merchandise is called **Purchases.** Suppose that Chou buys $4,000 worth of Barbie dolls on account from Mattel Manufacturing on July 6. The Purchases account records all merchandise bought for resale. Here's how this would be recorded if special journals were not used.

Purchases is a cost.
The rules work just like they were an expense.

Purchases	
Dr.	Cr.
4,000	

This account has a debit balance and is classified as a cost. Purchases represent costs that are directly related to bringing merchandise into the store for resale to customers. The July 6 entry would be analyzed and journalized as follows:

> If Chou's purchased a new display case for the store, it would not show up in the Purchase account. The case is considered equipment that is not for resale to customers.

Accounts Affected	Category	↑ ↓	Rules	T Account Update
Purchases	Cost	↑	Dr.	**Purchases** Dr. | Cr. 4,000 |
Accounts Payable, Mattel	Liability	↑	Cr.	**Acc. Payable** Dr. | Cr. | 4,000 — **Mattel** | 4,000

July	6	Purchases		4 0 0 0 00				
		Accounts Payable, Mattel				4 0 0 0 00		
		Purchases on account						

Keep in mind we would have to record to Mattel in the accounts payable subsidiary ledger. We will talk about the subsidiary ledger in Learning Unit 10-2.

PURCHASES RETURNS AND ALLOWANCES

Chou noticed that some of the dolls he received were defective, and he notified the manufacturer of the defects. On July 9, Mattel issued a debit memorandum indicating that Chou would get a $500 reduction from the original selling price. Chou then agreed to keep the dolls. The account that records a decrease to a buyer's cost is a contra-cost account called **Purchases Returns and Allowances.** The account lowers the cost of purchases.

Purchases Returns and Allowances

Dr.	Cr.
	500

← Normal balance is a credit.

Let's analyze this reduction to cost and prepare a general journal entry.

Accounts Affected	Category	↑ ↓	Rules	T Account Update	
Accounts Payable, Mattel	Liability	↓	Dr.	Acc. Payable Dr. | Cr. 500 | 4,000	Mattel 500 | 4,000
Purchases Returns and Allowances	Contra-cost	↑	Cr.	Purchases Ret. & Allow. Dr. | Cr. | 500	

July	9	Accounts Payable, Mattel		5 0 0 00		
		Purchases Returns and Allowances			5 0 0 00	
		Received debit memorandum				

When posted to general ledger accounts as well as recording to Mattel in the accounts payable subsidiary ledger, Chou owes $500 less.

PURCHASES DISCOUNT

Now let's look at the analysis and journal entry when Chou pays Mattel. Mattel offers a 2 percent cash discount if the invoice is paid within 10 days. To take advantage of this cash discount, Chou sent a check to Mattel on July 15. The discount is taken after the allowance.

$$\begin{array}{r} \$4,000 \\ -\ \ 500 \text{ allowance} \\ \hline \$3,500 \times .02 = \$70 \text{ purchases discount} \end{array}$$

The account that records this discount is called **Purchases Discount.** It, too, is a contra-cost account because it lowers the cost of purchases.

Purchases Discount

Dr.	Cr.
	70

← Normal balance is a credit.

Let's analyze and prepare a general journal entry:

Remember, for Mattel this is a sales discount, while for Chou this is a purchases discount.

Remember, purchases were a debit; purchases discounts are credits.

Accounts Affected	Category	↑ ↓	Rules	T Account Update
Accounts Payable, Mattel	Liability	↓	Dr.	Acc. Payable / Mattel — Dr.|Cr. 500|4,000 500|4,000 3,500| — Mattel 500|4,000 |3,500
Purchases Discount	Contra-cost	↑	Cr.	Purchases Discounts — Dr.|Cr. |70
Cash	Asset	↓	Cr.	Cash — Dr.|Cr. |3,430

	July	15	Accounts Payable, Mattel		3 5 0 0 00				
			Purchases Discount					7 0 00	
			Cash					3 4 3 0 00	
			Paid Mattel balance owed						

After the journal entry is posted and recorded to Mattel, the result will show that Chou saved $70 and totally reduced what he owed to Mattel. The actual — or net — cost of his purchase is $3,430, calculated as follows:

Purchases	$4,000
− Purchases Returns and Allowances	500
− Purchases Discounts	70
= Net Purchases	$3,430

Freight charges are not taken into consideration in calculating net purchases. Still, they are very important. If the seller is responsible for paying the shipping cost until the goods reach their destination, the freight charges are **F.O.B. destination.** For example, if a seller located in Boston sold goods F.O.B. destination to a buyer in New York, the seller would have to pay the cost of shipping the goods to the buyer.

If the buyer is responsible for paying the shipping costs, the freight charges are **F.O.B. shipping point.** In this situation, the seller sometimes will prepay the freight charges as a matter of convenience and will add it to the invoice of the purchaser.

Example:

Bill amount ($800 + $80 prepaid freight)	$880
Less 5% cash discount (.05 × $800)	40
Amount to be paid by buyer	$840

Purchases discounts are not taken on freight. The discount is based on the purchase price.

If the seller ships goods F.O.B. shipping point, legal ownership (title) passes to the buyer *when the goods are shipped.* If goods are shipped by the seller F.O.B. destination, title will change *when goods have reached their destination.*

F.O.B. stands for "free on board" the carrier.

F.O.B. Destination: Seller pays freight to point of destination.

F.O.B. Shipping Point: Buyer pays freight from seller's shipping point.

When does title change to goods shipped?

356

CH. 10 / SPECIAL JOURNALS: PURCHASES AND CASH PAYMENTS

LEARNING UNIT 10-1 REVIEW

AT THIS POINT you should be able to

◆ Explain and calculate purchases, purchases returns and allowances, and purchases discounts. (p. 354)
◆ Calculate net purchases. (p. 356)
◆ Explain why purchase discounts are not taken on freight. (p. 356)
◆ Compare and contrast F.O.B. destination with F.O.B. shipping point. (p. 356)

SELF-REVIEW QUIZ 10-1

(The forms you need can be found on page 332 of the *Study Guide and Working Papers.*)

Which of the following statements are false?

1. Net purchases = Purchases − Purchases Returns and Allowances − Purchases Discount.
2. Purchases is a contra-cost.
3. F.O.B. destination means the seller covers shipping cost and retains title till goods reach their destination.
4. Purchases discounts are not taken on freight.
5. Purchases Discount is a contra-cost account.

Solution to Self-Review Quiz 10-1

Number 2 is false.

Quiz Tip:

Buyer			*Seller*		
Purchase	Dr.	Cost	Sale	Cr	Revenue
PRA	Cr.	Contra-cost	SRA	Dr.	Contra-revenue
PD	Cr.	Contra-cost	SD	Dr.	Contra-revenue

LEARNING UNIT 10-2
Steps Taken in Purchasing Merchandise and Recording Purchases

Merchandising companies must take specific steps when they purchase goods for resale. Let's look at the steps Art's Wholesale Clothing Company took when it ordered goods from Abby Blake Company on April 3.

Step 1: Prepare a Purchase Requisition at Art's Wholesale Clothing Company

Authorized personnel initiate purchase requisition.

The inventory clerk notes a low inventory level of ladies' jackets for resale, so he sends a **purchase requisition** to the purchasing department. A duplicate copy is sent to the accounting department. A third copy remains with the department that initiated the request, to be used as a check on the purchasing department.

FIGURE 10-1
Purchase Order

```
PURCHASE ORDER NO. 1
ART'S WHOLESALE CLOTHING COMPANY
1528 BELLE AVE.
NEW YORK, NY 10022
```

| Purchased From: | Abby Blake Company 12 Foster Road Englewood Cliffs, NJ 07632 | Date: April 1, 19XX Shipped VIA: Freight Truck Terms: 2/10, n/60 FOB: Englewood Cliffs |

Quantity	Description	Unit Price	Total
100	Ladies' Jackets Code 14-0	$50	$5,000

Art's Wholesale
By: Bill Joy

Purchase order number must appear on all invoices.

Four copies of purchase order: (1) (original) to supplier, (2) to accounting department, (3) remains with department that initiated purchase requisition, (4) to file of purchasing department.

Step 2: Purchasing Department of Art's Wholesale Clothing Company Prepares a Purchase Order

After checking various price lists and suppliers' catalogs, the purchasing department fills out a form called a **purchase order.** This form gives Abby Blake Company the authority to ship the ladies' jackets ordered by Art's Wholesale Clothing Company (see Fig. 10-1).

Step 3: Sales Invoice Prepared by Abby Blake Company

Abby Blake Company receives the purchase order and prepares a sales invoice. The sales invoice for the seller is the **purchase invoice** for the buyer. A sales invoice is shown in Figure 10-2.

The invoice shows that the goods will be shipped F.O.B. Englewood Cliffs. This means that Art's Wholesale Clothing Company is responsible for paying the shipping costs.

The sales invoice also shows a freight charge. This means that Abby Blake prepaid the shipping costs as a matter of convenience. Art's will repay the freight charges when it pays the invoice.

Step 4: Receiving the Goods

When goods are received, Art's Wholesale inspects the shipment and completes a **receiving report.** The receiving report verifies that the exact merchandise that was ordered was received in good condition.

FIGURE 10-2
Sales Invoice

```
SALES INVOICE NO. 228
ABBY BLAKE COMPANY
12 FOSTER ROAD
ENGLEWOOD, CLIFFS, NJ 07632
```

| Sold To: | Art's Wholesale Clothing Co. 1528 Belle Ave. New York, NY 10022 | Date: April 3, 19XX Shipped VIA: Freight Truck Terms: 2/10, n/60 Your Order No: 1 FOB: Englewood Cliffs |

Quantity	Description	Unit Price	Total
100	Ladies' Jackets Code 14-0 Freight	$50	$5,000 50 $5,050

FIGURE 10-3
Invoice Approval Form

```
┌──────────────────────────────────────────────────────────┐
│                   INVOICE APPROVAL FORM                    │
│                  Art's Wholesale Clothing Co.              │
│ ┌──────────────────────────────────┬──────────────────┐   │
│ │ Purchase Order #                 │  ──────────────   │   │
│ │ Requisition check                │  ──────────────   │   │
│ │ Purchase Order check             │  ──────────────   │   │
│ │ Receiving Report check           │  ──────────────   │   │
│ │ Invoice check                    │  ──────────────   │   │
│ │ Approved for Payment             │  ──────────────   │   │
│ └──────────────────────────────────┴──────────────────┘   │
└──────────────────────────────────────────────────────────┘
```

Step 5: Verifying the Numbers

Before the invoice is approved for recording and payment, the accounting department must check the purchase order, invoice, and receiving report to make sure that all are in agreement and that no steps have been omitted. The form used for checking and approval is an **invoice approval form** (see Fig. 10-3).

Keep in mind that Art's Wholesale Clothing Company does not record this purchase until the *invoice is approved for recording and payment.* However, Abby Blake Company records this transaction in its records when the sales invoice is prepared.

THE PURCHASES JOURNAL AND ACCOUNTS PAYABLE SUBSIDIARY LEDGER

Let's look at how Art's Wholesale Clothing Company journalizes, posts, and records to the accounts payable subsidiary ledger. We will also look at the **purchases journal,** a multicolumn special journal Art's uses to record the buying of merchandise or other items on account, and the **accounts payable subsidiary ledger,** an alphabetical list of the amounts owed to creditors from purchases on account.

For example, on April 3 Art's Wholesale Clothing Company records in its purchases journal the following:

- ◆ Date: April 3, 19XX
- ◆ Account Credited: Abby Blake Company
- ◆ Date of Invoice: April 3
- ◆ Invoice Number: 228
- ◆ Terms: 2/10, n/60
- ◆ Accounts payable: $5,050; Purchases: $5,000; Freight-In, $50

See Figure 10-4 for complete purchases journal.

Note that the normal balance in the accounts payable subsidiary ledger is a credit.

As soon as the information is journalized in the purchases journal (see Fig. 10-4 on p. 360), you should:

1. Record to Abby Blake Co. in the accounts payable subsidiary ledger to indicate that the amount owed is now $5,050. When this is complete, place a (✓) in the PR column of the purchases journal.
2. Post to Freight-In, account no. 514, in the general ledger right away. When this is complete, record the 514 in the PR column under sundry in the purchases journal.

The posting and recording rules are similar to those in the previous chapter, but here we are looking at the buyer rather than at the seller.

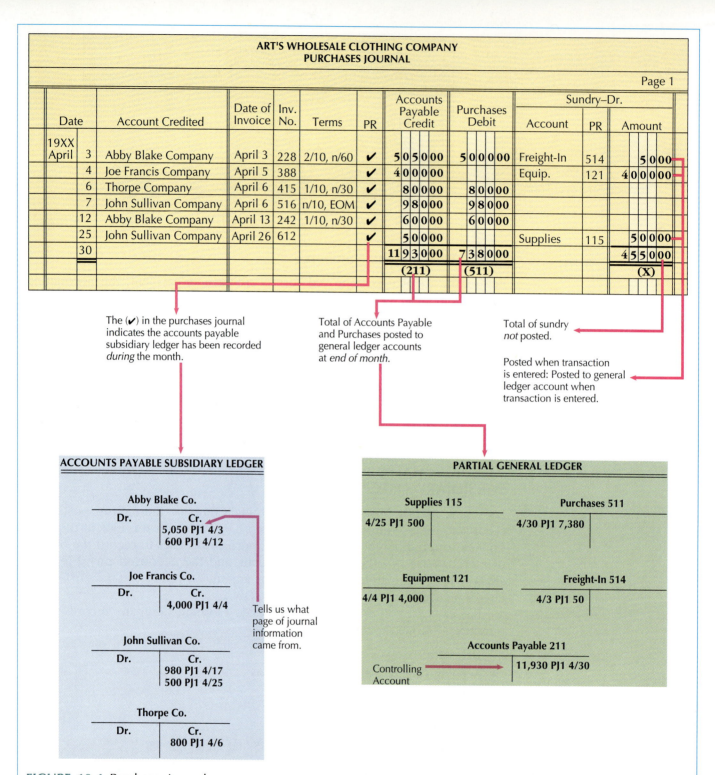

ART'S WHOLESALE CLOTHING COMPANY PURCHASES JOURNAL												
									Sundry–Dr.			Page 1
Date	Account Credited	Date of Invoice	Inv. No.	Terms	PR	Accounts Payable Credit	Purchases Debit		Account	PR	Amount	
19XX April 3	Abby Blake Company	April 3	228	2/10, n/60	✔	5 0 5 0 00	5 0 0 0 00		Freight-In	514	5 0 00	
4	Joe Francis Company	April 5	388		✔	4 0 0 0 00			Equip.	121	4 0 0 0 00	
6	Thorpe Company	April 6	415	1/10, n/30	✔	8 0 0 00	8 0 0 00					
7	John Sullivan Company	April 6	516	n/10, EOM	✔	9 8 0 00	9 8 0 00					
12	Abby Blake Company	April 13	242	1/10, n/30	✔	6 0 0 00	6 0 0 00					
25	John Sullivan Company	April 26	612		✔	5 0 0 00			Supplies	115	5 0 0 00	
30						11 9 3 0 00	7 3 8 0 00				4 5 5 0 00	
						(211)	(511)				(X)	

The (✔) in the purchases journal indicates the accounts payable subsidiary ledger has been recorded *during* the month.

Total of Accounts Payable and Purchases posted to general ledger accounts at *end of month*.

Total of sundry *not* posted.

Posted when transaction is entered: Posted to general ledger account when transaction is entered.

ACCOUNTS PAYABLE SUBSIDIARY LEDGER

Abby Blake Co.

Dr.	Cr.
	5,050 PJ1 4/3
	600 PJ1 4/12

Joe Francis Co.

Dr.	Cr.
	4,000 PJ1 4/4

Tells us what page of journal information came from.

John Sullivan Co.

Dr.	Cr.
	980 PJ1 4/17
	500 PJ1 4/25

Thorpe Co.

Dr.	Cr.
	800 PJ1 4/6

PARTIAL GENERAL LEDGER

Supplies 115
4/25 PJ1 500

Purchases 511
4/30 PJ1 7,380

Equipment 121
4/4 PJ1 4,000

Freight-In 514
4/3 PJ1 50

Accounts Payable 211
Controlling Account → 11,930 PJ1 4/30

FIGURE 10-4 Purchases Journal

THE DEBIT MEMORANDUM

In Chapter 9, Art's Wholesale Clothing Company had to handle returned goods as a seller. It did this by issuing credit memoranda to customers who returned or received an allowance on the price. In this chapter, Art's must handle returns as a buyer. It does this by using debit memoranda. A **debit memorandum** is a

FIGURE 10-5
Debit Memorandum

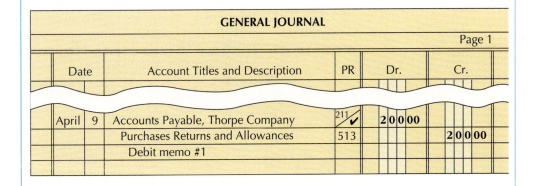

DEBIT MEMORANDUM			No. 1

Art's Wholesale
Clothing Company
1528 Belle Ave.
New York, NY 10022

TO: Thorpe Company   April 9, 19XX
    3 Access Road
    Beverly, MA 01915

WE DEBIT your account as follows:

Quantity		Unit Cost	Total
20	Men's Hats Code 827 – defective brims	$10	$200

piece of paper issued by a customer to a seller. It indicates that a return or allowance has occurred.

Suppose that on April 6 Art's Wholesale had purchased men's hats for $800 from Thorpe Company (p. 360). On April 9, 20 hats valued at $200 were found to have defective brims. Art's issued a debit memorandum to Thorpe Company, as shown in Figure 10-5. At some point in the future, Thorpe will issue Art's a credit memorandum. Let's look at how Art's Wholesale Clothing Company handles such a transaction in its accounting records.

Journalizing and Posting the Debit Memo

First, let's look at a transactional analysis chart.

Accounts Affected	Category	↑	↓	Rules
Accounts Payable	Liability		↓	Dr.
Purchases Returns and Allowances	Contra-cost	↑		Cr.

Next, let's examine the journal entry for the debit memorandum:

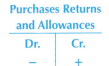

		GENERAL JOURNAL				
						Page 1
	Date	Account Titles and Description	PR	Dr.		Cr.
	April 9	Accounts Payable, Thorpe Company	211✓	2 0 0 00		
		Purchases Returns and Allowances	513			2 0 0 00
		Debit memo #1				

The two postings and one recording are:

1. **211** — Post to Accounts Payable as a debit in the general ledger account no. 211. When this is done, place in the PR column the account number, 211, above the diagonal on the same line as Accounts Payable in the journal.
2. **✓** — Record to Thorpe Co. in the accounts payable subsidiary ledger to show that Art's doesn't owe Thorpe as much money. When this is done, place a (✓) in

the journal in the PR column below the diagonal line on the same line as Accounts Payable in the journal.

3. 513 — Post to Purchases Returns and Allowances as a credit in the general ledger (account no. 513). When this is done, place the account number, 513, in the posting reference column of the journal on the same line as Purchases Returns and Allowances. (If equipment was returned that was not merchandise for resale, we would credit Equipment and not Purchases Returns and Allowances.)

LEARNING UNIT 10-2 REVIEW

AT THIS POINT you should be able to

◆ Explain the relationship between a purchase requisition, a purchase order, and a purchase invoice. (p. 358)
◆ Explain why a typical invoice approval form may be used. (p. 359)
◆ Journalize transactions into a purchases journal. (p. 360)
◆ Explain how to record the accounts payable subsidiary ledger and post to the general ledger from a purchases journal. (p. 360)
◆ Explain a debit memorandum and be able to journalize an entry resulting from its issuance. (p. 361)

SELF-REVIEW QUIZ 10-2

(The forms you need are on pages 333–335 of the *Study Guide and Working Papers.*)

Journalize the following transactions into the purchases journal or general journal for Munroe Co. Record to accounts payable subsidiary ledger and post to general ledger accounts as appropriate. Use the same journal headings we used for Art's Wholesale Clothing Company.

19XX

May 5 Bought merchandise on account from Flynn Co., invoice no. 512, dated May 6, terms 1/10, n/30, $900.

7 Bought merchandise from John Butler Company, invoice no. 403, dated May 7, terms n/10 EOM, $1,000.

13 Issued debit memo no. 1 to Flynn Co. for merchandise returned, $300, from invoice no. 512.

17 Purchased $400 of equipment on account from John Butler Company, invoice no. 413, dated May 18.

Solution to Self-Review Quiz 10-2

Page 2

Date	Account Credited	Date of Invoice	Inv. No.	Terms	PR	Accounts Payable Credit	Purchases Debit	Sundry–Dr.		
								Account	PR	Amount
19XX May 5	Flynn Co.	May 6	512	1/10, n/30	✔	9 0 0 00	9 0 0 00			
7	John Butler	May 7	403	n/10, EOM	✔	1 0 0 0 00	1 0 0 0 00			
17	John Butler	May 18	413		✔	4 0 0 00		Equip.	121	4 0 0 00
31						2 3 0 0 00	1 9 0 0 00			4 0 0 00
						(212)	(512)			(X)

MUNROE CO.
GENERAL JOURNAL

Page 1

Date	Account Titles and Description	PR	Dr.	Cr.
19XX May 13	Accounts Payable, Flynn Co.	212/✔	3 0 0 00	
	Purchases Returns and Allowances	513		3 0 0 00

ACCOUNTS PAYABLE SUBSIDIARY LEDGER

JOHN BUTLER COMPANY
18 REED RD.
HOMEWOOD, ILLINOIS 60430

Date	Explanation	Post. Ref.	Debit	Credit	Cr. Balance
19XX May 7		PJ2		1 0 0 0 00	1 0 0 0 00
17		PJ2		4 0 0 00	1 4 0 0 00

FLYNN COMPANY
15 FOSS AVE.
ENGLEWOOD CLIFFS, NEW JERSEY 07632

Date	Explanation	Post. Ref.	Debit	Credit	Cr. Balance
19XX May 5		PJ2		9 0 0 00	9 0 0 00
13		GJ1	3 0 0 00		6 0 0 00

Equipment   Account No. 121

Date	Explanation	Post. Ref.	Debit	Credit	Balance Debit	Balance Credit
19XX May 17		PJ2	4 0 0 00		4 0 0 00	

Accounts Payable   Account No. 212

Date	Explanation	Post. Ref.	Debit	Credit	Balance Debit	Balance Credit
19XX May 13		GJ1	3 0 0 00		3 0 0 00	
31		PJ2		2 3 0 0 00		2 0 0 0 00

Purchases   Account No. 512

Date	Explanation	Post. Ref.	Debit	Credit	Balance Debit	Balance Credit
19XX May 31		PJ2	1 9 0 0 00		1 9 0 0 00	

Purchases, Returns, and Allowances   Account No. 513

Date	Explanation	Post. Ref.	Debit	Credit	Balance Debit	Balance Credit
19XX May 13		GJ1		3 0 0 00		3 0 0 00

Quiz Tip:

Buyer	*Seller*
Receives Credit Memo	**Issues Credit Memo**
Issues Debit Memo	**Receives Debit Memo**
Dr. Accounts Payable	**Dr. SRA**
Cr. PRA	**Cr. Accounts Receivable**

LEARNING UNIT 10-3
The Cash Payments Journal and Schedule of Accounts Payable

Art's Wholesale Clothing Company will record all payments made in cash (or by check) in a **cash payments journal** (also called a *cash disbursements journal*). In many ways, the structure of this journal resembles that of the cash receipts journal discussed in Chapter 9. Now, however, we are looking at the outward flow of cash instead of the inward flow.

Art's conducted the following cash transactions in April:

19XX

April   2   Issued check no. 1 to Pete Blum for insurance paid in advance, $900.

         7   Issued check no. 2 to Joe Francis Company in payment of its April 5 invoice no. 388.

         9   Issued check no. 3 to Rick Flo Co. for merchandise purchased for cash, $800.

FIGURE 10-6 Cash Payments Journal Recording and Posting

CASH PAYMENTS JOURNAL Page 1

Date		Ck. No.	Account Debited	Post. Ref.	Sundry Accounts Dr.	Accounts Payable Dr.	Purchases Discount Cr.	Cash Cr.
19XX April	2	1	Prepaid Insurance	116	9 0 0 00			9 0 0 00
	7	2	Joe Francis Company	✔		4 0 0 0 00		4 0 0 0 00
	9	3	Purchases	511	8 0 0 00			8 0 0 00
	12	4	Thorpe Company	✔		6 0 0 00	6 00	5 9 4 00
	28	5	Salaries Expense	611	7 0 0 00			7 0 0 00
	30				2 4 0 0 00	4 6 0 0 00	6 00	6 9 9 4 00
					(X)	(211)	(512)	(111)

Recorded Daily
Individual debits to the accounts payable subsidiary ledger are recorded daily. (✔) is placed in PR column when posted.

Total Not Posted
Individual items posted during the month to the general ledger.

Total Posted
Totals posted to the general ledger at the end of the month.

PARTIAL GENERAL LEDGER

Cash   Account No. 111

Date		Explanation	Post. Ref.	Debit	Credit	Balance Debit	Balance Credit
19XX April	30		CRJ1	1 4 3 2 4 00		1 4 3 2 4 00	
	30		CPJ1		6 9 9 4 00	7 3 3 0 00	

Prepaid Insurance   Account No. 116

Date		Explanation	Post. Ref.	Debit	Credit	Balance Debit	Balance Credit
19XX April	2		CPJ1	9 0 0 00		9 0 0 00	

ACCOUNTS PAYABLE SUBSIDIARY LEDGER

NAME Abby Blake Co.
ADDRESS 12 Foster Rd., Englewood Cliffs, New Jersey 07632

Date		Explanation	Post. Ref.	Debit	Credit	Cr. Balance
19XX April	3		PJ1		5 0 5 0 00	5 0 5 0 00
	12		PJ1		6 0 0 00	5 6 5 0 00

NAME Joe Francis Co.
ADDRESS 2 Roundy Rd., Cincinnati, Ohio 45200

Date		Explanation	Post. Ref.	Debit	Credit	Cr. Balance
19XX April	4		PJ1		4 0 0 0 00	4 0 0 0 00
	7		CPJ1	4 0 0 0 00		– 0 –

FIGURE 10-6 (cont.)

Controlling Account →

Accounts Payable Account No. 211

Date	Explanation	Post. Ref.	Debit	Credit	Balance Debit	Balance Credit
19XX April 9		GJ1	200 00		200 00	
30		PJ1		11930 00		11730 00
30		CPJ1	4600 00			7130 00

Purchases Account No. 511

Date	Explanation	Post. Ref.	Debit	Credit	Balance Debit	Balance Credit
19XX April 9		CPJ1	800 00		800 00	
30		PJ1	7380 00		8180 00	

Purchases Discount Account No. 512

Date	Explanation	Post. Ref.	Debit	Credit	Balance Debit	Balance Credit
19XX April 30		CPJ1		6 00		6 00

Salaries Expense Account No. 611

Date	Explanation	Post. Ref.	Debit	Credit	Balance Debit	Balance Credit
19XX April 28		CPJ1	700 00		700 00	

NAME John Sullivan Co.
ADDRESS 18 Print St., Wellesley, Mass. 01980

Date	Explanation	Post. Ref.	Debit	Credit	Cr. Balance
19XX April 7		PJ1		980 00	980 00
25		PJ1		500 00	1480 00

NAME Thorpe Co.
ADDRESS 3 Access Rd., Chicago, Illinois 60430

Date	Explanation	Post. Ref.	Debit	Credit	Cr. Balance
19XX April 6		PJ1		800 00	800 00
9		GJ1	200 00		600 00
12		CPJ1	600 00		-0-

12 Issued check no. 4 to Thorpe Company in payment of its April 6 invoice no. 414 less the return and discount.
28 Issued check no. 5, $700, for salaries paid.

Posting and recording rules for this journal are similar to those for the cash receipts journal in Chapter 9.

The diagram in Figure 10-6 on pages 365–366 shows the cash payments journal for the end of April along with the recordings to the accounts payable subsidiary ledger and postings to the general ledger. Study the diagram; we will review it in a moment.

JOURNALIZING, POSTING, AND RECORDING FROM THE CASH PAYMENTS JOURNAL TO THE ACCOUNTS PAYABLE SUBSIDIARY LEDGER AND THE GENERAL LEDGER

Figure 10-6 shows how Art's Wholesale Clothing Company recorded the payment of cash on April 12 to Thorpe Company. The purchases journal shows that Art's purchased $800 of merchandise from Thorpe on account on April 6. The amount Art's owes is discounted 1 percent. The amount owed ($800 − $200 returns) is recorded in the accounts payable subsidiary ledger as soon as the entry is made in the cash payments journal. The payment reduces the balance to Thorpe to zero. Art's Wholesale Clothing Company receives a $6 purchases discount.

As explained in Chapter 9, Sundry is a miscellaneous accounts column that provides flexibility for reporting infrequent transactions that result in an inflow of cash.

At the end of the month the totals of the Cash, Purchases Discount, and Accounts Payable accounts are posted to the general ledger. The total of sundry is *not* posted. The accounts Prepaid Insurance, Purchases, and Salaries Expense are posted to the general ledger at the time the entry is put in the journal.

The cash payments journal of Art's Wholesale Clothing Company can be crossfooted as follows:

Remember, there is no discount on sales tax or freight.

$$\text{Debit} = \text{Credit Columns}$$
$$\text{Sundry} + \text{Accounts Payable} = \text{Purchases Discounts} + \text{Cash}$$
$$\$2,400 + \$4,600 \qquad = \$6 \qquad\qquad + \$6,994$$
$$\underline{\$7,000} = \underline{\$7,000}$$

Schedule of Accounts Payable

Now let's prove that the sum of the accounts payable subsidiary ledger at the end of the month is equal to the controlling account, Accounts Payable, at the end of April for Art's Wholesale Clothing Company. To do this, creditors with an ending balance in Art's accounts payable subsidiary ledger must be listed in the schedule of accounts payable (see Fig. 10-7). At the end of the month the total owed ($7,130) in Accounts Payable, the **controlling account** in the general ledger, should equal the sum owed the individual creditors that are listed on the schedule of accounts payable. If it doesn't, the journalizing, posting, and recording must be checked to ensure that they are complete. Also, the balances of each title should be checked.

FIGURE 10-7
Schedule of Accounts Payable

ART'S WHOLESALE CLOTHING COMPANY SCHEDULE OF ACCOUNTS PAYABLE APRIL 30, 19XX	
Abby Blake Co.	$5 6 5 0 00
John Sullivan Co.	1 4 8 0 00
Total Accounts Payable	$7 1 3 0 00

Trade Discounts

Trade discounts are reductions from the purchase price. Usually, they are given to customers who buy items to resell or to use to produce other salable goods.

Amount of Trade Discount = List Price − Net Price

Different trade discounts are available to different classes of customers. Often, trade discounts are listed in catalogs that contain the list price and the amount of trade discount available. Such catalogs usually are updated by discount sheets.

Trade discounts have *no relationship* to whether a customer is paying a bill early. Trade discounts and list prices are not shown in the accounts of either the purchaser or the seller. Cash discounts are not taken on the amount of trade discount.

For example, look at the following:

- List price, $800
- 30% Trade discount
- 5% Cash discount
- Thus: Invoice cost of $560 ($800 − $240) less the cash discount of $28 ($560 × .05) results in a final cost of $532 if the cash discount is taken.

The purchaser as well as the seller would record the invoice amount at $560.

> **Trade discounts are not reflected on the books.**

LEARNING UNIT 10-3 REVIEW

AT THIS POINT you should be able to

- Journalize, post, and record transactions utilizing a cash payments journal. (p. 365)
- Prepare a schedule of accounts payable. (p. 367)
- Compare and contrast a cash discount to a trade discount. (p. 367)

SELF-REVIEW QUIZ 10-3

(The forms you need are on pages 335–337 of the *Study Guide and Working Papers*.)

Given the following information, journalize, crossfoot, and when appropriate record and post the transactions of Melissa Company. Use the same headings as used for Art's Clothing. All purchases discounts are 2/12, n/30. The cash payments journal is page 2.

ACCOUNTS PAYABLE SUBSIDIARY LEDGER

Name	Balance	Invoice No.
Bob Finkelstein	$300	488
Al Jeep	200	410

PARTIAL GENERAL LEDGER

Account No.	Balance
Cash 110	$700
Accounts Payable 210	500
Purchases Discount 511	——
Advertising Expense 610	——

19XX

June 1 Issued check no. 15 to Al Jeep in payment of its May 25 invoice no. 410 less purchases discount.

8 Issued check no. 16 to Moss Advertising Co. to pay advertising bill due, $75, no discount.

9 Issued check no. 17 to Bob Finkelstein in payment of its May 28 invoice no. 488 less purchases discount.

Solution to Self-Review Quiz 10-3

MELISSA COMPANY
CASH PAYMENTS JOURNAL

Page 2

Date	Ck. No.	Account Debited	Post. Ref.	Sundry Accounts Dr.	Accounts Payable Dr.	Purchases Discount Cr.	Cash Cr.
19XX June 1	15	Al Jeep	✔		2 0 0 00	4 00	1 9 6 00
8	16	Advertising Expense	610	7 5 00			7 5 00
9	17	Bob Finkelstein	✔		3 0 0 00	6 00	2 9 4 00
30				7 5 00	5 0 0 00	1 0 00	5 6 5 00
				(X)	(210)	(511)	(110)

$75 + $500 = $10 + $565
$575 = $575

ACCOUNTS PAYABLE SUBSIDIARY LEDGER

NAME Bob Finkelstein
ADDRESS 112 Flying Highway, Trenton, New Jersey 08611

Date	Explanation	Post. Ref.	Debit	Credit	Cr. Balance
19XX June 1	Balance	✔			3 0 0 00
9		CPJ2	3 0 0 00		–0–

NAME Al Jeep
ADDRESS 118 Wang Rd., Saugus, Mass. 01432

Date	Explanation	Post. Ref.	Debit	Credit	Cr. Balance
19XX June 1	Balance	✔			2 0 0 00
1		CPJ2	2 0 0 00		–0–

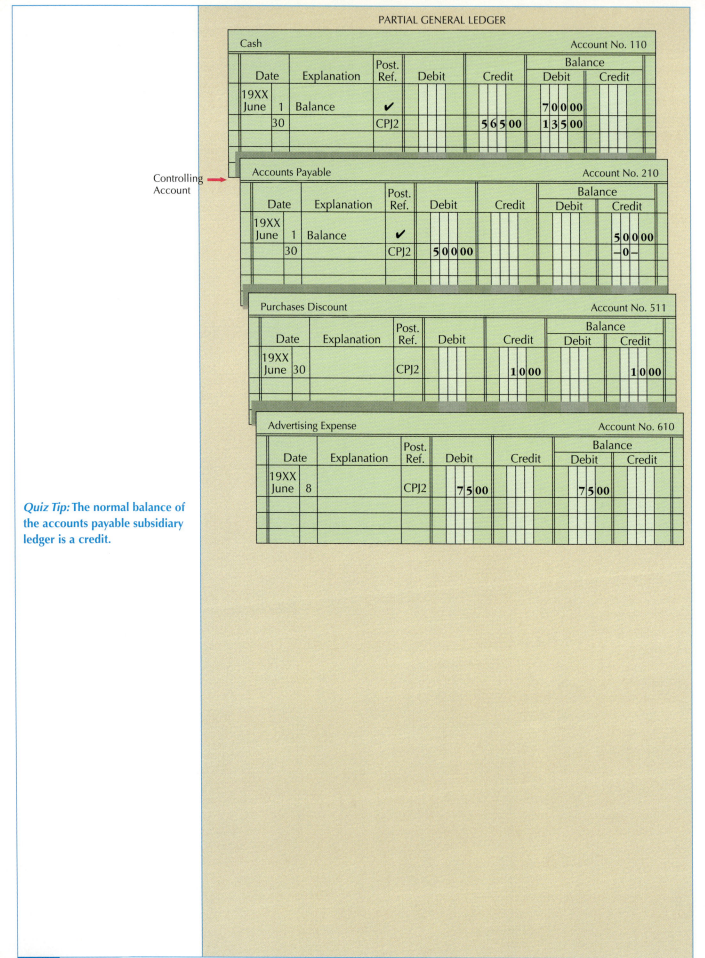

Cash — Account No. 110

Date		Explanation	Post. Ref.	Debit	Credit	Balance Debit	Balance Credit
19XX June	1	Balance	✔			700 00	
	30		CPJ2		565 00	135 00	

Accounts Payable — Account No. 210

Controlling Account →

Date		Explanation	Post. Ref.	Debit	Credit	Balance Debit	Balance Credit
19XX June	1	Balance	✔				500 00
	30		CPJ2	500 00			–0–

Purchases Discount — Account No. 511

Date		Explanation	Post. Ref.	Debit	Credit	Balance Debit	Balance Credit
19XX June	30		CPJ2		10 00		10 00

Advertising Expense — Account No. 610

Date		Explanation	Post. Ref.	Debit	Credit	Balance Debit	Balance Credit
19XX June	8		CPJ2	75 00		75 00	

Quiz Tip: **The normal balance of the accounts payable subsidiary ledger is a credit.**

COMPREHENSIVE DEMONSTRATION PROBLEM WITH SOLUTION TIPS

(The forms you need are on pages 338–340 of the *Study Guide and Working Papers*.)

Record the following transactions into special or general journals. Record and post as appropriate.

Note: All credit sales are 2/10, n/30. All merchandise purchased on account has 3/10, n/30 credit terms.

Solution Tips to Journalizing

		19XX	
CRJ	March	1	J. Ling invested $2,000 into the business.
SJ		1	Sold merchandise on account to Balder Co., $500, invoice no. 1.
PJ		2	Purchased merchandise on account from Case Co., $500.
CRJ		4	Sold $2,000 of merchandise for cash.
CPJ		6	Paid Case Co. from previous purchases on account, check no. 1.
SJ		8	Sold merchandise on account to Lewis Co., $1,000, invoice no. 2.
CRJ		10	Received payment from Balder for invoice no. 1.
GJ		12	Issued a credit memorandum to Lewis Co. for $200 for faulty merchandise.
CRJ		14	Received payment from Lewis Co.
PJ		16	Purchased merchandise on account from Noone Co., $1,000.
PJ		17	Purchased equipment on account from Case Co., $300.
GJ		18	Issued a debit memorandum to Noone Co. for $500 for defective merchandise.
CPJ		20	Paid salaries, $300, check no. 2.
CPJ		24	Paid Noone balance owed, check no. 3.

Record Accounts Receivable Subsidiary Ledger immediately.

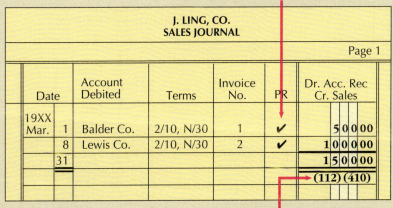

J. LING, CO.
SALES JOURNAL

Page 1

Date		Account Debited	Terms	Invoice No.	PR	Dr. Acc. Rec Cr. Sales
19XX Mar.	1	Balder Co.	2/10, N/30	1	✔	5 0 0 00
	8	Lewis Co.	2/10, N/30	2	✔	1 0 0 0 00
	31					1 5 0 0 00
						(112) (410)

Total posted at end of month to these accounts.

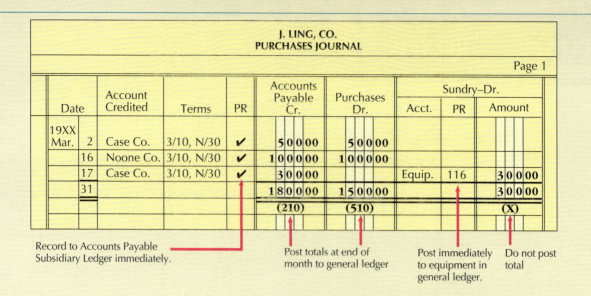

J. LING, CO.
PURCHASES JOURNAL

Page 1

Date	Account Credited	Terms	PR	Accounts Payable Cr.	Purchases Dr.	Sundry–Dr. Acct.	PR	Amount
19XX Mar. 2	Case Co.	3/10, N/30	✔	500 00	500 00			
16	Noone Co.	3/10, N/30	✔	1000 00	1000 00			
17	Case Co.	3/10, N/30	✔	300 00		Equip.	116	300 00
31				1800 00	1500 00			300 00
				(210)	(510)			(X)

Record to Accounts Payable Subsidiary Ledger immediately.

Post totals at end of month to general ledger

Post immediately to equipment in general ledger.

Do not post total

Post to capital immediately.

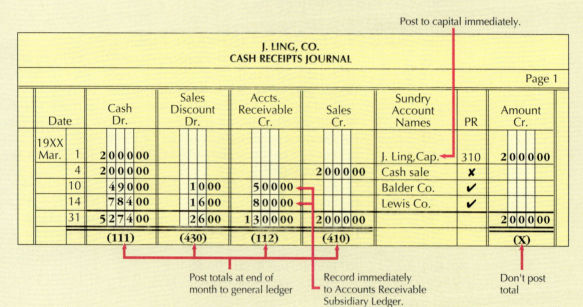

J. LING, CO.
CASH RECEIPTS JOURNAL

Page 1

Date	Cash Dr.	Sales Discount Dr.	Accts. Receivable Cr.	Sales Cr.	Sundry Account Names	PR	Amount Cr.
19XX Mar. 1	2000 00				J. Ling, Cap.	310	2000 00
4	2000 00			2000 00	Cash sale	✗	
10	490 00	10 00	500 00		Balder Co.	✔	
14	784 00	16 00	800 00		Lewis Co.	✔	
31	5274 00	26 00	1300 00	2000 00			2000 00
	(111)	(430)	(112)	(410)			(X)

Post totals at end of month to general ledger

Record immediately to Accounts Receivable Subsidiary Ledger.

Don't post total

Record immediately to Accounts Payable Subsidiary ledger.

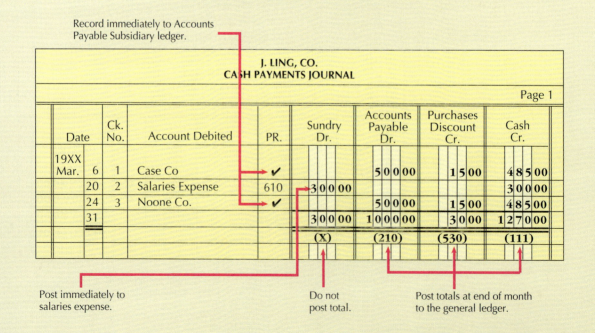

J. LING, CO.
CASH PAYMENTS JOURNAL

Page 1

Date	Ck. No.	Account Debited	PR.	Sundry Dr.	Accounts Payable Dr.	Purchases Discount Cr.	Cash Cr.
19XX Mar. 6	1	Case Co	✔		500 00	15 00	485 00
20	2	Salaries Expense	610	300 00			300 00
24	3	Noone Co.	✔		500 00	15 00	485 00
31				300 00	1000 00	30 00	1270 00
				(X)	(210)	(530)	(111)

Post immediately to salaries expense.

Do not post total.

Post totals at end of month to the general ledger.

GENERAL JOURNAL   Page 1

Date		Account Titles and Description	PR	Dr.	Cr.
19XX Mar.	12	Sales Returns and Allowances	420	200 00	
		Accounts Receivable, Lewis Co.	112 ✓		200 00
		Issued Credit Memo			
	18	Accounts Payable, Noone Co.	210 ✓	500 00	
		Purchases Returns and Allowances	520		500 00
		Issued Debit Memo			

Record and post immediately to Subsidiary and General Ledger.

ACCOUNTS RECEIVABLE SUBSIDIARY LEDGER

Balder Company

Date	PR	Dr.	Cr.	Dr. Bal.
19XX 3/1	SJ1	500		500
3/10	CRJ1		500	——

Lewis Company

Date	PR	Dr.	Cr.	Dr. Bal.
19XX 3/8	SJ1	1,000		1,000
3/12	GJ1		200	800
3/14	CPJ1		800	——

ACCOUNTS PAYABLE SUBSIDIARY LEDGER

Case Company

Date	PR	Dr.	Cr.	Cr. Bal.
19XX 3/2	PJ1		500	500
3/6	CPJ1	500		——
3/17	PJ1		300	300

Noone Company

Date	PR	Dr.	Cr.	Cr. Bal.
19XX 3/16	PJ1		1,000	1,000
3/18	GJ1	500		500
3/24	CPJ1	500		——

GENERAL LEDGER

Cash 111

3/31 CRJ1 5,274	1,270 3/31 CPJ1
Balance 4,004	

Sales 410

	1,500 3/31 SJ1
	2,000 3/31 CRJ1
	3,500 Balance

Accounts Receivable 112

3/31 SJ1 1,500	200 3/12 GJ1
Balance 0	1,300 3/31 CRJ1

Sales Returns + Allowances 420

3/12 GJ1 200	

Equipment 116

3/17 PJ1 300	

Sales Discount 430

3/31 CRJ1 26	

Accounts Payable 210		Purchases 510	
3/18 GJ1 500	1,800 3/31 PJ1	3/31 PJ1 1,500	
3/31 CPJ1 1,000			
	300 Balance		

J. Ling, Capital 310		Purchase Ret. + Allow. 520	
	2,000 3/1 CRJ1		500 3/18 GJ1

		Purchase Discount 530	
			30 3/31 CPJ1

		Salaries Expense 610	
		3/20 CPJ1 300	

Summary of Solution Tips

Chapter 9 — Seller	Chapter 10 — Buyer
Sales Journal	Purchases Journal
Cash Receipts Journal	Cash Payments Journal
Accounts Receivable Subsidiary Ledger	Accounts Payable Subsidiary Ledger
Sales (Cr.)	Purchases (Dr.)
Sales Returns + Allowances (Dr.)	Purchase Returns + Allowances (Cr.)
Sales Discounts (Dr.)	Purchase Discounts (Cr.)
Accounts Receivable (Dr.)	Accounts Payable (Cr.)
Issue a Credit Memo	Receive a Credit Memo
or	or
Receive a Debit Memo	Issue a Debit Memo
Schedule of Accounts Receivable	Schedule of Accounts Payable

When Do I Do What?

A Step-by-Step Walk-Through of This Comprehensive Demonstration Problem

Transaction	What to Do Step by Step
19XX	
March 1	*Money Received:* Record in Cash Receipts Journal. Post immediately to J. Ling, Capital, since it is in Sundry.
1	*Sale on Account:* Record in Sales Journal. Record immediately to Balder Co., in Accounts Receivable Subsidiary Ledger. Place a (✓) in PR column of Sales Journal when subsidiary is updated.
2	*Buy Merchandise on Account:* Record in Purchases Journal. Record to Case Co. immediately in the Accounts Payable Subsidiary Ledger.
4	*Money In:* Record in Cash Receipts Journal. No posting needed (Put an X in PR column.)
6	*Money Out:* Record in Cash Payments Journal. Save $15, which is a Purchase Discount. Record immediately to Case Co. in Accounts Payable Subsidiary Ledger (the full amount of $500).

Transaction	What to Do Step by Step
8	**Sales on Account:** Record in Sales Journal. Update immediately to Lewis in Accounts Receivable Subsidiary Ledger.
10	**Money In:** Record in Cash Receipts Journal. Since Balder pays within 10 days, they get a $10 discount. Record immediately to Balder in the Accounts Receivable Subsidiary Ledger, the full amount.
12	**Returns:** Record in General Journal. Seller issues credit memo resulting in higher sales returns and customers owing less. All postings and recordings are done immediately.
14	**Money In:** Record in Cash Receipts Journal:

$$\begin{array}{r} \$1,000 - \$200 \text{ returns} = \$800 \\ \times .02 \\ \hline \$\ 16 \text{ discount} \end{array}$$

Record immediately the $800 to Lewis in the Accounts Receivable Subsidiary Ledger.

16	*Buy Now, Pay Later:* Record in Purchases Journal. Record immediately to Noone Co. in the Accounts Payable Subsidiary Ledger.
17	*Buy Now, Pay Later:* Record in Purchases Journal in Sundry. This is not merchandise for resale. Record and Post immediately.
18	*Returns:* Record in General Journal. Buyer issues a debit memo reducing their Accounts Payable due to Purchases Return and Allowances. Post and Record immediately.
20	*Salaries:* Record in Cash Payments Journal, Sundry column. Post immediately to Salaries Expense.
24	*Money Out:* Record in Cash Payments Journal. Save 3 percent — $15, a Purchase Discount. Record immediately to Accounts Payable Subsidiary Ledger that you reduce Noone by $500.

End of Month: Post totals (except Sundry) of Special Journal to the General Ledger.

Note: In this problem at end of month (1) Accounts Receivable in the General Ledger, the controlling account, has a zero balance, as does each title in the Accounts Receivable Subsidiary Ledger. (2) The Balance in Accounts Payable (the controlling account) is $300. In the Accounts Payable Subsidiary Ledger, we owe Case $300. The sum of the Subsidiary does equal the balance in the controlling account at the end of the month.

SUMMARY OF KEY POINTS

Learning Unit 10-1

1. Purchases are merchandise for resale. It is a cost.

2. Purchases Returns and Allowances and Purchases Discount are contra-cost.

3. *F.O.B. shipping point* means that the purchaser of the goods is responsible for covering the shipping costs. If the terms were *F.O.B. destination,* the seller would be responsible for covering the shipping costs until the goods reached their destination.

4. Purchases discounts are not taken on freight.

1. The steps for buying merchandise from a company may include:
   a. The requesting department prepares a purchase requisition.
   b. The purchasing department prepares a purchase order.
   c. Seller receives the order and prepares a sales invoice (a purchase invoice for the buyer).
   d. Buyer receives the goods and prepares a receiving report.
   e. Accounting department verifies and approves the invoice for payment.
2. The purchases journal records the buying of merchandise or other items on account.
3. The accounts payable subsidiary ledger, organized in alphabetical order, is not in the same book as Accounts Payable, the controlling account in the general ledger.
4. At the end of the month the total of all creditors' ending balances in the accounts payable subsidiary ledger should equal the ending balance in Accounts Payable, the controlling account in the general ledger.
5. A debit memorandum (issued by the buyer) indicates that the amount owed from a previous purchase is being reduced because some goods were defective or not up to a specific standard and thus were returned or an allowance requested. On receiving the debit memorandum, the seller will issue a credit memorandum.

Learning Unit 10-3

1. All payments of cash (check) are recorded in the cash payments journal.
2. At the end of the month, the schedule of accounts payable, a list of ending amounts owed individual creditors, should equal the ending balance in Accounts Payable, the controlling account in the general ledger.
3. Trade discounts are deductions off the list price that have nothing to do with early payments (cash discounts). Invoice amounts are recorded *after* the trade discount is deducted. Cash discounts are not taken on trade discounts.

KEY TERMS

Accounts payable subsidiary ledger A book or file that contains in alphabetical order the name of the creditor and amount owed from purchases on account.

Cash payments journal (Cash disbursements journal) A special journal that records all transactions involving the payment of cash.

Controlling account The account in the general ledger that summarizes or controls a subsidiary ledger. Example: The Accounts Payable account in the general ledger is the controlling account for the accounts payable subsidiary ledger. After postings are complete, it shows the total amount owed from purchases made on account.

Debit memorandum A memo issued by a purchaser to a seller, indicating that some Purchases Returns and Allowances have occurred and therefore the purchaser now owes less money on account.

F.O.B. Free on Board, which means without shipping charge either to the buyer or seller up to or from a specified location. In the view of one or the other, the shipment is *free* on board the carrier.

F.O.B. destination *Seller* pays or is responsible for the cost of freight to purchaser's location or destination.

F.O.B. shipping point *Purchaser* pays or is responsible for the shipping costs from seller's shipping point to purchaser's location.

Invoice approval form The accounting department uses this form in checking the invoice and finally approving it for recording and payment.

Purchases Merchandise for resale. It is a cost.

Purchases Discount A contra-cost account in the general ledger that records discounts offered by suppliers of merchandise for prompt payment of purchases by buyers.

Purchase invoice The seller's sales invoice, which is sent to the purchaser.

Purchases journal A multicolumn special journal that records the buying of merchandise or other items on account.

Purchase order A form used in business to place an order for the buying of goods from a seller.

Purchase requisition A form used within a business by the requesting department asking the purchasing department of the business to buy specific goods.

Purchases Returns and Allowances A contra-cost account in the ledger that records the amount of defective or unacceptable merchandise returned to suppliers and/or price reductions given for defective items.

Receiving report A business form used to notify the appropriate people of the ordered goods received along with the quantities and specific condition of the goods.

QUESTIONS, MINI EXERCISES, EXERCISES, AND PROBLEMS

Discussion Questions

1. Explain how net purchases is calculated.
2. What is the normal balance of Purchases Discount?
3. What is a contra-cost?
4. Explain the difference between F.O.B. shipping point and F.O.B. destination.
5. F.O.B. destination means that title to the goods will switch to the buyer when goods are shipped. Agree or disagree. Why?
6. What is the normal balance of each creditor in the accounts payable subsidiary ledger?
7. Why doesn't the balance of the controlling account, Accounts Payable, equal the sum of the accounts payable subsidiary ledger during the month?
8. What is the relationship between a purchase requisition and a purchase order?
9. What purpose could a typical invoice approval form serve?
10. Explain the difference between merchandise and equipment.
11. Why would the purchaser issue a debit memorandum?
12. Explain the relationship between a purchases journal and a cash payments journal.
13. Explain why a trade discount is not a cash discount.

Mini Exercises

(The forms you need are on page 342 of the *Study Guide and Working Papers.*)

Overview

1. Complete the following table:

To the Seller		To the Buyer
Sales	↔	a. _____
Sales Returns and Allowances	↔	b. _____
Sales Discount	↔	c. _____
Sales Journal	↔	d. _____
Cash Receipts Journal	↔	e. _____
Credit Memorandum	↔	f. _____
Schedule of Accounts Receivable	↔	g. _____
Accounts Receivable Subsidiary Ledger	↔	h. _____

BLUEPRINT OF PURCHASES AND CASH PAYMENTS JOURNALS

Purchase of Merchandise or Other Items on Account

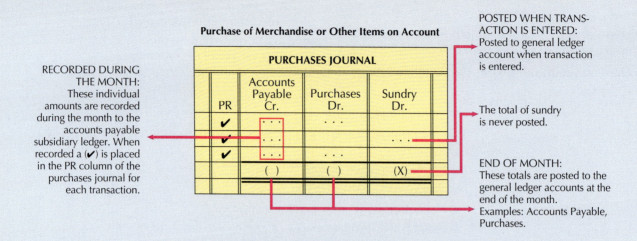

RECORDED DURING THE MONTH: These individual amounts are recorded during the month to the accounts payable subsidiary ledger. When recorded a (✔) is placed in the PR column of the purchases journal for each transaction.

POSTED WHEN TRANSACTION IS ENTERED: Posted to general ledger account when transaction is entered.

The total of sundry is never posted.

END OF MONTH: These totals are posted to the general ledger accounts at the end of the month. Examples: Accounts Payable, Purchases.

Issuing a Debit Memo (or Receiving a Credit Memo)

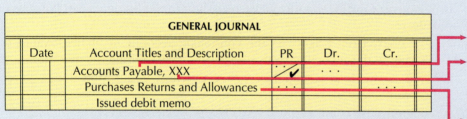

POSTED AND RECORDED WHEN TRANSACTION IS ENTERED Two postings and one recording:
1. Posted to Accounts Payable in the general ledger.
2. Recorded to XXX in the accounts payable subsidiary ledger. A (✔) indicates recording to the accounts payable subsidiary ledger is complete.
3. Posted to Purchases Returns and Allowances in general ledger.

Outward Flow of Cash

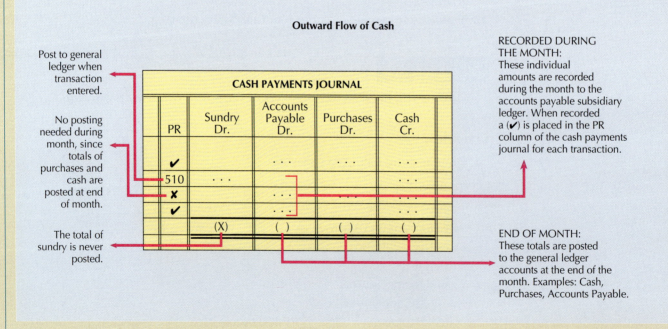

Post to general ledger when transaction entered.

No posting needed during month, since totals of purchases and cash are posted at end of month.

The total of sundry is never posted.

RECORDED DURING THE MONTH: These individual amounts are recorded during the month to the accounts payable subsidiary ledger. When recorded a (✔) is placed in the PR column of the cash payments journal for each transaction.

END OF MONTH: These totals are posted to the general ledger accounts at the end of the month. Examples: Cash, Purchases, Accounts Payable.

2. Complete the following table:

	Category	↑	↓	Temporary or Permanent
Purchases				
Purchases Returns and Allowances				
Purchases Discount				

Calculating Net Purchases

3. Calculate Net Purchases from the following: Purchases, $6; Purchases Returns and Allowances, $2; Purchases Discounts, $1.

Purchases Journal, General Journal, Recording and Posting

4. Match the following to the three journal entries (more than one number can be used).

> 1. Journalized into Purchases Journal.
> 2. Record immediately to Subsidiary Ledger.
> 3. Post totals from Purchases Journal (except Sundry total) at end of month to General Ledger.
> 4. Journalized in General Journal.
> 5. Record and post immediately to Subsidiary and General Ledger.

    a. Bought merchandise on account from Also Co., invoice no. 12, $20.

    b. Bought Equipment on account from Jone Co., invoice no. 13, $40.

    c. Issued debit memo no. 1 to Also Co. for merchandise returned, $4, from invoice no. 12.

Recording Transactions in Special Journals

5. Indicate in which journal each transaction will be journalized:

1. SJ   **4.** CPJ

2. PJ   **5.** GJ

3. CRJ

_____   **a.** Issued credit memo no. 2, $13.

_____   **b.** Cash sales, $20.

_____   **c.** Received check from Blue Co., $50 less 3 percent discount.

_____   **d.** Bought merchandise on account from Mel Co., $35, 1/10, n/30, invoice no. 20.

_____   **e.** Cash Purchase, $15.

_____   **f.** Issued debit memo to Mel Co., $15 for merchandise returned from invoice no. 20.

6. From the following prepare a schedule of Accounts Payable for AVE Co. for May 31, 19XX:

Accounts Payable Subsidiary Ledger

Rowe Co.

	5/7	PJ1	60

Bloss Co.

5/25	CPJ1	10	5/20	PJ1	50	

General Ledger

Accounts Payable

5/31	CPJ	10	5/31	PJ1	110	

Exercises

(The forms you need are on pages 343–345 of the *Study Guide and Working Papers*.)

10-1. From the accompanying purchases journal, please record to the accounts payable subsidiary ledger and post to general ledger accounts as appropriate.

PURCHASES JOURNAL

Page 1

Date	Account Credited	Date of Invoice	Terms	Post Ref.	Accounts Payable Credit	Purchases Debit	Sundry-Dr. Account	PR	Sundry-Dr. Amount
19XX June 3	Barr Co.	May 3	1/10, n/30		600 00	600 00			
4	Jess Co.	May 4	n/10, EOM		900 00	900 00			
8	Rey Co.	May 8			400 00		Equipment		400 00

Recording to the accounts payable subsidiary ledger and posting to the general ledger from a purchases journal.

Partial Accounts Payable Subsidiary Ledger

Barr Co.

Jess Co.

Rey Co.

Partial General Ledger

Equipment 120

Accounts Payable 210

Purchases 510

Journalizing, recording, and posting a debit memorandum.

10-2. On July 10, 19XX, Aster Co. issued debit memorandum no. 1 for $400 to Reel Co. for merchandise returned from invoice no. 312. Your task is to journalize, record, and post this transaction as appropriate. Use the same account numbers as found in the text for Art's Wholesale Clothing Company. The general journal is page 1.

Journalizing, recording, and posting a cash payments journal.

10-3. Journalize, record, and post when appropriate the following transactions into the cash payments journal (p. 2) for Morgan's Clothing. Use the same headings as found in the text (p. 365). All purchases discounts are 2/10, n/30.

ACCOUNTS PAYABLE SUBSIDIARY LEDGER

Name	Balance	Invoice No.
A. James	$1,000	522
B. Foss	400	488
J. Ranch	900	562
B. Swanson	100	821

PARTIAL GENERAL LEDGER

Account	Balance
Cash 110	$3,000
Accounts Payable 210	2,400
Purchases Discount 511	
Advertising Expense 610	

19XX

April 1 Issued check no. 20 to A. James Company in payment of its March 28 invoice no. 522.

8 Issued check no. 21 to Flott Advertising in payment of its advertising bill, $100, no discount.

15 Issued check no. 22 to B. Foss in payment of its March 25 invoice no. 488.

Schedule of accounts payable.

10-4. From Exercise 10-3, prepare a schedule of accounts payable and verify that the total of the schedule equals the amount in the controlling account.

F.O.B. destination.

10-5. Record the following transaction in a transaction analysis chart for the buyer: Bought merchandise for $9,000 on account. Shipping terms were F.O.B. destination. The cost of shipping was $500.

Trade and cash discounts.

10-6. Angie Rase bought merchandise with a list price of $4,000. Angie was entitled to a 30 percent trade discount, as well as a 3 percent cash discount. What was Angie's actual cost of buying this merchandise after the cash discount?

Group A Problems

(The forms you need are on pages 346–367 of the *Study Guide and Working Papers*.)

Journalizing, recording, and posting a purchases journal.

10A-1. Judy Clark recently opened a sporting goods shop. As the bookkeeper of her shop, please journalize, record, and post when appropriate the following transactions (account numbers are: Store Supplies, 115; Store Equipment, 121; Accounts Payable, 210; Purchases, 510):

19XX

Check Figure:

Total of Purchases Column $2,300

June 4 Bought merchandise on account from Aster Co., invoice no. 442, dated June 5, terms 2/10, n/30, $900.

5 Bought store equipment from Norton Co., invoice no. 502, dated June 6, $4,000.

8 Bought merchandise on account from Rolo Co., invoice no. 401, dated June 9; terms 2/10, n/30, $1,400.

14 Bought store supplies on account from Aster Co., invoice no. 419, dated June 14, $900.

10A-2. Mabel's Natural Food Store uses a purchases journal (p. 10) and a general journal (p. 2) to record the following transactions (continued from April):

19XX

Journalizing, recording, and posting a purchases journal as well as recording debit memorandum and preparing a schedule of accounts payable.

May 8 Purchased merchandise on account from Aton Co., invoice no. 400, dated May 9, terms 2/10, n/60, $600.

10 Purchased merchandise on account from Broward Co., invoice no. 420, dated May 11, terms 2/10, n/60, $1,200.

12 Purchased store supplies on account from Midden Co., invoice no. 510, dated May 13, $500.

14 Issued debit memo no. 8 to Aton Co. for merchandise returned, $400, from invoice no. 400.

17 Purchased office equipment on account from Relar Co., invoice no. 810, dated May 18, $560.

24 Purchased additional store supplies on account from Midden Co., invoice no. 516, dated May 25, terms 2/10, n/30, $650.

The food store has decided to keep a separate column for the purchases of supplies in the purchases journal. Your task is to

1. Journalize the transactions.

2. Post and record as appropriate.

3. Prepare a schedule of accounts payable.

ACCOUNTS PAYABLE SUBSIDIARY LEDGER

Name	Balance
Aton Co.	$ 400
Broward Co.	600
Midden Co.	1,200
Relar Co.	500

PARTIAL GENERAL LEDGER

Account	Number	Balance
Store Supplies	110	$ —
Office Equipment	120	—
Accounts Payable	210	2,700
Purchases	510	16,000
Purchases Returns and Allowances	512	—

Journalizing, recording, and posting a cash payments journal. Preparing a schedule of accounts payable.

Check Figure:

Total of Schedule of Accounts
Payable $1,900

10A-3. Wendy Jones operates a wholesale computer center. All transactions requiring the payment of cash are recorded in the cash payments journal (p. 5). The account balances as of May 1, 19XX, are as follows:

ACCOUNTS PAYABLE SUBSIDIARY LEDGER

Name	Balance
Alvin Co.	$1,200
Henry Co.	600
Soy Co.	800
Xon Co.	1,400

PARTIAL GENERAL LEDGER

Account	Number	Balance
Cash	110	$17,000
Delivery Truck	150	—
Accounts Payable	210	4,000
Computer Purchases	510	—
Computer Purchases Discount	511	—
Rent Expense	610	—
Utilities Expense	620	—

Your task is to

1. Journalize the following transactions.

2. Record to the accounts payable subsidiary ledger and post to general ledger as appropriate.

3. Prepare a schedule of accounts payable.

19XX

May 1 Paid half the amount owed Henry Co. from previous purchases of appliances on account, less a 2 percent purchases discount, check no. 21.

3 Bought a delivery truck for $8,000 cash, check no. 22, payable to Bill Ring Co.

6 Bought computer merchandise from Lectro Co., check no. 23, $2,900.

18 Bought additional computer merchandise from Pulse Co., check no. 24, $800.

24 Paid Xon Co. the amount owed less a 2 percent purchases discount, check no. 25.

28 Paid rent expense to King's Realty Trust, check no. 26, $2,000.

29 Paid utilities expense to Stone Utility Co., check no. 27, $300.

30 Paid half the amount owed Soy Co., no discount, check no. 28.

10A-4. Abby Ellen opened Abby's Toy House. As her newly hired accountant, your task is to

1. Journalize the transactions for the month of March.

2. Record to subsidiary ledgers and post to general ledger as appropriate.

3. Total and rule the journals.

4. Prepare a schedule of accounts receivable and a schedule of accounts payable.

The following is the partial chart of accounts for Abby's Toy House:

Comprehensive Problem: All special journals and the general journal. Schedule of accounts payable and accounts receivable.

Check Figures:

Total of Schedule of Accounts Receivable $7,600

Total of Schedule of Accounts Payable $9,000

Abby's Toy House Chart of Accounts

Assets
110   Cash
112   Accounts Receivable
114   Prepaid Rent
121   Delivery Truck

Liabilities
210   Accounts Payable

Owner's Equity
310   A. Ellen, Capital

Revenue
410   Toy Sales
412   Sales Returns and Allowances
414   Sales Discounts

Cost of Goods
510   Toy Purchases
512   Purchases Returns and Allowances
514   Purchases Discount

Expenses
610   Salaries Expense
612   Cleaning Expense

19XX

March 1 Abby Ellen invested $8,000 in the toy store.

1 Paid three months' rent in advance, check no. 1, $3,000.

1 Purchased merchandise from Earl Miller Company on account, $4,000, invoice no. 410, dated March 2, terms 2/10, n/30.

3 Sold merchandise to Bill Burton on account, $1,000, invoice no. 1, terms 2/10, n/30.

6 Sold merchandise to Jim Rex on account, $700, invoice no. 2, terms 2/10, n/30.

8 Purchased merchandise from Earl Miller Co. on account, $1,200, invoice no. 415, dated March 9, terms 2/10, n/30.

9 Sold merchandise to Bill Burton on account, $600, invoice no. 3, terms 2/10, n/30.
9 Paid cleaning service $300, check no. 2.
10 Jim Rex returned merchandise that cost $300 to Abby's Toy House. Abby issued credit memorandum no. 1 to Jim Rex for $300.
10 Purchased merchandise from Minnie Katz on account, $4,000, invoice no. 311, dated March 11, terms 1/15, n/60.
12 Paid Earl Miller Co. invoice no. 410, dated March 2, check no. 3.
13 Sold $1,300 of toy merchandise for cash.
13 Paid salaries, $600, check no. 4.
14 Returned merchandise to Minnie Katz in the amount of $1,000. Abby's Toy House issued debit memorandum no. 1 to Minnie Katz.
15 Sold merchandise for $4,000 cash.
16 Received payment from Jim Rex, invoice no. 2 (less returned merchandise) less discount.
16 Bill Burton paid invoice no. 1.
16 Sold toy merchandise to Amy Rose on account, $4,000, invoice no. 4, terms 2/10, n/30.
20 Purchased delivery truck on account from Sam Katz Garage, $3,000, invoice no. 111, dated March 21 (no discount).
22 Sold to Bill Burton merchandise on account, $900, invoice no. 5, terms 2/10, n/30.
23 Paid Minnie Katz balance owed, check no. 5.
24 Sold toy merchandise on account to Amy Rose, $1,100, invoice no. 6, terms 2/10, n/30.
25 Purchased toy merchandise, $600, check no. 6.
26 Purchased toy merchandise from Woody Smith on account, $4,800, invoice no. 211, dated March 27, terms 2/10, n/30.
28 Bill Burton paid invoice no. 5, dated March 22.
28 Amy Rose paid invoice no. 6, dated March 24.
28 Abby invested an additional $5,000 in the business.
28 Purchased merchandise from Earl Miller Co., $1,400, invoice no. 436, dated March 29, terms 2/10, n/30.
30 Paid Earl Miller Co. invoice no. 436, check no. 7.
30 Sold merchandise to Bonnie Flow Company on account, $3,000, invoice no. 7, terms 2/10, n/30.

Group B Problems

(The forms you need are on pages 346–367 of the *Study Guide and Working Papers*.)

Journalizing, recording, and posting a purchases journal.

10B-1. From the following transactions of Judy Clark's sporting goods shop, journalize in the purchases journal and record and post as appropriate:

Check Figure:
Total of Purchases Column
$2,200

19XX
June
4 Bought merchandise on account from Rolo Co., invoice no. 400, dated June 5, terms 2/10, n/30, $1,800.
5 Bought store equipment from Norton Co., invoice no. 518, dated June 6, $6,000.
8 Bought merchandise on account from Aster Co., invoice no. 411, dated June 5, terms 2/10, n/30, $400.
14 Bought store supplies on account from Aster Co., invoice no. 415, dated June 13, $1,200.

10B-2. As the accountant of Mabel's Natural Food Store (1) journalize the following transactions into the purchases (p. 10) or general journal (p. 2),
(2) record and post as appropriate, and (3) prepare a schedule of accounts
payable. Beginning balances are in your *Working Papers.*

19XX

May   8   Purchased merchandise on account from Broward Co., invoice no. 420,
dated May 9, terms 2/10, n/60, $500.

10   Purchased merchandise on account from Aton Co., invoice no. 400,
dated May 11, terms 2/10, n/60, $900.

12   Purchased store supplies on account from Midden Co., invoice no. 510,
dated May 13, $700.

14   Issued debit memo no. 7 to Aton Co. for merchandise returned, $400,
from invoice no. 400.

17   Purchased office equipment on account from Relar Co., invoice no.
810, dated May 18, $750.

24   Purchased additional store supplies on account from Midden Co.,
invoice no. 516, dated May 25, $850.

10B-3. Wendy Jones has hired you as her bookkeeper to record the following
transactions in the cash payments journal. She would like you to record
and post as appropriate and supply her with a schedule of accounts
payable. (Beginning balances are in your workbook or Problem 10A-3,
p. 355 in the text.)

19XX

May   1   Bought a delivery truck for $8,000 cash, check no. 21, payable to Randy
Rosse Co.

3   Paid half the amount owed Henry Co. from previous purchases of computer merchandise on account, less a 5 percent purchases discount,
check no. 22.

6   Bought computer merchandise from Jane Co. for $900 cash, check no.
23.

18   Bought additional computer merchandise from Jane Co., check no. 24,
$1,000.

24   Paid Xon Co. the amount owed less a 5 percent purchases discount,
check no. 25.

28   Paid rent expense to Regan Realty Trust, check no. 26, $3,000.

29   Paid half the amount owed Soy Co., no discount, check no. 27.

30   Paid utilities expense to French Utility, check no. 28, $425.

10B-4. As the new accountant for Abby's Toy House, your task is to

1. Journalize the transactions for the month of March.

2. Record to subsidiary ledgers and post to the general ledger as appropriate.

3. Total and rule the journals.

4. Prepare a schedule of accounts receivable and a schedule of accounts
payable.

(Use the same chart of accounts as in Problem 10A-4, p. 383. Your workbook has all the forms you need to complete this problem.)

19XX

March   1   Abby invested $4,000 in the new toy store.

1   Paid two months' rent in advance, check no. 1, $1,000.

1   Purchased merchandise from Earl Miller Company, invoice no. 410,
dated March 2, terms 2/10, n/30, $6,000.

3   Sold merchandise to Bill Burton on account, $1,600, invoice no. 1,
terms 2/10, n/30.

6 Sold merchandise to Jim Rex on account, $800, invoice no. 2, terms 2/10, n/30.

8 Purchased merchandise from Earl Miller Company, $800, invoice no. 415, dated March 9, terms 2/10, n/30.

9 Sold merchandise to Bill Burton on account, $700, invoice no. 3, terms 2/10, n/30.

9 Paid cleaning service, $400, check no. 2.

10 Jim Rex returned merchandise that cost $200 to Abby. Abby issued credit memorandum no. 1 to Jim Rex for $200.

10 Purchased merchandise from Minnie Katz, $7,000, invoice no. 311, dated March 11, terms 1/15, n/60.

12 Paid Earl Miller Co. invoice no. 410, dated March 2, check no. 3.

13 Sold $1,500 of toy merchandise for cash.

13 Paid salaries, $700, check no. 4.

14 Returned merchandise to Minnie Katz in the amount of $500. Abby issued debit memorandum no. 1 to Minnie Katz.

15 Sold merchandise for cash, $4,800.

16 Received payment from Jim Rex for invoice no. 2 (less returned merchandise) less discount.

16 Bill Burton paid invoice no. 1.

16 Sold toy merchandise to Amy Rose on account, $6,000, invoice no. 4, terms 2/10, n/30.

20 Purchased delivery truck on account from Sam Katz Garage, $2,500, invoice no. 111, dated March 21 (no discount).

22 Sold to Bill Burton merchandise on account, $2,000, invoice no. 5, terms 2/10, n/30.

23 Paid Minnie Katz balance owed, check no. 5.

24 Sold toy merchandise on account to Amy Rose, $2,000, invoice no. 6, terms 2/10, n/30.

25 Purchased toy merchandise, $800, check no. 6.

26 Purchased toy merchandise from Woody Smith on account, $5,900, invoice no. 211, dated March 27, terms 2/10, n/30.

28 Bill Burton paid invoice no. 5, dated March 22.

28 Amy Rose paid invoice no. 6, dated March 24.

28 Abby invested an additional $3,000 in the business.

28 Purchased merchandise from Earl Miller Co., $4,200, invoice no. 436, dated March 29, terms 2/10, n/30.

30 Paid Earl Miller Co. invoice no. 436, check no. 7.

30 Sold merchandise to Bonnie Flow Company on account, $3,200, invoice no. 7, terms 2/10, n/30.

REAL WORLD APPLICATIONS

10R-1.

Hint: $R = \dfrac{I}{PT}$

Angie Co. bought merchandise for $1,000 with credit terms of 2/10, n/30. Owing to the bookkeeper's incompetence, the 2 percent cash discount was missed. The bookkeeper told Pete Angie, the owner, not to get excited. After all, it was a $20 discount that was missed—not hundreds of dollars. Could you please act as Mr. Angie's assistant and show the bookkeeper that his $20 represents a sizeable equivalent interest cost? In your calculation assume a 360-day year. Make some written recommendations so that this will not happen again.

SALES JOURNAL		
Account	PR	
Blue Co.		4 8 0 0 00
Jon Co.		5 6 0 0 00
Roff Co.		6 4 0 0 00
Totals		16 8 0 0 00

PURCHASES JOURNAL		
Account	PR	
Ralph Co.		4 0 0 0 00
Sos Co.		6 0 0 0 00
Jingle Co.		8 0 0 0 00
Totals		18 0 0 0 00

GENERAL JOURNAL			
Sales Returns and Allowances		1 6 0 0 00	
Accounts Receivable, Jon Co.			1 6 0 0 00
Customer returned merchandise			
Accounts Payable, Jingle Co.		8 0 0 00	
Purchases, Returns, and Allowances			8 0 0 00
Returned defective merchandise			

CASH RECEIPTS JOURNAL*						
Cash Dr.	Sales Discount Dr.	Accounts Receivable Cr.	Sales Cr.	Sundry-Dr.		
				Account Name	PR	Amount Cr.
4 7 0 4 00	9 6 00	4 8 0 0 00		Blue Co.		
1 9 6 0 00	4 0 00	2 0 0 0 00		Jon Co.		
5 0 0 0 00			5 0 0 0 00	Sales		
20 0 0 0 00				Notes Payable		20 0 0 0 00
3 1 3 6 00	6 4 00	3 2 0 0 00		Roff Co.		
4 6 0 0 00			4 6 0 0 00	Sales		
39 4 0 0 00	2 0 0 00	10 0 0 0 00	9 6 0 0 00	Totals		20 0 0 0 00

* Note: This company's set of columns differs from that shown in the chapter.

CASH PAYMENTS JOURNAL					
Account	PR	Sundry	Accounts Payable	Purchases Discount	Cash
Sos Co.			3 0 0 0 00	6 0 00	2 9 4 0 00
Salaries Expense		2 6 0 0 00			2 6 0 0 00
Jingle Co.			4 0 0 0 00	8 0 00	3 9 2 0 00
Salaries Expense		2 6 0 0 00			2 6 0 0 00
Totals		5 2 0 0 00	7 0 0 0 00	1 4 0 00	12 0 6 0 00

10R-2.

Jeff Ryan completed an Accounting I course and was recently hired as the book-keeper of Spring Co. The special journals have not been posted, nor are *Dr.* and *Cr.* used on the column headings. Please assist Jeff by marking the Dr. and Cr. headings as well as setting up and posting to the general ledger and recording to the subsidiary ledger. (Only post or record the amounts, since no chart of accounts is provided.) Make some written recommendations on how a new computer system may lessen the need for posting.

 make the call

Critical Thinking/Ethical Case

10R-3.

Spring Co. bought merchandise from All Co. with terms 2/10, n/30. Joanne Ring, the bookkeeper, forgot to pay the bill within the first 10 days. She went to Mel Ryan, Head Accountant, who told her to backdate the check so it looked like the bill was paid within the discount period. Joanne told Mel that she thought they could get away with it. Should Joanne and Mel backdate the check to take advantage of the discount? You make the call. Write down your specific recommendations to Joanne.

ACCOUNTING RECALL

A CUMULATIVE APPROACH

THIS EXAM REVIEWS CHAPTERS 1 THROUGH 10

Your *Study Guide and Working Papers* has forms (pp. 372 and 379) to complete this exam, as well as worked-out solutions. The page references next to each question identify what page to turn back to if you answer the question incorrectly.

PART 1   Vocabulary Review

Match the terms to the appropriate definition or phrase.

Page Ref.

(212)	1. Checks outstanding	A. A contra-cost account
(356)	2. F.O.B. destination	B. Issued by a buyer to the seller
(360)	3. Purchases journal	C. Special journal that records
(319)	4. Sales journal	buying on account
(355)	5. Purchases discount	D. Sales on account
(314)	6. Credit memorandum	E. Seller pays cost of freight
(280)	7. 941	F. Form completed quarterly for
(360)	8. Debit memorandum	FIT, Social Security, and Medicare

(365)	9. Cash payments journal	G. Merchandise for resale
(354)	10. Purchases	H. Payment of cash
		I. Issued by seller
		J. Checks not yet processed by the bank

PART II   True or False (Accounting Theory)

(314)   11. Issuing a credit memo results in seller increasing its purchases returns and allowances.

(355)   12. Purchases discounts have a normal balance of a debit.

(248)   13. Medicare and Social Security have different rates.

(365)   14. Each creditor in the accounts payable subsidiary ledger usually has a debit balance.

(216)   15. Petty cash is an asset that will only be debited with establishment or when raising to a higher amount.

CONTINUING PROBLEM

Freedman was very happy to see the progress made by using the specialized journals. For the month of February he will add two additional journals (purchases journal and the cash payments journal). To assist you in recording the transactions, the following is an updated schedule of accounts payable as of January 31:

Schedule of Accounts Payable

Office Depot	$50
System Design Furniture	$1,400
Pac Bell	$150
Multi Systems	$450
Total Accounts Payable	$2,050

Assignment:

(See pp. 373–378 in your *Study Guide and Working Papers.*)

4. Journalize the transactions in the appropriate journals (cash payments, purchase journal, or general journal).

5. Record in the accounts payable subsidiary ledger and post to the general ledger as appropriate. A partial general ledger is included in the *Working Papers.*

6. Prepare a schedule of accounts payable as of February 28, 19XX.

The transactions for the month of February are:

Feb.   1   Prepaid the rent for the months of February, March, and April, $1,200; check #2585

4   Bought merchandise on account from Multi Systems (purchase order #4010), $450; terms are 3/10, n/30

8 Bought office supplies on account from Office Depot (purchase order #4011), $250; terms are n/30

9 Purchased merchandise on account from Computer Connection (purchase order #4012), $500; terms are 1/30, n/60

15 Paid (purchase order #4010) in full to Multi Systems; check #2586

21 Issued debit memorandum #10 to Computer Connection for merchandise returned from (purchase order #4012), $100

27 Paid for office supplies, $50; check #2587

COMPUTERIZED ACCOUNTING APPLICATION FOR CHAPTER 10

PART A: Recording Transactions in the Sales, Receipts, Purchases, and Payments Journals

PART B: Computerized Accounting Instructions for Abby's Toy House (Problem 10A-4)

Before starting on this assignment, read and complete the tasks discussed in Parts A, B, and F of the Computerized Accounting appendix at the back of this book and complete the Computerized Accounting Application assignments for Chapter 3, Chapter 4, the Valdez Realty Mini Practice Set (Chapter 5), and the Pete's Market Mini Practice Set (Chapter 8).

PART A: Recording Transactions in the Sales, Receipts, Purchases, and Payments Journals

What to Record in a Computerized Sales or Receipts Journal

The Sales and Receipts Journals in Simply Accounting are designed to work with the Receivables and General Ledgers modules in an integrated fashion. When transactions are recorded in the Sales and Receipts journals, the program automatically posts the customer's account in the accounts receivable subsidiary ledger, records the journal entry, and posts all accounts affected in the general ledger. However, the type of transactions recorded in the Sales and Receipts journals in Simply Accounting differ from the types of transactions recorded in these journals in a manual accounting system. An explanation of the differences appears in the following chart:

Name of Computerized Journal	Types of Transactions Recorded in Computerized Journal
Sales Journal	Sales of merchandise on account
	Sales returns and allowances (credit memos)
Receipts Journal	Cash receipts from credit customers
General Journal	Cash receipts from all sources other than credit customers

Computerized Schedule of Accounts Receivable

A Customer Aged Detail report (the computerized version of a schedule of accounts receivable) for The Mars Company appears below (terms of 2/10, n/30 are offered to all credit customers of The Mars Company):

The Mars Company: Customer Aged Detail As at 3/1/97

			Total	Current	31 to 60	61 to 90	91+
John Dunbar							
909	2/25/97	Invoice	500.00	500.00	—	—	—
Kevin Tucker							
911	2/26/97	Invoice	550.00	550.00	—	—	—
			1,050.00	1,050.00	—	—	—

What to Record in a Computerized Purchases or Payments Journal

The Purchases and Payments Journals in Simply Accounting are also designed to work with the Payables and General Ledgers modules in an integrated fashion.

When transactions are recorded in the Purchases and Payments journals, the program automatically posts the vendor's account in the accounts payable subsidiary ledger, records the journal entry, and posts all accounts affected in the general ledger. However, the type of transactions recorded in the Purchases and Payments journals in Simply Accounting differ from the types of transactions recorded in these journals in a manual accounting system. An explanation of the differences appears in the following chart:

Name of Computerized Journal	Types of Transactions Recorded in Computerized Journal
Purchases Journal	Purchases of merchandise and other items on account
	Purchase returns and allowances (debit memos)
Payments Journal	Cash payments to credit vendors
General Journal	Cash payments for all purposes other than payments to credit vendors

Computerized Schedule of Accounts Payable

A Vendor Aged Detail report (the computerized version of a schedule of accounts payable) for The Mars Company appears below:

The Mars Company: Vendor Aged Detail As at 3/1/97

			Total	Current	31 to 60	61 to 90	91+
Laurie Snyder							
567	2/27/97	Invoice	435.00	435.00	—	—	—
Pat Young							
789	2/25/97	Invoice	112.00	112.00	—	—	—
			547.00	547.00	—	—	—

Open the Company Data Files

1. Click on the Start button. Point to Programs; point to Simply Accounting; then click on Simply Accounting in the final menu presented. The Simply Accounting Open File dialog box will appear.

2. Insert your Student Data Files disk into disk drive A. Enter the following path into the **File name** text box: A:\student\mars.asc

3. Click on the **Open** button; enter 3/31/97 into the **Using Date for this Session** text box; then click on the **OK** button. Click on the **OK** button in response to the message "The date entered is more than one week past your previous **Using** date of 3/1/97." The Company Window for Mars will appear.

Add Your Name to the Company Name

4. Click on the Company Window Setup menu; then click on Company Information. The Company Information dialog box will appear. Insert your name in place of the text "Your Name" in the **Name** text box. Click on the **OK** button to return to the Company Window.

How to Record a Sale on Account

5. On March 1, 1997 sold merchandise to Kevin Tucker on account, $800, invoice no. 913, terms 2/10, n/30. Double-click on the Sales icon to open the Sales Journal dialog box. Note that the program automatically offers **Invoice** 913 as the invoice number for this transaction through the program's automatic invoice numbering feature. Click on the arrow button to the right of the **Sold to** text box to display a list of customers; then click on Kevin Tucker. Note that the company's standard payment terms of 2/10, n/30 are presented. Highlight the **Date** text box; enter 3/1/97; then press the TAB key until the insertion point is positioned in the **Amount** text box. Enter 800; then press the TAB key. The flashing insertion point will move to the **Acct** text box. Press the ENTER key to display the Select Account dialog box; then select 4110 Sales. Your screen should look like this:

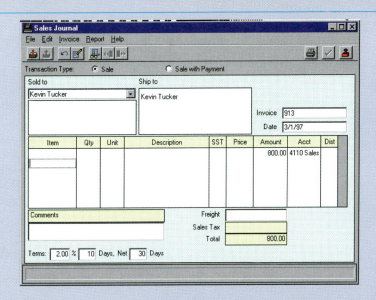

How to Review a Sales Journal Entry

6. Before posting this transaction, you need to verify that the transaction data are correct by reviewing the journal entry. To review the entry, click on the Sales Journal Report menu; then click on Display Sales Journal Entry. The journal entry representing the data you have recorded in the Sales Journal dialog box is displayed. Review the journal entry for accuracy noting any errors. Note that the program has automatically debited the accounts receivable account through its integration feature.

How to Edit a Sales or Purchases Journal Entry Prior to Posting

7. Close the Sales Journal Entry window. If you have made an error, use the following editing techniques to correct the error:

Editing a Sales or Purchases Journal Entry

◆ Move to the text box that contains the error by either pressing the TAB key to move forward through each text box or the SHIFT and TAB keys together to move to a previous text box. This will highlight the selected text box information so that you can change it. Alternatively, you can use the mouse to point to a text box and drag through the incorrect information to highlight it.

◆ Type the correct information; then press the TAB key to enter it.

◆ If you have associated the transaction with an the incorrect customer or vendor, reselect the correct customer or vendor from the customer or vendor list display after clicking on the arrow button to the right of the **Sold to** text box (customers) or **Purchased From** text box (vendors).

◆ If you have associated a transaction with an incorrect account, double-click on the incorrect account; then select the correct account from the Select Account dialog box. This will replace the incorrect account with the correct account.

◆ To discard an entry and start over, click on the close button. Click on the **Yes** button in response to the question "Are you sure you want to discard this journal entry?"

◆ Review the journal entry for accuracy after any editing corrections.

◆ **It is IMPORTANT TO NOTE that the only way to edit a journal entry after it is posted is to reverse the entry and enter the correct journal entry.** To correct journal entries posted in error, see Part C of the Computerized Accounting appendix at the back of this book.

How to Post a Sales Journal Entry

8. After verifying that the journal entry is correct, click on the **Post** icon to post this transaction. A blank Sales Journal dialog box is displayed, ready for additional Sales Journal transactions to be recorded.

How to Record a Credit Memo

9. On March 5, 1997 issued credit memorandum no. 14 to Kevin Tucker for returned merchandise that cost $50. Click on the arrow button to the right of the **Sold to** text box; then click on Kevin Tucker. Highlight the **Invoice** text box; enter Cm 14; then press the TAB key. Enter 3/5/97 into the **Date** text box; then press the TAB key until the insertion point is positioned in the **Amount** text box. Enter − 50 (don't forget the minus sign!); then press the TAB key. The flashing insertion point will move to the **Acct** text box. Press the ENTER key to display the Select Account dialog box; then select 4120 Sales Returns and Allowances. Your screen should look like this:

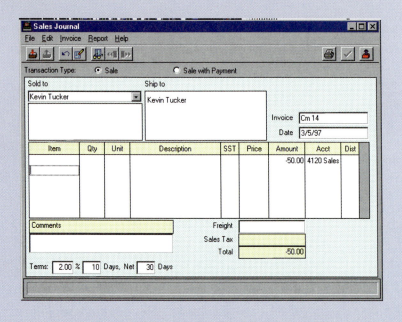

Review the Entry

10. Click on the Sales Journal Report menu; then click on Display Sales Journal Entry. Review the journal entry for accuracy noting any errors. Note that the program has automatically credited the accounts receivable account through its integration feature.

11. Close the Sales Journal Entry window; then make any editing corrections required.

Post the entry

12. After verifying that the journal entry is correct, click on the **Post** icon to post this transaction; then close the Sales Journal dialog box.

How to Record a Cash Receipt from a Credit Customer

13. On March 7, 1997 received check no. 1634 from Kevin Tucker in the amount of $735 in payment of invoice no. 913 ($800), dated March 1, less credit memorandum no. 14 ($50), less 2 percent discount ($16 − 1 = $15 net sales discount).

   Open the Receipts Journal dialog box by double-clicking on the Receipts Journal icon. Click on the arrow button to the right of the **From** text box; click on Kevin Tucker; then press the TAB key. Enter 1634 into the **No.** text box; then press the TAB key. Enter 3/7/97 into the **Date** text box; then press the TAB key. Click in the **Disc. Taken** field for invoice no. 913; click in the **Payment Amt.** field for invoice no. 913; click in the **Disc. Taken** field for Cm 14; click in the **Payment Amt.** field for Cm 14; then press the TAB key. Your screen should look like the one at the top of page 395.

How to Review a Receipts Journal Entry

14. Before posting this transaction, you need to verify that the transaction data are correct by reviewing the journal entry. To review the entry, click on the Receipts Journal Report menu; then click on Display Receipts Journal Entry. The journal entry representing the data you have recorded in the Receipts Journal dialog box is displayed. Review the journal entry for accuracy noting any errors. Note that the program has automatically debited the cash and sales

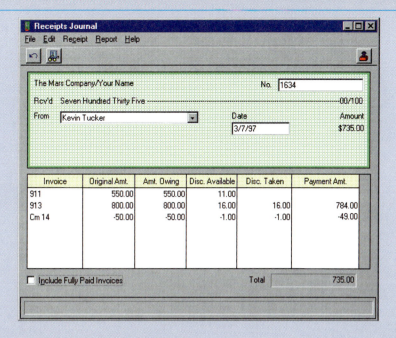

discounts accounts and credited the accounts receivable account through its integration feature.

How to Edit a Receipts or Payments Journal Entry Prior to Posting

15. Close the Receipts Journal Entry window. If you have made an error, use the following editing techniques to correct the error:

    Editing a Receipts or Payments Journal Entry

    ◆ Move to the text box that contains the error by either pressing the TAB key to move forward through each text box or the SHIFT and TAB keys together to move to a previous text box. This will highlight the selected text box information so that you can change it. Alternatively, you can use the mouse to point to a text box and drag through the incorrect information to highlight it.

    ◆ Type the correct information; then press the TAB key to enter it.

    ◆ If you have associated the transaction with an incorrect customer or vendor, re-select the correct customer or vendor from the customer or vendor list display after clicking on the arrow button to the right of the **From** text box (customers) or **To the Order of** text box (vendors). You will be asked to confirm that you want to discard the current transaction. Click on the **Yes** button to discard the incorrect entry and display the outstanding invoices for the correct customer or vendor.

    ◆ To discard an entry and start over, click on the close button. Click on the **Yes** button in response to the question "Are you sure you want to discard this journal entry?"

    ◆ Review the journal entry for accuracy after any editing corrections.

    ◆ **It is IMPORTANT TO NOTE that the only way to edit a journal entry after it is posted is to reverse the entry and enter the correct journal entry.** To correct journal entries posted in error, see Part C of the Computerized Accounting appendix at the back of this book.

How to Post a Receipts Journal Entry

16. After verifying that the journal entry is correct, click on the **Post** icon to post this transaction. A blank Receipts Journal dialog box is displayed, ready for additional Receipts Journal transactions to be recorded. Close the Receipts Journal dialog box.

How to Record a Purchase on Account

17. On March 15, 1997 purchased merchandise from Pat Young on account, $275, invoice no. 796, terms 3/15, n/30. Double-click on the Purchases icon to open the Purchases Journal dialog box. Click on the arrow button to the right of the **Purchased from** text box; then click on Pat Young. Note that Pay Young's stan-

dard payment terms of 3/15, n/30 are presented. Click on the **Invoice** text box; enter 796; then press the TAB key. Enter 3/15/97 into the **Date** text box; then press the TAB key until the insertion point is positioned in the **Amount** text box. Enter 275; then press the TAB key. The flashing insertion point will move to the **Acct** text box. Press the ENTER key to display the Select Account dialog box; then select 5100 Purchases. Your screen should look like this:

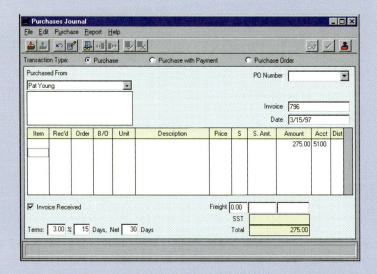

<table>
<tr><td>**How to Review a Purchases Journal Entry**</td><td>**18.**</td><td>Before posting this transaction, you need to verify that the transaction data are correct by reviewing the journal entry. To review the entry, click on the Purchases Journal Report menu; then click on Display Purchases Journal Entry. The journal entry representing the data you have recorded in the Purchases Journal dialog box is displayed. Review the journal entry for accuracy noting any errors. Note that the program has automatically credited the accounts payable account through its integration feature.</td></tr>
</table>

How to Review a Purchases Journal Entry

18. Before posting this transaction, you need to verify that the transaction data are correct by reviewing the journal entry. To review the entry, click on the Purchases Journal Report menu; then click on Display Purchases Journal Entry. The journal entry representing the data you have recorded in the Purchases Journal dialog box is displayed. Review the journal entry for accuracy noting any errors. Note that the program has automatically credited the accounts payable account through its integration feature.

19. Close the Purchases Journal Entry window; then make any editing corrections required.

How to Post a Purchases Journal Entry

20. After verifying that the journal entry is correct, click on the **Post** icon to post this transaction. A blank Purchases Journal dialog box is displayed, ready for additional Purchases Journal transactions to be recorded.

How to Record a Debit Memo

21. On March 17, 1997 returned merchandise to Pat Young in the amount of $75. Issued debit memorandum no. 27. Click on the arrow button to the right of the **Purchased From** text box; then click on Pat Young. Click on the **Invoice** text box; enter Dm 27; then press the TAB key. Enter 3/17/97 into the **Date** text box; then press the TAB key until the insertion point is positioned in the **Amount** text box. Enter − 75 (don't forget the minus sign!); then press the TAB key. The flashing insertion point will move to the **Acct** text box. Press the ENTER key to display the Select Account dialog box; then select 5120 Purchase Returns and Allowances. Your screen should look like the one at the top of page 397.

Review the Entry

22. Click on the Purchases Journal Report menu; then click on Display Purchases Journal Entry. Review the journal entry for accuracy noting any errors. Note that the program has automatically debited the accounts payable account through its integration feature.

23. Close the Purchases Journal Entry window; then make any editing corrections required.

Post the Entry

24. After verifying that the journal entry is correct, click on the **Post** icon to post this transaction; then close the Purchases Journal dialog box.

How to Record a Cash Payment to a Credit Vendor

25. On March 25, 1997 issued check no. 437 to Pat Young in the amount of $194 in payment of invoice no. 796 ($275), dated March 15, less debit memorandum

Purchases Journal

File Edit Purchase Report Help

Transaction Type: ● Purchase   ○ Purchase with Payment   ○ Purchase Order

Purchased From   PO Number [▼]

[Pat Young ▼]

Invoice [Dm 27]
Date [3/17/97]

Item	Rec'd	Order	B/O	Unit	Description	Price	S	S. Amt.	Amount	Acct	Dist
									-75.00	5120	

☑ Invoice Received   Freight [0.00] [   ]
                                                            SST   [   ]
Terms: [3.00] % [15] Days, Net [30] Days   Total [-75.00]

no. 27 ($75), less 3 percent discount ($8.25 − 2.25 = $6 net purchases discount).

Open the Payments Journal dialog box by double-clicking on the Payments icon. Click on the arrow button to the right of the **To the Order of** text box; click on Pat Young; then press the TAB key. Enter 437 into the **No.** text box; then press the TAB key. (The program has offered a default check **No.** of 435 which is the next check number in the program's automatic check numbering sequence. However, since certain cash payments are recorded in the General Journal and the checks used are not recorded in the Payments Journal the check **No.** needs to be advanced to the next check number in The Mars Company's checkbook.) Enter 3/25/97 into the **Date** text box; then press the TAB key. Click in the **Disc. Taken** field for invoice no. 796; click in the **Payment Amt.** field for invoice no. 796; click in the **Disc. Taken** field for Dm 27; click in the **Payment Amt.** field for Dm 27; then press the TAB key. Your screen should look like this:

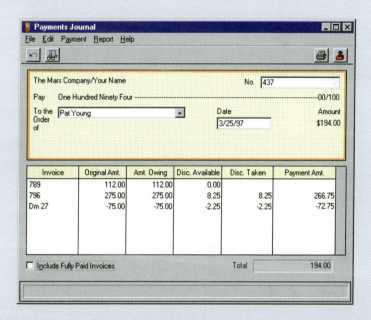

Payments Journal

File Edit Payment Report Help

The Mars Company/Your Name   No. [437]

Pay   One Hundred Ninety Four --------------------------------------00/100

To the [Pat Young ▼]   Date   Amount
Order   [3/25/97] $194.00
of

Invoice	Original Amt.	Amt. Owing	Disc. Available	Disc. Taken	Payment Amt.
789	112.00	112.00	0.00		
796	275.00	275.00	8.25	8.25	266.75
Dm 27	-75.00	-75.00	-2.25	-2.25	-72.75

☐ Include Fully Paid Invoices   Total   [194.00]

**How to Review a Payments
Journal Entry**

26. Before posting this transaction, you need to verify that the transaction data are correct by reviewing the journal entry. To review the entry, click on the Payments Journal Report menu; then click on Display Payments Journal Entry. The journal entry representing the data you have recorded in the Payments Journal dialog box is displayed. Review the journal entry for accuracy noting any errors. Note that the program has automatically debited the accounts payable account and credited the cash and purchases discount accounts through its integration feature.

27. Close the Payments Journal Entry window; then make any editing corrections required.

How to Post a Payments Journal Entry

28. After verifying that the journal entry is correct, click on the **Post** icon to post this transaction. A blank Payments Journal dialog box is displayed, ready for additional Payments Journal transactions to be recorded. Close the Payments Journal dialog box.

How to Display and Print a Customer Aged Detail Report

29. Click on the Company Window Reports menu; point to Receivables; then click on Customer Aged. The Customer Aged Report Options dialog box will appear asking you to define the information you want displayed. Click on the **Detail** option button, click on the **Select All** button; leave the As at date set at 3/31/97; then click on the **OK** button. Click on the Customer Aged Detail File menu; then click on Print to print the report.

How to Display and Print a Vendor Aged Detail Report

30. Close the Customer Aged Detail window; click on the Company Window Reports menu; point to Payables; then click on Vendor Aged. The Vendor Aged Report Options dialog box will appear asking you to define the information you want displayed. Click on the **Detail** option button, click on the **Select All** button; leave the As at date set at 3/31/97; then click on the **OK** button. Click on the Vendor Aged Detail File menu; then click on Print to print the report.

Print Reports

31. Close the Vendor Aged Detail window, then print the following reports:

a. General Journal (By posting date, All ledger entries, Start: 3/1/97, Finish: 3/31/97).

b. General Ledger Report (Start: 3/1/97, Finish: 3/31/97, Select All).

Note that by checking the **All Ledger Entries** check box in the General Journal Options dialog box, all transactions recorded in the Sales, Receipts, Purchases, and Payments Journals are reflected in the General Journal report.

Review your printed reports. If you have made an error in a posted journal entry, see Part C (Reversing an Entry Made in the Sales Journal, Receipts Journal, Purchases Journal, or Payments Journal Dialog Box) of the Computerized Accounting appendix for information on how to correct the error.

Exit from the Program

32. Click on the Company Window File menu; then click on Exit to end the current work session and return to your Windows desktop.

Complete the Report Transmittal

33. Complete The Mars Company Report Transmittal located in Appendix A of your *Study Guide and Working Papers*.

PART B: Computerized Accounting Instructions for Abby's Toy House (Problem 10A-4)

Open the Company Data Files

1. Click on the Start button. Point to Programs; point to Simply Accounting; then click on Simply Accounting in the final menu presented. The Simply Accounting Open File dialog box will appear.

2. Insert your Student Data Files disk into disk drive A. Enter the following path into the **File name** text box: A:\student\abby.asc

3. Click on the **Open** button; enter 3/31/97 into the **Using Date for this Session** text box; then click on the **OK** button. Click on the **OK** button in response to the message "The date entered is more than one week past your previous **Using** date of 3/1/97." The Company Window for Abby will appear.

Add your Name to the Company Name

4. Click on the Company Window Setup menu; then click on Company Information. The Company Information dialog box will appear. Insert your name in place of the text "Your Name" in the **Name** text box. Click on the **OK** button to return to the Company Window.

5. Record the following transactions using the General, Sales, Receipts, Purchases, and Payments journals:

1997

March   1 Abby Ellen invested $8,000 in the toy store.

         1 Paid three months' rent in advance, check no. 1, $3,000.

         2 Purchased merchandise from Earl Miller Company on account, $4,000, invoice no. 410, terms 2/10, n/30.

         3 Sold merchandise to Bill Burton on account, $1,000, invoice no. 1, terms 2/10, n/30.

         6 Sold merchandise to Jim Rex on account, $700, invoice no. 2, terms 2/10, n/30.

         9 Purchased merchandise from Earl Miller Co. on account, $1,200, invoice no. 415, terms 2/10, n/30.

         9 Sold merchandise to Bill Burton on account, $600, invoice no. 3, terms 2/10, n/30.

         9 Paid cleaning service $300, check no. 2.

       10 Jim Rex returned merchandise that cost $300 to Abby's Toy House. Abby issued credit memorandum no. 1 to Jim Rex for $300.

       11 Purchased merchandise from Minnie Katz on account, $4,000, invoice no. 311, terms 1/15, n/60.

       12 Issued check no. 3 to Earl Miller Co. in the amount of $3,920 in payment of invoice no. 410 ($4,000), dated March 2, less 2 percent discount ($80). (*Note:* Use the DELETE key to remove amounts in the **Disc. Taken** and **Payment Amt.** fields that do not apply to this payment.)

       13 Sold $1,300 of toy merchandise for cash. (*Reminder:* Cash sales are recorded in the General Journal.)

       13 Paid salaries, $600, check no. 4.

       14 Returned merchandise to Minnie Katz in the amount of $1,000. Abby's Toy House issued debit memorandum no. 1 to Minnie Katz.

       15 Sold merchandise for $4,000 cash. (*Reminder:* Cash sales are recorded in the General Journal.)

       16 Received check no. 9823 from Jim Rex in the amount of $392 in payment of invoice no. 2 ($700), dated March 6, less credit memorandum no. 1 ($300), less 2 percent discount ($14 − 6 = $8 net sales discount).

       16 Received check no. 4589 from Bill Burton in the amount of $1,000 in payment of invoice no. 1, dated March 2. (*Note:* Use the DELETE key to remove amounts in the **Disc. Taken** and **Payment Amt.** fields that do not apply to this payment.)

       16 Sold toy merchandise to Amy Rose on account, $4,000, invoice no. 4, terms 2/10, n/30.

       21 Purchased delivery truck on account from Sam Katz Garage, $3,000, invoice no. 111, (no discount). (*Reminder:* Purchases of merchandise and other items on account are recorded in the Purchases Journal.)

       22 Sold to Bill Burton merchandise on account, $900, invoice no. 5, terms 2/10, n/30.

       23 Issued check no. 5 to Minnie Katz in the amount of $2,970 in payment of invoice no. 311 ($4,000), dated March 11, less debit memorandum no. 1 ($1,000), less 1 percent discount ($40 − 10 = $30 net purchases discount).

       24 Sold toy merchandise on account to Amy Rose, $1,100, invoice no. 6, terms 2/10, n/30.

       25 Purchased toy merchandise, $600, check no. 6. (*Reminder:* Cash purchases are recorded in the General Journal.)

       27 Purchased toy merchandise from Woody Smith on account, $4,800, invoice no. 211, terms 2/10, n/30.

       28 Received check no. 4598 from Bill Burton in the amount of $882 in

payment of invoice no. 5 ($900), dated March 22, less 2 percent discount ($18).

28 Received check no. 3217 from Amy Rose in the amount of $1,078 in payment of invoice no. 6, dated March 24, less 2 percent discount ($22).

28 Abby invested an additional $5,000 in the business.

29 Purchased merchandise from Earl Miller Co., $1,400, invoice no. 436, terms 2/10, n/30.

30 Issued check no. 7 to the Earl Miller Co. in the amount of $1,372 in payment of invoice no. 436 ($1,400), dated March 29, less 2 percent discount ($28).

30 Sold merchandise to Bonnie Flow Company on account, $3,000 invoice no. 7, terms 2/10, n/30.

Print Reports

6. Print the following reports:

   a. Customer Aged report As at 3/31/97 (Detail, Select All).

   b. Vendor Aged report As at 3/31/97 (Detail, Select All).

   c. General Journal (By posting date, All ledger entries, Start: 3/1/97, Finish: 3/31/97).

   d. General Ledger Report (Start: 3/1/97, Finish: 3/31/97, Select All).

Review your printed reports. If you have made an error in a posted journal entry, see Part C of the Computerized Accounting appendix at the back of this book for information on how to correct the error.

Exit from the Program

7. Click on the Company Window File menu; then click on Exit to end the current work session and return to your Windows desktop.

Complete the Report Transmittal

8. Complete The Abby's Toy House Report Transmittal located in Appendix A of your *Study Guide and Working Papers.*

A

How Companies Record Credit Card Sales in Their Special Journals

Recording Bank Credit Cards

Example—Credit Card Sale of $100, Master Card: It is interesting to note that for bank credit cards (Master Card, Visa) the sales are recorded in the seller's Cash Receipts Journal, since the slips are converted into cash immediately. Bank credit cards are not treated as accounts receivable. The fee the bank charges, $2\frac{1}{2}$ to 6 percent, is usually deducted, and the bank credits the depositor's account immediately for the net. The end result for the seller is:

Accounts Affected	Category	↑	↓	Rule
Cash	Asset	↑		Dr. $94
Credit Card Expense	Expense	↑		Dr. 6
Sales	Revenue	↑		Cr. 100

		Cash Dr.	Credit Card Expense Dr.	Accounts Receivable Cr.	Sales Credited	Sales Tax Payable Cr.	Sundry Account Name	Amount Cr.	
Date									
		94 00	6 00		100 00				

Table title: CASH RECEIPTS JOURNAL

It is the responsibility of the credit card company to sustain any losses (bad debts) from customers' nonpayment. If the bank waits to take the discount until the end of the month, the seller makes a nonpayment entry in the cash payment journal to record the credit card expense; the end result would be credit card expense up and cash balance down. Usually, the bank would send the charge on the monthly statement. *Remember: bank credit cards are not treated as accounts receivable.*

RECORDING PRIVATE COMPANY CREDIT CARDS

Private companies such as American Express and Diners Club are considered by sellers as accounts receivable. The seller periodically summarizes the sales slips and submits them to the private credit card company for payment (which the company will pay quickly). Let's look at two situations to show how a company would handle its accounting procedures for these credit sales transactions.

Situation 1: On May 4, Morris Company sold merchandise on account of $53 to Bill Blank. Bill used American Express. Assume Morris Company has a low dollar volume and few transactions.

Note in Figure A-1 how the sale of $53 is recorded in the sales journal. Keep in mind that Morris is treating American Express, not Bill Blank, as the accounts receivable. In Figure A-2 we see on June 8 payment is received from American Express and results in

1. Cash increasing by $50.35.
2. Credit card expense rising by $2.65.
3. Accounts receivable being reduced by the $53 originally owed by American Express.

Situation 2: On March 31, Blue Company summarized its credit card sales for American Express. Payment was received on April 13 from American Express. Assume Blue Company has a high dollar volume and many transactions.

Note in Figure A-3 how each credit company has its own column set up. In the ledger there is an account set up for each as well; the posting to the ledger would be done at the end of the month. With high volume and the need to record many transactions, the use of these additional columns (versus Figure A-1) will result in increased efficiency. Figure A-4 shows the receipt of money from American Express less the credit card expense charge.

FIGURE A-1

						SALES JOURNAL													
		Date	Invoice	Description of Accounts Receivable	PR		Accounts Receivable Dr.			Sales Tax* Payable Cr.			Sales Cr.						
		May 4	692	American Express				5 3	00		3	00		5 0	00				
				(Bill Blank)															

* Assume a 6% sales tax.

FIGURE A-2

		Date	Cash Dr.			Sales Discount Dr.		Credit Card Expense Dr.			Accounts Receivable Cr.		Sales Tax Payable Cr.		Sundry				
															Account Name	PR	Amount Cr.		
						CASH RECEIPTS JOURNAL													
		June 8	5 0	35				2	65*		5 3	00			American Express				
															(Bill Blank)				

* Assume credit card expense of 5%. Note the $2.56 is 5% × $53.

BLUE COMPANY SALES JOURNAL

Date	Invoice Number	Description of Accounts Receivable	PR	Accounts Receivable Dr.	Credit Cards — American Express Dr.	Credit Cards — Diners Club Dr.	Sales Tax Payable Cr.	Credit Card Sales Cr.	Sales Cr.
March 31		Summary of American Express			1197 0 0 00	53 00	57 0 0 00	114 0 0 00	
					(112)	(113)		(401)	

BLUE COMPANY CASH RECEIPTS JOURNAL

Date	Cash Dr.	Sales Discount Dr.	Credit Card Expense Dr.	Accounts Receivable Cr.	Credit Card Accounts Rec. — American Express Cr.	Credit Card Accounts Rec. — Diners Club Cr.	Sales Cr.	Sales Tax Payable Cr.	Sundry — Account Name	Sundry — PR	Sundry — Amount Cr.
April 13	112 5 1 8 00		71 8 2 00		119 7 0 0 00				Summary of American Express payments		

INVENTORY* AND DEPRECIATION

LEARNING UNIT B-1
How to Assign Costs to Ending Inventory Items

The method one uses to assign costs to ending inventory will have a direct effect on the company's cost of goods sold and profit. Look at the accompanying diagram and note that in each column that ending inventory has a different value assigned to it. Note also how this affects gross profit in each of the four columns.

	A		B		C		D	
Net sales		$50,000		$50,000		$50,000		$50,000
Beginning Inventory	$ 4,000		$ 4,000		$ 4,000		$ 4,000	
Net Purchases	20,000		20,000		20,000		20,000	
Cost of Goods Available for Sale	24,000		24,000		24,000		24,000	
Ending Inventory	5,000		6,000		7,000		8,000	
Cost of Goods Sold		19,000		18,000		17,000		16,000
Gross Profit		$31,000		$32,000		$33,000		$34,000

If all inventory brought into a store had the same cost, it would be simple to calculate ending inventory, and we would not have to include this appendix in the book. Unfortunately, things are not that easy; often the very same products are purchased and brought into the store at different costs during the same accounting period. Over the years there have been developed four generally accepted methods to assign a cost to ending inventory. They are: (1) specific invoice, (2) weighted-average, (3) first-in, first-out, and (4) last-in, first-out. Each is based on the flow of costs, not the flow of goods (the actual physical movement of goods sold in a store).

SPECIFIC INVOICE METHOD

Jones Hardware sells rakes. At the end of the period 12 rakes remain unsold. Notice in the accompanying diagram that on January 1, at the start of the accounting period, 10 rakes were on hand, but during the period additional purchases of rakes were made. The price given in the chart at the top of the next page is the purchase price paid by the store — it is not the same as the selling price, which is what the store charges its customers for the rakes. The selling price is not involved here. At the bottom of the chart you can see that 44 rakes cost Jones Hardware $543.

In the **specific invoice method**, one assigns the cost of ending inventory by identifying each item in that inventory by a specific purchase price and invoice number. Items can be identified by serial number, physical description, or location. Using this method, Jones Hardware knew that six of the rakes not sold were from the March 15 invoice and the other six were from the August 18 purchase. Thus $150 was assigned as the actual cost of ending inventory. If the total cost of goods available

*See page 457 for appendix on Perpetual Inventory.

	Goods Available for Sale			Calculating Cost of Ending Inventory		
	Units	Cost	Total	Units	Cost	Total
January 1 Beg. Inventory	10 @	$10 =	$100			
March 15 Purchased	9 @	12 =	108	6 @	$12	$72
August 18 Purchased	20 @	13 =	260	6 @	13	78
November 15 Purchased	5 @	15 =	75			
	44		$543	12		$150

Cost of Goods Available for Sale	$543
Less: Cost of Ending Inventory	150
= Cost of Goods Sold	$393

for sale is $543 and we subtract the actual cost of ending inventory ($150), this method provides a figure of $393 for cost of goods sold.

Let's look at pros and cons of this method:

Pros	Cons
1. Simple to use if company has small amount of high-cost goods—for example, autos, jewels, boats, antiques, etc.	1. Difficult to use for goods with large unit volume and small unit prices— for example, nails at a hardware store, packages of toothpaste at a drug store.
2. Flow of goods and flow of cost are the same.	2. Difficult to use for decision-making purposes—ordinarily an impractical approach.
3. Costs are matched with the sales they helped to produce.	

WEIGHTED-AVERAGE METHOD

The **weighted-average method** calculates an average unit cost by dividing the *total cost* of goods available for sale by the total *units* of goods available for sale. Since we don't know exactly *which* items are left in ending inventory, we will calculate the average of all the goods we have available in order to come up with a fair approximation of the cost of the ending inventory.

	Goods Available for Sale		
	Units	Cost	Total
January 1 Beg. Inventory	10 @	$10 =	$100
March 15 Purchased	9 @	12 =	108
August 18 Purchased	20 @	13 =	260
November 15 Purchased	5 @	15 =	75
	44		$543

$\dfrac{\$543}{44} = \$12.34$ weighted-average cost per unit

12 rakes × $12.34 = $148.08

Cost of Goods Available for Sale	$543.00
Less: Cost of Ending Inventory	148.08
= Cost of Goods Sold	$394.92

The pros and cons of this method:

FIRST-IN, FIRST-OUT METHOD (FIFO)

In the **FIFO method,** one assumes that the oldest goods (rakes, in this case) are sold first. In other words, the first merchandise brought into the store tends to be sold first. Indeed, it is often the sale of these items that prompts the store to buy more of them — as they start to run out, the store purchases more. When costs are assigned in the FIFO method, the cost of the last items brought into the store is assigned to ending inventory and the inventory sold is assigned to cost of goods sold. For example, using our Jones Hardware situation, the ending inventory of 12 rakes on hand are assigned a cost from the last two purchases of rakes (purchases made on November 15 and some purchases made on August 8), $166. Using the FIFO method, it is always assumed that it is the most recently purchased merchandise that has not been sold. Look at how this works out in the accompanying table.

FIRST-IN, FIRST-OUT METHOD

	Goods Available for Sale			Calculating Cost of Ending Inventory		
	Units	Cost	Total	Units	Cost	Total
January 1 Beg. Inventory	10 @	$10 =	$100			
March 15 Purchased	9 @	12 =	108			
August 18 Purchased	20 @	13 =	260	7 @	$13 =	$ 91
November 15 Purchased	5 @	15 =	75	5 @	15 =	75
	44		$543	12		$166

Cost of Goods Available for Sale	$543
Less: Cost of Ending Inventory	166
= Cost of Goods Sold	$377

If you are having difficulty with this, think of the inventory as being taken from the bottom layer first, then the next one up, and the next one up, etc.

At the top of the next page are the pros and cons of this method.

LAST-IN, FIRST-OUT METHOD (LIFO)

Under the **LIFO method,** it is assumed that the rakes *most recently acquired* by Jones are sold first. In other words, the last merchandise brought into the store is the first to be sold. As an example of this method, think of a barrel of nails. It is the most recently purchased nails, which are at the top of the barrel, that are sold first — the nails at the bottom of the barrel are sold last. Note in the accompanying

Pros	Cons
1. The cost flow tends to follow the physical flow (most businesses try to sell the old goods first—for example, perishables such as fruit or vegetables).	1. During inflation this method will produce higher income on the income statement—thus more taxes to be paid. (We will discuss this later in this appendix.)
2. The figure for ending inventory is made up of current costs on the balance sheet (since inventory left over is assumed to be from goods last brought into the store).	2. Recent costs are not matched with recent sales, since we assume *old* goods are sold first.

diagram that the 12 rakes not sold were assigned costs based on the old inventory of January and March that totaled $124, giving Jones a cost of goods sold of $419.

LAST-IN, FIRST-OUT METHOD

	Goods Available for Sale			Calculating Cost of Ending Inventory		
	Units	Cost	Total	Units	Cost	Total
January 1 Beg. Inventory	10 @	$10 =	$100	10 @	$10 =	$100
March 15 Purchased	9 @	12 =	108	2 @	12 =	$ 24
August 18 Purchased	20 @	13 =	260			
November 15 Purchased	5 @	15 =	75			
	44		$543	12		$124

Cost of Goods Available for Sale	$543
Less: Cost of Ending Inventory	124
= Cost of Goods Sold	$419

These are the pros and cons of this method:

LIFO METHOD

Pros	Cons
1. Cost of goods sold is stated at or near current costs, since costs of *latest* goods acquired are used.	1. Ending inventory is valued at very old prices.
2. Matches current costs with current selling prices.	2. Doesn't match physical flow of goods (but can still be used to calculate flow of costs).
3. During periods of inflation this method produces the lowest net income, which is a tax advantage. (The lower cost of ending inventory means a higher cost of goods sold; with a higher cost of goods sold, gross profit and ultimately net income are smaller, and thus taxes are lower.)	

Now we will compare the methods that could be used by Jones Hardware to see the cost of ending inventory and the assigned cost of goods sold (see top of next page).

COMPARISON OF METHODS FOR JONES HARDWARE

	Cost of Ending Inventory	Cost of Goods Sold
Specific Invoice	$150.00	$393.00
Weighted-Average	148.08	394.92
FIFO	166.00	377.00
LIFO	124.00	419.00

All four methods are acceptable accounting procedures, and each has its own virtues:

1. The specific invoice method matches exactly costs with revenue — as we have noted before, this is very important in the accrual basis of accounting.

2. The weighted-average method tends to smooth out the fluctuations between FIFO and LIFO.

3. FIFO provides an up-to-date picture of inventory on the balance sheet, since it uses the latest purchases to calculate ending inventory.

4. When prices are rising, LIFO shows the highest costs of goods sold and thus provides some tax advantages.

LEARNING UNIT B-1 REVIEW

FIFO, LIFO, weighted-average.

PROBLEM (Solution at End of Appendix)

Regis Company began the year with 300 units of product B in inventory with a unit cost of $40. The following additional purchases of the product were made:

◆ April 1, 200 units @ $50 each

◆ July 5, 500 units @ $60 each

◆ Aug. 15, 400 units @ $70 each

◆ Nov. 20, 200 units @ $80 each

At end of year Regis Company had 400 units of its product unsold. Your task is to calculate cost of ending inventory as well as cost of goods sold by (a) FIFO, (b) LIFO, (c) weighted-average.

LEARNING UNIT B-2
Depreciation Methods

In this unit we will look at different methods for computing depreciation. If you want to check any of the concepts of depreciation, you can refer back to Chapter 4.

When a company calculates its periodic depreciation expense, different methods will produce significantly different results. Thus the method of depreciation chosen will affect the net income for current as well as future periods, as well as the **book value** (cost of asset less accumulated depreciation) of the asset on the balance sheet.

Let's assume that Melvin Company purchased a truck on January 1, 19XX, for $20,000, with a **residual value** of $2,000 and an estimated life of 5 years. The following are the four depreciation methods that Melvin Company could use:

Think of residual value as trade-in value at end of estimated life.

1. Straight-line method.   3. Sum-of-the-years'-digits method.

2. Units-of-production method.   4. Declining-balance method.

STRAIGHT-LINE METHOD

The **straight-line method** is simple to use, because it allocates the cost of the asset (less residual value) evenly over its estimated useful life. (At the time an asset is acquired, an estimate is made of its usefulness or **useful life** in terms of number of years it would last, amount of output expected, etc.) Let's look at how Melvin Company calculates its depreciation expense for each of the estimated 5 years of usefulness using the straight-line method. Take a moment to read the key points in the parentheses below the accompanying table.

The formula:

$$\frac{\text{cost} - \text{residual value}}{\text{service useful life in years}} = \frac{\$20,000 - \$2,000}{5} = \$3,600$$

End of Year	Cost of Delivery Truck	Yearly* Depreciation Expense	Accumulated Depreciation, End of Year	Book Value, End of Year (Cost − Accum. Dep.)
1	$20,000	$3,600	$ 3,600	$16,400
2	20,000	3,600	7,200	12,800
3	20,000	3,600	10,800	9,200
4	20,000	3,600	14,400	5,600
5	20,000	3,600	18,000	2,000
	↑	↑	↑	↑
	(Cost of machine doesn't change)	(Note that depreciation expense is the same each year)	(Accumulated depreciation increases by $3,600 each year)	(Book value each year is lowered by $3,600 until residual value of $2,000 is reached)

* The depreciation rate is 100 percent ÷ 5 years = 20 percent. The 20 percent is then multiplied times the cost minus the residual value.

UNITS-OF-PRODUCTION METHOD

Depreciation expense is directly related to use, not to passage of time.

With the **units-of-production method** it is assumed that *passage of time* does not determine the amount of depreciation taken. Depreciation expense is based on *use*, be it total estimated miles, tons hauled, or estimated units of production—for example, the number of shoes a machine could produce in its expected useful life. The accompanying table shows the calculations that Melvin Company makes for its truck using the units-of-production method (note that the truck is assumed to have an estimated life of 90,000 miles).

The formula:

$$\frac{\text{cost} - \text{residual value}}{\text{estimated units of production}} = \frac{\$20,000 - \$2,000}{90,000 \text{ miles}} = \$.20 \text{ per mile}$$

($.20) × (no. of miles driven) = Depreciation expense for period

End of Year	Cost of Delivery Truck	Miles Driven in Year	Yearly Depreciation Expense	Accumulated Depreciation, End of Year	Book Value, End of Year (Cost − Accum. Dep.)
1	$20,000	30,000	$6,000	$6,000	$14,000
2	20,000	21,000	4,200	10,200	9,800
3	20,000	15,000	3,000	13,200	6,800
4	20,000	5,000	1,000	14,200	5,800
5	20,000	19,000	3,800	18,000	2,000
		↑	↑		
		(After 5 years, truck has been driven 90,000 miles)	(Depreciation expense is directly related to number of miles driven)		

SUM-OF-THE-YEARS'-DIGITS METHOD

The **sum-of-the-years'-digits method** places more depreciation expense in the early years rather than the later years in order to better match revenue and expenses, since an asset's productivity may be reduced in later years. For this reason it is called an **accelerated depreciation** method. To use it, you multiply cost minus residual times a certain fraction. This fraction is made up of the following:

1. *The denominator:* The denominator is based on how many years the asset is likely to last (say 5). You then add the sum of the digits of 5 years (1 + 2 + 3 + 4 + 5), which equals 15; 15 is the denominator. [There is also a formula to use for the denominator: $N(N + 1)/2$, where N stands for number of years of useful life (in our case, 5 years). In our case the formula would look like this: $5(5 + 1)/2 = 15$.]
2. *The numerator:* The years in reverse order are the numerator (in our case, 5, 4, 3, 2, 1).

Thus in year 1 the fraction would be 5/15; in year 2, 4/15; in year 3, 3/15; in year 4, 2/15; in year 5, 1/15. And in each year you would multiply this fraction times cost minus residual to find the depreciation expense. This is shown in the accompanying table.

End of Year	$\begin{pmatrix} \text{Cost} \\ \text{Minus} \\ \text{Residual} \end{pmatrix}$	×	$\begin{pmatrix} \text{Fraction} \\ \text{for Year} \end{pmatrix}$	=	Yearly Depreciation Expense	Accumulated Depreciation, End of Year	Book Value, End of Year (Cost − Accum. Dep.)
1	$18,000	×	$\frac{5}{15}$	=	$6,000	$ 6,000	$14,000 ($20,000 − $6,000)
	(20,000 − 2,000)						
2	18,000	×	$\frac{4}{15}$	=	4,800	10,800	9,200
3	18,000	×	$\frac{3}{15}$	=	3,600	14,400	5,600
4	18,000	×	$\frac{2}{15}$	=	2,400	16,800	3,200
5	18,000	×	$\frac{1}{15}$	=	1,200	18,000	2,000
		↑			↑	↑	↑
	(Fraction for year is multiplied times cost minus residual)				(Depreciation expense in first year is highest)	(Each year depreciation accumulates by a smaller amount)	(Book value goes down each year until residual is reached)

Take a moment to make sure you see how the figures for these calculations are arrived at before moving on to the next method.

DOUBLE DECLINING-BALANCE METHOD

The **double declining-balance method** is also an accelerated method, in which a larger depreciation expense is taken in earlier years and smaller amounts in later years. This method uses twice the straight-line rate, which is why it is called the *double* declining-balance method.

A key point in this method is that *residual value* is *not* deducted from cost in the calculations, although the asset cannot be depreciated below its residual value. To calculate depreciation, take the following steps:

1. Calculate the straight-line rate and double it:

$$\frac{100\%}{\text{useful life}} \times 2$$

2. At the *end of each year* multiply rate times book value of asset at beginning of year.

Let's look at how Melvin Company calculates the depreciation on its truck using this method.

Note rate of .40 is not
changed (20% × 2)

End of Year	Cost	Accumulated Depreciation, Beg. of Year	Book Value Beg. of Year (Cost − Acc. Dep.)	Dep. Exp. (B.V. Beg. of Year × Rate)	Accumulated Depreciation, End of Year	Book Value, End of Year (Cost − Acc. Dep.)
1	$20,000		$20,000	$8,000 ($20,000 × .40)	$ 8,000	$12,000 (20,000 − 8,000)
2	20,000	$ 8,000	12,000	4,800 (12,000 × .40)	12,800 (8,000 + 4,800)	7,200
3	20,000	12,800	7,200	2,880 (7,200 × .40)	15,680	4,320
4	20,000	15,680	4,320	1,728 (4,320 × .40)	17,408	2,592
5	20,000	17,408	2,592	592	18,000	2,000

(Original cost remains the same)

(Depreciation is limited to $592, since the asset cannot depreciate below the residual value)

(The book value now equals the residual value)

Be sure to note the $592 in year 5 of depreciation expense. We could not take more than the $592, or we would have depreciated the asset below the residual value.

DEPRECIATION FOR TAX PURPOSES BEFORE THE TAX REFORM ACT OF 1986

Over the years, the methods we have discussed have been used for *financial* reporting; they have not been used for *tax* purposes. For tangible assets bought prior to 1981, tax law allowed companies to use the declining-balance or sum-of-the-years'-digits methods for tax reporting. Beginning in 1981, the Accelerated Cost Recovery System (MACRS) began to be used. The MACRS is a simpler system, meant to stimulate economic growth by faster cost recovery.

MACRS eliminates the concept of useful life and salvage value and establishes classes of depreciable property, dividing it into 3-, 5-, 10-, 18-, or 19-year property. The deductions for depreciation MACRS allows are shown in Table B-1 on page B9. Using this table, you can see that if Melvin Company used ACRS for its $20,000 truck (a light truck in the 3-year class) bought on January 1, the following depreciation would be recorded:

19X1   .25 × $20,000 = $ 5,000
19X2   .38 × 20,000 =   7,600
19X3   .37 × 20,000 =   7,400
$20,000

The important points to remember are:

1. ACRS is generally not acceptable in preparing financial reports, because it allocates depreciation over a much shorter period than estimated useful life.

2. ACRS for tax reporting defers payment of income tax, since large amounts of depreciation are charged to earlier years.

Note that Table B-1 is before the Tax Reform Act of 1986.

	For Property in the		
	Three-Year Class[1]	Five-Year Class[2]	Ten-Year Class[3]
1st year	25	15	8
2nd year	38	22	14
3rd year	37	21	12
4th year		21	10
5th year		21	10
6th year			10
7th year			9
8th year			9
9th year			9
10th year			9

[1] Three-year class includes autos, some tools, and light trucks.
[2] Five-year class includes most machinery and equipment.
[3] Ten-year class includes amusement parks, pipelines, and nuclear plants.

MACRS AFTER THE TAX REFORM ACT OF 1986 (GENERAL DEPRECIATION SYSTEM)

This tax act generally overhauls the depreciation setup of property placed in service after December 31, 1986. Look for a moment at Figure B-1. This is a chart that summarizes the Tax Reform Act update. As you can see, some new classes are introduced (7- and 20-year property); cars and light trucks are moved from the 3-year class to the 5-year class; and office equipment moves from the 5-year class to the 7-year class.

According to this act, classes 3, 5, 7, and 10 use 200 percent declining-balance, switching to straight-line, while classes 15 and 20 use 150 percent declining-

FIGURE B-1

Summary of Classes for the Tax Reform Act Update

The following classes use a 200 percent declining-balance, switching to straight-line:

◆ 3-year: Race horses more than two years old or any horse other than a race horse that is more than 12 years old at time placed into service; special tools of certain industries.

◆ 5-year: Automobiles (not luxury); taxis; light general-purpose trucks, semiconductor manufacturing equipment; computer-based telephone central office switching equipment; qualified technological equipment; property used in connection with research and experimentation.

◆ 7-year: Railroad track; single-purpose agricultural (pigpens) or horticultural structure; fixtures, equipment, and furniture.

◆ 10-year: The 1986 law doesn't add any specific property under this class.

The following classes use a 150 percent declining-balance, switching to straight-line:

◆ 15-year: Municipal wastewater treatment plants; telephone distribution plants and comparable equipment used for two-way exchange of voice and data communications.

◆ 20-year: municipal sewers.

The following classes use straight-line:

◆ 27.5-year: Only residential rental property.

◆ 31.5-year: Only nonresidential real property.

Recovery Year	3-Year Class (200% D.B.)	5-Year Class (200% D.B.)	7-Year Class (200% D.B.)	10-Year Class (200% D.B.)	15-Year Class (150% D.B.)	20-Year Class (150% D.B.)
1	33.00	20.00	14.28	10.00	5.00	3.75
2	45.00	32.00	24.49	18.00	9.50	7.22
3	15.00*	19.20	17.49	14.40	8.55	6.68
4	7.00	11.52*	12.49	11.52	7.69	6.18
5		11.52	8.93*	9.22	6.93	5.71
6		5.76	8.93	7.37	6.23	5.28
7			8.93	6.55*	5.90*	4.89
8			4.46	6.55	5.90	4.52
9				6.55	5.90	4.46*
10				6.55	5.90	4.46
11				3.29	5.90	4.46
12					5.90	4.46
13					5.90	4.46
14					5.90	4.46
15					5.90	4.46
16					3.00	4.46
17						

* Identifies when switch is made to straight-line.

balance, switching to straight-line. Both residential and nonresidential real property must use straight-line. Note that the recovery period is extended to $27\frac{1}{2}$ years for residential property and to $31\frac{1}{2}$ years for nonresidential property.

Let's use Table B-2 (which was developed for this tax law) to calculate depreciation on the purchase of a nonluxury car for $5,000 on March 19, 1987.

Using Table B-2 to figure our example, we get the following:

YEAR	DEPRECIATION
1	.20 × $5,000 = $1,000
2	.32 × $5,000 = 1,600
3	.1920 × $5,000 = 960
4	.1152 × $5,000 = 576
5	.1152 × $5,000 = 576
6	.0576 × $5,000 = 288

When we use this table, we do not have to decide which year we should switch from declining-balance to straight-line.

LEARNING UNIT B-2 REVIEW

PROBLEMS (Solution at End of Appendix)

Depreciation schedule.

1. Agor Co., whose accounting period ends on December 31, purchased a machine for $34,000 on January 1 with an estimated residual value of $4,000 and

estimated useful life of 10 years. Prepare depreciation schedules for the current as well as following year using (a) straight-line, (b) sum-of-the-years'-digits, and (c) declining-balance at twice the straight-line rate.

ACRS.

2. Jangles bought an amusement park for $200,000 on January 1, 19XX. Calculate his depreciation expense for tax purposes for the first three years using the Accelerated Cost Recovery System. (This is before the Tax Reform Act of 1986 came into effect.)

ACRS and Tax Reform Act of 1986.

3. Bill Moore Company bought a light general-purpose truck for $10,000 on March 8, 1987. Calculate the yearly depreciation using the ACRS method. (Remember that the Tax Reform Act of 1986 applies.)

4. On January 1, 19XX, a machine was installed at Zebrot Factory at a cost of $29,000. Its estimated residual value at the end of its estimated life of 4 years is $9,000. The machine is expected to produce 50,000 units with the following production schedule:

   ◆ 19X1: 8,000 units
   ◆ 19X2: 17,000 units
   ◆ 19X3: 15,000 units
   ◆ 19X4: 10,000 units

Complete depreciation schedules for (a) straight-line, (b) units of production, (c) sum-of-the-years'-digits, (d) declining balance at twice the straight-line rate.

Solution to Problem on Inventory

(See Learning Unit B-1 Review.)

		UNITS	COST PER UNIT		
Jan. 1	Beg. Inv.	300	$40	=	$12,000
Apr. 1	Purchased	200	50	=	10,000
Jul. 5	Purchased	500	60	=	30,000
Aug. 15	Purchased	400	70	=	28,000
Nov. 20	Purchased	200	80	=	16,000
		1,600			$96,000

a. FIFO

200 × $80	= $16,000	COGAFS	$96,000
200 × $70	= 14,000	− Cost of End. Inv.	30,000
Cost of End. Inv.	$30,000	COGS	$66,000

b. LIFO

300 × $40	= $12,000	COGAFS	$96,000
100 × $50	= 5,000	− Cost of End. Inv.	17,000
Cost of End. Inv.	$17,000	COGS	$79,000

c. WEIGHTED-AVERAGE

$$\frac{\$96,000}{1,600 \text{ units}} = \$60$$

400 × $60 = $24,000   Cost of Ending Inventory

COGAFS	$96,000
− Cost of End. Inv.	24,000
COGS	$72,000

Solution to Depreciation Problems

(See Learning Unit B-2 Review.)

1. a. Straight-line

$$\frac{\$34,000 - \$4,000}{10} = \frac{\$30,000}{10} = \$3,000$$

Year	Cost	Dep. Exp.	Acc. Dep. E.O.Y.	Book Value E.O.Y.
1	$34,000	$3,000	$3,000	$31,000
2	34,000	3,000	6,000	28,000

b.

Year	Cost Less Residual	×	Fraction for Year	=	Yearly Deprec. Expense	Acc. Dep. E.O.Y.	Book Value E.O.Y.
1	$30,000	×	10/55	=	$5,454.55	$ 5,454.55	$28,545.45
2	30,000		9/55	=	4,909.09	10,363.64	23,636.36

c.

DECLINING-BALANCE

Year	Cost	Acc. Dep. B.O.Y.	Book Value B.O.Y.	Dep. Exp.	Acc. Dep. E.O.Y.	Book Value E.O.Y.
1	$34,000	—	$34,000	$6,800	$ 6,800	$27,200
				(34,000 × .20)		
2	34,000	$6,800	27,200	5,440	12,240	21,760

2. Amusement Parks — Ten-Year Class

Year
1	.08 × $200,000 = $16,000
2	.14 × 200,000 = 28,000
3	.12 × 200,000 = 24,000

Total Depreciation for Three Years $68,000

3.
.20	× $10,000 =	$ 2,000
.32	× 10,000 =	3,200
.1920	× 10,000 =	1,920
.1152	× 10,000 =	1,152
.1152	× 10,000 =	1,152
.0576	× 10,000 =	576
		$10,000

4. a.

$$\frac{\$29,000 - \$9,000}{4 \text{ Years}} = \frac{\$20,000}{4} = \$5,000$$

End of Year	Cost of Equipment	Yearly Depreciation Expense	Acc. Dep. E.O.Y.	Book Value E.O.Y.
19X1	$29,000	$5,000	$ 5,000	$24,000
19X2	29,000	5,000	10,000	19,000
19X3	29,000	5,000	15,000	14,000
19X4	29,000	5,000	20,000	9,000

b.
$$\frac{\$29{,}000 - \$9{,}000}{50{,}000 \text{ units}} = \frac{\$20{,}000}{50{,}000} = \$.40 \text{ per unit}$$

End of Year	Cost of Equipment	Units Produced	Yearly Depreciation Expense	Acc. Dep. E.O.Y.	Book Value E.O.Y.
19X1	$29,000	$ 8,000	$3,200	$ 3,200	25,800
19X2	29,000	17,000	6,800	10,000	19,000
19X3	29,000	15,000	6,000	16,000	13,000
19X4	29,000	10,000	4,000	20,000	9,000

c.

End of Year	Cost Less Residual × Rate	=	Yearly Depreciation Expense	Acc. Dep. E.O.Y.	Book Value E.O.Y.
19X1	$20,000 × 4/10	=	$8,000	$ 8,000	$21,000
19X2	20,000 × 3/10	=	6,000	14,000	15,000
19X3	20,000 × 2/10	=	4,000	18,000	11,000
19X4	20,000 × 1/10	=	2,000	20,000	9,000

d.

End of Year	Cost	Acc. Dep. B.O.Y.	Book Value B.O.Y.	Dep. Exp.	Acc. Dep. E.O.Y.	Book Value E.O.Y.
19X1	$29,000	—	$29,000	$14,500 (29,000 × .50)	$14,500	$14,500
19X2	29,000	14,500	14,500	5,500	20,000	9,000

In year 2 we could only depreciate up to $5,500 so that Book Value does not go below Residual value of $9,000.

COMPUTERIZED ACCOUNTING

PART A
An Introduction

ccounting procedures are essentially the same whether they are performed manually or on a computer. The following is a list of the accounting cycle steps in a manual accounting system as compared to the steps in a computerized accounting system.

STEPS OF THE ACCOUNTING CYCLE

Manual Accounting System	Computerized Accounting System
1. Business transactions occur and generate source documents.	1. Business transactions occur and generate source documents.
2. Analyze and record business transactions in a journal.	2. Analyze and record business transactions in a computerized journal.
3. Post or transfer information from journal to ledger.	3. Computer automatically posts information from journal to ledger.
4. Prepare a trial balance.	4. Trial balance is prepared automatically.
5. Prepare a worksheet.	5. No worksheet is necessary.
6. Prepare financial statements.	6. Financial statements are prepared automatically.
7. Journalize and post adjusting entries.	7. Record adjusting entries in a computerized journal; posting is automatic.
8. Journalize and post closing entries.	8. Closing procedures are completed automatically.
9. Prepare a post-closing trial balance.	9. Trial balance is prepared automatically.

The accounting cycle comparison shows that the accountant's task of initially analyzing business transactions in terms of debits and credits (both routine business transactions and adjusting entries) is required in both manual and computerized accounting systems. However, in a computerized accounting system, the "drudge" work of posting transactions, creating and completing worksheets and financial statements, and performing the closing procedures is all handled automatically by the computerized accounting system.

In addition, computerized accounting systems can perform accounting procedures at greater speeds and with greater accuracy than can be achieved in a manual accounting system. It is important to recognize, however, that the computer is only a tool that can accept and process information supplied by the accountant. Each business transaction and adjusting entry must first be analyzed and recorded in a computerized journal correctly; otherwise, the financial statements generated by the computerized accounting system will contain errors and will not be useful to the business.

Before a business can begin to use a computerized accounting system, and specifically the Simply Accounting system, it must have the following items in place:

1. A computer system
2. Computer software
   a. Operating system software
   b. Applications software
      (1) Accounting applications software
      (2) Simply Accounting

COMPUTER SYSTEM

A computer system consists of several electronic components that together have the ability to accept user-supplied data; input, store, and execute programmed instructions; and output results according to user specifications. The physical computer and its related devices are the hardware, while the stored program that supplies the instructions is called the software.

To understand how a computer system works, we must first look at a conceptual computer that demonstrates the major components and functions of a computer system. The conceptual computer shown in Figure C-1 has four major elements — input devices, processing/internal memory unit, secondary storage devices, and output devices. The illustration also shows the flow of data into the computer and of processed information out of the computer.

Input devices are used to feed data and instructions into the computer. Once the data and instructions are entered, the computer must be able to store them internally and then process the data based on the instructions. Storage and processing occur in the processing/internal memory unit.

There are two types of internal computer memory: random-access memory (RAM) and read-only memory (ROM). RAM is the largest portion of the memory but still has limited capacity; consequently, secondary storage devices are needed. In addition, RAM is temporary — anything stored in RAM is erased when power to the computer is interrupted. Therefore, data stored in RAM must be saved to a secondary storage medium through the use of a secondary storage device before the power is turned off. ROM is permanent memory and consists of those instruction

FIGURE C-1
Conceptual Computer

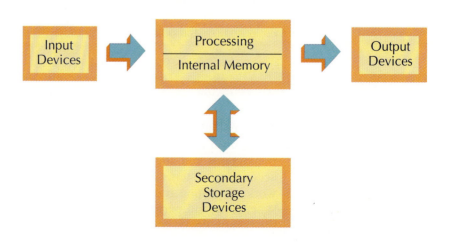

Monitor **Processing/Internal Memory Unit**
(housed inside box)

Floppy
Disk Drive

Hard Drive

CD-ROM Drive

Printer

Keyboard **Mouse**

FIGURE C-2
Typical Configuration of a
Microcomputer System

sets necessary to start the computer and receive initial messages from input devices. ROM takes up only a small portion of the total internal memory capacity of a computer system.

Finally, the results of processing must be made available to computer users through output devices. These components form a collection of devices referred to as computer hardware because they have physical substance.

In a typical microcomputer system (see Fig. C-2) a keyboard and mouse are used for input and a printer and monitor are used for output. The processing/internal memory unit is housed inside a box along with secondary storage devices consisting of a hard drive unit, one or more floppy disk drives, and a CD-ROM drive.

Computer hardware can do nothing without a computer program. Computer programs are supplied on floppy disks or CD-ROMs, which are secondary storage media used in floppy disk or CD-ROM drives. Figure C-3 shows an example of a floppy disk and of a CD-ROM.

To operate a particular computer program you must first load the program into the system's internal memory (RAM) through the use of a floppy disk or CD-ROM drive or by accessing the program that has been installed and stored on the system's hard drive. Once a program is accessed by RAM, the computer can execute the program instructions and process data as directed by the user through the keyboard or mouse. At the end of a processing session, the results may be viewed on the monitor, printed on the printer, and/or stored permanently on a floppy disk or hard drive.

COMPUTER SOFTWARE

The computer can do nothing without a computer program. Computer programs control the input, processing, storage, and output operations of a computer. Computer programmers write the instructions that tell the computer to execute certain

FIGURE C-3
Storage Media

CD-ROM **Floppy disk**

Write
Protect
Notch

Label

procedures and process data. There are two broad categories of computer software: operating system software and applications software.

Operating System Software

Operating system software provides the link between the computer hardware, applications software, and the computer user. It consists of programs that start up the computer, retrieve applications programs, and allow the computer operator to store and retrieve data. Operating system software controls access to input and output devices and access to applications programs. There are several popular operating systems for microcomputers. They include Windows 95, DOS, DOS combined with Windows 3.XX, OS/2, the Macintosh operating system, and UNIX.

Applications Software

Applications software refers to programs designed for a specific use. The five most common types of business applications software are database management, spreadsheets, word processing communications, and graphics. Spreadsheet software allows the manipulation of data and has the ability to project answers to "what if" questions. For example, a spreadsheet program could project a company's profit next year if sales increased by 10 percent and expenses increased by 6 percent. Word processing software enables the user to write and print letters, memos, and other documents. Graphics software displays data visually in the form of graphic images, and communications software allows your computer to "talk" to other computers. But to accomplish communications you need additional hardware: a modem to transmit and receive data over telephone lines. Database management software stores, retrieves, sorts, and updates an organized body of information. Most computerized accounting systems are designed as database management software. Accounting information is data that must be organized and stored in a common base of data. This allows the entry of data and the retrieval of information in an organized and systematic way.

Applications software is frequently linked with a particular operating system. Database management, spreadsheet, word processing graphics, communication, accounting, and other software applications are available in versions that work with most of the popular operating systems. For example, if your computer system is using Windows 95 you would purchase the Windows 95 version of a word processing program. If you were using a Macintosh computer and operating system you would purchase the Macintosh version of a spreadsheet program.

Accounting Applications Software   Most computerized accounting software is organized into modules. Each module is designed to process a particular type of accounting data such as accounts receivable, accounts payable, or payroll. Each module is also designed to work in conjunction with the other modules. When modules are designed to work together in this manner, they are referred to as integrated software. In an integrated accounting system each module handles a different function but also communicates with the other modules. For example, to record a sale on account, you would make an entry into the accounts receivable module. The integration feature automatically records this entry in the sales journal, updates the customer's account in the accounts receivable subsidiary ledger, and posts all accounts affected in the general ledger. Thus in an integrated accounting system, transaction data are only entered once. All of the other accounting procedures required to bring the accounting records up-to-date are performed automatically through the integration function.

Simply Accounting   The educational version of Simply Accounting has been selected for use in this text to demonstrate and help you learn how to use a computerized accounting system. It is easy to use, fully integrated, and is also available in versions that work with several different operating systems. Simply Accounting includes six modules: General, Receivables, Payables, Inventory, Payroll, and Project.

Two modes of operation are available in Simply Accounting: Ready and Not Ready. The Not Ready mode is used when you are converting a manual accounting system to a computerized accounting system. The Ready mode is used for regular accounting purposes. The educational version is the complete commercial program package with one restriction: The program will not accept dates after January 1, 1998. The payroll functions of the educational version are based on the federal and state tax laws in effect as of April 15, 1997.

WORKING WITH SIMPLY ACCOUNTING

Before you begin to work with Simply Accounting you need to be familiar with your computer hardware and the Windows 95 operating system. When you are running Windows 95, your work takes place on the desktop. Think of this area as resembling the surface of a desk. There are physical objects on your real desk and there are windows and icons on the Windows 95 desktop.

A mouse is an essential input device for all Windows 95 applications. A mouse is a pointing device which assumes different shapes on your monitor as you move the mouse on your desk. According to the nature of the current action, the mouse pointer may appear as a small arrow head, an hourglass, or a hand. There are five basic mouse techniques:

◆	Click	To quickly press and release the left mouse button.
◆	Double-click	To click the left mouse button twice in rapid succession.
◆	Drag	To hold down the left mouse button while you move the mouse.
◆	Point	To position the mouse pointer over an object without clicking a button.
◆	Right-click	To quickly press and release the right mouse button.

The Windows 95 Desktop

Figure C-4 shows a typical opening Windows 95 screen. Your desktop may be different, just as your real desk is arranged differently from those of your colleagues.

- ◆ **Desktop icons:** Graphic representations of drives, files, and other resources. The desktop icons that display will vary depending on your computer setup.
- ◆ **Start button:** Clicking on the Start button displays the start menu and lets you start applications.
- ◆ **Taskbar:** Contains the Start button and other buttons representing open applications.

FIGURE C-4
Windows 95 Desktop

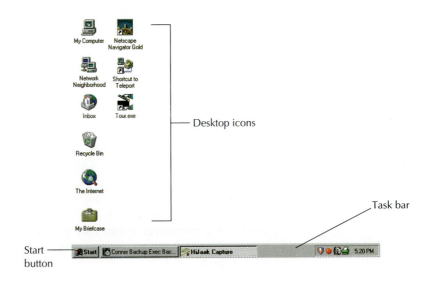

Applications Window (the Company Window)

As you work with Simply Accounting two kinds of windows will appear on your desktop: the application window (called the Company Window — see Fig. C-5), and windows contained within the Company Window (called dialog boxes). An application window contains a running application. The name of the application and the application's menu bar will appear at the top of the application window. Regardless of the windows that are open on your desktop, most windows have certain elements in common.

FIGURE C-5

Simply Accounting Application (Company) Window

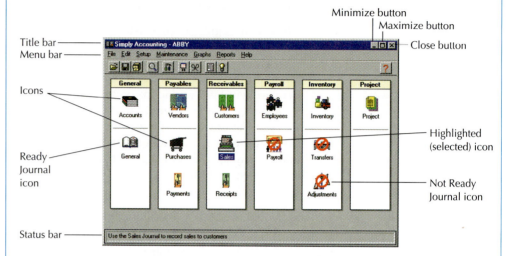

- ◆ **Minimize button:** Clicking on this button minimizes a window and displays it as a task button on the taskbar.
- ◆ **Maximize button:** Clicking on this button enlarges the window so that it fills the entire desktop. After you enlarge a window, the maximize button is replaced by a **Restore button** (a double box, not shown) that returns the window to the size it was before it was maximized.
- ◆ **Close button:** Clicking on this button will close the window.
- ◆ **Title bar:** Displays the name of the application.
- ◆ **Menu bar:** This window element lists the available menus for the window.
- ◆ **Icons:** The Company Window displays the icons that represent a company's accounting books — the full set of Ledgers and Journals that you use to record accounting transactions. The top row contains the Ledgers; the bottom two rows contain the Journals aligned vertically with their related Ledgers.
- ◆ **Highlighted (selected) icon:** The active icon in the Company Window.
- ◆ **Not Ready Journal icon:** A Journal icon is shown with a no-entry symbol if its status is Not Ready.
- ◆ **Ready Journal icon:** A Journal icon is shown without a no-entry symbol if its status is Ready.
- ◆ **Status bar:** A line of text at the bottom of many windows that gives more information about a field, button, or menu item. If you are unsure of what to enter in a field or what a button is for, point to it with your mouse and read the status bar.

Dialog Boxes

A dialog box appears when additional information is needed to execute a command. There are different ways to supply that information; consequently, there are different types of dialog boxes. Most dialog boxes (see Fig. C-6) contain options you can select. After you specify options, you can choose a command button to carry out a command. Other dialog boxes (see Fig. C-7) may display additional information, warnings, or messages indicating why a requested task cannot be accomplished.

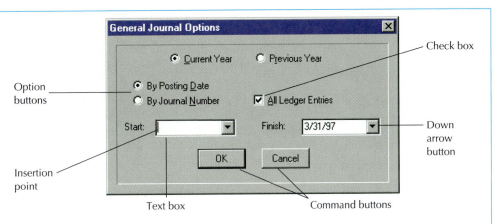

FIGURE C-6
Dialog Box 1

Option buttons

Check box

Down arrow button

Insertion point

Text box

Command buttons

◆ **Insertion point:** This element shows where you are in the dialog box. It marks the place where text will appear when you begin typing.

◆ **Check box:** A small square that represents an option. When you select an option (click on the empty check box), the check box contains an X; when you turn off the option (click on the check box to remove the X), it is blank.

◆ **Option buttons:** A small circle that represents an option. When you select (click on the button) an option from a group, that button contains a large black dot; the remaining buttons in the group are blank. Option buttons represent mutually exclusive options. You can select only one option button at a time.

◆ **Text box:** When you move to an empty text box, an insertion point appears at the far left-hand side of the box. The text you type starts at the insertion point. If the box you move to already contains text, this text is selected (highlighted), and any text you type replaces it. You can also delete the selected text by pressing the DELETE or BACKSPACE key.

◆ **Command buttons:** Choose (click) on a command button to initiate an immediate action such as carrying out or canceling a command. The **OK, Cancel, Yes, No,** and **Post** buttons are common command buttons.

◆ **Down arrow button:** Click on this button to display a list of choices.

FIGURE C-7
Dialog Box 2

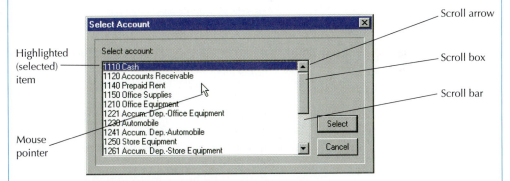

Highlighted (selected) item

Mouse pointer

Scroll arrow

Scroll box

Scroll bar

◆ **Highlighted (selected) item:** To highlight or select an item in a displayed list, click on the item.

◆ **Scroll bar:** A bar that may appear at the bottom and/or right side of a window or dialog box if there is more text than can be displayed at one time within the window.

◆ **Scroll arrow:** A small arrow at the end of a scroll bar that you click on to move to the next item in the list. The top and left arrows scroll to the previous item; the bottom and right arrows scroll to the next item.

◆ **Scroll box:** A small box in a scroll bar. You can use the mouse to drag the scroll box left or right, or up or down. The scroll box indicates the relative position in the list.

◆ **Mouse pointer:** The mouse pointer is shown as a small arrow head in this example.

Using Menus

Commands are listed on menus, as shown in Figure C-8. Each application has its own menus which are listed on the **Application menu bar.** To display a complete menu, click on the **Menu title.** When a menu is displayed, choose a command by clicking on it or by typing the **Underlined letter** to execute the command. You can also bypass the menu entirely if you know the **Keyboard equivalent** shown to the right of the command when the menu is displayed.

A **Dimmed command** indicates that a command is not currently executable; some additional action has to be taken for the command to become available. Some commands are followed by **Ellipses** (. . .) to indicate that more information is required to execute the command. The additional information can be entered into a dialog box, which will appear immediately after the command has been selected.

FIGURE C-8
Sample Menu

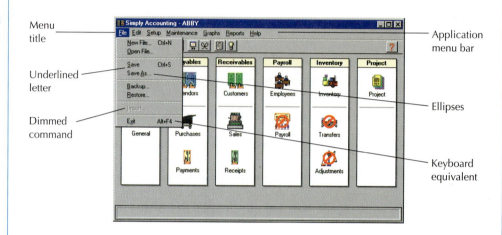

Working in the Windows 95 Environment

You can use a combination of mouse and keyboard techniques to navigate within the Windows 95 environment. For example, you can click on an item to select it, and then press the ENTER key to choose it, or you can just double-click on the item. Simply Accounting is designed for a mouse, but it also provides keyboard equivalents for almost every command. It may seem confusing at first that there are several different ways to do the same thing. You will find this flexibility useful. For example, if your hands are already on the keyboard, it may be faster to use the keyboard equivalent of a mouse command. Alternatively, if your hand is already on the mouse, it may be faster to use a mouse technique to carry out a command. When a procedure in an assignment says to select or choose an item, generally use whichever method you prefer. Alternative procedures are often provided as well. It is not necessary to memorize any particular technique, just be flexible and willing to experiment. As you gain experience with the program, you will develop personal preferences, and the various techniques will become second nature.

Windows 95 Tour

Windows 95 includes a tour to acquaint new users with mouse techniques and the Windows 95 operating environment. Use the following instructions to access the Windows Tour on your computer system.

1. Click on the Start button; then click on Run.

2. Type tour.exe into the **Open** text box; then click on the **OK** button.

3. Follow the instructions on your screen to complete the tour.

PART *B*
Installing Simply Accounting/Creating a Student Data Files Disk

This section of the appendix discusses several basic operations that you need to complete to install the Simply Accounting program and create a Student Data Files disk for use in completing the Computer Workshop assignments in this text.

SYSTEM REQUIREMENTS

The recommended minimum software and hardware your computer system needs to run both Windows and Simply Accounting successfully are:

- Microsoft Windows 3.1 or 3.11, or Windows 95.
- A personal computer with an 80486/33 processor.
- A hard disk with 12 MB of free disk space.
- One 3.5 inch high density floppy disk drive.
- A CD-ROM drive (optional, the Simply Accounting program and the Student Data Files are also available on 3.5 inch high density floppy disks).
- 8 MB of RAM.
- A VGA, or similar high-resolution monitor that is supported by Windows.
- A printer that is supported by Windows.
- A mouse that is supported by Windows.

CD-ROM CONTENTS

The Simply Accounting installation and program files (in condensed form) and the Student Data Files (not in condensed form) for use in completing the Computer Workshops are on the CD-ROM that accompanies this text.

Installation Procedures

To install Simply Accounting on your hard disk, follow these instructions:

1. Start Windows.
2. Make sure that no other programs are running on your system.
3. Insert the CD-ROM in your CD-ROM drive.
4. Click on the Start button; then click on Run.
5. Type d:setup and press the ENTER key. For d, substitute the letter of your CD-ROM drive.
6. Follow the step-by-step instructions as they appear on the screen. Enter your Name and your school's name as the Company when requested. Enter the following serial number when requested: 252160230500. Install all of the Simply Accounting components. Read the ReadMe text file; then click on the Close button.
7. Put your CD-ROM away for safekeeping.

Installing Simply Accounting on a Network

Simply Accounting can be used in a network environment as long as each student uses a separate Student Data Files disk to store his or her data files. Refer to the *Instructor's Resource and Solutions Manual for College Accounting,* seventh edition, for specific network installation instructions.

APP. C / COMPUTERIZED ACCOUNTING

C9

Students should consult with their instructor and/or network administrator for specific procedures regarding program installation and any special printing procedures required for proper network operation.

Creating a Student Data Files Disk

The Student Data Files for use in completing the Computer Workshops are on the CD-ROM that accompanies this text in a special folder called Student. You need to copy these files from the CD-ROM to a 3.5 inch high density floppy disk. You will need a blank, formatted 3.5 inch high density floppy disk labeled "Student Data Files Disk."

1. Insert the CD-ROM in your CD-ROM drive.
2. Insert your blank, formatted 3.5 inch high density floppy disk into your 3.5 inch disk drive.
3. Double-click on the My Computer icon on your Windows 95 desktop. The My Computer window will appear.
4. In the My Computer window double-click on the icon for your CD-ROM drive. The contents of the CD-ROM will be displayed.
5. Right-click on the Student folder; point to Send To; then click on the icon for $3\frac{1}{2}$ Floppy. The copying window will appear. When your system has finished copying the files, close the CD-ROM window, then close the My Computer window.
6. Put your CD-ROM away for safekeeping. Use your Student Data Files disk to complete the Computer Workshop assignments.

PART C

Correcting a Posted Transaction

Once a transaction is posted in Simply Accounting, the journal entry will be permanently reflected in the accounting records. This feature of Simply Accounting is designed to ensure that a good audit trail of all transactions is constantly maintained within the program. Consequently, the only way to correct a posted transaction is to reverse the original entry. After this is accomplished, the accounting records will be in the same position as if the transaction had not been posted in the first place, but a complete record of the original entry and the reversing entry will be maintained by the program. After the reversing entry is posted, enter the correct journal entry.

The term reversing entry as it is used here should not be confused with the optional way of handling certain adjusting entries. The optional reversing entry procedure for adjusting entries is designed to help prevent errors. Reversing an incorrect entry in a computerized accounting system is a required procedure designed to correct an error that has already occurred.

The following procedures for reversing an incorrect journal entry and re-entering the correct journal entry are not intended to be exhaustive, but to give you the general idea of how to correct transactions posted in error. It is impossible to predict the particular error or combination of errors you might make in an assignment.

REVERSING AN ENTRY MADE IN THE GENERAL JOURNAL DIALOG BOX: USE THE GENERAL JOURNAL

You will need to have a printed copy of a General Journal report listing the entry you intend to reverse on hand as you work through the following reversing and correcting procedures.

1. Open the General Journal; enter the word "Reverse" into the **Source** text box; press the TAB key; enter the **Using** date into the **Date** text box; press the TAB key; enter an explanation for the transaction into the **Comment** text box; then press the TAB key.

2. Refer to your printed copy of the General Journal report. With the flashing insertion point positioned in the **Account** text box press the ENTER key to bring up the Select Account dialog box. Double-click on the account that you credited in the incorrect journal entry; enter the amount used in the credit portion of the incorrect journal entry into the **Debits** text box; then press the TAB key.

3. If you are reversing a compound journal entry, skip this step and go to the next step. With the flashing insertion point positioned in the **Account** text box, press the ENTER key to bring up the Select Account dialog box. Double-click on the account that you debited in the incorrect journal entry; then press the TAB key to accept the default **Credits** amount.

4. If you are reversing a compound journal entry, press the ENTER key with the flashing insertion point positioned in the **Account** text box to bring up the Select Account dialog box. Double-click on the first account that you debited in the incorrect compound journal entry. The program will offer a default **Credits** amount and the **Credits** amount will remain highlighted. Override the default **Credits** amount by entering the amount used in the debit portion of the incorrect compound journal entry. Press the TAB key; then press the ENTER key to bring up the Select Account dialog box. Double-click on the second account that you debited in the incorrect compound journal entry. The program will offer a default **Credits** amount; press the TAB key to accept the default **Credits** amount.

5. Click on the General Journal Report menu; then click on Display General Journal Entry. Verify that the reversing entry is correct. The reversing entry should be the exact opposite of your incorrect journal entry. Accounts and amounts originally debited should be credited, and accounts and amounts originally credited should be debited.

6. Close the General Journal Entry Display window. Make editing corrections if necessary.

7. Click on the **Post** icon to post the entry.

8. Re-enter the journal entry correctly. Enter the word "Correct" in the **Source** text box to indicate that it is a correcting entry; enter the **Using** date into the **Date** text box.

NOTE: Simply Accounting will not accept duplicate invoice or check numbers in the Sales, Receipts, Purchases, Payments, or Payroll Journals. This feature of the program is designed to prevent the error of entering invoices and checks twice. Consequently, invoice and check numbers must be modified when reversing and correcting entries are entered. Insert the letter R after the invoice or check number to indicate a reversing entry. Insert the letter C after the invoice or check number to indicate a correcting entry.

REVERSING AN ENTRY MADE IN THE PAYROLL JOURNAL DIALOG BOX: USE THE PAYROLL JOURNAL

1. Click on the Company Window Setup Menu; then click on Settings. The Settings dialog box will appear. Click on the **Payroll** tab; click on the **Automatic Payroll Deductions** check box to de-select this option (the X will disappear from the check box); then click on the **OK** button.

2. Open the Payroll Journal; click on the arrow key to the right of the **To the order of** text box; select the employee from the list displayed; then press the TAB key.

3. Enter the check number into the **No.** text box inserting the letter R after the check number to indicate that this is a reversing entry; then press the TAB key.

4. Enter the Using date into the **Date** text box; then press the TAB key.

5. Accept the **Period Start** and **Period End** dates offered by pressing the TAB key.

6. Refer to your General Journal report listing the incorrect payroll journal entry. Enter amounts into the following text boxes overriding any default amounts offered:

Wages   Enter the amount debited to the Wages account as a negative number.

FIT   Enter the amount credited to the FIT Payable account as a negative number.

SIT   Enter the amount credited to the SIT Payable account as a negative number.

Medicare Tax   Enter the amount debited to the Medicare Tax Expense account as a negative number.

Soc Sec Tax   Enter the amount debited to the Social Security Tax Expense account as a negative number.

7. Press the TAB key; click on the Payroll Journal Report menu; then click on Display Payroll Journal Entry. Verify that the entry is correct. It should be the exact opposite of your incorrect payroll entry. Accounts and amounts originally debited should be credited, and accounts and amounts originally credited should be debited.

8. Close the Payroll Journal Entry window. Make editing corrections if necessary.

9. Click on the **Post** icon to post the entry.

10. Click on the Company Window Setup menu; then click on Settings. The Settings dialog box will appear. Click on the **Payroll** tab; click on the **Automatic Payroll Deductions** check box to re-select this option (the X will re-appear in the check box); then click on the **OK** button.

11. Re-enter the payroll journal entry correctly. Insert the letter C after the check number in the **No.** text box to indicate that this is a correcting entry; enter the **Using** date into the **Date** text box.

REVERSING AND CORRECTING ENTRIES MADE IN SPECIAL JOURNALS

You must know for certain which dialog box you originally used (Sales Journal, Receipts Journal, Purchases Journal, or Payments Journal) to record a transaction prior to attempting to use the reversing procedures described in the following sections for special journals. If you are uncertain about which dialog box you used to record the journal entry you wish to reverse and correct, print a Sales Journal, Receipts Journal, Purchases Journal, and Payments Journal report.

1. **To print a Sales Journal,** click on the Sales Journal icon to highlight the icon; click on the Company Window Reports menu; then click on Display Sales Journal. Enter 3/1/97 into the **Start** date text box; leave the **Finish** date text box set at 3/31/97; then click on the **OK** button. The Sales Journal Display window will appear. Click on the Sales Journal Display File menu; then click on Print to print the report. After you have printed the report, close the Sales Journal Display window.

2. **To print a Receipts Journal,** click on the Receipts Journal icon to highlight the icon; click on the Company Window Reports menu; then click on Display Receipts Journal. Enter 3/1/97 into the **Start** date text box; leave the **Finish** date text box set at 3/31/97; then click on the **OK** button. The Receipts Journal Display window will appear. Click on the Receipts Journal Display File menu; then click on Print to print the report. After you have printed the report, close the Receipts Journal Display window.

3. **To print a Purchases Journal,** click on the Purchases Journal icon to highlight the icon; click on the Company Window Reports menu; then click on Display Purchases Journal. Enter 3/1/97 into the **Start** date text box; leave the

Finish date text box set at 3/31/97; then click on the **OK** button. The Purchases Journal Display window will appear. Click on the Purchases Journal Display File menu; then click on Print to print the report. After you have printed the report, close the Purchases Journal Display window.

4. **To print a Payments Journal,** click on the Payments Journal icon to highlight the icon; click on the Company Window Reports menu; then click on Display Payments Journal. Enter 3/1/97 into the **Start** date text box; leave the **Finish** date text box set at 3/31/97; then click on the **OK** button. The Payments Journal Display window will appear. Click on the Payments Journal Display File menu; then click on Print to print the report. After you have printed the report, close the Payments Journal Display window.

Review each report to determine which report contains the journal entry you wish to reverse; then use the following chart to determine which set of instructions to use to reverse the journal entry and enter the correct entry.

If the journal entry you wish to reverse appears on the:	Use these instructions to reverse the entry and enter the correct entry:
Sales Journal	Reversing an Entry Made in the Sales Journal Dialog Box: Use the Sales Journal
Receipts Journal	Reversing an Entry Made in the Receipts Journal: Use the Sales Journal
Purchases Journal	Reversing an Entry Made in the Purchases Journal: Use the Purchases Journal
Payments Journal	Reversing an Entry Made in the Payments Journal: Use the Purchases Journal

Reversing an Entry Made in the Sales Journal Dialog Box: Use the Sales Journal

1. Open the Sales Journal; click on the arrow button to the right of the **Sold to** text box; select the customer from the list displayed; then press the TAB key until the Invoice text box is highlighted.

2. Enter the invoice number used in the incorrect entry into the **Invoice** text box followed by the letter R to show that you are reversing this entry; then press the TAB key.

3. Enter the Using date into the **Date** text box; then press the TAB key until the insertion point is positioned in the **Amount** text box.

4. Enter the same **Amount** as used in the incorrect entry, preceded by a minus sign if the incorrect amount was originally entered as a positive amount. Enter the amount as a positive amount if the original amount entered was negative. Press the TAB key.

5. Enter the same **Acct** number as used in the incorrect entry (do not use the Accounts Receivable account number); then press the TAB key.

6. Click on the Sales Journal Report menu; then click on Display Sales Journal Entry. Verify that the entry is correct. The entry should be the exact opposite of your incorrect entry. Accounts and amounts originally debited should be credited, and accounts and amounts originally credited should be debited.

7. Close the Sales Journal Entry window. Make editing corrections if necessary.

8. Click on the **Post** icon to post the entry.

9. Re-enter the journal entry correctly. Insert the letter C after the invoice number to show that this is a correcting entry; enter the **Using** date into the **Date** text box.

Reversing an Entry Made in the Receipts
Journal Dialog Box: Use the Sales Journal

1. Open the Sales Journal; click on the arrow button to the right of the **Sold to** text box; select the customer from the list displayed; then press the TAB key until the **Invoice** text box is highlighted.

2. Enter the customer's check number used in the incorrect entry into the **Invoice** text box followed by the letter R to show that you are reversing this entry; then press the TAB key.

3. Enter the Using date into the **Date** text box; then press the TAB key until the flashing insertion point is positioned in the **Amount** text box.

4. Enter the amount debited to the Cash account in the incorrect journal entry into the **Amount** text box; then press the TAB key.

5. Enter the Cash account number into the **Acct** text box; then press the TAB key.

6. If necessary, enter the amount debited to the Sales Discounts account in the incorrect journal entry into the **Amount** text box; then press the TAB key.

7. Enter the Sales Discounts account number into the **Acct** text box; then press the TAB key.

8. Click on the Sales Journal Report menu; then click on Display Sales Journal Entry. The entry should debit the Accounts Receivable account and credit the Cash account (and the Sales Discounts account, if necessary) for the amount of the entry you are reversing. Verify that the entry is correct.

9. Close the Sales Journal Entry window. Make editing corrections if necessary.

10. Click on the **Post** icon to post the entry.

11. Re-enter the customer's payment correctly using the Receipts Journal dialog box. Insert the letter C after the customer's check number to show that this is a correcting entry; enter the **Using** date into the **Date** text box. Enter amounts as necessary into the **Disc Taken** and **Payment Amt** text boxes to record the correct amount received from the customer.

Reversing an Entry Made in the Purchases
Journal Dialog Box: Use the Purchases Journal

1. Open the Purchases Journal; click on the arrow button to the right of the **Purchased From** text box; select the vendor from the list displayed; then press the TAB key until the flashing insertion point is positioned in the Invoice text box.

2. Enter the invoice number used in the incorrect entry into the **Invoice** text box followed by the letter R to show that you are reversing this entry; then press the TAB key.

3. Enter the Using date into the **Date** text box; then press the TAB key until the insertion point is positioned in the **Amount** text box.

4. Enter the same **Amount** as used in the incorrect entry, preceded by a minus sign if the incorrect amount was originally entered as a positive amount. Enter the amount as a positive amount if the original amount entered was negative. Press the TAB key.

5. Enter the same **Acct** number as used in the incorrect entry (do not use the Accounts Payable account number); then press the TAB key.

6. Click on the Purchases Journal Report menu; then click on Display Purchases Journal Entry. Verify that the entry is correct. The entry should be the exact opposite of your incorrect entry. Accounts and amounts originally debited should be credited, and accounts and amounts originally credited should be debited.

7. Close the Purchases Journal Entry window. Make editing corrections if necessary.

8. Click on the **Post** icon to post the entry.

9. Re-enter the journal entry correctly. Insert the letter C after the invoice number to show that this is a correcting entry; enter the **Using** date into the **Date** text box.

Reversing an Entry Made in the Payments Journal Dialog Box: Use the Purchases Journal

1. Open the Purchases Journal; click on the arrow button to the right of the **Purchased From** text box; select the vendor from the list displayed; then press the TAB key until the flashing insertion point is positioned in the **Invoice** text box.
2. Enter the check number used in the incorrect entry into the **Invoice** text box followed by the letter R to show that you are reversing this entry; then press the TAB key.
3. Enter the Using date into the **Date** text box; then press the TAB key until the insertion point is positioned in the **Amount** text box.
4. Enter the amount credited to the Cash account in the incorrect journal entry into the **Amount** text box; then press the TAB key.
5. Enter the Cash account number into the **Acct** text box; then press the TAB key.
6. If necessary, enter the amount credited to the Purchases Discount account in the incorrect journal entry into the **Amount** text box; then press the TAB key.
7. Enter the Purchases Discount account number into the **Acct** text box; then press the TAB key.
8. Click on the Purchases Journal Report menu; then click on Display Purchases Journal Entry. The entry should debit the Cash account (and the Purchases Discount account, if necessary) and credit the Accounts Payable account for the amount of the entry you are reversing. Verify that the entry is correct.
9. Close the Purchases Journal Entry window. Make editing corrections if necessary.
10. Click on the **Post** icon to post the entry.
11. Re-enter the payment issued to the vendor correctly using the Payments Journal dialog box. Insert the letter C after the check number to show that this is a correcting entry; enter the **Using** date into the **Date** text box. Enter amounts as necessary into the **Disc Taken** and **Payment Amt** text boxes to record the correct amount of the payment issued to the vendor.

PART *D*
How to Repeat or Start Over on an Assignment

You always have the option to repeat an assignment for additional practice or start over on an assignment. To repeat or start over on an assignment, make a new Student Data Files disk using the procedures listed in the Creating a Student Data Files Disk section of this appendix. Relabel your first Student Data Files disk "Student Data Files #1" and label your new copy "Student Data Files #2." Store your disk labeled "Student Data Files #1" in a safe place; then use the disk labeled "Student Data Files #2" to repeat the assignment or start over on the assignment.

After you have repeated or started over on an assignment, you can continue to use the disk labeled "Student Data Files #2" to complete the remaining assignments in this text.

PART E
How and When to Use the Backup Copy of a Company's Data Files

At certain times in the assignments you are asked to make a backup copy of a company's data files. There are several reasons why you might wish to access the backup copy of a company's data files. For example, you may not have printed a required report in an assignment before advancing the **Using** date to a new month, or you may want to start an assignment over at the point where the backup copy was made rather than at the beginning of an assignment.

To use the backup copy of a company's data files complete the following procedures. The backup data files for Valdez Realty for June are used to explain the process in the following procedures.

1. Click on the **Start** button. Point to Programs; point to Simply Accounting; then click on Simply Accounting in the final menu presented. The Simply Accounting-Open File dialog box will appear.

2. Insert your Student Data Files disk into disk drive A. Enter the following path into the **File name** text box: A:\student\valdjune.asc.

3. Click on the **Open** button; leave the **Using Date for this Session** set at 6/30/97; then click on the **OK** button. The Company Window for Valdjune will appear on your screen. If you only need to print reports for Valdez Realty for June, print those reports now; click on the Company Window File menu; then click on Exit to end the current work session and return to your Windows desktop. If you want to start the Valdez Realty assignment over at the point where you made the June backup copy (i.e., you completed the June transactions and adjusting entries correctly, but made an error in the June closing process and/or made errors in the July transactions) continue with the following instructions.

4. Click on the Company Window File menu; click on Save As; then enter the following new file name into the **File name** text box: A:\student\valdez.asc.

5. Click on the **Save** button. Click on the **OK** button in response to the question "Replace existing file?" Note that the company name in the Company Window has changed from Valdjune to Valdez.

6. Continue with the Valdez Realty Mini Practice Set starting with instruction #17 under Part A: The June Accounting Cycle.

If you want to use the backup copy of a company's data files in a situation other than that described in the preceding section, substitute the desired backup file name for valdjune. asc and the desired current data file name for valdez. asc into the procedures described in the preceding section. A summary of the substitutions appears at the top of page C17.

PART F
Print and Display Settings in Simply Accounting for Windows

When you install Simply Accounting, the program automatically installs the default printer established in Windows as the default printer for Simply Accounting. If you have not yet installed a default printer in Windows, you will need to do so prior to attempting to print any reports from the Simply Accounting program. Refer to your Windows manual for information on installing a printer. You do not need to re-install Simply Accounting for Windows. The next time you access Simply Accounting, the Windows default printer will automatically be established as the default printer for Simply Accounting.

Backup You Want to Use	Substitute in Prior Procedures	Using Date	Continue Assignment Starting With
1. valdjuly.asc	valdjuly.asc for valdjune.asc	7/31/97	Valdez Realty Mini Practice Set Part B, instruction #15
2. petejan.asc	petejan.asc for valdjune.asc pete.asc for valdez.asc	1/31/97	Pete's Market Mini Practice Set, instruction #20
3. petefeb.asc	petefeb.asc for valdjune.asc pete.asc for valdez.asc	2/29/97	Pete's Market Mini Practice Set, instruction #30
4. petemar.asc	petemar.asc for valdjune.asc pete.asc for valdez.asc	3/31/97	Pete's Market Mini Practice Set instruction #42
5. dressmar.asc	dressmar.asc for valdjune.asc dress.asc for valdez.asc	3/31/97	The Corner Dress Shop Mini Practice Set instruction #15

The installation process for the Windows default printer does not ensure that the default printer and display settings within Simply Accounting will work to your satisfaction; consequently, you must test and if necessary adjust your printer and display settings before you complete any of the assignments in the text. Once the print and display settings are adjusted, they will become the default printer and display settings for each set of company data files. You need only make these adjustments once.

How to test and adjust the default printer and display settings for Simply Accounting

1. Click on the **Start** button. Point to Programs; point to Simply Accounting; then click on Simply Accounting in the final menu presented. The Simply Accounting-Open File dialog box will appear.
2. Insert your Student Data Files disk into disk drive A. Enter the following path into the **File name** text box: A:\student\printest.asc
3. Click on the **Open** button. The program will respond with a request for the **Using Date for this Session**. Leave the **Using Date for this Session** text box set at 12/1/97; then click on the **OK** button. The Company Window will appear.
4. Click on the Company Window Setup menu; then click on Settings. The Settings dialog box will appear.
5. Click on the Display tab; then adjust the display features based on the following definitions and suggestions:

   ◆ **Display Font:** Click on the arrow button to the right of the **Display Font** text box to display a list of available fonts. Select the font you want to see on the screen when you display reports.
   ◆ **Size:** Click on the arrow button to the right of the **Size** text box to display a list of available type sizes. Select the type size you want to see on the screen when you display reports.
   NOTE: It is suggested that you adjust the display settings to agree with **Display Font** and **Size** used for the screen illustrations in the text. These settings are:
   ◆ **Display Font:** MS Sans Serif
   ◆ **Size:** 8

6. Click on the **OK** button to return to the Company Window. These display settings will become the new display settings for all sets of company data files.

7. Click on the Company Window Reports menu; point to Financials; then click on Trial Balance. The Trial Balance Options dialog box will appear. Leave the **As at** date set at 12/1/97; then click on the **OK** button. The Trial Balance report window will appear.

8. The scroll bar can be used to advance the display to view other portions of the report.

9. Click on the Trial Balance File menu; then click on Print to print the Trial Balance.

10. Click on the Close button to close the Trial Balance window and return to the Company Window.

11. Review your printed Trial Balance report. If the font, type size, and/or margins are not satisfactory continue with the following instructions. If the font, type size, and margins are satisfactory, click on the Company Window File menu; then click on Exit to end your current work session and return to your Windows desktop.

12. To adjust the printer settings, click on the Company Window Setup menu; then click on Printers. The Printers dialog box will appear.

13. Click on the Reports & Graphics tab; then adjust the printer settings as necessary based on the following definitions:

◆ **Printer:** Click on the arrow button to the right of the **Printer** text box to display a list of available printers. These are the printers you set up in Windows. If you want to use a printer that is not on the list, you must install the new printer in Windows. Select the printer you want to use.

◆ **Font:** Click on the arrow button to the right of the **Font** text box to display a list of available fonts. Select the font you want to use.

◆ **Size:** Click on the arrow button to the right of the **Size** text box to display a list of available type sizes. Select the type size you want to use. The larger the type size selected, the larger the type will appear on your printed reports. If no type size options appear, make sure that you have selected a font in the **Font** text box; then select the type size for the **Font** you have selected.

◆ **Top Margin:** Enter the amount you want the top margin of the text to be lowered or raised if your reports are being printed too high or too low on the page. The amount should be expressed in inches and decimal fractions of an inch (up to two decimal places). Positive amounts lower the top margin; negative amounts raise it.

◆ **Left Margin:** Enter the amount you want the left margin of the text to be moved to the right or left if your reports are being printed too far to the left or right. The amount should be expressed in inches and decimal fractions of an inch (up to two decimal places). Positive amounts move the left margin to the right, negative amounts move it to the left.

14. After you have established the desired printer settings, click on the **OK** button to return to the Company Window. These printer settings will become the new printer settings for all sets of company data files.

15. To test your adjusted printer settings, click on the Company Window Reports menu; point to Financials; then click on Trial Balance. The Trial Balance Options dialog box will appear. Leave the **As at** date set at 12/1/97; then click on the **OK** button.

16. Click on the Trial Balance File menu; then click on Print to print the Trial Balance.

17. Click on the Close button to close the Trial Balance window and return to the Company Window.

18. Review your printed Trial Balance report. If the font, type size, and/or margins are still not satisfactory go back to instruction #12 and make new adjustments. If the font, type size, and margins are satisfactory, click on the Company Window File menu; then click on Exit to end your current work session and return to your Windows desktop.

INDEX

posting from sales journal to, 319
subsidiary, 319
    accounts payable, 360
    accounts receivable, 319
Liability(ies), 11
  as real accounts, 161
  T account rules for, 40
Lookback periods, 275
Loss, net, 18

M

Maker, 209
Matching principle, 403
Medical insurance, 249
Medicare, 248
Memorandum:
  credit, 314
    journalizing and posting, 323
  debit, 360
    journalizing and posting, 360
Merchandise:
  bought for resale, 354
  defined, 354
  purchasing, 354
Merit-rating plan, 271

N

N/10, EOM, 314
Natural business year, 71
Net income, 17
Net loss, 17
Net pay, 249
Net purchases, 356
Net realizable value, 505
Net sales, 315
Nonsufficient Funds (NSF) checks, 212
Normal balance of an account, 40
NSF (Nonsufficient Funds) checks, 212

O

Office salaries expense, 251
Office supplies, adjustments for, 119
On account, buying assets on, 7
Operating expenses, 17
Order, purchase, 358
Original entry, book of. *See* Journal(s)

Outstanding checks, 212
Overtime, 238
Overtime pay, calculating, 238
Owner's equity, 5
  statement of, 17
    for merchandise company, 462
  subdivisions of, 17
  T account rules for, 40

P

Partnership, 2
Pay, net, 249
Payee, 289
Payment:
  cash, 364
    cash payments journal and schedule of accounts payable, 364
    purchasing merchandise and recording purchases, 354
Payroll:
  Fair Labor Standards Act (Wages and Hours Law) and, 237
  federal income tax withholding and, 238
  recording and paying, 250
  recording data in payroll register, 243
  state and city income taxes and, 249
  tax expense, 271
    Federal Insurance Contributions Act (FICA), 248
    Federal Unemployment Tax Act (FUTA), 285
    journalizing, 271
    State Unemployment Tax Act (SUTA), 271
  workers' compensation insurance and, 286
Payroll register, 244
Permanent vs. temporary accounts, 161
Petty cash fund, 216
  payments from vouchers, 217
  replenishing, 217
  setting up, 216
Petty cash record, auxiliary, 217
P&L statement. *See* Income statement
Post-closing trial balance, 171
Posting, 81
  adjusting entries, 158
  from cash payments journal to accounts payable ledger and general ledger, 365